The Uley Shrines

Excavation of a ritual complex on West Hill, Uley, Gloucestershire: 1977–9

English Heritage
Archaeological Report no 17

The Uley Shrines

Excavation of a ritual complex on West Hill, Uley, Gloucestershire: 1977–9

by Ann Woodward and Peter Leach

with contributions by
Justine Bayley, Sarnia Butcher, Lynne Bell, Graham Cowles, Andrew David, Brenda Dickinson, John Drinkwater, the late Maureen Girling, Margaret Guido, Mark Hassall, Martin Henig, Michael Heyworth, Elizabeth James, Catherine Johns, Bruce Levitan, Glenys Lloyd-Morgan, Beverley Meddens, Jennifer Price, Fiona Roe, Juliet Rogers, Richard Reece, Alan Saville, Lyn Sellwood, Vanessa Straker, Roger Tomlin and Alwyne Wheeler

English Heritage
in association with
British Museum Press
1993

English Heritage acknowledges with gratitude a generous grant from British Museum Press towards the production of this book

Published by English Heritage, Fortress House, 23 Savile Row, London, W1X 2HE

Typesetting output by Saxon Graphics Ltd, Derby

Printed in England by Page Bros, Norwich

A CIP catalogue record for this book is available from the British Library

ISSN 0953-3796
ISBN 1 85074 3037

Editor, Pamela V Irving
Graphics officer, Karen Guffogg
Principal illustrators: Susan Banks, Trevor Pearson and Joanna Richards

Preface

This report comprises four main parts: first the presentation of the basic stratigraphic and structural information in chapters 1--4, secondly a description of the finds in chapters 5–11, then analyses of biological and environmental data, chapter 12, and finally a section of synthesis and discussion in chapter 13. Additionally an appendix discusses Saxon, medieval, and post-medieval development of the area.

The very substantial programme of post-excavation was carried out through the Committee for Rescue Archaeology in Avon, Gloucestershire, and Somerset (CRAAGS), later renamed The Western Archaeological Trust (WAT), and subsequently through the Birmingham University Field Archaeology Unit (BUFAU). The work has involved input from many team members and the complex co-ordination of the necessary specialist contributions. Interim assessments of the excavation results were published following the 1977 season (Ellison 1978) and immediately after the completion of the excavations in 1979 (Ellison 1980). A discussion of the site phasing was presented to a meeting of the Society of Antiquaries of London in 1982 but it was decided that, owing to the complexities of site detail and interpretation that were emerging, it would be sensible not to publish that account, but to reserve a more final revision of the phasing for this full report of the excavations. The decision proved to have been a wise one, especially as it was only during preparation of the reconstruction drawings illustrating chapter 13, that the intricacies of the latest site phases were finally unravelled.

The text of the initial site descriptions has been written by Ann Woodward, but is based on matrix diagrams and archival area by area commentaries prepared by Peter Leach. The finds reports have been arranged and edited by Ann Woodward. Major contributions are by Roger Tomlin, Richard Reece, Martin Henig, Justine Bayley, and Sarnia Butcher and shorter reports have been provided by Brenda Dickinson, Mark Hassall, Michael Heyworth, Margaret Guido, Elizabeth James, Catherine Johns, Jennifer Price, Fiona Roe, and Alan Saville. The remainder of the descriptions of the finds have been prepared by the monograph authors, the items of iron and pottery by Peter Leach and the remainder by Ann Woodward. Chapter 12, the environmental analyses, is largely the work of Bruce Levitan, with shorter contributions from Vanessa Straker and the late Maureen Girling, Beverley Meddens, Lynne Bell, Juliet Rogers, Graham Cowles and Alwyne Wheeler. The final section, chapter 13, contains a discussion of the structures excavated and presents a series of reconstruction drawings which were conceived by Ann Woodward and executed by Joanna Richards. These drawings benefited very greatly from advice and inspiration provided by Warwick Rodwell, Martin Henig and Philip Rahtz. There follows a consideration of finds distributions on site, and a comparison of the major votive assemblage with other assemblages from Roman religious centres in the west, and with those from some local Roman domestic sites. Important aspects of the votive faunal remains are highlighted and a reconstruction of the changing environmental context of the site is attempted. The sequence of events presented is exciting and unusual in its detail; however the authors wish to emphasise that the conclusions are those that can be extracted most logically from the excavated data in the light of our present state of knowledge. Care has been taken to separate description from discussion, in order that these conclusions may be questioned and furthered as a result of future research into the early history of religion in Britain.

Acknowledgements

Both the excavation campaign and the preparation of this volume have involved a very large number of people and we are pleased to be able to express our thanks to them here. All the archaeological work was undertaken by closely integrated teams, and a very high standard of workmanship was achieved throughout; but above all we are grateful to the landowners, Major and Mrs C A Goldingham, who not only afforded us every facility and kindness during the excavation seasons, but most generously have donated all the resulting finds to the British Museum. The excavations were sponsored by English Heritage (then the Directorate of Historic Buildings and Monuments, Department of the Environment), the British Museum, the Society of Antiquaries of London and the Bristol and Gloucestershire Archaeological Society; the post-excavation programme was funded by English Heritage through WAT and BUFAU and this report has been published by English Heritage in conjunction with the British Museum. The British Museum also took responsibility for the conservation of the many complex finds, in particular the lead tablets.

In and around Uley we are extremely grateful to the many local residents who supplied hospitality and accommodation to members of the team, and to archaeologists who shared their detailed knowledge of the area: Lionel Walrond of Stroud Museum, Eddie Price at Frocester Court, and Ted Swain and Mary Parris of the Kingscote Archaeological Association. On site, supervisory roles were taken by Howard Davies, Eric Elias, Terry Pearson, Geoff Perry, Elizabeth James, Beverley Meddens, Robert Read and Jane Wadham. Sarah Adams and Helen Humphries were in charge of finds processing and Sebastian Rahtz acted as finds recording supervisor and site photographer. Surveying was expertly undertaken by Bill Ellison and Richard McDonnell, and environmental sampling was supervised by Bruce Levitan. Judy Davies supplied healthy food, and administrative tasks were eased by constant assistance from Sally Smallridge. For academic advice and encouragement during the excavations we are pleased to extend thanks to Warwick Rodwell and Richard Savage (then of CRAAGS), Ian Longworth and Catherine Johns of the British Museum, Christopher Young and Stephen Dunmore (of the then Department of the Environment), Philip Rahtz, Charles Thomas, Graham Webster, Martin Henig, Peter Fowler, Richard Reece, Michael Fulford and Mark Hassall. John Drinkwater wishes to thank M Costen of Bristol University, and D Smith, archivist at the Gloucester Records Office for help and advice during the preparation of his contribution; Michael Heyworth is grateful to Leo Biek, Justine Bayley, Michael Cable, Ian Freestone, and Julian Henderson for discussions and suggestions during the course of his work. Fiona Roe wishes to thank P Jackson, H P Powell and R R Howell, and also Prof J Dewey of the Dept of Earth Sciences, University of Oxford for the use of facilities which enabled her to carry out work for her contribution. Vanessa Straker would like to thank Wendy Carruthers for her comments and for allowing a quote from an unpublished report, Mark Robinson for his constructive suggestions, and Martin Bell.

Bruce Levitan wishes to thank Susan Banks, Annie Grant, Tony Legge, Rosemary Luff, Terry O'Connor and Sebastian Payne for help of various kinds over the ten years he worked on the animal remains.

The post-excavation and publication programmes have been monitored by Paul Gosling and Stephen Johnson, and the editing has been carried out by Pamela V Irving for English Heritage. We are indebted to them for their constant care and concern throughout the intricacies of a complex project. Conservation of the finds was completed with speed and efficiency by Simon Dove in the Department of Prehistoric and Romano-British Antiquities at the British Museum. Cataloguing and archive drawing were undertaken by a series of Job Creation and other teams funded by the Manpower Services Commission. The principal illustrators for the project were Joanna Richards, Helen Humphries and Susan Banks (for WAT) and Trevor Pearson (BUFAU). Other substantial contributions have been made by Charlotte Cane, Tish O'Connor, Elizabeth James and Jane Wadham. The text was expertly processed onto disc by Ann Humphries and Jackie Pearson. We are especially grateful to all the authors of specialist contributions to this volume; their many names are recorded on the title page. Some have worked in close association with the project for many years and we are indebted particularly to Martin Henig, Richard Reece, Bruce Levitan and Justine Bayley for their endless patience and continuing interest. The project has benefited throughout from our keen interest in ancient religion and post-Roman problems, inspired by many years of digging and discussion with Philip Rahtz.

We finally wish to thank the Trustees of the British Museum for permission to reproduce photographs supplied by the British Museum.

Contents

List of illustrations

List of tables

Contents of fiche

Fiche 1: Finds

Fiche 2: Environmental

Summary

The excavations at the prehistoric, Romano-British and post-Roman religious site on West Hill, Uley between 1976 and 1979 involved the meticulous dissection of 2150 sq m of complex stratification and has led to the definition of a series of some 20 structures, originally executed in stone, timber and turf. From the remains of their destruction were recovered over 8,000 small finds, 67,000 sherds of pottery weighing 480kg and a quarter of a million animal bones. This extensive and carefully recorded pool of data has allowed the reconstruction of a sequence of ritual activities on West Hill extending from prehistory to at least the seventh or eighth century AD.

The earliest phase of use was represented by standing stones or massive posts forming the focus of an open-ended oval enclosure, probably of Neolithic date. Towards the end of the Iron Age the site, which probably occupied a sacred woodland clearing, was modified and developed to form a sequence of ditched and palisaded enclosures which contained two shrines of timber construction, and were associated with deep pits containing ritual deposits. The artefacts derived from this phase include important assemblages of iron weaponry, bone and antler tools, and votive ceramics.

The central timber shrine was replaced, probably in the early second century AD, by a stone Romano-Celtic temple, on the same alignment. The temple was of unusual plan and was extended in the mid-fourth century. Ranged around the temple were sets of buildings constructed in stone and, later, in timber. These buildings were extended, modified and rebuilt during 300 years of use and may be interpreted as living quarters, guest accommodation, and shops associated with the use of the temple. A substantial range of finds indicate that activity centred around a cult of the god Mercury. These items include fragments of a limestone cult statue, figurines, altars, and a major series of lead tablets, many of them inscribed. The latter also have provided important evidence concerning religious formulas, language, and handwriting. The animal bone assemblage contains substantial percentages of sacrificial remains of goat, sheep, and cockerels which also may be associated with the cult of Mercury.

Following partial collapse and demolition of the temple towards the end of the fourth century, the temple was modified and a remnant of it reused for a short period. Pagan finds were associated with this reuse, but at some time in the early fifth century, all temple remains were obliterated, and votive objects were spread or deliberately buried in particular sectors of the site.

Over the temple site, and once again on the same alignment, a timber hall or basilican church was constructed, along with its north-western annexe or baptistery, and the whole was enclosed by a perimeter bank of turf. Later the timber building was dismantled and replaced by a smaller multi-phased structure built in stone. The complex was still enclosed by a bank, while the stone-floored annexe or baptistery survived as a free standing feature. All these post-temple buildings incorporated important votive material such as figurines, altars, or selected portions of statuary, which had been buried within their foundations at the time of construction, and it is suggested that they were Christian in character. Associated with their demolition phases were fragments of red-streaked window glass of seventh or eighth-century date. Following the construction of a further series of more ephemeral structures in timber, the site was abandoned and given over to agriculture.

The discussion section attempts to place the finds in their context and concentrates on four main themes: the use and reuse of sacred sites over long time spans, the plan and supposed cult activities of the Roman temple, the modification of such temples towards the end of the Roman period, and the impact of early Christianity.

Résumé

Au cours des fouilles, entreprises entre 1976 et 1979 sur le site de West Hill, à Uley, site à occupations préhistorique, romano-britannique et post-romaine, on s'est livré à un examen méticuleux de 2150 métres carrés de strates complexes et on a été amené à identifier une suite de quelques 20 structures, construites, à l'origine, en pierres, en bois et en mottes de terre. De ce qui restait après leur destruction, on a retiré plus de 8000 petites trouvailles, 67,000 tessons de poterie, et 250,000 ossements d'animaux. Cette vaste banque de données, soigneusement répertoriées, a permis de découvrir que des activités rituelles s'étaient succédées sur West Hill depuis la préhistoire jusqu'au moins au septième ou huitième siècle après J-C.

Les vestiges de la phase d'occupation la plus ancienne consistaient en pierres dressées et en poteaux massifs formant le point focal d'une enceinte ovale ouverte à une extrémité, datant probablement du Néolithique. Vers la fin de l'Age du Fer, le site, qui se situait dans la forêt, probablement dans une clairiére sacrée, fut agrandi et transformé en une succession d'enceintes entourées de fossés et de palissades qui renfermaient deux sanctuaires construits en bois et qui s'accompagnaient de fosses profondes contenant des dépôts rituels. Les objets provenant de cette phase consistaient en d'importantes collections d'armes en fer, d'outils en os ou en bois de cerfs et de céramiques votives.

Le sanctuaire central en bois fut remplacé, probablement au début du deuxième siècle après J-C, par un temple Romano-celte, en pierres, construit sur le même alignement. Le plan du temple était inhabituel, on l'agrandit au milieu du quatrième siècle. Répartis autour de ce temple se trouvaient des groupes de bâtiments construits d'abord en pierres, puis, plus tard, en bois. Ces édifices furent agrandis, modifiés, reconstruits au cours des trois cents ans d'occupation et on peut considérer qu'ils consistaient en habitations, logements pour visiteurs et ateliers et étaient liés à la fréquentation du temple.

Une part substantielle des trouvailles indique que les activités se concentraient autour du culte du dieu Mercure. Parmi ces objets, on a trouvé des fragments d'une statue cultuelle en pierre calcaire, des figurines, des autels et une importante série de tablettes en plomb, dont un grand nombre portent des inscriptions. Ces dernières nous ont également fourni d'importants renseignements sur les formules religieuses, la langue et l'écriture. La collection d'ossements d'animaux comprend un pourcentage élevé de restes de chèvres, moutons et coqs utilisés pour des sacrifices, découverte que l'on peut également rapprocher du culte de Mercure.

A la suite de l'effondrement et de la démolition d'une partie du temple, vers la fin du quatrième siècle, celui-ci fut modifié et une partie en fut réutilisée pendant une courte période. On a associé à cette réutilisation certaines trouvailles païennes; cependant, à un moment quelconque au début du cinquième siècle, tout ce qui restait du temple a été anéanti, et les objets votifs ont été éparpillés ou délibérément enterrés dans certains secteurs du site.

A l'emplacement du temple, et à nouveau orienté dans le même sens, on a construit une salle ou basilique à usage d'église, en bois, on lui a adjoint, au nord-ouest, une annexe ou baptistère; l'ensemble était entouré par un talus herbeux sur tout son périmètre. Plus tard, l'édifice en bois fut démantelé et remplacé par une structure de pierres plus petite et construite en plusieurs étapes. Ce complexe était toujours entouré par un talus, mais l'annexe ou baptistère, dont le sol était en pierre, constituait maintenant un élément séparé et indépendant. Tous les bâtiments postérieurs au temple recelaient d'importants objets de culte, tels que figurines, autels et morceaux choisis de statues, qui avaient été ensevelis dans les fondations au moment de leur construction, et on suggère que ces trouvailles étaient caractéristiques de la période Chrétienne. On a associé aux phases de démolition de ces bâtiments des fragments d'un vitrail veiné de rouge datant du septième ou du huitième siècle. Après la construction d'un nouveau groupe de structures plus éphémères, en bois, le site a été abandonné et est devenu terre agricole.

La section consacrée à la discussion essaie de replacer les trouvailles du site dans leur contexte et se concentre sur quatre thèmes principaux: l'utilisation et la réutilisation des sites sacrés sur une longue période de temps, le plan et les éventuelles activités religieuses du temple romain, les transformations subies par de tels temples vers la fin de l'époque romaine et l'impact du début du christianisme.

Zusammenfassung

Die Ausgrabungen auf der vorgechichtlichen, romano-britischen und nachrömischen Kultstätte auf West Hill, Uley schlossen zwischen 1976 und 1979 die äußerst sorgfältige Untersuchung von 2150 qm verworrener Stratifikation ein und haben zu der Festlegung einer Folge von ungefähr zwanzig Bauten, die ursprünglich aus Stein, Holz und Grassoden errichtet waren, geführt. Aus den durch Abbruch entstandenen Trümmern wurden über 8000 Kleinfunde, 67,000 Keramikscherben und eine Viertelmillion Tierknochen sichergestellt. Diese weitreichende und sorgfältig aufgenommene Datenansammlung erlaubte die Rekonstruktion der Abfolge in der kultischen Aktivität auf West Hill, welche von der vorgeschichtlichen Zeit bis wenigstens in das siebte oder achte Jahrhundert n. Chr. reichte.

Die früheste Nutzungsphase bestand aus Steinsetzungen oder massiven Holzpfosten, die den Kern einer ovalen Einfriedung mit offenem Ende, wahrscheinlich neolithischen Datums, bilden. Gegen Ende der Eisenzeit wurde die Fundstätte, die wahrscheihlich auf einer Rodung innerhalb eines heiligen Hains lag, umgestaltet und in eine Reihe von mit Gräben und Palisaden versehenen Einfriedungen umgewandelt, die zwei Holzschreine enthielten. Dazu gehörten tiefe Gruben mit Votivgaben. Die Funde, die dieser Phase entstammen, schließen bedeutende Ansammlungen von Eisenwaffen, Knochen- und Hirschhornwerkzeuge und Votivkeramik ein.

Der zentrale Holzschrein wurde wahrscheinlich im frühen zweiten Jahrhundert n. Chr. durch einen romano-keltischen Steintempel mit gleicher Ausrichtung ersetzt. Der Tempel hatte einen ungewöhnlichen Grundriß und wurde in der Mitte des vierten Jahrhunderts vergrößert. Um den Tempel herum lagen Gebäudegruppen angeordnet, die zuerst in Stein, dann später in Holz errichtet wurden. Diese Gebäude wurden während der 300 Jahre ihrer Nutzung erweitert, umgeändert und neugebaut und können als Wohnquatiere, Gastunterkünfte und Läden, die mit der Nutzung des Tempels in Verbindung standen, angesehen werden. Eine ansehnliche Fundansammlung deutet darauf hin, dabß die Kulthandlungen der Verehrung des Gottes Merkur gewidmet waren. Unter den Funden befinden sich Fragmente eines Kultstandbildes aus Kalkstein, Figurinen, Altäre und eine bedeutende Reihe von Bleitäfelchen, von denen viele beschriftet waren. Diese letzteren haben obendrein wichtige Informationen über religiöse Formeln, über Sprache und Handschrift geliefert. Die Tierknochenansammlung enthält hohe Prozentsätze an Opfern von Ziegen, Schafen und Hähnen, Gaben, die mit dem Kult des Merkur verbunden sind.

Nach seinem teilweisen Einsturz und der teilweisen Abtragung gegen Ende des vierten Jahrhunderts wurde der Tempel umgeändert und seine Reste für kurze Zeit weiterbenutzt. Heidnische Funde sind mit dieser Neunutzung verbunden, aber irgendwann im frühen fünften Jahrhundert wurden alle Reste des Tempels ausgelöscht, die Kultgegenstände verstreut oder absichtlich an bestimmten Punkten der Fundstelle vergraben.

Über der Tempelstelle und wieder in gleicher Ausrichtung wurden eine Hallen- oder Basilikakirche aus Holz mit Anbau oder Taufkapelle im Nordwesten errichtet und das Ganze wurde dann mit einem Umgebungswall aus Grassoden eingefaßt. Der Holzbau wurde dann später abgebrochen und durch ein kleineres mehrphasiges Steingebäude ersetzt. Der Komplex war weiterhin von einem Wall umgeben, während das mit einem Steinfußboden versehene Nebengebäude oder Baptisterium als freistehender Bau weiterbestand. Alle diese dem Tempel nachfolgenden Gebäude enthielten wichtiges Kultmaterial wie etwa Figurinen, Altäre und bestimmtel Teile von Bildwerken, die während des Baues in die Fundamente eingefügt worden waren, und man nimmt an, daß sie christlichen Charakters sind. Zu den Abbruchphasen gehören Fragmente von rotgestreiftem Fensterglas aus dem siebten oder achten Jahrhundert. Nachdem an dieser Stelle weitere Folgen von leichten Holzbauten errichtet worden waren, wurde diese Örtlichkeit verlassen und dem Pflug übergeben.

Die sich anschließende Diskussion versucht die Funde in ihren Zusammenhang einzuordnen und konzentriert sich dabei auf vier Hauptthemen: die Nutzung und erneute Nutzung von Kultplätzen über lange Zeitspannen hin, der Grundriß und die mutmaßliche kultische Aktivität des römischen Tempels, die Veränderungen in solchen Tempeln gegen Ende der römischen Zeit und der Einfluß des frühen Christentums.

1 The site

Introduction

The religious complex on West Hill, Uley is located at a high point near to the edge of the Cotswold escarpment in southern Gloucestershire (Fig 1). It lies adjacent to one of the largest hillforts in the county, Uley Bury, and close by in the next field are the upstanding remains of Hetty Pegler's Tump, which is probably the best known of all the Severn-Cotswold tombs of the early Neolithic period. These sites lie in the heartland of the dense concentrations of prehistoric and Roman sites on the Cotswolds, which have already been described in detail by the Royal Commission on Historical Monuments (RCHM 1976). However, prior to pipeline construction in 1976, the complex site which forms the subject of this volume was known only from a handful of Roman coins and a few objects of metal and baked clay which formed part of a group of surface finds collections donated to Stroud Museum.

Thus, when the Severn Trent Water Authority commenced the laying of a water main in a trench through the northern sector of Uley parish, an archaeological response by the Committee for Rescue Archaeology in Avon, Gloucestershire, and Somerset (CRAAGS) concentrated on a watching brief and limited excavations on the line of the pipe trench, which ran along the north-eastern defences of the Iron Age hillfort of Uley Bury (Saville and Ellison 1983). The watching of works in the field north of the Bury and the road was a necessary postscript. The results of a few days of intensive recording by a small team of archaeologists, in close co-operation with a most helpful gang of pipe layers, surpassed all expectations and formed the prologue for a major campaign of excavation during the following three summers. The pipe line contained traces of Iron Age and Roman occupation, including pits, quarries, mortared stone walls and a single coffined burial. Associated with the main stone built structure were a series of votive finds which indicated the presence of a Roman religious site. These finds included rolled lead tablets bearing inscriptions (*defixiones*, see chapter 7), miniature votive pots (see chapter 8) and a fragment of a copper alloy figurine (Fig 86, no 1).

In view of the continuous damage to the site during agricultural operations and the danger of destruction of the archaeological deposits by treasure hunters, it was felt that a more extensive rescue excavation should be mounted. Negotiations with the Department of the Environment (now English Heritage), the landowner Major C A Goldingham, various funding bodies and

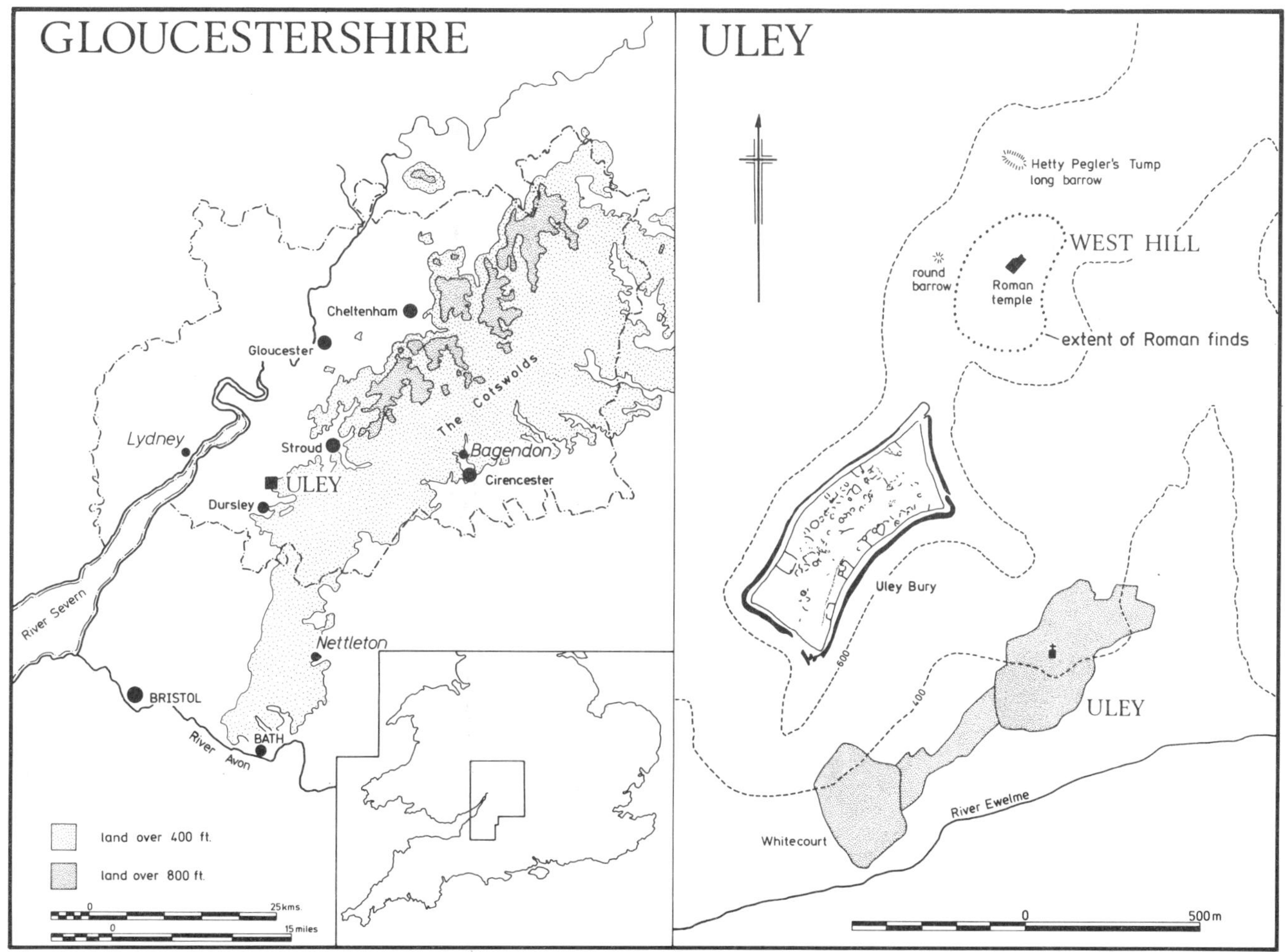

Fig 1 Site location, scale 1:20,000

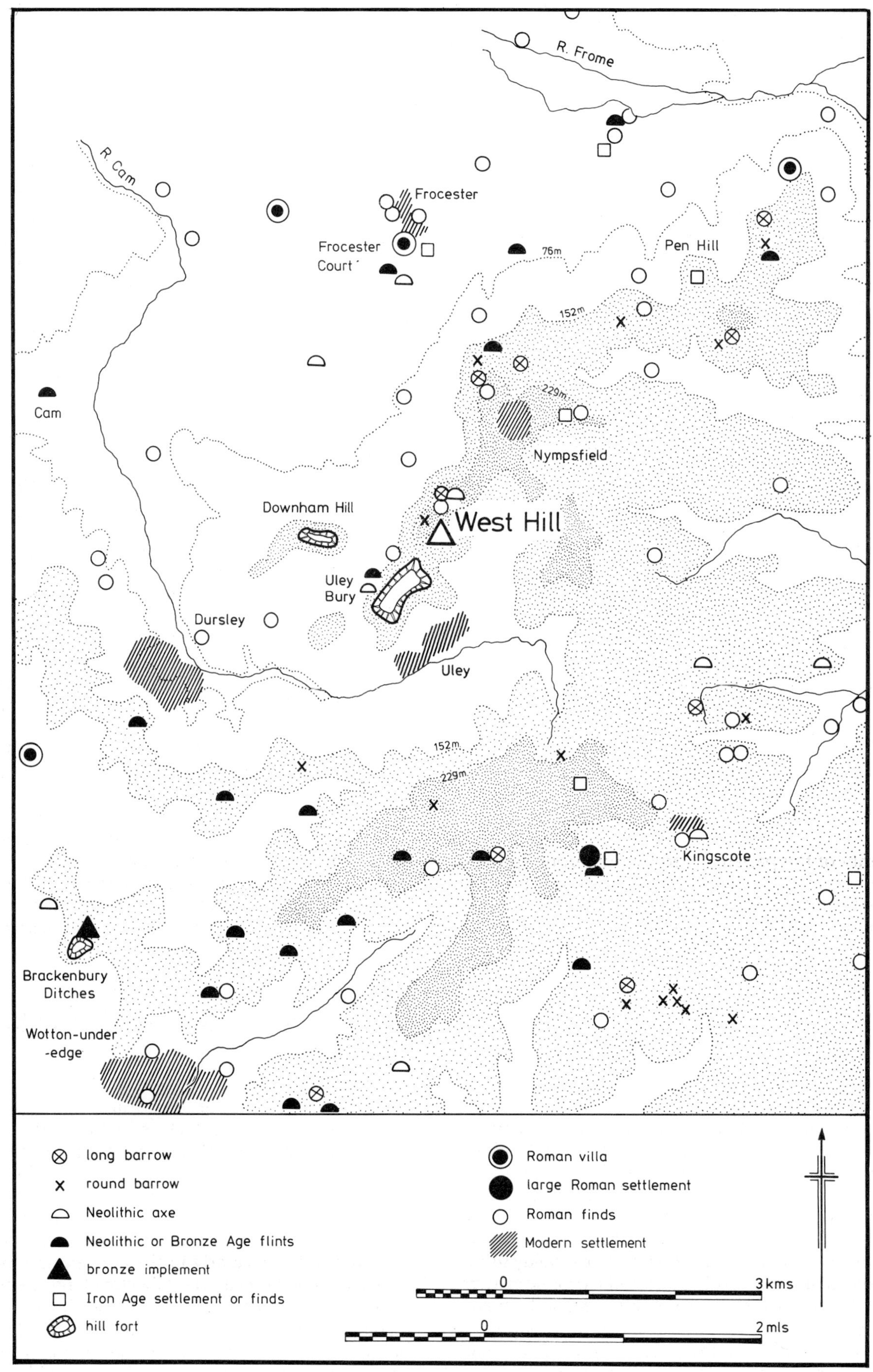

Fig 2 Prehistoric and Roman sites in the region

local institutions were initiated, and major campaigns of excavation were undertaken in 1977, 1978, and 1979. The success of these campaigns was due to the generosity and kindness of the landowner, the sponsors, and many local residents, and to the continuing enthusiasm and loyalty of a very hard working team of excavators, supervisors, finds processors, and visiting consultants. The main aims of the excavation programme were to define the central zone of the expected Roman religious complex, to investigate the nature and building history of the Roman buildings, to seek any traces of a pre-Roman precursor to the Roman shrine and, by careful site recording, to dissect the latest remains and observe any indications of post-Roman modifications or reuse. In addition, it was intended to record the positions of as many of the finds as possible, in order that the distributions of votive and other material could be analysed, and to pay particular attention to the recovery of biological and environmental data. Happily, each of these aims was achieved during the three seasons of excavation, and the present volume summarises the results of a major programme of analysis relating to all these important themes. It is hoped that the results published here will demonstrate the enhanced information concerning religious sites which may be recovered by the application of rigorous techniques of excavation and recording.

Geology and geography

by John Drinkwater

The village of Uley lies along the lower slopes of a valley which cuts north-eastwards into the Cotswold escarpment (Figs 1 and 2). It is a sheltered situation with the protective upland ring broken only on the south-west. The River Ewelme, the *raison d'être* for the medieval prosperity of the parish, is fed by numerous springs, and flows through the valley to the west. It is possible to show how the geology and topography have played an important part in fashioning the agricultural practices of the parish, and how the natural resources have been used industrially.

The spur of escarpment which forms the northern edge of the parish, under which the village nestles, is a ridge of Upper Inferior Oolite. Broken by a gap at Crawleys Shard, it constitutes the two flat areas of Uley Bury and West Hill. Although now continuously utilised as arable land, the soils on this escarpment plateau are thin and dry. In the late 16th century the interior of Uley Bury was referred to as Heatherland and during the medieval period the downlands of the escarpment were extensively employed as sheepwalks.

A band of Lower Inferior Oolite surrounds the upland mass and runs around the rim of the valley to the south and east. This band supported a prolific growth of beech trees, of which considerable areas still remain. During the medieval period thickets of woodland still existed, intermixed with the arable, a 'haystall of wood' being a common expression in the indentures for this period. These woods provided a valuable source of building material and fuel and the beechmast was utilised as pig food. The oolite escarpment once stretched much further west into the Severn Valley but over the course of time it has eroded along its western edge. This has produced outliers, detached remnants of oolite, cut off from the main escarpment. In the parish of Uley, Downham Hill (Fig 2) is an example of this type of feature.

As we descend the scarp slope beneath the oolite, we enter the region of the Upper Lias Cotteswold Sand. The soils above this layer constitute the arable land of the parish. Spreading from the lower scarp slopes out across the valley, around and past Downham, this area has long been under cultivation. Fertile and well drained in the higher levels, the land becomes heavier and less well drained towards the river. In the bottom of the valley the river has cut its way down through the Middle Lias strata into the Lower Lias clays. As a consequence the land bordering the river has heavy soils which are prone to waterlogging. This region constitutes the 'meads' or meadows, the permanent pasture land of the parish.

By reason of its situation and geology the parish is capable of supporting a balanced agricultural economy, with upland grazing, woodland, a fertile arable area below the scarp, with a copious water supply and lush pasture in the valley bottom. This water supply, combined with other environmental and geological factors, provided the basis for the wool processing industry, which from the medieval period onwards brought affluence to Dursley, Uley, Stroud, and other local valley settlements. The erosion effect on the escarpment edges has produced a steep scarp slope, where the rain water percolating through the limestone has hollowed out the clay stratum beneath. The boundary between the oolite and the lias clays is marked by a spring line along which the village is situated. Between the Cotteswold Sands and the Durham Silts and Clays is a layer of Middle Lias Marlstone Rock. This is an aquifer, its water-holding properties controlling the seepage of water through the sandy beds, and ensuring a constant water supply. This constancy, together with the pressure of water from a scarp face, and the chemical suitability of the water, were prime factors for the development of the medieval wool processing industry.

Prehistoric and Roman sites in the region

The religious complex at West Hill, lies within a landscape rich in the remains of prehistoric and Romano-British activity. The distribution of various categories of these sites is demonstrated in Figure 2. The earliest evidence shown comprises scatters of flint artefacts, mainly of Neolithic or Early Bronze Age date but sometimes includes forms of Mesolithic type. These are concentrated particularly in the area around Wotton-under-Edge where surface collectors have been active during this century. A very fine collection of flint and stonework derives from the interior of Uley Bury hillfort. This includes polished axe fragments of flint and stone and may denote major occupation of the hilltop during the Neolithic period. Indeed, this may have been the site of a Neolithic enclosure similar to that known through excavation at Crickley Hill,

Coberley (Dixon 1979), although any traces of such an earthwork have been masked by the massive defences of Iron Age date. Late Neolithic settlement is represented by the storage pits excavated at Cam, near Dursley, which contained a varied assemblage of domestic items (Smith 1968). Peterborough pottery of Mortlake and Fengate styles was associated there with a perforated stone mace head of local rock, fragments of daub, and the bones of both domestic and wild animals.

Many long barrows of early Neolithic date are found in the vicinity, including the well known examples of 'The Toots' on Selsley Common, the Bown Hill and Nympsfield barrows and Hetty Pegler's Tump. These barrows, varying in length from 30m to over 60m, belong to the group of Severn-Cotswold tombs, which has been discussed most recently in Darvill 1982. Most contained burial chambers constructed in stone, and many excavated examples have been shown to have developed through several building phases. Multiple stone chambers can be seen both at Nympsfield and Hetty Pegler's Tump, and it is thought that the number of chambers in each case may reflect the number of social units that existed in the barrow building community (eg Fleming 1973). At Nympsfield the chambers contained the remains of disarticulated human skeletons, pottery bowls in the late Neolithic Mortlake and Ebbsfleet styles, two leaf shaped flint arrowheads, and other flint tools (Saville 1979). Hetty Pegler's Tump was excavated in the nineteenth century, principally by Thurnam, and was found to contain at least 15 skeletons and various items such as a perforated boar's tusk (Thurnam 1854; Clifford 1966). This tomb lies within a few 100m of the religious site on West Hill (see Figs 1 and 4) and it is interesting to note that both at Nympsfield and Hetty Pegler's Tump, the finding of Roman coins in blocking material indicated that the tombs had been opened during the Roman period.

Situated on the scarp edge, not far from the Nympsfield long barrow, is a large round cairn known as the Soldier's Grave. This enclosed a central boat-shaped rock-cut pit lined with drystone walling. This contained a mass of human and animal bones and some pottery which was probably of late Neolithic or Beaker date (Clifford 1937, pl XI, B and D). The distribution of other round barrows in the area is shown in Figure 2. Where excavated, these barrows have been found to date from the Bronze Age. Grave goods are rare, but in the Uley region, include a Beaker from a barrow near Woodchester, part of a Collared Urn from Nailsworth (O'Neil and Grinsell 1960, fig 4) and fragments of Beaker pottery from the Lechmore barrow, Nailsworth (Clifford 1937, pl XI). Many round barrows have been flattened almost totally by ploughing, including an example recently identified by John Drinkwater in the field south of Hetty Pegler's Tump and opposite the West Hill Roman site.

The Early Iron Age in Gloucestershire is characterised by earthwork types similar to those current in Wessex. These fall into two main types: the large hilltop enclosures such as those indicated at Nottingham Hill or Norbury Camp, which may have functioned as defended food stores and stock enclosures, and the much smaller defended settlement sites (Darvill 1987, 126). Several promontories in the Stroud area are cut off by cross-ridge dykes to form protected areas which may have been similar in function to the large hilltop enclosures. The earthwork on Pen Hill, King's Stanley (Fig 2) is one of these cross-ridge dykes, but it is unexcavated and undated. A good example of the smaller defended sites is Brackenbury Ditches, North Nibley. This is a strongly defended hillfort situated on a spur of the escarpment. It is unexcavated and although covered by trees, is the best preserved Cotswold hillfort still extant. Elsewhere, such defended sites are known to contain round or rectangular houses and four-post structures.

By the Middle Iron Age, larger hillforts with multiple fortifications were being constructed. At Uley Bury, an area of 13 hectares was enclosed by the visually impressive ramparts, which enhance the defensive nature of the existing spur. The ramparts are known to have been constructed by a simple system of terracing and revetment, and excavation at one of the minor entrances produced a copper alloy ring headed pin, a penannular brooch, fragments of shale vessels and two spit-shaped currency bars (Saville and Ellison 1983). The interior is unexcavated, but air photographs have provided evidence of a complex palimpsest of compounds, ditches and circular structures indicative of intensive settlement (Hampton and Palmer 1977, fig 1). The finding of Dobunnic coins during surface collection suggests that occupation continued into the Late Iron Age. Some of the smaller hillforts were remodelled, amongst them Brackenbury Ditches where some of the banks appear to be secondary. Also dating from the Middle Iron Age is a series of open settlements; the best excavated example of these lies in our area at Frocester Court. Located in the Severn Valley it was a ditched enclosure, containing up to six round-houses which probably dated from the second century BC. It produced evidence for metalworking as well as for domestic activities. An agrarian base is suggested by the presence of contemporary field boundaries around it (Price 1983). Such farms and larger agricultural complexes or villages continued to be the main settlement forms in the Late Iron Age. At Frocester Court, minor remodelling of the enclosure was undertaken in the first centuries BC and AD and three small enclosures or gardens were added. The presence of coins and imported Gaulish pottery demonstrate that the occupants had access to the continental trade links that had transformed the economy by this period.

The developing economic system was associated with the closer definition of territorial ethnic groups, each characterised by their own pottery styles and coins. In the Gloucestershire area, the local tribe was the Dobunni. The farmers and craftsmen were ruled and co-ordinated by a growing elite, who may have occupied and controlled the larger hillforts, which were still in use, and the newly constructed large enclosures defined by discontinuous dykes. As mentioned above finds of Dobunnic staters from the interior of Uley Bury suggests that occupation continued there, while the ditch system on Minchinhampton Common, just south of Stroud, bears morphological similarities to the larger enclosure of Bagendon (Clifford 1961). Excavations at Bagendon have provided evidence for four phases of intensive occupation, metalworking, and coin production. It is near, or within, such centres that religious foci are likely to be found, and the complex on West Hill, just outside Uley Bury, is the first of these to be defined and investigated within Dobunnic territory.

Roman Gloucestershire is dominated by the two towns of Glevum (Gloucester) and Corinium (Cirencester). The countryside around these centres was densely populated and intensively exploited, with the rural communities occupying a variety of settlements ranging from small farmsteads to large rural complexes possessing some urban characteristics. The settlement area at Kingscote falls into this latter category, with evidence of paved roads, opulent stone buildings, craft activities and, probably, a religious focus (Swain 1975–79). Of the smaller farmsteads, 45 or 50 in the county show evidence of having been rich establishments, usually classed as villas. In the area local to Uley, the most well known are the long-lived farmhouse with courtyard, formal gardens, dovecote and baths excavated at Frocester Court (Gracie 1970, Gracie and Price 1980) and the very large villa, which might better be described as a palace, at Woodchester. The rich estates seem to have been established around the beginning of the fourth century AD, possibly due to an influx of wealthy individuals who were leaving the towns at this time, or who had possibly emigrated from Gaul (McWhirr 1981, 104).

Although no structural remains of Roman temples or shrines have been recovered within Gloucester or Cirencester, several rural religious sites have been investigated within the county. Small square temples are known from Wycomb and Chedworth (McWhirr 1981, 152), and at Chedworth there is also evidence of a water shrine in an angle of the extensive villa buildings. It may be that the villa itself fulfilled some religious functions, but this hypothesis remains unproven. What is certain is that the water shrine or *nymphaeum* was converted to Christian use, with the rim of its octagonal reservoir being inscribed with a *chi-rho* symbol (Goodburn 1976, 24). Most impressive was the religious complex excavated by Wheeler at Lydney Park. Here a Romano-Celtic temple of unique plan was surrounded by a large courtyard house, a bath suite and a row of small rooms, all contained within the confines of an earlier Iron Age promontory fort (Wheeler and Wheeler 1932). The excavations produced a massive array of votive finds and evidence of dedication to Nodens, a god of water and healing. The Iron Age defences were remodelled in the post-Roman period, and no doubt the temple was subjected to some continuing use in the fifth and sixth centuries. Other indications of religious sites, in the form of votive depositions or groups of stone altars are known from Lower Slaughter, Daglingworth, King's Stanley, and Bisley (McWhirr 1981, 159). It is within this multi-faceted ideological context that our study of the West Hill religious complex must be set.

Geophysical survey

by Andrew David

The purpose of the geophysical survey was to attempt to trace unexcavated archaeological features extending beyond the limits of the then current excavations, and also to look for postulated features related to the temple, such as a temenos ditch. In addition, the survey was designed to look further afield for any other indications of buried remains which might add to the understanding of the archaeological context of the site under excavation. Both magnetometer and resistivity surveys were undertaken, following the establishment of a 30m grid across the field.

Magnetometer survey

The majority of the field was surveyed with a fluxgate gradiometer which was carried systematically across the survey grid along 30m traverses repeated at 1m intervals, the instrument signal being plotted simultaneously on a chart recorder. A subjective interpretation of the resulting magnetometer plots is shown on Fig 3 (see also AM Lab report no 2879).

Experience has shown that magnetometer survey can be particularly effective on sites underlain by Jurassic limestone, a parent rock which generates soils with a magnetic susceptibility (MS) very favourable to the detection of archaeological features. Uley has proved to be no exception to this, with anomalies of archaeological origin consequently well defined, if often of indeterminate pattern and confused amongst a profusion of weaker and less distinct anomalies.

Immediately to the north of the recent excavations there is considerable magnetic disturbance, which can be related to Structure X, recognised in this area from the aerial photographs. The anomalies here are too densely concentrated to indicate more than a series of conjoined linear features of approximately the same orientation as the cropmark. Such strong positive anomalies are unlikely to relate specifically to walls, but more probably to the silting between them, the magnetic response from which has probably been enhanced by local occupational activity and perhaps burning.

To the east of this 'building', and of the excavation, a curving linear feature appears to have been detected. The orientation of the magnetometer traverses here, as well as local magnetic interference, both obscure what may be a significant ditch alignment, perhaps the only candidate for a temenos boundary. Such an interpretation must be highly speculative however, in view of the incomplete nature of the anomaly and the difficulties of making sense of the magnetic data in such a restricted area.

Further to the north, in the corner of the field, the survey was increasingly restricted by the pipe to the west and the hedge and plough-bank to the east. There are nevertheless several significant anomalies. Of these, some are strongly magnetic and relatively discrete, perhaps indicating the presence of pits containing occupational material or refuse. The more pronounced anomalies could be responses to kilns or other industrial structures (marked K on Fig 3). There also appear to be several lengths of ditch in this area.

Turning southwards, there is considerable evidence for buried remains, not least of which is the complex of anomalies about 30m south-east of the temple. This is composed of anomalies of the same strength and character as those noted immediately north of the excavation trench and could therefore also be assumed to relate in some way to the presence of building foundations. A sample of Roman mortar from the excavations

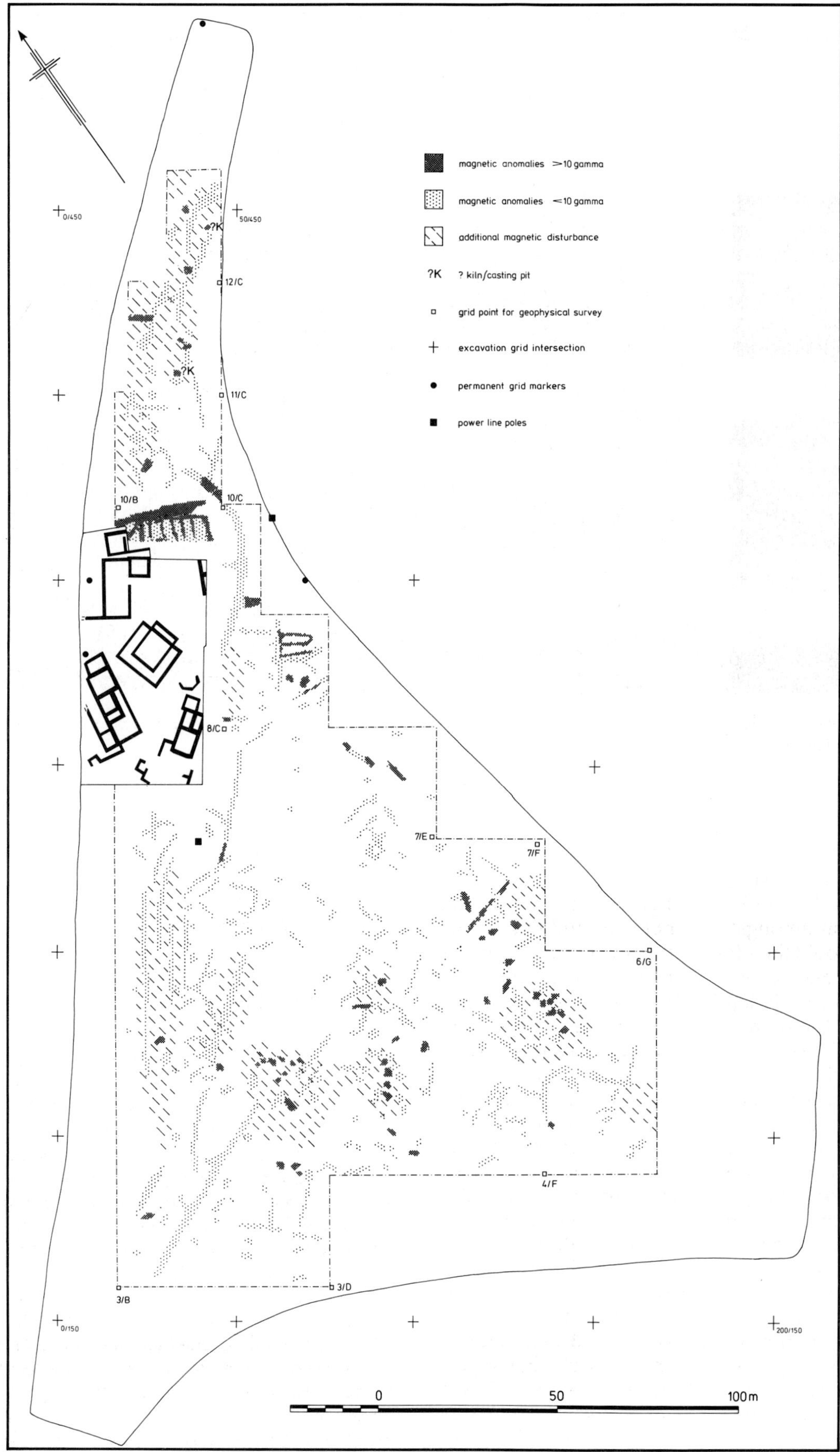

Fig 3 Excavated features and results of the archaeomagnetic survey, scale 1:1666

Fig 4 Excavation of the Roman temple, Structure II view from the south towards Hetty Pegler's Tump (top left) (1977). (Photo: Peter Leach)

gave an MS value of 15.5×10^{-8} SI/kg. Such a low value, combined with that for the native stone, contrasts significantly with the substantial magnetic enhancement of the topsoil (124×10^{-8} SI/kg) from this area. Soil accumulation amongst a complex of building debris and walls would therefore result in a disjointed pattern of magnetic anomalies corresponding with equivalent undulations in soil depth. Other features detected in this area (to the south-east of the excavations) include lengths of ditch and further anomalies consistent with pits or hearths.

The remainder of the survey covers much of the field that extends southward on a level with the site, and sloping to the east. Throughout this area there appears to be an extensive scatter of archaeological features. With the exception of groups of prominent anomalies suggestive of pit-like features and portions of ditch, most of the remaining anomalies are weak and difficult to interpret. Many are near the limit of detectability (ie less than 5nT) and the suggested interpretation on Fig 3 can only be accepted as both partial and generalised. There is an impression of widespread occupational activity of varying intensity, thin in parts, but apparently more substantial where the stronger pit-like anomalies congregate. There appear to be numerous ditches over the area, although only detected here and there, or merely as faintly discernible trends of discontinuity, blending with less linear and more diffuse areas of anomalous readings. South-west of the excavated area there are apparently two or more parallel ditches, suggested by a lengthwise displacement of the accompanying magnetometer traces. These could be interpreted as road ditches, especially as they are directed towards the temple site, and are disposed parallel to the modern road.

Resistivity survey

In the time available, two areas were selected for area survey by resistivity, with a Martin-Clark meter. The Twin Electrode configuration was used, with a probe-spacing and reading interval of 1m.

The first area covered the zone immediately north of the excavation in the hope of elucidating details of the building, Structure X, indicated on the aerial photograph and by magnetometer survey. The results were disappointing, however: discontinuous high resistance anomalies were found, almost certainly relating to building foundations, but with no clear pattern. The extremely stony nature of the soil may have the effect of obscuring all but the best preserved of the features.

The second area, down slope to the south-east of the temple, includes the group of magnetic anomalies mentioned above. The resistivity data shows a clear band of high readings suggestive of building debris. On filtering, greater detail is visible (see AM Lab rep no 2879), with a hint of rectilinearity amongst clusters of high readings, again though a definitive pattern is elusive.

Fig 5 Excavation in progress in 1977, Structure X as a cropmark, right. (Photo: Colin Pennycuick)

Fig 6 Maximum extent of excavations in 1978, view from the south.(Photo: Sebastian Rahtz)

Conclusions

If not establishing a particularly clear or coherent pattern, the survey findings have at least demonstrated the extent and density of archaeological activity on this part of West Hill. The area in the northern corner of the field, where the temple precinct is situated, has revealed anomalies confirming the presence of buildings and other features in the vicinity of the excavation. There is little indication, however, of the exact nature of the buried remains responsible for the somewhat confused magnetic plots, or for the relationship between anomalies and excavated structures. A temenos boundary cannot be confidently inferred from the geophysical evidence alone, nor, for instance, can the possible existence of burials. These latter are usually undetectable owing to the lack of magnetic or moisture contrast between their filling and the surrounding subsoil.

Both resistivity and magnetometer readings indicate archaeological activity south-eastwards and down slope from the main site, and anomalies here suggest important and hitherto unsuspected remains.

The quantities of significant magnetic anomalies distributed widely over the remainder of the field may, or may not, be related to the temple site – one can only note the very long-lasting attraction that this plateau has had from prehistoric times onwards. Although widespread, the anomalies are on the whole rather weak for an area where background magnetic susceptibility can be very high. This might suggest that occupational activity, whilst likely to be represented by these anomalies, was perhaps of relatively slight intensity here, ie anomalies from the prolonged and concentrated use of substantial pits, hearths and living areas seem to be absent or indistinguishable. Further work would be needed to qualify this interpretation, and to fully and objectively describe all the anomalies involved. Without widespread resistivity coverage, the presence of stone buildings cannot be inferred at these further limits of the field.

Fig 7 Aerial view from the south-east of areas excavated in 1979. (Photo: Colin Pennycuick)

Fig 8 Excavation and recording procedures in progress (1979). (Photo: Sebastian Rahtz)

In conclusion, over ten years after this survey was undertaken it is worth emphasising that subsequent developments in archaeological geophysics would now almost certainly allow a very considerable improvement in quality and detail beyond that which it was then possible to achieve. Total coverage of the field with the higher resolution of the resistivity and magnetic instruments now available, alongside improved data treatment and presentation, would undoubtedly be repaid. A detailed magnetic susceptibility area survey would also be informative, especially over outlying parts of the field. Such an approach, now a prospect for some future research project, would provide a valuable refinement in our understanding of the archaeological environs of the site as presented by the survey work to date.

Strategies for excavation and recording

Three major seasons of excavation involved the dissection of a series of adjoining areas which occupied a high point of the hill top, and coincided with a particularly dense concentration of structural remains cut by the water pipe trench. An area of 2150 square metres was excavated almost totally. The northern sector of the temple was uncovered in 1977 (Figs 4 and 5) but detailed excavation of these complex deposits was not undertaken until 1978 (Fig 6). The deepest ditch segment (F264) lay across the boundary of the 1977 and 1978 excavation areas and the southern portion, which had been examined only in part in 1977, was fully excavated in 1979 (Fig 7).

In the first two seasons the modern ploughsoil was removed by mechanical means, but hand excavation of the topsoil over Structures IX and XIV in 1979 (16.7% of the total area excavated) demonstrated that the occurrence of finds within it was minimal. The upper spit of ploughsoil contained few finds and more than half of these were undiagnostic fragments of iron nails. The lower spit, immediately above the structural remains contained twice as many finds, but again nail fragments were most common, followed by small fragments from glass vessels. The coins and other diagnostic finds only occurred in areas above the demolition deposit of Structure XIV and the plough-disturbed tessellated floor of Structure IX. Also in 1979 a campaign of sieving was mounted, in order to test the degree of recovery of small finds and biological data by hand excavation in the various contexts. The results of these experiments have been published separately (Levitan 1982a).

Structural remains and stratification were removed mainly by trowel, and the techniques of dissection combined the use of major cumulative sections, and the careful selection of standing sections, located to attempt to resolve specific structural problems. Mortared stone walls were not removed in case it were decided in the future to display the buildings. Visible elevations were drawn but some details of construction and, in particular, of earlier features such as Iron Age post holes beneath them, were therefore not recovered. In 1977 two buildings (Structures II and IV) were excavated by removing opposed quadrants of the fill in each room, while Structure I was recorded by drawing cumulative sections. In 1978 the front of the Roman temple (Structure II) was excavated using the cumulative section method. There was no doubt that this latter method recorded more information, and in a more comprehensive manner during excavation, than the quadrant method. Separate numbering systems for section drawings were used in each season. These have been retained in the present report to avoid any confusion in cross referencing to the archive. The OD heights for published sections are to be found in the archive. The detailed planning of rubble spreads proved invaluable in the elucidation of the post-Roman phases and the rigorous recovery of the available environmental data has made a significant contribution to the overall interpretation of the site. The field had usually been planted with cereals, by the direct drilling method, but every five years or so a shallow ploughing was undertaken. Following such a ploughing in September 1978, the opportunity was taken to collect surface finds from the disturbed soil, and these results are compared with those of the geophysical survey.

All finds except pottery and animal bones were recorded at least two dimensionally, and during the third season, the scatters of bone, pottery and tile fragments were also recorded in detail from the top of the plough soil downwards (Fig 8). The finds were plotted onto distribution sheets on site; these were at the same scale as the plans of structures and features and all were checked exhaustively. All context details and finds were recorded using a suite of *pro formae* and the files containing these sheets form the basis of the site archive, along with the site and post-excavation graphics. Selected indexes are recorded in computer files, namely the index of small finds, pottery analysis sheets, an index of painted wall plaster and abbreviated context descriptions. The archive and all the finds are to be housed in the Department of Prehistoric and Romano-British Antiquities of the British Museum.

Phasing summary

The structures and boundary features excavated on West Hill have been ascribed to eight major phases spanning eight centuries AD and, possibly, two millennia BC. The scheme of site phasing is shown in Fig 9 where a series of simplified phase plans are set alongside a time chart. The dates for Phases 2 to 7 have been derived from the analysis of the many thousands of coins undertaken by Richard Reece (see chapter 5).

Phase 1, prehistoric Two round-bottomed ditches F179 and F382 may have formed part of an open-ended oval enclosure or, possibly, the quarries for a long barrow. North of these were various pits which may have held standing stones or massive posts.

Phase 2a–c, early-first century AD Ditches F179 and F382 were recut and formed the southern portion of a major enclosure defined to the north and west by ditches F584 and F816 and, on the east, by deep ditch segment F264. Outside the enclosure pit F836 may have been one of a series of votive structures and in the centre of the enclosure a timber fence or wall defined a square, Structure XVI, which probably functioned as a shrine. The votive pit F251 was cut into the edge of F264 in Phase 2c, and was associated with a series of palisades and posts set into the primary fills within the ditch segment F264.

Phase 2d, mid-first century (*c* AD 50) The ditches of the northern sector of the main enclosure continued in use, as did Structure XVI and the pit F836. In F264, the palisades were dismantled and a layer of silting developed.

Phase 3a(i), late-first century AD The western ditched palisade F593 continued in use, while F816 was dismantled in order that the trapezoidal Structure XVII might be built. Pits F836 and F251 were still open, and F251 was partially recut; the central Structure XVI remained in use and this and Structure XVII were associated with the deposition of human infant burials.

Phase 3a(ii), late-first century AD Palisade F593, Structures XVI and XVII and pit F836 continued in use. Within the upper fillings of F264, the palisades and post holes of Structure XVIII were inserted.

Phase 3b, late-first or early-second century AD The remaining palisades were dismantled, along with Structure XVIII and, probably, Structure XVII.

Phase 3c, late-first or early-second century AD The hollows overlying the surrounding ditches and palisade trenches were infilled with debris containing pottery and bone. The upper portion of pit F836 was also infilled and there may have been a brief period of abandonment. Structure XVI, the central shrine, probably survived, even if it was not in use at this time.

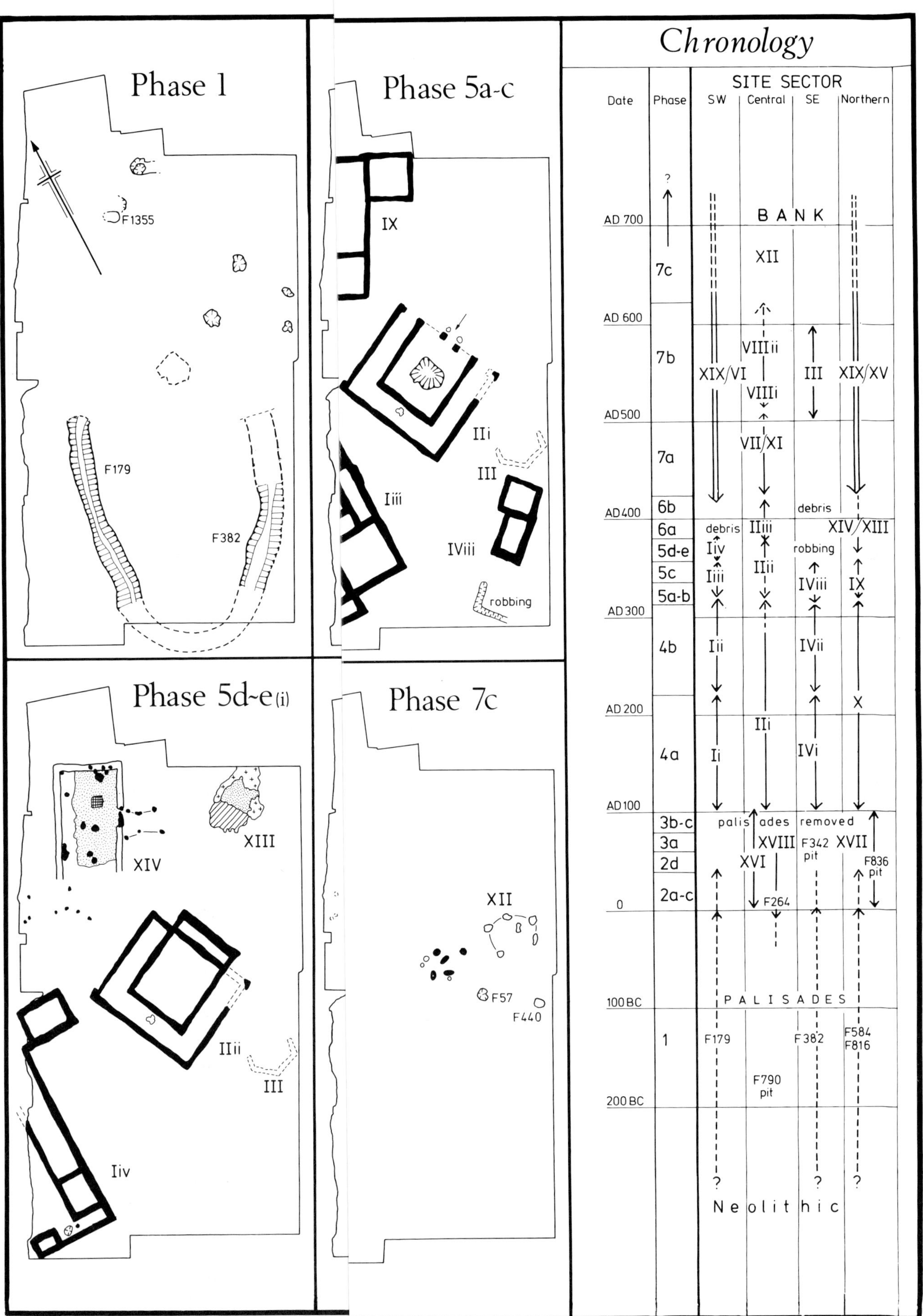

Fig 9 Schematic phase plans and chronological

Phase 4a, second century (*c* AD 100 to 200) The major stone Structures I (Rooms B,C,F and H), IV (Rooms B/C and D), X and the temple, Structure II, were now constructed and between Structures II and X the cobbled courtyard was laid. Structure III possibly originated at this time as a replacement for pit F342.

Phase 4b, third and early-fourth century (*c* AD 200 to 310 or 317) Structure I was extended by the addition of Rooms D,E and G, while Rooms A and F were added to Structure IV. Towards the end of this phase Structure X and most of Structure IV were demolished, but the temple (Structure II) and its courtyard continued in use.

Phase 5a, early-fourth century (*c* AD 310/317 to 330) Structure I was extended again with Rooms J and K being built at its southern end. The temple and courtyard continued in use and, partly replacing Structure X, a new stone Structure IX(i) was built.

Phase 5b, early to mid-fourth century (*c* AD 330 to 345) Structures I, II and the courtyard continued in use, but Structure IX was rebuilt and extended by the addition of Room A. The front half of Room B, and Room A, of former Structure IV formed a small free standing building in this phase.

Phase 5c, mid-fourth century (*c* AD 345 to 353) Structure IX was demolished.

Phase 5d, mid to late-fourth century (*c* AD 353 to 360) The front of the temple fell and was reconstructed with a projecting portico. Structure I was reduced in size to Rooms A, D and E only with the latrine, Room K left free standing, and the remains of the walls of Structure IV were robbed. North of the temple two new buildings principally constructed in timber were provided: Structure XIV over the former Structure IX and Structure XIII on the demolition rubble of Structure X.

Phase 5e(i), late-fourth century (*c* AD 360 to 370) Structure I was finally demolished; Structures II, XIV and XIII continued in use.

Phase 5e(ii), late-fourth century (*c* AD 370 to 380) Hollows over the demolished remains of Structure I were filled with deposits of votive debris, probably cleared out from the temple.

Phase 6a, end of the fourth century (*c* AD 380 to 400) Following further collapse, the temple was modified and a remnant of it reused for a short period. A wooden annexe was constructed against one of the surviving ambulatories. Structures XIII and XIV may have contined in use.

Phase 6b, early-fifth century (*c* AD 400 to 420) The modified temple, II(iii), was demolished and its rubble spread over its former site and that of Structure IV. Structures XIII and XIV were probably demolished als. Thus, the site was cleared totally.

Phase 7a: mid to late-fifth century (after AD 420) The hall or basilican church, Structure XI was constructed, mainly of timber, along with its north-western annexe or baptistery, and the central area was enclosed by a perimeter bank of turf, Structure XIX, which was provided with at least two entrances of timber constructio, Structures VI and XV.

Phase 7b(i), early-sixth century Structure XI was dismantled and replaced by a stone building, Structure VIII(i), with Structure III possibly re-established, or still functioning, to the south. The complex was still enclosed by the bank, Structure XIX, and the baptistery, Structure VII, survived as a free standing feature.

Phase 7b(ii), later-sixth to early-seventh century Structure VIII was extended by the addition of an apse on the north-eastern side. Structures VII, XIX and possibly III continued in use. Deposition of the head of the Roman cult statue (Fig 72) was associated probably with the extension of Structure VIII, but could belong equally to Phase 7b(i).

Phase 7c, seventh century or later Structures III, VIII and XIX decayed and the central area was now taken up with timber Structure XII, two irregular settings of post holes above the site of the former temple, and a pit containing a piece of antler.

Phase 8, medieval and modern The final timber buildings decayed and became buried by deposits of medieval and modern ploughsoil.

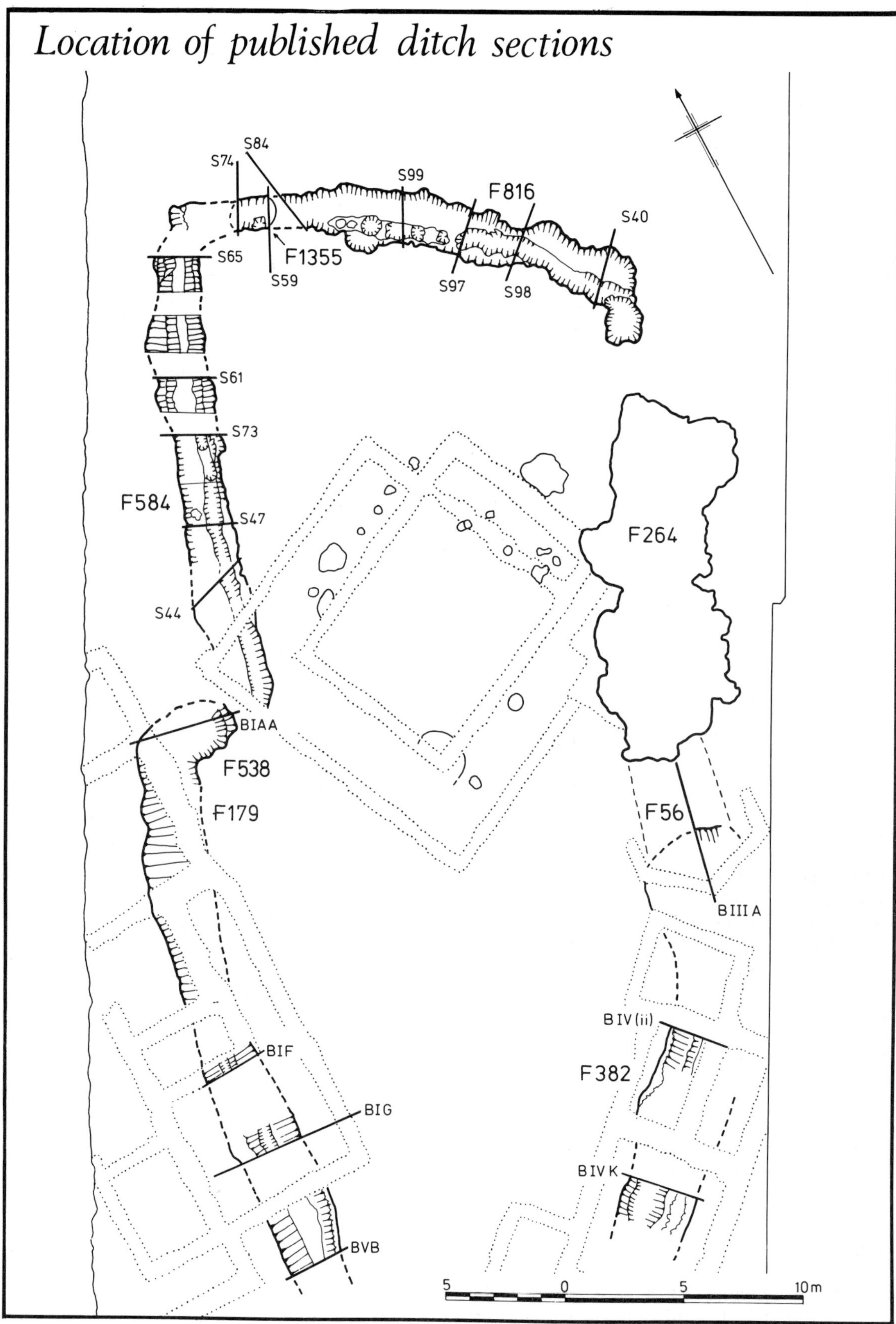

Fig 10 Early features, scale 1:240

2 The prehistoric enclosure and shrines

Ditch F179, Phases 1–2

Beneath the Roman building range, Structure I, and terminating between it and the site of the later temple (Structure II) ran a ditch of considerable dimensions (Figs 10 and 11). It varied in width from 2.40m to 3.40m and in depth from 1.0m to 1.70m. Although the length exposed was not excavated in its entirety (see Fig 10), it appeared that the ditch was shallower towards the middle of its run (Fig 12, section BI F) and deeper at its northern terminal (Fig 12, section BI AA) and towards a southern end which was not reached within the excavated area (Fig 12, section BV B).

The main run of the ditch was V-profiled and the sides and bottom were very weathered. A shallow, rock-cut slot, F190, along the ditch base was recognised in places (Fig 12, section BI F). Primary weathering detritus context 191 (Fig 12, section BI F) occurred along the ditch sides but had not filled this possible palisade slot. Most of the infilling appears to have dated from a later phase when the postulated palisade was removed, as major deposits of rubble and soil, containing pottery, tile fragments, and other finds occur as extensive disturbed spreads throughout the excavated ditch segments, contexts 139 and 180 (Fig 12, sections BI G and BI F), contexts 534, 535, and 537 (Fig 12, section BV B). The finds from these layers include charcoal, animal bone, pottery, a bone pin fragment, a whetstone, an iron stylus, and from context 356, a Nauheim derivative brooch (Fig 123, no 1). The northern terminal F538 was characterised by a more rounded profile (Fig 12, section BI AA, and Fig 15). The major fills were once again of disturbed rubble, context 521 containing a piece of copper alloy strip and the higher deposit, context 516, a penannular brooch (Fig 125, no 9) dating from the first half of the first century AD.

Following removal of any remains of the postulated palisade belonging to a primary ditch, which may well have dated from pre-Iron Age times, the ditch was possibly recut and reused in the first centuries BC and AD. The disturbed fillings, which incorporated substantial amounts of domestic and personal debris, may represent a sequence of ritual deposits rather than structural infill. Indeed, above these rich layers, the levelling fills connected with the construction of Roman Structure I, such as context 519 (Fig 12, section BV B), were relatively devoid of finds, although this particular layer did contain a trumpet brooch (Fig 124, no 10) which was probably of second-century date.

Ditch F382, Phases 1–2

Beneath the foundations of Roman Structure IV lay a further substantial ditch, similar in dimensions to that investigated beneath Structure I (Fig 14).

As with ditch F179, the full extent of ditch F382 was not established but it's northern terminal, F56, was partly excavated (Fig 10). The V-profiled ditch possessed heavily weathered sides and the shallow, rock-cut slot in its base (Figure 12, section BIV K) may also have been designed to hold a palisade. As in the case of ditch F179, the presence of the soft ditch fills had caused the builders of the Roman buildings to construct deep and substantial foundations where walls crossed the line of the ditch (Fig 12, elevation BI V(ii), and Fig 14).

The main rubble fillings: context 383 (Fig 12, elevation BIV (ii), context 370 (Fig 12, section BIV K), and context 40 (Fig 12, section BIII A) contained no metal finds, but the presence of early Roman pottery types suggests that this ditch may have been cleaned out for reuse in the same way that the Phase 2 ditch F179 had been . A steep sided, deeper terminal, F56, cut through the ditch F382 (Fig 12, section BIII A), but its primary fill context 39, was only partially revealed beneath the later Structure III. Feature F56 almost certainly relates to the activities of Phase 2 (Fig 15), although no finds or deposits of a specifically votive character were recognised from the excavated sample. The continuation north of ditch F382 (largely unexcavated) was terminated by the later cut of ditch F264, but its original line was re-established by the shallower recut ditch F965 (Figs 22 and 23), which may have linked ditch F264 with the terminal F56 later in Phase 2 or in Phase 3. Later still was a pit, F342, cut into the fills of F56 (Figs 22 and 23), which contained an assemblage of abundant early second-century pottery with charcoal, suggestive of ritual deposition and perhaps comparable to and contemporary with the Phase 3 structures and deposits immediately to the north (eg Structure XVIII, Fig 22). The adjacent contemporary and later deposits forming context 35 (Fig 12, section BIII A), continue north as context 963 (Fig 65, section S58), infill the depression above the ditches F382 (Fig 15) and F965 (Fig 22), and equate with deposits of Phase 4 and later above F264 (Fig 12, section BIII A, and Fig 65, section S58).

Ditch F584, Phases 2–3

Beneath the western corner of the later stone temple, and running below the alignment of Structure IX (Fig 9), lay the infilled remains of a third major ditch F584 (Fig 15). The southern portion was totally excavated, except where it ran below the stone foundations of the temple building Structure II, while the northern sector was excavated by alternate segments (Fig 10). The ditch was much smaller than ditches F179 or F382 and presented a square-cut flat based profile rather than a V-shaped one (Fig 16, sections S44, S47, S61, S65, S73). The ditch varied in width from 1.95m to 2.10m; the depth averaged 0.65m towards the southern end, and 0.55m in the northern sector. The fill of the main ditch was a thick deposit of stony clay soil, context 580; this was cut along the length of the ditch by narrow, vertical-sided slot F593, which usually had been cut below the base level of the wider ditch F584. This slot was filled with context 581, a primary deposit of loose rubble packing and clay soil (Fig 16, sections S44, S47, and S73), which may have supported a timber palisade. Most of the postulated palisade trench was filled however with a mixed rubble and soil deposit context 594, which contained early Roman pottery. This probably

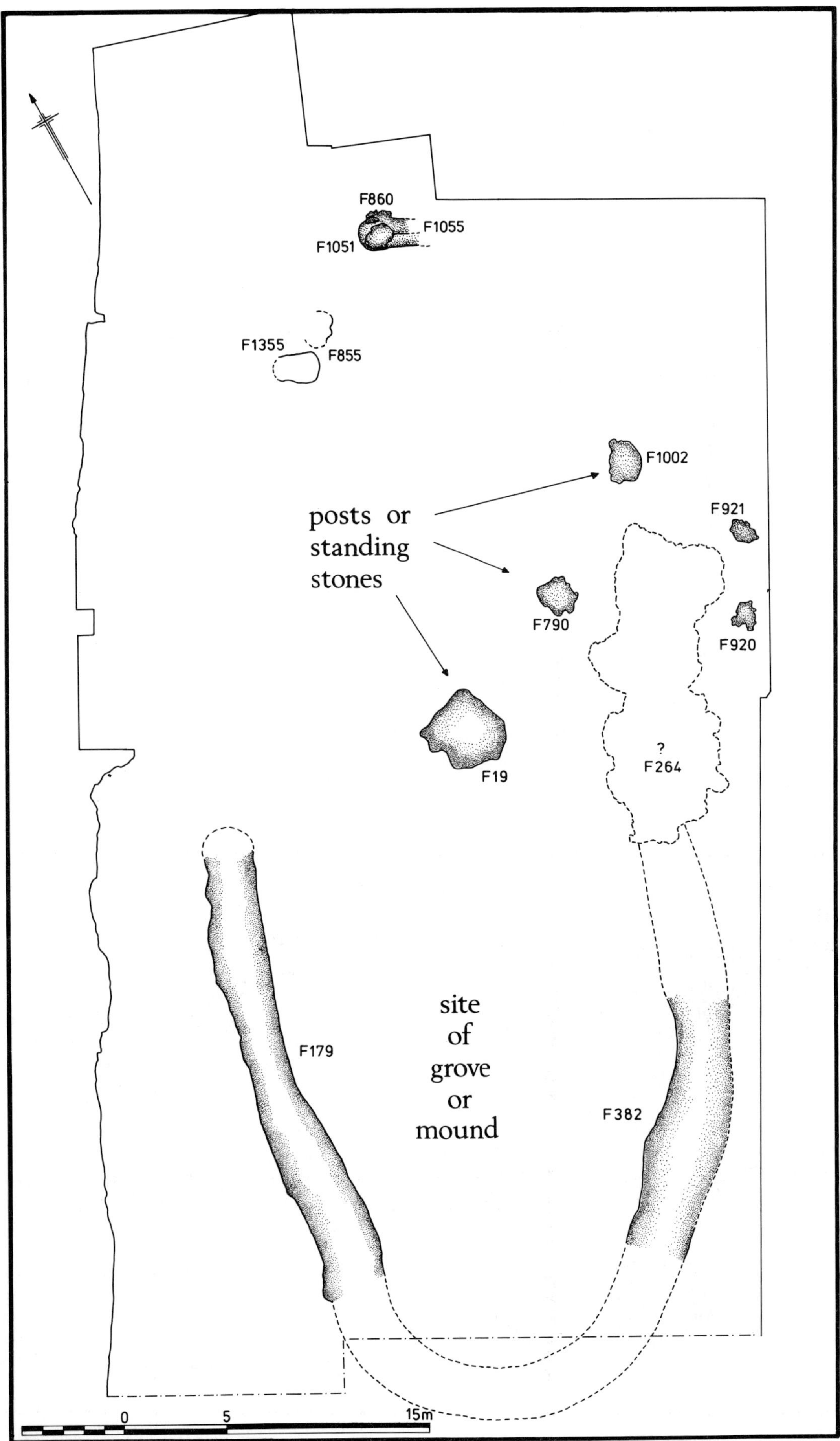

Fig 11 Phase 1 plan: ?Neolithic, scale 1:280

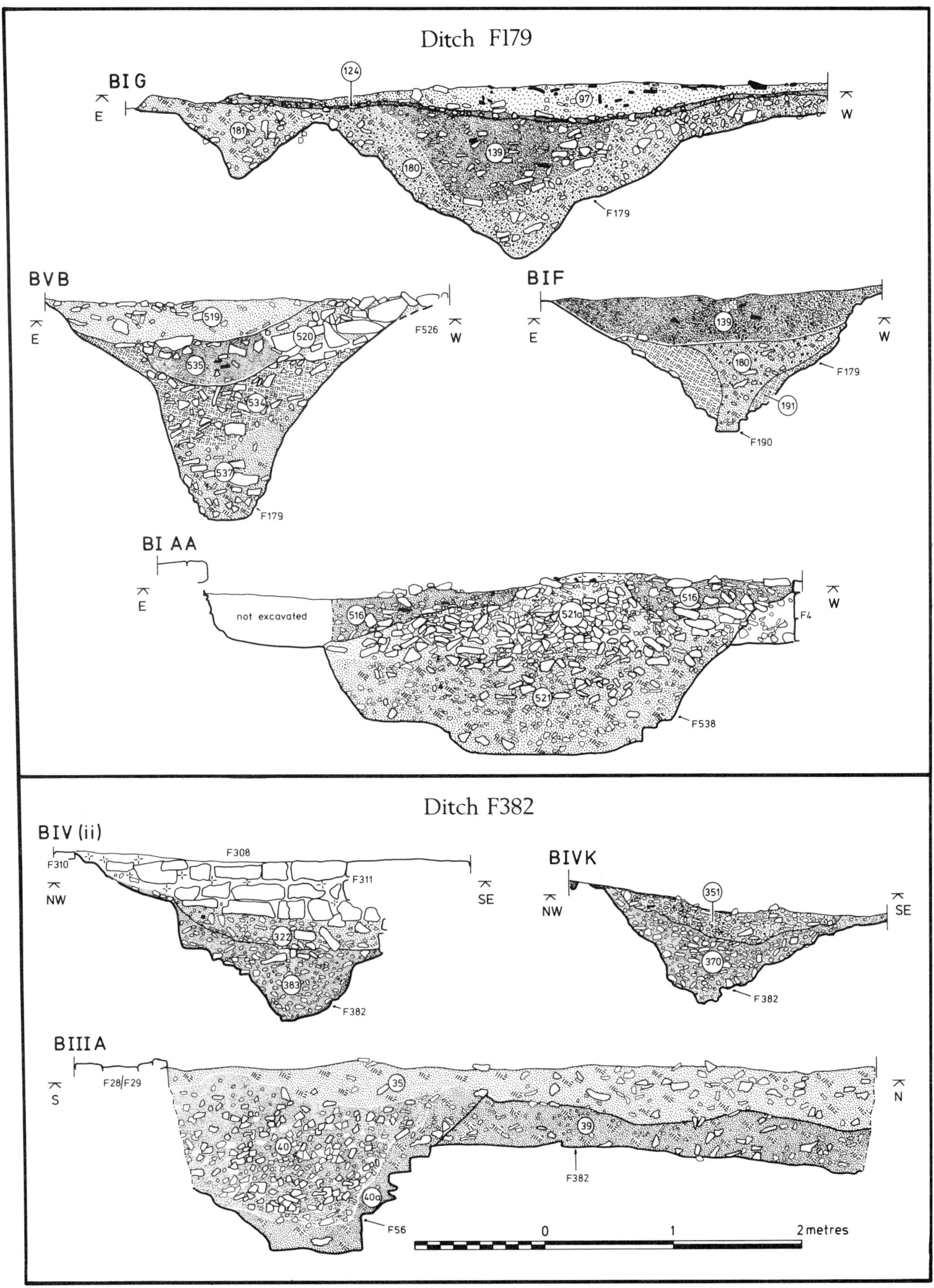

Fig 12 Phases 1–2, sections of ditches F179 and F382, scale 1:40

represented a phase of destruction, as did the thick spreads of clay, rubble and debris occupying the upper levels of the whole ditch, contexts 579 and 1315 (Fig 16, sections S44, S47, S61, S65, and S73). The occasional observation of the possible positions of vertical posts, such as that shown in Figure 16, section S73, suggested that the destruction phase may have involved careful vertical withdrawal of the posts, rather than generalised digging out. No true post pipes, indicative of decay *in situ*, were seen in the many transverse and longitudinal sections that were recorded.

Towards the northern end, where there was a shallow square-ended terminal, the ditch depth decreased (Fig 16, sections S61 and S65) and any junction with the ditch F816, running at right angles from this terminal, was obscured by the foundations of the Roman Structure IX. It is possible however that these two ditches, which were morphologically very similar, were of a similar date. Finds from ditch F584 were few, the primary fills producing one flint core only. The palisade fill, context 594 (Fig 16), contained a further flint core and a Colchester brooch of the late first century AD (Fig 123, no 8). The ultimate fill, context 579, included more worked flints, fragments of Roman glass, pottery, and an iron hobnail. On the western side of the ditch there were extensive traces of a soily layer containing small fragments of Iron Age pottery. This may have been an original ground surface or the remnant of an external bank. In the southern sector less substantial remains of a similar layer were located, also to the east of the ditch.

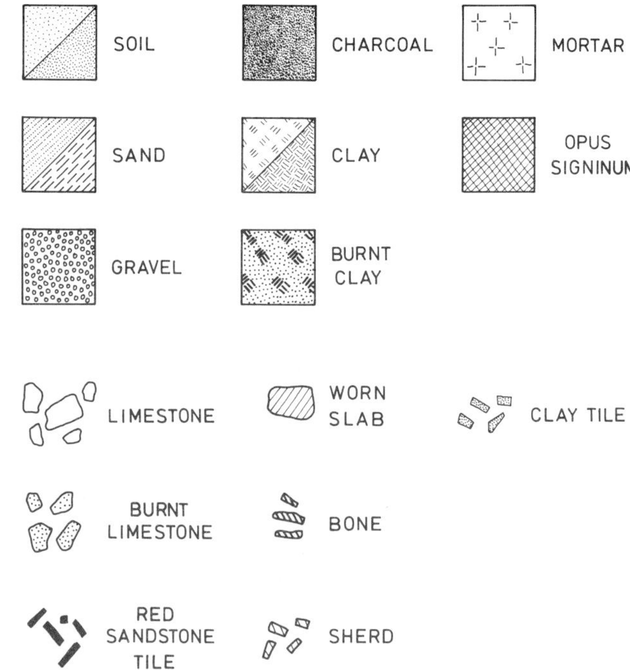

Fig 13 Key to publication conventions used on plans and sections

Ditch F816 Phases 1–2

On the northern margin of the excavated area ran the fourth major linear ditch F816 (Figs 10, 15, and 17).

Fig 14 Ditch F382 segment excavated beneath the wall foundations of Room B, Structure IV, from south west (1977). (Photo: Peter Leach)

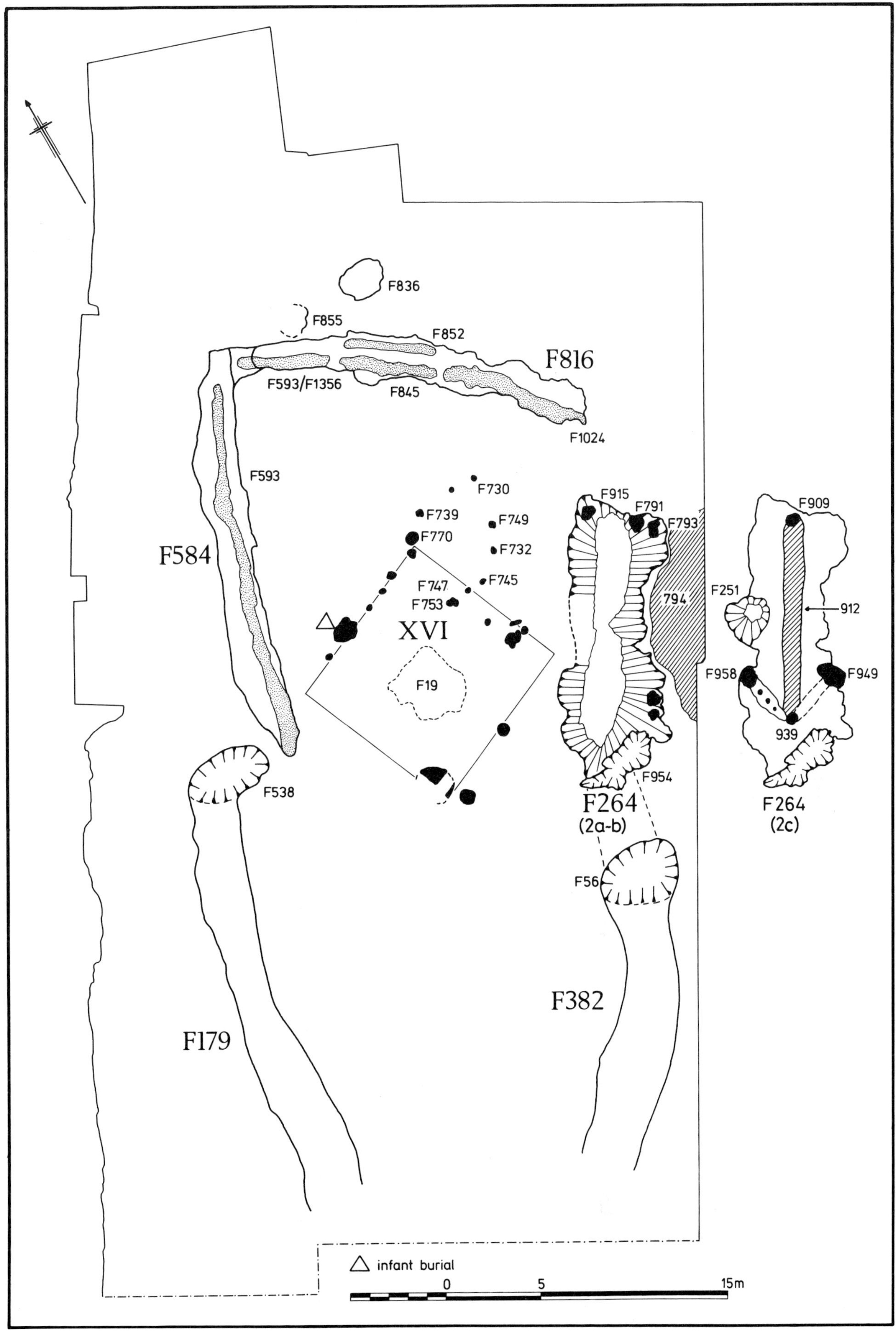

Fig 15 Phase 2 plan, first century AD, scale 1:280

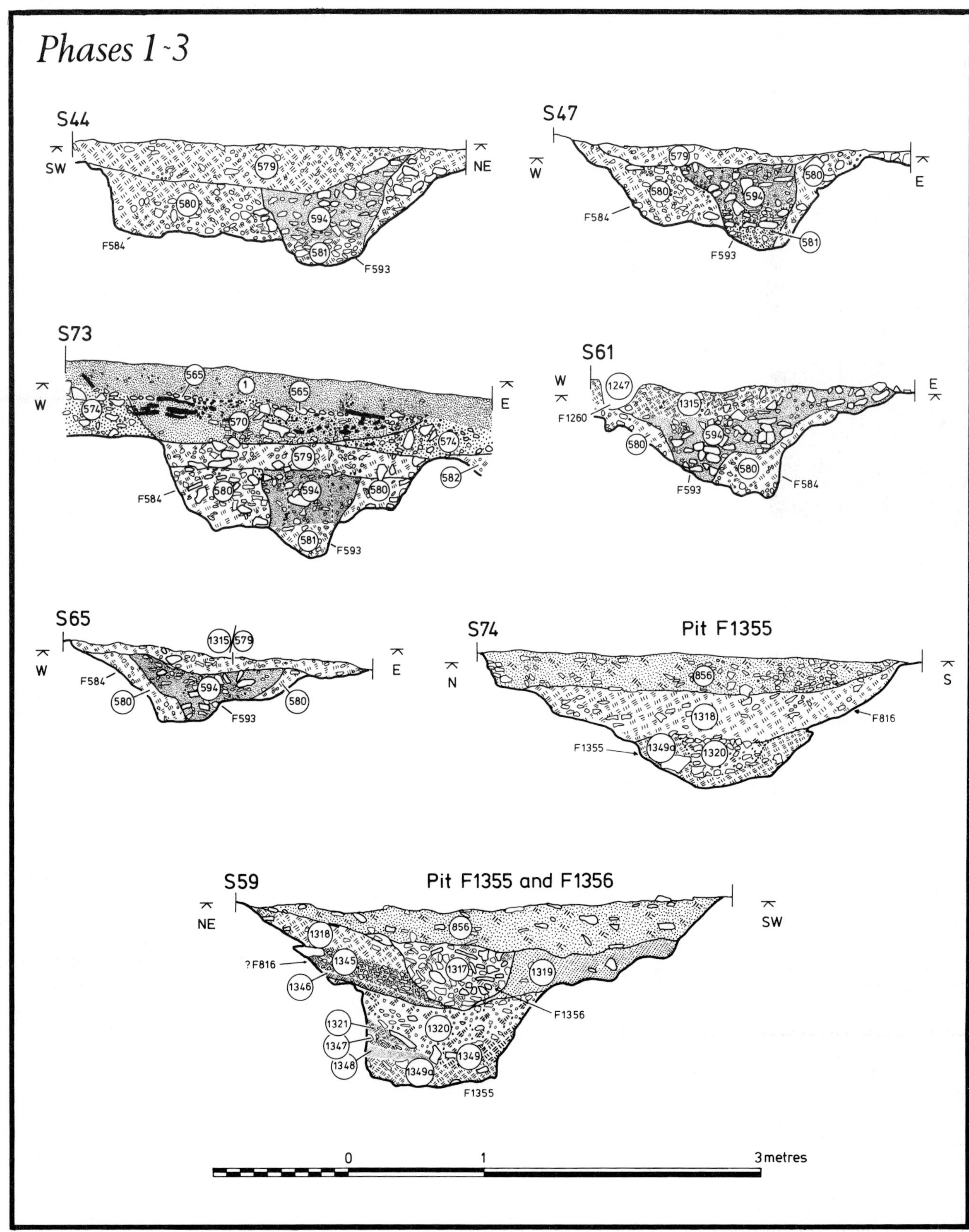

Fig 16 Sections of ditch F584/F816, scale 1:40

Fig 17 Pit F836 and ditch F816 (centre), fully excavated 1978, view from the north. (Photo: Sebastian Rahtz)

However, the earliest feature recognised along its line was pit F1355 which was probably circular in shape and 1.25m deep (Figs 10 and 16, sections S59 and S74). The lower fills comprised the succession of sterile clays, sandy silts, and rubble of contexts 1320, 1321, 1347, 1348, and 1349 (Fig 16, section S59), and the feature may be of Phase 1 earlier prehistoric origin. Adjacent to it, the partly excavated feature F855, filled with the rubble and soil of context 856 (Figs 15 and 18, section S84) may be a similar pit.

The main ditch F816 was on average 1.90m wide, flat bottomed and relatively shallow, 0.40–0.60m deep, (Figs 16 and 18). There may have been an entrance way between its expanded eastern terminal and the northern end of ditch segment F264 (Fig 15). A series of palisade settings within the ditch may have been primary features, as was apparently the case with palisade cut F593 in ditch F584. At the eastern end of ditch F816, a linear cut occupied the southern sector of ditch F1024 (Fig 15). This was a U-shaped cut which was shallower in places than F816, the main ditch (Fig 18, sections S40, S97, and S98), and filled with the loose stony fills of contexts 858 and 1002. Further west two further segments of possible palisade cut were F845 and F593/F1356, while segment F852 ran parallel to F845 on its northern side (see Fig 15). Palisade cuts F845 and F852 were filled with the rubble and soil of contexts 844, 846, and 853 (Fig 18, sections S84 and S99). Context 846 contained evidence of burning and intentional deposition of material. None of the trenches showed traces of post positions in any of the many longitudinal and transverse sections recorded; any posts appear to have been withdrawn, as in the case of the other palisades discussed above. At the western end, trench F1356, cutting the primary fills of ditch F816, above the earlier pit F1355 (Figs 15 and 16, section S59), probably equates with the palisade cut F593.

The primary fillings of ditch F816 were context 849 (Fig 18, sections S84 and S97–S99) and contexts 1318, 1319, 1345, and 1346 (Fig 16, sections S59 and S74); they contained no finds apart from a few flint artefacts and scraps of unidentified metal. The palisade trench fills included a scatter of small Iron Age sherds, a fragment of iron, and from near the top of cut F1024 (Fig 15), a Theodosian coin. This area of the ditch lay beneath the post-Roman Phase 7 bank and this late coin is presumably related to disturbance of the upper fills during this period of activity. The more irregular slot F1008 (Fig 18, section S40) was cut from a higher level and filled with burnt limestone debris; it is dated to the post-Roman period and will be considered further in chapter 4.

The removal and abandonment of the palisades, which must have preceded the construction of the northern side of Structure XVII in Phase 3, was marked by clay and rubble deposits above the previous fillings. These deposits included context 803 (Fig 18, sections S97–9). An equivalent to the west was context 856 (Fig 16, sections S59 and S74). In contrast to the final filling layers of the other three ditches F179, F382, and F584, those in F816 contained no finds.

Ditch F264 and pit F251, Phases 2–3

A complex of slots, gullies and pits was contained within a major ditch segment F264 (Fig 19), which was located north of ditch F382/F56 (Fig 15). It appears to have been constructed later than ditch F382 at the beginning of Phase 2, and throughout this phase and the next, internal features were added and modified.

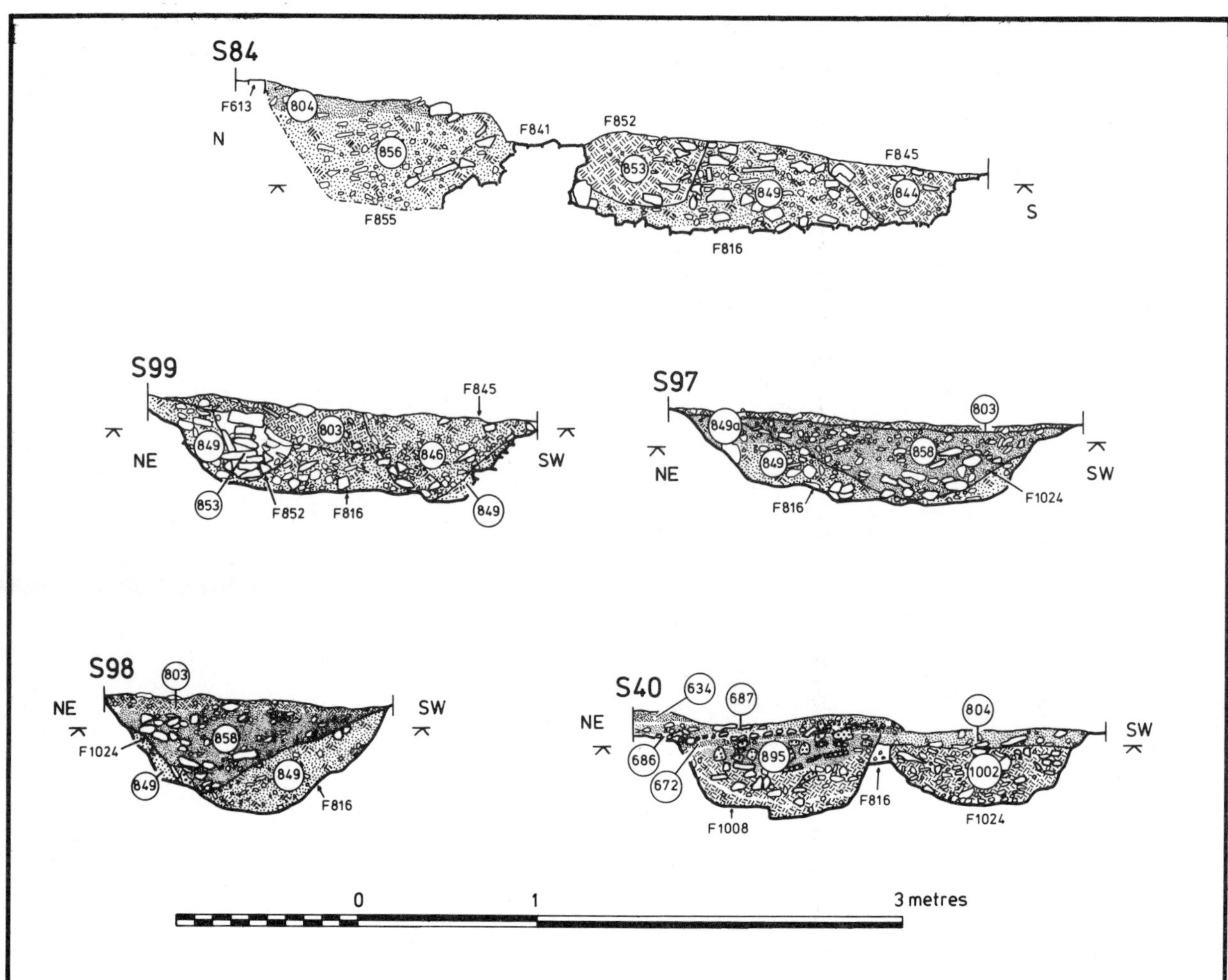

Fig 18 Phases 1–2, sections of ditch F816, scale 1:40

The sequence of pits and structures appears to have functioned alongside the timber enclosure or building, Structure XVI, lying nearby to the west. The ditch was totally excavated over three seasons, but locally the stratification had been truncated and disturbed quite severely by the insertion of Structure II, the Roman temple, and the later post-Roman stone Structure VIII of Phase 7 (see Figs 23 and 29).

Phase 2a

The truncation of the northern end of ditch F382 by the cut F954 at the southern termination of ditch segment F264, and the morphological similarity of these cuts with the Phase 2–3 square cut ditches F584 and F816 of the northern enclosure (Fig 15) suggests that F264 belongs to this phase rather than with the more weathered ditches to the south, which have been dated to Phase 1. The configuration of the ditch with its uneven edges and irregular shelving sides is shown in Figures 20 and 21. Primary deposits included context 794, thick remnants of bank material on the outer, eastern lip (Figs 15 and 21, section S100), context 767, layers of primary weathering detritus in the ditch base (Fig 21, sections S54 and S100; Fig 65, sections S1 and S38), and context 953 (Fig 65, sections S58). These contained one unretouched flint flake only. Fairly soon after initial construction, three post pits were dug at the northern end of the ditch F915 (Figs 15 and 20), and on the higher platform ledge of F791 and F793. The last two pits possessed fillings which incorporated flecks of charcoal. At the south-east end, further post pits F950 and F952 (Figs 20 and 65, section S47) were located similarly on a platform ledge and probably were contemporary.

Phase 2b

Following construction, initial phases of use were evidenced by the deposits of weathering debris and apparently deliberate dumps of mixed rubble and soil of context 925 (Fig 21, section S100) and context 267 (Fig 65, sections S1 and S38). Context 925 and other similar deposits contained two iron projectile heads (including Fig 112, no 1), a riveted copper alloy strip and an antler tool (Fig 146, no 4). Later deposits in the same series included deliberate spreads of pottery, charcoaly soil and animal bone at the northern end, eg context 928 (Fig 21, section S54). A comparable deposit, context 955, at the southern end within the depression F954 (Fig 20) contained animal bones and a shale bracelet fragment.

Phase 2c

Cutting the major deposits of Phase 2b (contexts 267 and 767) context 912, a longitudinal trench filled with rubble, was constructed possibly to support a timber

Fig 19 Ditch F264 (north east portion) and pit F251, fully excavated 1978, view from the east. (Photo: Sebastian Rahtz)

palisade (Fig 15, plan; Fig 21, sections S54 and S100; Fig 65, section S1). No individual post holes were recognised apart from F909 at the northern end. The southern end had been disturbed by post-Roman Structure VIII, but terminated at a narrower palisade trench, F938, aligned south-east to north-west (Fig 65, sections S1 and S38). This held a deep post pit, F958 (Figs 20 and 64, section S1) at its north-western limit and context 939, a possible post setting, at its junction with context 912 (Fig 15). A second arm of narrow palisade trench may have extended from context 939 north-eastwards to another large post pit, F949, cut into the eastern margin of F264 (Figs 15 and 65, section S47). The main rubble packing, context 912, may have derived from the initial digging of pit F251 (Figs 15, 20, and 21, section S82) which took place during this phase. Context 912 contained a flint flake, an iron projectile head (Fig 112, no 3), and bone and antler tools (Fig 146, nos 3 and 7), while post pits F949 and F958 produced Iron Age potsherds and a fragment of iron.

Within pit F251, which was dug at a roughly central location cutting the western margin of F264, a short interval of rapid primary weathering, context 927 (Fig 21, section S82), was followed by the early deposits of contexts 924 and 926 (Fig 21, section S82) and context 931 (not illus). These deliberate deposits contained an iron projectile head (Fig 112, no 2) and bolt heads (Fig 113, nos 1–3); a rosette brooch (Fig 123, no 4) and a penannular brooch (Fig 125, no 8), both of which can be dated to the first half of the first century AD.

Following some deposition associated with the longitudinal palisade, the northern terminal-post F909 (Fig 15) and, probably the posts of the major palisade itself, were removed and their fills, contexts 908 and 912, sealed by a second phase of weathering and other deposits. At the northern end of F264 these included contexts 757 (not illus) and 758 (Fig 21, sections S54 and S100) as well as, over the fill of F909, deposits 786 and 907 (Fig 21, section S54). Contexts 757 and 758 contained Iron Age pottery, four flint artefacts, eight iron projectile heads (including Fig 112, nos 5, 6, 8, and 9; Fig 113, no 5), two Dobunnic coins and scraps of copper alloy sheet. No equivalent horizon was traced beyond the disturbance caused by Structure VIII unless the context 262 (Fig 65, section S38) represents a conflation of the two layers 733 and 758 (Fig 21, sections S54 and S100), which were more easily distinguished in the northern sector of F264.

Phase 2d

A temporary phase of abandonment in this area, or at least a cessation of deposition, is suggested by the substantial weathering detritus, context 733 (Fig 21, sections S54 and S100). This deposit contained a flint flake, three iron projectile heads (Fig 112, nos 4 and 7; Fig 113, nos 4 and 6), other fragments of iron and a penannular brooch pin (Fig 125, no 8). Context 262 may be the equivalent of this in the southern half of ditch F264 (Fig 65, sections S1 and S38), but this contained only some pottery. The possibly multi-phased deposit context 956, also divorced by Structure VIII from deposits further north, probably continued this horizon fur-

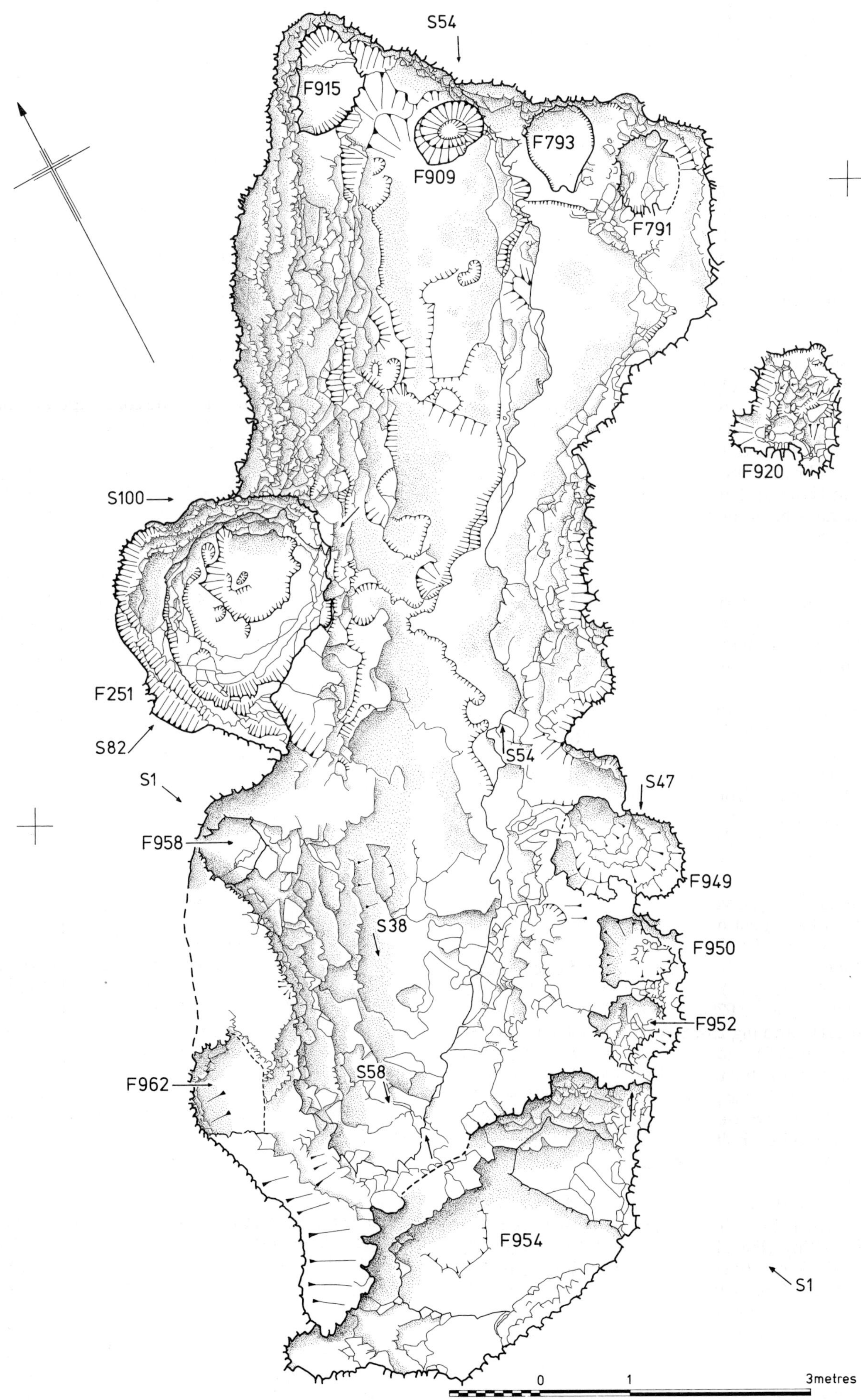

S54
F915
F909
F793
F791
F920
S100
F251
S82
S54
S47
S1
F958
F949
S38
F950
F952
F962
S58
F954
S1
0
1
3metres

ther south above depression F954 to the south termination of ditch F264 (Fig 65, section S58). Pit F251, context 923, which contained Iron Age pottery and animal bone, was probably contemporary with these more widespread deposits (Fig 21, section S82).

Phase 3a

Activities in the ditch F264 area now may be divided into two sub-phases, denoted 3a(i) and 3a(ii). In Phase 3a(i) deposition of weathering products, soil, and artefacts, continued over the northern sector of F264, context 726 (Fig 21, sections S54 and S100). This was darker than the underlying layer 733 and contained later pottery, along with an early first-century AD coin, two iron projectile heads (Figs 112, no 10; and 113, no 17), a copper alloy spiral-headed pin (Fig 131, no 2), a bone spindle whorl (Fig 143, no 6) and various objects of copper alloy and iron. No precise equivalent continuation south of the foundations of the post-Roman Structure VIII was defined. Context 461 (Fig 65, sections S1 and S47) at the southern end was a deposit containing pottery and bone and may have been contemporary, as also may have been the upper part of context 262 (Fig 65, section S38).

Further deposition within the focal pit F251 lay above the secondary weathering, context 923, which may have been recut in part (Fig 21, section S82). Context 910 contained many artefacts, apparently ritually deposited, with context 911 above producing early Roman pottery and animal bone. The finds from context 910 included Roman pottery, bone, charcoal, eight iron projectile heads (including Figs 112, no 11; and 113, nos 11–16 inclusive), a quern fragment, and a whetstone. The latest deposit of this phase in F251 was context 258, largely composed of weathering debris, and containing two iron bolt heads (Fig 113, nos 7 and 8) and other fragments of iron. Thus the focal pit had been filled and covered over prior to the remodelling of features in the depression remaining over ditch F264 during Phase 3a(ii).

This remodelling involved the insertion of a further series of gullies, post holes and stone settings which have been grouped as Structure XVIII (Figs 22 and 23). Parallel slightly curved alignments of drystone footings F788 and F789 (Fig 23) lay immediately north of two short ditch segments F756a and F756b (Fig 21, sections S54 and S100, and Fig 23). Segment F756b cut into the top fills of pit F251 and contained large fragments of amphora, possibly the remains of a complete vessel set into this feature. These pits, which appear to have been designed to receive deposits rather than posts, also contained two iron bolt heads (Fig 113, nos 9 and 10) and scraps of copper alloy, and between them lay a patch of concentrated charcoal and ash. Running at right angles to ditch segments F756a and F756b ran a longer ditch, F751, which displayed clear traces of a palisade setting (Fig 21, sections S54 and S100), the small pit F913 may have been associated (Fig 23). The latter contained early Roman pottery, animal bones, and charcoal, and was cut by the footings of the post-Roman Structure VIII.

Fig 20 Phase 2, plan of ditch segment F264, scale 1:60

In the southern sector of the almost filled ditch F264, a large pit F945 (Fig 23) had been cut by the south walls of Structure VIII (Fig 65, section S58) and was probably of this sub-phase. Further south-west a gully or palisade trench, F965, continued towards the pit F342, which lay below the footings of post-Roman Structure III (Fig 23). The gully F965 was sealed by the clay layer context 456, similar to context 461 and to context 255 within the confines of the Structure VIII wall footings (Fig 65, sections S1 and S58).

Within the confines of the wall footings of the later Structure VIII was a single deposit of clay, context 255 (Figs 22 and 23), probably belonging to Phase 3a(ii). Such a dating would be upheld by the finds which included three late first-century AD coins, a Nauheim derivative brooch (Fig 123, no 2) and three 'South-western' type brooches (Figs 123, no 10; and 124, nos 1 and 5), all of late first-century date, and one coin of the early second century AD. This thick homogeneous deposit is quite distinct from the contemporary fillings of F264 to its north and south and one possibility is that the clay represents the lining and silting within a feature, perhaps a pool of water, confined by timber, the construction subsequently having been totally destroyed by the foundations of Structure VIII, laid almost exactly over it. Such a postulated feature might have survived through Phases 4 and 5a–b (see Figs 29, 33, and 35). However, if this were the case, then any finds datable to these later phases must have been contained in contexts that were totally destroyed when the floor and footings of Structure VIII were inserted during Phase 7. Outside this forerunner of Structure VIII, to the south and south-west, context 942, a thin deposit of gritty mortar, may mark a building level associated with the erection of both this structure and the temple, Structure II of Phase 4. This deposit, and the sequence above it of contexts 451, 454 and 456 (Fig 65, sections S1 and S58), provide further clues to the existence of a structure here although all these contexts were devoid of diagnostic finds (see chapter 3).

Pit F836 Phases 2–3

Outside the confines of the Phase 2 and 3 ditch F816 and the subsequent palisades, the only area to be excavated to pre-Roman levels was the area lying below Room A of Roman Structure IX. Here was found and excavated deep circular pit F836 (Figs 15 and 24), which was similar in many respects to the pit F251, associated with the later phases of use of the ditch segment F264 described above. A close dating to Phase 2 or 3 cannot be attempted owing to the lack of any clear relationship with the ditch F816. Immediately north of the pit lay a series of shallow oval scoops and pits which continued unexcavated beyond the eastern confines of the later Room A of Structure IX.

The pit was roughly oval in plan with vertical or undercut sides (Fig 24, plan and section); it measured 2.40 × 2.0m and was 1.80m deep. Above a layer of primary weathering detritus in the base of the pit context 851 were a series of deposits containing probably votive material. The mixed, often banded and multi-coloured layers of contexts 842, 847, 848, and 850, included orange and grey-green clay bands interspersed with ash and charcoal. Unlike pit F251, the

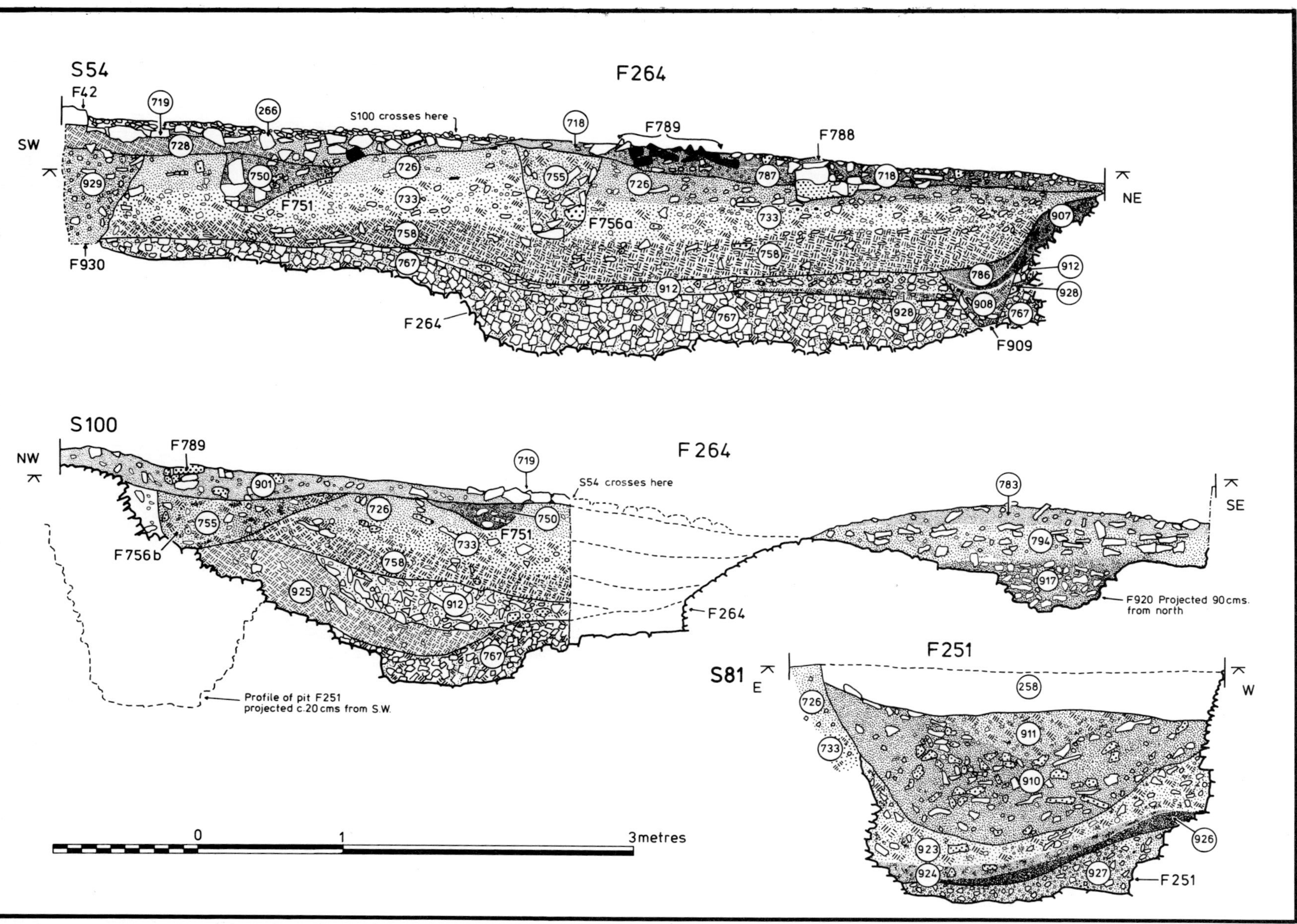

Fig 21 Phases 2–3, sections of ditch segment F264, scale 1:40

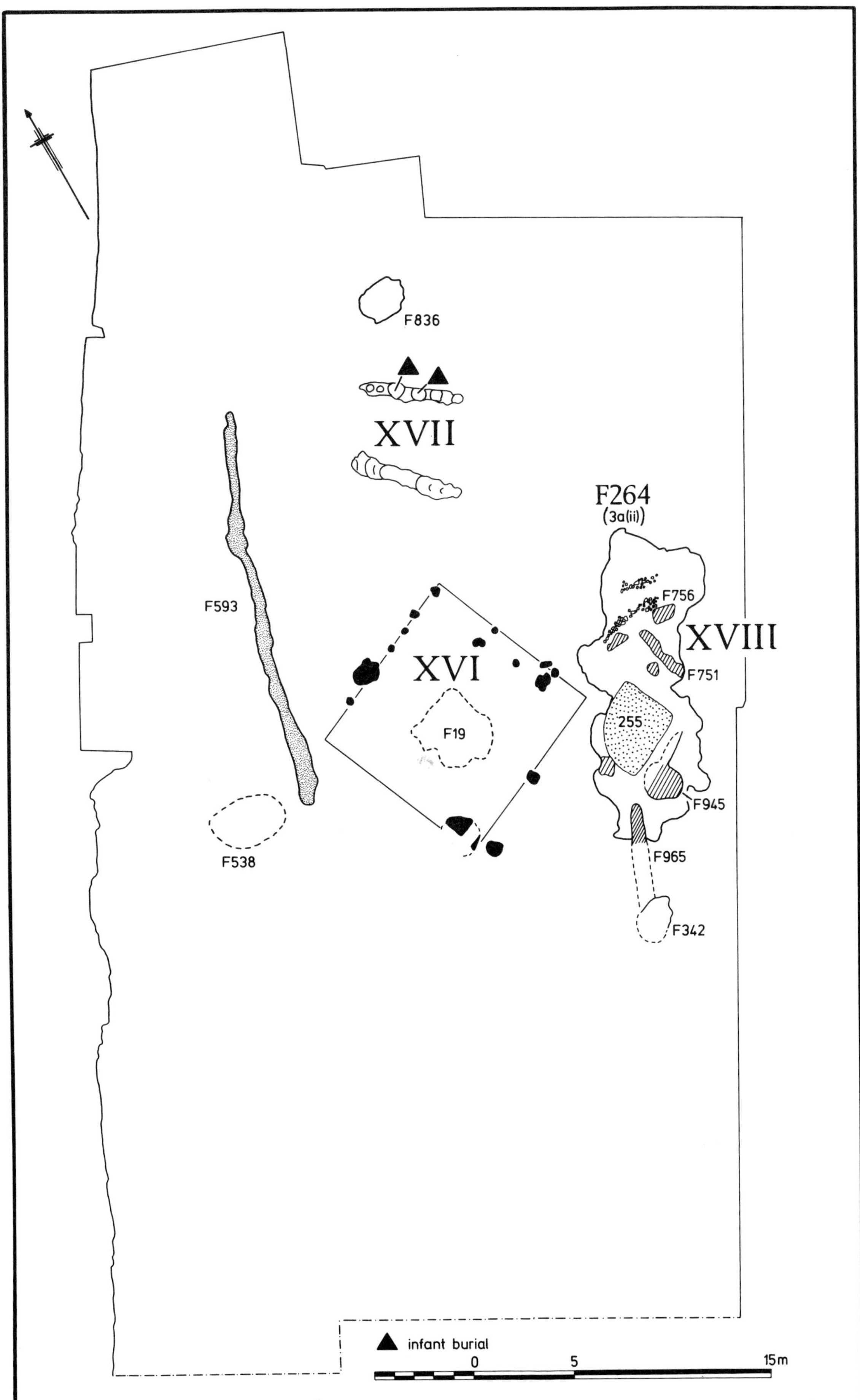

Fig 22 Phase 3 plan, late first to mid-second century AD, scale 1:280

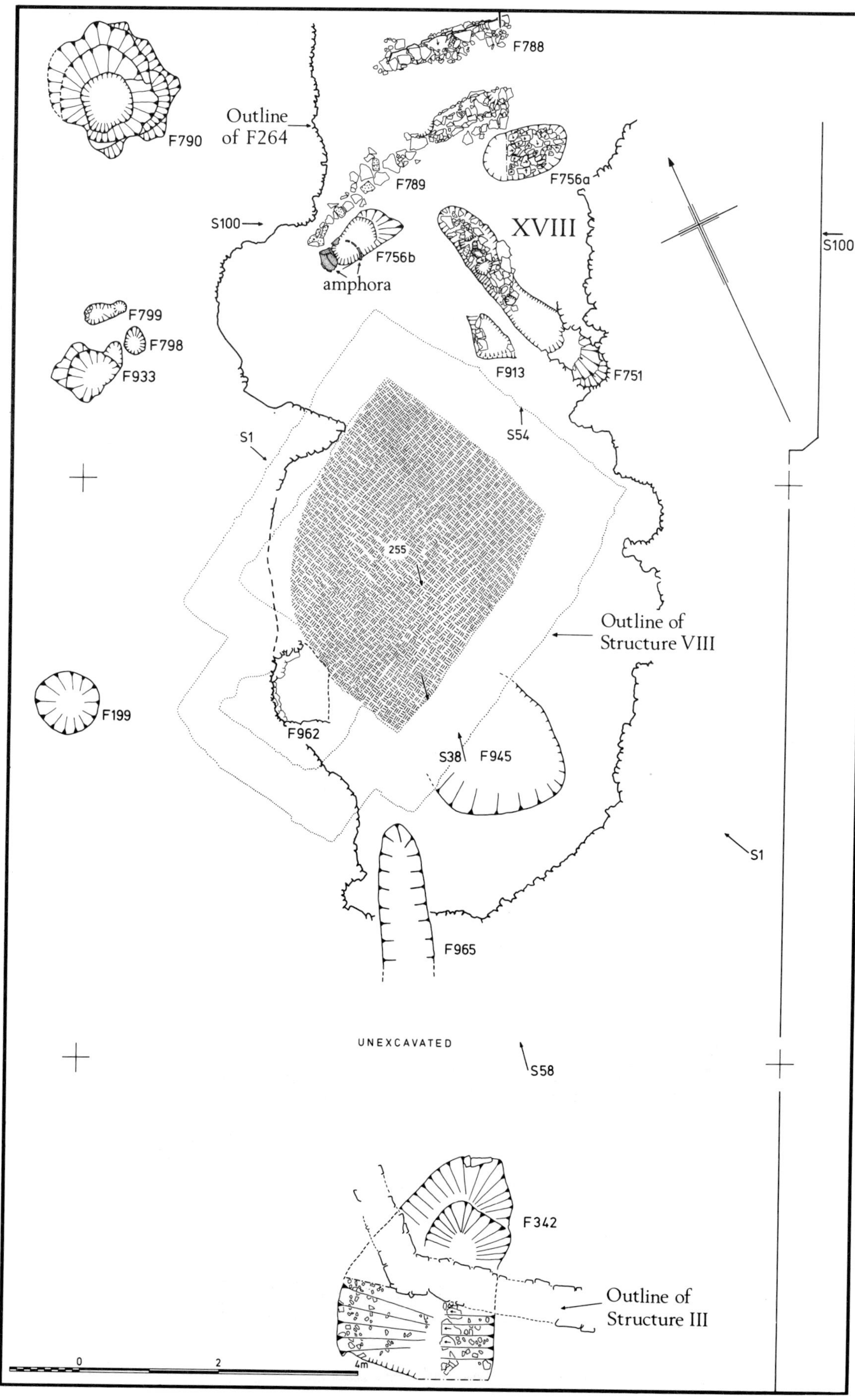

Fig 23 Phase 3, plan of ditch segment F264 and Structure XVIII, scale 1:80

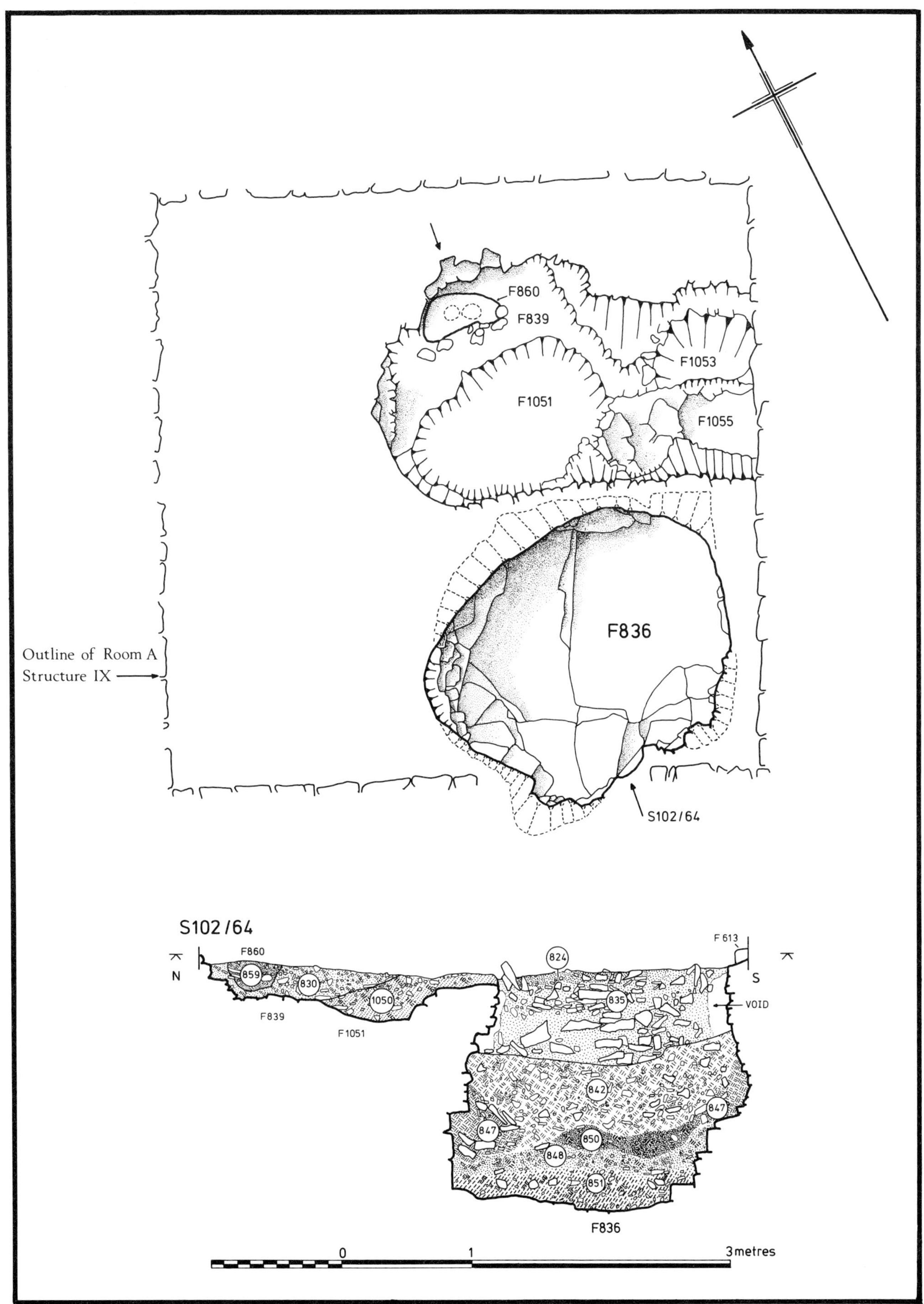

Fig 24 Phases 2–3, pit F836, scale 1:60

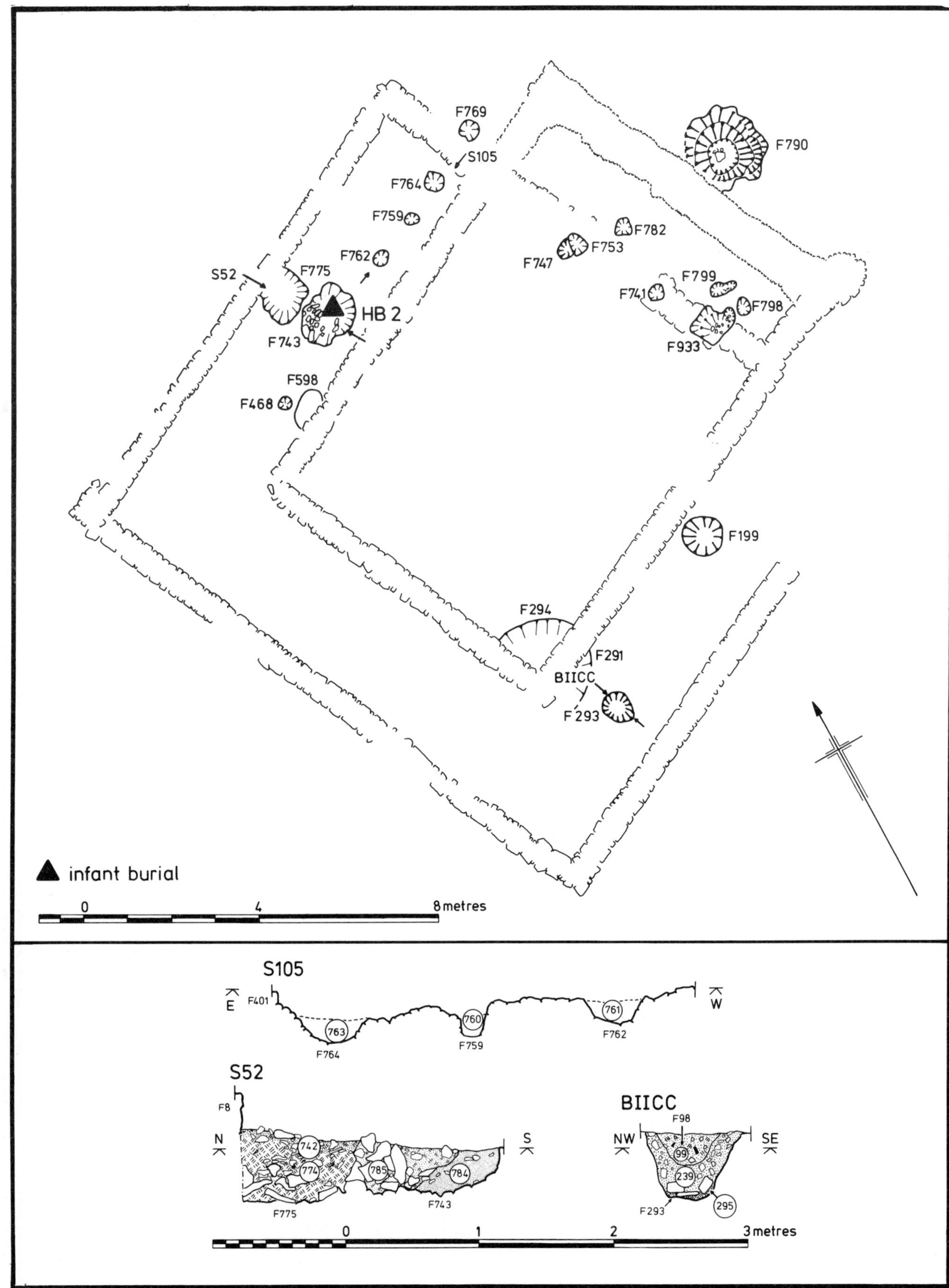

Fig 25 Phases 2–3, Structure XVI, scale 1:40

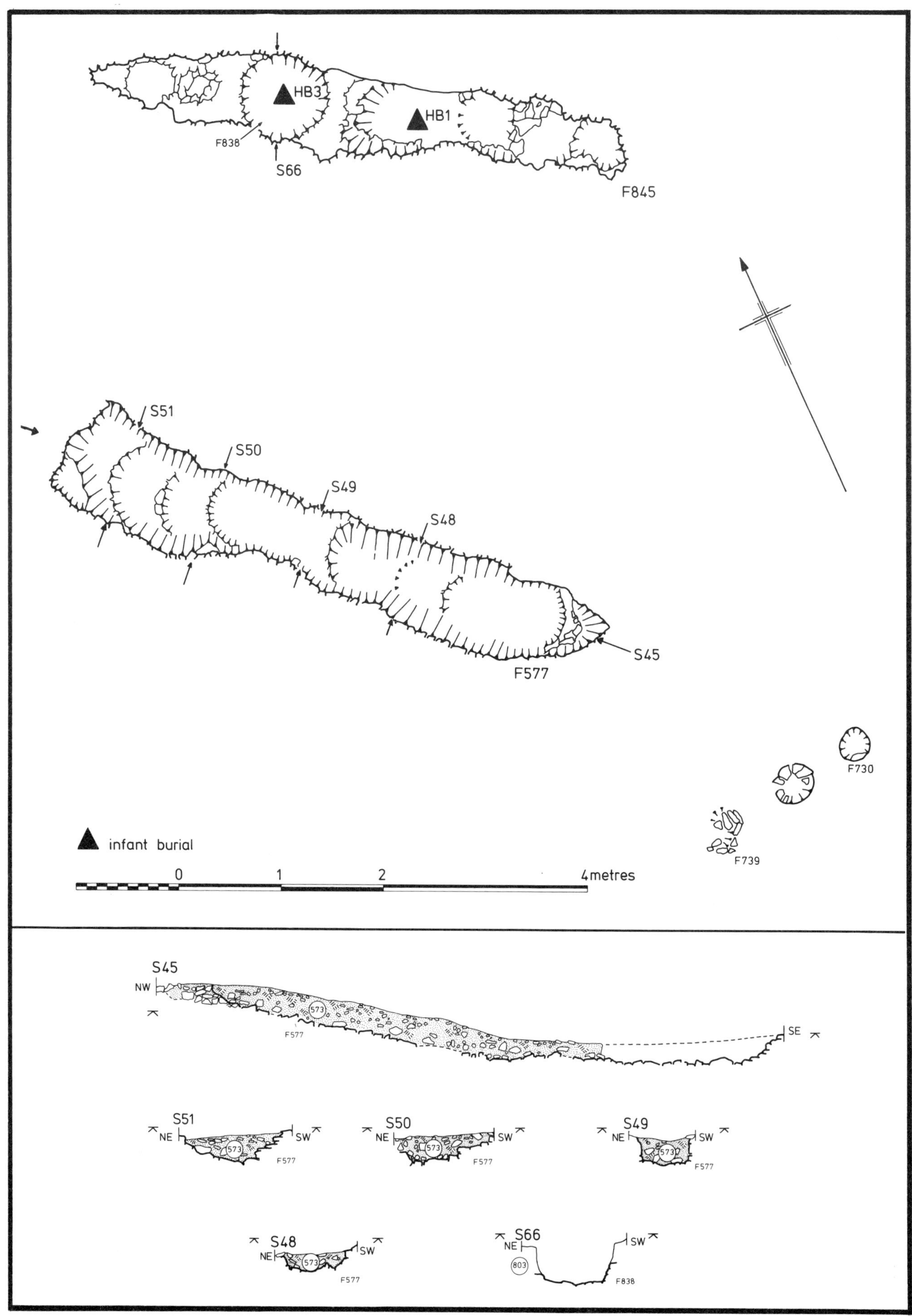

Fig 26 Phase 3, Structure XVII, scale 1:50

lower deposits contained no artefacts except a fragment of iron, but a copper alloy toilet article (Fig 135, no 8), was found in the uppermost rubbly clay of context 842. Above the clay layers was a thick deposit of very loose large limestone rubble blocks, context 835. This contained fragments of iron and two copper alloy brooches: one of first-century date and one pre-Flavian (Fig 123, nos 5 and 7). This rubble deposit may mark a stage of abandonment or obliteration of the pit.

The use of pits and scoops to the north of the pit may have been contemporary with, or earlier than, the functioning of pit F836, although clear relationships have not survived (Fig 24). Earliest was F1051, a circular scoop whose fill, context 1050, was cut by ditch F1055, which in turn was cut by a minor pit F1053. The early pit, F1051, was also cut, or rather recut in part, by shallow circular pit F839, filled by context 830 (Fig 24, section), which in turn contained a deeper portion, F860, filled by context 859, a mixture of Jurassic fossils, flint and pebbles, possibly originally set around a post (Fig 24, section). The flints included two scrapers, a further possible scraper, a piercer, a core, and 18 unretouched flakes; the diagnostic items were of Neolithic to Early Bronze Age type (Saville, in archive). Their presence may indicate that these shallow features were rather earlier than the pit, of the first century AD, located next to them and they have been allocated to Phase 1 (Fig 11).

Above the rubble deposit context 835 in pit F836, and continuing above context 1050 in F1051, was a layer of stony silt context 824 (Fig 24). This contained a 'South-western' type brooch of *c* AD 100 (Fig 124, no 3), a glass melon bead of Claudian to Antonine date (Fig 126, no 7), a probable iron stylus, and a decorated copper alloy strip (Fig 153, no 10). Thus, the main pit appears to have gone out of use during the first century AD and to have been obliterated fairly soon thereafter.

Structure XVI, Phases 2–3

Beneath the remains of the Roman temple, Structure II, a series of post holes and shallow pits were found, cut into the weathered natural limestone surface. These formed two sides of a square or rectangular enclosure or structure, which possessed a similar alignment to that of the later Roman temple, Structure II (Figs 25 and 29). Below the floor of the later western ambulatory was a row of six post holes, F759, F762, F764, and F769, and two cut within F743 and F468, which were on average, 0.20m deep (Fig 25, plan and section S105). At right angles to this row, and lying below the foundations of the later temple portico was a double row of more shallow holes: F741, F747 or F753, F782, F798, F799, and F933. On the eastern side of the later temple site a few larger holes of varying depth were located (Fig 25, plan and section BII CC). Reconstruction of any building is difficult but the most economical hypothesis involves a postulated square structure or, more likely, owing to the slightness of the post holes, an enclosure, with sides measuring 8.20m. In this case the post rows on the southern and eastern sides might underlie the equivalent walls of the cella of the later temple, which were not removed during the excavation. Four of the post holes, F759 and F764 on the west; F799 and F933 to the north, contained fragments of Final Iron Age pottery, and post hole F933 also yielded an iron projectile head (Fig 113, no 20) similar to those found in deposits within pit F251 located nearby (see Fig 15). One of the western post holes, F743, filled by context 785, cut the eastern of a pair of adjacent sub-circular pits (Fig 25, section S52). The slightly smaller pit, F775, contained a little Late Iron Age pottery and a piece of burnt flint, while its neigbour, F743, had been used for the deposition of a human infant burial (HB2, Fig 183) and an almost complete carinated Dobunnic jar (Fig 166, no 75), together with some animal remains. The pits appear to have predated Structure XVI, but may have been dug immediately prior to its construction in order that the infant inhumation might serve as a foundation deposit.

Immediately north of the proposed square enclosure lay a deep irregular rock-cut pit F790 (Figs 25 and 34, section BIIC). This contained charcoal flecks only and may be considerably earlier than the Late Iron Age structure just described. Similar but more shallow rock-cut features, F920, F921, and F1002, lay immediately north and east of F264 (Fig 11). The latter F920 was sealed by a layer of possible bank material associated with early phases of the use of the ditch segment F264 (Fig 21, section S100), and the features are therefore provisionally assigned to Phase 1.

Further north were a series of shallow post holes which produced no finds but were sealed by the cobbled surfaces of the Roman Structure II temple forecourt. The position of these holes F730, F732, F739, F745, F749, F770, and F747 or F753, is shown in Figures 15 and 25. They form a roughly penannular setting which may have supported the posts of a circular building. However, the relationship between the intercutting post holes F747 and F753, and thus the relationship between this small building and the square Structure XVI, could not be established.

Structure XVII, Phase 3

Cutting the fills of former ditch F816 and, in particular, the line of the southern palisade slot F845 (Fig 15), was a line of poorly defined post holes (Fig 26). The clearest individual post pit, F838, was 0.83m in diameter and 0.40m in depth (Fig 26, section S66). It contained in its base the inhumation of a human infant (HB3) and the remains of a second infant burial (HB1) was recovered further east within the secondary fillings of F845 (Fig 27). To the south of this row of substantial post holes was a gully of similar length but lying at a slight angle to F845. This gully, F577, was fairly regular in depth (*c* 0.25m) but ran down the line of slope (Fig 26, plan and section S45). The impressions of a series of adjacent timbers were visible in its base. Taken together, these two slots or gullies may have contained the posts supporting a trapezoidal structure 3.80m wide on the west and flaring to a width of 4.60m on the east side. No associated floor or exterior levels had survived.

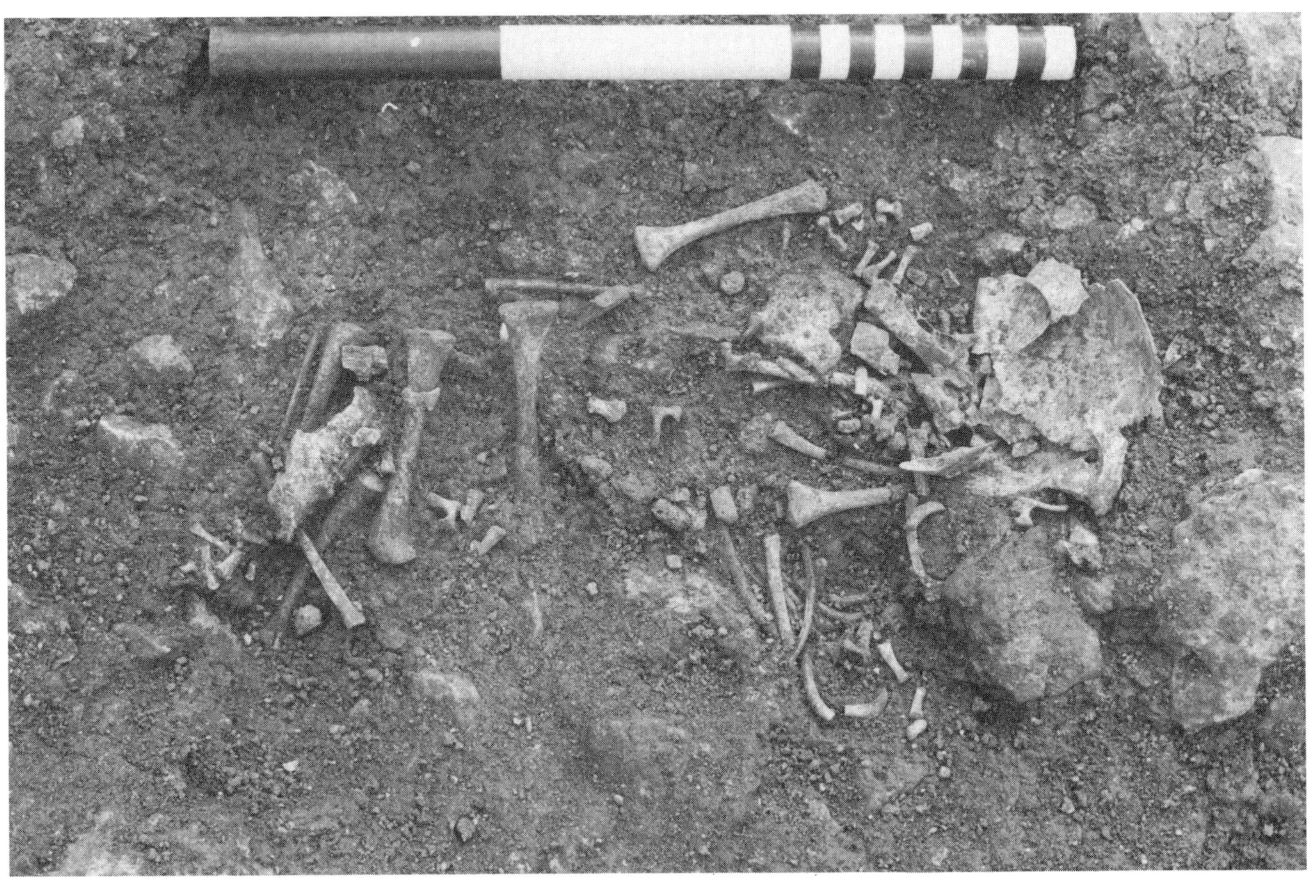

Fig 27 Infant burial HB1 in secondary fill of F845, view from the south. (Photo: Sebastian Rahtz)

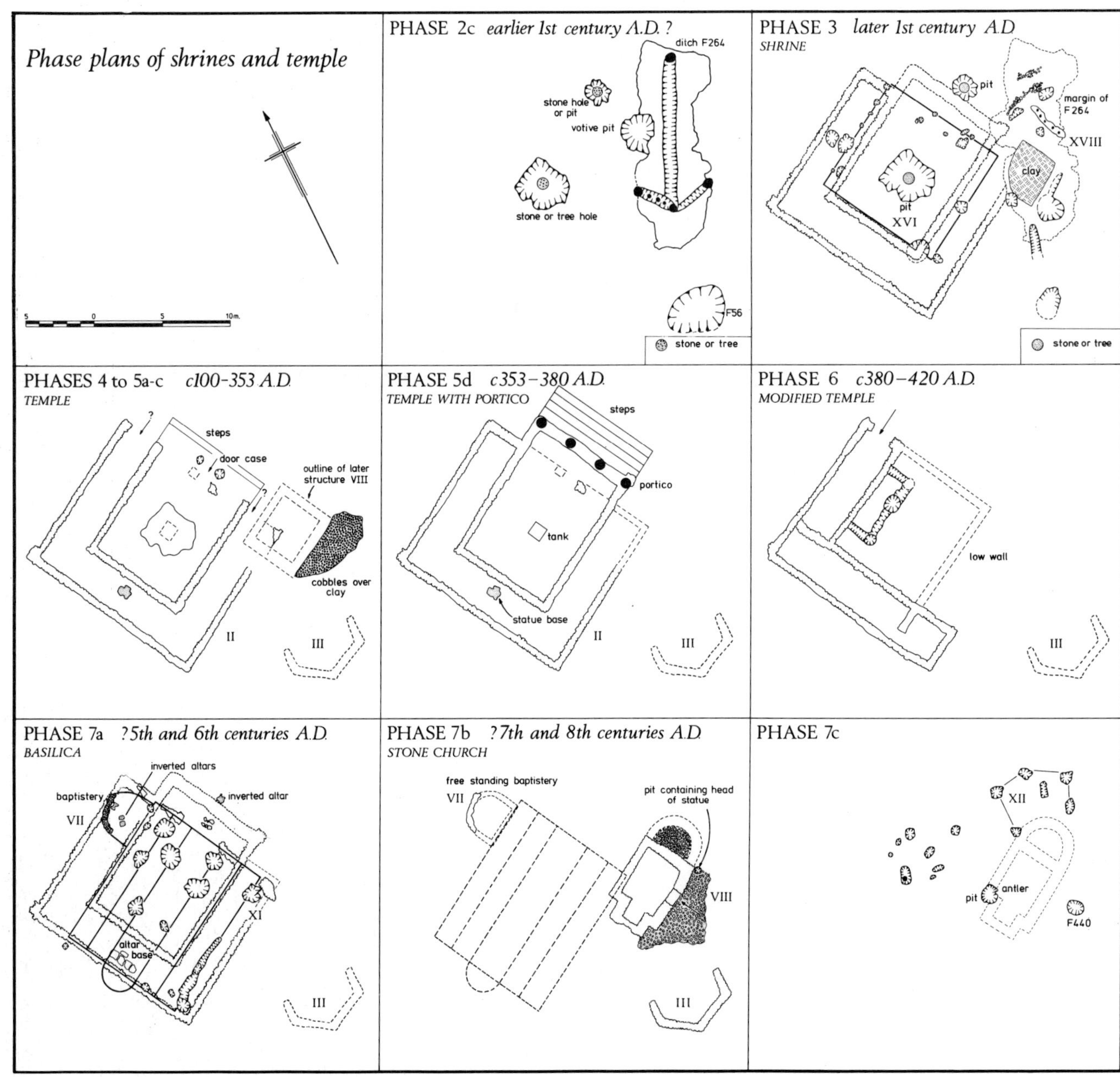

Fig 29 Phase plans of shrines and temple (Structures XVI, II, III, VII, and XII), scale 1:500

3 The Romano-British temple complex

Structure II

Phases 4 and 5a–c

The compilation of a full archaeological description of the temple building, Structure II (Fig 28) is hindered by the almost total absence of stratification relating to its construction and first stages of use. There is circumstantial evidence from other buildings, and from the finds, to be discussed in detail below, which suggests that the temple was constructed in the second century, probably immediately following the dismantling of the Final Iron Age shrine (Structure XVI) at the end of the first, or the beginning of the second century AD. The floor and activity layers that did survive within the temple area relate to further phases of use in the final years of the fourth century and beyond (Phases 6 and 7), while the main Roman floor surfaces and levels appear to have been destroyed prior to the modifications carried out in Phase 6. The situation can best be appreciated by studying the reconstructed profile through the temple (Fig 30) which shows that the temple was constructed on a considerable slope. Assuming that the internal floor was level, and not stepped, then that level would have been 0.30m above the modern ground surface in the centre of the cella, and 0.65m above it in the area of the Phase 5d portico.

The first stone temple, Structure II (see Figs 29, 32, 33, and 35) comprised an almost square building (14 × 12m externally) which possessed a rectangular cella (7 × 8m internally) flanked, on three sides only, by ambulatories which were 2.30m in width. The cella (Room E) and ambulatories on the west (Room C), south (Room A), and east (Room D), were supported by stone walls whose footings survived to a maximum of three courses. These were of squared mortared oolitic limestone facing blocks, enclosing a randomly distributed rubble core. Where there were no underlying earlier features the footings had been inset into the weathered clay and limestone natural ground surface. The walls of the cella and ambulatories were of similar thickness, averaging 0.60m wide.

The west ambulatory (Room C) was bounded by walls F8 to the west, and F16 to the east, and was terminated to the north by wall F401, which ran into the south ambulatory (Room A/B). This was defined by the walls F3 and F7 to the north and south respectively, while at the junction of walls F8 and F7 there was an additional exterior foundation. This may have been the site of a corner buttress to provide extra support above the fill of the Iron Age ditch F584, or it may represent the only surviving trace of a system of exterior pilasters. The third side of the ambulatory (Room D) was bounded by walls F9 and F10 to the east and west, but no traces of any north end-wall, or footings for one were found. However the north-east corner of the temple had been destroyed almost completely by the construction of the stone built Structure VIII in Phase 7 (Figs 29 and 32). Within this later building, a fragment of foundation material and corner walling, context 436, survived and was subsequently buttressed by F232. This fragment

Fig 28 Structure II, the temple, extent of the excavation in 1977, view from the south. (Photo: Peter Leach)

could have been the junction of the eastern outer ambulatory wall, F9, and a north end wall to the eastern ambulatory, but no trace of any wall foundation or trench was found in the area surviving between the cella wall, F10, and the west wall of Structure VIII. It may be that there was an original entrance located here (see Fig 35), but in this case one would have expected a balancing doorway into the northern end of the other side ambulatory (Room C). The northern wall, F401, of Room C (Fig 32) could have been a later insertion, although there was no indication from the surviving courses of masonry to suggest that this was so. However, a rebuild of the northern end of the cella wall, F16, in Phase 5d (see below), associated with the construction of the portico, might indicate bonding-in with a new terminal wall for the western ambulatory at that time.

The remains of the original north-east corner is represented by some layers of foundation material context 436 (Figs 32 and 65, section S1) set on the lip of ditch segment F264, but the original wall courses have not survived. Any link between these contexts and F9 was later severed by the insertion of the walls of Structure VIII and the later pit F57. Outside the temple was a layer of mixed debris and weathering detritus, context 963, which probably accumulated while Structure II stood during Phases 4 and 5 (Fig 65, section S58). Similar deposits survived north of the later site of Structure VIII, and all these layers represent further deposition of material in the hollow surviving over the infilled ditch complex F264. They contained two iron projectile heads (Fig 112, no 12), possibly residual from ditch section F264; an iron bolt head (Fig 113, no 19); a bone pin (Fig 131, no 15); and a lead fitting (Fig 155, no 13). Within the confines of the later Structure VIII no definite Phase 4 or 5a–c deposits survived between the make-up layer context 255, dated by coins and brooches to the late first or early second century AD, and the foundation levels of Structure VIII (Fig 65, sections S1 and S38). However if the mortar spread, context 942, marked the construction of the temple, then the overlying clay and rubble layer 456, south of the later Structure VIII, may be later than context 255 and belong to Phase 4 (Figs 35 and 65, section S1). This clay and rubble layer contained fragments of iron only. It was subsequently sealed by a series of cobbled surfaces, contexts 451 and 454 (Figs 33 and 65, section S58), succeeded by context 444 (Fig 65, section S1), distinguishable above the soft fills of ditch segment F264, south-east of the later Structure VIII.

There is no stratification within the confines of the later Structure VIII to match these Phase 4 and 5 deposits of building debris and exterior surfaces. The clay layer 255, dated to the late first or early second century (Phase 3), reaches to the same level as the exterior surfaces just described, and the dichotomy in the stratification within and outside the walls of the later Structure VIII raises the possibility that these zones were always separated from each other. This could mean that a small building or room stood roughly on the site of the later Structure VIII during Phases 4 and 5. Any existing traces of the foundations of such a building would have been destroyed totally during the erection of Structure VIII. The outline of this postulated structure or room is shown on the phase plan (Fig 33). If such a room did exist, then the temple plan would have been irregular indeed, and no parallels for primary annexes occupying such an unbalanced position are known. For the purposes of the reconstruction drawings (Figs 212–4) this postulated annexe has been omitted, but its possible existence should not be discounted, and it is shown on the final reconstruction (Fig 228).

The inner ambulatory walls F3, F10, and F16 defined three sides of the cella (Room E) which measured 8 × 7m internally. Wall F3 alone had been set within a construction trench, F91, filled with context 92 silt and mortar (Fig 34, section BII C). This context contained the heads of a copper alloy stud and pin. Details of the fourth, northern, side of the cella were much obscured by later rearrangements, but the footings of a primary entrance structure were distinguishable (Figs 35 and 33). These comprised a pair of massive mortared stone plinths, set approximately 1.40m apart in the centre of the northern side of the cella. The eastern plinth F713 was set within a foundation trench F741, packed with the stone rubble of context 902. A small portion of its western end had been robbed away leaving a rubble fill, context 740, within part of the foundation trench F741. Context 902, the rubble fill, contained a single large iron nail head. The western plinth had been totally robbed, leaving an elongated trench, F737, containing context 736 rubble. This rubble incorporated a cylindrical iron object. In line with the plinths, but approximately 1m to the north, were a pair of post pits, F720 and F724 (Figs 31 and 32) which were on average 0.50m in diameter, 0.40m deep and contained no finds. The set of plinths and post holes probably supported a small porch or, more likely, a doorcase in classical style. There were no traces of walls or timber partitions which might have linked this structure to the end walls of the flanking ambulatories, but the later Phase 6 and 7 walls would have destroyed any such evidence. Such partitions surely must have existed and F747, a single posthole just west of the robbed plinth F737 (Fig 32), could mark the line of one of them.

The only feature surviving within the cella that might have been primary to the temple structure was the centrally placed irregular pit F19 (Figs 32 and 35), which penetrated the upper weathered levels of the natural limestone. This pit was cut by later post pits and post holes of Phase 7 and its main filling had been disturbed substantially during the modifications of the area in Phase 6 (Fig 34, sections BII C and BII D). It was, on average, 3.0m across and sloped gently, but unevenly, to a maximum surviving depth of 0.70m. The lowest layers of infilling, contexts 18 and 208, contained cast copper alloy rings (Fig 114, nos 5 and 16) and groups of coins similar to those found in the main fill, context 17 above. Thus no primary deposits appear to have survived. The sharply angled corners which survived at the south-west, and by projection, on the north-west limits of the pit, might indicate that it had been designed to hold a square or rectangular container, perhaps a water tank. However, if such a tank was to have been of any depth, its maximum length could not have been more than 1.45m (see Fig 30). The heavily weathered profile of the pit suggests prolonged exposure after removal of the postulated tank, or that it had been sunk into the fill of an earlier feature. Thus pit F19 might have marked the presence of a pre-existing focus, central to the Iron Age shrine, which could have

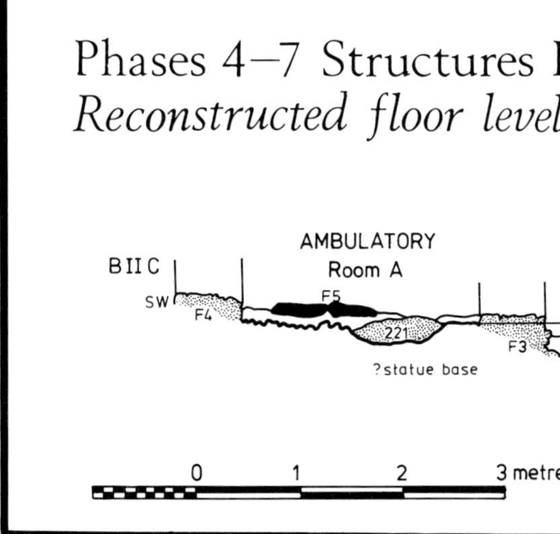

Fig 30 Reconstructed section, scale 1:75

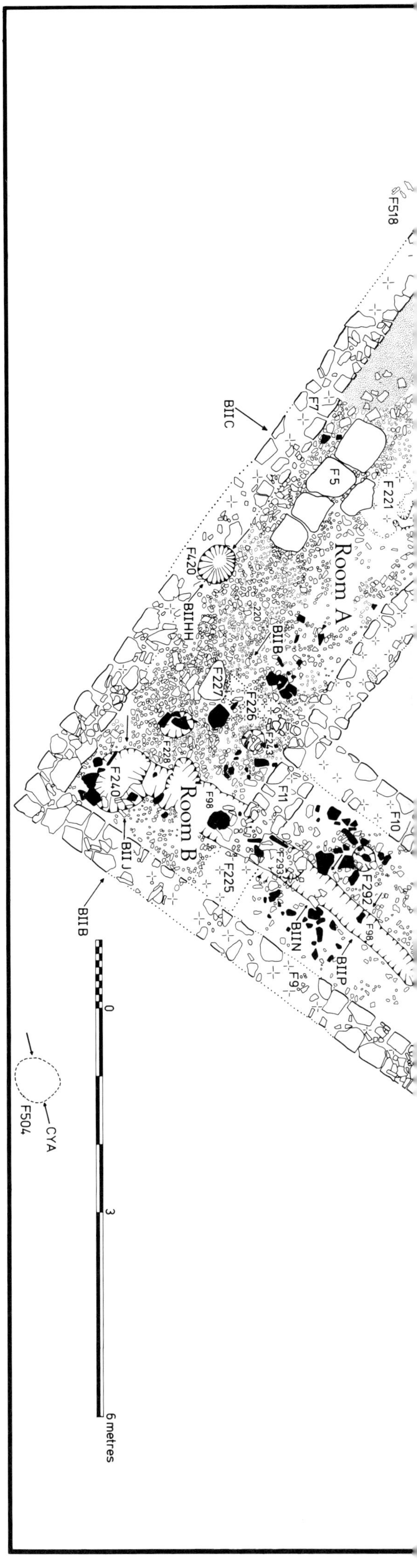

Fig 32 Phases 4–7, plan of Structures II, XI and VII, scale 1:80

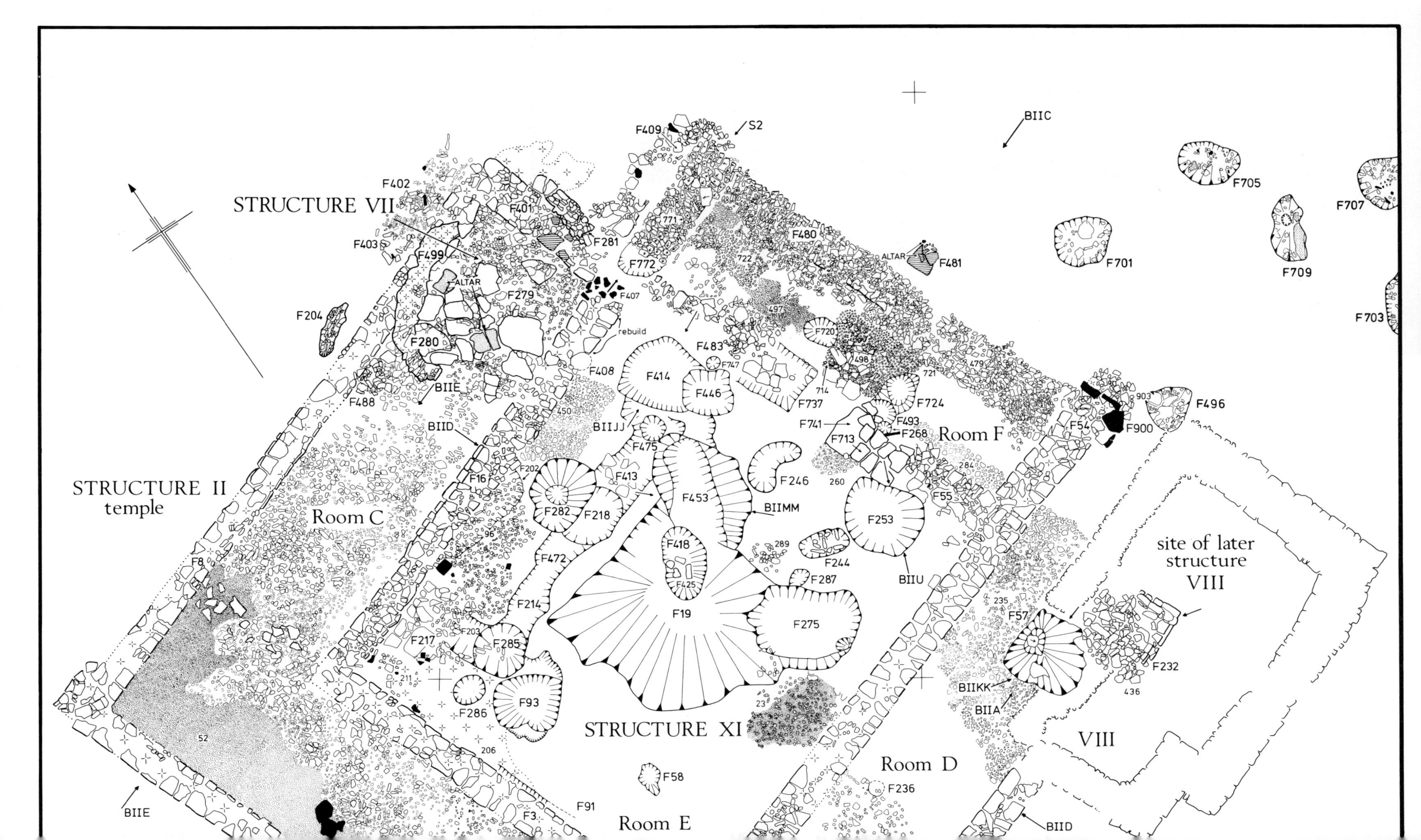
STRUCTURE VII
STRUCTURE II
temple
Room C
STRUCTURE XI
Room E
Room D
Room F
site of later
structure
VIII
VIII
ALTAR
ALTAR
rebuild
BIIE
BIIE
BIID
BIID
BIIJJ
BIIMM
BIIU
BIIKK
BIIA
BIIC
S2
F402
F403
F499
F401
F281
F279
F280
F204
F407
F408
F488
F409
F772
F480
F481
F701
F705
F707
F709
F703
F414
F446
F483
F747
F737
F720
F724
F741
F713
F493
F268
F54
F900
F496
F16
F202
F282
F218
F413
F475
F453
F418
F425
F19
F246
F253
F244
F287
F275
F472
F214
F217
F203
F285
F286
F93
F58
F236
F55
F57
F232
F8
F3
F91
771
722
497
498
479
721
714
903
450
96
211
206
52
260
284
289
235
436
23

Fig 31 Structure II, north-east entrance arrangements, view from the south-west (1978). (Photo: Sebastian Rahtz)

taken the form perhaps of a standing stone or, indeed, a substantial living tree.

Within the flanking ambulatories traces survived of worn limestone cobbled surfaces, which represent some of the original temple floor levels (Figs 30 and 32). In Room C, the cobbled surface context 89 was virtually complete (Fig 36, section BII E). At the south-west corner it merged with a similar surface, context 220, in Room A (Fig 34, section BII C). These cobbles also rested upon a clayey footing. Both floors had subsided above the infill of the Late Iron Age ditch F584, and the presence of this underlying ditch may also have necessitated the thickening of the wall junction between F7 and F8 mentioned above, and the insertion of deep drystone rubble foundations into its fills (Fig 36, elevation, Room A/C).

Finds from probably original floor and sub-floor levels included; in Room C, a copper alloy finger ring, a limestone spindle whorl (Fig 143, no 1), and a whetstone (Fig 147, no 5); and in Room B, scraps of copper alloy, iron, and one intrusive fourth-century coin.

Midway along the southern ambulatory the cobbles were interrupted by F419, a circular pit 0.90m in diameter, containing context 221, hard packed mortar and some stone rubble (Fig 34, section BII C). Much of the upper surface of this mortar was visible as a clear area within the surrounding floor, and it may represent an original feature of the building. Its position and morphology suggest a function as a foundation for a statue plinth or other similar structure within the temple, although interpretation as a mortar mixing pit, associated with construction of the temple, cannot be ruled out entirely. No cobbling survived in Room D, apart from a small rectangular patch near the northern end. Two post holes, F236 and F292, located in this ambulatory, may have been contemporary and could have supported internal features (Fig 32). Context 237, the fill of post hole F236, contained an inlaid enamel disc (Fig 126, no 2).

Phase 5d

Following a long period of use the doorcase was dismantled, and the entrance area was remodelled and extended to provide a projecting area (Room F) measuring 7 × 1m internally. The most likely hypothesis seems to be that these projecting foundations supported a portico in classical style; the floor area of such a portico would have been 8.2 × 2.00m (Fig 29). The extension was accomplished by a lengthening of the two inner ambulatory walls, F10 and F16, a further 2.0m to the north and then linking these with a wall across the new front (Fig 32). Whether the plinths for the previous entrance, and the associated partitions, were still in existence to provide a closing wall to the cella cannot be proven, but it seems extremely likely that they were. It should be noted that the new portico gave access only to the cella and not to the flanking ambulatories which still remained as separately accessible components within the existing temple plan. The nature of the footings of all three new sections of wall suggested a more massive construction than that of the primary temple. The wall extending on from F16 on the west had been robbed down to its lower foundation courses of pitched unmortared limestone packing, context 771, set within F772, a construction trench (Figs 32 and 34, section S2).

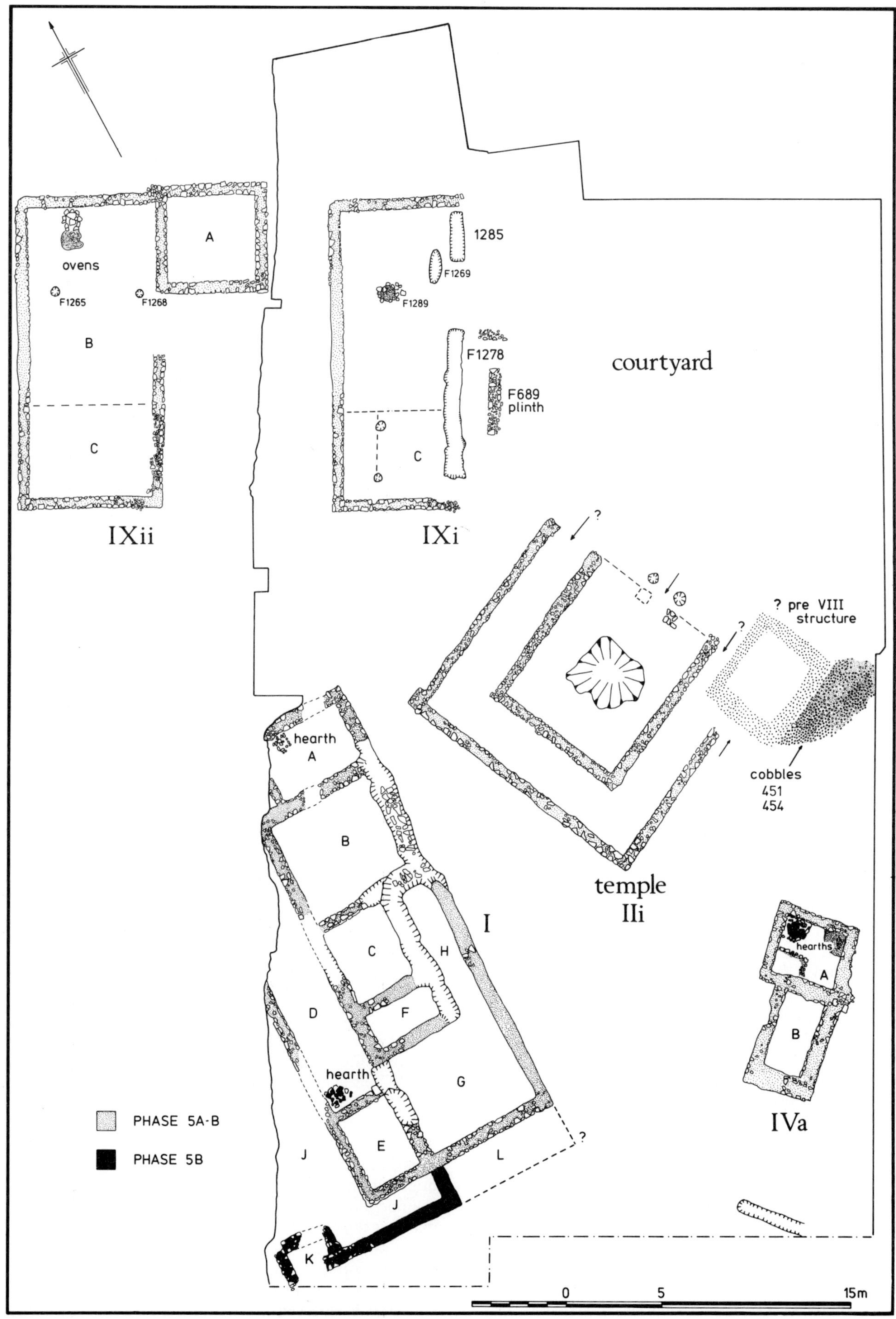

Fig 33 Phase 5a–b plan, earlier mid-fourth century AD, scale 1:280

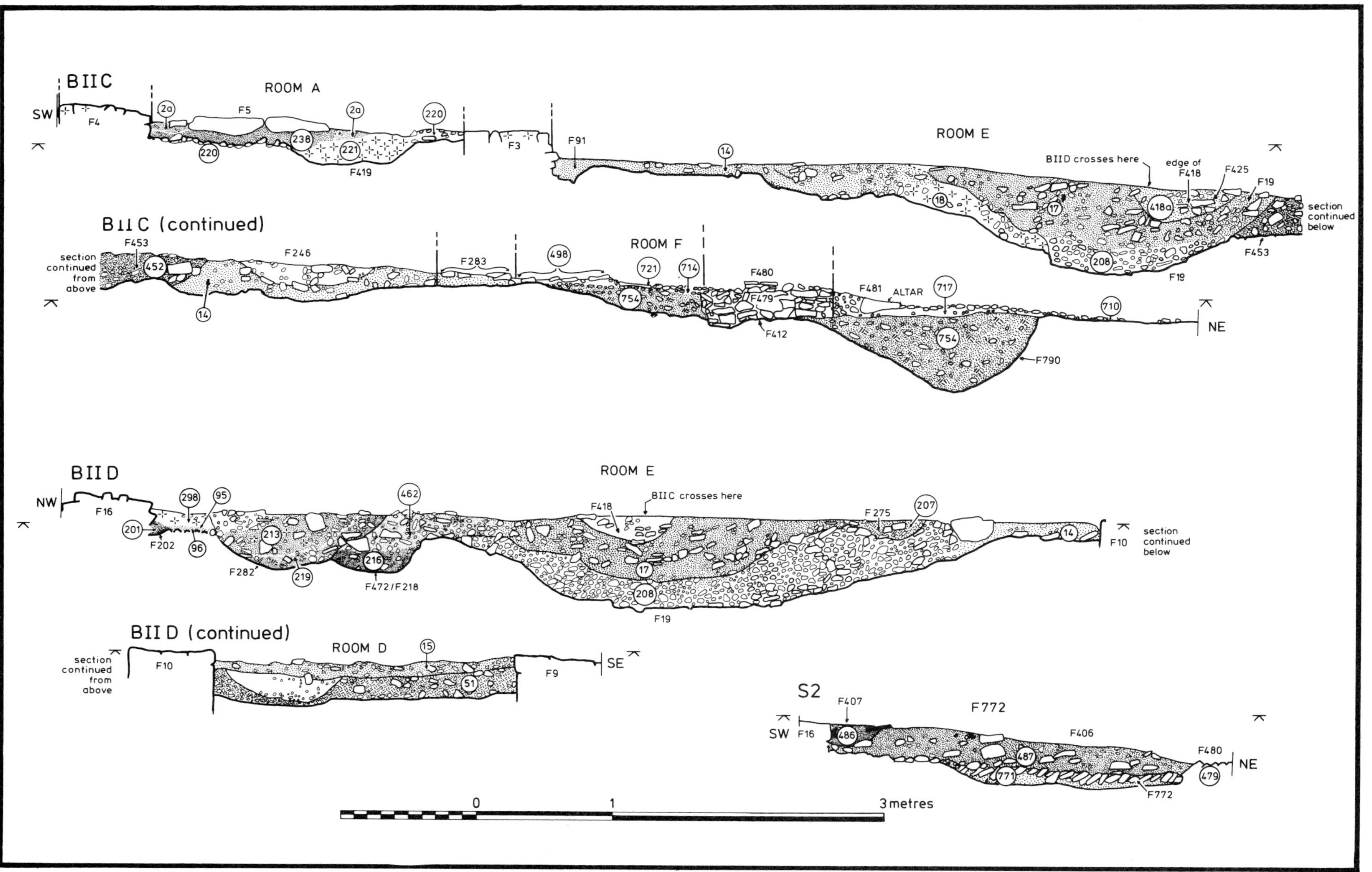

Fig 34 Phases 4–7, sections of Structures II and VII, scale 1:40

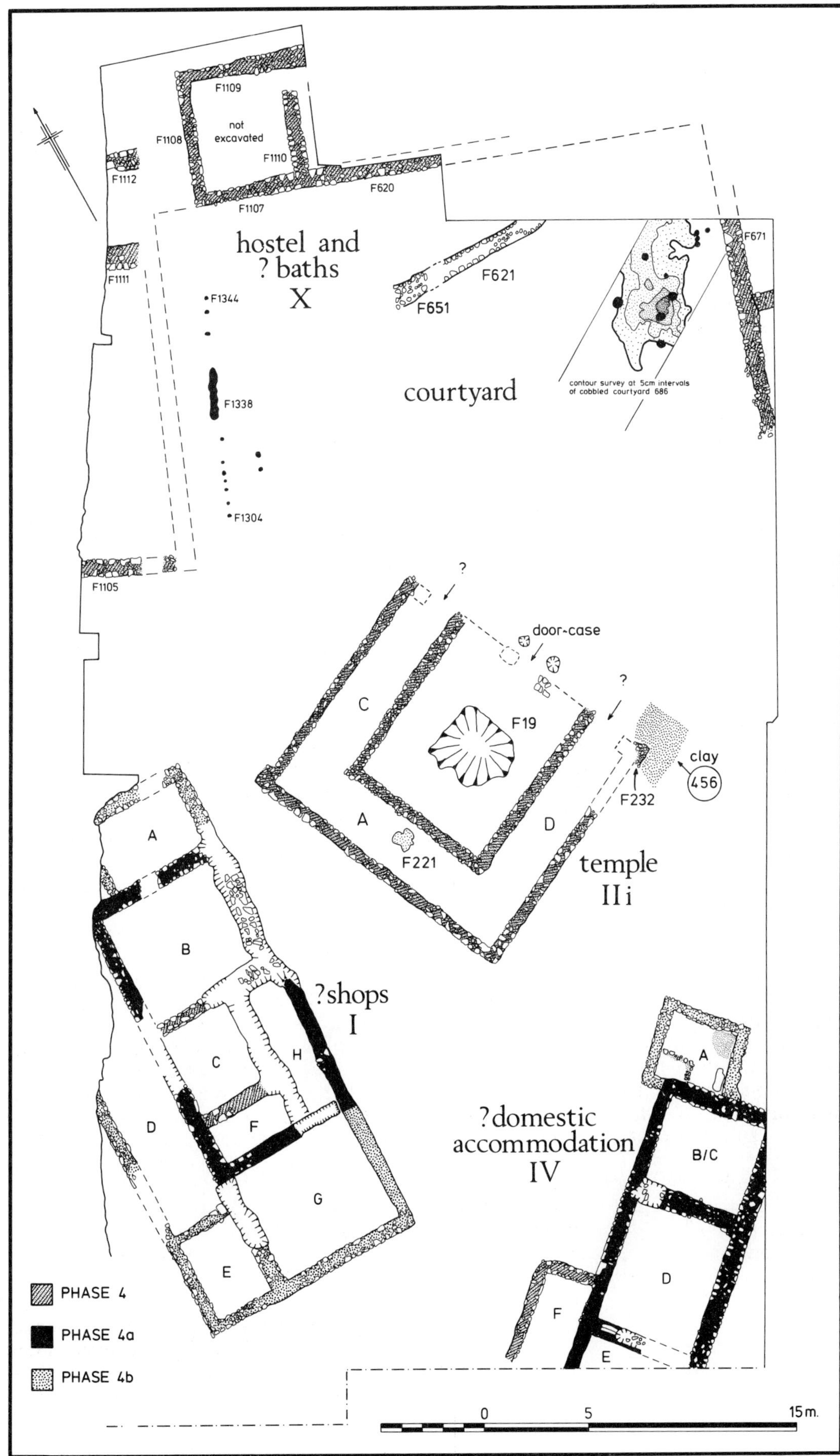

Fig 35 Phase 4 plan, second to early fourth century AD, scale 1:280

The packing material contained only one residual flint flake. To the east the corresponding wall, extending from F10, had survived to its lowest mortared course, F54. Here the proximity of the early votive pit F251 (Fig 29) had necessitated the construction of very substantial footings, founded within the soft infilling layers over the pit. Pitched unmortared limestone blocks had been set into a construction trench, and at its northern termination, to ensure further reinforcement at this potentially unstable corner, the footings were thickened with a mortared sill of sandstone tiles packed around with rubble, context 903 (Fig 32), which formed the foundation for a buttress F900. The rubble context 903 contained a silver coin of AD 77–8 which probably derived from the upper fills of pit F251, which would have been disturbed during the construction of the portico foundations. The linking wall between these two extensions was also set deeply within construction trench F412 which varied in depth according to the presence of underlying features, and the level of more solid bedrock beneath the weathered surface (Figs 32 and 34, section BII C). Pitched drystone footings, F479, were tied in with those of the two side walls and supported a small portion of the lowest mortared course of the wall F480 (Fig 34, section BII C). A coin of AD 350–60 was recovered from these footings.

No details of the threshold arrangements survived, although, as suggested above, the eastern plinth F713 (Fig 32) remained as an upstanding fragment, and may still have been in use as part of the support of the partition walls and door posts between portico and cella. If the floor level of the portico was the same as that in the cella then a flight of steps would have been necessary to reach the portico from the courtyard below. One possible arrangement, involving a flight of four steps, is shown in the reconstructed profile across the temple (Fig 30). The only clear dating evidence for the construction of the portico is a coin of AD 350–60 recovered from the pitched footings of the front wall. This suggests that reconstruction did not take place before AD 350. However, too great a reliance on a single coin found within a poorly sealed context would be unwise. In fact the portico may have been constructed rather earlier and thus have been contemporary, at least in part, with the main floruit of the surrounding stone buildings of Phase 5a–b.

No features or deposits within the ambulatory could be assigned to Phase 5d although is is assumed that it did continue in use throughout this phase. The northern end of the ambulatory wall F16 was rebuilt and packed around with a strengthened bond with the new portico wall. As noted above, this may have been to enable construction of a blocking wall across an original entrance in the north end of the west ambulatory. Within the cella, no contemporary floor levels survived but, as in Phases 5a–c, the primary fill of the central pit F19, although much disturbed, may have been related to its use as the setting for a water container or small pool.

Structure X

Phase 4a–b

During the excavation season of 1977 oblique aerial photographs of the site showed up the clear crop mark of a substantial building located just north of the temple (Fig 5). This building showed as a major range of rooms aligned roughly east–west, with one room projecting slightly to the north (Fig 9, Phases 4a and b, and Fig 42). East of this projecting room were marks indicating the presence of substantial walls defining a dense block of small square and rectangular rooms. There were also traces of an eastern wing, one wall of which was later exposed within the excavated area, although the main east–west range and this eastern wing were not excavated. The walls facing the temple courtyard were exposed in part however, as were portions of the exterior occupation levels and demolition deposits. On the western side of the structure were the remains of a balancing west wing, or of a contemporary, but separate, structure in this location. These had been destroyed almost totally during the construction of Structure IX in Phase 5a, as well as by the pipe trench in 1976. Despite this damage a few stubs of walls, a line of post holes, and some stratification survived in this area, and these have provided some useful structural and chronological information.

West of the pipe trench there remained small lengths of three massively constructed mortared stone walls F1105, F1111, and F1112 (Fig 35). All were truncated by the pipe trench and could not be traced further east. It seems probable that the remains of an eastern wall for the range had lain roughly along the line of the 1976 trench and wall F1103 of Structure IX (Fig 48), and had been destroyed by them. Limited excavation within the confines of these walls identified sequences of soil and cobbled surfaces. These layers contained no diagnostic finds apart from a fragment of an oolitic limestone sphere (Fig 81, no 4). Above these floor and occupation levels were deposits of demolition rubble which contained nails.

Beneath the construction deposits of Structure IX, and cutting the upper fills of the Late Iron Age and early Roman ditch F584, was a line of post or stake holes and a timber slot running parallel to the postulated eastern wall of the western wing of Structure X (Fig 35). The line commenced with post hole F1304 at the south end, and continued with further post holes at short intervals towards a central slot F1338, which itself contained three more post holes. Beyond this were three other, less closely spaced post holes which may also have been related. The single post holes, which were on average 0.13m deep, contained no finds, but a third or fourth-century coin was recovered from one of the post holes within the slot F1338. It is possible that the post holes and slot could have held the foundations for a porch or verandah associated with the west wing of Structure X.

The demolition of the west wing is most probably represented by deposits of burnt soil and rubble, contexts 1231 and 1224, sealed beneath the construction levels of Structure IX, and immediately east of the proposed verandah alignment described above (see Fig 49, section S2). These layers contained four late third-century coins; small copper alloy studs and fittings; iron nails and fittings; and a shale bracelet fragment. A demolition date of *c* AD 300 seems to be indicated.

The main east–west range of Structure X was not excavated but various wall components were exposed and their surface features recorded. The main south wall F620 (Fig 35) was massively constructed and sim-

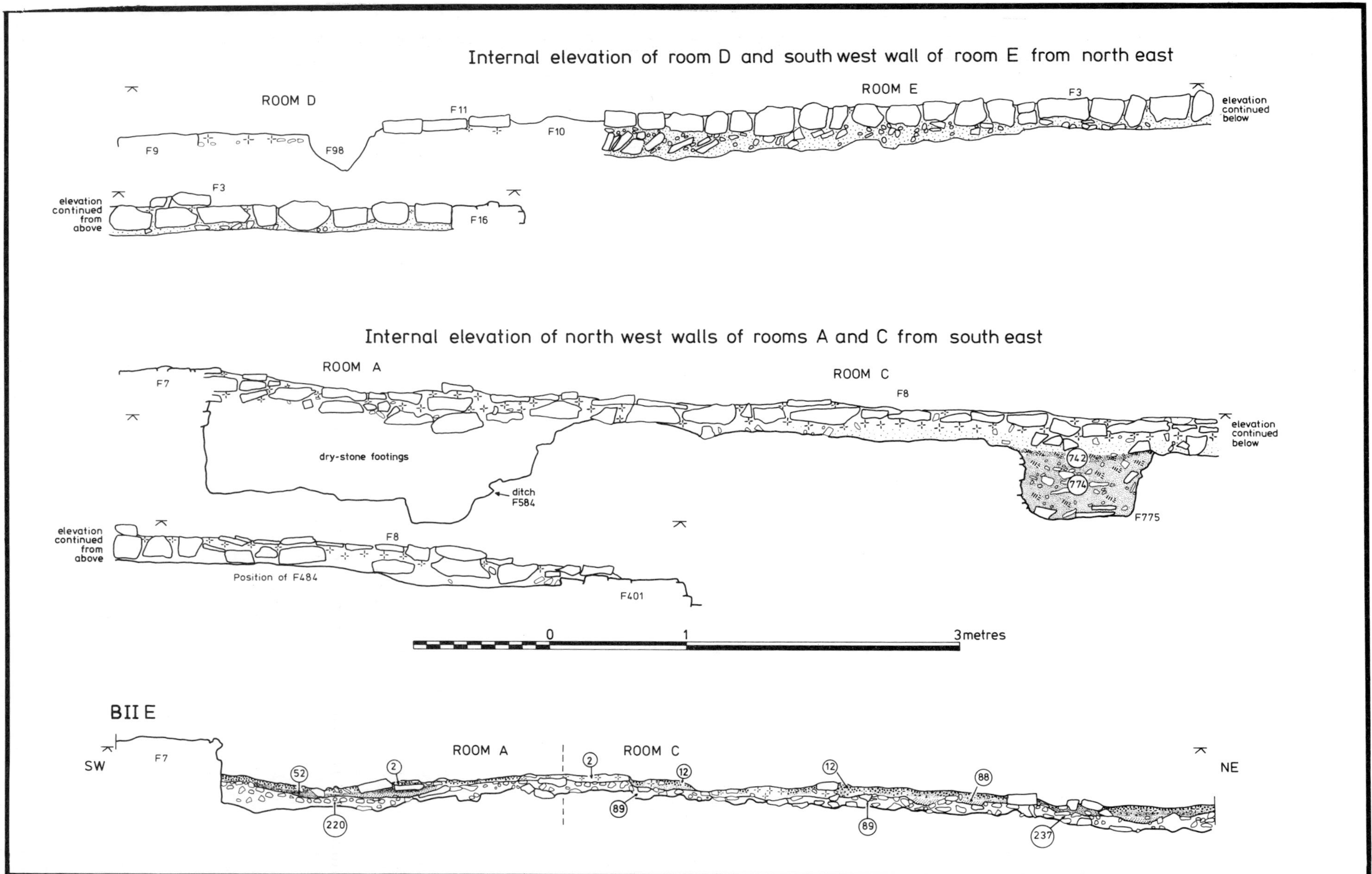

Fig 36 Phases 4–5, Structure II, wall elevations and sections, scale 1:40

ilar in build to the cross walls of the west wing, F1110, F1111, and F1112, excavated beyond the pipe trench. Within the spread of demolition rubble south of wall F620 were the traces of another substantial wall F621, lying on a different alignment. This wall continued westwards as F651 below the construction levels of Structure IX, Room A, and to the west it became a deposit of dispersed rubble, context 685 (Fig 49, section S13). Associated with wall F651 was a disturbed floor level, context 682, lying above deposits of stony soil and rubble including context 823 (Fig 49, section S13). Finds from these contexts include glass, and iron fittings (including Fig 153, no 24). The diagonal wall F621/F651 must belong to another building extending beyond the northern limit of the excavated area. No clear dating evidence was recovered for this building, but it seems likely that it predated Structure X and may therefore have been standing in the late first to early second centuries AD.

Although the east–west range and east wing of Structure X were not excavated, inspection of the surfaces of some of the walls suggested that it was a complex structure of several phases. At the western end of the main range the original wide wall footings (eg F620) had been reused in part as a base for the narrower walls of a square room comprising F1107, F1108, and F1109, and a partition wall F1110 had been inserted, butting against F620/F1107 on the south (Fig 35). Similarly, in the north-eastern corner of the excavated area, a partition wall had been butted against the main west wall of the eastern wing. These modifications may have occurred in Phase 4, or perhaps in Phase 5, such that the small unexcavated room lying north of Structure IX, may have been contemporary with it.

Apart from the very fragmentary remains of the western wing of this building, which survived below the later Structures IX and XIV, none of the interior of Structure X was excavated. A large area of limestone rubble, lying in the northern zone of the excavation area, was presumed to derive from the demolition or collapse of Structure X, and it was decided to test the nature and dating of these deposits by excavating a portion of them. Thus a transect 4m wide was excavated, partly below the site of the Phase 5d–e Structure XIII which lay upon the platform of rubble (see Fig 35). The stratification was recorded in great detail so that, in the case of a possible future excavation of Structure X, these results could be incorporated into the report of any further work. The detailed descriptions are held in the archive, but the general sequence of deposits is illustrated in Figure 55, section S32.

The bank of material, up to 0.45m in thickness, contained layers relating to the use and destruction of Structure X above a continuous cobbled surface, context 686 (Fig 55, section S32), which probably represented the northern zone of the temple courtyard laid out when Structure X was built. The surface was uneven and occasionally disturbed, but its main feature was a distinct sub-circular depression, well demonstrated by the results of the contour survey shown in Figure 35. The courtyard surface, and any earlier contexts, were not explored in this area as it was thought that a larger area of the exterior of Structure X should be investigated before disturbing the cobbles and any contained features. However, it does seem likely that the marked depression reflected the position of yet another Late Iron Age or early Roman feature, perhaps a circular pit similar to F836 excavated beneath Room A of Structure IX. Indeed it is not impossible that the excavated pit and this postulated second example might be part of a series of ritual pits encircling the ditched enclosure on this northern side.

Cutting the cobbled courtyard surface were numerous small patches of soil, some of which may have been the fills of post holes and the distribution of these is shown in Figure 35. They were not excavated but may have represented the position of supports for features associated with Structure X, either porches or a verandah, or booths and stalls placed within the courtyard. Immediately above the cobbles was a complex succession of small deposits of sand, clay, ashy lenses, laid rubble, and mortar patches, all probably associated with the occupation of the adjacent Structure X. These included mortar context 629, limestone rubble context 890, and rubble in soil context 1009 (Figure 55, section S32). Finds from these deposits are few, but include a perforated copper alloy disc (Fig 151, no 6); a fragment of iron spiral tube (Fig 153, no 23) and many other fragments of iron.

Phase 4b

Above these occupation layers lay a second complex sequence of rubble, mortar, and burnt layers, presumably reflecting the process of the demolition of Structure X. The most extensive layers were dumps of massive limestone blocks, context 694, which formed a loose deposit of rubble, containing many air spaces (Fig 55, section S32). A similar, although unexcavated, rubble spread continued westwards towards the site of Structure IX and all appear to derive from the collapse or demolition of a very substantial stone and mortar building. Beneath the excavated rubble a primary phase of the demolition process is represented by further spreads of rubble and mortar, contexts 800 and 810, and below these, context 813, more restricted spreads of rubble in soil, plaster, and mortar, and context 820a, soil containing considerable quantities of charcoal. The latter may be related to the primary destruction of Structure X or to sub-phases of building modification, extension or repair during its period of use. Finds were more numerous than in the underlying layers, but again mainly consisted of fragments of iron; with the addition of a green glass bead; the shaft of a bone pin; and a whetstone. The iron objects included many large nails or bolts and fittings, which would have been derived from the fabric of the stone building which had been demolished. Further layers of silt and rubble, eg context 695 (Fig 55, section S32), lying against the major demolition deposits, may date from Phases 4b or 5a–c.

Structure I

Phases 4–5

Structure I was a substantial stone building cut along it entire length by the water pipe trench in 1976 (Fig 37). It was aligned roughly along the path of the underlying

Late Iron Age and early Roman ditch F179 (Fig 9). No definite dating evidence for its period of construction was recovered but, as will be argued below, it appears to have been a complex multiphase structure originating in the second or third century AD. The building was totally excavated except for its western margin which lies below the modern road. From north to south Rooms A to K were distinguished (Fig 38).

Room A was defined on its north and east sides by wall footings F25 and F26 (Figs 38 and 39, section BI B) contained in construction trenches, but the former contained no finds. The east wall F25 was robbed at its southern end and its junction with the walls of Room B destroyed. Wall F27 divided Room B from Room A, and footings F34, F147, with robber trenches F64 and F65 defined Room B on its other three sides (Fig 38). The east wall survived only as the massive deep footings F112, within the robber trench F64, set into the upper fill of the ditch F179 (Fig 39, sections BI C and BI A). The small rectangular Room C was bounded partly by fragments of wall footings F34, F46, and F81, but otherwise on the east by the wide robber trench F157. This contained fragments of deep footings F157 (similar to F112), founded in the upper fills of the ditch F179. To the south lay the smaller Room F, also bounded by F46 and F81, but with the eastern wall robbed out (robber trench F166), and most of the south wall F83 also robbed (trench F84). Rooms C and F were flanked on the west by the long rectangular Room D, severely damaged by the pipe trench (Fig 39, section BI N). This was bounded by walls F47 and F49 to the south and west; the postulated north wall is assumed to lie beneath the modern road. A narrow corridor (Room H) flanked Rooms C and F on the other side, its walls almost totally robbed out (robber trenches F64, F144, F157, and F166). To the south lay a large sub-square room (G), its eastern wall almost completely robbed (traces of mortar and stone fragments were found in context 67) but its south wall F50 survived to one course in its foundation trench. The north and west walls, F46 and F83, survived only as fragments, with associated robber trenches F74 and F84 respectively. Contexts connected with levelling for construction beneath Rooms F and G contained a few finds, including a miniature pot (Fig 119, no 4), a green glass bead, and two late fourth-century coins, which may have been intrusive. West of Room G, and continuing the line of Room D, was Room E defined by walls F47, F49, F50, and the fragment F46 running into robber trench F74. Room J may have been a further corridor or verandah attached to the south-west corner of the building. A fragment of its southern wall F102 survived; otherwise it was defined by the robber trenches F103 and F104. In the extreme south-western corner lay Room K, a small square structure, enclosing a deep pit (probably a latrine) and defined by walls F102, F105, F152, and F153. Room J continues as a much larger room for an unknown distance to the north beneath the modern hedge and road. A fragment of robber trench F527 and some possible floor make-up to the south of Room G may indicate the former presence of a further room in the south-east corner of Structure I.

Occupation deposits

Most rooms possessed carefully laid limestone cobbled floors (Fig 38), although these had been disturbed or

Fig 37 Excavation in progress in 1977, south end of Structure I, view from the south-west. (Photo: Peter Leach)

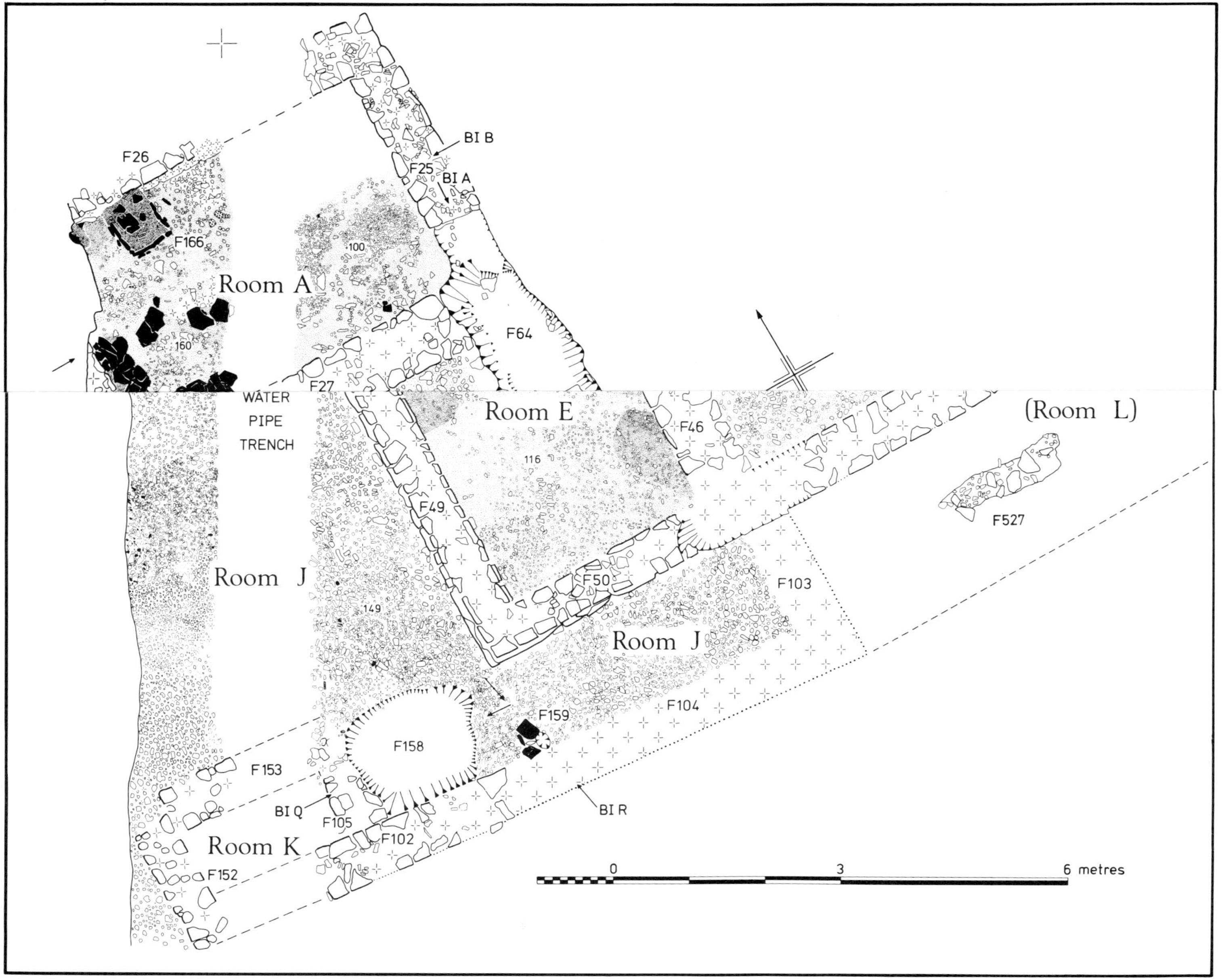

Fig 38 Phases 4–5, plan of Structure I, scale 1:80

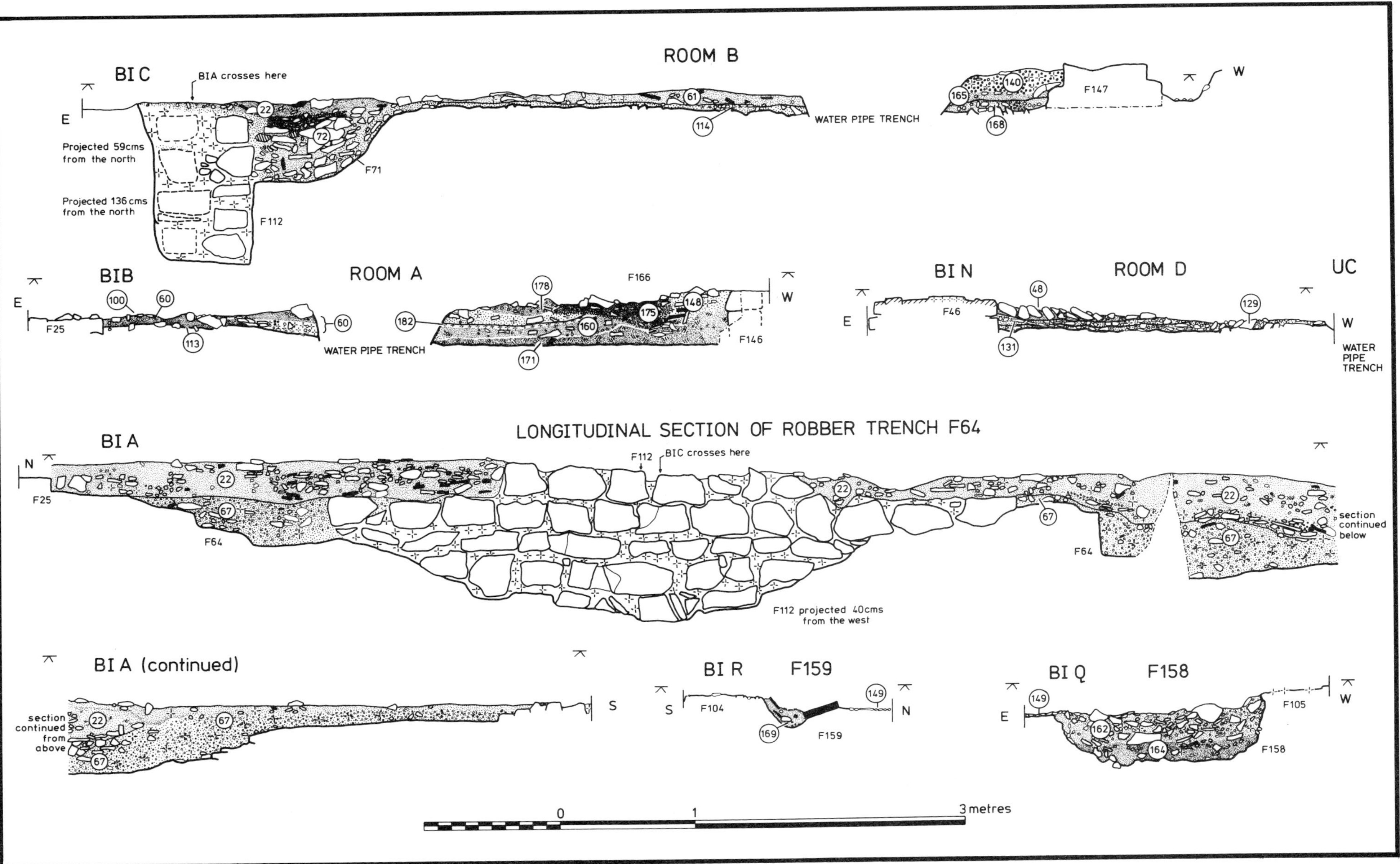

Fig 39 Phase 5, sections of Structure I, scale 1:40

worn away in places. Occupation levels had survived only rarely, and such deposits were restricted mainly to Rooms A and B where the stratification was thicker (Fig 39, sections BI B and BI C).In Room A, a rectangular hearth F166 (Fig 40, centre) lay on the worn surface of the floor, context 171. A layer of ash and charcoal, context 175 (Fig 39, plans and section BI B), lay against the occupation deposits of context 160 (Fig 38 and 39 section BI B). This was sealed by a later cobbled floor level, context 182, which continued east of the pipe trench as context 113 (Fig 38, section BI B), and the hearth F166 appears to have been refurbished and reused in this second stage of occupation. Context 160, belonging to the first phase of occupation, contained the head of a votive iron spear; a bone ring (Fig 115, no 22); a blue glass bead; and a copper alloy mount; along with six coins dating from the late third and early fourth centuries. The secondary floor level, context 113, produced a spiral fragment of copper alloy.

Some disturbed occupation layers (eg context 165) survived above contexts 114/168, the cobbled floor in Room B (Fig 39, section BI C), and contained a fragment of a miniature pot. In Rooms C and F, two layers of cobbling survived in part, and occupation debris in Room C contained a glass bead. In Room D context 129, the primary cobbled surface (Fig 39, section BI N) was sealed by further small cobblestones of context 131, which were in turn sealed by context 48, an area of massive pitched limestone blocks and limestone fragments lying against wall F46. Adjacent to context 48 was a contemporary deposit of ashy soil. In the southwest corner of Room D was a multi-phased hearth F119 (Figs 38 and 40, top). This comprised two major surfaces, one of limestone, and the second of reused sandstone roof tiles, constructed above a shallow pit. The cobbled floor of Room E, context 116 (Fig 38), survived almost intact and upon it were three areas of burning. In Room G, the cobbles forming context 124 had sunk over the underlying ditch F179, and thus survived well along its line. The occupation layer 170 (not illus) contained a fragment of a lead tablet. Room J also possessed a well preserved cobbled floor, comprising contexts 149/170, which was cut by a large pit F158 (infilled by soil and rubble contexts 162 and 164) and adjacent post hole F159 (containing sandstone tile packing and soil context 169), (Figs 38 and 39, sections BI Q and BI R). Both these features related to post-demolition activities, and their fills will be further considered below. Room K, a latrine or cess pit, contained an organic fill in a rock-cut pit. This fill contained plant and animal remains (see chapter 12) and a series of votive objects relating to a later stage of use of Structure I, probably in Phase 5b.

Building Sequence

A study of the occurrence of multiple floor levels, the morphology of the wall footings and the occurrence of possible and probable butt joints has indicated that Structure I originated as a compact rectangular building which was extended at least twice, and also subdivided. The thickest and most carefully constructed walls are those defining a central rectangular area later occupied by Rooms B, C, F, and H (Fig 35). The slighter walls forming Rooms C and F were probably butted against wall F46, and thus represent inserted later partitions. Room A, with its more irregular, and slightly narrower wall footings was probably added later although the main junctions were disturbed by robbing and could not be analysed in detail. Similarly the shallower foundations of Rooms D, E, and G suggest that they were also extensions, on the south and west sides. Finally the narrow Room J, and the latrine, Room K, appear to have been added in the south-west corner of the structure, the former possibly continued to the south-east as a room of slighter build, Room L (Fig 33). These final additions may date from Phase 5b. The multiple occupation deposits and reused hearths excavated in Rooms A, D, and E, together with the degree of survival of their wall footings, suggest that these rooms continued in use after the main eastern core of Structure I had been demolished. Thus these three rooms, and probably Room J and the latrine pit, may have continued in use during Phases 5c and 5d, and the pit F158 and post hole F159 may have been constructed in this same occupation phase (Fig 41). It may be that the original core had collapsed on the east side due to subsidence over the fills of ditch F179 below. A modification within the northern wall of Room E, which survived as an area of carefully laid reused sandstone roof tiles, may represent the threshold of a doorway inserted to allow access between the surviving Rooms D and E (see Fig 40, wall elevations and Fig 41). A further late threshold may be represented by a zone of very worn stone blocks within the wall fragment F46; this would have provided a new access from the outside into Room D, and the pitched cobbles, context 48 (Fig 39, section BI N), were probably associated with this threshold. In Room A piles of sandstone roof tiles, presumably from the demolished sector of the building, had been utilised to form a rough bench inside the western and southern walls (Fig 38).

Demolition, Phases 5c–d and 5e(i)

All rooms contained layers of demolition debris up to 0.02m in thickness, and many of the walls on the eastern side of the building were robbed out. It may be that worked stone from these footings was used to refurbish the fabric of Rooms A, D, and E which continued in later use. However, none of the demolition or robbing contexts were associated with coins dated later than AD 378 and it is therefore concluded that the whole structure had been demolished by *c* AD 380. Domestic and votive small finds were found in the demolition deposits throughout the building. Full lists are available in the archive; illustrated items are indicated below. The sequence of robbing was sometimes complex. For example, in Room B the primary demolition deposits contexts 61/140 (Fig 39, section BI C) were cut by the robber trench F64 and backfilled with rubble context 67 (Fig 39, section BI A). Subsequently a second robbing pit F71 (Fig 39, section BI C) was cut, presumably to gain access to the deep foundations of F112. The finds from the various robber trench fills are summarised below. The coins from the demolition deposits are of the late third century and the first half of the fourth century, whilst those in the fills of the robber trenches are almost entirely of the mid-fourth century AD. It is this phase of robbing that may be linked to the refurbishment of Rooms A, D, and E during the final phase of use postulated for Structure I.

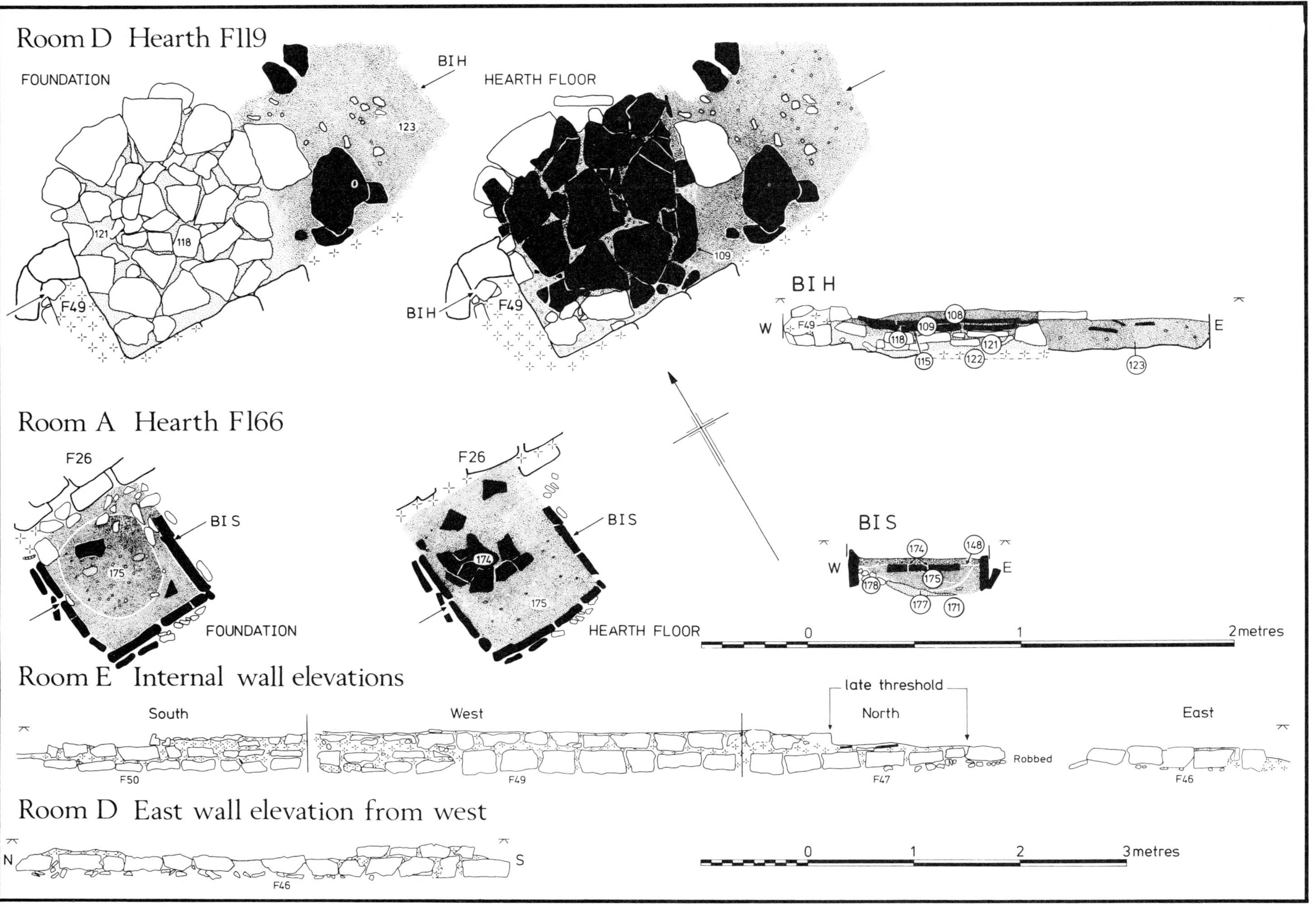

Fig 40 Phase 5, Structure I, Room D, hearth F119, Room A, hearth F166, Room E internal wall elevations, scale 1:50

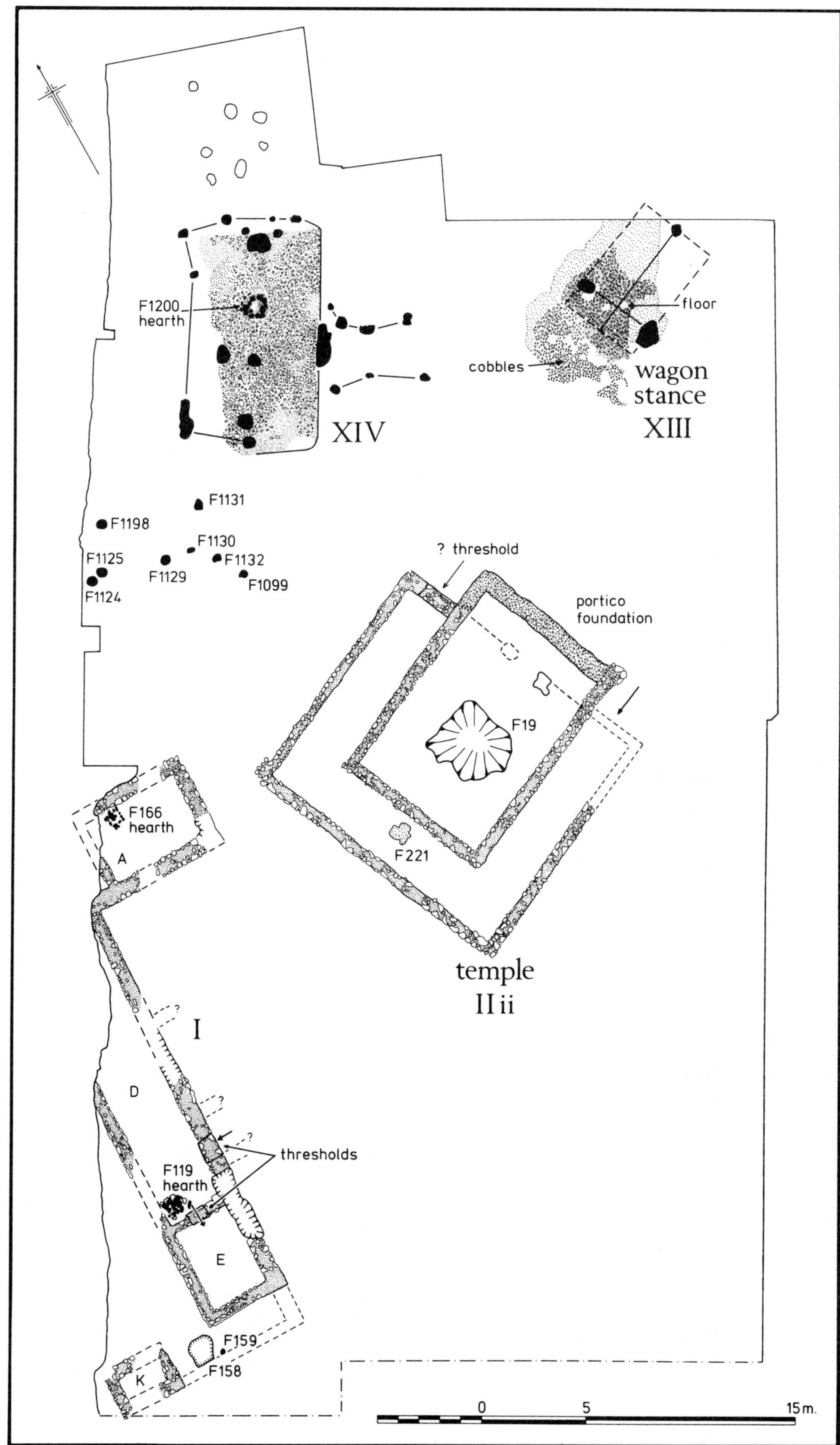

Fig 41 Phase 5d–e plan, late-fourth century AD, scale 1:280

Diagnostic finds from the demolition contexts

Room A
demolition rubble
Context 60/148: five coins with a date range of 270–90; a copper alloy *caduceus* (Fig 89, no 2)
robber trenches
Trench F64, fill, context 67: five coins of the mid-fourth century; a lead tablet; an iron ring (Fig 154, no 10); copper alloy fragments
Trench F71, fill, context 72: a fragment of copper alloy

Room B
demolition rubble
Context 140/61: six coins with a date range of 217–360; a miniature pot (Fig 119, no 8); a copper alloy chain fragment (Fig 133, no 6)
robber trench
Trench F65, fill, context 68: a coin of 350–60; a shale bracelet fragment (Fig 129, no 9); a bone pin (Fig 131, no 22); a fragment of a lead or pewter vessel (Fig 157, no 3)

Room C
demolition rubble
Context 70: nine coins with a date range of 270–360; a miniature pot (Fig 118, no 2); a copper alloy bracelet fragment
robber trench
Trench F66, fill, context 69: 16 coins with a date range of 270–370; a copper alloy bead and a fitting

Room D
demolition rubble
Context 45: a miniature pot; two glass beads (including Fig 126, no 12); a copper alloy nail cleaner (Fig 135, no 5)
robber trench
Trench F90, fill, context 37: four coins with a date range of 270—350; six lead tablets (including Tablets 23–5); a glass bead; a copper alloy fragment

Room E
demolition rubble
Context 63:a lead tablet; a miniature pot
robber trench
Trench F74, fill, context 73: a miniature pot

Room F
demolition rubble
Context 80: 58 coins with a date range of 270–350; a lead tablet; a copper alloy coiled strip (Fig 153, no 5)
robber trench
Trench F85, fill, context 86: two coins with a date range of 350–60

Room G
demolition rubble
Context 97: eight coins with a date range of 270–350; a lead tablet; three miniature pots; a copper alloy pin shaft; a bone and iron razor or knife (Fig 136, no 11)
robber trench
Trench F84, fill, context 82: ten coins with a date range of 307–360

Room H
demolition rubble
Context 120: a coin of 270–73

Room J
demolition rubble
Context 106: an iron projectile; two miniature pots (including Fig 119, no 5); a bone pin shaft; a copper alloy lock plate (Fig 151, no 1), an awl, a furniture boss; an iron staple

Later contexts
Pit F158
three lead tablets; two miniature pots (Fig 117, nos 4 and 5); two bone pins (Fig 131, nos 12 and 25)
Room K, Cess pit
Context 187: a second-century coin; five coins with a date range of 293–378; 28 lead tablets (including Tablets 69–71); 19 miniature pots (including Figs 118, no 9 and 119, no 9); a bone pin

Deposits of votive material (Phase 5e(ii))

Following the final demolition of the remnant of Structure I, Rooms A, D, and E, *c* AD 380, the area of the former building was used for deposition of substantial quantities of debris, which included many objects of votive character. This debris seems to have derived from the temple Structure II, possibly in association with a major collapse or demolition and the subsequent modification of the temple building which took place at this time. The deposit over the demolished remains of Structure I was probably a uniform one, but has survived best in the hollows which developed above the fills of the various robber trenches. This is shown best in Figure 39, sections BI A and BI C, where a debris deposit, context 22, lies above fill contexts 67 and 72, in robber trenches F64 and F71. Towards the unploughed hedge bank the overall deposit survived much better, and here the layer was particularly characterised by dense concentrations of animal bones, including many horn cores of goats (see chapter 12). The distribution of these deposits is shown in Figure 42, where contexts 22, 32, 38, and 62 reflect the positions of robber trenches F64/F71, F65, F66, and F74 below them. The general layer, context 20, which lay immediately under the ploughsoil and above the remains of Structure I, probably represents the last remnant of a deposit of votive debris which originally covered this whole area. The diagnostic small finds from all these layers are summarised below; full lists of all the finds are available in the site archive. The distribution of coins includes many issues of late third and fourth-century date up to AD 360, as in the underlying robber trench fills, but also present are significant numbers of coins of the House of Valentinian, indicating that this deposit of debris must date to the late AD 370's. Indeed it must have immediately post-dated the final demolition of the remnant of Structure I. The small finds include most classes of votive object found on the site: a figurine, lead tablets, decorated plaques, miniature pots, brooches, glass beads, and spoons, along with other fittings from pieces of furniture. In addition, all these deposits contained very large quantities of potentially sacrifical animal bones.

Diagnostic finds from deposits of votive material above the demolition contexts

over robber trenches
Context 22: 46 coins with a date range of 270–360, plus a 'hoard' of four with a date range of 360–80; the copper alloy Sol bust (Figs 82 and 85, no 1); three lead tablets

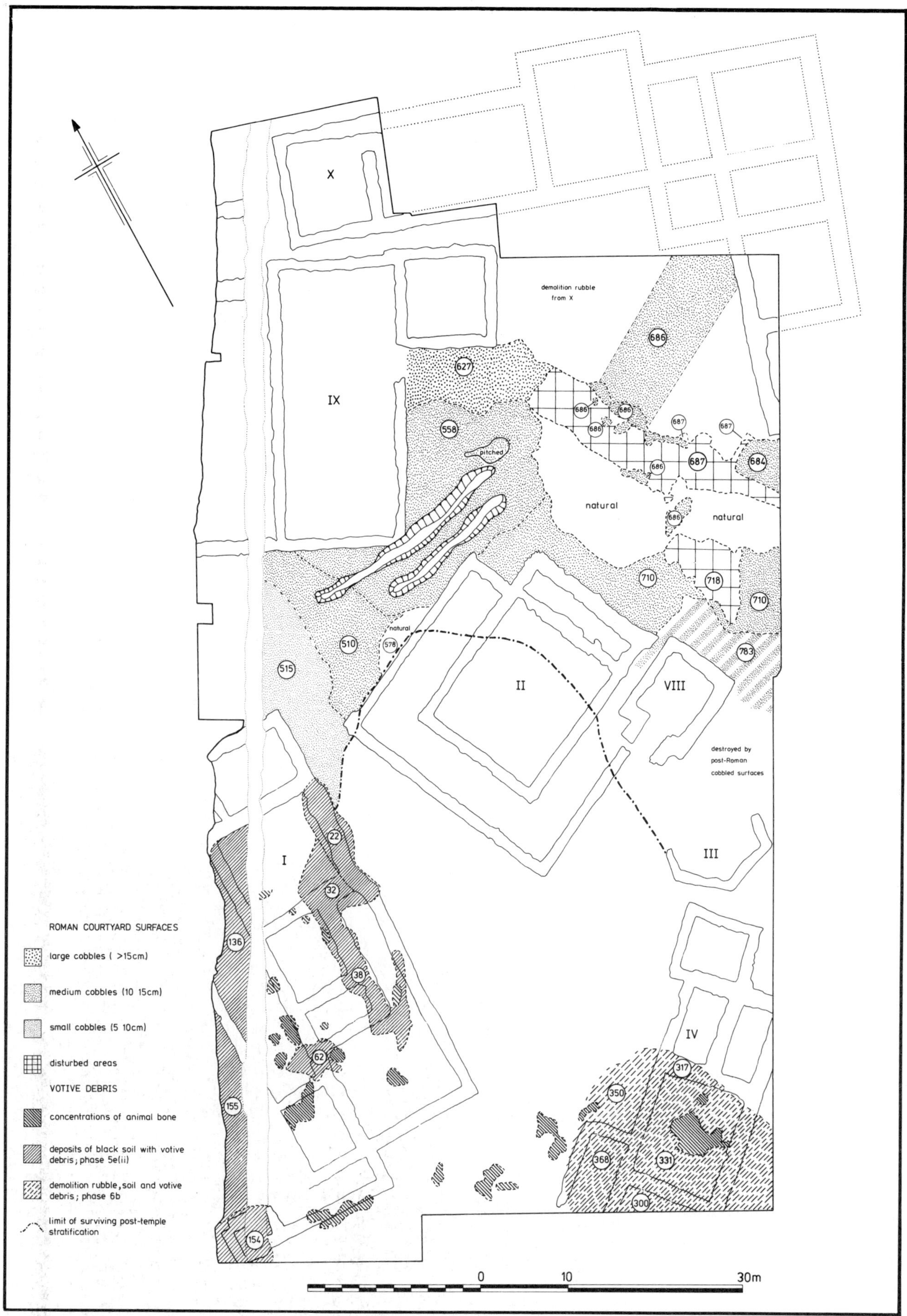

Fig 42 Plan showing the extent of courtyard surfaces and deposits of votive debris, scale 1:600

(including Tablet 22); a copper alloy votive leaf (Fig 92, no 1), a leaf fragment (Fig 92, no 8); an iron catapult bolt (Fig 113, no 24); a copper alloy cast ring (Fig 114, no 15); a miniature pot; a bracelet fragment (Fig 128, no 1), a spoon handle (Fig 134, no 5); a knife fragment (Fig 144, no 2), a ring; bone inlay (Fig 150, no 3); a copper alloy spiral rod (Fig 153, no 6), a washer (Fig 154, no 5)

Context 32: 14 coins with a date range of 270–360, three with a date range of 360–80; four lead tablets (including Tablet 35); a copper alloy cast ring (Fig 114, no 24); an iron knife (Fig 144, no 4); a copper alloy stud (Fig 150, no 13), a decorated strip (Fig 153, no 11), a furniture boss fragment; an iron handle (Fig 157, no 10)

Context 38: 51 coins with a date range of 270–360, ten with a range of 360–80; miniature spears (Fig 110, nos 1 and 4); a miniature pot; a copper alloy brooch (Fig 125, no 2), a bracelet fragment (Fig 127, no 28), a spoon handle (Fig 134, no 6), a spoon bowl (Fig 134, no 7), a furniture boss fragment; an iron fitting

Context 62: six coins with a date range of 270–360; 13 lead tablets (including Tablets 5, 36, 47–52, 53(ii), and 54); a miniature pot; an iron staple; a bone pin (Fig 131, no 17); a curled copper alloy strip (Fig 153, no 2)

overall layer
Context 20: 58 coins with a date range of 270–360, four with a range of 360–80; 12+ lead tablets (including Tablets 21, 27–33, and 43); 10 miniature pots (including Figs 118, nos 3 and 4; 119, no 7); a copper alloy buckle (Fig 135, no 11); a glass bead; an iron fitting; a whetstone (Fig 147, no 11)

towards the hedge bank
Context 136: a coin of 270–360; a lead tablet; two miniature pots; copper alloy fragments

Context 155: three coins with a date range a 270–360; a lead tablet; a miniature pot

above Room K
Context 154: a lead tablet; a fragment of copper alloy furniture boss

Structure IV

Phases 4 and 5a–b

Structure IV was situated south of the temple in the south-eastern corner of the excavated area (Fig 43). Only its western and northern sectors were examined; it is suspected that further rooms extended east beyond the edge of the excavated area, and it was demonstrated, by clearance of plough soil, that a substantial range of rooms continued to the south-west. The extent of these rooms, which were not excavated, is shown in Figure 3. The wall foundations were all of mortared limestone blocks, surviving to a height of two or three courses, laid over pitched foundations which were particularly deep where wall lines crossed the underlying ditch F382 (see Fig 45, section BIV D). The whole building seems to have been aligned according to the line of this Late Iron Age and early Roman ditch, just as Structure I appears to have been aligned above ditch F179. Rooms A, B, and C were totally excavated, as well as three quadrants of Room D, and the north-eastern portion of Room F (Fig 44). Room A was defined by walls F305, F306, and F307, which were butted on to wall F308, the north-eastern wall of Room B. This room contained three hearths, a stone door step, and complex occupation deposits, indicative of the two main phases of use. Rooms B and C were enclosed by walls F308, F310, F318, F321, and F362, with wall F311 dividing B from C. Walls F310 and F321 continued, F310 as F361, to form the north-western and south-eastern walls of Room D, which was enclosed on the south-west by the walls F358 and F359 of Room F. These were in turn butted on to the robbed remnant F352 of wall F361. All excavated rooms were found to have carefully laid cobbled floors, and Room D had sandstone tile hearth F367 set against its north-eastern wall. This was filled with context 366, ash, and context 360, rakeout from the fire, which had spread out over the cobbles of the floor (Figs 44 and 45, section BIV G). Walls F311 and F318, belonging to Rooms B and C, had been set in foundation trenches cut through the upper fills of the underlying ditch F382. The fill of foundation trench F364, context 322 (Fig 44, section BIV D) contained second and third-century pottery; otherwise no dating evidence for construction of the building was recovered. Occupation deposits survived only in Rooms A and D. In Room D these comprised the context 360 rakeout, derived from the tile hearth F367 already mentioned. This deposit contained three bone pin shafts and a copper alloy rivet (Fig 152, no 9). The disturbed floor level of Room B (context 320) included two glass beads, a copper alloy finger ring (Fig 132, no 17) and a whetstone (Fig 147, no 2). Also from this disturbed context were 16 coins, mainly of the late third century, but including three fourth-century types.

The floor of Room A, context 329 (Fig 45, section BIV B), contained a cast ring (Fig 114, no 23), and a copper alloy bracelet fragment. The layer of rakeout and the secondary floor level, context 302 (Fig 45, section BIV B, and Fig 46) included a copper alloy earring (Fig 127, no 12); a glass bead; five fragments of shale and jet bracelets (Figs 129, nos 15, 16, and 18; and 130, nos 1 and 7) and two pieces of jet hair pin (Figs 131, nos 9 and 11). This layer also contained four late third-century coins. A compact area of cement outside this room, and partly beneath Structure III, may represent mortar mixing for its construction, but this deposit contained no finds. Exterior layers of gravel and rough cobbling were probably contemporary with the use of Room A. The sequence of hearths is shown in Figure 45, sections BIV B and BIV C, and in Figure 46. In the first phase of use, a rectangular hearth F328 was bounded by a mortared limestone wall, while in the opposite corner another hearth F337 was composed of successive layers of gravel and mortar, with a fill of ash, context 335 (Fig 46, section BIV E). The hearth F328 was remodelled by the incorporation of a capping of gravel and mortar, containing an ash and charcoal deposit, context 315 (Fig 45, section BIV B). Following the build up of the secondary floor level, context 302, two new hearths were built. Over the remains of F328 a smaller setting of reused sandstone roofing tiles, F314 (Figs 44, 45, section BIV B, and Fig 46), was inserted in the corner of the room, whilst in the northern corner a new sub-circular hearth F326, built from limestone and sandstone fragments, was inserted (Fig 45, section BIV C, and Fig 46).

Fig 43 Structure IV, Rooms A,B,C and D, extent of excavation in 1977, view from the north-west. (Photo: Peter Leach)

Building sequence

Observation of butt joints demonstrates that Room A was added to wall F308 and that Room F was annexed to wall F352 (Fig 44). In addition wall F318 was an inserted partition between walls F310 and F321, and wall F311 was subsequently inserted to partition Room B from Room C. This evidence, taken together with consideration of the thickness and morphology of the various walls, suggests that the building originally comprised a rectangular block, later occupied by Rooms B, C, D, and E, and which possibly extended eastwards beyond the limits of the cutting (Fig 35). A partition wall between Rooms B/C and D was then inserted; whether wall F356 between Rooms D and E was also an insertion cannot be determined due to the damage caused by later robbing. Dating evidence, to be discussed below, shows that the main range of Structure IV was demolished *c* AD 310 and the main phase of use is therefore assigned to Phase 4: the first rectangular structure to Phase 4a and the addition of Rooms A, and probably F, to Phase 4b. The presence of late third-century coins in the rakeout, context 302, in Room A suggests that the second phase of hearths and occupation may have belonged to the early fourth century. The presence of a few fourth-century coins in the disturbed floor level of Room B, and the secondary insertion of wall F311, further indicate that Room B may have survived the period of general demolition. Thus the adjacent Rooms A and B may have survived and been refurbished to function as a freestanding two room unit during Phase 5a–b (Fig 33).

Demolition

All rooms, with the exception of Room A, contained thick deposits of demolition rubble incorporating limestone blocks, mortar, plaster and fragments of sandstone roof tiles (Fig 45). The major contexts were contexts 309 and 312 in Room B, contexts 332 (and 348 not illus) in Room D, context 347 in Room E, and context 369 (not illus) in Room F. The identifiable small finds recovered from these deposits are summarised below. The coins suggest that the major part of the structure was demolished early in the fourth century AD. The finds from these layers are presumed to relate to the former use of Structure IV and of adjacent buildings. The concentration of votive objects, such as the miniature pots, lead tablets, and, in particular, the worn limestone statue head (Fig 77, no 2) must signify ritual activity on the site in the years preceding AD 310, and provide some of the clearest evidence that the temple must have been in use during the third, and probably also the second, centuries AD. Robbing of walls in Room D took place a little later, according to the coin evidence from context 346 (see below) while, as argued above, Rooms A and B probably still stood, and were in full use, until the mid-fourth century. Thus, a later layer of demolition rubble, context 317 over Room B, contained coins which included issues of Theodora (AD 337–40) and Helena (AD 337–41).

The latest deposits over part of the site of Structure IV are rubble spreads which probably derive from the final demolition of the temple in Phase 6b (Fig 42). These will be discussed in detail in chapter 4.

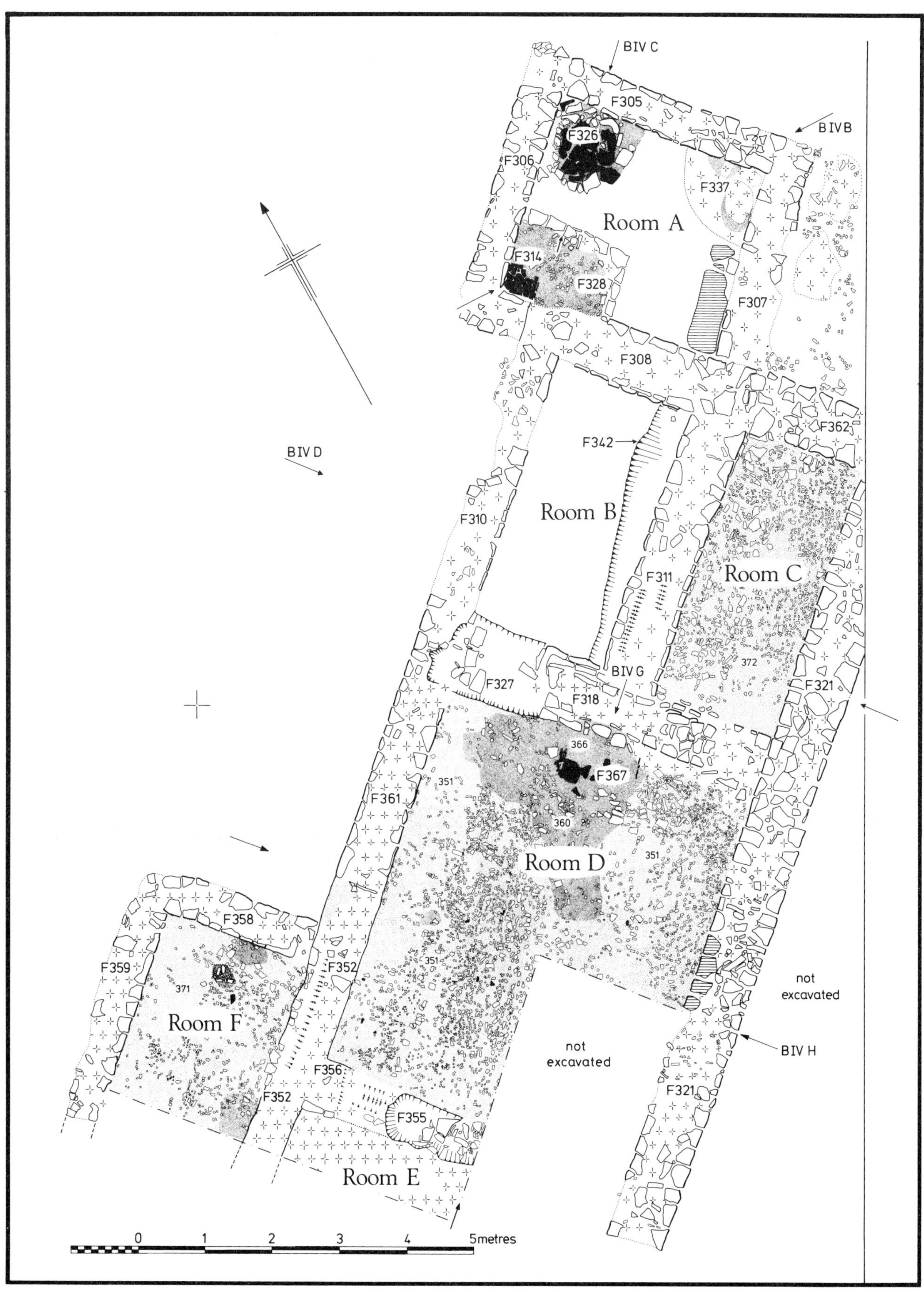

Fig 44 Phases 4 to 5a–b, plan of Structure IV, scale 1:80

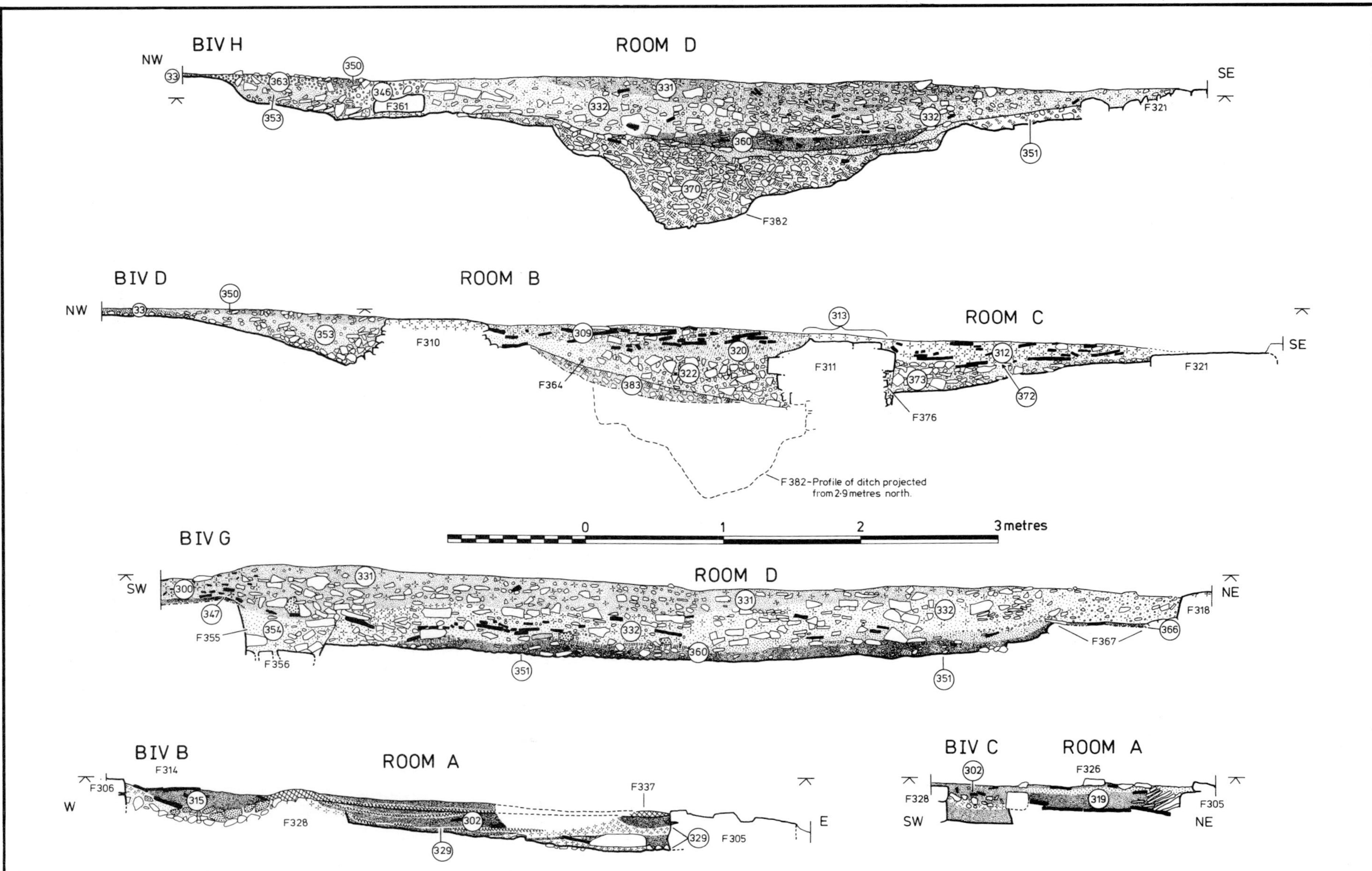

Fig 45 Phases 4 to 5a–b, sections of Structure IV, scale 1:40

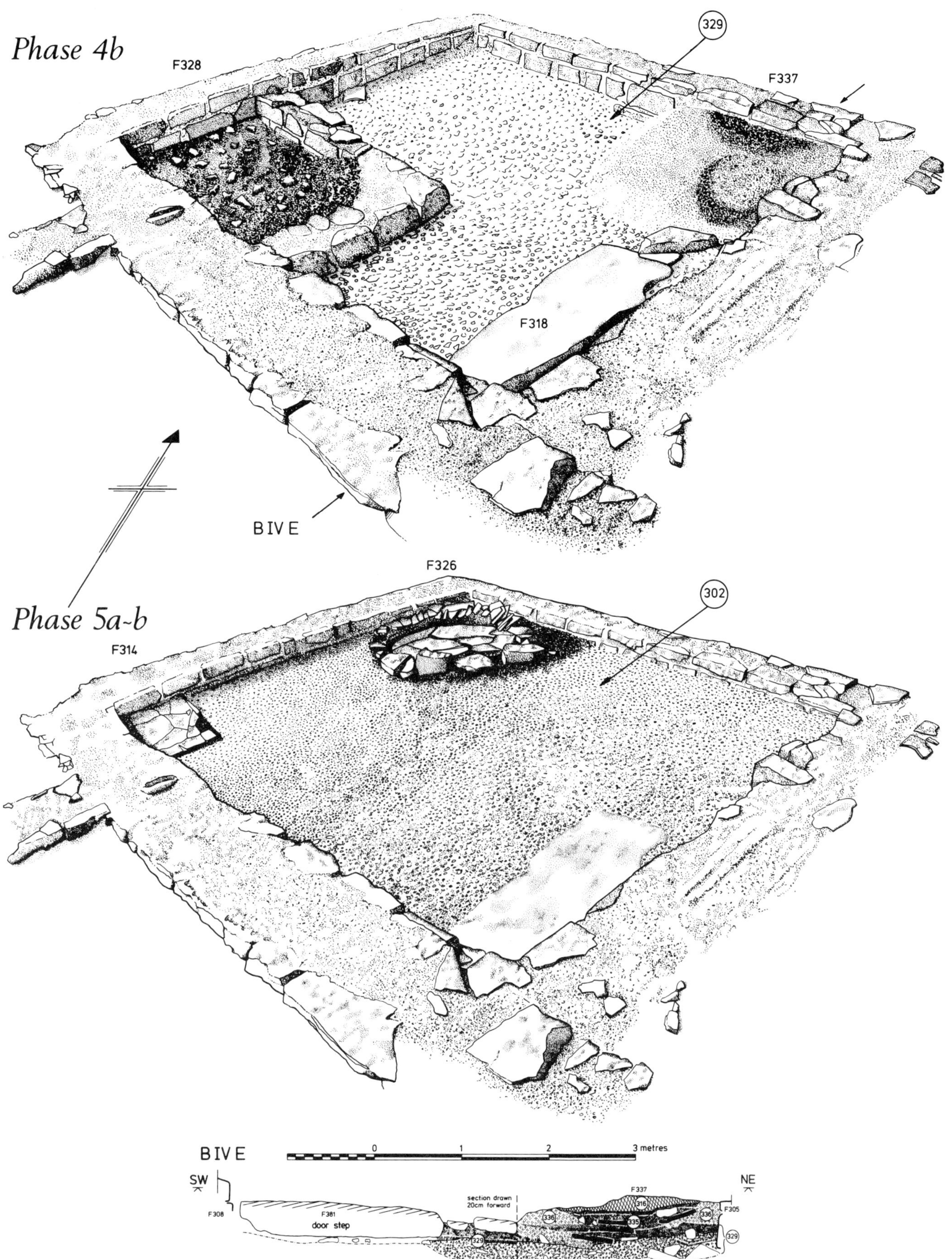

Fig 46 Structure IV, Room A, isometric views and section, scale 1:60

Diagnostic finds from the demolition contexts

Room B
first demolition
Context 309/312: six coins with a date range of 260–313; a lead tablet; a miniature pot; a jet/shale bead (Fig 127, no 3); a bracelet fragment (Fig 129, no 7); a whetstone (Fig 147, no 4); copper alloy tubing

second demolition (Rooms A and B only)
Context 317: five coins with a date range of 193–341

Room D
first demolition
Context 332/348: seven coins with a date range of 238–307; a worn statue head (Fig 77, no 2); two lead tablets (including Tablet 62); six miniature pots (including Fig 118, nos 1, 7, 11, and 12); a copper alloy bracelet fragment (Fig 127, no 17); a jet/shale bracelet fragment (Fig 130, no 2); a bone pin (Fig 131, no 14); a key ring (Fig 132, no 10); iron keys (Fig 139, nos 2 and 6), fittings; a needle (Fig 145, no 2)
robber trench
Context 346: two coins with a date range of 293–345; two miniature pots (Fig 117, nos 6 and 7); a glass bead

Room E
first demolition
Context 347: inscribed lead tablet 57; a miniature pot

Room F
first demolition
Context 369: a coin of 270–90; a lead tablet; two miniature pots (including Fig 118, no 8)

Fig 47 Structure IX, Rooms B and C, below Structure XIV, view from the south (1979). (Photo: Sebastian Rahtz)

Structure IX

Phase 5a

Following the demise of Structure X, the area occupied by its former south-west wing was taken up as the site for a new stone building, Structure IX (Fig 47). Coin evidence suggests that initial construction took place around or just after AD 300. The first Structure, IX(i), was rectangular in shape and was subsequently replaced by the slightly larger and L-shaped Structure IX(ii) (Fig 33).

The first structure, measuring *c* 16 × 8m, was defined by stone wall footings F1102, F1103, and F1104 (Figs 48 and 49) to south, west, and north. The original east wall was represented by a largely robbed wall, F1286, surviving as a fragment within its rock-cut foundation trench F1278, which had been enlarged by robbing (Fig 48 and Fig 49, section S46). The line of wall F1286 continued north as a strip of rubble, context 1285 (Fig 33), lying within a trench which was not excavated. The character of the junction between this rubble and the north wall footings F1104 suggested that they had been bonded, whilst the junction between the footings F1104 and the east wall F614 of Structure IX(ii) definitely had been reconstructed. The junction of wall F1286 with wall F1102 to the south had been destroyed by robbing and later ploughing, although it should be noted that the robber trench F1278 did not extend quite as far as wall F1102. A 2m gap between the wall F1286 and the rubble strip, context 1285, suggested that an original entrance lay on the east side. The fragment of wall foundation F698 may have been connected with an entrance structure, as also may a short north–south section of wall, F814, which subsequently became incorporated into the east wall of Structure IX(ii) (Fig 48). Further east lay a further isolated strip of wall footing, F689, parallel to wall F1286 but 1.60m in front of it. No associated features such as post holes were located, but the plinth may have supported a verandah south of the entrance, or have provided the foundation for a free-standing screen.

The interior was subdivided into two unequal parts by context 1234, a short strip of rubble and roof tile fragments running east–west (Figs 48 and 49, section S2); this may reflect the former line of a slight partition wall. Certainly the deposits north and south of it were markedly distinct. Deposits in Room C, south of the rubble layer context 1234, were characterised by deposits of stone rubble and tile (perhaps from the demolition of Structure X); context 1231, ash and burnt soil (Fig 49, section S2), was sealed by context 1220 compact soil containing many ceramic tile fragments. This formed a base for context 1217, the mortar bedding of a plain tessellated pavement, F1216. To the east all these deposits had been ploughed away. No tesserae survived in the western sector of the room either, and this may reflect the original extent of the floor, and possibly a subdivision of the room, or the removal of part of the floor during the modifications accompany-

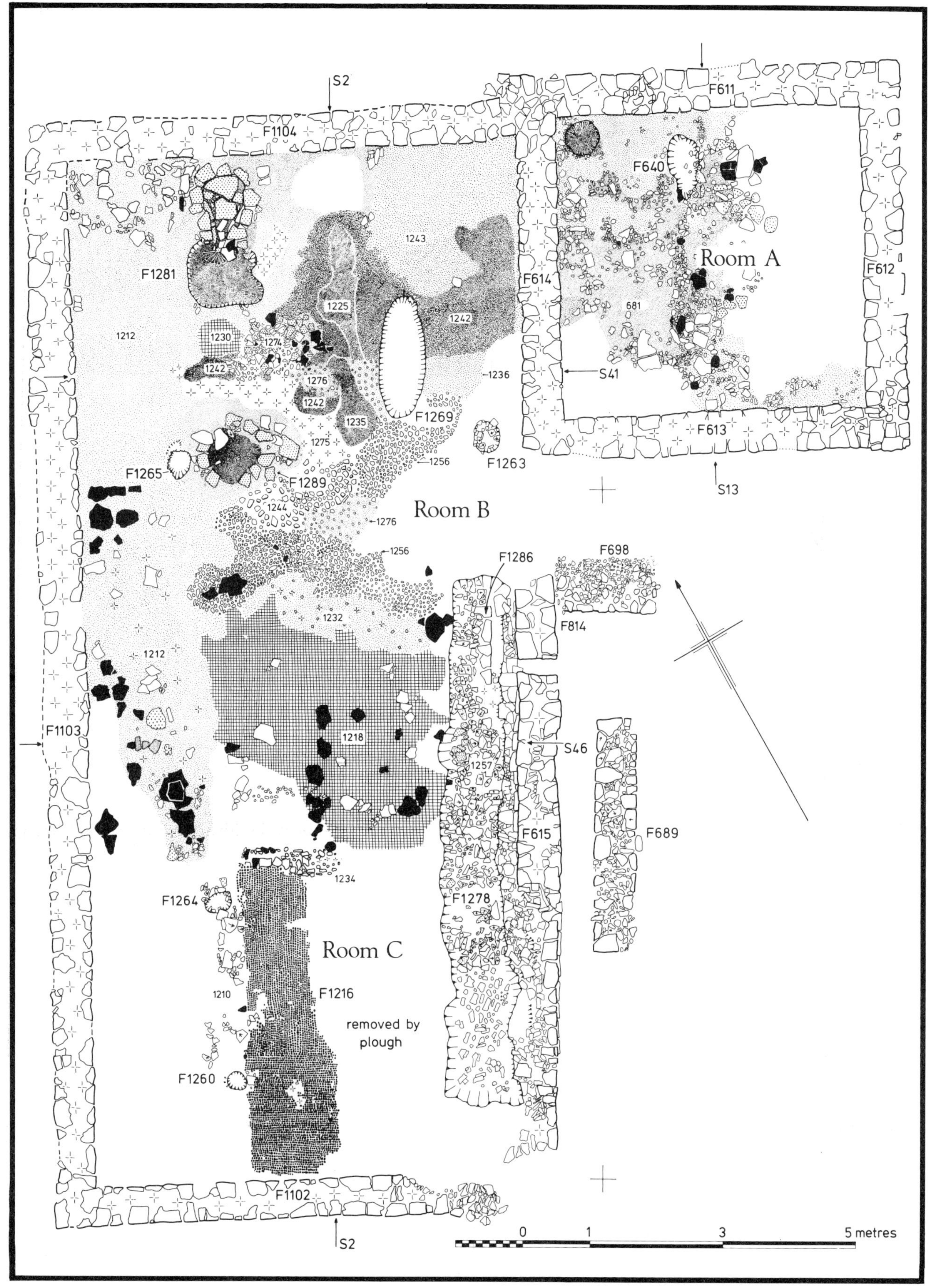

Fig 48 Phase 5a–c, plan of Structure IX, scale 1:80

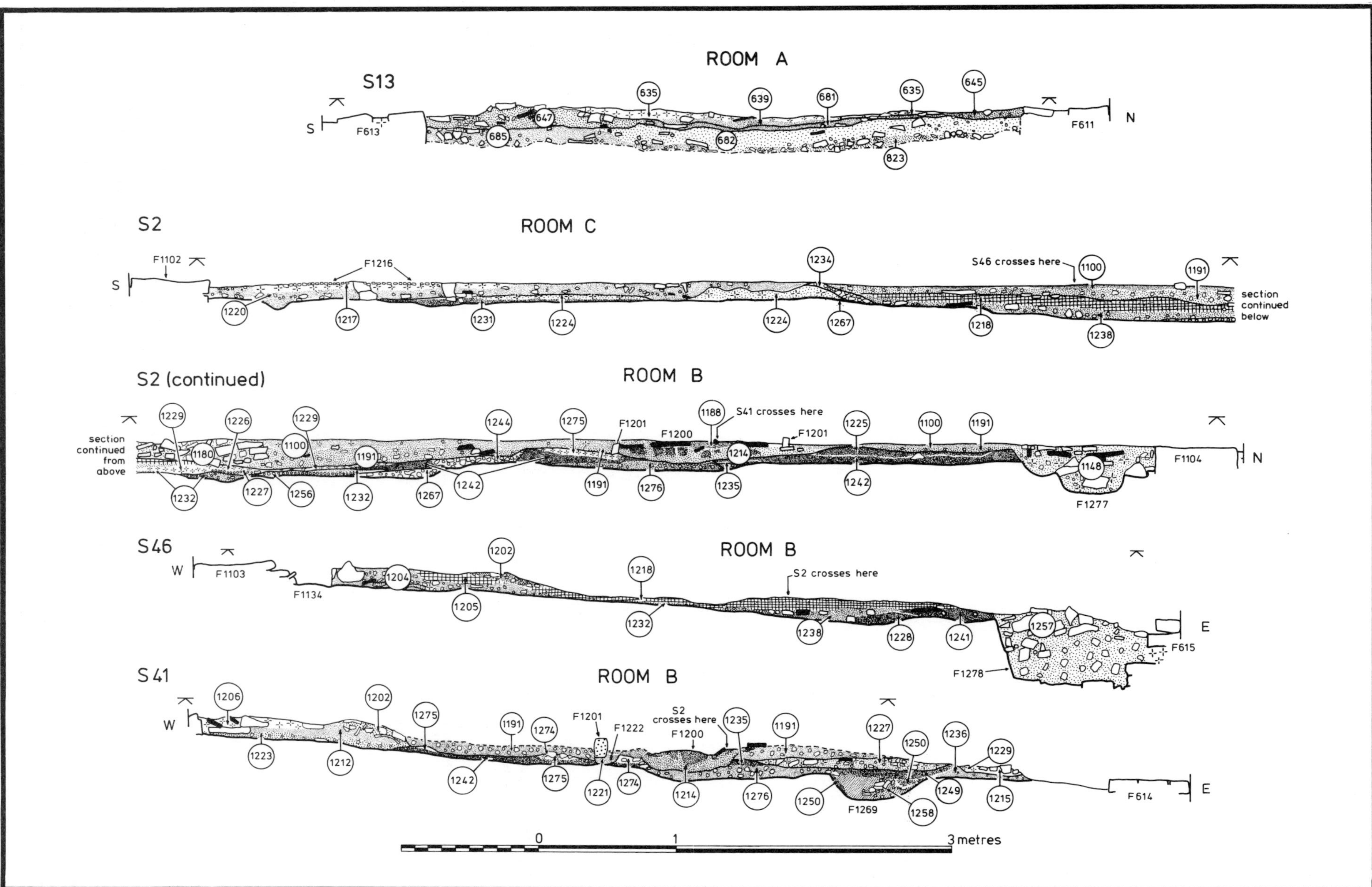

Fig 49 Phase 5, sections of Structures IX and XIV, scale 1:40

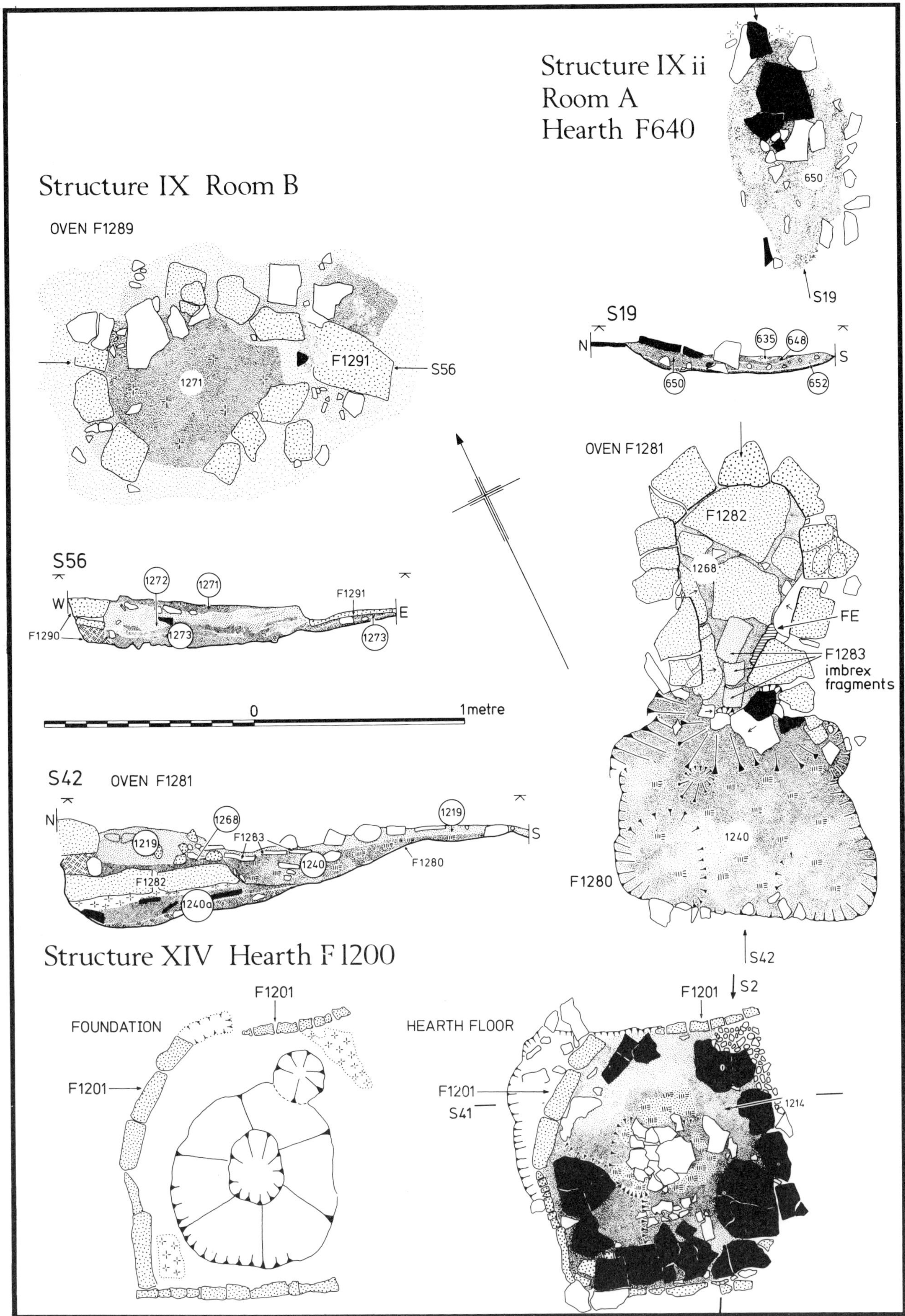

Fig 50 Phase 5, Structures IX and XIV, ovens and hearths, scale 1:25

ing the construction of Structure IX(ii). Twenty-five coins (many from the foundation for the tessellated floor) dated from the later third century. Room C also produced a shale bracelet fragment (Fig 130, no 3), a glass counter (Fig 135, no 14), four bone pin fragments, small metal objects and a blob or dribble of copper alloy.

The northern end of the building (Room B) contained a succession of hearths and ovens. The earliest of these was a pit containing ash and burnt soil fills, which was cut by an elongated hearth F1269 (Fig 48), which was filled with a sequence of burnt deposits, contexts 1259, 1250, and 1258 (Fig 49, section S41). A more substantial stone-lined oven to the south-west, F1289 (Fig 48), was set in construction pit F1290 (Figs 48 and 50, section S56). This contained burnt fills contexts 1271, 1272, and 1273 and the remains of a tiled horizontal draught flue F1291. A smaller pit nearby held the remains of an *in situ* coarse ware vessel. Spreads of burnt soil and debris around these features included contexts 1236 and 1276 (Fig 49, section S41). Two intermittent cobbled areas (eg context 1256, Fig 49, section S2) and an area of stone paving probably represented portions of the contemporary floor levels at this end of the building. The soil spread context 1232 (Fig 49, section S2) probably also belonged to this phase. Room B produced one mid-fourth-century coin; a fragment of a clay vessel (Fig 121, no 2); a bone pin (Fig 131, no 27) and a copper alloy spoon bowl (Fig 134, no 3).

Phase 5b

During the early part of the fourth century, the building was modified by the reconstruction of the east side and the addition of a further room, Room A, at the north-eastern corner. The new east wall F615 was laid on pitched footings and it was aligned with the west wall of Room A, F614 (Fig 48). The corner of the new room was joined to the original north wall of Structure IX(i), F1104, by an irregular section of new stonework. The central eastern entrance position was maintained, and the subdivision into two major rooms continued. In addition, a line of disturbed rubble, context 1210, and two post holes F1260 and F1264 may represent a distinct sub-partition within Room C (Fig 48). Finds in this room now included five late third-century coins and a copper alloy earring (Fig 127, no 13).

The larger Room B continued to be taken up with hearths, ovens and associated deposits. The main new feature in Phase 5b comprised a pear-shaped oven F1281 (Figs 48, 50, and 51), with a firebox pit F1280, filled with ashy soil, on its south side, context 1240 (Fig 50). It backed onto F1104, the northern wall of the building and contained fills of ash and burnt soil, context 1240a (Fig 50, section S42), beneath burnt floor F1282 of limestone and sandstone flags. This was enclosed by a drystone chamber of burnt limestone, which also contained a clay tile flue F1283 and a fill of burnt soil and ash, context 1268. Finds from the oven and rakeout layers included a mid-fourth-century coin, a fragment of the base of a limestone column (Fig 138, no 1), a baked clay whorl (Fig 143, no 5), and a bone handle (Fig 144, no 8).

Areas of burnt soil and ash occurred as patches elsewhere in Room B (including contexts 1225, 1230, 1235, 1242, and 1243, Figs 48 and 49, section S2). Also there were patches of cobbled surfaces, although these may never have formed a uniform and even floor. An area of rough worn cobbles context 1274 (Fig 48) set in mortar lay close to the earlier oven F1289. Two successive cobbled surfaces, context 1227 (Fig 49, section S41) set into context 1229 mortar, followed by cobbles of context 1203, occupied a more extensive area inside the eastern entrance. Two post holes F1263 and F1265 (Fig 48) may represent later arrangements within Room B, possibly a further partition following the abandonment of hearths F1269 and F1289. The cobbled surfaces produced fragments of metal and glass and a shale bracelet fragment (Fig 129, no 22).

The four walls of Room A, F611, F612, F613, and F614 defined an almost square room measuring 5.80 × 5.60m extending eastward from the north-east corner of the main block (Fig 48). All were bonded together and wall F611 was linked to wall F1104 by an irregular segment of new footings. A dump of hard mortar, soil, and stone rubble in mortar against the exterior footings of wall F613 probably represented surplus mortar and building debris from the time of construction. Part of an original floor of worn limestone blocks lay close to the surviving footings of wall F621, part of Structure X (Fig 35). Extensive deposits of silty soil, context 681 (Fig 48) and context 639 (Fig 49, section S13) covered much of the floor, along with context 645, a strip of stonier silt, around the edges of the room. (Fig 49, section S13).

The main hearth F640 (Figs 48 and 50) was cut into deposit 645 in the north-west corner of the room. An oval pit was filled with a sequence of ash and burnt soil, contexts 648, 650, and 652, capped by sandstone and limestone blocks. In the south-east corner of the room a layer of rubble and dark soil, context 647, (Fig 52) may have accumulated during the operation of the hearth and continued in use as a surface in Phase 5d–e. Construction deposits in Room A contained one late third-century coin, while the interior levels included an iron ring (Fig 154, no 12) and the rim fragment from a copper alloy vessel (Fig 156, no 5).

Fig 51 Structure IX, oven F1281, view from the west (1979), scale 0.30m. (Photo: Sebastian Rahtz)

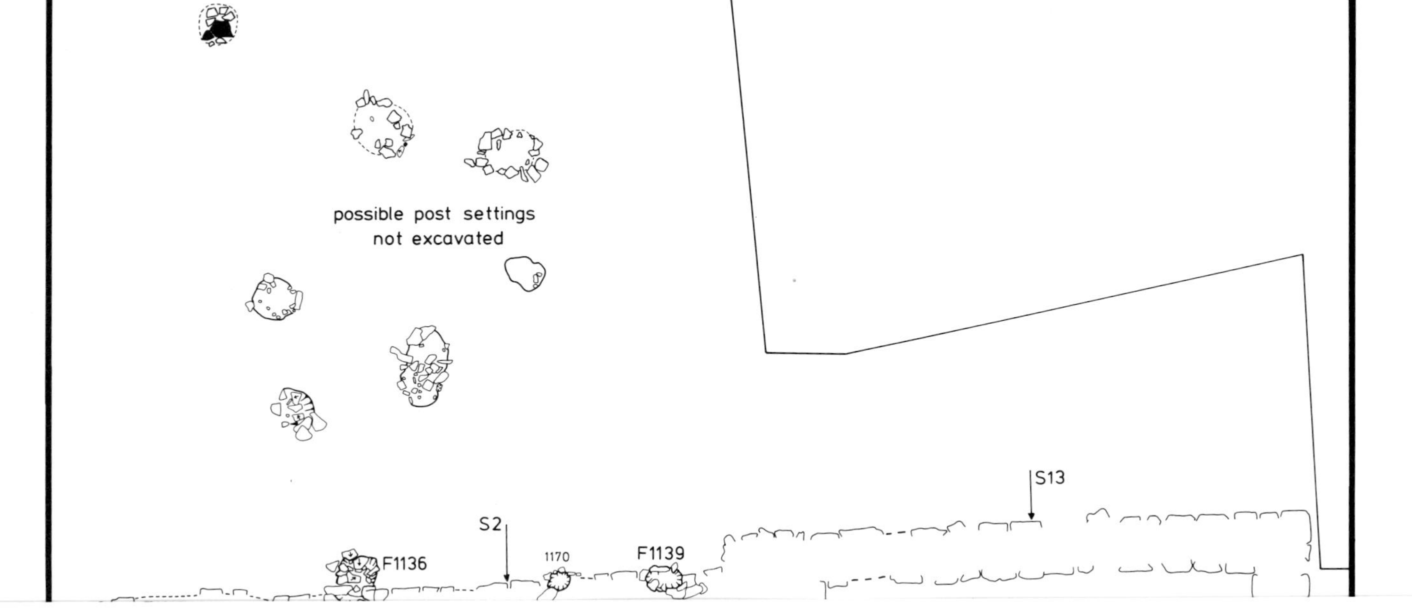
possible post settings
not excavated
S13
S2
F1136
1170
F1139

Phase 5c

The most extensive demolition deposits surviving in the area of Structure IX, contexts 1204 and 1206, were located immediately outside the south end of the building and along the west interiors of Room C (Fig 49, section S46) and Room B (Fig 49, section S41) respectively. The latter, context 1206, sealed context 1212, another extensive dump, mainly of mortar and finer rubble, and context 1223 composed of large rubble. A separate patch of similar materials, context 1238 (Fig 49, section S2), lay further east over the floors of Room B. Demolition deposits over most of Room B were destroyed during the construction of Structure XIV, but a few patches remained above the abandoned ovens F1281 and F1289, context 1219 (Fig 50, section S42). Further deposits of building rubble, mortar and soil lay immediately outside the east wall F615. The finds from these demolition levels are summarised below. The coins contained within them indicate that demolition may have occurred around AD 350. Only context 1204 produced coins of second-century date and this dump may have included residual rubble from the underlying Structure X.

Diagnostic finds from the demolition rubble

Context 1204: four second-century coins, five third-century coins, nine coins with a date range of 300–350; copper alloy cast rings (including Fig 114, nos 2 and 14); two brooches (Fig 125, nos 6 and 7); a shale bracelet fragment (Fig 129, no 17); copper alloy tweezers (Fig 135, no 1); an iron spoon (Fig 135, no 3); a glass counter (Fig 135, no 15); an iron chisel (Fig 145, no 11); and a whetstone (Fig 147, no 6).

Context 1206: two third-century coins, one with a date range of 300–50; a copper alloy *caduceus* (Fig 89, no 1); fragments of an antler and copper alloy bracelet (Fig 130, no 13); an iron tool (Fig 145, no 8)

Context 1208: two copper alloy blobs; a melon bead (Fig 126, no 8)

Context 1213: two third-century coins, and one with a date range of 300–50

Context 1223: three third-century coins, and three with a date range of 300–35; an iron knife (Fig 144, no 1), a blade fragment; a hook or catch (Fig 153, no 1)

Context 1238: a coin with a date range of 300–50

Context 1245: a third-century coin

Structure XIV

Phase 5d–e

Soon after the demolition of Structure IX, around AD 350, the site was used for the foundations of a timber-framed building, Structure XIV (Figs 41 and 52). This comprised a rectangular structure aligned with its predecessor and defined by post holes, slots and a terraced platform cut into the floor of Structure IX, Room B. The new building covered an area 11 × 5m, with an eastern porch measuring 5 × 3m. Difficulties were encountered in the definition of some of the post holes relating to this structure, but the extent is well indicated by the more positive holes, the slots and the limits of the terraced floor level. The whole terrace was filled by a dark ashy soil, context 1191 (Fig 53), which indicated destruction by burning. The resultant ash had become mixed with the final floor deposits, and as the posts had burned *in situ*, variations in soil characteristics were difficult to determine.

Just outside the western terraced edge, a line of cuts and post settings ran parallel with, but just inside, the former west wall of Structure IX, F1103. At the southern end, an elongated cut F1134 (Fig 49, section S46, and Fig 52) was 0.12m deep and further north lay a series of soil and rubble patches, a post hole F1135 and, at the corner junction, a large terminal post setting F1145. Post hole depths are summarised in Figure 53, left. The northern wall line was more clearly marked by post holes, some of which cut the wall footings F1104. From west to east these comprised post holes F1136, F1354, 1170, F1144, and F1139. Along the east side the walls may have been supported upon the footings of walls F614 and F615, with at least one post hole F1143, cutting F614. The south end of the building was marked by the pronounced edge of a terrace which ran approximately along the line of the former partition between Rooms B and C of Structure IX. Post hole F1142 and post setting 1181 may have held central supports on this wall line. The location of a central ridge line may be represented by post holes F1142 (at the south end), F1141, F1146, F1149, and F1354. Indicators of activities within the building comprised a pit or bin, F1277 (Fig 49, section S2), with a stone capping and fill, context 1148, at the north end, and a large square hearth, F1200, located a little north of centre (Fig 49, sections S41 and S2, Figs 52 and 54). An area of rubble, context 1180, formed a platform further to the south (Fig 52). A dump of wall plaster apparently functioned as floor footings towards the south end. A roughly rectangular porch was defined on the north-east side by post holes F662, F665, F674, and F1143 (Fig 52), cutting the south wall of the former Room A of Structure IX. The southern row of posts was supported in post holes F644, F676, and F691. Between the two lines of post holes an area of pitched limestone and tile fragments was set into mortar; this formed a distinct floor level.

The post hole fills contained many small items of metal and glass including numerous nails, scraps of copper alloy sheet and a copper alloy blob. The fills of hearth F1200 and the bin F1277 produced further metal fragments, many hobnails, pieces of glass, and a finger

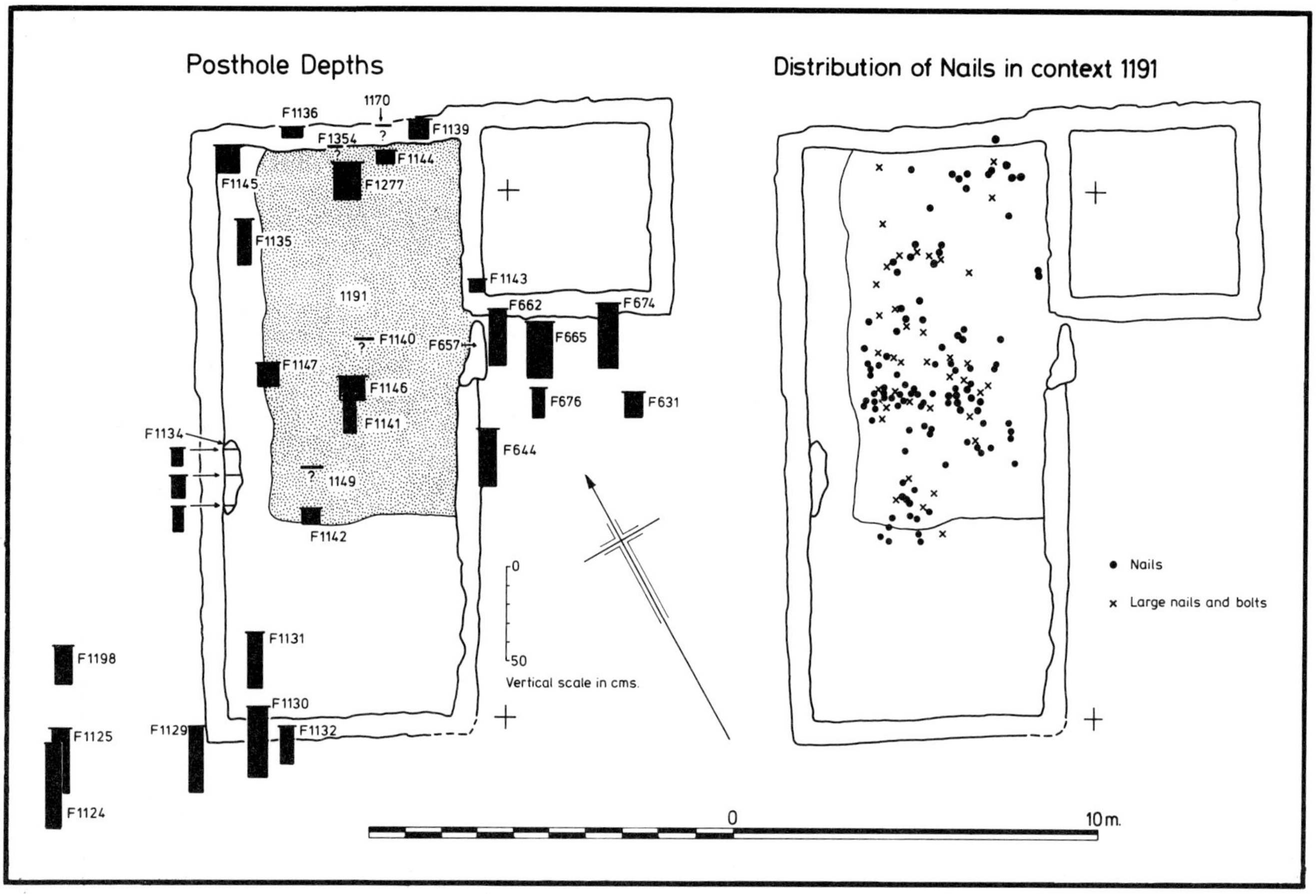

Fig 53 Structure XIV, posthole depths and distribution of nails in context 1191, scale 1:200

ring (Fig 132, no 3). The patches of flooring within the building contained five fourth-century coins, dating from AD 310 to 375, small metal items and a coiled terminal of iron (Fig 153, no 26).

To the south-west of the main area of Structure XIV, a further group of features may represent another building at right angles, or a west wing attached to the main structure (Figs 41 and 53). Context 1202 (Fig 52), a strip of rubble along the western terraced edge of Structure XIV, extended further south to cut the earlier tessellated floor of Structure IX, Room A. This rubble may have formed a footing both for the west wall of Structure XIV and the east wall of the western wing extension. A possible shallow beam slot may have marked the eastern margin of this wing. Post holes connected with it were remarkably deep (see Fig 53) and included post holes F1130, F1131, and F1132 within the former area of Structure IX and postholes F1124, F1125, F1129, and F1198 further to the west. The rubble layer, context 1202 contained 16 coins dating from AD 270 to 360 and obviously comprised material derived from the demolition of Structure IX. It also produced an enamelled brooch (Fig 124, no 8), a millefiori mount (Fig 126, no 4), a finger ring (Fig 132, no 18); an iron chisel or spoke-shave (Fig 145, no 9); and a bone sleeve (Fig 150, no 1).

Fig 54 Structure XIV, hearth F1201, view from the north-east (1979), scale 1m. (Photo: Sebastian Rahtz)

The interior of the main area of Structure XIV was occupied by the distinctive layer of black ashy soil, context 1191, referred to above. The concentration of debris and artefacts within this deposit suggests that it represented occupation levels as well as destruction deposits. Of the 64 coins found in the context, 56 were of mid-fourth-century date (320–378) and seven were of the late third century. Only one coin was a possible Theodosian issue, and this might indicate a destruction date of *c* 380, or just possibly within Phase 6 (very early fifth century). Other objects found comprised 14 objects of copper alloy, including a sheet leaf (Fig 92, no 9), a cast ring (Fig 114, no 4), and a bracelet fragment (Fig 127, no 19). There were also three bone pins, part of a bone bracelet (Fig 130, no 11); shale bracelet fragments; a glass counter (Fig 135, no 17); and 25 iron items, including a fitting (Fig 138, no 9), a candlestick (Fig 149, no 2), and a stud (Fig 150, no 18). Possible evidence for metalworking included two blobs or dribbles of copper alloy and three pieces of fuel-ash slag. The deposit contained many iron nails (their distribution is plotted in Fig 53). They appear to concentrate in the centre of the proposed building and the roughly linear patterns may reflect the positions of major roof timbers that fell during the conflagration that consumed the structure.

Rubble make-up context 647 and the remains of a mortar surface context 635 (Fig 52) may be remnants of exterior surfaces relating to Structures XIV, XIII or other structures situated beyond the limits of excavation. Alternatively, the mortar level may be an interior surface, associated with a building supported in part by the six post holes, above interpreted as having held the timbers for a porch attached to Structure IV.

Structure XIII

Phase 5d–6a

Traces of a structure built over the levelled demolition rubble of Structure X included floor foundation deposits and three probable post holes (Fig 55). The main floor context 608 consisted of large pitched limestone blocks, which were only slightly worn, laid in soil above a very hard base of creamy-yellow mortar context 628. On the north side the pitched stones had been disturbed by ploughing and the loose rubble and mortar of context 632 probably represents its disturbed remains. To the south of context 608 was a further area of pitched limestone cobbles, context 630, which was

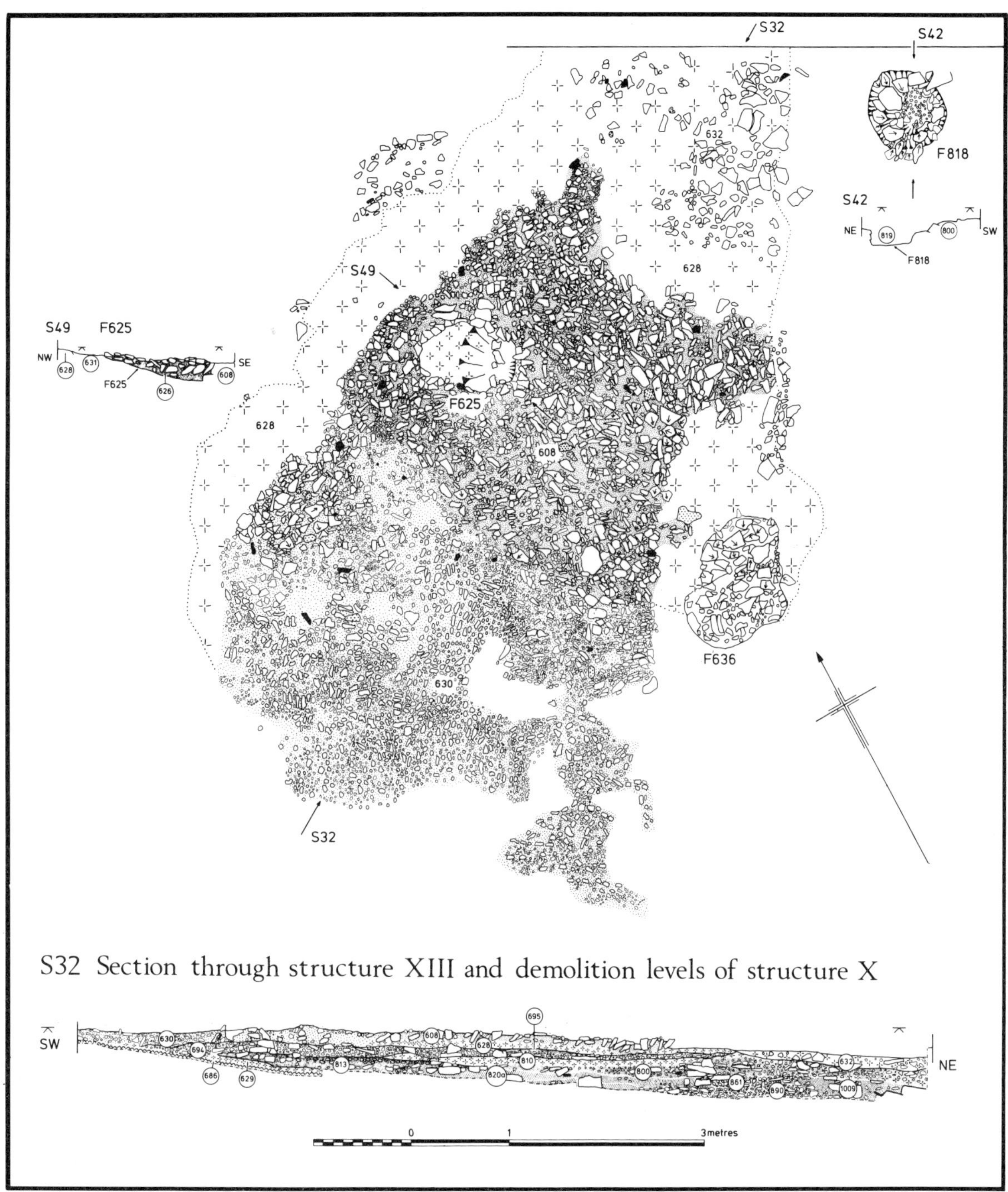

Fig 55 Phase 5d–6a, Structure XIII, scale 1:60

slightly worn. Three shallow post sockets were 0.80 to 1.35m in diameter and on average, 0.20m deep (Fig 55). Sockets F625 and F636 could have been situated near the front of a rectangular building measuring 4.8 × 4m with socket F818 holding a central roof support at the back (Fig 41). However the main floor, context 608, extended south of the two front post sockets, perhaps indicating the existence of an overhanging roof or porch belonging to a building with overall dimensions of 6.2 × 4m. It is suggested that this slight timber structure may have functioned as a shed to provide shelter for animals, stores or vehicles.

The post sockets included no finds in their fills but the mortar foundation, context 628, incorporated a coin of AD 350–60, and the floors, contexts 608 and 630, contained three coins of AD 350–60, one Theodosian coin; a copper alloy finger ring (Fig 132, no 13); one glass bead; and a number of iron hobnails.

The courtyard

Phases 4–6

The temple buildings were surrounded by a carefully laid courtyard surface comprising worn and rounded limestone cobbles laid tightly together. In general the stones were not pitched or arranged in lines, as was often the case with the cobbled surfaces and floors of the post-Roman phase. The extent of surviving courtyard surfaces is shown in Figure 42. The main area lay between Structures IX, X and II, immediately north of the temple entrance, but the single layer of medium sized cobble stones was worn completely away in the base of the depression between the temple and Structure X. Cobbles of larger size were found in the area around the entrance to Structure IX, and a pair of deep cart ruts ran through the narrow gap between Structures IX and II. The edge of the northern rut cut the corner foundation of Structure IX, suggesting that at least in its later phases of use, the track post-dated the demolition of Structure IX. This period of use could have been contemporary with the currency of Structure XIV in the later fourth century.

To the east of the temple, any Roman courtyard layers had been destroyed by the foundations of the stone platforms around the post-Roman Structure VIII. South-west of the temple, a distinctive area of smaller cobbled surface (stones averaging 50 to 100mm in diameter) was cut by the wall trenches of Structure I. A small portion of similar cobbles ran beneath the foundations of part of the eastern wall of Structure I and these smaller cobbles may represent the remnants of an earlier courtyard surface dating to the earlier part of Phase 4. In the area between Structures I and IV no stratification of Roman or post-Roman date survived.

4: The latest Roman and post-Roman shrines

Structure II

Phase 6

The third major phase of use for Structure II involved activities in parts of the former temple building and the construction of certain modifications and additions (Figs 29, 32, and 56). The portico and eastern ambulatory (Rooms F and D) appear to have gone out of use, with no stratification surviving. Modifications to the other ambulatories (Rooms A and C), the survival of occupation debris within them, and the construction of Room B indicate that these survived, whilst a lean-to annexe against Room C, in the area of the former cella, also belongs to this period of use. Thus the Phase 6 structure consisted of an L-shaped stone building, probably with its original roofs, and with a timber-framed addition filling part of the angle (Fig 56). The existence of the timber-framed annexe implies that the cella was no longer roofed and it appears that the portico, cella and eastern ambulatory either had been demolished or, more likely, had been cleared of debris following a collapse of the north-east corner of the edifice which overlaid the fill of the large Iron Age ditch segment F264 (Fig 29). The remaining portions of the structure were tidied up and modified to form the sanctuary of Phase 6, a strange structure indeed, but containing various deposits and features indicative of function. The outline of the area in use is reflected by the distribution of Theodosian coins found in Phase 6 deposits (Fig 224 in chapter 13).

Rooms A and C

The former west and south ambulatories were floored with worn limestone cobbles contexts 220 and 89 (Fig 36, section BII E). While context 220 may be the reused floor of the temple, context 89 slopes well below the postulated level of the temple floor (see Fig 30) and was probably laid in Phase 6. Above the floors a series of deposits survived comprising dark soil, stones, plaster fragments and ash and incorporating votive objects in some quantity in contexts 52 and 88 (Fig 36, section BII E) and contexts 2a and 238 (Fig 34, section BII C)). Against the outer wall of Room C a patch of burnt limestone blocks F488 (Fig 32) may have been the base of a hearth or altar.

Room A had been separated from Room C by an inserted partition wall. Traces of its footings survived as a zone of scattered stone blocks (Fig 32) and a bed of mortar, part of context 2 (Fig 36, section BII E), but whether it had been broken by an entrance could not be ascertained. Worn stones within the footings of the north wall of Room C suggest the position of an entrance there in this phase. Finds from the associated deposits included 26 coins, of which five were Theodosian issues; a votive iron miniature spear; cast copper alloy rings (Fig 115, nos 2 and 3); a disc brooch (Fig 125, no 4); glass beads; bone inlay (Fig 150, no 4); copper alloy-headed studs; and iron bolts and fittings.

Room B

At the eastern end of Room A, partition walls were inserted to block the access to the site of the former eastern ambulatory and create a small square room, Room B (Figs 32, 56, and 57). The blocking wall between F3 and F9 was supported on a substantial stone and mortar foundation, F11/F225, surviving to two courses, which had been cut through by the timber slot F98 of the later Structure XI of Phase 7 (Figs 29 and 32). The partition wall consisted of a less substantial construction of mortar and smaller stone blocks F226 (Fig 58, section BII B) with large slab F227 (Fig 32) possibly marking the jamb of an entrance from Room A. No diagnostic finds were recovered from this room.

Timber-framed annexe

A three-sided structure was inserted against wall F16 in the former cella area (Fig 56). A rectangle 4.7 × 1.5m, defined by post pits and wall trenches, it was cobble floored. To the south, wall trench F203 linked the face of wall F16 to a corner post pit F285 (Fig 32). Running north, trench F214/F472 (Fig 32) was interrupted by a further pit F218 (Fig 34, section BII D), while the site of a probable third post pit had been destroyed by the pit F414 of Phase 7. The wall trench did not return to meet wall F16 and this north end may have had an entrance to the annexe. The limestone cobbles of contexts 96 and 450 (Fig 32) formed the floor. Against F16 there were traces of an area of intense burning, F202, associated with the layers of ash and other debris of contexts 95 and 201 (Fig 34, section BII D) and context 449 (not illus). Over the fill of trench F203 were some large slabs F217 (Fig 56); these may have been the threshold for a later entrance, or laid after demolition.

It is thought that the timbers had not decayed *in situ*; indeed they must have been removed to allow the structural developments of Phase 7. Finds from the slots and pits must therefore relate both to previous destruction, and subsequent construction activities in the area. They include 40 coins (of which five were Theodosian issues), four lead tablets (including Tablet 3), and a disc brooch (Fig 125, no 3). The north sector of the wall trench F472 was dug in spits so that the dating evidence could be assessed more accurately, and it is relevant that two Theodosian coins, recovered from the base fill, may relate to the construction rather than to the demolition of the timber structure. Further evidence is provided by the finds from the activity deposits inside the building. The occupation levels, contexts 95 and 499, produced two further Theodosian coins and a votive cast copper alloy ring; the ash layer context 201 contained burnt objects including a broken copper alloy pin and the figurine of Mercury wearing a cloak (Fig 85, no 4).

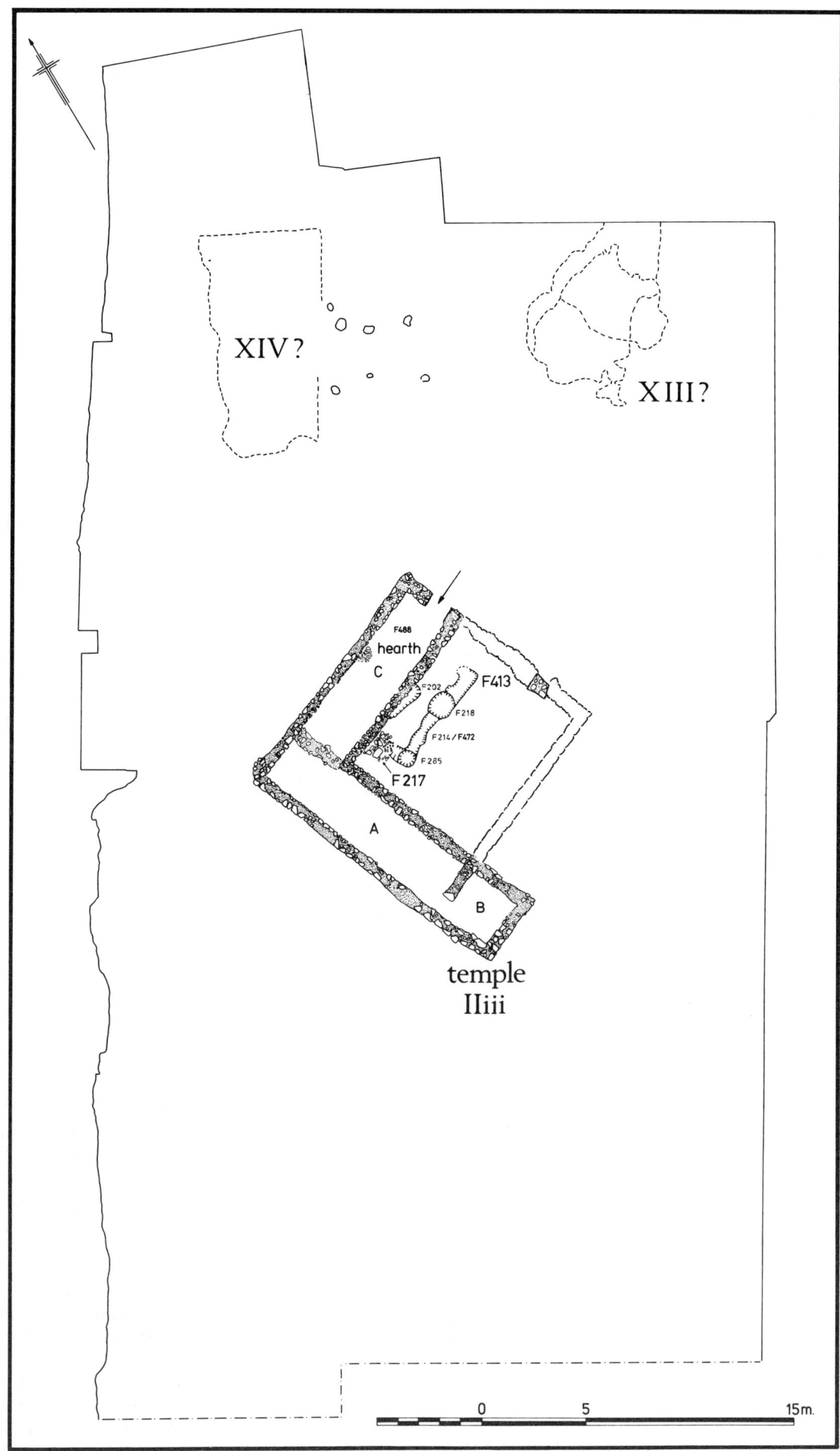

Fig 56 Phase 6 plan, final fourth and fifth centuries AD, scale 1:280

Fig 57 Foundation paving (F5) above Structure II, south ambulatory (Room A), Room B above, view from the north-west (1977). (Photo: Peter Leach)

Phase 6b: demolition of the modified temple

The modified temple building (Structure II) of Phase 6a was demolished, probably during the fifth century, and the resulting rubble and debris were levelled above the temple foundations and over the demolished remains of Structure IV. In the temple area, demolition deposits were identified over all former rooms except the porch. These comprised context 2 above Room A (Fig 34, section BII C, and Fig 36, section BII E), context 6 above Room B (Fig 58, section BII B), context 12 over Room C (Fig 36, BII E), context 15 above Room D (Fig 34, BII D) and context 14 in the cella (Fig 34, section BII C). The uppermost filling of the central pit F19, context 17 (Fig 34, sections BII C and BII D), was indistinguishable from these demolition deposits. A few deposits of loose clean demolition rubble were recorded in the cella area over the former porch, and also spilling into the courtyard to the north. The extensive finds from the major demolition contexts above the temple are summarised below. The large number of coins included 683 late-Roman issues, mainly *Fel Temp Reparatio* copies, which may have derived from one or more single hoards offered up in the temple, and a significant total (68) of Theodosian coins. These latter coins must have related to the use of the modified temple in Phase 6a. Their presence indicates that demolition took place after AD 402, but how long into the fifth century the modified temple survived cannot be established with certainty (see chapter 5).

A second spread of demolition rubble, similar in character to those described above, and containing a comparable range of coins, sealed the demolition contexts of Structure IV from Room D southwards (Fig 42), thickening in that direction to obscure all sign of the earlier building. The main deposit over Structure IV Room D, context 331 (Fig 45, section BIV G), continued over the west wall as contexts 340 and 350 (Fig 42). This was contiguous with context 317 above the robber pit F327 (Figs 42 and 44), and context 368 above Room F, and was also continued above Room E and the unexcavated wing as contexts 300 (see Fig 42) and 301 (not illus). Within the rubble there were concentrations of votive material including major deposits of animal remains (Fig 42), lead tablets, miniature pots, and objects of copper alloy (see below). The metal objects here were mainly items of jewellery, but in the deposits above the former temple, votive objects were incorporated into the rubble (see below). These included a silver *caduceus*, a face mask, a detached wing, 12 copper alloy rings and, from context 14, the remarkable repoussé sheet embellished with Christian scenes (Figs 95 and 96).

Diagnostic finds from the final demolition over the temple

Room A
Context 2: 30 coins: one pre-fourth-century, four early fourth-century, 17 late fourth-century, eight Theodosian; two lead tablets; copper alloy cast rings (Fig 115, nos 4, 7, and 8), a toilet article (Fig 135, no 7); a glass bead; copper alloy furniture fittings (Fig 151, nos 12 and 13)

Room B
Context 6: eight coins: one pre-fourth-century, two early fourth-century, five late fourth-century; inscribed lead tablet 26

Room C
Context 12: 21 coins: four early fourth-century, 14 late fourth century, three Theodosian; copper alloy cast rings (Figs 114, nos 17 and 18, and 115, nos 5 and 6), and a brooch (Fig 125, no 11)

Room D
Context 15: 13 coins: one pre-fourth-century, ten early fourth-century, two late fourth-century; copper alloy and a millefiori mount (Fig 126, nos 5 and 6)

Room E (cella)
Context 14: 300 coins: 57 pre-fourth-century, 18 early fourth-century, 190 late fourth-century, 35 Theodosian; a silver *caduceus* (Fig 89, no 4); a copper alloy mask (Fig 88, no 5), votive leaves (Fig 92, nos 2–4), sheet (Fig 93, nos 9 and 11), repoussé sheet (Figs 95 and 96); six lead tablets (including Tablets 39 and 63–65); a miniature spear (Fig 110, no 7); iron projectiles (Figs 112, no 14; 113, no 21); a glass bead; cast rings (Figs 114, nos 7 and 8; and 115, no 9); a miniature pot; bracelets of copper alloy (Fig 127, nos 18 and 25) and jet and shale (Fig 129, no 10); a

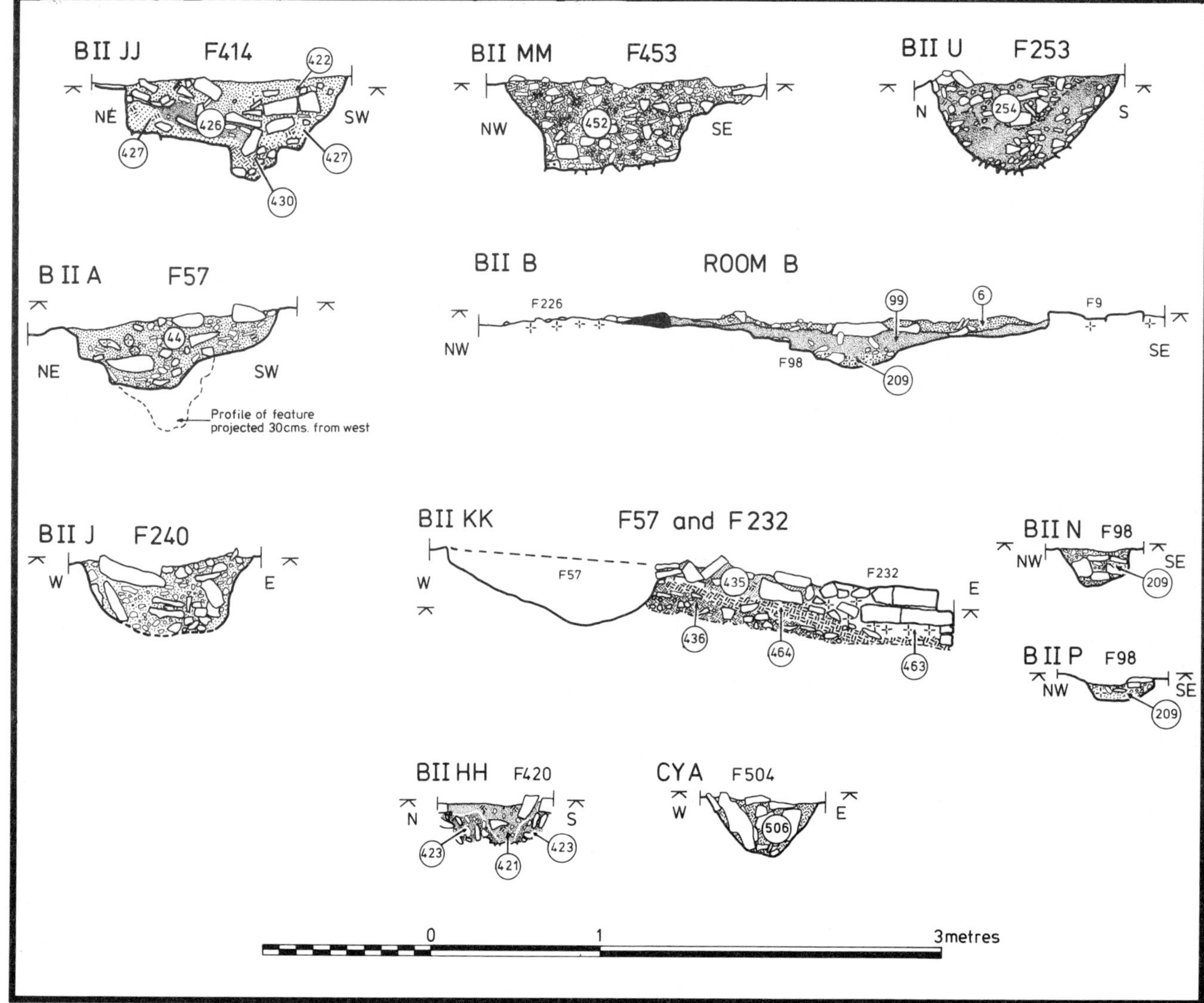

Fig 58 Phase 7, sections of Structures VII and XI, scale 1:40

buckle (Fig 135, no 10), a stylus (Fig 143, no 15), a strip (Fig 153, no 12), and a ring (Fig 154, no 11)

Pit F19
Context 17: 383 coins: 24 pre-fourth-century, 38 early fourth-century, 199 late fourth-century, 22 Theodosian; seven lead tablets (including Tablets 34 and 37–39); a copper alloy wing (Fig 88, no 2), a cast ring (Fig 114, no 26); a miniature pot; a glass bead; a bracelet (Fig 128, no 2)

Diagnostic finds from the rubble spread above the demolition deposits of Structure IV

over Room D
Context 350/340/331: five coins with a date range of 335–420; three lead tablets (including Tablet 55); a copper alloy brooch (Fig 124, no 2); a glass bead; a copper alloy bracelet fragment (Fig 128, no 7); and a jet/shale finger ring (Fig 133, no 1)

over Room E
Context 300/301: 35 coins with a date range of 260–402; three lead tablets; an iron bolt; three miniature pots; three glass beads (including Fig 126, no 18); copper alloy bracelets (Fig 128, nos 4 and 5), a finger ring (Fig 132, no 14), and a spoon (Fig 134, no 10)

over Room F
Context 368: four coins with a date range of 260–378; copper alloy fragments; iron fragments; a bone pin (Fig 131, no 18)

Structures XI and VII

Phase 7a

Following demolition of the final remaining portions of the modified temple and the levelling of the debris not removed, a further series of structures were built. The elements of these included a series of major post pits, mainly situated in the former area of the cella, a beam slot, stone wall footings, bonded together with a mixture of reused mortar and wall plaster, and two areas of slab flooring or foundation (Figs 29 and 59). In interim publications these features were interpreted as the components of two successive buildings: rectangular Structure VII aligned north-west/south-east with an off-centre apsidal extension to the north-west, followed by a larger rectangular building, Structure XI

Fig 59 Structure XI (basilica) remains over Structure I, view from the north-west (1977). (Photo: Peter Leach)

(Ellison 1980, figs 15.3 and 15.4). More detailed analysis has led to the conclusion that a single building is represented: a rectangular construction of five bays, with an attached annexe on the north-west, which incorporates all the elements mentioned above. The components will first be described in groups, followed by an exposition of the detailed plan of the building.

Post pits and slot

Cutting through context 14, the demolition and levelling deposits related to the destruction of the Phase 6 modified temple in the northern sector of the former cella, were a series of five major post pits (Figs 29, 32 and 59). These formed a rectangle of two pairs: pits F414 and F282 on the west and pits F253 and F275 to the east, with the fifth pit, F453, which was more oval in outline, occupying a roughly central position. Their average diameter was 1.3m and their surviving depths ranged from 0.15m to 0.4m. Those furthest north, F414 and F253, were noticeably the deeper. No traces of post positions were detected during excavation but all the fillings contained substantial amounts of disturbed packing material consisting mainly of limestone building blocks reused from the former temple buildings,and including fragments of the Mercury statue (Figs 60 and 72–6). Some of the pits displayed a simple rounded profile eg F253 (Fig 58, section BII U and Fig 60), F275, and F282 (Fig 34, section BII D), whilst others were more vertically sided, eg F453 (Fig 58, section BII JJ) and F414 (Fig 58, section BII MM). Two pits, F453 and F275, cut the Phase 6 filling of the central pit F19 (Figs 32 and 34, sections BII C and BII D) while pit F282 cut through the post pit F218 and slot F472 of the timber annexe structure, also of Phase 6. Pit F453, in turn, was cut by a later post hole F425, and by a stone setting F418 (Figs 32 and 34, section BII C), the edge of pit F414 was cut by a later post hole F446 (Fig 32). Further south within the former cella area were two slighter and shallower post holes F93 and F58 (Fig 32), while to the

Fig 60 Structure XI (basilica) post hole F253 with a statue fragment (Fig 75, no 6) in the packing, view from the west (1977), scale 0.20m. (Photo: Peter Leach)

east and occupying the south-west corner of the later Structure VIII, was a substantial post pit (F57), which lay in line with pits F253 and F414. This reached a maximum depth of 0.68m and was roughly square in shape, each side measuring 1.2m (Fig 58, section BII A). In its final form pit F57 was seen to cut F231 and F234, the adjacent walls of Structure VIII (Fig 58, section BII KK and Fig 66,), but it was probably a feature of two phases, the earlier possibly a post hole pre-dating Structure VIII.

Where the post pits described above lay in a line, the lines were in alignment with the rectangular layout of the former temple walls. The timber slot F98 (Fig 32) and its associated post hole F240, set out south of post pit F57 roughly on the centre line of the former eastern ambulatory (Rooms B and D), also conformed to this layout. Circular pit F240 was 0.43m deep (Fig 58, section BII HH) and the trench varied in depth from 0.25m near F240 (Fig 58, section BII B) through 0.21m (Fig 58, section BII N) and 0.12m (Fig 58, section BII P), petering out to nothing at a distance 5.4m north from the centre of F240. West of F240 were three further small post holes, F243, F228, and F420 (Fig 32), the latter cutting the edge of wall F7, located amongst a scatter of large red sandstone roof tile fragments, which were probably used in packing or supporting the wall footings. Further west still lay the setting of five large limestone slabs F5 and context 57 (Figs 32 and 34, section BII C) which had been laid level above the Phase 6 demolition debris in the former Room A. West of F5 and in line with post pits F414 and F282 was a setting of three sandstone roof tiles laid flat, while outside the wall F7, and in line with wall F16 of the former cella, was a small square post-setting F518.

Wall footings

Immediately north of post pits F414 and F253, and in line with the former northern limit of the cella, two sections of rough wall footings were inserted (Fig 32). On the east side footing F55 was butted against the earlier plinth F713, linking it to the former wall F10 and set within a construction trench F934 (not illus). Further west a much more fragmentary length of wall footings, F483, was built between trench F737 and former wall F16. Both lengths of wall foundation survived as roughly laid courses, poorly bonded with a mixture of lime and reused wall plaster. Confirmation of a central entrance between these wall sections was provided by an area of worn limestone paving, context 498 (Figs 29, 32, and 61) just to the north, and worn cobbling extending over the demolished footings of the former portico F480. At this point a large fragment of Roman altar had been laid face down to provide a ramp sloping up towards the threshold gap (Fig 62). One post hole, F493, immediately north of F713, may have been connected with further entrance arrangements, or have been dug later. The remnant corner of stonework, F232, which survived within the later Structure VIII comprised three courses, in a matrix of crushed reused mortar (Fig 58, section BII KK, Figs 64, 65, section S1, and 66). This was in line with the other wall foundation fragments described above, but could be interpreted alternatively as a later addition to the wall foundation remnant context 436 of Structure II; an attempt at buttressing this corner of the ambulatory prior to its collapse in Phase 5e (see chapter 3).

Structure VII, north-western annexe

A semicircular area of worn limestone paving slabs and cobbles F279, lay immediately north-west of the post rows and above the former western ambulatory of the temple (Figs 29, 32, 61, and 63). Two damaged altars were incorporated in this floor, one the complete but defaced altar of Mercury (Fig 63) and the other comprising two joining top and back fragments from an altar (Fig 79), the base of which had been incorporated in the threshold of the timber building described above. The floor F279 lay on a rubble foundation, context 484 (not illus) which contained five fourth-century coins and a copper alloy fitting (Fig 156, no 2). The paved area was bounded on the north, south, and west by surviving portions of pitched and horizontally laid limestone rubble, in a matrix of crushed wall plaster and reused mortar F281, F280, and F499 (Fig 32). Similar fragments probably deriving from this former wall had fallen northwards, and one such deposit contained small metal objects, including a further copper alloy fitting (Fig 156, no 3). Three post holes F403, F408, and F407 cut through the demolition rubble and apparently were associated with the structure; none of the fillings contained finds.

The fragile remains of this structure survived immediately below the ploughsoil and were in a remarkable state of preservation. Immediately to the south a major deposit of plain, thick, white wall plaster was found to overlie the demolition deposits context 12 within former Room C (Fig 36, section BII E) and it seems likely that this derived from the facings of the walls of the paved structure described.

Interpretation

The pits, post holes, gullies, dry-stone footings and paved areas considered above may be grouped together as the elusive traces of a major building built during the fifth or sixth centuries AD (Figs 29 and 61). The post pits and timber gullies may have supported a timber hall of five bays, Structure XI, entered from the north by means of a stepped approach over the former porch of the temple. Two of the rows of timber supports would have been carried on the surviving wall foundations of the cella, and the large paving stones F5 would have assumed a central position opposite the proposed entrance. On the north-west, an apsidal paved extension or annexe (Structure VII) was surrounded by dry-stone walling of a similar kind, but with smaller sized stones than the remnants of the stone based facing wall along the northern limit of the main building. It will be argued below that this building may have been a timber basilica, with the altar at the western end, and an attached north-western baptistery.

The well-preserved state of the fragile remains of the baptistery walls suggest that this part of the structure was one of the last surviving features on the site. It may therefore have outlived the timber basilica to be refurbished and modified as a free-standing building, to

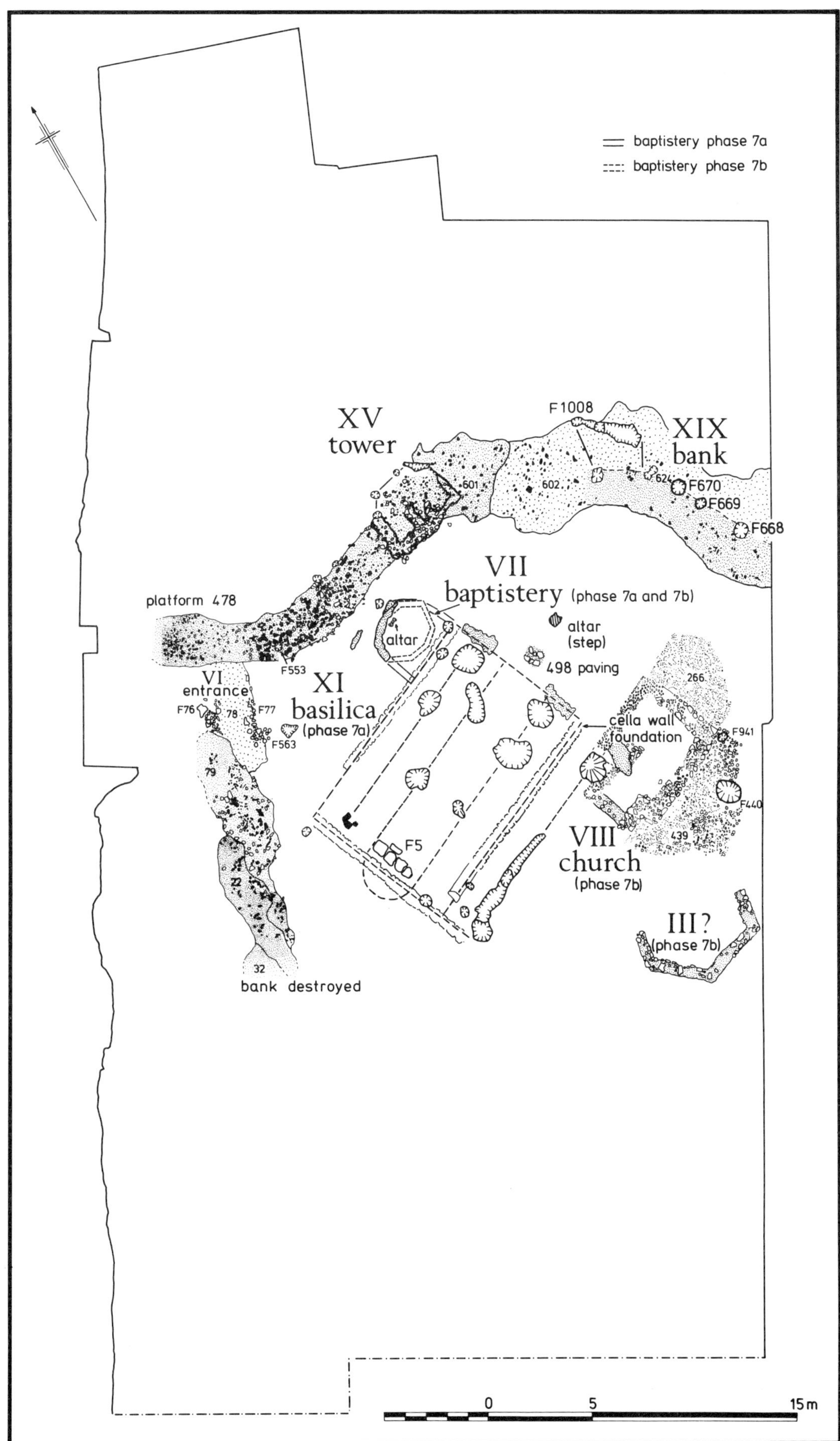

Fig 61 Phase 7 plan, ?sixth to seventh centuries AD, scale 1:280

Fig 62 Mercury altar (Fig 80), reused as a step, F281, at the entrance to Structure XI, view from the south-west (1978), scale 0.30m. (Photo: Sebastian Rahtz)

function in concert with the stone walled Structure VIII of Phase 7b described below. In this later phase, the angled wall fragments might indicate that the tank was octagonal in shape, with a temporary cover, perhaps of leather or canvas, supported by timbers held in post holes F403 and F408 (Fig 32) (see Fig 220).

Structure VIII

Phase 7b

The wall foundations of a stone building, measuring a maximum of 5.50m by 4.25m, survived as one course of flat mortared limestone blocks above unmortared pitched stone footings up to 1.18m deep (Figs 29, 61, 65, and 66). These had been built through the fillings of ditch segment F264, down to bedrock, in order to provide a sound footing for what must have been a tall and substantial stone structure. The walls were on average 0.85m in width, greater than that of any of the wall foundations provided for the Roman temple (Structure II). Only the north wall F42 (Fig 66) possessed a clear construction trench, but this was detected only on the outer side of the footings. This north wall also had the deepest footings, although they were shallower to the east where they reached the edge of the pre-Roman ditch. They were bonded with the footings of the east wall F41, comprising pitched rubble context 448 (Fig 65, sections S1, S58, S38). The western footings for wall F231 were also bonded in with the north wall F42, but no mortared upper course survived here (Fig 65, west wall elevation). To the south the footings decreased in depth as they reached the west

Fig 63 Structure VII, baptistery floor, context 279, and other remains over Structure II, Room C, view from the north-east (1977). (Photo: Peter Leach)

Fig 64 Structure VIII, cut into Structure II ambulatory, Room D, view from the south-east (1977). (Photo: Peter Leach)

sloping side of the pre-Roman ditch F264 beneath. The footings F231 were cut to the south by the later pit F57 (Fig 66).

To the south the width of the building had been constricted to form a slightly narrower annexe or entrance passage. On its west side, footings F234 with some traces of mortar, cut the floor of the former temple ambulatory and its outer wall F9. Its eastern limit was formed by an offset extension of wall F41, apparently of a single build with it. The slighter rubble foundation, F43, may have supported a wall or threshold. The eastern wall F41 was less well defined in its centre portion and the presence of a threshold in this position may also be indicated.

The interior of Structure VIII possessed a well laid cobbled limestone floor, and multi-phased laid stone platforms extended north and east from the exterior wall faces. All these surfaces were characterised by closely set, worn, limestone fragments, laid on edge to form very compact and durable floors. This cobbling technique was quite different from that employed in the interior floors and courtyard surfaces of the Roman phases described above. Inside Structure VIII, the cobbled floor, context 233 (Fig 66), showed signs of extensive wear. It was founded upon context 249, a base of loose rubble lying above the clay of layer 255 (Fig 65, sections S1 and S38). The floor, context 233, contained two late fourth-century coins; the foundation, context 249, a coin of the late third-century. The corner of stonework, F232, must have been visible, and may have been reused as the base for some internal fitting (Fig 66).

Outside the northern wall F42, context 728, a clay deposit, sealed F930, the top of the wall's foundation trench (Fig 21, section S54) and then thinned out to the north. This layer may have incorporated clay dug out from the clay layer 255, during the construction of the building, and contained fragments of the Roman cult statue, including the body of the cockerel (Fig 75, no 5) and two silver finger rings (Fig 132, nos 23 and 24). The adjacent outer wall footings of F42 incorporated two leg fragments from the deity himself (Figs 67 and, 73, nos 2 and 3). Above the clay foundation context 728 was a heavy rubble platform, context 719, which contained yet another fragment of the cult statue, the body of the ram (Fig 21, section S54 and Fig 74, no 4). This platform functioned as a foundation for a cobbled surface, context 266 (Fig 66), a carefully laid and well defined area that appeared to represent an interior floor rather than an exterior yard. However, no clear traces of any boundary walls were present, so any superstructure would have had to have been supported by timber framing.

In contrast, the sequence of platforms east of Structure VIII was more variable, patched and weathered, and seemed to be the remnant of a heavily used exterior courtyard surface. There were two major constructional phases. The pit F940, which contained the head of the cult statue of Mercury (Figs 29, 66, 68, and 72) was cut through the Phase 4–5 context 444 cobbles, and the pit filling, context 941, was sealed by the foundations of an exterior platform to the south. This substantial platform was supported on rubble foundations contexts 439 and 438 (Figs 66 and 65, sections S1 and

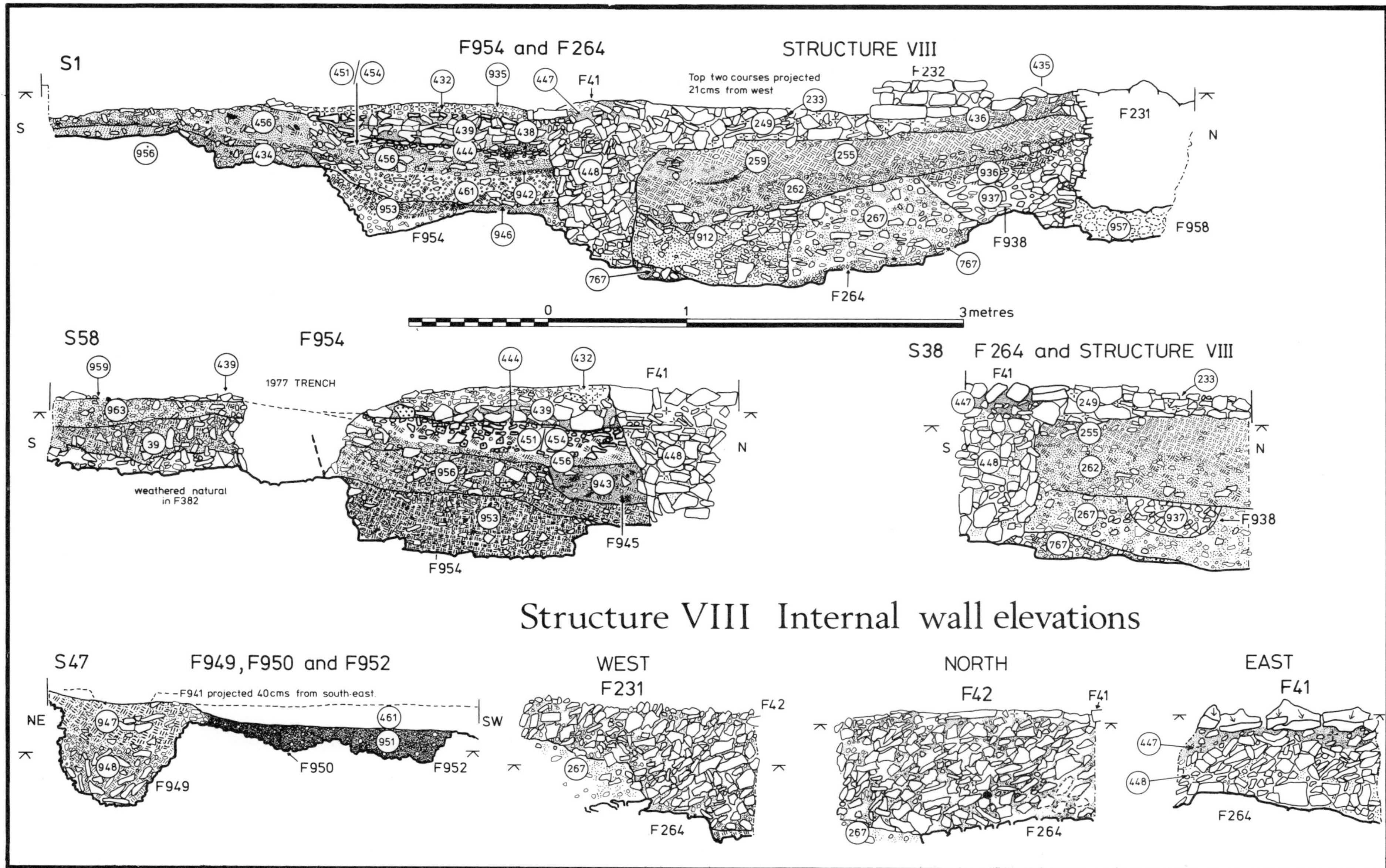

Fig 65 Phases 2–7, sections of ditch segment F264 (south-west) and Structure VIII, scale 1:40

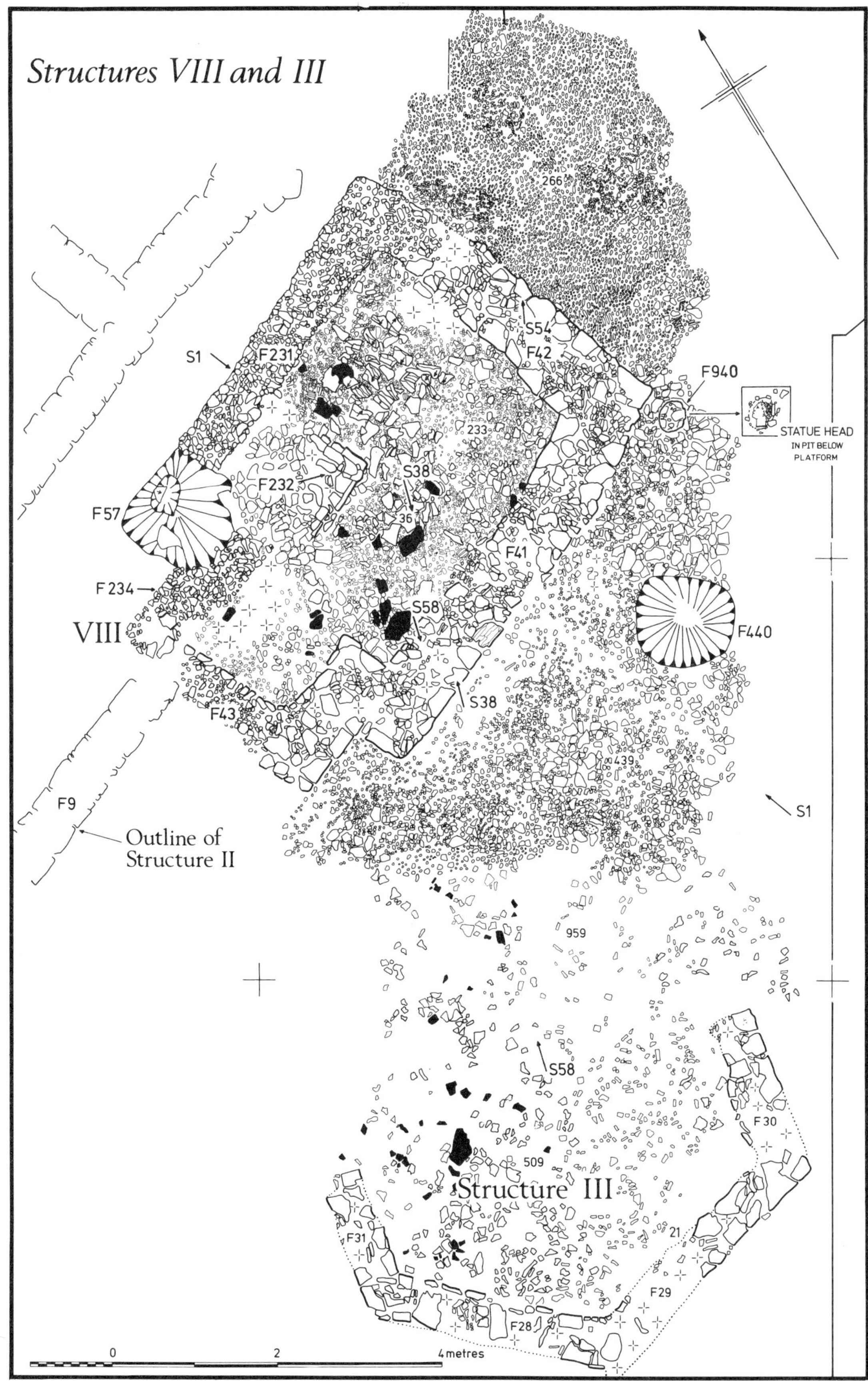

Fig 66 Phase 7, plan, scale 1:70

Fig 67 Statue fragments (Fig 73, nos 2 & 3) built into wall foundations (F41) of Structure VIII, view from the north-east (1978). (Photo: Sebastian Rahtz)

S58) which linked to another platform foundation (context 719 below context 266), north of Structure VIII (Fig 21, section S54). On these foundations lay a worn, cobbled surface context 432 (Fig 65, section S58), which was the stratigraphic equivalent of the floor context 266. Pit F440 had been cut from the latest exterior level, but may belong with pit F57 in Phase 7c (below). The fill of pit F440, context 439, contained some iron hobnails and a glass bead, while a group of 24 coins and a lead tablet may have derived from the same context. This suggests that some votive debris from the temple phases became incorporated within this rubble foundation, and that the date of the coins: 16 of the late fourth-century plus six Theodosian issues, can by no means be taken to date the laying down of the exterior cobbled surface of context 432. Continuing south from these cobbles was a further intermittent layer of cobbling, context 959 (Figs 66 and 65, section S58), which may have been contiguous with context 509 running north from Structure III (Fig 66). Context 959 contained a residual later first-century AD brooch of Polden Hill type (Fig 123, no 9).

The evidence summarised above can be interpreted in terms of a two phase structure. Firstly, the simple rectangular structure with its southern annexe was built, possibly with an entrance midway along the eastern side. In a second phase the cobbled floor, context 266, was added to the north, possibly for a timber-framed apsidal extension, and the doorway could have been moved to the western end. The substantial stone platform context 432 was added also to raise the exterior ground level on the east side. According to this interpretation, the insertion of the statue leg fragments and the head of Mercury would belong to the first phase, the burying of the stone bodies of cockerel and goat to the second, although it should be borne in mind that the temporal separation between these two structural phases may have been quite brief.

As stated above, the coins from the rubble foundation contexts 438/439 cannot be taken as dating evidence for construction, nor can the coins from the interior floor level context 233. The remarkable point concerning the interior of Structure VIII is that so few finds were recovered. Indeed, the absence of Theodosian coins may well indicate that construction took place very much later than their currency, which was during the use of the modified temple of Phase 6.

Rubble from the destruction of Structure VIII survived in patches over the eastern exterior platform; the cobbled floor context 266 beyond it; above the former temple courtyard to the north; and as a scatter of large pieces of worked stone and sandstone roof tiles sealing the floor, context 233, in the building. Some of this debris, context 36, is shown in Fig 66. In its northern sector there were distinct lines of pitched, evenly-sized limestone blocks, suggesting that a door or a window arch may have fallen rather than been demolished piece by piece. It may be, therefore, that the building was left to become a ruin, with most of the building material gradually removed from the site. The surviving foundations and floors appeared to have been exposed to the elements for a great length of time, compared with the sharp-edged and un-eroded temple foundations. The surviving areas of destruction rubble contained eleven late fourth-century coins, an iron staple, a glass bead, two lead tablet fragments, and a copper alloy rivet cover (Fig 150, no 14).

Structure III

Phase 7b?

Approximately four metres south of Structure VIII were the foundations of an open sided stone-walled building, Structure III (Fig 66). These foundations comprised four short segments of mortared wall footings, all bonded together but with only one course surviving. There were no traces of any continuing wall lines, either in stone or timber, extending further to the north. The central segments, footings F28 and F29, were 3.20m long; the northern arms, footings F30 and F31, extending 1.90m only. An interior surface, context 21, was contiguous with a rough worn exterior rubble surface, context 509, which may have linked with context 959 extending south from the latest exterior platform around Structure VIII (Fig 66). Below contexts 21 and 509 was a cobbled surface, context 539 (not illus), which probably equated with context 444 of Phase 4–5 (Fig 65, section S1). These associations suggest that Structure III was still in use during the life of Structure VIII but that its origin may lie in Phases 4 or 5. The foundations and precise stratigraphic relationships of Structure III were not fully explored in excavation, although there appeared to be similarities with the mortared foundations of Structure VIII. The contexts of Structure III produced no coins at all and only one identifiable find, a bone spindle whorl (Fig 143, no 7).

Fig 68 Head of the cult statue Mercury (Fig 72) in situ as excavated, Structure VIII, view from the north-west (1979). (Photo: Sebastian Rahtz)

Structural features later than Structure VIII

Phase 7c

Cutting the foundations of Structure VIII were F496 (Figs 29, 32, and 69), a post hole which probably belonged to the post setting of Structure XII described below, and the pit F57 (Fig 66). This pit was one of the first features to be recognised on removal of the modern ploughsoil. It was 0.80m in diameter and its maximum depth was 0.65m (Fig 58, section BII A). The filling was quite different from those of the post pits belonging to Structure XI above, with few stones and a deliberately placed fragment of antler. Pit F57 also contained a copper alloy disc (Fig 152, no 2) and one Theodosian coin. The pit F440, cutting context 432, the platform east of Structure VIII, may also be of this phase and is of similar dimensions to pit F57.

Within the area of the former cella were a further series of post holes, some of which cut the post pits of Structure XI (Fig 29, Phase 7c, and Fig 32). Five of these were of medium size, F246 and F418, cutting F453 (Fig 34, section BIIC); double post hole F244 (Fig 32), F446, cutting F414, and F493; these may have functioned together. An arrangement of four smaller stone-edged post settings, F287, F413, F425 cutting F418, and F475 (Figs 29 and 33) were probably the latest features and could have supported a very slight trapezoidal structure. Of the first group, post hole F246 contained two fourth-century and one Theodosian coin, post hole F446 contained two mid fourth-century coins and post hole F493 contained a fragment of iron. The later group of post settings were devoid of finds, apart from one late third-century coin and copper alloy fragments in setting F287.

Structure XII

Phase 7c

Just within the bank designated Structure XIX (Fig 61), a group of large post pits indicated the site of a roughly semicircular timber building (Fig 29). These pits F701, F703, F705, F707, and F709 (Fig 69) cut through the Roman courtyard levels and another of them, pit F496, cut the corner of the foundations of Structure VIII. The pits were, on average, 1.0m in diameter and from 0.2 to 0.4m deep. Several were oval in outline and they all contained packing stones, some of which were of considerable size, eg that in F709 (see Fig 69). A patch of crushed mortar and limestone fragments, F491 extending northwards from pit F496, may be the remnant of a floor level associated with this building. Finds associated with this structure included one late fourth-cen-

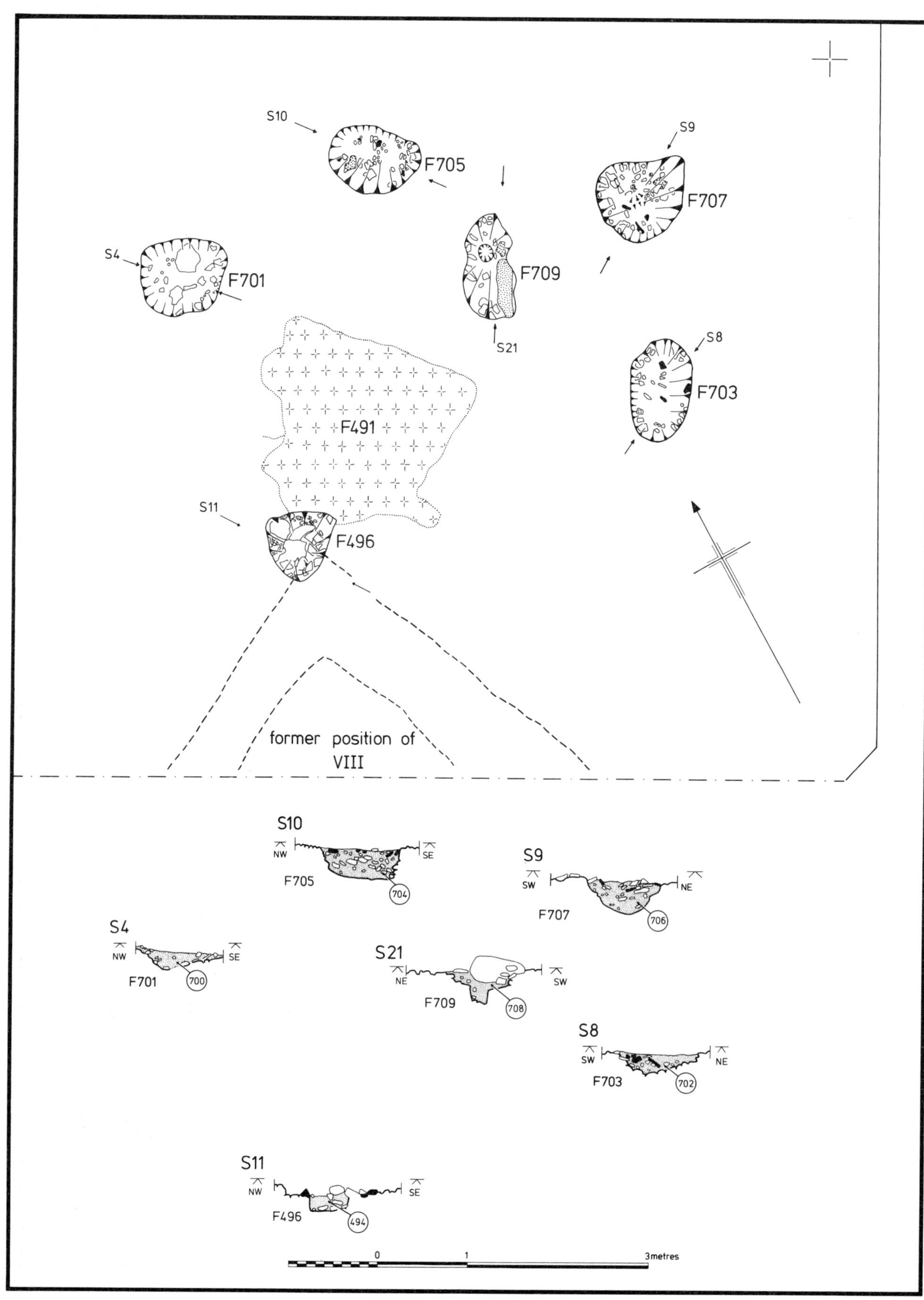

Fig 69 Phase 7, Structure XII, scale 1:60

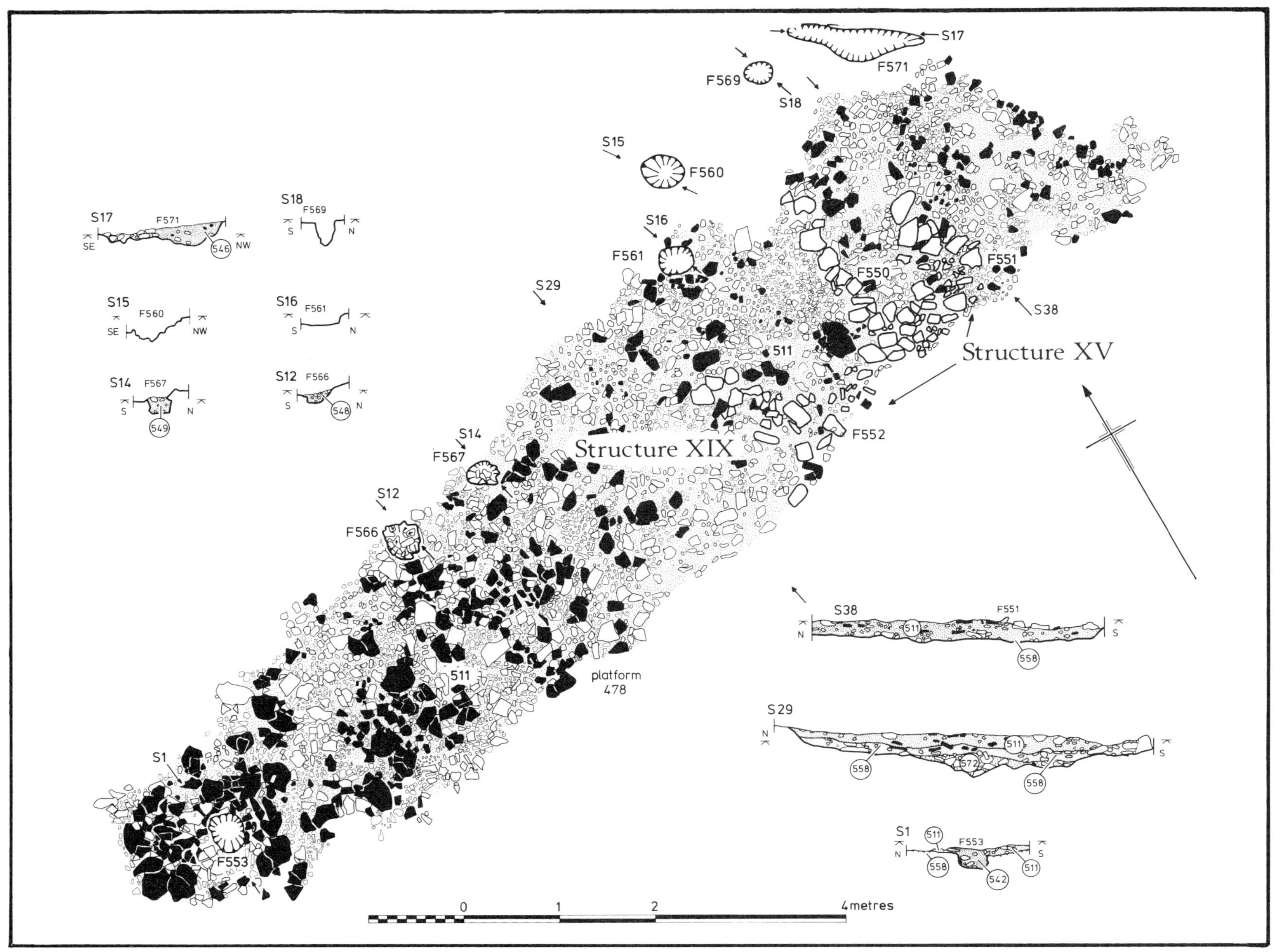

Fig 70 *Phase 7, Structure XV and XIX, scale 1:60*

tury coin from the mortar floor and another from the fill of post pit F703. Otherwise the post pit fillings produced only one fragment of glass and a piece of flint. The sparseness of these finds, and the fact that pit F496 cut the foundations of Structure VIII, imply a very late date for this enigmatic structure.

Structure XIX, the perimeter bank

Phase 7

Over the trackway between the former Roman Structure IX, and the site of the temple, Structure II, and lying in the hollow in front of the former temple, was a wide arc of dark soil filled with votive debris, associated with structural elements of worked stone and reused roof tile. These have been interpreted as the remains of a turf bank, partly supported on a stone and tile foundation, and revetted by timbers supported in a series of post holes, which cut the temple courtyard.

Between former Structures IX and II, a platform, context 478, composed largely of reused sandstone roof tiles and limestone rubble, was laid along the axis of the Roman hollow way F554, presumably in order to level up the ruts (Fig 70). This extended *c* 8m to the north-east, towards a group of stone footings and post holes interpreted as the footings for a rectangular platform or tower, Structure XV (Fig 70). These comprised three sections of unmortared limestone footings F550, F551, and F552, with the northern edge of the structure defined by post holes F560, F561, and F569, and an elongated slot F571. Taken together, these features indicate the former existence of a rectangular building, perhaps a tower, Structure XV, with a curved or three sided northern frontage projecting beyond the line of the context 478 platform. The original front of the bank is suggested by the presence of post holes F566 and F567, located in the edge of the tile and stone platform.

Above these structures was context 511, a linear spread of very dark soil up to 0.20m thick (Fig 70, sections), which was filled with a mass of diagnostic finds, including 398 coins and many metal and other objects of votive character. This dark soil probably represented the remains of bank material which appears to have been largely composed of turf. The votive material may have been incorporated intentionally, or perhaps more likely, was contained within the turves, which might have been cut from immediately around the modified temple building of Phase 6. East of the tower, Structure XV, the dark soil deposit continued, albeit in a more spread form, as a series of humic layers in the hollow of the former Roman courtyard: contexts 601 and 602 (Fig 61). Within these deposits there were various post holes or groups of packing stones which may have held a revetment for the proposed turf bank in this area. These included context 624, a packing layer which marked a possible double post setting, and post holes F668, F669, and F670 (Fig 61). The timber slot F1008 was probably of this phase also and may have served to define the eastern side of an entrance which was marked on the west by the stone-based tower or platform, Structure XV. Few of these individual features contained any finds, but two post holes produced coins: one late fourth-century coin from F571 of Structure XV and one late fourth-century and one Theodosian issue from post packing context 624.

At the south-western end of the context 478 platform, and near its inner edge, lay a deep post hole F553, which probably paired with F563, located 4m to the south (Figs 61 and 70). Immediately west of these probable gate support holes were two parallel lines of loose limestone footings, F76 and F77, separated by a rough, slightly worn rubble surface, context 78 (Fig 61). These footings of Structure VI may have been constructed to support an elaborate entrance feature, perhaps another tower similar to Structure XV. However, there is no evidence to suggest whether the two entrances observed were subsequent or contemporary. South of Structure VI a strip of very worn rubble and roof tile fragments, context 79, ran south towards the site of the Roman Structure I, where the dark matrix merged with contexts 22 and 32, deposits of votive debris preserved within the hollows over the robbing trenches on its eastern side. All these dark deposits may represent the last remains of a turf bank on the western side of the post-temple structures. The bank also continued beyond the northern flank of the proposed western entrance, Structure VI, as indicated by the presence of deep humic deposits south of the site of Structures IX and XIV. These contexts (gridded and prefixed 03, 04, and 05 in the site archive) contained even greater densities of finds than the bank deposits further east. The occurrence of certain categories of objects, especially of metal, are summarised in Table 1.

Table 1: selected finds categories from the post-Roman bank, Structure XIX

Contexts:	*601 to 605*	*478 and 511*	*Grid Sqrs 03 to 05*	*Total*
Coins				
late 3rd century	12	2	7	21
early 4th century	48	10	32	90
late 4th century	126	45	46	217
Theodosian	46	8	16	70
total				398
copper alloy items	99	39	66	204
iron items	37	25	39	101
glass	65	25	119	99
hobnails	49	20	39	108
glass beads	4	1	3	8
bone items	2	3	10	15

The large number of coins recovered included a significant proportion of Theodosian issues (18%), indicating that the bank was constructed within or after the fifth century AD. There were particularly high numbers of fragments of vessel glass, iron hobnails and well preserved votive objects of silver, copper alloy, and iron.

Illustrated or catalogued items from the bank material contexts include fragments of statuary (Fig 81, nos 1, 2, and 3); copper alloy figurines (Fig 85, nos 5 and 6), a votive leg (Fig 88, no 8); inscribed lead tablets (Tablets 77–81); fragments of two *caducei* (Fig 89, nos 5 and 6); three votive leaves (Fig 92, nos 5–7); many pieces of copper alloy sheet plaque, (Fig 93, nos 1–8, 10, and 12), including one (Fig 93, no 6) depicting a deity; a silver amulet case (Fig 97, no 2); miniature votive spearheads (Fig 110, nos 8 and 11) and the very fine ritually bent example of silver (Fig 110, no 5, and Fig 111), and an iron spearhead (Fig 112, no 15); eight votive copper alloy rings (Fig 114, nos 10, 19, and 20, Fig 115, nos 10–14). Personal items and jewellery included copper alloy necklace fasteners (Fig 127, nos 9 and 10), bracelet fragments (Figs 127, nos 21, 26, and 27; 128, nos 8–13; pieces of shale bracelets (Fig 130, nos 5 and 6); a copper alloy pin (Fig 131, no 6); and three finger rings (Fig 132, nos 25–27). There was also an antler handle (Fig 145, no 10) and six pieces of antler inlay (Fig 150, nos 6–8, and 10–12). Fittings of copper alloy were also well represented (Figs 151, nos 8, 9, and 11; 152, no 1; 153, nos 3, 4, 7, 8, 13–17, 19 and 20); and finally an iron fitting (Fig 154, no 16).

5 The coins

by Richard Reece

Coin list in chronological order

Notes

References are given to RIC, HK or CK

RIC = *Roman Imperial Coinage*, Mattingly, Sydenham, Sutherland and Carson, London 1923ff

HK = *Late Roman Bronze Coinage*, Carson, Hill and Kent, London 1960, part I

CK = the same, part II

Where the coin described corresponds exactly to the reference it is described as RIC 66.If it is not completely legible, but corresponds in most details to the reference it is described as 'as RIC 66'. When the coin is a copy of an official product of the central mint it is described as 'copy of RIC 66' if it corresponds in all details, and 'copy as RIC 66' if some of the details are obscure or omitted. The borderline between regular coins and copies is subjective and undefined: this is highly unsatisfactory but in the present state of knowledge, and short of illustrating every coin, this is all that can be attempted in the time available. The general principle is that at least one aspect of a coin must be irregular for the coin to be classed as a copy: thus the flan may be either highly irregular in shape, or smaller than the regular issue, the lettering may be erratic, illegible, or illiterate, the portrait may be unusual.

3	**British**	Probably Dobunnic (3)
2	**Claudius** I	RIC copy as 66, copy as 69
1	Vitellius	*Sestertius* reverse illegible
2	Vespasian	RIC 109, 752
1	Domitian	RIC 248
2	Trajan	RIC as 494, *Dupondius*, reverse illegible
8	Hadrian	RIC 562.a, 577.b; *Sestertii* (3), *Dupondii* (2), *As* (1), reverses illegible
5	Antoninus Pius	RIC 546, as 617, 635, 942, *As* reverse illegible
6	Marcus Aurelius	RIC (Antoninus Pius) 1263; (Marcus Aurelius) as 798, as 812, 911, as 960, *Sesterius* reverse illegible
1	Lucius Verus	RIC as 1396
5	Faustina II	RIC (Marcus Aurelius) 1645, 1692, *Asses* reverses uncertain (1 cast and 2 struck)
3	Lucilla	RIC (Marcus Aurelius) 1756 (2), *Sestertius* reverse illegible
1	Commodus	RIC 497
1	Crispina	RIC 665
1	Clodius Albinus,	RIC as 52
1	Septimius Severus	RIC 693
1	Elagabalus	RIC 67
2	Julia Soemias	RIC 241, 243
1	Julia Maesa	RIC 272
1	Severus Alexander	Denarius, reverse illegible
1	Gordian III	RIC 89
30	Gallienus	RIC 157, 160 (2), 163 (2), 176, 207, 210, 226 (2), 229, 230, 236 (2), 245, 267, 280 (2), 283 (3), 287, 297, 317, 470, copy as 615, reverses illegible (4)
2	Salonina	RIC copy as 23, 66
29	Claudius II	RIC 19, 33, 34, 45, 46 (2), 54, 56, 62, 80, 85, 86 (2), 103, 169, 195, 261 (7), 266 (4), reverses illegible (2)
1	Quintillus	RIC 26
2	Aurelian	RIC 47, 138
3	Tactius	RIC 65, 69, 89
3	Probus	RIC 175, 203, 712
3	Postumus	RIC 311, 325, reverse illegible
19	Victorinus	RIC 46, 59, 67 (3), 71 (2), 78 (2), 89, 114 (5), 117, 118, *Divo Victorino* 85, reverse illegible
53	Tetricus I	RIC 56 (3), 79, 80 (6), 87 (5), 88 (3), copy as 88, 90, 100 (5), as 100 (3), 101 (4), 109, 120, 121, 126 (2), 132 (5), as 132, 136, 142, 146 (2), copy of 146, reverses illegible (5)
18	Tetricus II	RIC 254, 255, as 255, 260 (2), copy as 260, 270 (6), copies as 270 (2), 272 (2), reverses illegible (2)
15	Carausius	RIC 98, copy as 98, as 101, as 121 but mint-mark F/O/ML, 252, 807, 855, 878 (2), 878 overstruck on ?Valerian I, 878 reverse brockage, 895, 909, 983, as 1083
5	Allectus	RIC 33, 79, 96, 105, 128
6	Radiates	Regular: reverses from *Genius*, *Hilaritas*, illegible (4)

173		Barbarous: reverses from *Aeternitas*, Altar, Candelabrum, *Fides* (2), *Fortuna* (4), *Hilaritas* (3), *Invictus* (7), *Juppiter*, *Laetitia* (3), *Pax* (47), *Pax Augusti*, *Princ Iuvent*, Sacrificial Implements (7), *Salus* (lO), *Spes* (13) *Victoria* (4), *Virtus* (9), very odd (2), lead flan but illegible reverse, illegible and uncertain (55)
1	Diocletian	RIC 6 *Ticinum* 36.a
3	Maximian I	RIC 6 London 90; Trier 573; Rome 104
2	Galerius	RIC 6 Lyon 38.b, 180.a
1	Licinius I	RIC 7 Nicomedia 44
1	Licinius II	RIC 7 Arles 142
12	Constantine I	RIC 6 London 121.a (3), 281, 284; Trier 870 (3), 873 (2), 890, 899
24		RIC 7 London 8, 33, 137, 154 (2), 159, 222, 293, as 293; Trier 213, 303 (2), 316, 341 (2), 342, 435, 449, 504, 509; Lyon 1, 214; Arles 57; *Ticinum* 140
14		HK 54, 61, 62 (3), 98, 238, 373 (2), 378, 398, 405, superb copy of 405, 1374
8	Constantine II	RIC 7 London 181, 198 (2), 255; Trier 353, as 463, 505; *Siscia* 176
33		HK copies as 49 (4), copies as 63 (2), 68 (2), 81 (2), 82, 88, copy as 88, 93 (7), 126, copy of 181, 187, copies of 187 (4), 198, 232, 247, 399 (2), 936
4	Crispus	RIC 7 London 115; Trier 347, 477; *Ticinum* 170
1	Delmatius	HK 237
56	*Urbs Roma*	HK as 51 (4), copies as 51 (17), 58 (3), copy of 58, 65 (3), copies of 65 (2), 76, 85 (2), copy of 85, copies of 184 (4), 190 (3), copies of 190 (9, one of them very good), 200, 205 (2), 376, copy of 376, 546
67	Constantinopolis	HK as 52 (3), copies as 52 (41), 59 (3), copies of 59 (2), copy of 66, 77 (4, one cut down), 86, copies of 185 (7), copies of 191 (4), 541
1	*Populus Romanus*	HK 1066
8	Helena	HK 104, 112 (3), as 112 (2), copy as 112, 128
10	Theodora	HK 105, 113 (3), as 113 (2), 129 (4)
2	Constantius II	RIC 7 Trier 506 (2)
54		HK as 50, 57 (4), 64, 74, 89, as 89, 94 (4), as 100, 116 (2), 126 (4), as 135, 137 (2), as 137, 139 (2), 140, 141, 145, 147 (2), 151, 151.a, 161 (2), 182, copy of 183, as 194, 199, 250, 256, 263, 266, 273, 370 (2), 407, 441 (2), 453, 744, 837, as 1064, 2033
39		CK 28, 30, 32 (3), 38, 39, as 40, 72, 75, as 76, 141, copy of 183, 189, 253 (2, one cut down), as 253 (2), copies as 253 (2), copy as 254, 256 (8), as 256 (5, one cut down), 452, 464, 689, 1218, as 1893
140	Constans	HK as 90, 127 (3), 131, 133 (9), copies of 133 (2), 138 (8), as 138, copies as 138 (9), 140 (7), 140.a, 142, 144, 148 (11), copies of 148 (2), 149 (7), 150 (15), 154 (4), 155 (3), 158 (2), 159 (4), 160 (22), 163, 164 (3), 227, copy of 243, 244, 253, 255, 261, 387, 401, 421 (2), 440, 442, 450, 457 (4), 638, 748, 856, 1065, 1290
32		CK 33 (11), as 33, 35 (13), 36, 39, 43, 182.a, 457, 604, 607
2	House of Constantine	RIC 7 London copy as 154; 310–317 otherwise illegible
117		HK as 48 (2), copies as 48 (17), copy of 49, copy of 49 but head left, copy as 49, copy as 53, as 57, copy of 62, as 87 (4), copies as 87 (46), as 88 (2), copies as 88 (2), copy as 89, copy as 110, copy as 112, as 132, copy of 132, copy as 132, copy of 133, copy as 133, as 137 (8), copies as 137 (5), copy as 180, copies of 181 (2), copy as 181, copy of 186, copy as 249, copy as 352, copy of 405, as 429, as 963 Hybrids obverse 51/reverse 52 (2), obv 52/rev 48, obv 52/rev 87 (2), obv 52/rev 145 – very important, obv 88/rev 52
809		CK *Fel Temp Reparatio* Fallen Horseman copies based on CK 25 (804), copies of 25 overstruck on Constantinopolis as HK 52, *Gloria Exercitus* as HK 48 (3), *Providentiae Augg* as RIC 7 London 293
225		Minims, less than 12mm diameter likely to be *Fel Temp Reparatio* copies but not certain (225)
31		Copies of the Constantinian period but otherwise illegible (31)
51	Magnentius	CK as 5, copies as 5 (5), 7, 8 (2, one cut down), copies as 8 (27), 10, 15, as 19, 50 (2), 58, copy as 58, 66, copies of 217 (2), copy as 217, copy of 219, copy of 221, copy as 221, copy as 233
1	Decentius	CK 9
2	Julian	Copper core of silver *siliqua* reverse VOT/V/MVLT/X mint-mark illegible; CK 270
114	Valentinian I	Silver RIC 9 Thessalonika 12.a: Bronze CK as 96 (4), 273, 275, as 275 (5), 281, 284, 290 (2), 300, 307, 317 (2), as 317 (7), 321 (7), 330 (2), 334 (2), 338 (3), 477, 479 (8), as 479, 481 (3), as 481, as 482, 491, 496, 501, 508, 512 (4), 514 (8), 518, 521 (2), 525 (4), 527 (14), 965, 967, 1011 (3), as 1011, 1014 (4), 1017 (2), 1358, 1408, 1409, 1414 (2), 1418, 1420 (2), 1702
164	Valens	CK as 97 (8), 121.A, 123, 276 (2), 277 (3), as 280, as 282 (3), 289, as 291, 303 (4), 309 (5), 319 (3), as 319 (3), 322 (4), 332 (4), 340 (9), 348, 365, 368, 480 (7), as 480 (2), 483 (15), as 483, 489 (2), 492 (2), as 497, 502, 504, 510 (3), 513 (2), 516 (7), as 516 (2), 520, 523 (3), 524, 526 (2), 528 (19), 532 (3), 535, 537, 542 (2), 713 (3), 720, 725 (2), 966, 968 (2), 972 (3), 985, 987, 999, 1012 (2), as 1012 (2), 1015, 1021 (2), 1031 (3), 1417, 1427, 1429, 1717

98	Gratian	a) Silver RIC 9 Trier 27.f (2): Bronze CK as 98 (2), 304, as 318 (2), 320 (3), as 320 (2), 323, as 323, 331 (2), 335 (2), 339, 341, 343, 351, 364 (2), 371 (4), as 371, 378 (5), as 378, 503 (2), as 503 (5), 517 (8), as 517 (2), 523.a (6), as 523.a (2), 529 (22), as 529, 531, 533 (4), 540, as 723, 726 (2), 1411, 1412, 1413, 1421, brockage of obverse, reverse illegible
1		b) CK 545
49	House of Valentinian	CK as 96 (26), as 275 (9), possible copy as 275, as 279, as 317 (3), as 319, as 322, as 344, as 525, as 1454, reverses illegible(4)
1	Valentinian II	a) CK 729
3		b) CK 789 (2), 1083 cut down
22		CK as 162 (7), 389, 562 (7), 796 (2), as 796, 799 (2), 1105 (2)
3	Theodosius I	b) CK as 749 halved, 792, 1081
30		c) CK 163 (2), as 163 (5), 166, 169, 391 (5), 565 (9), as 565, 797 (2), as 797 (2), 1106, as 1106
7	Magnus Maximus	Silver RIC 9 Trier 84.b: Bronze CK 156 (2), 387, 560 (3)
1	Eugenius	CK 393
32	Arcadius	CK 164 (4), as 164 (17), 167 (2), 392 (2), 566 (6), 1107
8	Honorius	Silver RIC 9 *Aquileia* as 59: Bronze CK 174, as 174 (2), 396, 570, 806 (2)
6	House of Theodosius	b) CK as 144, as 782 (2), as 789 (3)
169		c) CK as 162 (92), as 168 (2), as 389 (2), as 562 (11), as 796 (55), as 799 (2), as 807, as 1105, reverses illegible(3)
67	third-fourth century	otherwise illegible (67)
59	fourth century	otherwise illegible (59)

The Celtic coins

by Lyn Sellwood

Dobunnic silver piece; Allen class B; Mack 378, Van Arsdell 1042–1, Dobunnic B, *Find 3612, context 33, south courtyard, Phase 4–6*
Dobunnic (?), new type, base AR, *Find 5864, context 758, ditch F264, Phase 2d*
Dobunnic (?), new type as above, very base AR(?), heavily patinated, *Find 5753, context 757, ditch F264, Phase 2d*

The first coin is part of the Dobunnic regular series, classified by Van Arsdell (1989) as 1042–1, Dobunnic B, and attributed by him to Corio, date range 30–15 BC.

The other two coins may be of an 'irregular' Dobunnic type related to both regular and irregular Dobunnic issues but not ancestral to either. They may represent an issue complementary to, and possibly contemporary with Van Arsdell 1010–3, Dobunnic A (Mack 68), proposed date 35–30 BC. They may be products of a mint located in central and eastern Wiltshire, (Robinson 1977) although this is questioned by Van Arsdell (1989, 268). (see Fiche 1 for further discussion).

Discussion

The coin list is unusual in several ways and it will perhaps be easiest to work out from the particular to the more general. It may be that some of the coins found at Uley are occurring for the first time on an archaeological site in Britain but the comparative material is neither well enough gathered, nor well enough arranged to attempt any sort of objective check. On a more subjective level there are a few coins which are seen very rarely as site-finds and these include the coin of Delmatius and the *Restitutor Reipublicae* reverse of Valentinian I (CK 1702). Neither of these coins is of the highest scarcity in numismatic terms, but they are so rarely found in excavations that they are worth noticing. Unfortunately, once they have been noticed, there is little more that can be said, for each is a totally normal part of large issues, whose rarity resides only in knowledgeable, detailed, literate inspection. Their users would almost certainly not have been aware of their unusual nature and therefore no motives may be read back into either their use or their loss.
The irregular coins, those flans prepared and struck in Britain or North Gaul in imitation of the products being sent out from the central mints, are more interesting. The barbarous radiate coins struck between about AD 270 and 290 show a considerable range of diversity in style and subject matter: the reverse showing a candelabrum is most unusual, and at least two reverses are so definite in their execution, but so far from their prototypes that they at present defy description and can only be classed as 'very odd'. The whole series is presently under study by John Davies and it is to be hoped that when his present work is completed he will be able to work on more groups of site-finds such as these. Copies produced under the House of Constantine, about 324–355 are numerous and include one coin which is of considerable use. This copy (Hybrid obv HK 52/rev 145) shows an obverse of the Constantinopolis type, which was often copied in the 340's, but combines it with the reverse of two victories struck between 346 and 348. This two victories issue is only rarely copied compared with the earlier coins, and it is generally thought that the issue brought the period of closure at the official mints (and therefore the corresponding period of copying) to an end. This copy shows how coins of the early 330's were still being copied after the new issues had arrived from the continent after 346.

Over one thousand coins have been classed either as copies of the Fallen Horseman reverse of 350–55, or as minims (small illegible copies), and these must be an important source if Richard Brickstock's work on this series (Brickstock 1987) is followed up with a die study. At present they form no more than a bulge in the overall statistics, and will be considered in this context below.

A second unusual feature of the complete list is its possible continuity. It stretches from pre-Roman issues which, from the evidence available at Cirencester and Bagendon, were distinctly rare in Roman contexts soon after the conquest of AD 43, to the latest issues of the House of Theodosius minted in the West (395–400). The list is not uniform in its density throughout the whole period, but part of this variation is the overall variation which will be seen on every site in Britain. Thus coins of the period AD 40–240 are always less common than coins of the later third and fourth centuries.

The presence of the British coins suggests activity on the site during the first century AD. Of course this is well attested from other types of evidence such as the pottery but at present it is best to keep the types of evidence separate to see what different pictures may emerge. It is impossible to pin-point this activity with any more precision because it may, or may not, conform to the rules of Romanized coin use. Thus, if the people who lost the British coins, or deposited them, did so in full awareness of and participation in the coin use of Romanized Britain, the coins were deposited by AD 60 at the latest. But if these people were unaffected by Romanized coin use the coins may have been available for deposition well into the second century. We can never know this for sure because an absence of correlation with Romanization, either in coins, pottery, or brooches, remains undatable.

Until the end of the second century most of the Roman coins are very well worn and had probably been in circulation for some considerable time before being deposited. It is possible to feel a fair degree of certainty here because we know the excellent condition in which the coins of the first two centuries were issued from the mint. This does not apply to the coins of the later fourth century. It would be unusual for Claudian copies (produced *c* AD 43 to 64) to be still in circulation after the end of the first century because they were replaced fairly quickly by the new regular issues of Nero which entered the country in some numbers after AD 64, and the coins of Vespasian and Domitian might seem less worn that those of the early second century. It might therefore be possible to see one period of coin-loss in the 70's and 80's which would account for the first eight coins of the list, not including the sestertius of Vitellius, and then a gap in coin use, or coin loss, or coin deposition, until about the year 200. Some of the second-century coins must have seen more than half a century of wear before deposition, and such worn coins are typical of losses of the early third century. While all the coins after Domitian could have been lost after the year 200 there is nothing which specifically insists on this interpretation, and coin loss may have gone on gently throughout the second century. Such coins were still available to Postumus (260–8) to be overstruck, and they occur in hoards of the 260's, but they seem to have disappeared by the 280's, and it may be no accident that **some of the Barbarous Radiates produced between about 270–90 appear to be struck in the yellow brass of the old sestertii.**

The concentration of coins from 190–225 is unusual in view of the small number of earlier coins, and this would be enough evidence in itself of a rise in coin use on the site early in the third century. But this rise, which need be no more than an intensification of Romanization, rather than an intensification of activity, does not lead on to the great glut of radiate coins of 260–296 which might properly be expected. The regular radiate coins which form a prolific part of all coin lists in Britain are there, but their numbers are not great: it is perhaps in the local or national productions of the Barbarous Radiates that the best evidence of activity can be seen.

These irregular coins together with the regular issues from the official mints from 294–324 make it clear that there is activity on the site around the year 300 at a level at least equal to that around 200. This coin loss seems to increase through the first half of the fourth century, a normal characteristic of British sites, until it reaches a peak with the irregular issues of around 350–60. The House of Valentinian is very well represented, and the House of Theodosius shows continued activity to at least the period 395–400 with the issues of Honorius. No coin on the site can be dated to after AD 402, but this is to do no more than confirm that Uley has a normal coin pattern, for there are virtually no sites in the west of Britain with coins after 402. This says nothing at all about activity on the site and, just as I have earlier suggested that the rise and fall in coin loss in the early years is due more to waxing and waning Romanization, so the end of coin supply need be seen as no more than the withdrawal of one aspect of Romanization.

The important point here is to try to achieve some logic in the use of coins for dating after the last datable coin has entered the site. While coin use continues, and coin supply is maintained then the proportion of the latest coins to the general circulation pool will gradually rise. Thus an important point in any phase is the proportion of coins of the House of Theodosius to earlier coins. While this proportion is still rising it is likely that coin supply to the site is continuing. This stage must come to an end shortly after the western mints ceased large scale supply about 402. From this point onwards there is no clear reason for the balance of coins in the circulation pool to change unless some sorting by size or weight takes place. Two points need to be noted here: the state of the late coins cannot be taken as evidence for wear, and therefore for length of circulation, and there is absolutely no evidence whatsoever for any form of local coin production after official supplies ceased.

These points deserve expansion. The coins of the House of Theodosius can be dated between the main issue dates of 388 and 402 by the emperors who are mentioned on the coins. Thus Valentinian II died in 392, Theodosius I in 395, and coins of Honorius are common only after 394. It is possible therefore to isolate hoards buried between 388 and 394 (coins of Valentinian II but none of Honorius) in which none of these later coins may have been in circulation for more than six years. Yet some of these coins have very little detail and virtually no relief so that they appear very badly worn; it is clear that they themselves have not been worn, but they have been struck from dies that have been heavily used and on which most detail has been obliterated. The moment these coins gain an archaeological patina they are indistinguishable from coins that have seen half a century of wear, although they may have changed hands only once and have been minted only six months before deposition. It is important to note therefore that where we do not know the state of a coin when it was newly minted, we cannot judge its age at deposition by its appearance.

One of the most noticeable points about this particular coin list is the great number, variety, and freshness of the irregular coins, the copies. It is clear that from the Barbarous Radiates (280) to the Fel Temp copies (360) Uley is in touch with centres of unofficial coin production. It is also clear from the condition of many of these copies that they were deposited in a fairly fresh condition for their high relief and excellent detail could not have survived much handling. These copies were therefore deposited often as current coins rather than as worn out rubbish and there need be no suggestion that imitation coins are being offered in a religious setting rather than their more valuable regular counterparts. The particular point at issue is that Uley is in the main-stream of coin use, and is close to centres of coin copying, which seems to happen in times of shortage of suitable regular coin.

The most surprising feature of this coin copying is the point at which it did not happen, that is, at the end of the fourth century. The last coins to be supplied from the Gallic mints were the small issues of the House of Theodosius and these are not copied. Perhaps it would be safer to say that all the coins of the House of Theodosius on the site seem to belong to one integral series, and there is at present no reason whatever to separate out some of these coins as copies of the others, which would then be deemed regular. Working backwards from the last flourishing period of coin supply (388–402) there is on every British site a gap in coin loss, and therefore presumably in coin supply, from 378–88. The common issues before that, of the House of Valentinian, are very well represented, and there is only one coin out of about 400 which might be a copy. The assumption must be that the commonly supplied, used, and lost coins of 364–78 were not copied in the period of short supply from 378–88. In contrast the periods of short supply from 273–94, 341–48, and 348–64 resulted in many copies being made of the last coins commonly supplied and in use.

It might be objected that the only absence that has been demonstrated is the absence of copies of the coins of the House of Theodosius; other types of copies may well have been struck after 402, and copying may have been rife without any reference to coins of 388–402. This suggestion is superficially attractive and has always been seen as a possible answer to the sudden cessation of coin use in the early fifth century, but, at Uley, it can be easily refuted. If there are copies of the early fifth century then they should be distinguishable by their content or their style, but, with discussion of styles the whole matter becomes subjective and personal, and little hard evidence can be expected to emerge.

More open to logical argument is the stratigraphical position of these copies, for they ought to appear only in the levels which accumulated after the latest regular coins had entered the site. Inspection of the phased coin lists shows that there are no classes of coin which congregate in those latest phases, that coins of all classes occur in layers which must have been deposited throughout the coin-using phases of the site, and that there are therefore no candidates for classification as fifth-century copies. This leaves the question of how long the latest fourth-century coins continued in circulation and use. The danger here is twofold – that we project back on the fifth century our own anachronistic view that no-one can do without coin, and that we study the problem on sites which were occupied in the fourth century. If we are to resolve the problem we must approach it without any preconception as to whether money was or was not desirable in the later Roman period in Britain. If coins seem, on archaeological evidence, to drop out of use very quickly after continental supplies ceased then coins were apparently thought little of; if there is good archaeological evidence for the continued production and use of coins after regular supplies ceased then coin use was presumably important.

There is at present no hard evidence to suggest either the production, or the use of coins in Britain after the earliest years of the fifth century. Clear evidence can only come from sites without fourth-century debris, where the problem of residuality does not occur. Such sites, whether cemeteries or early Saxon dwelling sites, do sometimes have a few Roman coins amongst their finds, but such finds are so rare that they have never been taken to indicate coin use. Where they are found in cemeteries they occur more often as decoration that as practical coin, for they are often pierced and worn as bracelets or necklaces.

On sites already full of fourth-century debris, fifth-century activity, where it can be demonstrated rather than facilely assumed, must inevitably disturb earlier rubbish in any construction or demolition, and the incorporation of redeposited rubbish cannot be taken as diagnostic of coin use.

Finally, the coins which are re-incorporated into post-400 layers seldom show a progression from the continually evolving coinage pool of the fourth century, but usually form a random selection from coinage already lost on the site.

From these impressions, and they cannot be claimed as more than that, what might be expected is a series of layers in which the later coins of the fourth century were seen gradually coming into circulation. These layers would reach a point at which the latest coins had attained a maximum presence, and it is likely that these would be the latest layers to provide evidence of coin using on the site. Such layers would probably date to around 400–20. After this there might well be layers deposited during periods in which coins were rarely lost – a post-coin phase, but these layers would be disrupted by any major earth-moving, which would begin an unintentional and random process of redistribution of Roman coins from earlier levels.

If such coinless layers and phases exist they are, by definition the province of the excavator and not the numismatist. Both the numismatist, and the Roman coins themselves, have no power to assist in dating any archaeological sequence after about AD 420.

Coins and phasing

These notes cannot form more than a subjective impression of the dates which might be taken from the coins attributed to them. It would be possible to make firm numismatic statements, but these would be immediately obvious to anyone consulting the phased coin list in the computer archive, which gives dates for each coin, and it would be wrong to suggest that the phasing of the site, or the attribution of coins to phases, can ever be as certain as the use of dates to delimit the reign of a Roman emperor. The dates suggested are therefore impressions derived from consideration of all the coins in any one phase, and the relationship of coin groups to one another.

Phase 2d. The two British coins, and no Roman coins might suggest a date near to AD 50.

Phase 3. The coins from these phases (3a–c) are so scarce and erratic that no safe conclusions can be drawn.

Phase 4a. Over twenty coins which reach up to the Barbarous Radiate period make a sensible sequence which ought to end by the year 300.

Phase 4b. Another group of over 20 coins continues to 310–17 and so forms an obvious continuation from Phase 4a.

Phase 5a. Context 1220, a floor foundation, seems to stop at the date of Phase 4a, – *c* 300 – , and the other coins represent continued build-up towards the middle of the century.

Phase 5b. Coins which continue towards 345.

Phase 5c. About 80 coins with the five latest giving a firm date after 345 but before 355. In this case the absence of the very common coins of the mid-350's seems to set the end of Phase 5c clearly before 353.

Phase 5d. The coins from this phase form the natural continuation from Phase 5c and spread into the later 350's but not later.

Phase 5e. This phase contains coins struck after 364 but they are in a minority – 3 out of 126 in Phase 5e(i) and 24 out of 153 in Phase 5e (ii). This suggests a date within five years of 375 when the coins of the House of Valentinian were still entering the site.

Phase 6a. This phase already contains coins of Honorius and ought therefore to date after 394. Coins of the House of Theodosius are still in a clear minority so it suggests that coin supply is continuing. A date between 390 and 400 seems likely.

Phase 6b. Coins of the House of Theodosius are now common, but they are still in a minority. This may be the last phase in which a progression of gradual ageing of the circulation pool can be seen and may therefore belong to the period 400–20.

Phase 7a. The coinage in this phase is more mixed than before and this probably suggests disturbance and re-deposition. It does not seem to form a smooth progression from the earlier phases and might mark the end of Romanized coin use. If this is so it is likely to be after about 420.

Later phases. Once the progression is broken the coins higher in the stratigraphy must be assumed to be residual. In fact their composition becomes totally erratic and it seems likely that they can be used as nothing more than indicators of the disturbance of earlier layers.

Uley and other sites

The comparison of this site with other sites in Britain, as regards coin loss, has been investigated elsewhere in detail and need only be mentioned in summary here

Table 2: Coin quantification

period	*coins*		*group 2*	*deviation*			*corrected values*	
	no	*per 1000*	*per 1000*	*from mean*	*%*	*per 1000*	*devi-ation*	*%*
to AD 41	3	1	4± 8	−3	−38	2	−2	+25
41–54	2	1	8± 19	−7	−37	1	−7	+37
54–69	1	1	4± 10	−3	−30	1	−3	+30
69–96	3	1	14± 19	−13	−68	2	−12	−63
96–117	2	1	8± 10	−7	−70	1	−7	−70
117–138	8	3	7± 7	−4	−57	4	−3	−43
138–161	8	3	9± 11	−6	−55	4	−5	−45
161–180	12	4	5± 7	−1	−14	6	+1	+14
180–192	3	1	2± 3	−1	−33	2	–	–
192–222	5	2	7± 10	−5	−50	3	+4	−40
222–238	1	1	3± 6	−2	−33	1	−2	+33
238–259	1	1	4± 5	−3	−60	1	−3	−60
259–275	163	57	105± 40	−48	−120	86	−19	−48
275–294	199	69	81± 37	−12	−31	105	+24	+65
294–317	23	8	20± 20	−12	−17	12	−8	−40
317–330	37	13	39± 32	−26	−81	20	−19	−59
330–348	501	175	278±118	−103	−87	265	−13	−11
348–364	1190	415	110± 51	+305	+598	110	–	–
364–378	426	148	161± 75	−13	−17	226	−65	−87
378–388	20	7	6± 8	+1	+12	11	+5	+63
388–402	262	91	128±135	−37	−27	139	−11	−8
total		2870	*legible coins*					
		126	*uncertain*					
		2996	*overall total*					

(Reece 1980). The method involves summarising the coins which can be assigned to chronological periods of about twenty years and then comparing the coins in each of these periods with a selection of other rural sites in Britain. Table 2 gives the summary details extracted from the chronological list. Only the 126 coins listed as uncertain have to be left out of the calculations, and, in a total of 2996 coins this need cause little worry. These coins are all of the late third or fourth century and the 4.2% which they represent should probably be divided between the nine periods between 259 and 402. This suggests that it is most unlikely that they cause an actual error of 1% in any value.

In Table 2 the actual numbers of coins assigned to each period are given, and this is followed by that value expressed as coins per thousand. This simply avoids the use of the decimal point which would be necessary in percentages. In the third column the values show the mean for a collection of 49 sites in Roman Britain, excluding the larger towns, and, together with the mean, the variation within which the majority of those sites lie. In mathematical terms this is the mean for each period of the values from the 49 sites with one standard deviation. If the coin finds from British sites followed a normal distribution the standard deviation would include two out of every three sites leaving one of the three outside this variation. But it seems certain that the finds are not, technically, part of a normal distribution so that this rule does not apply. The fourth column shows the deviation of Uley from the rural mean. Thus, in period one the mean is 4 coins per 1000, the Uley value is 1 coin per 1000, which is three below the mean and so a deviation of −3. British rural sites vary from the mean by a value of 8, thus from 0–12; a deviation of −3 is 3 out of a permitted 8 variation, or 38% allowed variation. The fifth column therefore shows a percentage deviation of −38%. These figures can be combined in one diagram, see Fig 71, 1, where the mean is the centre line, the variation from the mean is shown above (+) or below (−). and 100% represents the permitted variation (or one standard deviation).

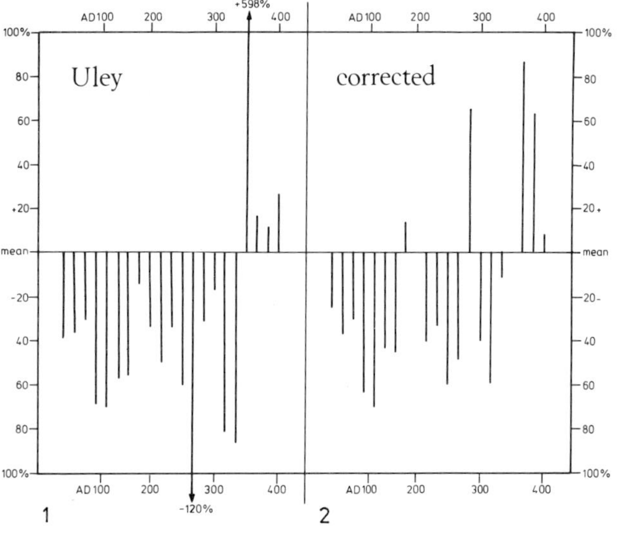

Fig 71 Chronological distribution of Roman coins

Fig 71, 1 shows quite clearly the major problem involved in interpreting the Uley coins in any comparative sense, for the period from 348–64 is far in excess of any British values known. This means that for the total of nearly 3,000 coins there are about five times more of this period than on any other site. Either this should be taken to mean that the results are right, and this site is extraordinary among British sites between 348–64, or that the results are somehow wrong, and that no site can really be that unusual. The simplest way in which the results can be wrong is in the failure to spot a hoard of coins, and to allow for this in the calculations.

If what we are looking at in a coin list is the results of a series of individual events occasioning either, the loss, or intentional deposition of a coin, then the assumption has to be that the results are very roughly equal, so that they usually concern only one coin, or occasionally, a small number. This assumption does not affect the value of the event: thus by dropping one gold coin by a shrine a considerable 'event' could take place, which to the treasurers would far outweigh a number of smaller 'events', yet to us as observers of individual coins it would number simply as one. If, instead of one gold coin the visitor deposited the same value in small bronze coins, say a bag of one thousand pieces, then instead of one unit deposited, one thousand units might have been hung up in a bag on a convenient nail. Whereas a gold coin was negotiable at a later date, one thousand *Fel Temp Reparatio* copies were almost certainly not, and the worthless metal objects which were literally *anathema* (that which was hung up in honour of a pagan god, and therefore, to Christians became untouchable) would be cleared out of the shrine by later adherents either of the same religion or of a different one.

These coins do occur commonly in the material which is thought to be redeposited after a clearing out of the temple and it may well be that they are parts of a very scattered hoard. If this is the case then they should be judged to represent one 'event' in any comparative study, for in all the other 49 rural sites in Britain hoard material has been rigorously excluded. But since the contents of the hoard (or hoards) are scattered they cannot be identified in detail.

It is worth looking at Fig 71, at this point, to see what effect this aberrant period has on the rest of the interpretation of the site. The attribution of 41.5% of the coins from the site to one period has made that period heavily over-represented and therefore all other periods under-represented. The impression given by the diagram, that Uley is strangely always below the British mean, is therefore partly an illusion. While we cannot isolate the actual coins which made up this possible hoard, as opposed to other coins of exactly the same type which were lost at the same time, and in the same places, we do know what the average value of coin loss on rural sites at this period was. We could attempt to return Uley to normality by bringing the period 348–64 back down to this value (11%) and adjusting the other periods accordingly. With the revision of the coin list this has now been done more accurately than in Reece 1980 so that, with the elimination of an earlier error, the resulting diagram, Fig 71, 2, is different from the earlier version.

Using the 'corrected' values Fig 71, 2 shows strong differences from the values which might include the hoard in Fig 71, 1. All values have now come nearer to the mean, the mid-second-century value is now just

above average, rather than just below, the period containing the Barbarous Radiate copies (275–96) is well above average, though still in the normal range, but the values consistently above average remain firmly in the late fourth century.

There is no way whatever of knowing whether the corrected values, in which the possible hoard has been removed, are to be preferred to the straight values. It is perhaps best to see the process of 'correcting' as a normal mathematical step in which, in any set of information, exceptional values are noted, and then in a second step are set aside so that the rest of the values can be seen more easily. The question at issue is whether a thousand pilgrims to a shrine each deposited one small coin over a period of time, or one pilgrim deposited a bag of a thousand coins at one instant, a bag which after years of hanging on the wall burst and deposited its now worthless contents over a broken floor. If we had a deposit in its original state, as in the spring at Bath, we could see the succession of events and the interleaving of one type of coin with another, but the Uley material has been redeposited. The coins themselves cannot give us such detail because the thousand pilgrims and the one could have brought their offerings from the same monetary pool.

Further work

Although substantial effort has been expended already on an analysis of the coins from Uley, there are many more aspects of the material which need to be studied. One clear failure in this report is the absence of a proper commentary on the irregular coinage, especially the Barbarous Radiates, the copies of the House of Constantine, and the Fallen Horseman copies. They need to be compared one with another to see how homogeneous a group they are, and they need to be compared with collections from nearby sites to see what types are regional, and which nationally distributed.

A second subject which would certainly repay study, perhaps using the computer, is the pattern of occurrence of certain coins in certain deposits, and the significance of the different compositions of different groups of coins. Related to this is the intriguing question of how far it is possible to unravel the sequence of deposition from objects of known dates excavated in a well recorded sequence. Perhaps the coins could be used to 'unpick' the stratigraphic sequence, so that by extracting redeposited material stage by stage, we could reconstitute the groups of material as originally deposited.

The coins and the site records are fully preserved, and can be consulted (see chapter 1) so these studies could be attempted in the future.

Summary

The coins from Uley form an unusually large group excavated in well-recorded contexts. Few of the coins are of importance in themselves, but, studied as a group they can be made to throw light on the sequence of the site, and the place of the site among the other rural and religious sites of Roman Britain.

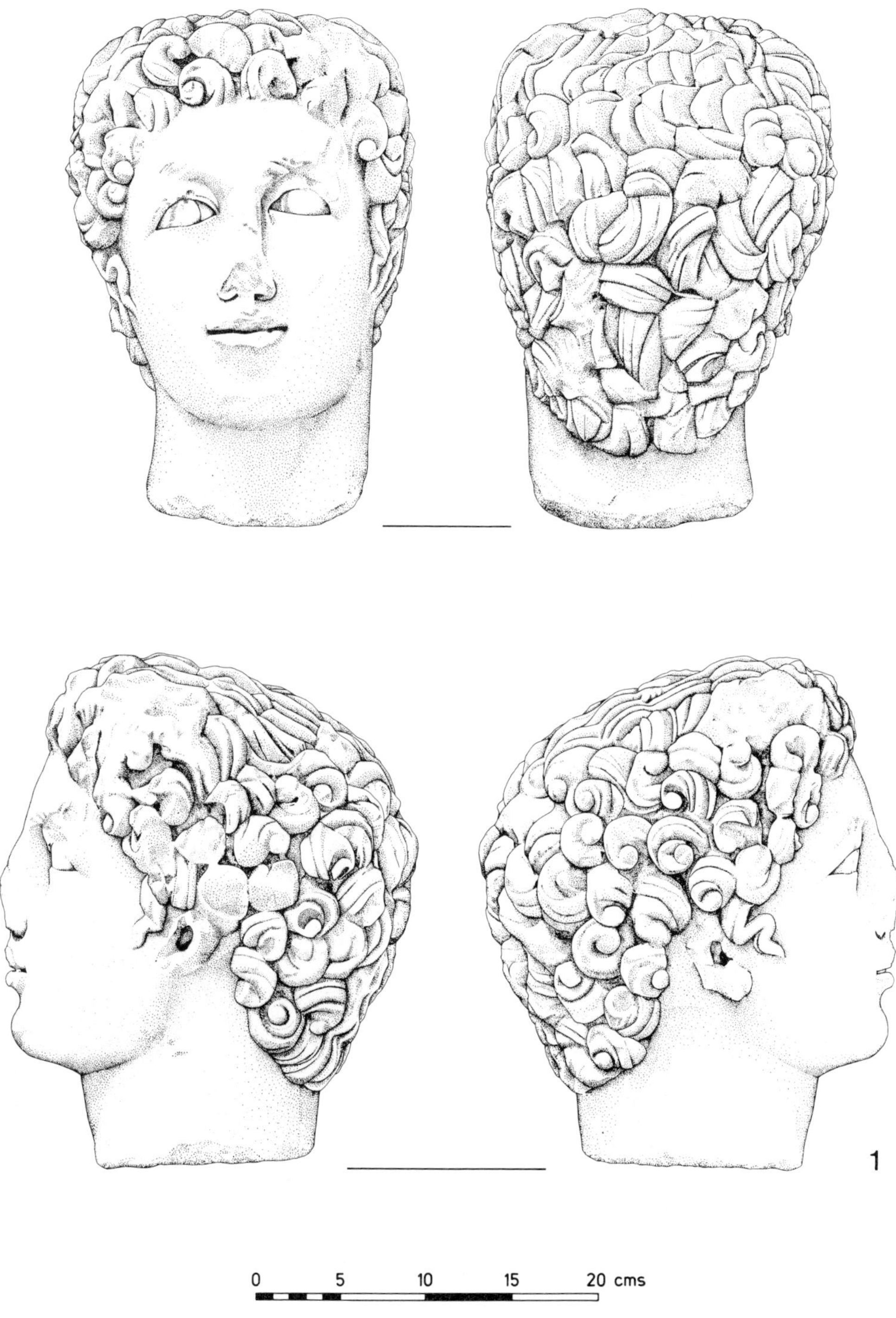

Fig 72 Limestone head from the cult statue, scale, 1:4

6 Votive objects: images and inscriptions

by Martin Henig
with contributions by Mark Hassall and Justine Bayley

Sculpture in stone

Statuary

All fragments were carved in the local oolitic limestone except where stated

The head, fragments of the left thigh, the lower right leg, and accompanying ram and cockerel, of a cult image of Mercury were recovered. The torso was not found and may have been broken up for use during building work and subsequently lost, or it may still be deposited in an area not excavated. The head, however, was carefully buried in the post-Roman period (see chapter 4).

Fig 72, and front cover
1 The head of the statue is carved in a highly accomplished manner, the more remarkable when it is remembered that the medium is not fine grained marble. When viewed from the front, the face seems rather bland and even mask-like, but the nose and lips were damaged in antiquity and the colour with which the statue would have been painted, now lost, would have enhanced the naturalness of the expression and in particular, given life to the eyes. In profile the head is dignified, the physiognomy composed and attractive, and the hair richly textured, with curling scroll-like locks, *Find 7902, context 940, Structure VIII, Phase 7*

In terms of Romano-British sculpture, this is a masterpiece, even superior to the much praised head of Mercury from Cirencester (Toynbee 1962, 131f, no 19, pl 29). That head may also derive from a cult image, although it was not itself found in a temple

Fig 73
2 Left thigh of the figure, including the knee, height 0.35m. On its left side is the stub of a strut of square section, 20 × 20mm, by which the statue would have been given additional support, in the form perhaps of a tree trunk or column. Such supports are frequently found with Roman statues, which tend to be less well balanced than their Greek prototypes, or are stone adaptations of bronzes better fitted to stand by themselves (Bieber 1977, 41; Deonna 1912, 339), *Find 5889, context 728, Structure VIII, Phase 7*
3 Lower right leg, including knee, height 0.38m, *Find 5890, context 728, Structure VIII, Phase 7*

Fig 74
4 Lower right leg and torso of a ram, height 0.18m. A large fragment, which joins the lower right leg fragment (no 3 above), comprising a small section of the lower right leg and the body of a ram, its head and most of its legs are missing, *Find 8351, context 719, Structure VIII, Phase 7*

Fig 75
5 Body of a cockerel, height 0.16m. Fragment of the left lower leg (ankle), attached to a substantial part of the figure of a cockerel, its body turned three quarters to the front, and its wings partially displayed. The head and neck of the bird, and much of its wings, are lost, *Find 5891, context 719, Structure VIII, Phase 7*

6 Fragment of drapery, *Find 8348, context 254, Structure XI, Phase 7* 7 Fragment of drapery, *Find 2976, context 14, Structure II, Phase 6b*

It is clear that the statue was of high quality and based on a late classical prototype, probably by Praxiteles. The sculptor may have been forced to simplify in rendering details (for instance the curls on the head) because of the relative coarseness of the local oolitic limestone used, compared with marble.

In contrast to the Cirencester Mercury and others like it (for example a head from Heidelberg: Espérandieu **8**, 1922, 151, no 6109), there is no *petasos* and the head is covered in a mass of tight curls, with a looser tress hanging down in front of each ear. Two stubs towards the front of the head, may represent wings. At a miniature scale we may compare it to the impression of a profile bust, probably of Mercury, taken from a gem found at Charterhouse on Mendip (Henig 1978, 308 and pl xxx, no app 151) and a similar but certain head of the god (with a wing in his hair) on an intaglio from Avenches (Guisan 1975, 8 and pl 1.3).

The figures of cult animals are both shown at approximately the same size, and that of the ram in particular is very small in relation to the figure of Mercury. It can be computed that the statue itself was slightly larger than life size (*c* 1.8m, or 6ft 10in high) and the stub of a strut on the remaining thigh shows, as stated above, that a tree stump, column or some other support was provided for stability. This varying treatment of scales, observable in other representations of Mercury with his animal attributes, including those on altars from this site (see below), is a simple device by which the size and importance of the god might be augmented and emphasised.

Although Roman statues of Mercury display a medley of influences from the time of Polykleitos onwards, the gentle humanity of the Uley head is Praxitelean and brings the great Olympia Hermes to mind (Lawrence 1972, 186 and pl 47a). Indeed the head of this statue is covered by a mass of curls, albeit arranged in a less regular manner. The general configuration of the statue type is, however, closer to the Hermes of Andros, a Roman copy of another Hermes by Praxiteles (Rizzo 1932, 76 and pls 113 and 114b) – the curls are here much more richly executed than on the Greek work and correspond more closely with those on the Uley statue (also see Comstock and Vermeule 1976, 102, no 156, for

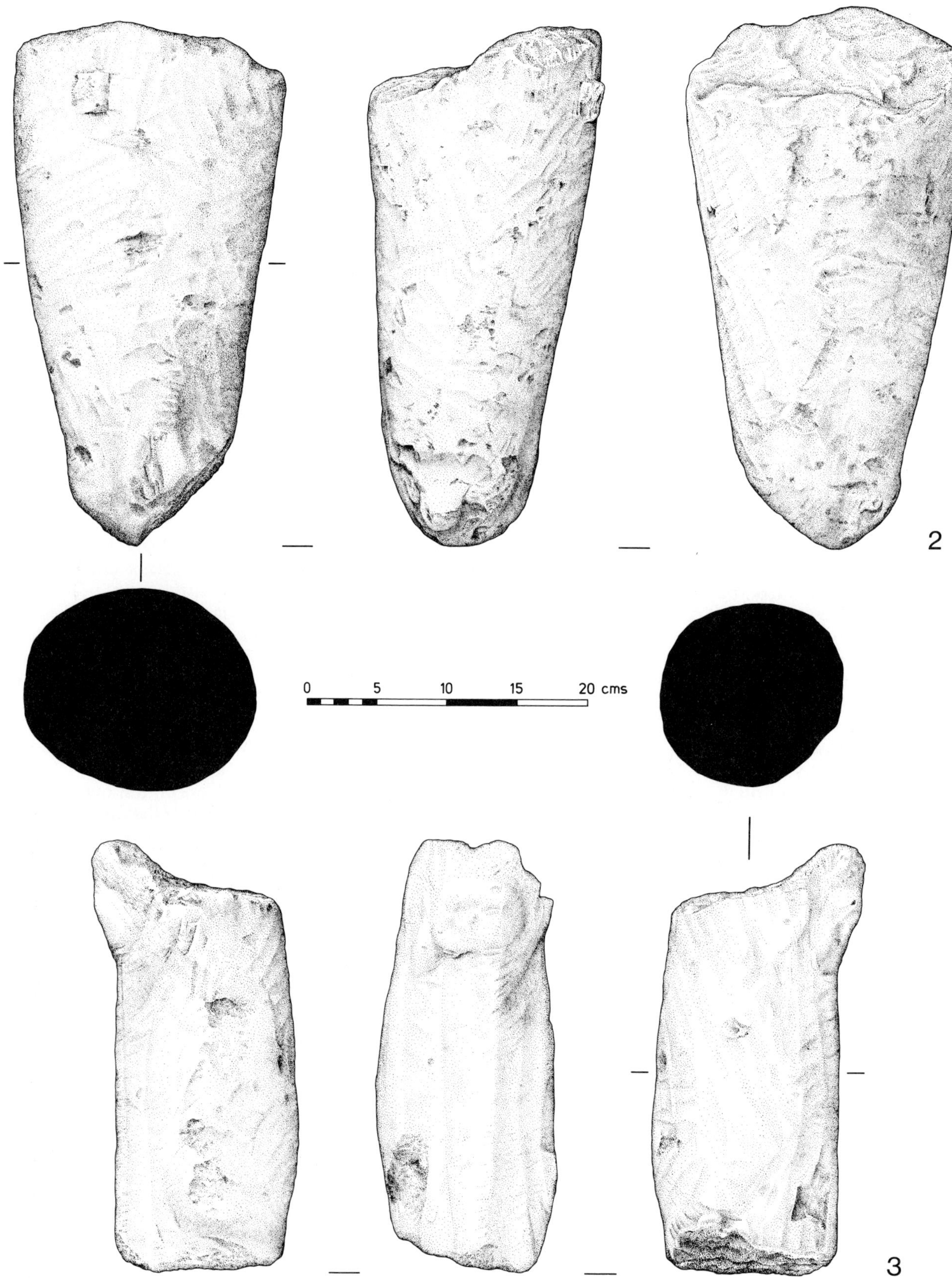

Fig 73 Limestone leg fragments from the cult statue, scale 1:4

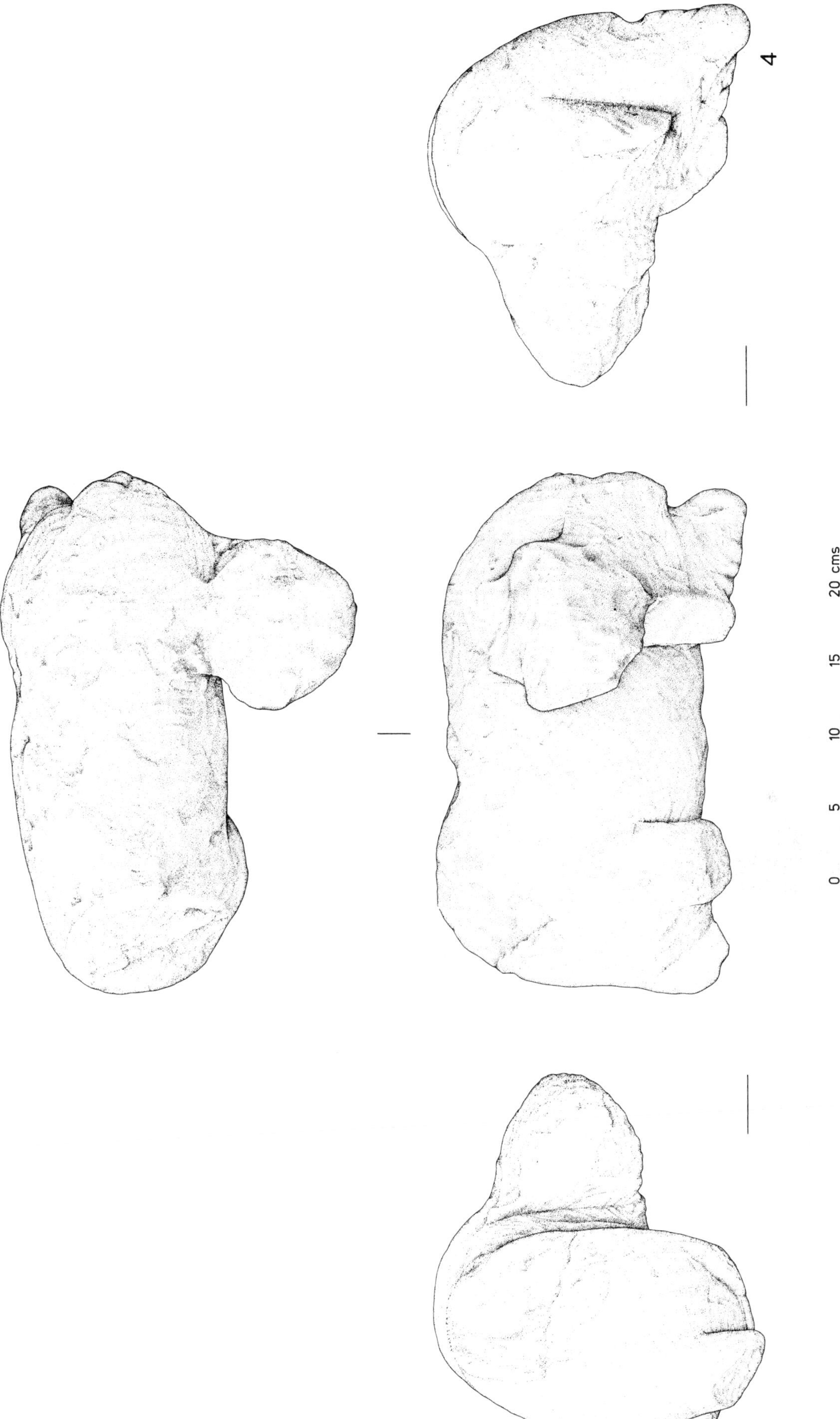

Fig 74 Limestone torso of a ram from the cult statue, scale 1:4

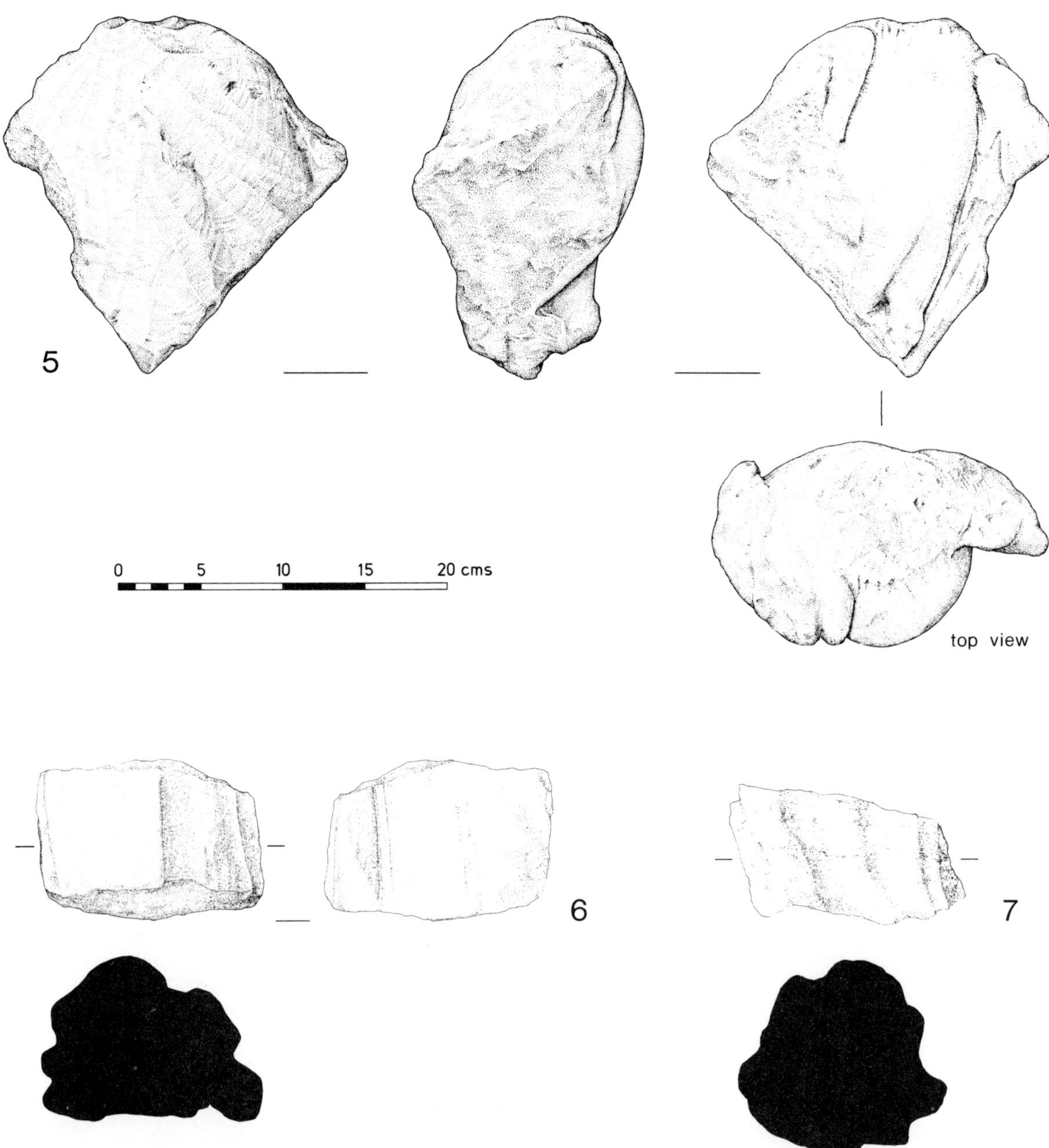

Fig 75 Body of a cockerel and drapery fragments from the cult statue, scale 1:4

another head of the Andros type). The same elaborate treatment of curls is to be seen over the forehead of the bronze portrait of Hadrian from London (Toynbee 1964, 50 and pl vi) but the overall elaboration of the coiffure and the evident use of the drill to create a rich texture is especially reminiscent of the youthful portraiture of Marcus Aurelius (Wegner 1939, 191 and pl 15; 195 and pl 14). The apparent outlining of the eyes and pupils also indicates a second-century date.

The Uley cult image, then, was made in Antonine, probably mid-Antonine, times and in a highly romanised milieu. Unlike the Antenociticus head from Benwell (Toynbee 1964, 106–7, pl xxviiia; Henig 1980b, pl 5, II), the main non-Classical element here is the use of a local stone, although the exuberant coiffure with its medley of curls may have some links, at least aesthetically, to Celtic curvilinear art (S-scrolls). The statue fragments indicate an amazingly high standard of workmanship for a figure carved in limestone. Presumably the sculptor came from a workshop in Bath or, more probably, Cirencester. Certainly the fragments of god and cult animals bring to mind the type of votive relief of Mercury from the city (Toynbee 1964, 156 and pl 40a; and see the report on the Uley altars below).

The reconstruction drawing presented here (Fig 76) was researched and drawn by Joanna Richards. It is largely based on the Praxitelean Hermes of Andros and, to a less extent, on the Olympian statue, which I believe is an original work by Praxiteles himself. In both these works the head is rather more inclined than seems to be the case at Uley but physiognomy and coiffure are very similar. The wings are an added feature, characteristic of Hellenistic and Roman figures of Mercury. Two small fragments which seem to represent drapery, perhaps covering a tree stump, make it possible to restore a *chlamys* as on the Andros Hermes. That there was such a support as a column or tree stump, here restored, is indicated by the stub on the left thigh.

Fig 76 Conjectural reconstruction of the cult statue of Mercury. (Drawn by Joanna Richards)

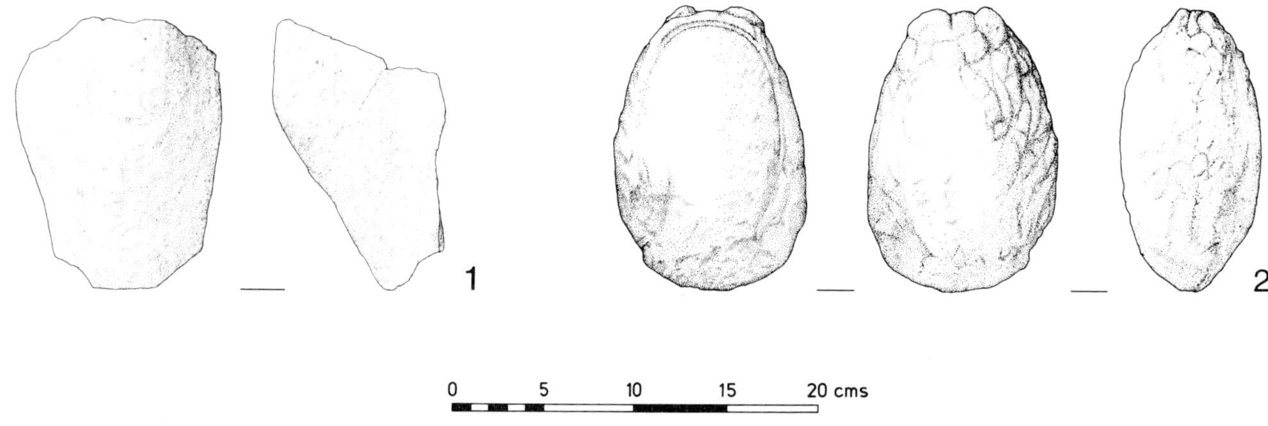

Fig 77 Fragments of other cult statuary, scale: 1:4

The money bag and *caduceus* are attributes of most ancient portrayals of Mercury, including small bronzes and votive reliefs from this site. Our only liberty is to represent the *caduceus* as of metal, which may, or may not, be justified. The ram and cockerel appear likewise on the altar reliefs described below but the former is frequently replaced by a goat on bronze groups etc (see figurines Finds 1949 and 1417, Fig 88, nos 3 and 4). Here though, the animal certainly looks like a ram.

Like many other Roman representations of the god from Gaul and Britain, this statue is not a slavish copy of a Greek statue but demonstrates artistic vitality and cultural interaction of a high order. Continuing Greek influence is demonstrated in the first century AD by Zenodorus' colossal bronze statue of Mercury produced for the *civitas* of the Arverni (Pliny *Naturalis Historia* **xxxiv**, 45).

For earlier publications see Henig 1980a, Ellison and Henig 1981 and Henig 1984, pl 18.

Fig 77
1 Fragment of a knee, from a different, smaller statue, *Find 2976, context 14, Structure II, Phase 6b*
2 Head, almost certainly also a head of Mercury, with curled hair and ovoid face, now very much abraded. It was, presumably, also part of a cult or votive figure, *Find 2710, context 332, Structure IV, Phase 4b*

Altars

Fig 78
Complete altar, defaced, one of three certain, figured altars (ie with reliefs from the front). This one is in reasonably good condition although the highest relief has been sheared away. The carving shows Mercury flanked by ram and cockerel. The style and iconography match the relief from Cirencester cited above (Toynbee 1964, 156 pl xla) very closely and the altar may have been produced in the same studio, *Find 2761, context 279, Structure VII, Phase 7*

Figs 79 and 80
Base of altar and joining fragments of lower relief. This second altar is more fragmentary and the relief is smaller. The subject is again Mercury with ram and cockerel. According to an inscription on the base the sculptor was Searigillus, son of Searix (Hassall below).

Fig 78 Complete oolitic limestone altar with defaced figure of Mercury flanked by ram and cockerel, scale 1:4. (Photo Sebastian Rahtz)

The base on which the inscription appears is ornamented with a frieze of leaves which may represent the metal votive leaves which are such a feature of votive material from this and other shrines (see below). It may be suggested that these would perhaps sometimes have been displayed on the raised pedestal or *suggestus* of the cult image, *Find 8352, context 481, Structure II, Phase 7*

Fig 79 *Reconstruction of the fragmentary limestone altar, scale 1:4. (Drawn by Joanna Richards)*

Fig 80 Base of an oolitic limestone altar to Mercury with inscription and ornamental frieze. (Photo: Sebastian Rahtz)

The inscriptions
based on notes supplied by Mark Hassall

The base carries two inscriptions, the first (a), has been cut immediately below the sculptured relief and is separated from the second, (b), by a panel, outlined by a simple chiselled groove and containing a row of four contiguous stylised leaves.

(*a*) SEARIGILLVSSẸẠRIGISFEC
Searigillus Searigis (filius) fec(it)
'Searigillus (son) of Searix made this'

For the names of the sculptor and his father *cf* Suarigillus Vasilli fil *CIL* **13**, 4433, Metz (not in Holder, Alt-celtischer Sprachschatz) derived, like Suarica, *ibid*, 5532, Dijon, from Suarix, – igis.

(*b*) .]OVERNIVṢ[ ]POṢIT VSL[
L]overnius pos(u)it v(otum) s(olvit) l(aetus)*
'Lovernius set this up and joyfully paid his vow'
*or libens; *willingly*

Lover(n)ios, 'son of the fox' was the name of the father of Bituitos defeated by Rome in BC 121 (Strabo iv 2.3). The name Lovernianus, derived from it, is already attested in the province (*J Roman Stud* **59** (1969) 239, no 23) on a pewter platter from Appleford, Oxfordshire. See *Britannia* **12** (1981) 370 for a previous reading of the Uley fragment.

Two additional joining fragments formed a broken section of the top of an altar with indentation and knot. These were of the same width as the fragments described above, and may have formed the back of the same piece, *Context 279, Structure VII, Phase 7*

Fig 81
1–2 Two fragments from a third altar in very fragmentary condition. They consist of the right leg and nude torso of Mercury, and a fragment of one top corner only, *Find 4661, context 482, Structure II, Phase 7*, and *Find 7763, context 0510, Structure XIX, Phase 7*

The most interesting observation to be made on the iconography of these three altar reliefs is how closely it seems to be based on and conditioned by that of the cult image, Figures 72–6 above.

3 Fragments of sculpture, possibly from an altar (not the same rock as Fig 81, nos 1–2 above). The curled motif could be part of a stylised *caduceus* or the horn of a ram, *Find 6619, context 0406, Structure XIX, Phase 7* 4
4 Fragment of carved hemisphere which could represent the globe of Victory or Fortuna, *Find 8485, context 1331, Structure X, Phase 4a*
5 Fragment of marble relief which is of interest as it is a piece of Italian marble. It is best interpreted as a cornucopia and drapery, although there is not enough remaining for certainty. Perhaps the goddess Fortuna, *Find 3834, context 1, Phase 8*

We may note another marble *ex voto*, previously published as Diana with her hound, but now identified as Bacchus with his panther, from the Roman temple

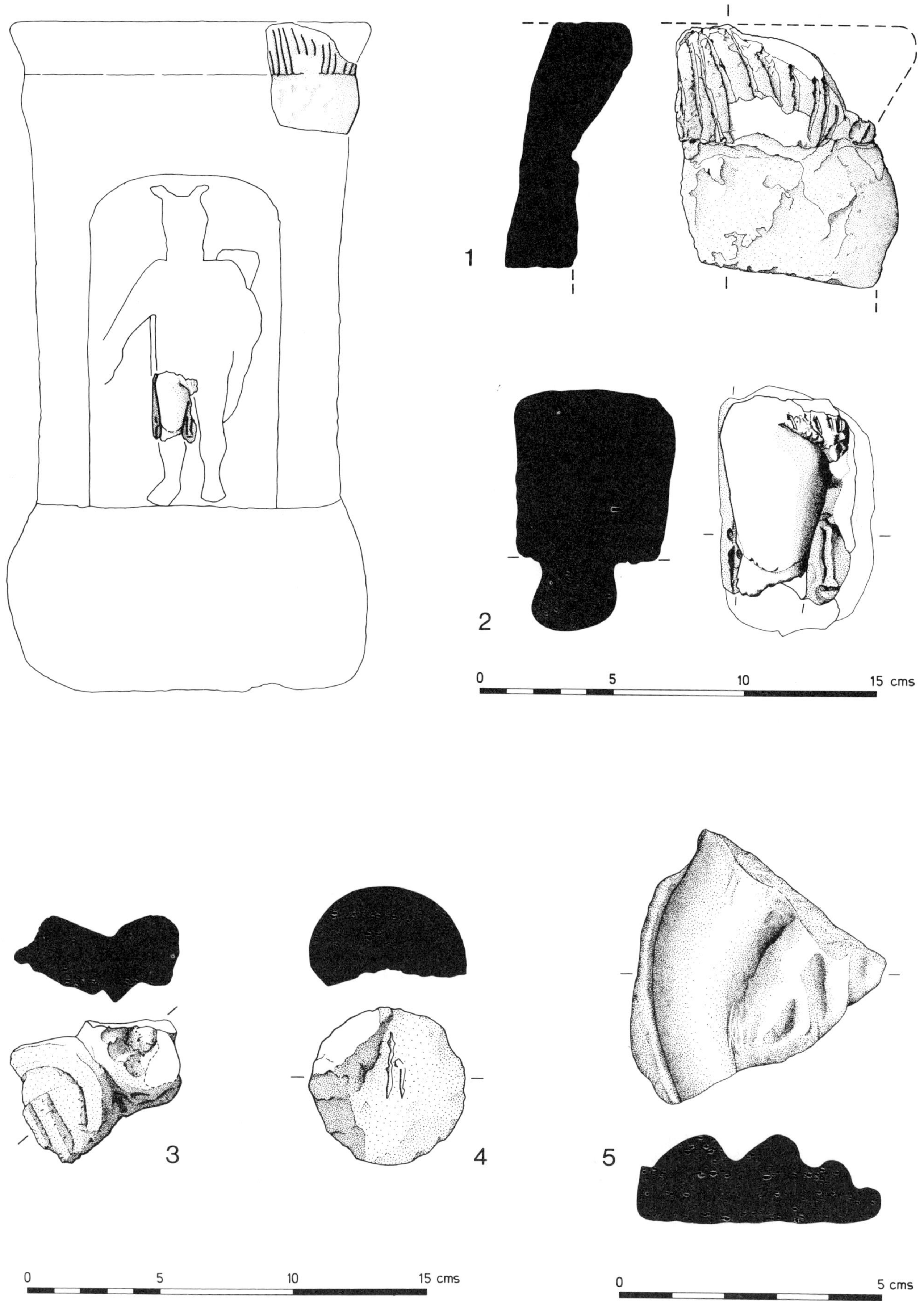

Fig 81 Fragments of a limestone altar (nos 1 and 2), , scale 1:2, statue (nos 3 and 4) and marble relief (no 5), scale 1:1

Fig 82 Copper alloy bust of Sol, scale 2:1. (Photo: Gordon Kelsey)

Fig 84 Copper alloy figurine of Mercury, scale 1:1. (Photo: Gordon Kelsey)

Fig 83 Copper alloy bucket mount with a horned figure bust, scale 1:1. (Photo: Gordon Kelsey)

at Maiden Castle (Cunliffe and Fulford 1982, 26, no 98, pl 26; Henig 1983a). The presence of such imported marble figurines at rural shrines is an indication of wealthy patrons amongst the worshippers; patrons who helped to keep the temples alive as flourishing concerns to the end of the fourth century.

Figurines

For this and all the following chapters, where actual alloy names are used, they derive from qualitative X-ray fluorescence (XRF) analyses by Justine Bayley. All items are copper alloy except where stated

Fig 85

1 and Fig 82, Bust of Sol of leaded bronze, less accomplished than the bust of Jupiter, Find 36 (Fig 88, no 6 below), and not from the same set, but also an ornamental fitting, *Find 709, context 22, over Structure I, Phase 5e (ii)*

Compare this with Henig in Taylor 1985, 31 and fig 13, no 187, from Cottenham; also note the Jupiter syncretised with Sol from Felmingham Hall, Norfolk (Gilbert 1978, 165, no 5).

2 and Fig 83, Bust of leaded bronze/gunmetal, with horned head, flanked by debased curvilinear ornament on a trapezoid plaque with notched border. Four rivet holes for attachment are present. The horns are knobbed bull's horns and the mask like face possesses almond shaped eyes, *Find 260, context 2, Structure II, Phase 6b*

This is probably a bucket mount. Compare Megaw

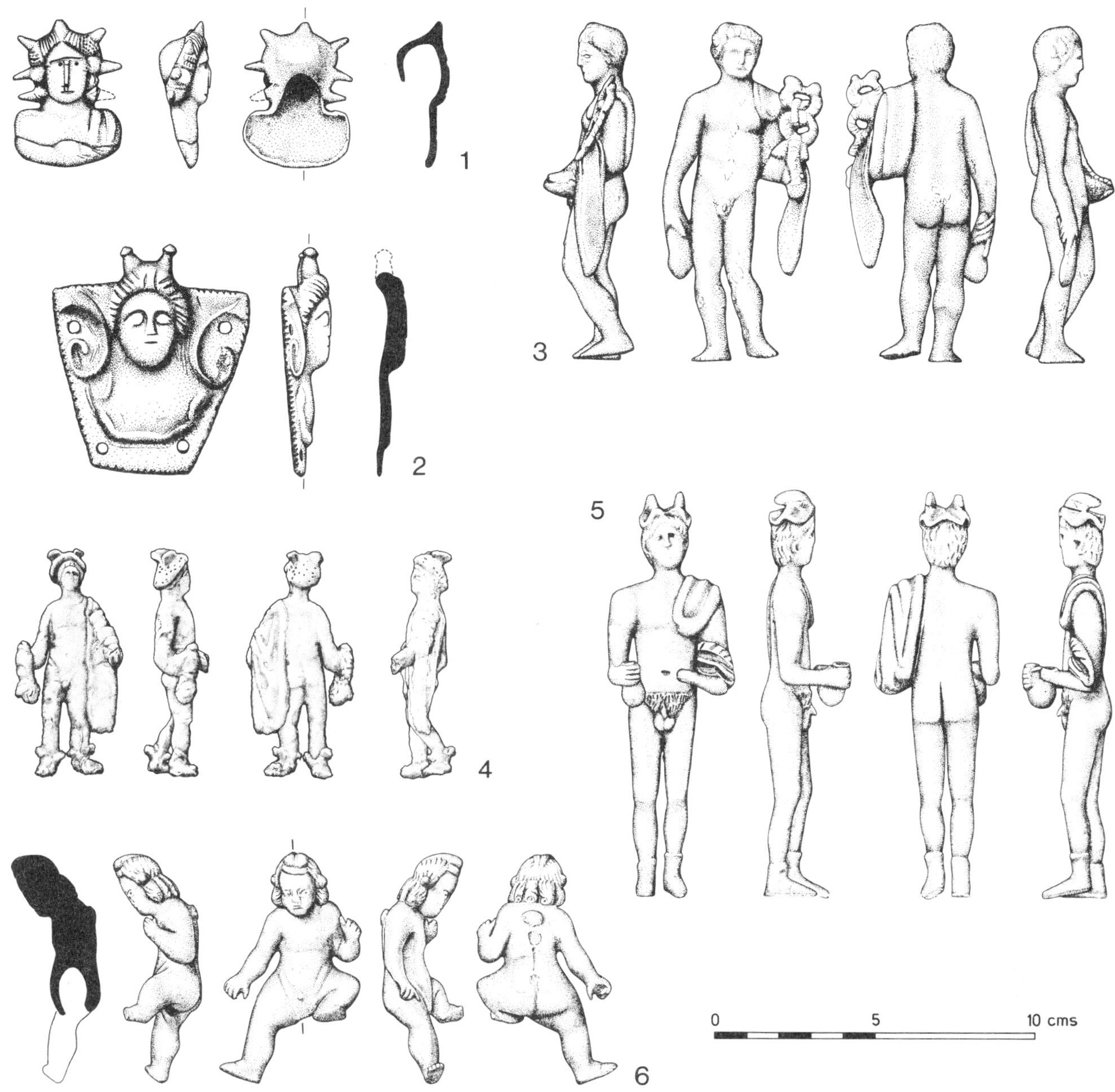

Fig 85 Figurines of Sol, a horned figure, Mercury and the infant Bacchus, scale 1:2

1970, 133, no 210 (Boughton Aluph near Ashford, Kent); Bushe-Fox 1932, 79, no 17, pl x (Richborough) and the Baldock bucket mounts (Stead 1971a, 252–4, figs 1 and 2). It is the sole figured bronze whose form is not entirely Roman, but as it is a portable object there is no way of telling whether it depicts the god worshipped on West Hill or not.

3 and Fig 84, Figurine of Mercury, leaded gunmetal, nude apart from *paenula* draped over left arm and hanging over shoulder. A standing figure, money bag in right hand, *caduceus* in left hand. See Boucher 1976, 106–8, figs 179–81 for this very common type. It approximates to the much finer Verulamium, King Harry Lane figurine *Britannia* **3** (1972) 330 and pl xxv b and c; Lindgren 1980, pl 19; see also Taylor 1985, 31 and fig 13, 185 from Cottenham, *Find 1567, context 2, Structure II, Phase 6b*

4 Figurine of Mercury, of copper/bronze, with winged *petasos* and boots. The *paenula* entirely envelops the god's left arm and shoulder but does not completely cover his body as seemed to be the case when the figurine was examined prior to cleaning (*Antiq J* **58** (1978) 369, pl lxxi b). See Boucher 1976, 101 and 116, figs 142–7; Kaufmann-Heinimann 1977, 34, no 28, pl 19 (Augst). Type modelled on a statue by Polykleitos, *Find 1749, context 201, Structure II, Phase 6a*

5 and Fig 86, Figurine of Mercury, of brass, similar to no 3 above but Mercury wears a winged *petasos* on his head and boots on his feet. The *caduceus* is now missing. The modelling of the figure is more distinctively provincial, being ornamented with markedly linear detail (eg on *paenula*, also pubic hair). Compare Lindgren 1980, pl 3 (London) and 18 (St Donats Castle, Glamorgan, Wales); Kaufmann-Heinimann 1977, 32–3, no 24, pl 14 (Augst), *Find 5542, context 478, Structure XIX, Phase 7*

6 and Fig 87, Mount of leaded gunmetal, in the form of a naked child with long hair, a fringe of locks descending to his shoulders. He is almost certainly the divine child Bacchus succoured by Mercury. Compare

Fig 86 Copper alloy figurine of Mercury, scale 1:1. (Photo: Sebastian Rahtz)

Fig 87 Copper alloy putto mount, probably the infant Bacchus, scale 1:1. (Photo: Sebastian Rahtz)

Fleischer 1967, 172, no 236, pl 118; Zadoks-Josephus-Jitta, *et al* 1969, 18–19, no 8 for Bacchus as a child; also for Mercury holding the infant Bacchus: Boucher 1976, 116–7, fig 193, recalling Praxiteles' famous statue at Olympia (Richter 1970, 199, fig 711), *Find 8066, context 0406, Structure XIX, Phase 7*

Fig 88

1 Wing, detached from a leaded bronze figurine, of a Cupid or Victory, well modelled with good linear detailing of the feathers. It is possible that this was deliberately broken from a figurine to serve as an *ex voto*. The use of wings as *ex votos* is attested at Matagne-la-Grande (Rober 1983, 31–2, nos 66 and 68). At Uley the reference would be to Mercury as a swift messenger, with winged *petasos* and winged shoes, *Find 0143, context 1, Phase 8*

2 Detached bronze curving wing, perhaps originally part of a sphinx support (as for example Henig 1970, 185, no 2, pl xxv c, presumably also an *ex voto* as with no 1 above, *Find 933, context 17, Structure II, Phase 6*

3 Figurine of a goat in leaded bronze, *cf* Kaufmann-Heinimann 1977, 89, no 95, pl 94 (Augst), see also references below, *Find 1949, context 210, Structure II, Phase 5e–d*

4 Figurine of a cockerel, in leaded bronze/gunmetal *cf* one from Vindolanda (Birley 1973, 122, no 23, pl xxi), *Find 1417, context 17, Structure II, Phase 6*

As we have seen, nos 3 and 4 above are models of cult animals associated with the god, and they may well have been intended to stand on pedestals flanking Mercury figurines; *cf* a figurine with a cock and ram, from King Harry Lane, Verulamium (*Britannia* **3** (1972) 330, pl xxv, b and c); one with a stand with goat and tortoise from Augst, (Kaufmann-Heinimann 1977, 105, no 155, pls 103–4); one with goat and tortoise from Vicus de Pommeroeul, Hainaut (Faider-Feytmans 1979, 198, no A3, 1); a goat and a cockerel from the Gallo-Roman temple at Matagne-la-Petite, (*ibid*, 197, A2, 1–3; De Boe 1982, 26 and 30, fig 9) together with a *caduceus* of similar form to Finds 1141 and 6632, (Fig 89, nos 1 and 5 below).

5 Mask of brass with a lead-rich backing, a youthful facing mask; the physiognomy is more classically organised than the Woodeaton example (Pitts 1979, 100, no 235); perhaps from a casket, *Find 407, context 14, Structure II, Phase 6b*

6 Bust of Jupiter, of brass with a drapery hanging over the left shoulder. This is probably an ornamental fitting which portrays Jupiter as one of the deities of the week, for a close parallel *cf* one from Lydney (Wheeler and Wheeler 1932, 91, no 141, pl xxx); also one from Caerleon (Toynbee 1964, 65, pl xiii a and b), *Find 36, context 1, Phase 8*

7 Part of a gunmetal model leg, the foot, which is missing may have been formed from a separate piece of metal, *Find 1427, context 17, Structure II, Phase 6*

8 Leg with foot, made of gunmetal. The exaggerated forward curve of the upper leg renders it unsuitable as part of a figurine, and it must be a purpose-made medical *ex voto*, *Find 7248, context 0406, Structure XIX, Phase 7*

9 Part of a leaded gunmetal model leg, without a foot, *Find 395, context I, Phase 8*

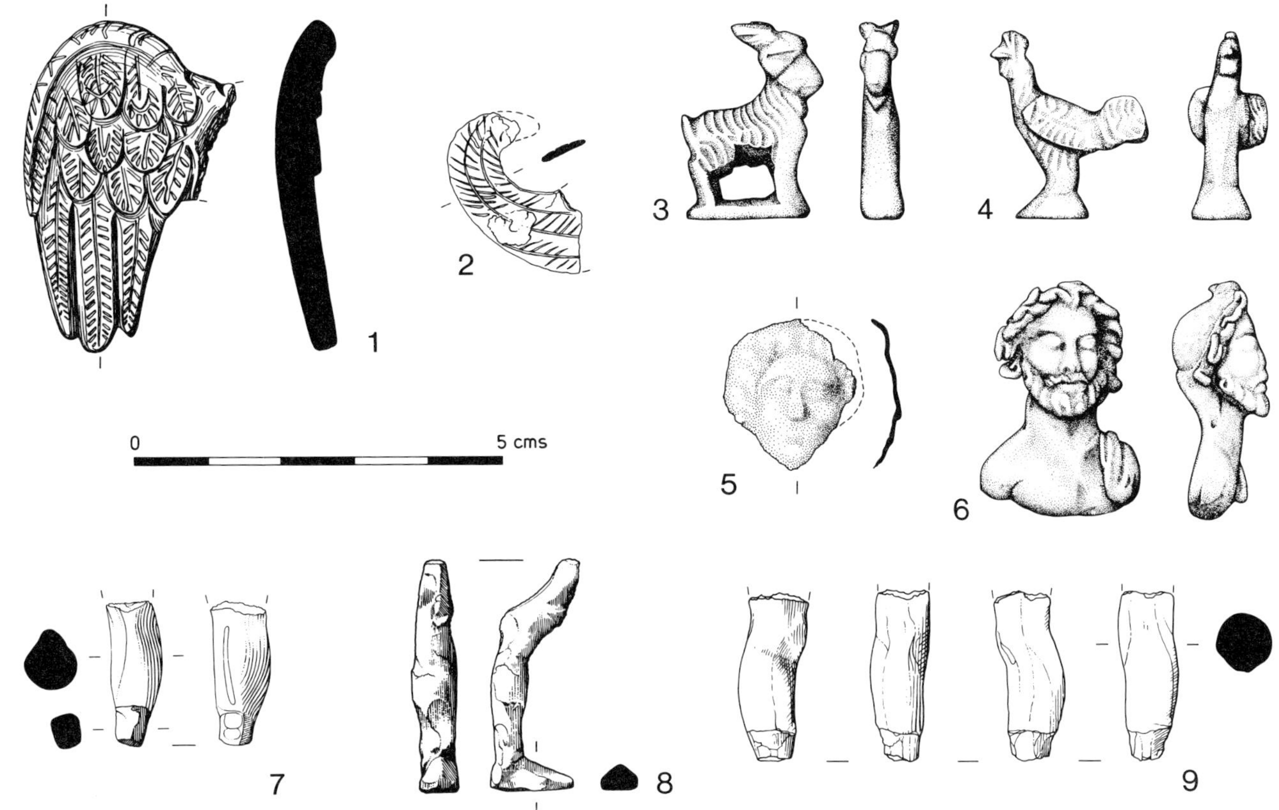

Fig 88 Copper alloy wings, goat, cock, mask, Jupiter head, and model legs of lead and copper alloy, scale 1:1

A clay leg was found at Muntham Court, Sussex (Burstow and Holleyman, 1957, 102); and a copper alloy leg has been found at Winchester (information Martin Biddle). It is attached to a ring, and intended to be either worn as an amulet, or used as a votive object at a shrine. Like the plaque, Find 3932 (Fig 93, no 5) with a foot shown in relief upon it, this alludes to Mercury as the god of wayfarers. In this connection the copper alloy votive legs from the Great St Bernard Pass (Leibundgut 1980, 109–10, nos 127–30) where Jupiter Poeninus had his temple, may be cited for this was certainly a traveller's sanctuary. At Uley, Mercury must have been regarded as an appropriate deity to cure diseases and sprains impeding movement which must have been prevalent and worrying in a peasant community, as well as being an occupational hazard for pilgrims and wayfarers in general, (compare Jackson (1988, 160) commenting on the prevalence of terracotta foot votives at Ponte di Nona).

Qualitative analyses of the figurines

by Justine Bayley

Fifteen objects were analysed qualitatively by energy dispersive X-ray fluorescence (XRF). The results are incorporated in the object descriptions, with the alloy names applied as described above and in chapter 9. The analytical results show that a wide range of copper alloys were used for the figurines and that no specific alloy seems to be associated with a particular type of figure. For example, the three Mercury figurines, Finds 1567, 1749, and 5542 (Fig 85, nos 3–5) are made of quite different alloys which would have had different colours in an unpatinated state. Most of the objects appear to be cast although Find 407 (Fig 88, no 5) is definitely wrought and Find 933 (Fig 88, no 2) may be wrought. These two pieces are, as expected, unleaded.

Craddock (1978) analysed larger statues but found only two objects with over 1% zinc and concluded that '... zinc was never deliberately added to ... statuary bronze'. Indeed, Oddy and Craddock (1986) say that Roman statues were normally leaded bronzes with 15–30% lead. Of the items from Uley, only Find 709 (Figs 82 and 85, no 1) and Finds 143 and 1417 (Fig 88, nos 1 and 4) are likely to have such high lead contents.

More directly comparable results to those presented here are contained in the work of Picon *et al* (1966, 1967, 1968 and 1973) and Beck *et al* (1985) who have both analysed large numbers of Roman figurines now in museums in France. Both showed that a wide range of copper alloys were used for figurines, but with no one alloy being preferred for any particular deity.

Condamin and Boucher (1973) summarise their previous work and identify geographical variations in the numbers of figurines which contain over 2% zinc. These objects would have compositions described above as leaded or unleaded brass, gunmetal or bronze/gunmetal. The proportion varies from only 14% for the finds in the museum at Vienne to 33% at Autun and 53% in the Rhineland (after Zadoks-Josephus-Jitta *et al* 1967 and 1969). If one accepts that the museum collections reflect local finds and (possibly) local manufacture, then there are regional variations in the alloys used for figurines. The work of Beck *et al* (1985) seems to bear this out as they too detected regional variations in preferred alloys (*ibid*, table 5). They found 50% of all figurines were leaded bronzes and a further 36% leaded gunmetals, with an overall figure of 41% containing significant amounts of zinc (ie brasses or gunmetals with or without lead).

The sample from this site is small but the proportions appear rather different to those of the French analyses. Only eight of the fifteen objects are leaded bronzes or gunmetals (*cf* 86% from Beck *et al* 1985) and eleven of them contain significant amounts of zinc, about double the average French figure. Without more analyses of British finds for comparison it is difficult to know how to interpret these differences. They could be a reflection of British taste, manufacturing practice, the the availability of different metals, the fact that Uley was a temple site, or just a chance variation, a product of the small number of objects analysed.

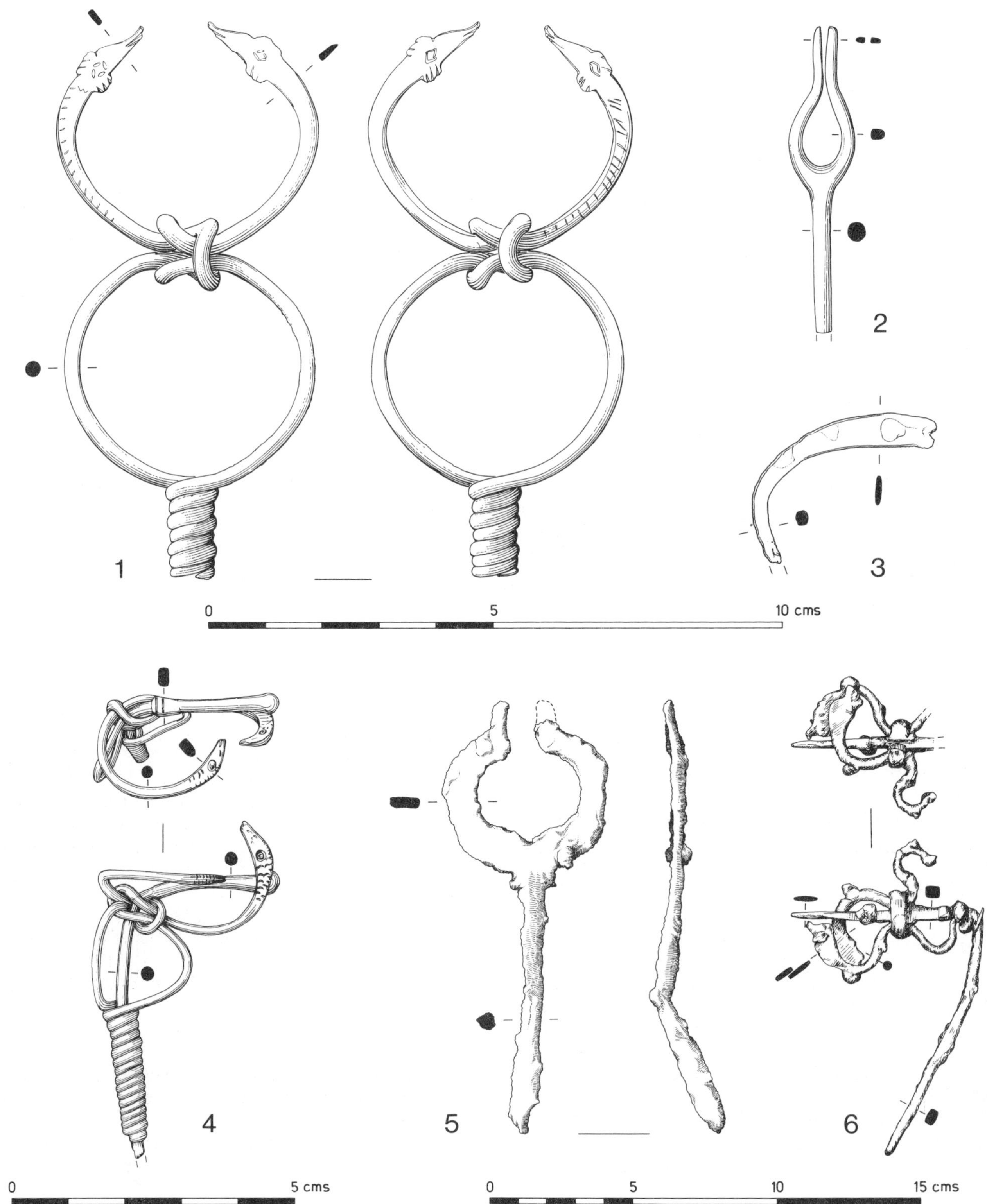

Fig 89 caducei *of copper alloy, except no 4 of silver, scale 1:1, and nos 5 and 6 of iron, scale 1:2*

Caducei

Fig 89
1 *Caduceus, Find 7828, context 1206, Structure IX, Phase 5c*
2 Simplified *caduceus, Find 1141, context 60, Structure I, Phase 5e(i)*
3 Serpent's head, detached from a *caduceus, Find 6722, context 410, Structure XIX, Phase 7*
4 and Fig 90, Silver *caduceus*, bent, *Find 1126, context 14, Structure II, Phase 6b*
5 Iron simple *caduceus, Find 6632, context 0401, Structure XIX, Phase 7*
6 Iron *caduceus*, bent, *Find 5198, context 557, Structure XV, Phase 7*

Finds 7828 (Fig 89, no 1) and 1126 (Figs 89, no 4; and 90) both have Hercules knots in the centre and serpent terminals. Find 6722 (Fig 89, no 3) is a serpent from a similar *caduceus.* A figure of Mercury from the treasure of Mercury's temple at Berthouville in France, Babelon 1916, 73–4, pls i–iii holds a *caduceus* of the same form. Find 1126 has been bent, probably deliberately in order to 'kill' it, and hence present it, as it were, sacrificially to Mercury, as has Find 5198 (Fig 89, no 6) an iron *caduceus* with simple binding at the centre. Such a practice implies that these objects were votives.

Separate *caducei* (ie not associated with figurines) are recorded at various sites, amongst them Richborough (Bushe-Fox 1949, 132, no 147) and Braughing (Stead 1970, 43f, fig v, no i).

Finds 1141 and 6632 (Fig 89, nos 2 and 5) are *caducei* of the simplified 'tuning fork' shape; the latter is of iron and has a flattened ring-like shape open at the top. The 'tuning fork' form is found at the Matagne-la-Petite temple (de Boe 1982, fig 9 and fig 10, no 40). It indicates that the nature of the *caduceus* as a staff with serpent terminals was not always realised.

See also chapter 8, the miniature votive spears

Votive plaques

All of copper alloy The inscriptions on Finds 3548, 1858, 1157, and 26 based on notes by Mark Hassall

Fig 91
1 Pieces of thin sheet, probably from a votive plaque. The sheet has been broken, probably as the result of folding in antiquity, into two major and six minor pieces, which may have come from a scale-shaped plaque with a curved top, *Find 3548, context 428, Structure XI, Phase 7*

It is similar to one from Niederbieber, *cf* in general Toynbee 1978, 129–47, and for the Niederbieber example *ibid*, 136–7, no 16 and fig 5.2. The sheet carries a punched inscription:
DEO | MERCV|[.]IOSEVERΛ[..]|PIOSV
V[...]|FELIXḶ[.
Deo Mercu[r]io Severa [..]PIOSV V.[.et] Felix e[t
'To the god Mercury, Severa and ... and Felix ...'
(See *Britannia* **17** (1986) 429–30 for a previous reading)

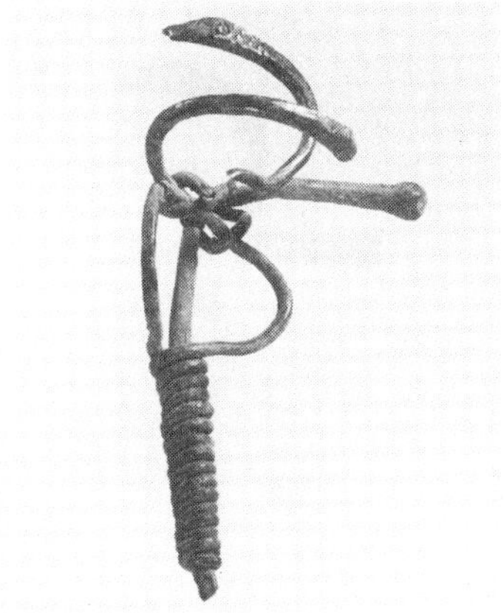

Fig 90 *Silver* caduceus *delibertely bent, scale 1:1. (Photo: Sebastian Rahtz)*

2 Fitting with two nail-holes, which terminates with a broken hinge, and perhaps formed the attached half of a small hinged clasp of a box, *Find 1858, context 33, southern courtyard, Phase 4–6*

Just below the broken hinge three small letters have been incised,
MER
Mer(curio)
'For Mercury'
(*Britannia* **17** (1986) 443)
3 Part of a pierced roundel, originally 60mm in diameter and 4mm thick, reading
.]PTIMẸ[... in openwork, *Find 1157, context 20, over Structure IX, Phase 7*

It can be restored with confidence from a virtually complete roundel from Silchester, Boon 1974, 66–7, fig 8, no 3, in the centre of which was an eagle framed by the letters,
O]ptime [Maxime con(serva)
'(Jupiter) Best (and) Greatest protect (us)'
(*Britannia* **10** (1979) 349, no 24)

The full motto, as found on a complete set of military belt fittings, will have read: optime maxime, con(serva) numerum omnium militantium *Jupiter) Best (and) Greatest protect (us) a troop of fighting men all*

No complete set has been found in Britain, but individual attachments or parts of them, have been found at various sites including Silchester, High Rochester, and Aldborough. For a discussion with full bibliography see Boon 1974, 66–8, 309, n 7, and fig 8, no 3.
4 Piece of sheet from the right hand end of an oblong mounting. There are a series of closely spaced nail-holes round the three original edges of the object, and in the surviving piece, a single, centrally placed nail-hole which was probably matched by at least one other hole, *Find 26, ploughsoil over Structure I*

Along the top and bottom edge of the mounting run a series of letters forming a two line votive inscription produced in repoussé. A ring produced in the same technique surrounds the central nail-hole. The inscription reads

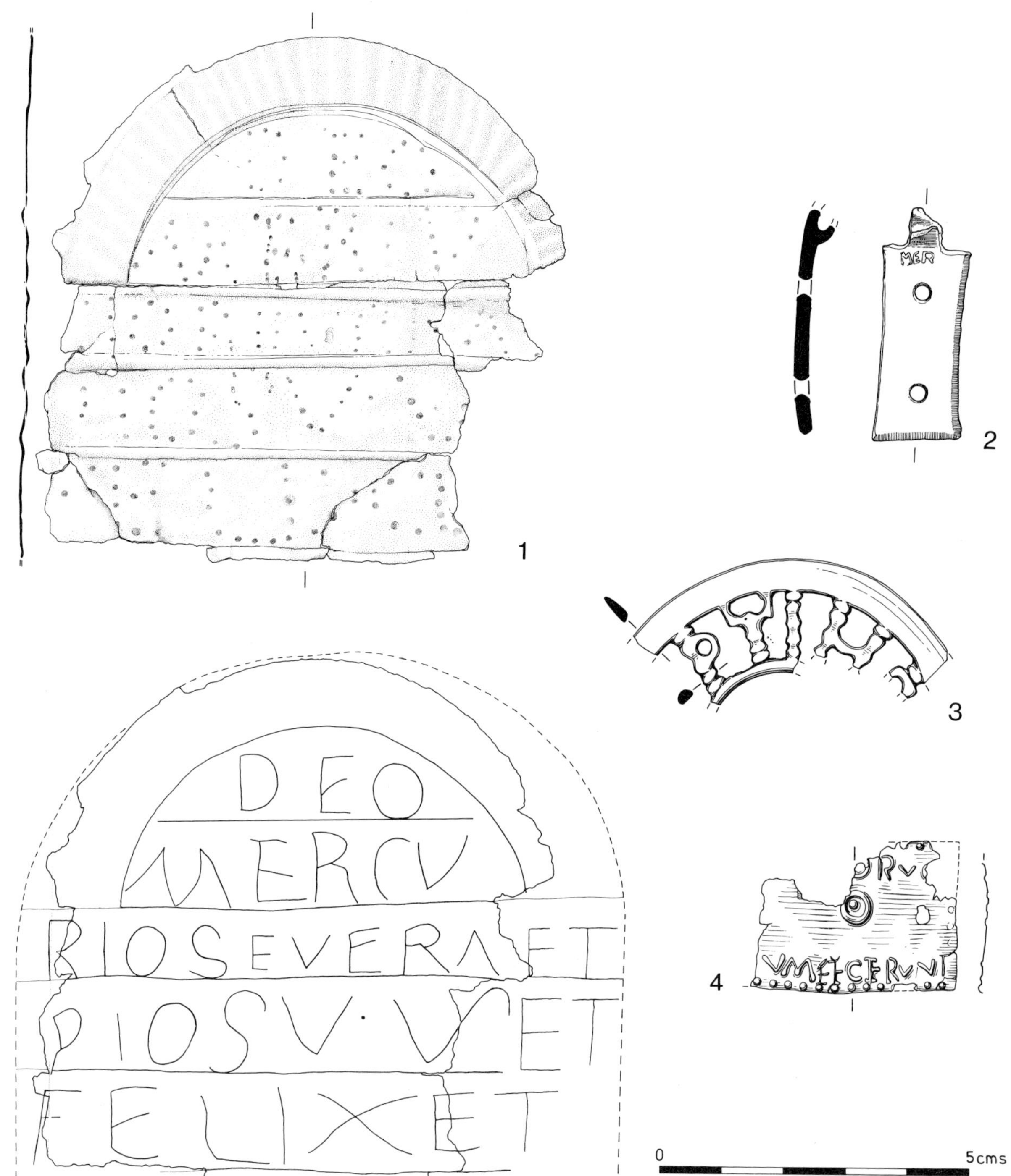

Fig 91 Inscriptions of copper alloy, scale 1:1

]ORV[.|...]VMFECERVNT
...oru[s | ...]um fecerunt
'...orus ... made this'

The first line presumably began with the name of the deity, perhaps Mercury, to whom the object had been given followed by the names of one of the dedicators, probably FL]ORV[S. The second line will have contained the name of a second dedicator, followed by a word describing the object presented, perhaps SACR]VM FECERVNT 'made the offering' (*cf RIB* 151), though other expansions are possible, eg VOT]VM or DON]VM. (*Britannia* **11** (1980) 411–2)

Fig 92

1 Sheet leaf with tip broken away, decorated with repoussé dots, 'feather' lines and corrugated borders, *Find 1061, context 22, Structure I, Phase 5e (ii)*

2 Fragment from a sheet leaf, with repoussé veining, *Find 1257, context 14, Structure I, Phase 6b*

3 Two fragments of a sheet leaf, with corrugated borders, *Find 656, context 14, Structure II, Phase 6b*

4 Fragments of sheet leaf, with repoussé veining, *Find 409, context 14, Structure II, Phase 6b*

5 Two fragments of sheet leaf, with incised veining, *Find 6464, context 0402, Structure XIX, Phase 7*

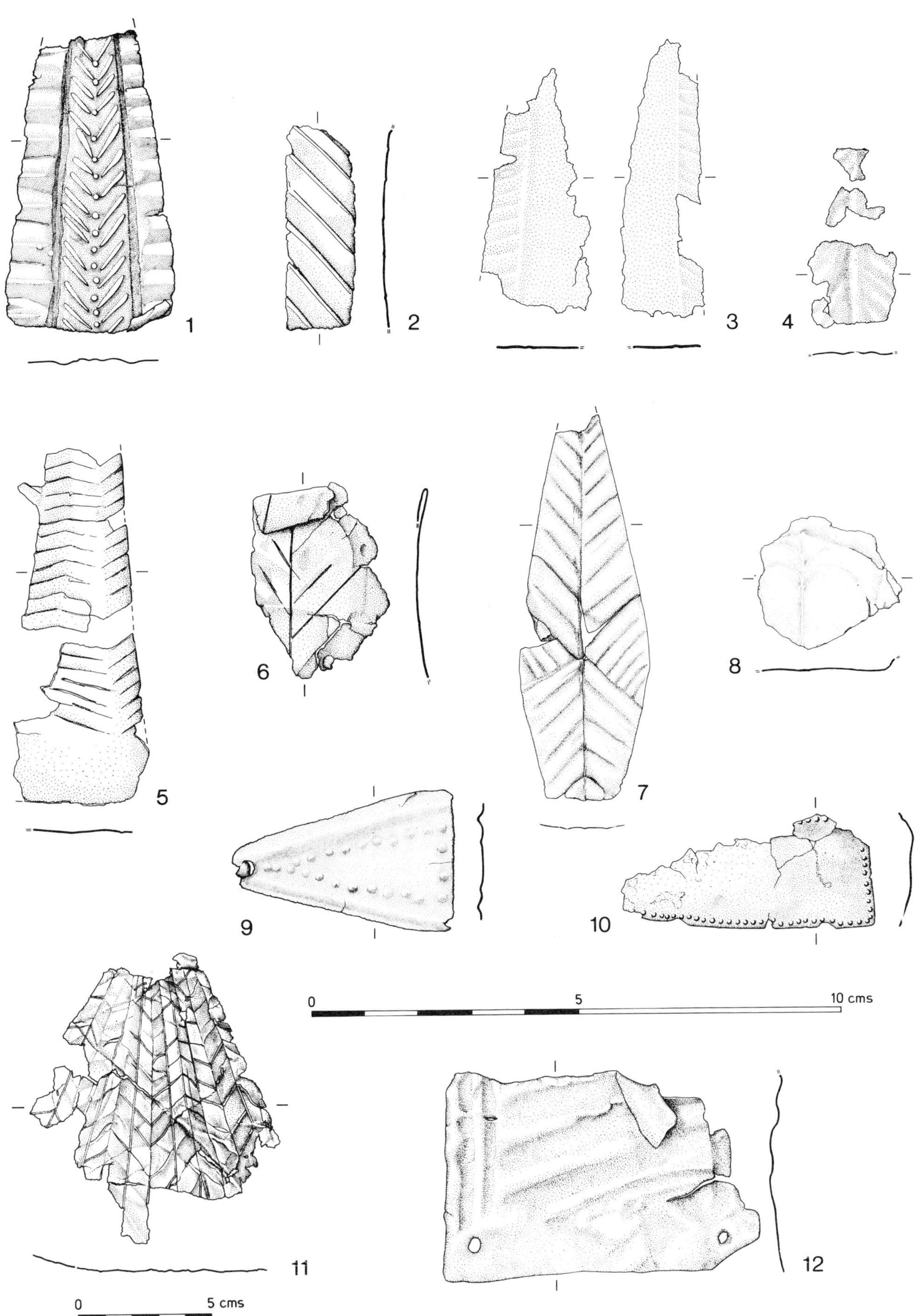

Fig 92 Leaves and plaques of copper alloy, scale 1:1

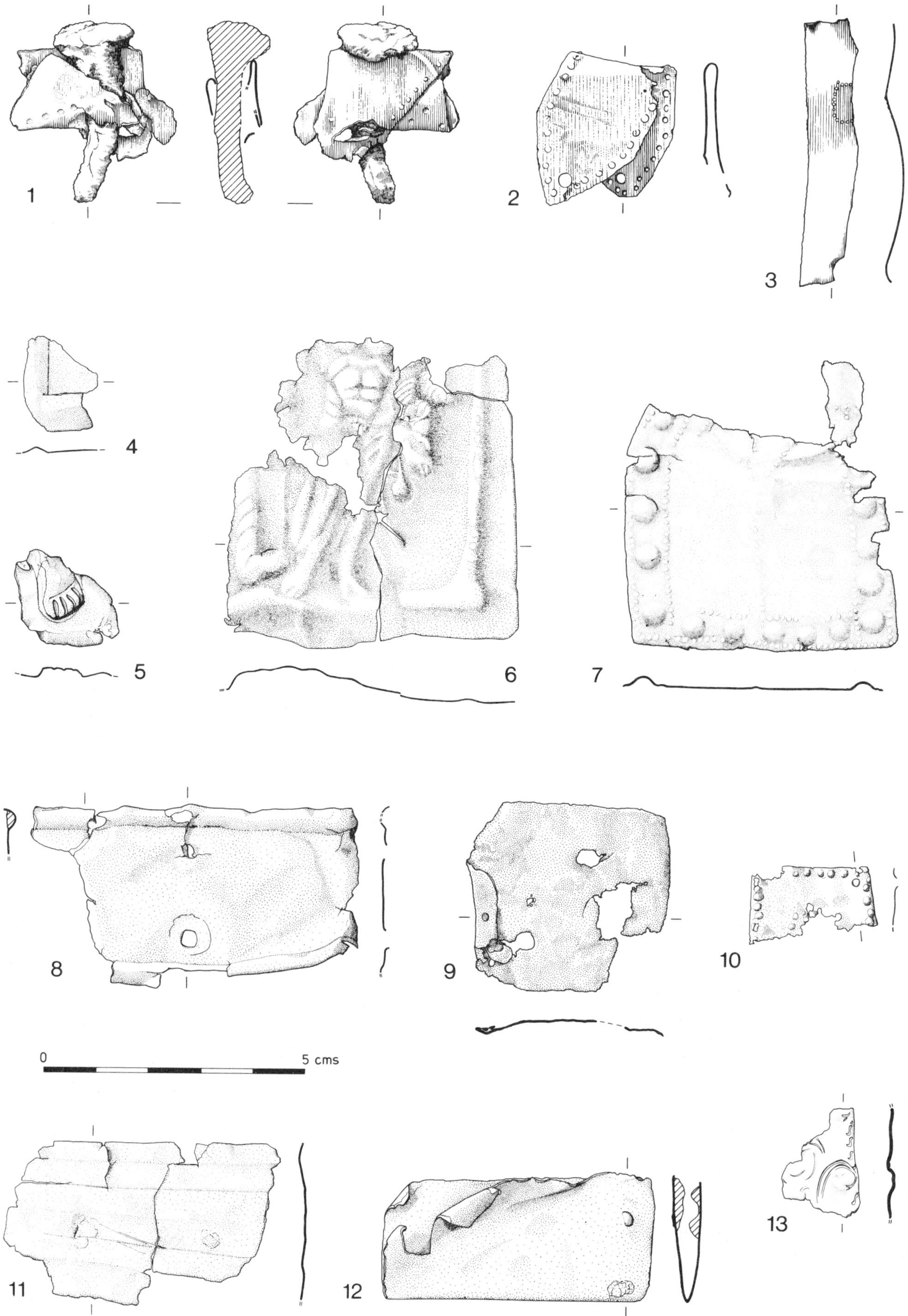

Fig 93 Plaques of copper alloy; no 1 pierced by an iron nail, scale 1:1

6 Bent fragment of a sheet leaf, with incised veining, *Find 4073, context 601, Structure XIX, Phase 7*
7 Sheet leaf, tip missing, with repoussé veining, *Find 5054, context 478, Structure XIX, Phase 7*

for an additional example of a votive leaf see Fig 160, no 2

8 Fragment of a plaque of unknown shape, with arched repoussé ornament resembling vegetation, *Find 1692, context 22, over Structure I, Phase 5e (ii)*
9 Triangular plaque, with repoussé border, lines, and small bosses, *Find 7297, context 1191, Structure XIV, Phase 5d–6b*
10 Fragment of a rectangular plaque, with a border of small repoussé bosses, *Find 4611, context 488, Structure II, Phase 6a*
11 Fragment, found folded, with incised line decoration; possibly part of a large leaf, *Find 5030, context 402, Structure VII, Phase 7*
12 Part of a square or rectangular plaque, with corner rivet holes and geometric repoussé decoration, *Find 4968, context 409, Structure II, Phase 6b*

Fig 93
1 Fragment of a folded sheet, pierced by an iron nail, and with boss decoration, *Find 6800, context 0412, Structure XIX, Phase 7*
2 Rectangular plate, bent in two, with pointed ends, terminal rivet holes, and small perforations around the margin, *Find 7259, context 0410, Structure XIX, Phase 7*
3 Fragment of a plaque, bearing part of a pricked motif, possibly a letter, *Find 8019, context 0406, Structure XIX, Phase 7*
4 Corner fragment of a plaque with a raised border, *Find 3896, context 511, Structure XIX, Phase 7*
5 Fragment from a plaque, probably silvered or tinned, and bearing a repoussé foot, *Find 3932, context 511, Structure XIX, Phase 7*
6 Joining fragments of a rectangular plaque, bearing a repoussé depiction of a standing male figure, nude apart from drapery, a *chlamys*, or just possibly, an animal skin, over his left arm. The former is far more likely, and in this case the subject is Mercury; but if it is an animal skin being worn then it would be Hercules. The figure stands within a raised border, hatched on the left side, probably the sides of an *aedicula*, *Find 4281, context 601, Structure XIX, Phase 7*

7 Part of a gabled plaque, ornamented with bosses, and containing a pricked-out object, perhaps a *caduceus*, *Find 8042, context 0406, Structure XIX, Phase 7*
8 Part of a rectangular plaque, with raised border and pierced holes, *Find 4137, context 601, Structure XIX, Phase 7*

9 Sub-square sheet with pierced holes, *Find 2160, context 14, Structure II, Phase 6b*
10 Part of a small plaque, with marginal bosses, and traces of a central motif made up of similar bosses, *Find 5162, context 478, Structure XIX, Phase 7*
11 Fragment of a sheet, a ?leaf with repoussé groove decoration, *Find 547, context 14, Structure II, Phase 6b*
12 Square plaque, plain and bent in two, *Find 4501, context 603, Structure XIX, Phase 7*
13 Fragment of a sheet, with marginal rocker tracer motifs, and curvilinear spiral or vegetative designs, *Find 370, context 1, Phase 8*

Fig 94
1 Fragment from the centre of a plaque, with a large repoussé boss surrounded by circles, and with radiating lines of smaller bosses, probably a breast with *areolar* glands, enlarged as during pregnancy (information from Dr K Knowles), if so it is a medical votive, *Find 1634, context 67, Structure I, Phase 5e (i)*

Although the connection between Mercury and gynaecology is not an obvious one Pamela Irving points out to me that pregnancy was a hazardous undertaking, for the child there would be a need for protection in its journey through the birth canal, and for the mother there would be a need to achieve a safe delivery (as graphically demonstrated in Jackson 1988, ch 4), so it is possible that Mercury could have appeal to both parties in the birth process. In addition in Cotswold sculpture Mercury sometimes has a female consort associated with fecundity conventionally described as 'Rosmerta' (Hunter 1981, 91–8), though she does not appear on the surviving sculpture from Uley. For a copper alloy breast from Bath see Cunliffe, ed 1988, 8, no 5.

2 Fragments of a rectangular plaque with raised margin and mounting holes, *Find 172, context 1, Phase 8*

3 Folded sheet fragment, *Find 6177, context 0215, Phase 8*

One of the most widespread means of making offerings to the gods was by means of plaques of silver or, as here, of copper alloy. Only a single example, Find 4281 (Fig 93, no 6) portrays Mercury *en repoussé* and this is not entirely certain, but another, Find 3548 (Fig 91, no 1) carries a pricked out dedication under a hemicycle. Compare Toynbee 1978, 136–7, no 16 (also La Baume 1977, fig 3) for one from Niederbieber showing Mercury; Toynbee 1978, 141, no 37, fig 8, for a dedication to Abandinus, in a roundel, from Godmanchester; showing that the West Hill inscription (Find 3548) may have been part of a leaf or feather.

The silvered or tinned bronze foot, Find 3932 (Fig 93, no 5) and the silvered plaque, Find 1634 (Fig 94, no 1) which may be a breast, are probably medical votives like the legs described above. The piece with more native style curvilinear ornamental design, Find 370 (Fig 93, no 13) can be matched at Lydney (Wheeler and Wheeler 1932, 90, pl xxix, 138–9). Amongst other plaques note one, Find 7297 (Fig 92, no 9) of triangular shape, comparable with examples from Woodeaton (Kirk 1949, 43, no 4 and plate vi a, 6). Many are of leaf or feather-like forms, sometimes ornamented, Finds 1061, 1257, 656, 0402, 4073, 5054 and 5030 (Fig 92, nos 1–7 and 11). These are very common on temple sites (*ibid*, 43–4; Rober 1983, 31–2, no 65, fig 16).

See also Fig 160, no 2, for another repoussé decorated plaque

Figs 95 and 96
A fragment of copper alloy sheet found folded tightly into four (i), which was subsequently unfolded by staff of the British Museum Conservation Department

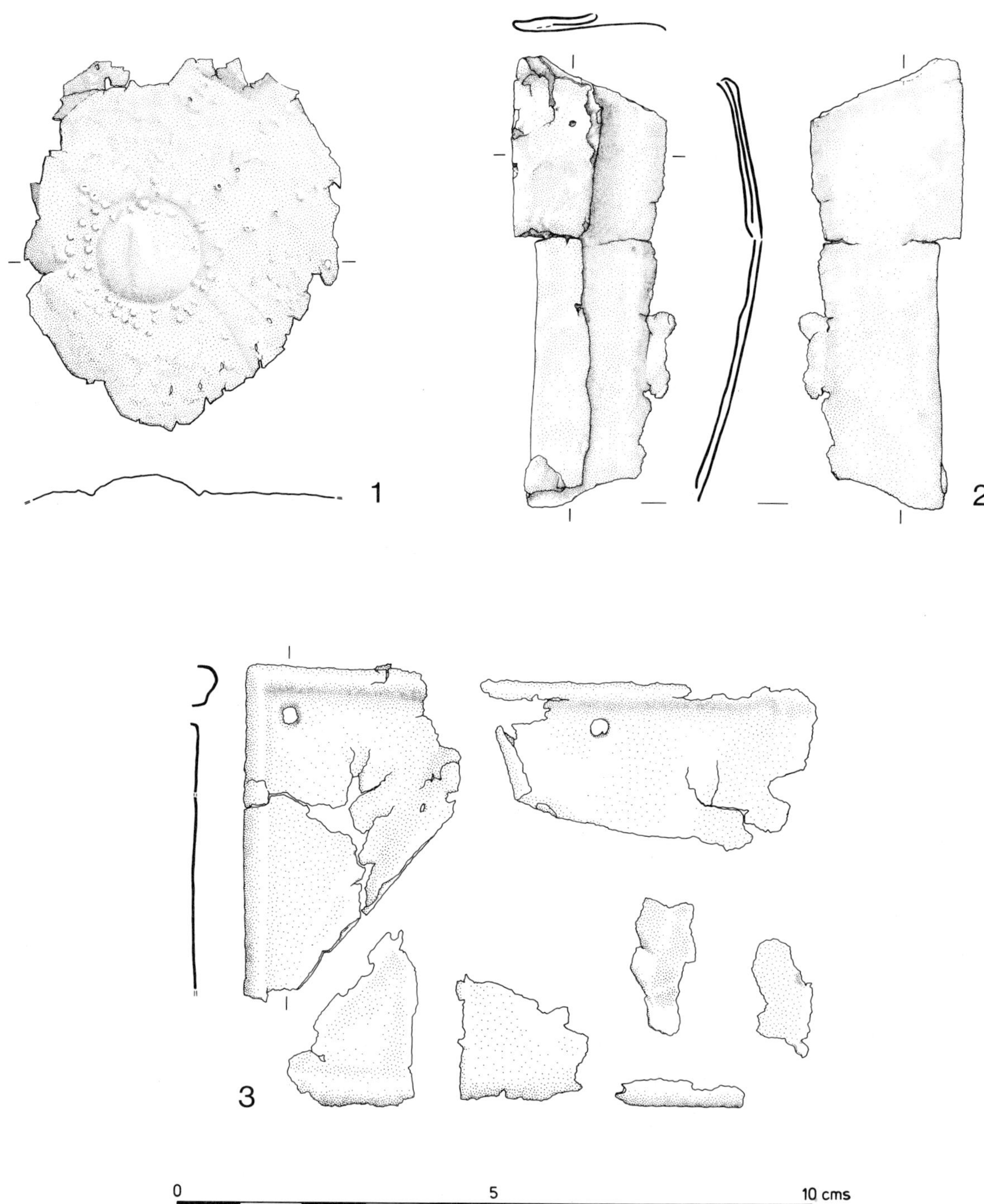

Fig 94 Plaques of copper alloy, scale 1:1

The sheet of metal was at first thought to be a figured plaque. It was carefully folded as though to 'kill' it or render it appropriate for deposition in a *favissa* (a pit for the reception of sacred items no longer needed but still dedicated to a deity). Since straightening out, it can be seen to be part of the sheeting from a casket; it bears figured scenes of which four remain, though there may well have been more originally, as only the bottom seems to have original edging, *Find 477, context 14, Structure II, Phase 6b*

The subject matter of the four scenes of this plaque are startlingly not pagan but Christian. Two of them, indeed, can be matched precisely on the sheeting of the casket from *Intercisa* now in Budapest (Buschhausen 1971, 132–6 no A 65, pls 80–81). The plaque was presumably produced by hammering the metal into a matrix or negative die, such as the Hellenistic example, now in the Metropolitan Museum, New York, used to make votive plaques (Reeder 1987, 423–40). Such a use of dies showing different scenes would allow for the different choice and ordering of episodes on the *Intercisa* casket.

The two superimposed scenes on the left are separated from the two on the right by two bands of beading, while a single beaded line divides the two upper scenes from the two lower ones. Exactly the same method of division may be seen on a plaque, found in Cologne and now in Bonn, depicting deities (Buschhausen 1971, 155–6 no A83, pls 94 (right) and 95).

Description

Figs 95 (ii) and 96

a) Top left, a large figure wearing a *himation* and ?boots. In front of him a smaller figure in a military tunic, flourishes a knobbed stick in his left hand and a sword in his right hand. The stick is to be identified as the centurion's *vitis* and the scene interpreted as Christ and the centurion who came to him to seek healing for his servant (Matthew 8: 5–13) – 'and Jesus said unto the centurion, Go thy way; and as thou hast believed, so be it done unto thee. And his servant was healed in the self same hour' (v 13). This is rather rare in early Christian art but Leclercq (in Leclercq and Cabrol 1925, cols 3259–60, fig 2345) illustrates a sarcophagus from Vienne with the centurion kneeling at Christ's feet.

b) Top right, on the right side the same large figure touches the eyes of an approaching nude figure, evidently with a wrinkled and deformed visage, perhaps to emphasise that he is blind, for this scene is to be interpreted as Christ healing the blind man, (Mark 8 : 22–25 and John 9, especially v 6, in John blind from birth) which is fairly common in early Christian art. It is shown on the bottom right of the *Intercisa* plaque (Buschhausen 1971, 134, pl 81), iconographically the same. It also appears on a casket from Mainz now in Bonn (*ibid*, 107–10, no A54, pls 62, 63, esp 110) where the blind man is more certainly clothed.

c) Bottom left, Jonah reclines under the gourd. In its branches at least one bird can be seen. By his side is the *ketos* (sea-monster) which in early Christian art swallows and later disgorges him (*cf* a mosaic floor, from the basilica of Bishop Theodore at Aquileia, dated AD 308–19: Henig 1983b, 123, pl 96). The scene appears identically on the *Intercisa* sheet (bottom left, Buschhausen 1971, 133 pls 80, 81).

d) Bottom right, 'Sacrifice of Isaac' (Genesis 22). Abraham stands to the front and looks to the right. In his right hand he holds a knife or sword. Below is a tree or bush, on his left is an altar with a fire burning upon

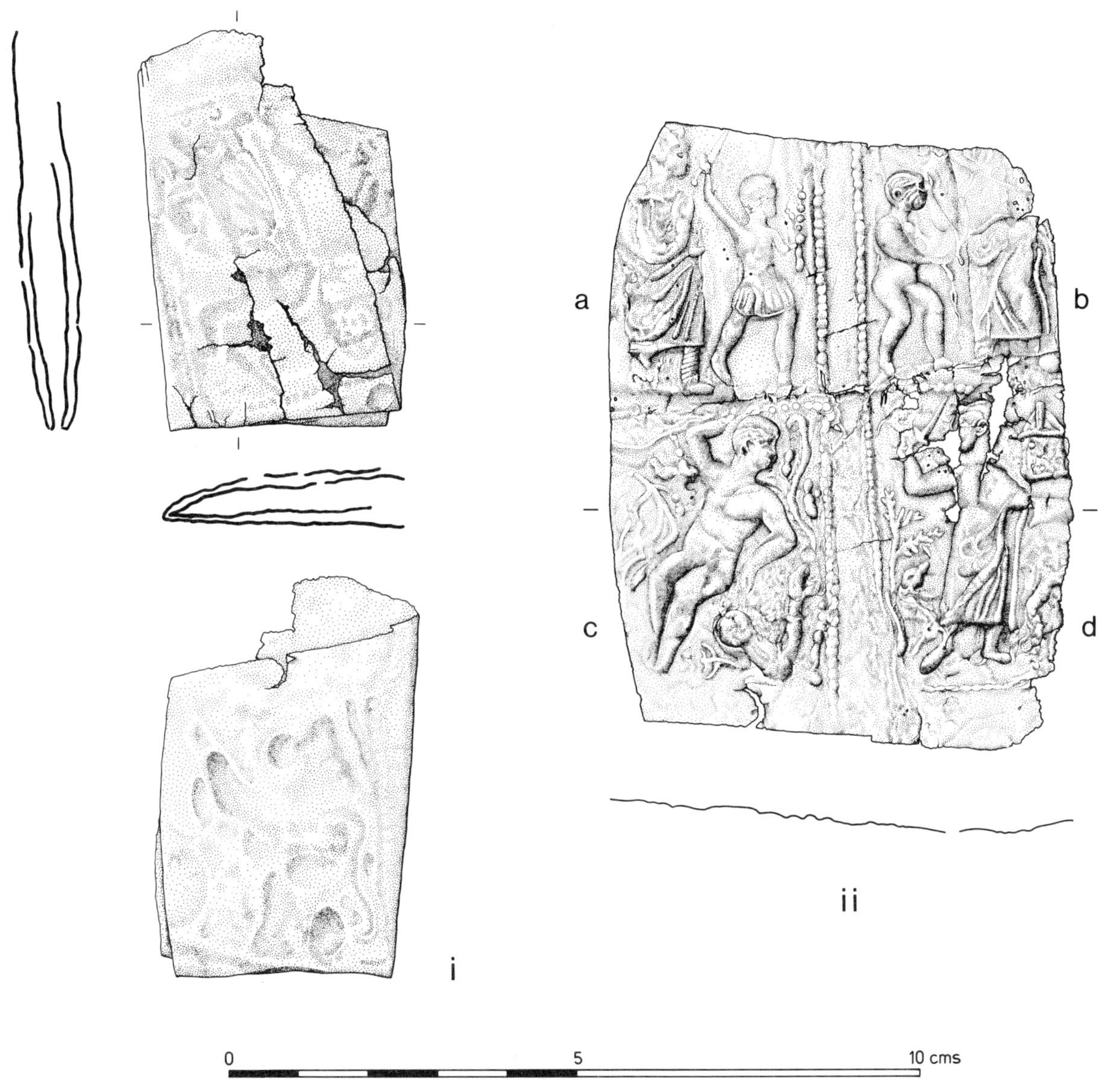

Fig 95 Copper alloy casket sheeting depicting biblical scenes, scale 1:1

Fig 96 Copper alloy casket sheeting depicting biblical scenes, scale 1.5:1
(Photo: British Museum)

it, and below that is a ram caught in a thicket. The theme is common in early Christian art and occurs on the *Intercisa* sheet (*ibid* 1971, 133) though on it and elsewhere Isaac is generally more prominent. The stance of Abraham on the box from Mainz (*ibid*, 109–10, pl 64) is closely comparable.

It is suggested that scenes were arranged on the Uley box in two registers, New Testament scenes above and Old Testament ones below. All four of the scenes here preserved have the theme of complete faith in God.

The *Intercisa* casket evidently had portraits of Crispus and Fausta above the lockplate and thus should be dated within the first half of the fourth century. The casket, which also bears images of Orpheus, Jupiter, Minerva, Mars, and Mercury, illustrates the complexity of religious observance at this time and it is by no means certain that the Uley sheet illustrates active Christian belief. It may well have belonged to people who felt that the new faith, under Imperial patronage, and therefore very powerful, could be integrated with the old. I have proposed that the Chi-Rho on the Frampton pavement, with its complex iconography, is another possible representation of this ambivalent stance (Henig 1986, 163–4). Nevertheless it is highly satisfactory to record some examples of Christian iconography, new to Roman Britain and to remind ourselves that little boxes such as this, both pagan and Christian, were ancestral to the reliquaries which were later to accumulate in church treasuries.

See also Fig 160, no 1 for a further figured sheet

Miscellaneous, probably votive, objects

Fig 97

1 Ovoid hollow shell, probably an amulet case, *Find 2351, context 154, Structure I, Phase 5e (ii)*

2 Silver shell of a conical amulet case, with side piercings, *Find 3973, context 511, Structure XIX, Phase 7*

3 Harness mount, about a third of a circular flat wheel shaped object. One lozenge shaped spoke remains, ornamented with an ovoid boss on which a single groove has been scored, representing a female *pudenda*, *Find 7269, context 1191, Structure XIV, Phase 5d–6b*

For other harness mounts see Oldenstein 1976, 282–4 eg no 1134 from Zugmantel. The *pudenda* bosses generally occur on separate, often lozenge-shaped, studs from leather work, *ibid*, 248, 267–72; Zadoks-Josephus-Jitta, *et al* 1973, 50–51, nos 72–6; Brown 1986, 44, fig 28, no 199; Bidwell 1985, 119 and fig 40, 18.

4 Sheet plate, cut in a pointed arch shape, embellished with cut out spirals; pierced by two studs with iron cores. Possibly part of a component of a head dress, *cf* a diadem from Hockwold (Toynbee 1962, 178, no 128). Alternatively it may have been affixed to a casket, *cf* one from Lydney (Wheeler and Wheeler 1932, 90 and pl xxix, nos 134 and 135), *Find 5028, context 601, Structure XIX, Phase 7*

Discussion

The votive objects provide a clear indication of the nature of the cult in Roman times. The Romanisation of religion at this site entailed the identification of the god worshipped as Mercury, an identification established for as long as the pagan temple lasted, by the cult image, which shows him as a virile *ephebe*. His external attributes are the ram (or goat) and cockerel which would certainly have had more meaning in rural Britain than the tortoise or scorpion also associated with him.

Indications of an earlier, more martial aspect of the deity in Iron Age times, is suggested by the continued offering of spears (now in the form of models, see chapter 8). *Defixiones* indeed confirm that there was some confusion of dedication between Mars and Mercury (see chapter 7). However we should not suppose that the classical aspect of the cult was simply a veneer, any more than we can for example, discuss Apollo's greatest sanctuary at Delphi, in mainland Greece, in terms of Python whom he replaced. Mercury, friend of mankind, succourer and healer of travellers and solver of disputes became pre-eminent on West Hill as the splendid cult statue proclaims. The presence of the figurine identified as Bacchus, Find 8066 (Fig 85, no 6) is further evidence that Mediterranean influences were far from absent. Against this we can set the rather simplified form of one sort of *caduceus*, Finds 1141 and 6632 (Fig 89, nos 2 and 5), perhaps the result of misunderstanding, and one rather doubtful rendering of Mercury as a horned god, Find 260 (Fig 85, no 2). Is this a misunderstanding of Mercury's wings or does it hark back to some pre-Roman Celtic deity?

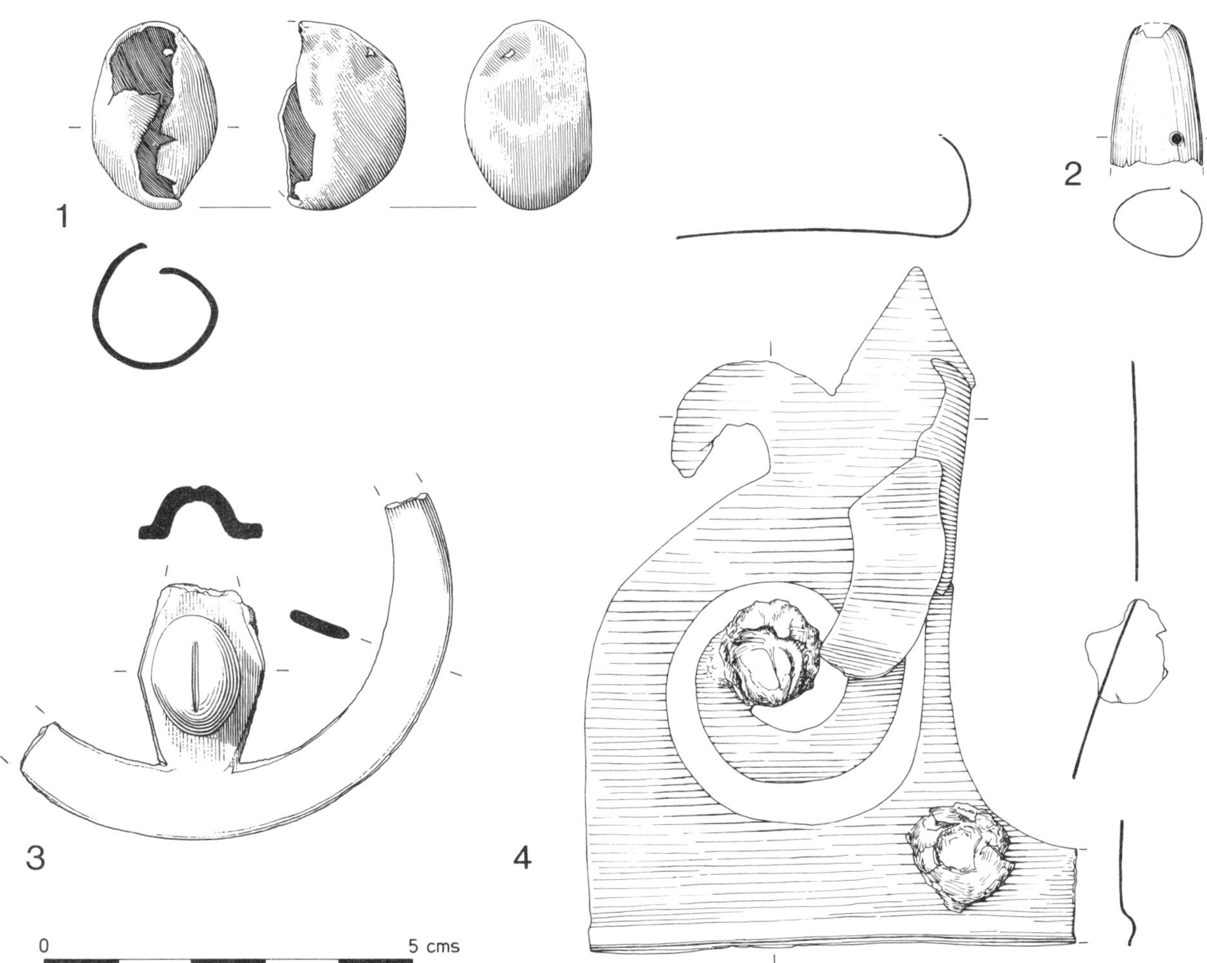

Fig 97 Objects of copper alloy, scale 1:1

Comparison may be made with the sanctuary of Sulis Minerva at Bath. In both places important figured works demonstrate the part played by the artist in changing the native's perception of deity (see Henig 1984, ch 3). The wealth of Bath does not need stressing but the number of silver objects (although these have not been analysed there are at least 12), the fragment of a marble figurine, Find 3834 (Fig 81, no 5), the soldier's badge, Find 1157 (Fig 91, no 3), and the other fitting from a military harness, Find 7269 (Fig 97 no 3) demonstrate that at Uley also there was a rich, and to some extent, cosmopolitan element in the clientele. The presence of medical models, inscribed lead tablets and other *ex votos* provides a further link between practices at the two temples.

The presence of such a large group of figurines is not, however paralleled at Bath, and this is indeed an important group of material to be recovered from a temple site in Britain. It may be compared to the collection of mounted Mars figurines from Brigstock (Greenfield 1963; Taylor 1963) and the figurines of miscellaneous deities from Lamyatt Beacon (Leech 1986). The consistency of the image of Mercury on the votive altars, Finds 2761 and 8352 (Figs 78 and 79) and in the three copper alloy figurines, Finds 1567, 1749, and 5542 (Fig 85, nos 3–5) demonstrate the strong influence which the cult image seems to have had on the iconography of later offerings at the sanctuary. The majority of the votaries were probably poor however and the miniature ceramic items (chapter 8) such as the clay stand or 'altar', Find 3412 (Fig 122), perhaps given with a little incense burning upon it (presumably at considerable expense to the impoverished countryman who presented it), and the many miniature pots (chapter 8, Figs 117–21), some very crudely made, which may well have held purely symbolic offerings, a few grains of cereal or a small quantity of wine or beer, all tell a story of simple faith and touching piety, as do the copper alloy rings (chapter 8, Figs 114–15) which may possibly symbolically represent notional offerings of precious rings or even torques.

7 Votive objects: the inscribed lead tablets

Introduction

by Ann Woodward

A total of 140 lead tablets were recovered during the excavations and 86 of them proved to have been inscribed on one or both sides. Most tablets had been rolled and then flattened and, on discovery, were in a generally poor state of preservation. Advice on conservation was provided promptly by the British Museum and, in due course, the tablets were conserved and unrolled by Simon Dove of the Department of Prehistoric and Romano-British Antiquities. The methods used by him have been published previously (Dove 1981). Some of the tablets bearing clear inscriptions were duplicated by producing silicone rubber moulds which were used to produce a few electrotypes. Three tablets were studied and read by Mark Hassall and Roger Tomlin (*Britannia* **10** (1979) 341–44, and Ellison 1980, appendix 2, and figs 15.7 and 15.8). Subsequently the difficult task of reading and translation was taken on by Dr Roger Tomlin, who had been working for some time on the group of inscribed lead tablets from the sacred spring at Bath. However, it was estimated that production of a full report on all the inscribed tablets from Uley would take several years, and for the purposes of the present volume, it was decided to prepare a full description of five inscribed items, brief descriptions of the remainder, and a discussion of the general character and potential of the assemblage. It is hoped that a full report can be prepared for publication in the future.

Lead tablets were found in all sectors of the excavated area, and in contexts of all phases from Phase 4 onwards. However, most derived from deposits dating from Phase 5, or were unstratified. Furthermore, within Phase 5, most tablets were found in the deposits of votive material which had been spread over the demolished and robbed remains of Structure I in Phase 5e(ii). This concentration is demonstrated clearly in the figures below, which summarise tablet occurrence by phase:

Phase	*context*	*total*
4	Structure IV occupation and demolition	5
5a–d	Structure I, late occupation	2
5d–e	Structure II, cella	6
5e(i)	Structure I, demolition	7
5e(ii)	votive material above Structure I	47
6	Structure II, converted temple	11
6b	rubble above Structure IV	4
7a	post pit fillings of Structure VII/XI basilica	9
7b	platform east of Structure VIII	1
8	unstratified/ploughsoil	47
	total	140

Apart from the preponderance of occurrences in Phase 5 deposits, it is also important to note that tablets were in use during Phase 4, when several items became incorporated into deposits within Structure IV. It may be concluded, on stratigraphic evidence, that the tablets were in use at Uley during the second to fourth centuries AD. Minor usage may have continued into

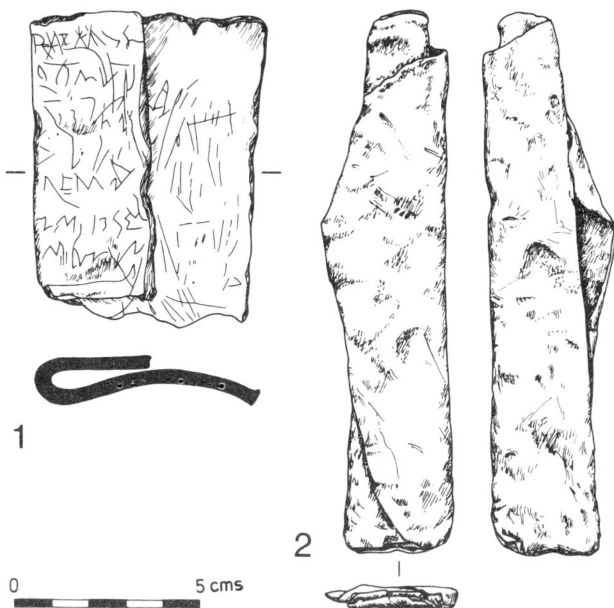

Fig 98 Examples of typical folded and rolled lead tablets, scale 1:2

Phase 6, but the items found within post fillings and deposits of Phase 7 may be considered to be residual. As stated above, many of the tablets had been rolled and flattened (Figs 98 and 99). Within the total of 140 items, 76% (109) tablets had been treated in this way. Of the remainder, 3.6% (5) were rolled but not flattened and 6.4% (9) had not been rolled at all. In 17 cases, the original form of the tablet could not be determined. It appears that most of the tablets had been subjected to a similar sequence of physical treatment, with the flat and rolled items possibly representing tablets which were in the process of preparation, although a few thicker examples (eg Fig 98, no 2) may have been designed to remain flat or were folded once only.

The inscribed lead tablets: an interim report

by R S O Tomlin

Many of the lead tablets from the temple of Mercury at Uley were not inscribed at all, or at least no text or trace of letters is now visible. Eighty-seven, however, still bear an inscription, even if it is often incomplete. The total is thus comparable with that from the sacred spring of Sulis at Bath, *c* 70 texts or considerable fragments, and *c* 50 minor fragments. These have now been published in Cunliffe 1988, 59–277, and separately in Tomlin 1988 (cited here as *Tab Sulis*, for tablet number). This report is only an interim, important texts remain unpublished; the collection as a whole rivals that from Bath, and merits full publication in due course.

Fig 99 Example of typical lead tablet prior to treatment at the British Museum, scale 3:4. (Photo:British Museum)

Introduction

The Uley tablets are difficult to decipher, not because of the intrinsic difficulty of the handwriting, but because of their physical condition after 1500 years and more of burial. (It also seems likely that they were not buried immediately, since when they occur in a stratified context, this context is usually later, sometimes a century later, than their likely date palaeographically). After being inscribed, most tablets were rolled up or folded. This treatment usually damaged them, but it may well have contributed to their preservation. The folding (and modern unfolding) has stressed the lead: lines of text are often lost or reduced to illegibility in the flaking and cracking of the surface at a fold, and sometimes the brittle metal has broken there entirely. On the other hand, rolling up a tablet protected its inner surface from corrosion by dissolved salts. It is notable how often a rolled tablet has lost the two ends of the cylinder to corrosion, resulting in two ragged edges when it is unrolled. Occasionally the inner surface of a tablet is miraculously preserved by a reddish-brown or dark-brown patination, presumably a film of lead oxide or dioxide. Tablet 72 is an example. Usually, however, the inner surface has been invaded by patches of corrosion, probably lead carbonate, which at first forms a protective skin, but then takes up moisture and expands. The resulting hydrocerussite (hydrated lead carbonate) destroys the metallic structure, and with it the fragile letters scratched by the stilus.

The inscribed text must often be recovered from quite slight traces, and experience is needed to distinguish stilus marks from casual or chemical damage. The Uley tablets as a whole are in a worse state than those from Bath. It may be that the Bath tablets, grievously damaged though they often are, benefited from being entirely waterlogged; and it certainly seems that their high tin content, while sometimes making them brittle, protected them from chemical decay. But both collections often present the same problems of decipherment, and experience with Bath has been invaluable at Uley.

Uley and Bath

The Uley tablets resemble those from Bath in many ways. (This resemblance extends to the inscribed lead tablets found at other temple sites in the area of the Severn estuary: Caerleon, Lydney, Brean Down and Pagans Hill, see Tomlin 1988, 61). The tablets are pieces of sheet lead (at Bath, often tin/lead alloy) inscribed with a sharp point, probably that of a stilus. The handwritings are broadly similar: Old Roman Cursive (ORC) of the second and third centuries, New Roman Cursive (NRC) of the fourth century, or capital letters, either neat 'bookhand' or, more often, clumsy copies of 'monumental' hand. Only two tablets, one from Uley and the one from Caerleon, are written in an early Old Roman Cursive (early second century?); most cursive texts are written in a distinctive, 'clerical' hand.

There is a physical difference between the Bath tablets and those from other sites. The Bath tablets are the only ones analysed, and they turn out to be usually made of a tin/lead alloy; this may have been a by-product of the local pewter-making. They tend to be thinner than the tablets from other sites (less than 1mm thick); often they seem to have been cast under pressure, a technique which produced a smooth surfaced, almost paper thin sheet. At Uley and elsewhere, lead seems to have been melted and poured onto a hard flat surface, a paving stone perhaps. The flat blob which resulted was then hammered out, to make it thinner and to give it a smooth surface for inscribing. Hammer marks can quite often be seen, and there is often a characteristic scalloped outline, where the soft metal has splayed out under the blows; sometimes the piece was roughly trimmed with a knife, or even cut into an irregular rectangle or strip.

The Bath tablets are therefore more sophisticated in appearance, but otherwise there are striking similarities in all the tablets from the area of the Severn estuary. The texts are almost always Latin, the only exceptions being lists of personal names (of Latin form) and three or four puzzling tablets from Bath and Uley which may be British Celtic transliterated. The Latin is remarkably uniform: it is full of formulas, repeated phrases, found at the different sites; it contains a sub-stratum of the spoken, 'vulgar' language. Thus, for example, the interesting word *baro* (man) is found at Bath, Brean Down and Uley. These similarities have been tabulated in Tomlin 1988, 63–79, and this interim report can be read as a summary *addendum*.

The content of the tablets is also broadly similar. Typically they are complaints of theft, addressed to a god. The god is asked to secure the return of stolen property, often by being 'given' the property, or the thief himself. The Uley tablets add some new misdemeanours, embezzlement for example, and seem to encompass a different range of stolen property than at Bath. This will be discussed below: it is tempting to see this as reflecting a difference between the two sites, an urban temple at a great healing shrine, and a rural temple with a more restricted clientele. It will be interesting to see whether the language of the texts also reflects this difference, since it may be possible to contrast, cautiously, the Latin of an urban community with that of the countryside. At first sight, however, the contrast is not striking (which may be significant in itself), but this question must await further examination.

The god of Uley

Cult objects and inscriptions recovered during the excavation have made it clear that the god worshipped at Uley was Mercury. This conclusion is richly confirmed by the tablets themselves, at least 18 of which are addressed to Mercury, usually *deo Mercurio*, but occasionally *deo sancto Mercurio* or *divo Mercurio* (the title *sanctissima* is applied to Sulis at Bath, and at Lydney Nodens is addressed as *devo*, *RIB* 306). It is well known, however, that the Roman god Mercury was the usual identification of a major Celtic god (*cf* Caesar, *Bell Gall* vi 17). The Uley tablets throw some light on this identification locally. Tablet 2 (below) was originally inscribed *deo Marti Silvano*, and *deo Mercurio* was written over it, but *deo Silvano* was retained later in the same text. Two other tablets are addressed to Mars, *deo Marti* (Tablet 84) and *divo Marti* (Tablet 24). This suggests that the god of Uley had attributes which made it possible to identify him as Mars or Silvanus, just as both these identifications were made of the Celtic god Cocidius in north-west Britain. More interesting than this, however, is a title which is applied to Mars in both those tablets, and to Mercury in four other tablets (28, 40, 62 and 78). Its use confirms that the same god is meant. It occurs in two cognate forms, of Celtic etymology like other cult titles of Mercury in Britain and Gaul, and was certainly of local significance, since another tablet (Tablet 75) refers to 'the temple of Mercury' at a place name which incorporates the same word. Unfortunately the reading and its etymology require further study, and it would be premature to publish it here. In due course it will be possible to make a minor addition to the toponymy of Roman Britain, and even to make a guess at the Celtic name of the god of Uley.

Formulas

The texts from Uley contain many words and phrases used repeatedly in the Bath tablets, which can thus be regarded as formulas. Most of them are found in other British curse tablet texts, but only occasionally in texts from other provinces; sometimes parallels can be found in Latin literary or legal texts. These formulas have been listed in Tomlin 1988, 63–8, by key word; the following are found in the Uley tablets:

donec, until, *cf nisi*
dono, I give, as *donavi, donatur*
exigas, you are to exact, as *exsigat*
fraudem, wrong, as *qui mihi fraudem fecerit*
inveniat, discovery of the thief
involare, steal
maiestas, majesty
nisi, unless, *cf donec*
nomen furis, the name of the thief
numen, divinity
perdidi(t), have/has lost, as *per(didi)t*
non permittas, you are not to allow
queror, conqueror, I complain
redemare sanguine suo, buy back with his own blood
sanitatem, health (with many variants)
si ... si, mutually exclusive alternatives
templum, fanum, temple

The *si ... si* formulas are particularly common at Uley, all the common variants being well attested: *si servus si liber* 'whether slave or free', *si baro si mulier, si mascel si femina, si vir si mulier, si vir si femina*, 'whether man or woman', and *si puer si puella*, 'whether boy or girl'. They were evidently so commonplace that they were confused – hence the inept *si vir si mascel* – and even abbreviated: *SB SM* (*si baro si mulier*), *SP SP* (*si puer si puella*). There are also many variants of the *sanitatem* formula, in which the thief is forced by ill health to return the stolen property; they include a new variant, the denial of 'hope and breath' (*nec spem nec spiritum*), and an abbreviation, from the tablet just cited: *nec dormire nec vig(ilare) nec sed(ere) nec iacere*.

There is now a second instance of a unique Bath formula, *Tab Sulis* 10, *ut [1–2]um dea Sulis maximo letum [a]digat*, 'that the goddess Sulis inflict death upon ...(?)', which makes it possible to resolve this textual crux. The new text (Tablet 43) reads: *rogo te ut e‹x›os maximo leto adigas*, 'I ask you to inflict maximum death upon them'. *Tab Sulis* 10, lines 10–12, can now be restored as *ut [e]um dea Sulis maximo letum* (sic) *[a]digat*, and the possibility that *maximo* is a personal name can be rejected. Both texts use *adigat/adigas* as if it meant 'to inflict someone (accusative) with death (ablative)'; whereas its usage is the reverse: 'to inflict death (accusative) upon someone (dative)'. *Tab Sulis* 10 has introduced a confusion of its own, the ungrammatical expression *maximo letum* (for *maximo leto*). But there is more to it than this. Both tablets are written in the same elegant 'rustic capitals', perhaps even by the same hand. This would raise an interesting question of authorship: was the same scribe active at both shrines? If so, it would imply, despite the multiplicity of hands found at Bath (see Tomlin 1988, 86, 99–101), that there were indeed professional scribes who drafted and inscribed tablets for petitioners. However, the author of *Tab Sulis* 10 is called *Docilianus*, and the author of Tablet 43 *Docilinus*. The names both belong to a group noticeable at Bath (see Tomlin 1988, 96, 261), 'Roman' names derived from the Celtic name *Docca*. It is possible that the same (anonymous) scribe wrote tablets at the two shrines for two petitioners with almost identical names; but a more economical hypothesis is that scribe and petitioner were one, and that he spelled his colourless name in two ways.

Three formulas not found at Bath now receive confirmation. Two are noted in the texts which follow: the 'gift' of a proportion of the stolen property to the god to secure his intervention (see note to Tablet 2, lines 10–11), and the technical term *repraesentare* (to pay at once, see note to Tablet 1, lines 11–12). The third is the 'literary' phrase *iteratis precibus* (with renewed prayers) in Tablet 72, otherwise found only in a Pagans Hill text (*Britannia* **15** (1984) 339, no 7) but already suspected of being a formula, since it occurs in Cyprian, *De mortalitate*, **18** (*CSEL* **3**, 308).

Language

The language of the Bath tablets, with its 'vulgar intrusions into would-be correct Classical Latin' (Smith 1972, 936), has been listed in Tomlin 1988, 74–9. At first sight (and there has been no time for a second), the same can be said of the Uley texts. Firm conclusions would be unwise while readings are still tentative, but with this proviso, some preliminaries can be offered.

Syntax

nessi me intercedente: Conflation of conditional clause and ablative absolute. *rogatum te habeo*: For classical *te rogavi*. This use of *habeo* as an auxiliary verb to express a perfect tense is already found in Plautus, but it is typical of Vulgar Latin and passes into the Romance languages.

Celtic substratum

donator for *donatur*: See note to Tablet 5, lines 4–5. *sacto* for *sancto*: See Jackson 1953, 406–7, and *cf* Hamp 1975, 155–6: an instance of the substitution of British ϰt for Latin *nct*.
Personal names of Celtic etymology also occur, as at Bath, eg *Senovarus* (*cf Tab Sulis* 9, *Senovara*). There are two or three texts like *Tab Sulis* 14 (which one of them resembles in script), where the language does not seem to be Latin; just possibly it is a transcription of British Celtic.

Unusual words

capit(u)larem, cap, *cf Tab Sulis* 55
carta, tablet, *cf Tab Sulis* 8
commonitorium, memorandum
co(n)scientiam, intended for forgiveness
gabatas, plates
hospitiolo, house, *cf Tab Sulis* 99
lintiamen, linen
resculas, chattels

Divergent spellings

capitlarem, for *capitularem*
coscientiam, for *conscientiam*
consortiam, for *concordiam?*
donator, for *donatur*
exsigat, for *exigat*
frenem, for *frenum*
invalavit, for *involavit*
lintiamen, for *linteamen*
maiet, for *meiat*
nissi, *nessi*, for *nisi*
ofero, for *offero*
perdederunt, for *perdiderunt*
Petroneus(?) for *Petronius*
prolocuntur(?) for *proloquuntur*
que, for *quae*
sacto, *sanco*, for *sancto*
representaverit, for *repraesentaverit*
sangun[e] sua, for *sanguine suo*
serus, for *servus*
tuor, for *tueor*

The influence of the spoken language can be seen in most of these, but *lintiamen* and *tuor* are forms so well attested as to be considered collateral rather than divergent, *maiet* is probably a slip (an anagram corruption), and *invalavit* (occuring three times) defies explanation.

Stolen goods

The five tablets (1–5) published here in full were all prompted by theft. Another tablet (68) complains of 'the theft which has been done me'. Many others contain fragments of formulas relating to theft, *si servus si liber*, the verb *involare*, and so forth. The Uley tablets thus resemble those from Bath, and indeed most British tablets (see Tomlin 1988, 60), in being aimed at thieves. In effect they are petitions to the divine: details are given of a theft, and action is requested against the thief. There are three interesting exceptions from Uley, all of which however request divine intervention against wrongdoers. Docilinus (Tablet 43) complains of harm done to his beast (*pecori meo*) by three named persons. An anonymous writer complains of 'those who plan evil against me' (Tablet 76). The third tablet (78) is the first instance from Britain of a crime well known elsewhere in the Empire, the embezzlement of a deposit: the writer consigns to Mercury the named person 'who has defrauded me of the *denarii* which he owed me'. All three texts continue with the usual formulas aimed at thieves: the guilty parties are to be forced by ill health to make reparation. Like the mass of British inscribed tablets, they are quasi-legal petitions addressed to a supernatural patron (see Tomlin 1988, 70–71).

In an action for theft, according to the jurist Ulpian (*Digest* XLVII 2.19), the object stolen must be identified. The Uley tablets, like those from Bath (see Tomlin 1988, 79–81), are not only a dossier of petty theft but a catalogue of personal possessions. Perhaps the most remarkable are 'the two wheels and the cows which I keep and several chattels from my house' lost by Honoratus (Tablet 72). There is a draught animal (Tablet 1), a bridle (Tablet 5), perhaps a sheep (Tablet 9), and certainly some wool (Tablet 58). The woman Saturnina lost some linen (Tablet 2). Household goods include vessels (Tablet 24), two pewter plates (Tablet 84), and what seems to be cash from a strongbox (Tablet 75). A gold ring is mentioned (Tablet 3), and a sum of money expressed in *denarii* (Tablet 21). There may be a reference to standing grain (Tablet 75). These tantalising glimpses contrast with the picture gained from Bath. Here fifteen items of clothing are named in twelve tablets (Tomlin 1988, 80), whereas at Uley only one tablet (Tablet 62) has yet been found to refer to clothing. At Bath small sums of money were lost, and pieces of jewellery, surely stolen at the baths like the items of clothing. Their owners, arguably, were visitors to the sacred spring, and their petitions a reflection of urban literacy. At Uley we glimpse an equally sophisticated literacy, but one which seems to belong to a modestly prosperous peasant community.

Handwriting

The handwriting of the Uley tablets, as already noted, is broadly similar to that found at Bath. It may be divided into three types, Capitals (both 'rustic capitals' and the various crude copies of 'monumental' capitals), Old Roman Cursive (ORC), and New Roman Cursive (NRC). A few texts contain cursive and capitals.

type	*Bath*		*Uley*	
Capitals	29	25%	23	26%
ORC	62	54%	55	63%
NRC	18	16%	8	9%
illiterate	5	4%	1	1%
total	114		87	

Many of the Bath texts are mere scraps, but they all seem to be from different tablets. Only a fraction of the deposit was recovered from the sacred spring, but since the votive objects were thrown into a sort of quicksand, what was found can be regarded as a random sample. The Uley deposit has also been disturbed, but is likely to be more complete.

It is noticeable that the proportions of the three types of script are broadly similar at Bath and Uley, with ORC texts preponderating. The date at which ORC was succeeded by NRC is still a problem, but current opinion would put it towards the end of the third century (see Tomlin 1988, 87–8). This is almost the only criterion for dating both the Bath and Uley tablets. There is one internal date at Bath, the 12th of April (*Tab Sulis* 94). At Uley there is a little more evidence. Two of the tablets (57 and 62) were found in a second-century context, but it is not clear whether this will be much help. Tablet 58 can be dated early: its ORC is unique in British inscribed tablets, except for *RIB* 323 (Caerleon), and resembles that found in stilus writing-tablets of the period *c* AD 75–125 from Britain. But the mass of ORC texts found at Uley is unstratified, or at least from contexts too late to be relevant, and its script is fairly homogeneous. It is too soon to say whether more than one tablet was written by the same hand. This script is typically a practised, 'clerical' hand which resembles one found in Dura papyri of the first half of the third century, apart from a 'late' E and S, which occur only in Tablet 80. It is the dominant hand at Bath and Uley, and it can reasonably be dated to the period *c* AD 175–275.

The ORC texts from Uley, and at least some of the capital-letter texts, can therefore be regarded as residual from the predecessor(s) of the fourth-century temple. The only difficulty is raised by Tablet 78, which alludes to the sum of 100,000 *denarii* 'given' to Mercury. It is not clear whether this is the whole sum lost, or only a fraction promised to the god. This is by far the largest sum mentioned by a British inscribed tablet, rivalled only by the 3000 *denarii* in the longest (ORC) text from Pagans Hill (*Britannia* **15** (1984) 339, no 7). The beginning of this tablet is lost, and with it the context of the money. These two sums dwarf the various moneys lost at Bath, 5 *denarii*, 2 *argentioli* (ORC texts), 6 *argentei* (NRC text), and 6 *argentioli* (capital-letter text), but the difference cannot be stressed, since the latter were probably lost from bathers' pockets, the 6 *argentei* explicitly 'from my purse' (*Tab Sulis* 98). By contrast, the figure from Uley must be a capital sum, money lent or deposited, money comparable with a coin hoard. The difficulty is whether such a sum could have circulated in a British rural community in the third century, the date of an ORC text. In AD 301 Diocletian's Prices Edict fixed the price of gold bullion at 72,000 *denarii* a pound (*Edict*, 28.1), and within a short time the government was levying gold at the rate of 100,000 *denarii* a pound (*P Oxy* 2106). Both figures will have been lower than the real exchange-rate, but we have some control in a papyrus of AD 324 (*P Oxy* 1430), from which we can deduce a gold price of 308,000 *denarii* to the pound.

These documents make it clear that, even after the rampant inflation of the third century, which continued unchecked in the fourth, '100,000 *denarii*' would still have been a substantial sum in the first quarter of the fourth century. *Denarii* were still being used as a unit of account in Italy in AD 323 (*ILS* 9420). It is tempting, therefore, to date Tablet 78 to the fourth century. But what of the ORC script? It is clear from *Tab Sulis* 66 that there was a period of transition, in which both ORC and NRC were used, and it is possible that scribes who learned to write ORC in the later third century continued to use it into the fourth century. The time lag might have been longer in somewhere as remote as the Cotswolds. At all events, until more evidence accumulates, this possibility must be borne in mind.

Names

The Bath tablets preserve more than 150 names (see Tomlin 1988, 95–8), most of them however in lists of names, a document hardly found at Uley. Names are also comparatively scarce in the Uley tablets at present simply because they are difficult to read with certainty. At first sight the mix resembles that from Bath, about twenty names, half of them Celtic, and half of them Latin *cognomina*. The Celtic names are rare or unique; among them is *Biccus* (Tablet 4), *Cenacus* (Tablet 1), and *Senovarus*, son of *Senovirus* (Tablet 62), which recalls *Senovara* at Bath. This is the only name explicitly of patronymic form, and it is interesting to see that it occurs in one of the two texts to be found in a second-century context. It would support the hypothesis put forward (in Tomlin 1988, 97) that this peregrine nomenclature, appropriate to a period before the mass of the population became Roman citizens, belongs to texts of the second century.

There is, as at Bath, no name borne by a Roman citizen. The Latin names are *cognomina*, usually developed from simpler *cognomina* (eg *Vitalinus* and *Natalinus*). Unlike the Celtic names, they are not distinctive. They may include names of concealed Celtic etymology: *Docilinus* (*cf Docca*) has been mentioned already. The most interesting of these Romanised Celtic names is, of course, the as yet unresolved place-name of the temple itself.

Texts: Tablets 1–5

Five inscribed tablets, with full text and commentary. Tablets 1—3 were first published in *Britannia* **10** (1979) 341–4 from electrotypes, which have now been re-examined. The originals of Tablets 1 and 2 have not yet been examined, but the reading of Tablet 3 has been corrected from the original. Tablet 4 is published in *Britannia* **19** (1988) 485–7. Tablet 5 appears in *Britannia* **20** (1989) 327–30.

Tablet 1

Figs 100–1
Irregular oblong, inscribed short-axis in ORC on both sides (not seen), measuring 85 × 135mm folded. There are patches of corrosion, but the text is well preserved. Published in *Britannia* **10** (1979) 340–2, no 2, from an electrotype and here revised; the original has not yet been examined, *Find 1180, context 62, over Structure I, Phase 5e (ii)*

Fig 100 Tablet no 1, 'Cenacus complains': (a) obverse, scale 1:1. (Photo: British Museum, Drawing: M W C Hassall)

transcript

(*a*) deomercurio *vacat*
cenacusquẹṛịtur
deuitalinoetnata
linofilioipsiusḍ
iument1–2quodeịrap
tumest e.rogat
deummercurium
utnecantesa
nitatem

restored text

(*a*) deo Mercurio
Cenacus quẹṛịtur
de Vitalino et Nata-
lino filio ipsius ḍ(e)
iument[o?] quod eị rap-
tum est e[t] rogat
deum Mercurium
ut nec ante sa-
nitatem

Fig 101 Tablet no 1, 'Cenacus complains': (b) reverse, scale 1:1. (Photo: British Museum, Drawing: M W C Hassall)

(b) habeantnissi
nissi(*deleted*)repraese[...]
tauerintmihi[...]
mentumquodrạ
pueruntetdeo
deuotione.quạ[...]
ipseabhisex
postulauerit

(b) habeant nissi
<nissi> repraese[n]-
taverint mihi [iu]-
mentum quod ra-̣
puerunt et deo
devotione[m] quạ[m]
ipse ab his ex-
postulaverit

Cenacus complains to the god Mercury about Vitalinus and Natalinus his son concerning the draught animal which has been stolen from him, and asks the god Mercury that they may have neither health before/unless they return at once to me the draught animal which they have stolen, and to the god the devotion which he has demanded from them himself.

Line 2 *Cenacus*: this Celtic personal name seems to be unattested, but is clearly cognate with a group of samian potters' names found in *CIL* **12** and **13**: Cennatus (Cenatus), Cenicus, Cenno (Ceno).

queritur: it is not clear from the electrotype whether some strokes are casual damage; by excluding them, it is possible to read *queritur* (only the dotted letters are uncertain). This is supported by the context; *cf* also *Tab Sulis*, 47 (*queror*), *ibid* 59 (*conqueror*).

Lines 3–4 *de Vitalino et Natalino*: both names are typical of the name-stock of Bath and Uley, being developed from common Latin cognomina (*Vitalis* and *Natalis*).

Lines 4–5 *d(e) iument[o?]*: there is no trace of the first *e* on the electrotype, nor any sign of significant damage, so it may have been omitted in error; the ablative *iumento* is required, but surviving traces on the electrotype and the spacing suggest *iument[um]*.

Line 8 *nec*: this redundant conjunction suggests that the scribe had in mind, or miscopied, a formula such as *nec somnum nec sanitatem* (see Tomlin 1988, 65–6). The thief is to be forced by ill health to return the stolen property, as in Tablets 2 and 4 below.

Line 10 *nissi*: repeated in error; the divergent spelling (of *nisi*) is also found in Tablet 2, Tablet 4, lines 10 and 14 below, in *Tab Sulis* 32, *cf ibid* 65, and *Britannia* **15** (1984) 339, no 7 (Pagans Hill), *nessi*. The gemination of *–ss–* should perhaps be seen as a hyper-correction.

Lines 11–12 *repraese[n]taverint*: this technical term, which occurs in two other Uley tablets, meaning 'to pay at once' or 'in ready money', is typical of the quasi-legal language found in British curse tablets.

Lines 13–14 *rapuerunt*: strict grammar would require the perfect subjunctive *rapuerint* appropriate to a relative clause within an indirect command; since this nicety is ignored (*cf* also *circumvenit* in Tablet 2 below), the verbal ending *–erit/–erint* in this and other tablets should be understood as a future perfect. See Tomlin 1988, 69–70.

Line 15 *devotione[m]*: in the sense of 'respect' owed to the god, not in its specialised sense of being made subject to the god's vengeance by a spell; for this see *Tab Sulis* 10, line 5, *devoveo* (with note).

Fig 102 Tablet no 2, 'Saturnina': (a) obverse; (b) reverse, scale 1:1. (Photo: British Museum)

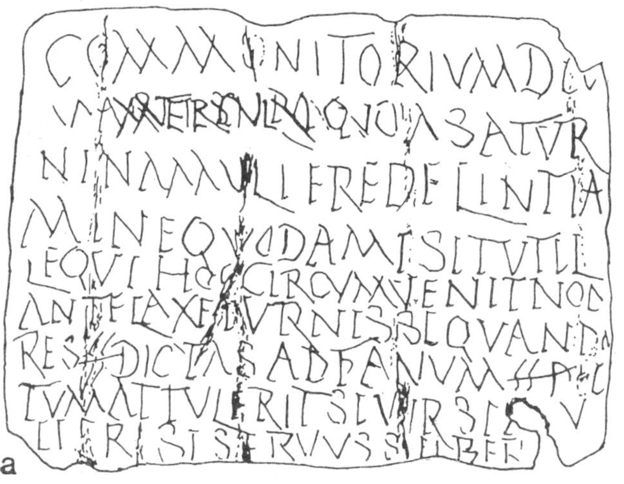
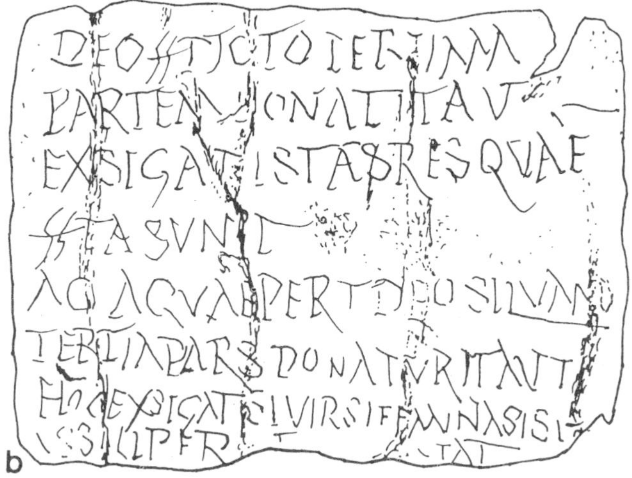

Fig 103 Tablet no 2, 'Saturnina': (a) obverse; (b) reverse, scale 1:1. (Drawing: M W C Hassall)

Tablet 2

Figs 102–3
Rectangle cut from lead sheet (not seen), measuring 83 × 60mm, folded. Inscribed both sides in capitals, damaged at the folds and at the corners, but otherwise complete and in good condition. Published in *Britannia* **10** (1979) 343, no 3, from an electrotype and here revised; the original has not yet been examined, *Find 2169, context 62, over Structure I, Phase 5e (ii)*

Line 1 *commonitorium*: for this technical, quasi-legal term, found here for the first time in a curse tablet text, see *TLL* s v. It does not occur before the fourth century, when it becomes quite common, sometimes in the special sense of a petition to a superior (eg Symmachus, *epistulae*, **i** 68), which would seem to be the sense here.
Line 2 *Mercurio*: written over *Marti Silvano* (but *deo Silvano* has been retained in line 14), suggesting an alternative Roman 'identification' of the god of Uley; he is 'identified' as Mars in Tablet 3, line 1 (below, with note). The Celtic god Cocidius was variously 'identified' with Mars (*RIB* 602, 993, 2015, 2024) and with Silvanus (*RIB* 1578).
Line 3 *muliere*: why the sex (or status?) of Saturnina is specified is not clear. Sulis received texts from women identified only by their names (*Tab Sulis* 59, 60, 61, 97), and it does not follow that a (male) scribe is writing for Saturnina.
Line 5 *circumvenit*: unique in curse tablet texts as a synonym for the usual *involavit*; for the (perfect indicative) tense, *cf* Tablet 1, line 13, *rapuerunt* (above, with note).
Lines 5ff *non ante laxetur* (etc): a unique variant of the common formula (see Tomlin 1988, 65–6) that the thief is to be forced by ill health to return the stolen property. *ante* is redundant, unless *quando[o]* is intended for *quam*, when *nissi* would be redundant.
Line 6 *nissi*: for the divergent spelling, *cf* Tablet 1, line

	transcript		*restored text*
(a)	commonitoriumdẹọ	*(a)*	commonitorium dẹọ
	mercurio (*over* martisiluano) asatur		Mercurio a Satur-
	ninamulieredelintia		nina muliere de lintia-
	minequodamisitutil		mine quod amisit ut il-
	lequiho.circumuenitnon		le qui ho[c] circumvenit non
	antelaxeturnissiquand.		ante laxetur nissi quand[o]
	ress̄s̄dictasadfanums̄s̄d1-2		res s(upra)dictas ad fanum s(upra)d[ic]-
	tumattul.ritsiuirsi.u		tum attul[e]rit si vir si [m]u-
	lieṛ siseruussịḷịber		lieṛ si servus sị ḷịber
(b)	deos̄s̄dictoterṭiam	*(b)*	deo s(upra)dicto terṭiam
	partem.onatitaut *vacat*(?)		partem [d]onat ita ut
	exsigatistasresquae		exsigat istas res quae
	s̄s̄tasunt *vacat*		s(upra)s(crip)ta sunt
	acaquaepertdeosiluano		ACA quae per(didi)t deo Silvano
	tertiaparsdonaturitaut		tertia pars donatur ita ut
	hocexsigatsịuirsif̣ẹminasis..[.]		hoc exsigat sị vir si f̣ẹmina si s[erv]-
	ussiliber[*c*2].[*c*7].at		us si liber [*c*2].[*c*7].at

A memorandum to the god...Mercury (over *Mars Silvanus*) *from Saturnina a woman, concerning the linen cloth which she has lost. (She asks) that he who has stolen it should not have rest before/unless/until he brings the aforesaid property to the aforesaid temple, whether man or woman, whether slave or free. She gives a third part to the aforesaid god on condition that he exact this property which has been written above. A third part...what she has lost is given to the god Silvanus on condition that he exact it, whether man or woman, whether slave or free...*

10 (see above, with note).

Line7 *s(upra)dictas*: for the abbreviation *cf deo s(upra)s(crip)to*, from Ratcliffe-on-Soar (*J Roman Stud* **53** (1963) 123); and *s(...) s (upra)s(crip)ti* from Eccles (*Britannia* **17** (1986) 430, fig 1). It seems to be 'clerical' language, like *infrascriptis* in *Tab Sulis* 8 (and see Tomlin 1988, 64). *ad fanum*: for the formula that stolen property should be returned to the temple, *cf* Tablet 4, line 10 (below, with note) and *ibid*, 68.

Lines 8–9 *cf* lines 16–17 below. These formulas are common in British curse tablets (see *ibid*, 67).

Line10 *deo s(upra)dicto*: see note to line 7.

Lines 10–11 *tertiam partem [d]onat*: *cf* line 15, *tertia pars donatur*: the 'gift' of a proportion of the stolen property to the god to secure his intervention is also found in Tablets 4 and 84 (below). The formula is not found at Bath, but also occurs in *RIB* 306 (Lydney) (one-half), *Britannia* **15** (1984) 339, no 7 (Pagans Hill) (one-half), and *J Roman Stud* **53** (1963) 123 (Ratcliffe-on-Soar) (one-tenth).

Line 12 *exsigat*: the formula, the exaction of a debt by the god (who has been made part-creditor), is also found at Bath, Pagans Hill, and Ratcliffe-on-Soar (see Tomlin 1988, 64). The Vulgar spelling is also found in *Tab Sulis* 34.

Line 13 *s(upra)s(crip)ta*: see note to line 7.

Line 14 *ACA quae per[didi]t:* it is not clear from the electrotype whether there was another letter between *ac* and *a* and between *per* and *t* but it seems there was not. *ACA quae* might be understood as *ac a quibus*, but the conjunction *ac* (instead of *et*) is otherwise unknown in British curse tablet texts, and the grammar of *a quae ... tertia pars* is very harsh. The sense must be *rerum ... tertia pars*. *per(didi)t* for *PERT* makes sense (for the formula see Tomlin 1988, 65), and the verb seems to have attracted copying errors, *cf* Tablet 4, line 3 (with note). *perit* is found in *Britannia* **17** (1986) 431, no 2 (Eccles), but, unless it is corrupt, in the sense of the *thief* 'perishing'.

deo Silvano: see note to line 2.

Line 15 *tertia pars*: see note to lines 10–11; presumably the same one-third, the god's name 'Silvanus' being retained in error.

Line 16 *exsigat*: see note to line 12

Lines 16–17 *cf* lines 8–9 above (with note). The last word is almost lost; evidently it was a verb in the present tense, third person singular, but there is no obvious candidate

Fig 104 Tablet no 3, scale 1:1. (Photo: British Museum)

Tablet 3

Figs 104–5
Fragment of a long strip cut from sheet lead, measuring 98 × 54mm, folded. Inscribed long-axis with a sharp point, with five lines of 'rustic capitals'. Published in *Britannia* **10** (1979) 344, no 4, and here revised. There is a small conjoining fragment, apparently uninscribed. Part survives of the top and bottom edges, but both left and right edges are broken; however, since *deo* (line 1) is likely to have been the first word, the left margin may survive, but the discontinuities of sense suggest that the missing right portion was extensive, *Find 2055, context 215, Structure II, Phase 6a*

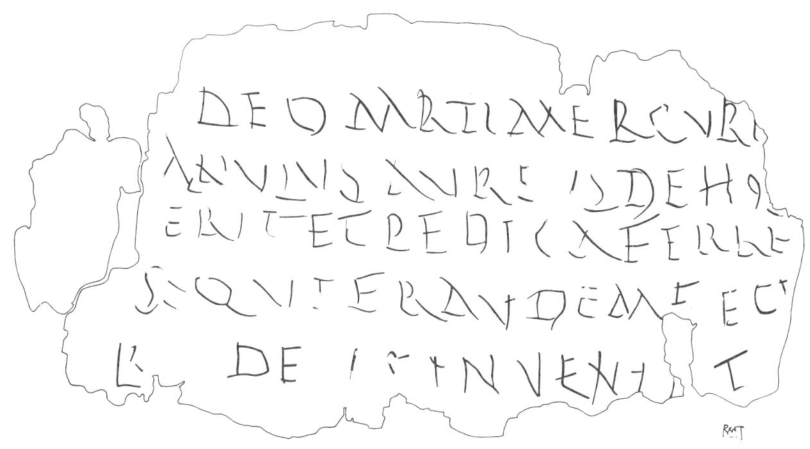

Fig 105 Tablet no 3, scale 1:1. (Drawing: R S O Tomlin)

transcript	*restored text*
deomrtimercurị[...]	deo M(a)rti Mercurị[o ...]
anulusaụreusdehoṣ[...]	anulus aureụs de hoṣ[pitiolo? ...]
er2–3etpedicaferre[...]	er[it?] et pedica ferre[a ...]
s.quifraudemf̣ecị[...]	s. qui fraudem f̣ecị[t ...]
ṛ[..]deụṣinueni.t *vacat*	ṛ[..] deụṣ inveni[a]t

To the god Mars/Mercury ... gold ring from ... [house] ... and iron fetter ... who did wrong ... let the god discover.

Line 1 *M(a)rti Mercuri[o]*: the *a* was omitted by haplography with the second half of the preceding *m*. This is the only tablet to couple Mars with Mercury, but Mercury has displaced Mars in Tablet 2, line 2 (above), and Tablets 24 and 84 (below) were also addressed to Mars.

Line 2 *anulus aureus*: the gold ring presumably had been stolen, *cf Tab Sulis* 97 (a silver ring), *RIB* 306 (a gold ring), but the nominative case, instead of the usual accusative, is a puzzle.

de hos[pitiolo?]: the trace of the final letter excludes *c*; the restoration suggested is borrowed from Tablet 72 (below), *cf Tab Sulis* 99, *de hospitio suo*. The next word would have been the possessive pronoun, *suo* or *meo*.

Line 3 *er[it?]*: this can be read by assuming that the vertical stroke after *r* is an error; if so, it is a verbal ending (eg *involaverit*, *perdiderit*, etc), rather than the future of *esse*.

et pedica ferre[a]: unparalleled and obscure; perhaps a rhetorical conceit, an iron fetter to punish the theft of a gold ring.

Line 4 There may be a letter between *s* and *q*, doubtfully *e* or *i*, but neither makes much sense.

qui fraudem feci[t]: this quasi-legal phrase, with the addition of *mihi*, is found in Tablet 78 (below) and *Tab Sulis* 32, line 5 (with note of parallels there, see also Tomlin 1988, 64).

5 *deus inveni[a]t*: for this phrase *cf Tab Sulis* 44, *qui rem ipsam involavit deus inveniat*, and *ibid* 99, *quicumque r[es] deus illum inveniat*. There is an uninscribed space after *inveni[a]t*, too brief for certainty, which suggests that it was the end of the text.

Fig 106 Tablet no 4, 'Biccus', scale 1:1. (Photo: British Museum)

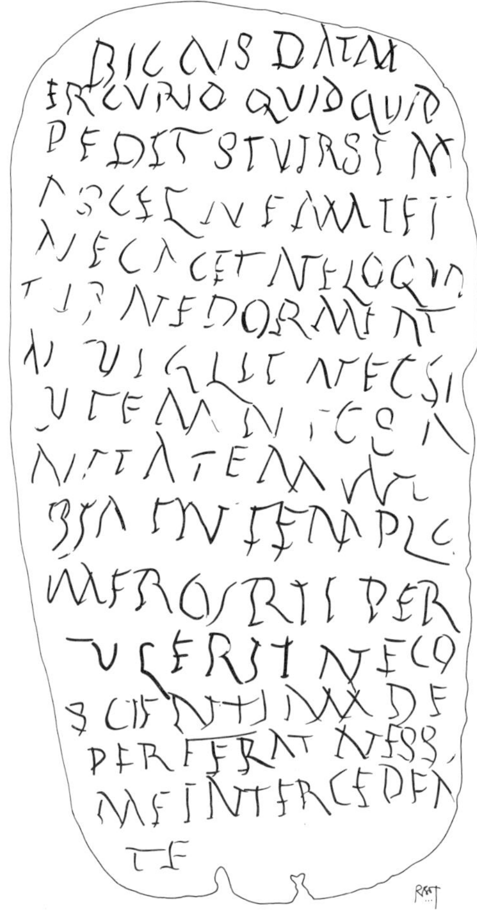

Fig 107 Tablet no 4, 'Biccus', scale 1:1. (Drawing: R S O Tomlin)

Tablet 4

Fig 106–7
Rounded oblong cut from sheet lead, measuring 66 × 124mm, folded. Published in *Britannia* **19** (1988) 485–6, no 2. Inscribed short-axis with sixteen lines of 'rustic capitals', lines 1–12 with a blunt point (W profile), lines 12–16 (from *ne*) with a sharp point (V profile), by the same hand throughout. There are patches of corrosion, especially at the edges, but the text is well preserved, *Find 5050, unstratified*

The text is full of half-understood formulas (noted below), as might be expected from all the evidence of faulty transcription. There are three copying mistakes, *pe(r)d(id)it* (line 3), *maiet* (line 4), *nessa* (lines 9–10); and the use of *quidquid* (line 2) may be due to mechanical copying of a formulary. *Ne taceat* may have been omitted after *ne loquatur*; there is certainly an omission after *de* (line 13), and probably of *habeat* in line 9 and of a subject (the thief) for the string of verbs. The formula *si vir si mascel* (lines 3–4) is confused, and like the malapropism *co(n)scientia* (lines 12–13) raises the question of whether the scribe understood what he was writing. Yet his hand is practised and implies a good standard of literacy. His language also contains traces of the Vulgar, spoken Latin, in *nessi* (lines 9–10, 14), *co(n)scientia* (lines 12–13), and in the inept use of *in* (line 10) and *de* (line 13). By implication, therefore, he was familiar with Latin both written and spoken; but he was handling formulas he only half understood, or which perhaps were too familiar to retain much meaning.

Line 1 *Biccus*: Celtic personal name, already attested in *CIL* **13** 5366a (Vesontio). Probably a variant of *Beccus* (*CIL* **12** 2514) or *Becco* (*CIL* **12** 5381, Tolosa), the childhood cognomen of M Antonius Primus of Tolosa, meaning 'beak' (Suetonius, *Vitellius* 18). *Beccus* (beak) is one of the few Celtic loan-words to be taken into Romance (Elcock 1975, 196).

dat: British inscribed tablets regularly 'give' the stolen property or the thief himself to the god, although *donare* is the usual verb (see Tomlin 1988, 63–4).

Line 2 *quidquid*: the object 'lost' is often specified (as in Tablets 1, 2, and 5), or there may be a reference to property *(rem* or *res)*. Here it is possible that the scribe was mechanically transcribing a formulary and forgot to specify whatever it was, or that he meant to write *quicumque*: see below, lines 4–5.

Line 3 *pe(r)d(id)it*: an error in transcribing a verb formulaic in British curse tablet texts (see Tomlin 1988, 65), a verb also garbled in *Tab Sulis* 6, *EERIDID* (*perdidi*) and

transcript	*restored text*
biccus datm	Biccus dat M-
ercurio quidquid	ercurio quidquid
pedit siuirsi m	pe(r)d(id)it si vir si m-
ascelnemaiet	ascel ne meiat (*transposed*)
necacet neloqụa	ne cacet ne loqụa-
ṭụrnedormiat	ṭụr ne dormiat
n.uigịletnecs.	n[e] vigịlet nec s[a]-
.utemnẹcsa	[l]utem nẹc sa-
nitatemnẹ	nitatem nẹ-
ssa intemplọ	ss[i] in templọ
mercurii per	Mercurii per-
ṭulerit neco	ṭulerit ne co(n)-
scientiamde	scientiam de
perferat ness.	perferat ness[i]
meinterceden̩	me interceden̩-
te	te

Biccus gives Mercury whatever he has lost (that the thief), whether man or male (sic), *may not urinate nor defecate nor speak nor sleep nor stay awake nor* [have] *well-being or health, unless he bring (it) in the temple of Mercury; nor gain consciousness* (sic) *of (it) unless with my intervention.*

Tab Sulis 103, *PEDRE* (*perdere*), and probably here in Tablet 2, line 14 (above).

Lines 3–4 *si vir si mascel*: the scribe has conflated two variants of the 'whether man or woman' formula common in British curse tablets (see Tomlin 1988, 67–68), *si vir si femina* and *si mascel si femina*

Lines 4–5 *ne meiat ne cacet*: the anagram *MAIET* is another transcription error. This is the first occurrence of the formula, but a variant is found in *Tab Sulis* 41, *nec adsellare nec [meiere]*. The subject of the verbs (and of *ne loquatur*, etc) is not explicit, but must be the thief; either this must be understood, or *fur, qui involavit* (etc) has been omitted in error; alternatively, *quidquid* (line 2) is an error for *quicumque*, *perdere* (cause loss to) being used in the sense of *involare* (steal) as in *Tab Sulis* 99.

Line 5–6 *ne loquatur*: the first occurrence of this formula in a British curse tablet, but *cf* Audollent 1904, no 270 (Hadrumetum) *non dormiat neque sedeat neque loquatur*. Another tablet (*RIB* 7) from London also silences its victim, but the context is unclear. Since the other formulas in this Uley text fall into contrasting pairs, as usual, it is possible that *ne taceat* has been lost, perhaps because it was confused with *ne cacet*.

Lines 6–7 *ne dormiat n[e] vigilet*: the formula is also found in Tablet 75 (below) and *Britannia* **3** (1972) 363 (Wanborough), *cf* Audollent 1904, no 270. Interdiction of sleep (*somnum*) and health (*sanitatem*) is often found in the Bath tablets: see Tomlin 1988, 65–6.

Lines 7–8 *nec s[al]utem nec sanitatem*: understand *habeat*, unless this was omitted in error, or the scribe's mechanical grasp of Latin was so weak that he thought this pair of nouns was another pair of verbs. The two nouns are also coupled in Tablet 62 (below) and in *Britannia* **17** (1986) 431, no 2 (Eccles).

Lines 9–10 *ness[i]*: the scribe wrote *nessa*, no doubt by confusion with the initial letters of *nec salutem* and *nec sanitatem* just before; the first *s* seems to be, not a corrected *c* but a confusion between cursive and capital forms; the second *s* is cursive. For this Vulgar spelling of *nisi cf* Tablet 1, line 10 (above, with note).

Lines 9–12 The thief is to be forced by ill health to return the stolen property, as in Tablets 1 and 2. For this common formula, see Tomlin 1988, 65–6. The tense of *pertulerit* is probably future perfect: see *ibid*, 69–70.

Lines 10–11 *in templo Mercurii*: *templo* alone (dative) would be better, or better still *ad templum*, but the uncertain use of prepositions, and a preference for simple prepositions like *in* and *de* instead of the Classical case-ending, are typical of Vulgar Latin. *cf Tab Sulis* 97, *Basilia donat in templum Martis anilum argenteum*. For the formula that stolen property should be returned to the temple, *cf* Tablet 2, line 7 (above, with note).

Lines 12–13 *ne co(n)scientiam*: perhaps an error by haplography for the less abrupt *nec co(n)scientiam*. The assimilation of medial *ns* to *s* in *co[n]scientiam* is typical of spoken Latin, and occurred very early. An instance from Britain is probably *RIB* 876, *Co(n)s[tant...]*.

co(n)scientiam: the context demands the sense 'forgiveness' or 'pardon', which is not found in Latin *conscientia*, which means variously 'complicity', 'consciousness', 'conscience'. The writer may have been groping for the very rare and post-classical *ignoscentia* (forgiveness), a synonym of the Classical *venia* or *indulgentia* (see *TLL* sv).

Line 13 *de*: the noun governed by this preposition, *hoc* (this), *furto* ((his) theft) or similar, has been omitted in error. The use of *de*, instead of the Classical genitive, is typical of Vulgar Latin.

Lines 14–16 *ness[i] me intercedente*: the context requires the sense 'unless I intervene', but the syntax is certainly not Classical, and does not seem to be Vulgar Latin either. It might be saved by supposing the loss of a final verb (eg *deus placetur*), on the lines of *Codex Iustinianus* x 34.2 (Krùger, 1963), *nisi ... ordinis intercedente decreto ... causa probetur* (unless permission is given by decision of the town council); much more likely, however, the writer did not know how to construct a conditional clause without a formula to guide him, and may indeed have confused *nessi* (*nisi*) with *sine* or even *non*.

intercedente: the sense of 'intercede', although familiar in English, seems to have been introduced by Christian writers (see *TLL* sv *intercedere*, 2156, 47ff.); here it is probably being used in a more strictly legal sense, to 'intervene' or 'interpose'. This is the first instance of the verb in a curse tablet text; they often contain quasi-legal language.

Fig 108 Tablet no 5, scale 1:1. (Photo: British Museum)

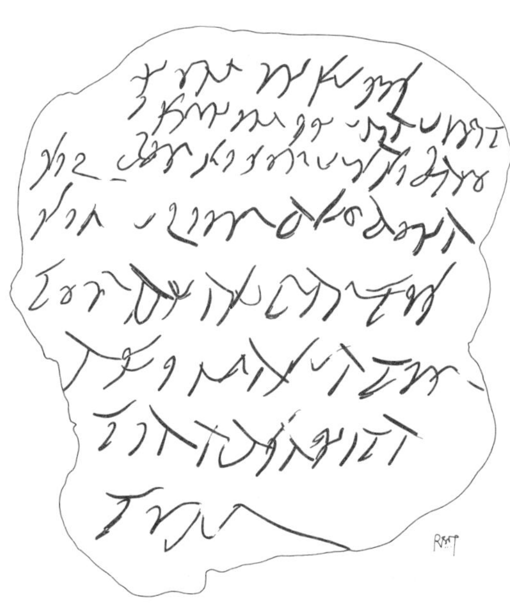

Fig 109 Tablet no 5, scale 1:1. (Drawing: R S O Tomlin)

transcript

nọmenmfuris *vacat*

[*c*2] ifrẹneminụọlauerit

sil[.] berṣiseruussibaro

siṃụlierdeodona-

tor (*over* .) u (*over* n) as (*over* u) partes

afiṃasuater

tiaadsanita *vacat*

tem

restored text

nọmen furis

[qu]i frenẹm invọlaverit

si l[i]ber ṣi servus si baro

si ṃụlier deo dona-

tor duas partes

AFIṂA sua ter-

tia ad sanita-

tem

The name of the thief who has stolen (my) bridle, whether free or slave, whether man or woman, is given to the god (...) two parts from his wife(?), a third to (his) health.

Tablet 5

Figs 108–9
Rounded rectangle trimmed from lead sheet which bears marks of hammering, measuring 70 × 72mm, not folded, previously published in *Britannia* **20** (1989) 327–30. Surface damage in the top left corner, but otherwise complete and in good condition. Inscribed on one side in ORC by a practised hand using an instrument which has sometimes left a thick line (W profile), perhaps a metal nib rather than a stilus. In this script *o*, *e*, and ligatured *i* can sometimes only be distinguished by context, *Find 2161, context 62, over Structure I, Phase 5e(ii)*

Lines 1ff *nomen furis* (etc): for the formula, *cf Tab Sulis* 16, *nomen furis qui [involaverit] donatur*.
Line 2 *frenem*: the reading is unavoidable, neither *e* (and certainly not the second *e*) resembling *u* elsewhere in this text. The scribe surely intended *frenum* (bridle), but either his eye was caught by the second syllable of *nomen* immediately above, or, more likely, he confused his declensions in a way typical of Vulgar Latin.
Lines 3–4 These formulas are common in British curse tablets: see Tomlin 1988, 67.
Lines 4–5 *donator*: the reading is certain; since the legal term *donator* (donor) is excluded by the syntax, and since the formula requires *donatur*, this is clearly what was intended. The divergent spelling may be due to a tendency by British Celtic speakers to confuse Latin $\bar{o}$ and $\bar{u}$: for other instances, see *Tab Sulis* 102 and Tomlin 1988, 75.
duas partes: *duas* has been written over an earlier text, presumably a mistake. The reference to 'two parts', ie two-thirds (*cf tertia*), suggests a formula by which a proportion of the stolen property is 'given' to the god to secure his intervention (*cf* Tablet 2, line 15, above with note), but the syntax is defective.
Line 6 *AFIMA sua*: presumably a copying error, letters omitted or misread; *a femina sua* (from his wife) is a plausible restoration, but is not certain.
tertia: this ought to be the proportion of the stolen property 'given' to the god (*cf* above, Tablet 2, line 15 with note), but the syntax is defective. The scribe seems to have miscopied a formula (see also next note)
Lines 7–8 *ad sanitatem*: as it stands, this (like the whole of lines 5–8) makes no sense. The scribe may have confused two formulas (for which see Tomlin 1988, 65–6 and 68), the interdiction of health (*sanitatem*) to the thief until his return of the stolen property to the temple (*ad templum*)

Descripta: Tablets 6–87

A summary catalogue is given below of all the other inscribed tablets found at Uley, which have now been examined, but whose text has not been fully deciphered and studied. Since this report was written Tablet 43 has been published (*Britannia* **20** (1989) 329–31. It is hoped to publish the rest in due course in a publication like the *Tabellae Sulis* from Bath. The tablets are of sheet lead, sometimes bearing marks of hammering, sometimes roughly trimmed to a rectangle. Almost all are damaged or quite badly corroded; condition has not been noted in detail. Most tablets are inscribed on one side only; this can be assumed to be so, unless stated otherwise, when reference will be made to side (*a*) and (*b*). The abbreviations ORC (Old Roman Cursive) and NRC (New Roman Cursive) are used. Dimensions (in millimetres) are given by the axis of writing, horizontal axis first

6 *Britannia* **4** (1973) 324, no 2, measuring 31 × 18mm. Fragment inscribed on both sides in ORC. The published reading is not certain: (*b*) lines 1–2 looks as if it may be a doublet of (*a*) lines 2–3, and what is read as *la*, side (a) line 2, looks more like *ad* or *ab*, *Surface find in 1972, remaining in private possession* (not seen)
7 measuring 58 × 115mm
(*a*) sixteen lines of well formed 'rustic capitals' with serifs
(*b*) two lines of the same
The text does not seem to be Latin, *cf Tab Sulis* 14, which it resembles, *Find 10, context 1, Phase 8*
8 measuring 120+ × 160+mm. Six fragments of a large tablet bearing a long ORC text, now badly worn, *Find 48, context 1, Phase 8*
9 measuring 92 × 79mm
(*a*) seven lines of ORC addressed *divo Mercurio*, perhaps referring to the theft of a sheep (*ovem*)
(*b*) five lines of ORC
Find 92, context 1, Phase 8
10 measuring 90+ × 60mm, still corrugated and difficult to read. Inscribed in strange angular letters, perhaps a pseudo-inscription, *cf Tab Sulis* 112–6, *Find 103, context 1, Phase 8*
11 five conjoining fragments and six small pieces, still rolled, of a tablet inscribed in ORC, *Find 104, context 1, Phase 8*
12 measuring 75+ × 120+mm, three fragments, two conjoining, of a long ORC text (now mostly lost) written short-axis on a long rectangular strip. The formula *si puer si puella* can be recognized. A nail was driven through the tablet after it had been folded up, *Find 112, context 1, Phase 8*
13 measuring 67 × 49mm,
c six lines of ORC, almost entirely obscured by corrosion, *Find 114, context 1, Phase 8*
14 measuring *c* 185 × 62mm, six lines of ORC, written long-axis on a long strip, badly corroded, *Find 122, context 1, Phase 8*
15 measuring 37 × 38mm, fragment preserving the left margin of a tablet inscribed in small ORC letters, badly corroded, *Find 134, context 1, Phase 8*
16 measuring 130 × 30mm, rectangular strip cut from lead sheet, one end rounded, the other end lost. Bears traces of one line of ORC written long-axis. Perhaps a tag or label, rather than a curse tablet, *Find 138, context 1, Phase 8*
17 measuring 103 × 82mm, long, closely written ORC text, on an undulating and corroded surface. Doubtfully legible, *Find 140, context 1, Phase 8*
18 measuring 46 × 52mm, fragment preserving two sides of a rectangular tablet.
(*a*) nine lines of ORC, shallowly inscribed and almost illegible (*b*) five lines of the same, with a line drawn below, *Find 141, context 1, Phase 8*

19 measuring 54 × 80mm, ten lines of capitals, largely lost in corrosion, *Find 167, context 1, Phase 8*
20 measuring *c* 90 × 130mm,
(*a*) ORC text mostly lost to corrosion
(*b*) ORC text in part legible; begins with the personal name *Cunovinna* and refers to lost property
Find 246, context 1, Phase 8
21 measuring 83 × 81mm
(*a*) symbol(?)
(*b*) twelve lines of ORC, shallowly inscribed and corroded; contains *denarii* sign followed by a numeral,
Find 729, context 20, over Structure IX, Phase 7
22 measuring 90 × 90mm, six lines of irregular ORC, shallowly inscribed and badly corroded, *Find 799, context 22, over Structure I, Phase 5e(ii)*
23 measuring *c* 70 × 45mm (largest fragment). One large and nine small fragments of a tablet inscribed on both sides in bold ORC. Some letters are legible despite the dense network of cracks, but the text may be too fragmentary to recover whole words, *Find 809a, context 37, over Structure I, Phase 5e(ii)*
24 measuring 125 × 92mm
(*a*) two lines of clumsy capitals
(*b*) *divo Marti* ... in capitals, followed by a long text in clumsy ORC perhaps legible with difficulty; it seems to be a complaint of the theft of vessels (*vasa*),
Find 809b, context 37, over Structure I, Phase 5e(ii)
25 measuring 100+ × 62mm, four conjoining fragments of a long strip inscribed long-axis, probably in ORC. Fragments still rolled and deeply corroded; probably illegible, *Find 809d, context 37, over Structure I, Phase 5e(ii)*
26 measuring 97 × 84mm
(*a*) random cuts and perhaps a deeply incised *D*
(*b*) a medley of letters, variously capitals and (apparently) NRC, in *c* seven lines subsequently defaced by repeated blows of a spike,
Find 838, context 6, Structure II, Phase 6b
27 measuring 34 × 41mm, fragment bearing six lines of ORC, badly worn and corroded, *Find 852, context 20, over Structure IX, Phase 7*
28 measuring 77 × 166mm, long strip bearing a long ORC text inscribed short-axis.
Text begins *d[eo] Mercurio* ..., but is badly corroded and almost illegible, *Find 859, context 20, over Structure IX, Phase 7*
29 measuring *c* 155 × 70mm, three fragments, probably conjoining, and many small fragments, of an irregular and damaged strip. A few letters, probably clumsy capitals, are visible of a text inscribed long-axis, *Find 866, context 20, over Structure IX, Phase 7*
30 measuring 49mm wide, two fragments of a strip inscribed long-axis with five lines of large irregular capitals, almost illegible, *Find 866b, context 20, over Structure IX, Phase 7*
31 measuring *c* 65 × 30mm, corroded fragment bearing trace of one letter, probably capital *E*, *Find 866c, context 20, over Structure IX, Phase 7*
32 measuring 62 × 39mm, fragment preserving part of the left margin. Traces of five lines of ORC, almost illegible, *Find 868, context 20, over Structure IX, Phase 7*
33 measuring 70 × 76mm, six lines of capitals, apparently two names of Celtic etymology (the first probably *Lugula*) each followed by a name in the genitive case, *Find 915, context 20, over Structure IX, Phase 7*
34 measuring 53 × 88mm,
eighteen lines of ORC, corroded at the edges but otherwise quite well preserved. Begins *Genitus Mercurio* and requires the return of stolen property, *Find 936, context 17, Structure II, Phase 7*
35 measuring 59 × 109mm, sixteen lines of ORC, complete and in fairly good condition. The text does not seem to be Latin, *Find 1036, context 32, Structure I, Phase 5e(ii)*
36 measuring 66 × 50mm
(*a*) six lines of ORC, badly corroded and almost illegible; nine lines have been scored across them diagonally, from left to right
(*b*) six lines of ORC, badly corroded and almost illegible
Find 1188, context 62, over Structure I, Phase 5e(ii)
37 measuring *c* 60 × 80mm
(*a*) illegible traces of letters, perhaps NRC; struck by a hammer after inscribing
(*b*) illegible traces of letters
Find 1423, context 17, Structure II, Phase 7
38 measuring *c* 70 × 40mm, four conjoining fragments, badly corroded, bearing traces of letters, perhaps irregular capitals, *Find 1484, context 17, Structure II, Phase 7*
39 measuring 92 × 101mm
(*a*) nine lines of ORC, with another line of ORC written at right angles on the left. Some letter forms (eg *e* and *u*) indistinguishable; no clear text
(*b*) nine lines of ORC, with two lines of ORC afterwards written upside down at the top,
Find 1573, context 14, Structure II, Phase 6b
40 measuring 52 × 111mm, fifteen lines of ORC, shallowly inscribed and badly corroded. Text begins *deo Me[r]{p23}curio* ..., but is only partly legible, *Find 1625, context 75, Structure II, Phase 5d–e*
41 measuring 89 × 61mm
(*a*) seven lines of irregular ORC, shallowly inscribed and badly corroded. Text probably begins *si quis* ...
(*b*) three lines of irregular ORC, shallowly inscribed and badly corroded, with uninscribed space below,
Find 1761, context 97, over Structure I, Phase 5e(ii)
42 two large and many smaller fragments of a tablet inscribed on both sides in ORC with a blunt point. The surface is a network of cracks, and the text is almost illegible, *Find 1900, context 61, over Structure I, Phase 5e(ii)*
43 measuring 84 × 98mm, thirteen lines of well formed 'rustic capitals' similar to those of *Tab Sulis* 10, and even perhaps by the same hand (now published in *Britannia* **20** (1989) 329–31). Docilinus complains to Mercury of the harm done to his beast (*pecori meo*) by three named persons, and asks that they be forced by death or ill health to make recompense, *Find 1913, context 206, Structure II, Phase 6b*
44 measuring *c* 48 × 50mm, one large and three small fragments, badly corroded, bearing traces of capitals, *Find 1941, context 204, Structure II, Phase 5d–e*
45 measuring 84 × 48mm, six lines of clumsy ORC, badly corroded, ending in *–us* or *–a*; probably a list of personal names, *Find 2109, context 123, Structure I, Phase 5a–d*
46 measuring 61 × 33mm, two conjoining fragments, and two other fragments, of a badly corroded tablet. Six lines of ORC, almost illegible, *Find 2122, context 207, Structure II, Phase 7*

47 measuring *c* 80 × 51mm, two conjoining fragments of a long strip, inscribed long-axis in ORC, badly corroded and almost illegible.
(*a*) six lines, including *conqu[e]ror* in line 2
(*b*) trace of six lines
Find 2169b.1, context 62, over Structure I, Phase 5e(ii)
48 measuring *c* 70 × *c* 40mm, two conjoining fragments.
(*a*) six lines of ORC, mostly illegible
(*b*) seven lines of ORC, mostly illegible
Find 2169b.2, context 62, over Structure I, Phase 5e(ii)
49 measuring *c* 50 × 58mm, nine lines of capitals between layout lines. Personal names, including *Vicarianus* in line 2, *Find 2169b.3, context 62, over Structure I, Phase 5e(ii)*
50 two conjoining fragments (i) measuring 46 × 43mm; and a third (ii) measuring 45 × 39mm, probably conjoining, from the left end of a long strip. Four lines of neat capitals, written long-axis, with an uninscribed space below, *Find 2169b.5, context 62, over Structure I, Phase 5e(ii)*
51 measuring *c* 75 × 165mm, irregular tablet, perhaps complete. *c* seven lines of confused letters, badly corroded. Only the last line (in NRC) is legible: *deuendi*, perhaps the end of a Celtic personal name, *Find 2169c.1, context 62, over Structure I, Phase 5e(ii)*
52 measuring 95 × 86mm, twelve-line text, with patches of corrosion, and obscured by consolidant. The cursive script is peculiar, but seems to be a clumsy NRC, *Find 2169d.1, context 62, over Structure I, Phase 5e(ii)*
53 (i) measuring *c* 80 × 55mm is not inscribed, and seems to be another tablet.
(ii) measuring *c* 150 × 52mm, is three conjoining fragments from the end of a long strip, inscribed long-axis in NRC. *si femina* can be read at one end, *Find 2169d.2, context 62, over Structure I, Phase 5e(ii)*
54 measuring 30 × 30mm, fragment bearing traces of four lines of ORC. *invola[ ]* can be read in line 2, *Find 2172, context 62, over Structure I, Phase 5e(ii)*
55 measuring 60 × 95mm, six lines of ORC beginning *deo Mercurio ...*, corroded at the edges, but otherwise in quite good condition, complete, *Find 2210, context 331, Structure IV, Phase 6b*
56 measuring 57 × 73mm, eight lines of crude capitals, lost to corrosion except for the left edge, *Find 2213, context 242, Structure II, Phase 7*
57 measuring 71 × 54mm, bottom left-hand corner of a tablet, inscribed in ORC. Part survives of six lines, the text ending in *habeat*, found in a second-century context (*cf* Tablet 62), *Find 2332, context 347, Structure IV, Phase 4b*
58 measuring 120 × 71mm, nine lines of ORC beginning *Mercurio*, apparently relating to the theft of property, ie wool (*res id est lanam*). The script resembles that found on stilus writing tablets of *c* AD 75–125, and is unique at Uley and unparalleled at Bath. It is thus probably the earliest tablet of the collection, its only equal among British curse tablets being the Caerleon tablet (*RIB* 323), *Find 2342, context 1, Phase 8*
59 measuring 57 × 44mm, oval tablet inscribed both sides in irregular capitals
(*a*) single letter, probably *Q*
(*b*) four lines accommodated to the curving edge, or perhaps written concentrically. The text is not obviously Latin,
Find 2349, context 1, Phase 8
60 measuring 83 × 74mm, three lines of capitals, lines 1 and 3 illegible. Accompanied by four small fragments, not conjoining, only one of them inscribed, *Find 2672, context 162, fill of F158, Structure I, Phase 5a–d*
61 measuring 83 × 94mm, eight lines of irregular capitals, somewhat damaged, *Find 2676, context 162, fill of F158, Structure I, Phase 5a–d*
62 measuring 89 × 128mm
(*a*) one line of ORC, title of Mercury
(*b*) seventeen-line ORC text, damaged by corrosion and obscured by consolidant, but more or less complete. Senovarus son of Senovirus asks Mercury to recover stolen property, apparently a cloak (*pallium*) and other clothing. From a second-century context (*cf* Tablet 57 above), *Find 2920, context 332, Structure IV, Phase 4b*
63 four fragments, not necessarily conjoining, inscribed in ORC. Only a few letters are legible, *Find 3336, context 14, Structure II, Phase 6b*
64 measuring 91 × 34mm, strip cut from thin lead sheet, left end lost. Inscribed long-axis by two hands:
(i) with a broad point, two or three lines of ORC;
(ii) with a fine point, one line of ORC at the bottom, followed by a second line of ORC above,
Find 3344, context 14, Structure II, Phase 6b
65 measuring 32 × 55mm, fragment of a tablet inscribed in NRC. The left margin and part of five lines survive, *Find 3407, context 14, Structure II, Phase 6b*
66 measuring 62 × 56mm, five short lines of irregular capitals, perhaps a pseudo-inscription, *cf Tab Sulis* 112–6, *Find 3485, context 428, Structure II, Phase 7*
67 measuring 91 × 30mm, strip cut from thin lead sheet, left end lost. Inscribed,
(i) at the bottom with two uneven lines of ORC
(ii) above them and overlying them, with clumsy ORC letters. No obvious text,
Find 3544, context 1, Phase 8
68 measuring 47 × 38mm, tablet inscribed on both sides in NRC with a broad nib-like point (W profile)
(*a*) seven lines beginning *deo sancto Mercuri[o]* relating to theft (*de furto*)
(*b*) seven lines beginning *nec* (and thus presumably continuing (*a*), but made almost illegible by corrosion, *Find 3652, context 451d, Structure VIII, Phase 6–7a*
69 measuring *c* 72 × 112mm, irregular tablet bearing traces of a few ORC letters, *Find 3676, context 187, Structure I, Phase 5e(ii)*
70 measuring 58 × 159mm, irregular strip, probably incomplete, inscribed on both sides with two texts
(*a*) at least nine lines of ORC written short-axis, very worn and almost illegible. On the same side, at right-angles, four lines of clumsy capitals beginning *dovo* (sic) *Mercurio*, also very worn
(*b*) two lines of clumsy capitals, written short-axis on the outside, at one end: *Severino|dona*,
Find 3684, context 187, over Structure I, Phase 5e(ii)
71 measuring *c* 56 × 46mm, irregular tablet inscribed on both sides in small ORC letters, now very faint. Text begins *[deo?] Mercurio ...*, *Find 3721, context 187, over Structure I, Phase 5e(ii)*
72 measuring 76 × 131mm, sixteen lines of ORC, complete and in good condition. Honoratus complains to Mercury of losing 'two wheels and the cows which I

keep and several chattels from my house'. He asks that the thief should have no health until he returns the stolen property, *Find 3740, context 1, Phase 8*
73 measuring *c* 15 × 18mm, fragment bearing part of two lines of ORC, *Find 3755, context 1, Phase 8*
74 measuring 80 × 53mm, upper portion of a tablet bearing six lines of irregular ORC, shallowly inscribed, worn and corroded. Text begins *deo Merc[u]ri[o] …, Find 3883, unstratified*
75 measuring *c* 110 × 59mm, ten lines of capitals, complete, but damaged by folding, and corroded. 'Gift' of stolen property, apparently cash *d[e] arca* and standing grain (*frumenta*), with the request that the thief be made to return it to the temple of Mercury at Uley. The formulas are abbreviated (eg *s(i) b(aro) s(i) m(ulier)*); the place-name is romanised but of Celtic etymology, *Find 4305, context 600, over Structure XIX, Phase 8*
76 measuring 79 × 75mm
(*a*) eight lines of ORC, damaged. Anonymous complaint to Mercury of 'those who plan evil against me'
(*b*) three lines of ORC continuing the formulas of (*a*); a fourth and final part-line may have been lost,
Find 4465, context 13, over Structure XIX, Phase 8
77 measuring 58 × 50mm
(*a*) text of unknown length in irregular NRC, badly worn and almost entirely lost
(*b*) *c* three lines of irregular NRC beginning *quos* (and thus presumably continuing (*a*)), but otherwise almost illegible,
Find 4629, context 605, Structure XIX, Phase 7
78 measuring 63 × 144mm, long strip, both edges corroded and broken, inscribed on both sides short-axis in ORC. Damaged at the folds; some letters obscured by consolidant
(*a*) seventeen lines of ORC. Mercury is entrusted with the person 'who has defrauded me of the *denarii* he owed me' (the only instance in British inscribed tablets of a denied deposit). The sum of one hundred thousand *denarii* is 'given' to Mercury, to ensure its return…
(*b*) thirteen lines of ORC … on pain of elaborate ill health, 'half-naked, toothless, tremulous, gouty' (etc), *Find 4714, context 601, Structure XIX, Phase 7*
79 measuring 90 × 84mm, nine lines of ORC beginning *deo Mercurio*, shallowly written, corroded and rather worn. Most of the text is probably illegible, *Find 4723, context 602, Structure XIX, Phase 7*
80 measuring 72 × 42mm, seven lines of ORC, complete, but obscured by consolidant. The script seems to have some NRC features. Text begins *carta qu(a)e Mercurio dona|tur*: for *carta* (page) *cf Tab Sulis* 8, *Find 4781, context 601, Structure XIX, Phase 7*
81 measuring 88 × 42mm, major portion of a tablet, badly corroded, with only isolated letters legible
(*a*) Seven lines of ORC
(*b*) Seven lines of ORC
Find 5061, context 478, Structure XIX, Phase 7
82 two conjoining fragments bearing traces of ORC; and four smaller fragments, *Find 5103, unstratified*
83 measuring 54 × 111mm, damaged and badly corroded strip inscribed short-axis with twelve lines of capitals. *[in]volavit* can be read, *Find 5911, from fieldwalking*
84 measuring 84 × 134mm
(*a*) ten lines of capitals. Anonymous complaint to Mars (bearing a title also borne by Mercury at Uley) of the theft of property defined as 'two pewter plates'
(*b*) twelve lines of ORC, continuing (*a*). The thief is to suffer ill health; 'half' the plates are given to the god, for him to exact the stolen property,
Find 5939, unstratified
85 measuring 69 × 77mm, ten lines of capitals, complete, but rather faint. Perhaps personal names, *Find 5948, unstratified*
86 measuring 89 × 105+mm, major portion of a rectangular tablet, with many small fragments perhaps from another tablet. Inscribed with one line of capitals, a personal name, *Find 6480, context 1100, Structure XIV, Phase 7–8*
87 measuring 87 × 82mm, *c* six lines of ORC, badly corroded and almost illegible, *Find 8353, unstratified*

8 Votive objects: weapons, miniatures, tokens, and fired clay accessories

Miniature spears

by Martin Henig

The giving of miniature weapons to a deity may have received added impetus in the Roman period by the provisions of the *Lex Iulia de Vi Publica* (*Digest* 48, 6, *cf* Henig 1984, 206) forbidding civilians to carry arms except for hunting; examples of miniature weapons from Frilford, previously thought to be of Iron Age date (Harding 1974, 103–5, fig 25A), may well be Roman (Harding 1987, 13–16). Final Iron Age deposits of full-size weapons were, of course, present in earlier phases at Uley, see below. The iron pin piercing a bone, Find 8266 (Fig 110, no 2) may be related to the miniature spears and, if so, is suggestive of other rituals as well as bending.

Find 4002 (Fig 110, no 5) is of silver, and is pierced for the insertion of a small ring, perhaps to make it rattle like the pole tip from Brigstock (Greenfield 1963, 249, no 7), the Felmingham Hall sceptre head (Gilbert 1978, 179–80, fig 3A) and the 'rattle' from Baldock (Stead and Rigby 1986, 153 and fig 66, no 523). The object has been ritually 'killed' by bending. The rest are all of iron, mainly with twisted shank and some have been bent.

Several iron spears with twisted shanks have been found at Lamyatt Beacon (Leech 1986, 303–4, nos 43–6, and probably nos 66–73); another example is recorded at Camerton (Wedlake 1958, 272, no 18, fig 56). A number of copper alloy spears have been found at Woodeaton (Kirk 1949, 40f, nos 6–12, pl iii d; fig 9, 1; Green 1975, 64); Lydney (Bathurst, 1879, pl xxv, no 10); and Baldock (Stead and Rigby 1986, 136 and fig 60, no 580). There is some evidence that Mars was venerated at Woodeaton, and the *defixiones* show that at Uley there was some confusion between Mercury and Mars (see chapter 7).

all objects are of iron, unless otherwise stated

Fig 110

1 Miniature spear with head broken, *Find 1754, context 38, over Structure I, Phase 5e (ii)*

2 Ring headed point piercing distal left humerus of a goat, *Find 8266, context 1255, Structure IX exterior, Phase 6*

3 Head of a miniature spear, broken, *Find 3106, context 160, Structure I Phase 5a–d*

4 Head of a miniature spear, broken, *Find 801, context 38, over Structure I, Phase 5e (ii)*

5 and Fig 111, Miniature spearhead of silver with the shaft twisted in two zones. The head has an off centre circular perforation, *Find 4002, context 511, Structure XIX, Phase 7*

6 Miniature spear, slightly bent, *Find 1398, context 52, Structure II, Phase 6a*

7 Miniature spear with twisted shaft, bent, *Find 344, context 14, Structure II, Phase 6b*

8 Miniature spear, severely corroded and with shaft broken, *Find 4101, context 601, Structure XIX, Phase 7*

9 Bar of rectangular section with one section twisted, possibly shafting for spears in process of manufacture, *Find 5172, context 472, Structure II, Phase 6a*

10 Spear with damaged head and with a shaft bearing two zones of twisting, *Find 4848, context 602, Structure XIX, Phase 7*

11 Shaft of spear with zone of twisting, *Find 4860, context 604, Structure XIX, Phase 7a*

12 Twisted spear shaft, broken and bent round on itself with much damaged head, *Find 2384, context 277, Structure II, Phase 8*

13 Twisted spear shaft with rough knob terminal, head end broken away, *Find 3851, context 1, Phase 8*

14 Spear, head broken, with massive shaft of square section, *Find 6278, context 0246, over Structure XIV, Phase 8*

Full-size weapons

A substantial number of normal sized iron weapons were recovered from all phases, but in particular from deposits in the immediately pre-conquest ditch (F264) and the associated votive pit (F251) of the first century AD (see chapter 2). The two main classes of weapon represented were spearheads and catapult-bolt heads, along with one example of a sword blade.

Iron spearheads have most recently been reviewed by Manning (1985, 160–170) with reference to the Durden collection in the British Museum, and in particular to the extensive and well provenanced material from Hod Hill in Dorset (*ibid*). Among the West Hill collection examples of four sub-groups appear to be represented:

Group I: small-bladed spearheads with blades normally 45–65mm long and 20–30mm wide. These are subdivided according to their sockets into IA – closed and welded, and IB – with rolled over flanges; this latter type are often more crudely made.

Group II: somewhat larger, ranging between 80–100mm in length and 20–30mm wide, divided into sub-groups IIA and IIB on similar criteria to those in Group I.

Iron catapult-bolt heads have also been reviewed recently with reference to the British Museum collection (*ibid*, 175–6). Examples of two classes appear to be present here:

Type I: possessing a square-sectioned pyramidal or diamond shaped head, and generally, a welded conical socket. None of the few specimens of this type from the site were complete.

Type II: the majority of the bolt heads present were of Type IIB, with flat blades and flanged sockets, and in most instances of relatively crude manufacture.

Damage or corrosion to a number of specimens has caused difficulties in attributing them to a type, and few of these spear or bolt head fragments are illustrated (except in archive), or appear to derive from primary contexts on site.

The military associations of both these classes of weapon, so frequently demonstrated when they are

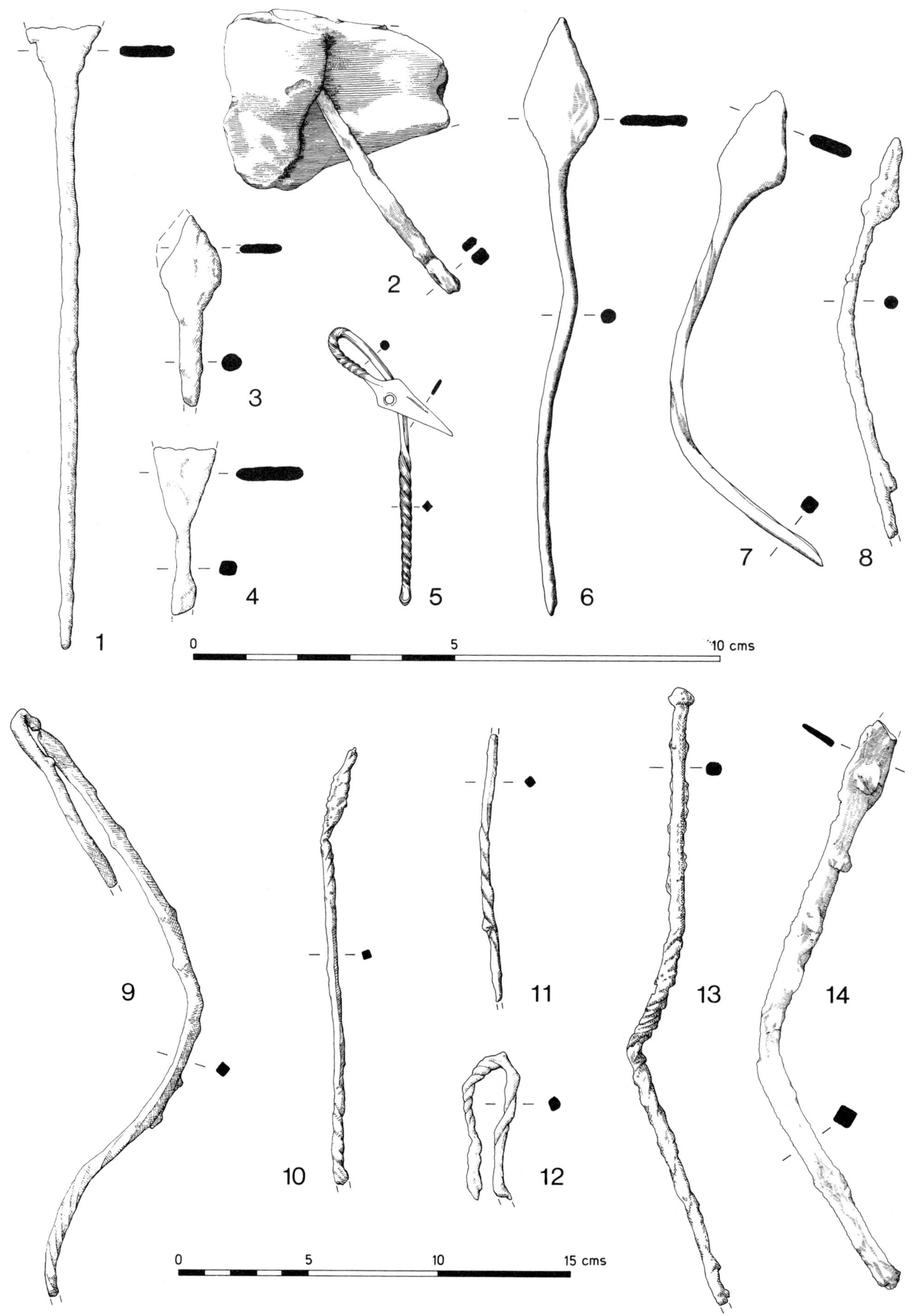

Fig 110 Miniature spearheads of iron (except no 5 of silver), scale 1:2

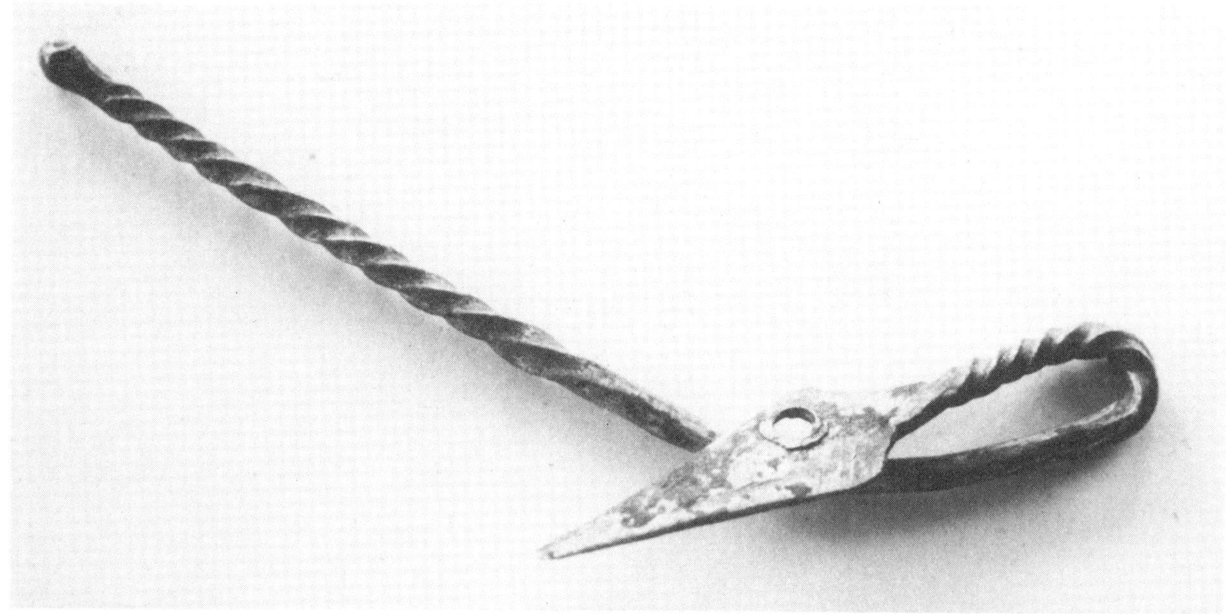

Fig 111 Silver miniature spearhead, deliberately bent, scale 3:1. (Photo: Sebastian Rahtz)

recovered from sites elsewhere in Britain, are for the most part of the mid to late first century AD. This accords well with the site contexts here, most of which should at least originate in that period, and which also contain other material (especially pottery) of early post-conquest date. By far the largest groups originate from the fills of a large rock-cut ditch segment (F264) and associated votive pit (F251), adjacent to the contemporary religious building, Structure XVI (see chapter 3). Several other specimens recovered were associated with Structure XVI, confirming their chronology and associations.

In the absence of a demonstrable early military presence at, or in the immediate vicinity of the site, the origin of these weapons is uncertain. More apparent is their site context, which strongly favours an interpretation involving religious votive deposition within a timber shrine and associated pit and ditch (see chapter 2). There was no evidence of the wooden shafts to which the spear and bolt heads would have been attached, but it is tempting to speculate that complete weapons may have been ritually broken before deposition, in parallel with the frequent bending or breaking of miniature weapons in similar circumstances (see above and Fig 110). Those few specimens recovered from elsewhere on the site, usually in later contexts, probably derive originally from Structure XVI and F264/F251, a hypothesis which is supported by their frequently damaged or fragmentary nature.

The finds of weapons were concentrated in Phases 2 and 3 , with a scatter of residual items occurring in the later phases. Within Phase 2 they derive mainly from Phases 2c and 2d, dating from immediately before and contemporary with the Roman conquest, whilst in Phase 3 all weapons were found in deposits of Phase 3a, the later first century AD. Most items had been deposited as deliberate offerings in the votive pit (F251) or in the adjacent infill of the associated ditch segment (F264).

Table 3 does however indicate an interesting chronological pattern of the finds. Most of the spearheads were found in Phase 2c or 2d deposits and only one example came from the votive pit (F251). On the other hand, two-thirds of the catapult-bolt heads came from Phase 3a and a substantial number were contained within F251. Thus, it may be that the spearheads were of pre-conquest type.

Table 3: The occurrence of iron projectile heads by phase

Phase	*2b*	*2c*	*2d*	*3a*	*4–5*	*6*	*7–8*	*total*
Spearheads								
Group IA	-	1	2	-	-	1	1	5
Group IB	-	1	2	2	1	-	-	6
Group II	1		1	-	1	-	-	3
Ungrouped	1	-	2	-	1	1	1	6
Bolt-heads								
Group I	-	-	-	1	1	1	-	3
Group IIB	-	3	3	12	1	1	1	21
total	*2*	*5*	*10*	*15*	*5*	*4*	*3*	*44*

Unfortunately it is difficult to separate Iron Age from Roman spearheads on typological grounds, those from undisputed Iron Age contexts such as Glastonbury and Meare, Somerset (Bulleid and Gray 1917, pl 62a; Gray and Bulleid 1953, pl 50) or Grimthorpe, Yorkshire (Stead 1968, figs 11 and 13) resembling very closely the main categories of Roman spearhead. A more likely hypothesis is that through time bolt heads became the preferred votive artefact.

Spearheads

all of iron

Fig 112

1 Spearhead, two incomplete fragments of blade and socketed shaft, Group IIA? (Manning 1985, 165–6, and pl 78), *Find 5785, context 905, ditch F264, Phase 2b*

2 Spearhead, blade tip missing, flange-socketed shaft, Group IB (*ibid*, 162–5 and pl 77–8), *Find 5837, context 924, ditch F264, Phase 2c*

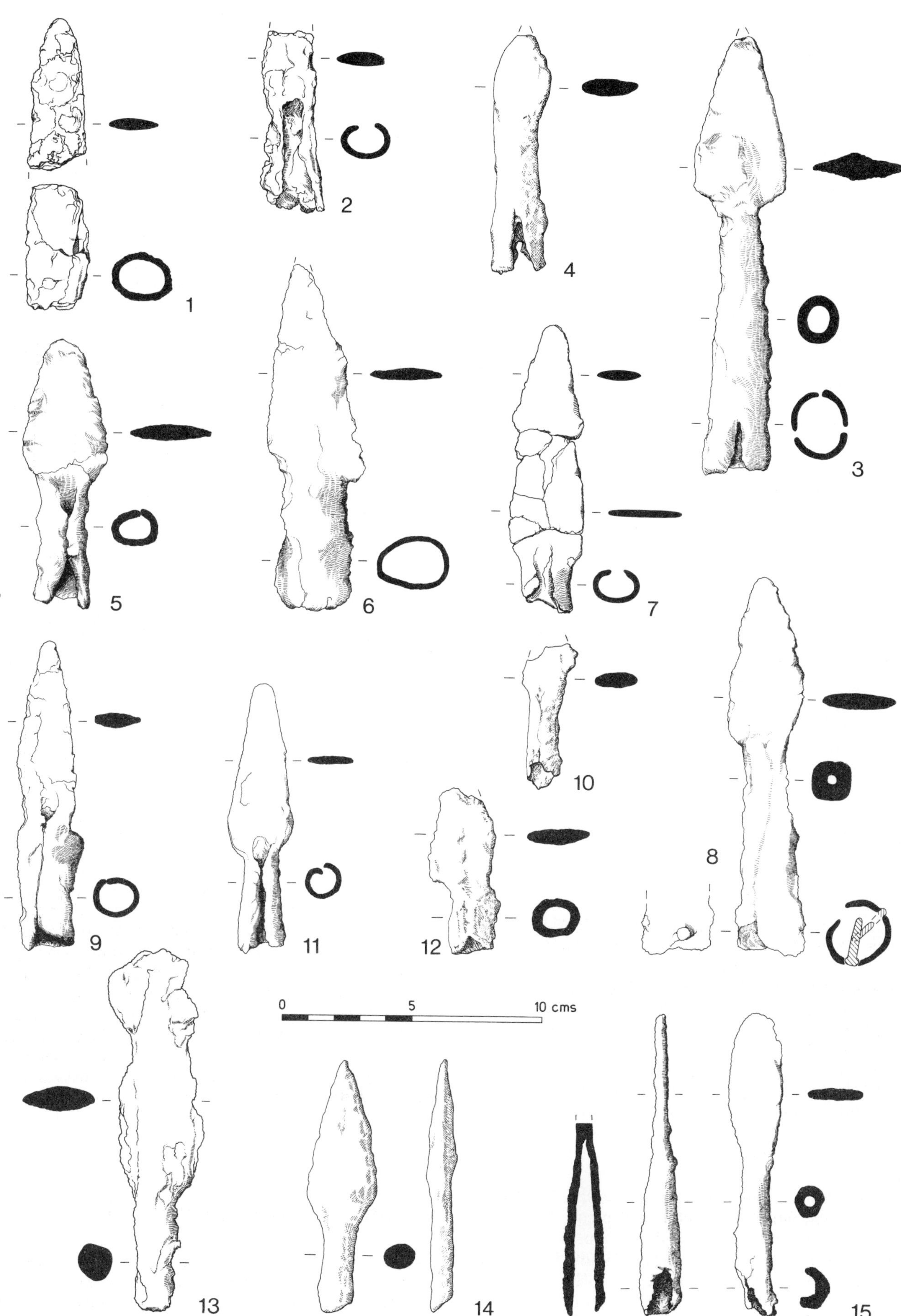

Fig 112 Spearheads of iron, scale 1:2

3 Spearhead, complete blade and socketed shaft, Group IA (*ibid*, and pl 76–7), *Find 5902, context 912, ditch F264, Phase 2c*
4 Spearhead, incomplete blade and socketed shaft, Group IA/B? (*ibid*, and pl 76–78), *Find 5579, context 733, ditch F264, Phase 2d*
5 Spearhead, complete blade and flange-socketed shaft, Group IB (*ibid*, and pl 77–8), *Find 5727, context 757, ditch F264, Phase 2d*
6 Spearhead, complete blade and socketed shaft, Group IA (*ibid*, and pl 76–7) *Find 5784, context 758, ditch F264, Phase 2d*
7 Spearhead, complete fragmented blade, flange-socketed shaft incomplete, Group IIB (*ibid*, 165–6 and pl 78–9), *Find 5859, context 733, ditch F264, Phase 2d*
8 Spearhead, complete blade and socketed shaft, the latter pierced by two fixing rivets, Group IA (*ibid*, 162–5 and pl 76–7), *Find 5866, context 758, ditch F264, Phase 2d*
9 Spearhead, complete blade and flange-socketed shaft, Group IB (*ibid*, and pl 77–8), *Find 5876, context 758, ditch F264, Phase 2d*
10 Spearhead, base of blade and flange-socketed shaft, Group IB? (*ibid*), *Find 5664, context 726, ditch F264, Phase 3a*
11 Spearhead, complete blade and flange-socketed shaft, Group IB (*ibid*), *Find 5828, context 910, ditch F264 (F251 fill), Phase 3a*
12 Spearhead, blade and flange-socketed shaft incomplete, Group IB (*ibid*), *Find 5361, context 718, ditch F264, Phase 4–5*
13 Spearhead, complete blade and socketed shaft, Group IIA (*ibid*, 165–6 and pl 78), *Find 5789, context 820A, Structure X, Phase 4b*
14 Spearhead, complete blade and socketed shaft, Group IA? (*ibid*, 162–5 and pl 76–7), *Find 2013, context 14, Structure II, Phase 6b*
15 Spearhead, complete blade and socketed shaft, Group IA (*ibid*), *Find 6329, context 0301, Structure XIX, Phase 7*

Bolt heads

all of iron

Fig 113
1 Catapult-bolt head, complete, Type IIB (*ibid*, 175–6 and pl 85), *Find 5836, context 924, ditch F264 (F251 fill), Phase 2c*
2 Catapult-bolt head, complete, Type IIB (*ibid*), *Find 5838, context 924, ditch F264 (F251 fill), Phase 2c*
3 Catapult-bolt head, complete, Type IIB (*ibid*), *Find 5857, context 931, ditch F264 (F251 fill), Phase 2c*
4 Catapult-bolt head, corroded head, Type IIB (*ibid*), *Find 5685, context 733, ditch F264, Phase 2d*
5 Catapult-bolt head, complete, Type IIB (*ibid*) *Find 5767, context 757, ditch F264, Phase 2d*
6 Catapult-bolt head, complete, Type IIB (*ibid*), *Find 5860, context 733, ditch F264, Phase 2d*
7 Catapult-bolt, head missing, Type I (*ibid*, 170–175 and pl 82–85), *Find 5763, context 258, ditch F264, Phase 3a*
8 Catapult-bolt head, complete, Type IIB (*ibid*, 175–6 and pl 85), *Find 5769, context 258, ditch F264 (F251 fill), Phase 3a*
9 Catapult-bolt head, complete, Type IIB (*ibid*), *Find 5786, context 755, fill of F756, ditch F264, Phase 3a*
10 Catapult-bolt head, complete, Type IIB (*ibid*), *Find 5816, context 755, fill of F756, ditch F264, Phase 3a*
11 Catapult-bolt head, complete, Type IIB (*ibid*), *Find 5819, context 910, ditch F264 (F251 fill), Phase 3a*
12 Catapult-bolt head, heavily corroded, Type IIB (*ibid*), *Find 5834, context 910, ditch F264 (F251 fill), Phase 3a*
13 Catapult-bolt head, complete, Type IIB (*ibid*), *Find 5844, context 910, ditch F264 (F251 fill), Phase 3a*
14 Catapult-bolt head, complete, Type IIB (*ibid*), *Find 5845, context 910, ditch F264 (F251 fill), Phase 3a*
15 Catapult-bolt head, complete, Type IIB (*ibid*), *Find 5846, context 910, ditch F264 (F251 fill), Phase 3a*
16 Catapult-bolt head, complete, Type IIB (*ibid*), *Find 5847, context 910, ditch F264 (F251 fill), Phase 3a*
17 Catapult-bolt head, complete, Type IIB (*ibid*), *Find 5856, context 726, ditch F264, Phase 3a*
18 Catapult-bolt head, complete, Type IIB (*ibid*), *Find 5873, context 726, ditch F264, Phase 3a*
19 Catapult-bolt head, complete, Type IIB (*ibid*), *Find 5776, context 901, Structure II, exterior, fill above ditch F264, Phase 3b–5*
20 Catapult-bolt head, complete, Type IIB (*ibid*), *Find 5884, context 932, fill of F933, Structure II, Phase 2–3*
21 Catapult-bolt head, distorted, Type IIB (*ibid*), *Find 1223, context 14, Structure II, Phase 6b*
22 Catapult-bolt, head missing, Type I? (*ibid*, 170–176 and pls 82–85), *Find 1829, context 201, Structure II, Phase 6a*
23 Catapult-bolt head, complete, Type II B (*ibid*, 175–6, pl 85), *Find 2433, context 277, Structure II, Phase 8*
24 Catapult-bolt, head missing, bent shaft, Type I (*ibid*, 170–75, and pls 82–85), *Find 1092, context 22, Structure I, Phase 5e (ii)*
25 Catapult-bolt, head missing, Type I or Type IIB? (*ibid*), *Find 5603, context 682, Structure X, Phase 4a*

Sword

26 Iron *spatha*, slightly tapered flat blade, tip missing, complete tang, total length 0,56m. (*ibid*, 149–152), *Find 6462, context 1100, Structure XIV, Phase 7–8*

The sword is a rare site find in Roman Britain, particularly from a non-military context. The *spatha* type, of which this appears to be an example, is usually associated with auxiliary units in the Roman army but was eventually adopted more widely from the third century onwards. Its late context in the burnt debris of Structure XIV suggests a weapon in current use at the end of the fourth, if not during the fifth century AD. Late Roman parallels are few and comparison with similar weapons from Germanic/Anglo-Saxon graves in fifth-century Britain may be more apposite.

Rings

by Justine Bayley and Ann Woodward

The excavations produced over 50 rings, all of copper alloy, which it is thought may have been made on the site and possibly used as tokens in a votive context. They were examined to investigate their mode of manufacture and analysed to see if any one alloy had been

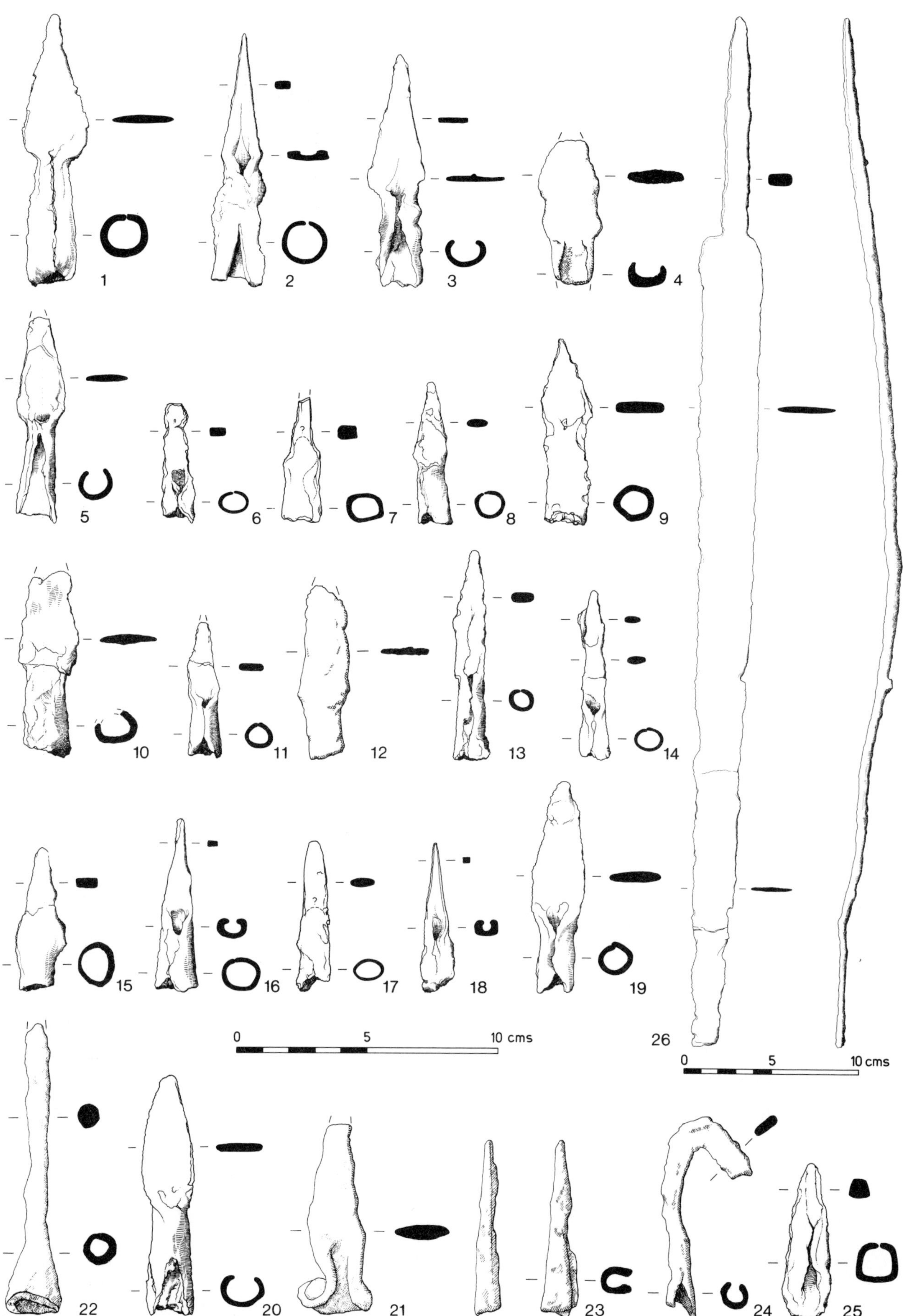

Fig 113 Bolt heads, scale 1:2, and sword of iron (no 26), scale 1:3

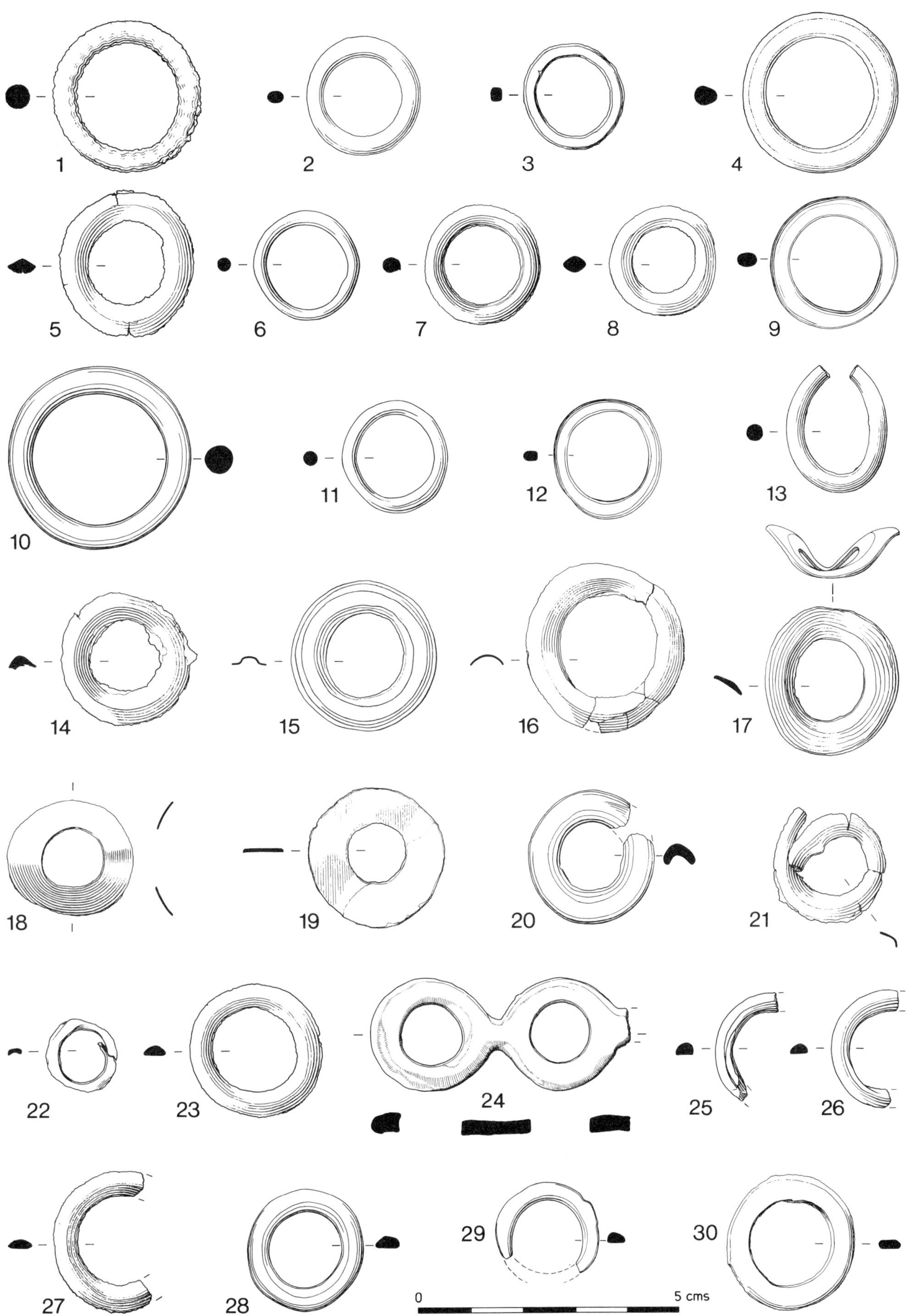

Fig 114 Copper alloy rings, scale 1:1

preferentially used. They were divided into four classes on the basis of their morphology.

Class I: Rings which were probably cast. They have varied cross sections: round, oval or ovolo, none of which could have been produced by a one piece mould so they were probably made in two piece moulds although no trace of casting flashes or other signs of their method of manufacture survive. Some are far from uniform in cross section which suggests they may have been at least partly hammered or filed to shape rather than cast. One in particular Find 4552, (Fig 114, no 12) shows evidence of extensive cold working.

Fig 114

1 Not analysed, *Find 3468, context 257, Structure II, Phase 4/5a—c*

2 Brass, *Find 7773, context 1204, Structure IX, Phase 5c*

3 Leaded bronze, *Find 1917, context 210, Structure II, Phase 5d–e*

4 Leaded brass/gunmetal, *Find 7054, context 1191, Structure XIV, Phase 5d–6b*

5 Bronze, *Find 628, context 18, Structure II, Phase 6*

6 Leaded gunmetal, *Find 1720, context 95, Structure II, Phase 6a*

7 Leaded brass/gunmetal, *Find 389, context 14, Structure II, Phase 6b*

8 Leaded gunmetal, *Find 416, context 14, Structure II, Phase 6b*

9 Leaded bronze, *Find 4663b, context 484, Structure VII, Phase 7a*

10 Leaded brass/gunmetal, *Find 4830, context 601, Structure XIX, Phase 7a*

11 Leaded brass/gunmetal, *Find 100, context 1, Phase 8*

12 Gunmetal, *Find 4552, context 13, over bank XIX, Phase 8*

13 Gunmetal wire or rod, *Find 6046, context 0263, over bank XIX, Phase 8*

Class II: Rings made from sheet metal which was cut and shaped (perhaps stamped in a die) and then filled with lead or lead-tin solder to give them weight and to help them retain their form. The two thin, washer like, perforated discs, Finds 1791 and 7853 (Fig 114, nos 18 and 19) may be blanks from which these rings were made. Find 1057 (Fig 114, no 15) has a rounded cross section rather than the typical triangular one and may be only part manufactured, a suggestion which is supported by its lack of filling.

14 Brass, *Find 7818, context 1204, Structure IX, Phase 5c*

15 Brass, *Find 1057, context 22, over Structure I, Phase 5e(ii)*

16 Bronze, *Find 3552, context 208, Structure II, Phase 5d–e*

17 Brass, *Find 288, context 12, Structure II, Phase 6b*

18 Bronze, *Find 1791, context 12, Structure II, Phase 6b*

19 Bronze, *Find 7853, context 0410, Structure XIX, Phase 7a*

20 Leaded bronze/gunmetal, *Find 4621, context 604, Structure XIX, Phase 7a*

21 Brass, *Find 21, context 1, Phase 8*

22 Sheet metal offcut of brass, *Find 206, context 1, Phase 8*

Classes III and IV: These rings were cast, most probably in open (one piece) moulds and were finished by filing the backs to flatten the worst of the irregularities produced by this method of manufacture. This shows particularly well on Find 1486 (Fig 115, no 2) but is noticeable on many other pieces too. Two rings, Finds 287, and 3737 (Fig 115, nos 5 and 16) retain traces of the tongues of metal that connected them to an adjoining ring, showing that they were cast in multiples, and one piece, Find 740 (Fig 114, no 24) is two rings joined in this way – and with a further tongue, suggesting this was the end part of a longer strip. Most of these rings are not very well or carefully finished; they appear to have been crudely mass produced. These rings have either a D-shaped or rectangular cross section (Class III) or a triangular section (Class IV) and would only have looked attractive from the front/top. Neither type would stand close examination or handling; they must have been made to be seen from a distance.

Class III

23 Leaded bronze/gunmetal, *Find 2205, context 329, Structure IV, Phase 4a*

24 Gunmetal(?), *Find 740, context 32, over Structure I, Phase 5e(ii)*

25 Gunmetal, *Find 542, context 17, Structure II, Phase 6*

26 Leaded gunmetal, *Find 988, context 17, Structure II, Phase 6*

27 Bronze/gunmetal, *Find 185, context 1, Phase 8*

28 Gunmetal, *Find 3764, context 1, Phase 8*

29 Gunmetal, *Find 3808, context 1, Phase 8*

30 Gunmetal, *Find 6318, context 0288, Phase 8*

Class IV

Fig 115

1 Gunmetal(?), *Find 5602, context 805, ditch F816, Phase 3c*

2 Bronze/gunmetal, *Find 1486, context 52, Structure II, Phase 6a*

3 Bronze, *Find 1595, context 52, Structure II, Phase 6a*

4 Leaded gunmetal, *Find 222, context 2, Structure II, Phase 6b*

5 Brass/gunmetal, *Find 287, context 12, Structure II, Phase 6b*

6 Bronze/gunmetal, *Find 377, context 12, Structure II, Phase 6b*

7 Leaded bronze, *Find 1430, context 2, Structure II, Phase 6b*

8 Leaded bronze/gunmetal, *Find 1542, context 2, Structure II, Phase 6b*

9 Bronze/gunmetal, *Find 3364, context 14, Structure II, Phase 6b*

10 Leaded bronze, *Find 4780, context 601, Structure XIX, Phase 7a*

11 Gunmetal, *Find 4859, context 602, Structure XIX, Phase 7a*

12 Bronze/gunmetal, *Find 4885, context 602, Structure XIX, Phase 7a*

13 Leaded gunmetal, *Find 4900, context 602, Structure XIX, Phase 7a*

14 Bronze, *Find 6771, context 0409, Structure XIX, Phase 7a*

15 Brass/gunmetal, *Find 39, context 1, Phase 8*

16 Brass, *Find 3737, context 1, Phase 8*

17 Gunmetal, *Find 4068, context 600, over bank XIX, Phase 8*

18 Gunmetal, *Find 4297, context 1, Phase 8*

19 Bronze/gunmetal, *Find 4496,context 600, Phase 8*

20 Leaded gunmetal, *Find 6021, context 0237, Phase 8*

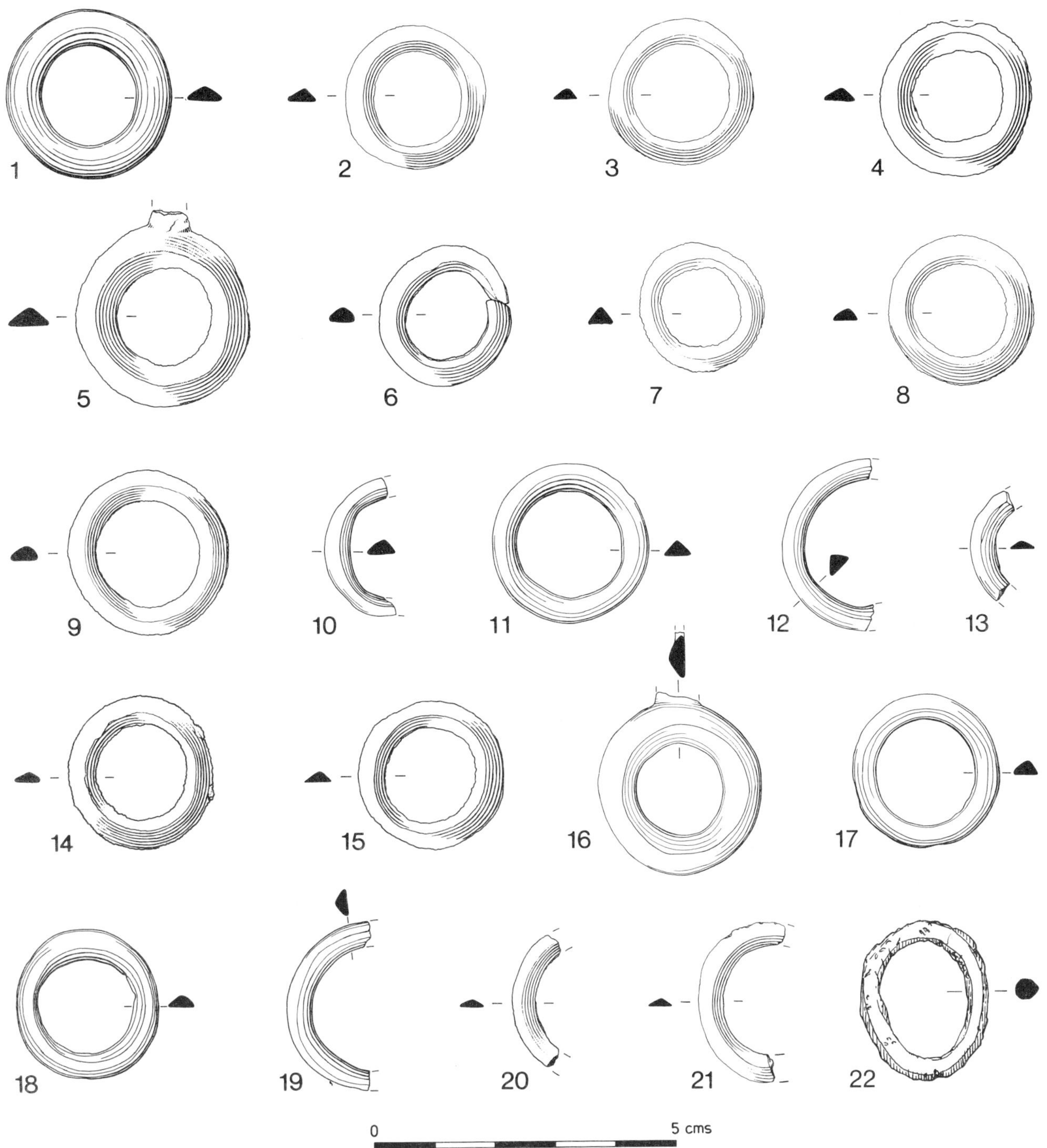

Fig 115 Copper alloy rings, scale 1:1

21 Gunmetal, *Find 6050, context 0232, Phase 8*
not illustrated
Leaded bronze/gunmetal, Class I, *Find 689, con- text 13, over Structure XIX, Phase 8*
Bronze, Class II, *Find 1831, context 12, Structure II, Phase 6b*
Brass, Class II, *Find 6808, context 0410, Structure XIX, Phase 7*
Leaded bronze, Class III/IV, *Find 2553, context 277, over Structure II, Phase 8*

Ring of antler
22 A roughly ovoid ring with rough surfaces (probably unfinished) and a subcircular cross section, ?deer antler. It bears some morphological resemblance to the crudely executed copper alloy rings described above, *Find 2719, context 160, Structure I, Phase 5a–d*

Dimensions of the rings

External and internal diameters and the maximum thickness of all measurable rings are listed in the archive and in fiche. A plot of the incidence of maximum diameters (Fig 116) shows some interesting patterns. The more complex and variable cast rings of Class I show the greatest size range. By contrast the Class II sheet rings are more restricted in size. The two classes of cast rings manufactured in open moulds, Classes III

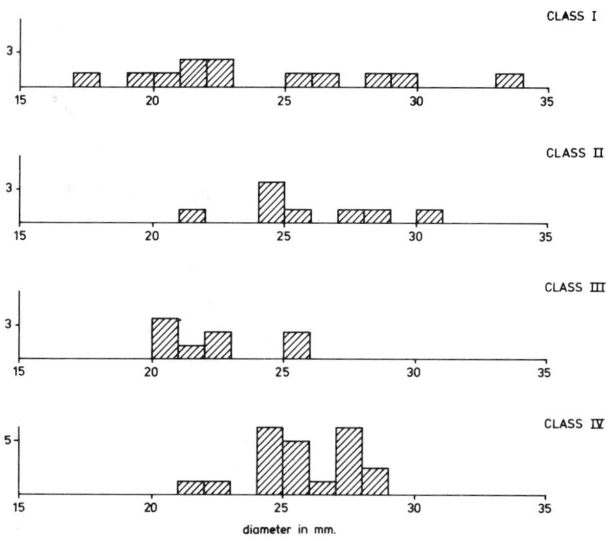

Fig 116 Dimensions of flat copper alloy rings

and IV, were defined on the basis of the shape of their cross sections (D-shaped or rectangular and triangular respectively). It can be seen that these classes are also separated to a large extent by their size ranges, Class III with a peak in the 20 to 23 mm range and Class IV examples tending towards diameters in excess of 24mm.

Analysis

The analytical results have been incorporated in the catalogue above, and summary tables are given in fiche. The lead content of the leaded rings is in some cases considerably higher than for the leaded bracelets (see chapter 9 below). Nearly two-thirds of the rings are of mixed alloys, ie they contain significant amounts of both tin and zinc, as compared with under a quarter of the bracelets. The Class II sheet metal rings are exceptions in being either brass or bronze. These two metals would have been different colours when well polished so it is interesting to speculate on whether they had different values or whether this variation in appearance was expected and accepted as inevitable. The rings that were cast, Classes I, III and IV, have very varied compositions in both the proportion of tin to zinc and the lead content. This suggests that the metal was not carefully selected but that anything that came to hand was used. The lack of precision and attention to detail is also reflected in the finish of the rings, some of which are very crudely executed. When method of manufacture, alloy use and final appearance are considered together, the overall impression is one of cheap mass production and not of craftsmanship of a high standard. These rings cannot have been valuable items and may well have served as tokens of some sort though, as mentioned above, they were most probably intended to be seen rather than handled. Classes III and IV and probably Class II rings were almost certainly being made on the site; the unfinished examples mentioned above are good evidence for this. These types of rings are not normally found in domestic contexts and so it is reasonable to relate them to the ritual use of this site. Type I rings are found on other temple sites, eg Harlow (France and Gobel 1985, 87–88, fig 45, 90–95) and so were probably items in normal circulation which may have had the same generalised function here or may have been used in the same way as the rings of Classes II to IV.

Following this analysis, it was felt that Find 628 (Fig 114, no 5) would be better classified as of Class II, and Finds 288 and 4621 (Fig 114, nos 17 and 20) as Class III/IV. This applies particularly to Find 4621 as it is made from a leaded alloy, rather than from the brass or bronze typical of Class II.

Chronology

When the distribution of alloys and types is considered relative to the phasing of the contexts that produced the rings, no clear pattern emerges (Table 4, fiche). The two early rings (Phases 3 and 4) are of Classes III and IV and eight rings of almost all types come from Phase 5. The majority however are Phase 6 and later and seem to concentrate in the area of Structure II (the temple), and, to a lesser extent, in the bank material of Phase 7, Structure XIX.

Table 4: The occurrence of copper alloy rings by phase

Phase	*3c*	*4*	*5*	*6*	*7*	*8*	*total*
Class I	-	-	4	4	2	3	12
Class II	-	-	3	3	2	2	10
Class III	-	1	1	2	-	4	8
Class IV	1	-	-	8	5	7	21
total	1	1	8	17	9	16	52

Discussion

Dr Henig, in his discussion of the finger rings (chapter 9), has highlighted the occurrence of some flimsy examples which may have been bought as trinkets on the temple site, and further notes a possible connection with the silver rings sometimes associated with depictions of Mercury. Alternatively, the sheet and cast rings may have served to represent 'ring money', tokens used as offerings to Mercury in his role as the patron for commerce and marketing.

Rings of Classes II, III and IV are not known from other temple sites in Britain, although as mentioned above a group of varied copper alloy rings, roughly equivalent to our Class I, was found at Harlow, Essex (*ibid*). Individual rings at the Harlow temple were recovered from contexts belonging to Periods I, V and VI, spanning the whole Roman period. The only close parallels for the cast rings of Classes III and IV that have been identified are finds from Alésia in France, from a deposit next to a temple building (Rabeisen and Menu 1985, 160–161) and, as Dr Henig points out, from the *favissa* of a Romano-Celtic temple at Mesnil de Baron-sur-Odon (Calvados) in Gaul (Bertin 1977, 81–2 and fig 13).

Miniature pots

A total of 94 miniature pots were found, although many were in a fragmentary and highly abraded state. Thirty-four complete or almost complete examples are illustrated in Figs 117 to 119 and a further twelve are

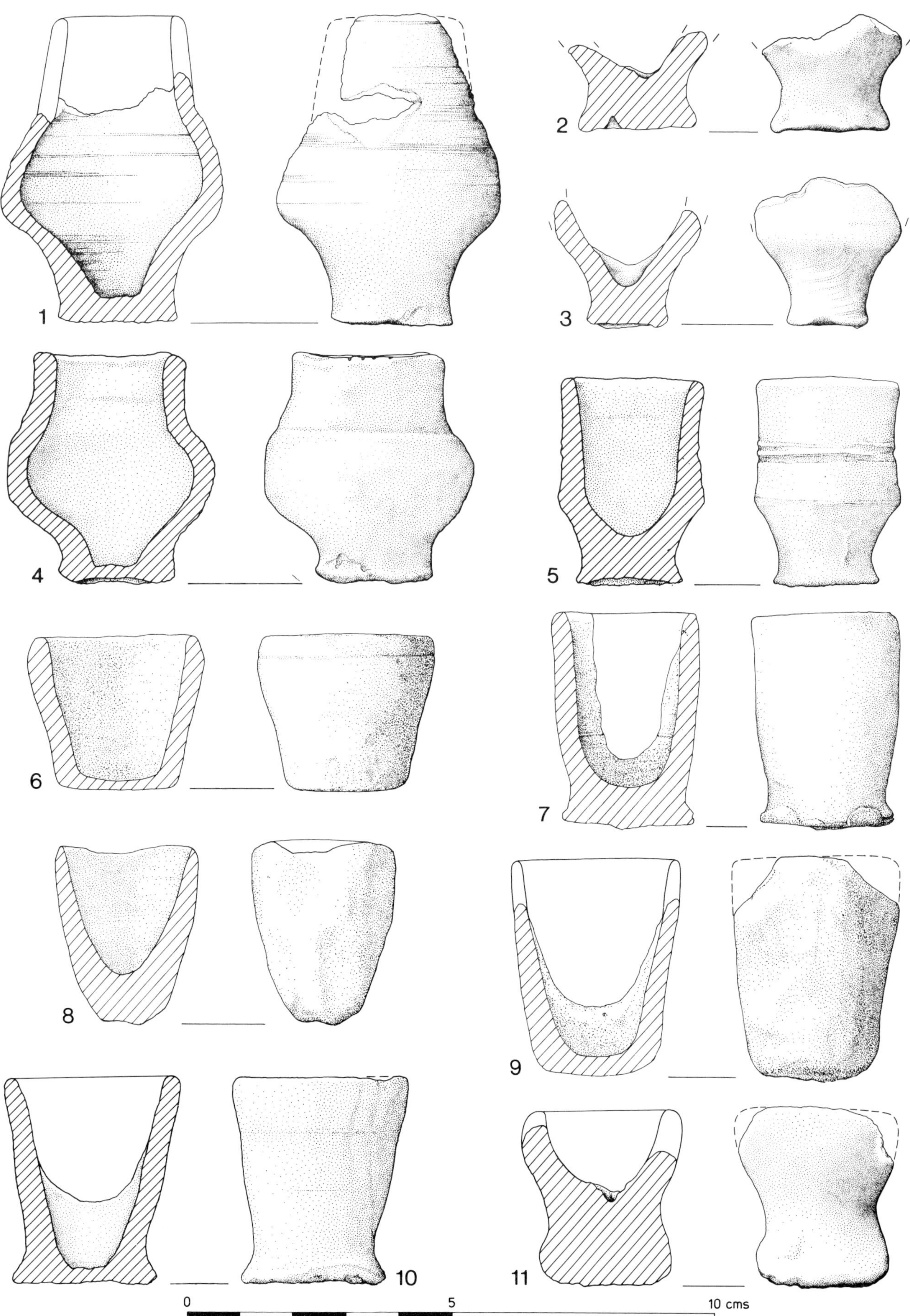

Fig 117 Miniature clay pots of Classes I (nos 1–5), II (nos 6–10) and III (no 11), scale 1:1

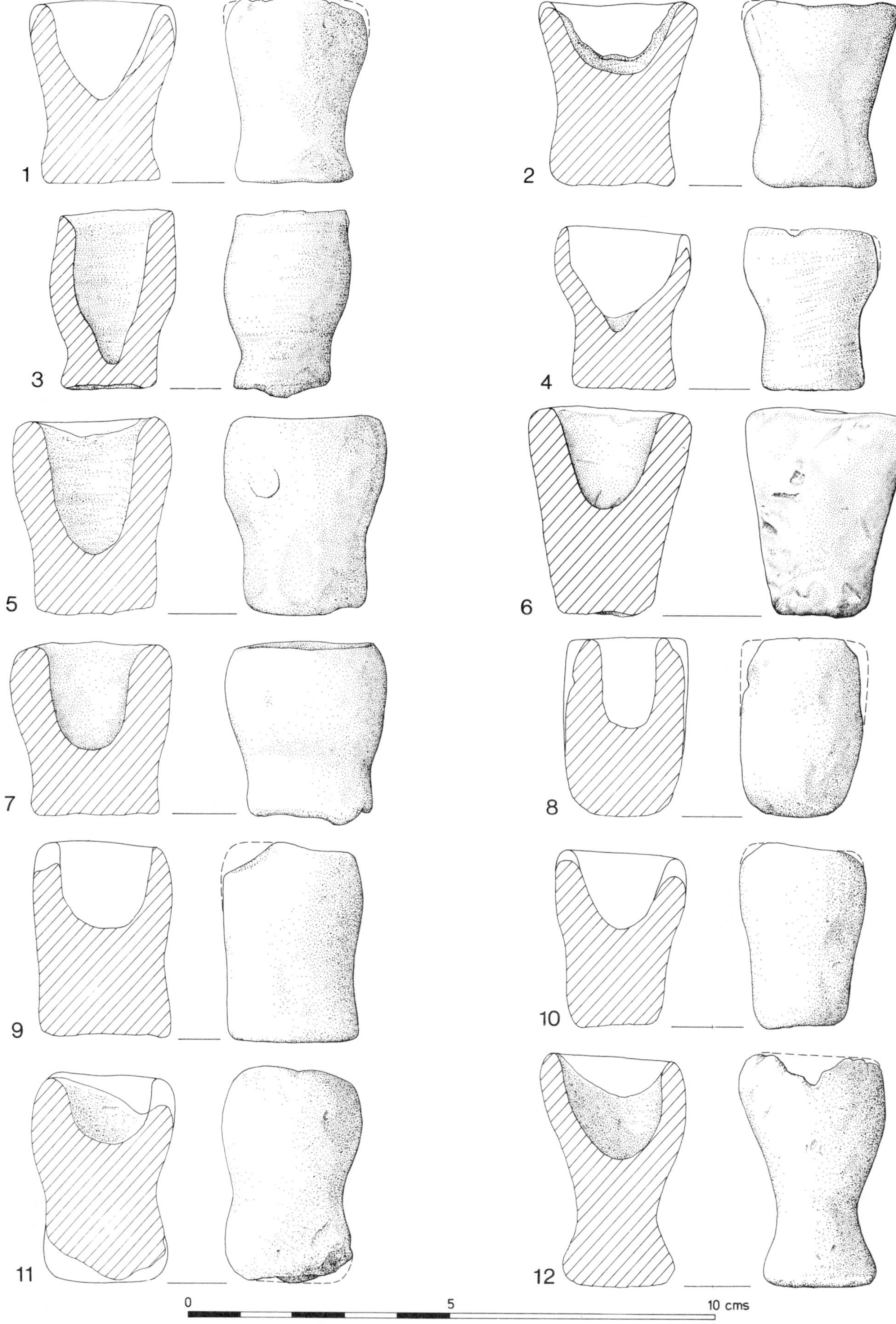

Fig 118 Miniature clay pots of Classes III (nos 1–5), IV (nos 6–11) and V (nos 11–12), scale 1:1

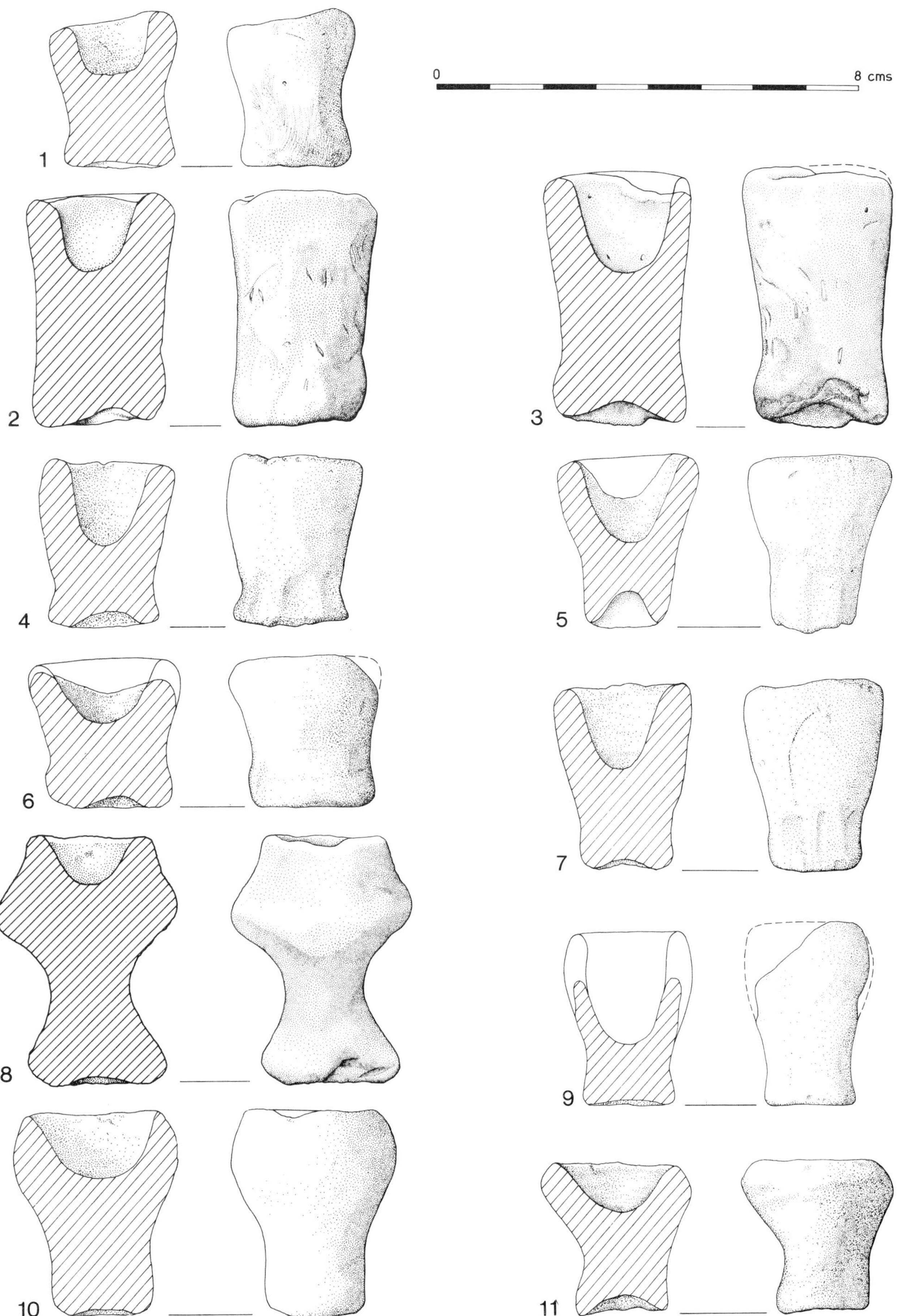

Fig 119 Miniature clay pots of Classes V (no 1), VI (nos 2–7) and VII (nos 8–11), scale 1:1

illustrated in the fiche section. As the vessels are often irregular in form each drawing shows a complete external view together with a full cross-section and where possible one view of the interior surface. Most were made by hand in a very soft, micaceous sandy, semi-oxidised fabric which does not equate closely with any of the coarse pottery type fabrics identified from the site. A few eg Finds 0117, 2767, 3236, 3237, 6637 (Fig 117, nos 1, 4, 6, 7, and 10) were of a harder and more reduced sandy matrix, approximating more closely to pottery fabric type 16 (see chapter 11), these examples may also have been thrown. No petrological analysis of these fabrics has been undertaken. The style of the vessels and the material used suggest a very local source and origin of manufacture. The vessels were mainly simple 'thumb pots' but had been formed into a variety of shapes. This variation has allowed the formulation of a classification into seven groups, as follows:

Class I: miniature copies of standard full-size vessel forms

Fig 117

1 *Find 0117, context TF5, Structure I, Phase 5e(ii)*
2 *Find 0125, context TF5, Structure I, Phase 5e(ii)*
3 *Find 0144, context TF5, Structure I, Phase 5e(ii)*
4 *Find 2767, context 162, fill of F158, over Structure I, Phase 5e(ii)*
5 *Find 2984, context 162, fill of F158, over Structure I, Phase 5e(ii)*

Class II: deep, straight sided cup with flat base

6 *Find 3236, context 346, Structure IV, Phase 5d*
7 *Find 3237, context 346, Structure IV, Phase 5d*
8 *Find 1937, context 210, Structure II, Phase 5d-e*
9 *Find 1052, context 20, over Structure IX, Phase 7*
10 *Find 6637, context 1101, over Structure XIV, Phase 7–8*

Class III: deep cup, slightly waisted, with deep expanded base

11 *Find 0115, context TF5, Structure I, Phase 5e(ii)*

Fig 118

1 *Find 2377, context 332, Structure IV, Phase 4b*
2 *Find 1205, context 70, Structure I, Phase 5e(i)*
3 *Find 1059, context 20, over Structure IX, Phase 7*
4 *Find 932, context 20, over Structure IX, Phase 7*
5 *Find 2179, context 1, Phase 8*

Class IV: shallow cup, straight sided, with deep cylindrical base

6 *Find 0127, context TF5, Structure I, Phase 5e(ii)*
7 *Find 3035, context 332, Structure IV, Phase 4b*
8 *Find 3269, context 369, Structure IV, Phase 4b*
9 *Find 3682, context 187, Structure I, Phase 5e (ii)*
10 *Find 4238, context 600, over Structure XIX, Phase 8*

Class V: shallow cup, slightly waisted, with deep expanded base

11 *Find 3008, context 332, Structure IV, Phase 4b*
12 *Find 2883, context 332, Structure IV, Phase 4b*

Fig 119

1 *Find 1433, context 300, over Structure IV, Phase 6b*

Class VI: shallow cup, slightly waisted, with indented expanded base

2 *Find 0128, context TF5, Structure I, Phase 5e (ii)*
3 *Find 0130, context TF5, Structure I, Phase 5e (ii)*
4 *Find 2181, context 128, Structure I, Phase 5a-d*
5 *Find 2346, context 106, Structure I, Phase 5e (i)*

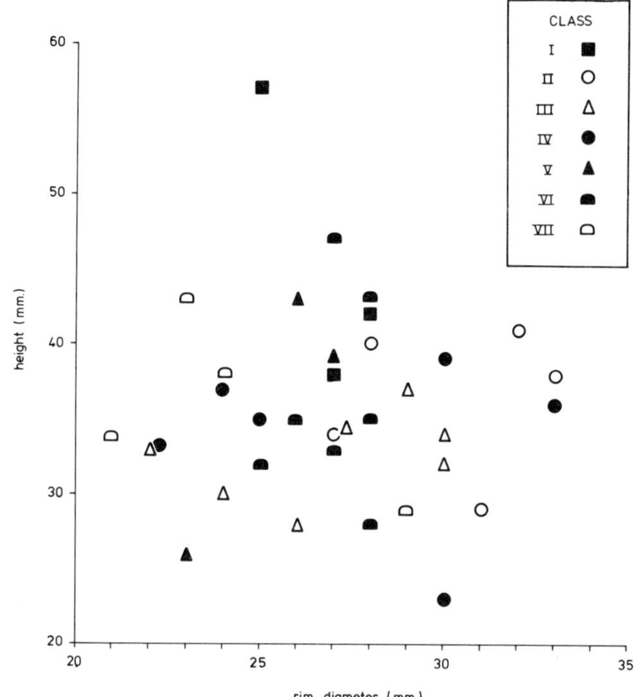

Fig 120 Dimensions of miniature clay pots

6 *Find 2735, context 136, Structure I, Phase 5e (ii)*
7 *Find 1177, context 20, over Structure IX, Phase 7*

Class VII: shallow cup, very waisted, indented base

8 *Find 2688, context 140, Structure I, Phase 5e (i)*
9 *Find 3661, context 187, Structure I, Phase 5e (ii)*
10 *Find 1860, context 33, southern courtyard, Phase 4–6*
11 *Find 2277, context 341, over Structure III, Phase 6–7*

An analysis of the sizes of the various classes of vessel (see Fig 120) indicates no clear separations. Thus there is no evidence on the basis of size, or indeed of shape, for suggesting any variations in function for the different classes or to imply that different classes may have been designed to contain differing commodities.

Miniature pots occurred in contexts dating from Phases 4 to 8, but there was a marked concentration of finds in Phases 4 and 5, and, in particular, Phase 5e (see Table 5). This strongly suggests that, while miniature pots were an active component of the assemblage associated with the temple complex in its major phases of use, they were no longer used in connection with the modified temple building, Structure II, of Phase 6. A further analysis of the occurrence of the vessel classes through time (in the archive) showed no clear patterning of any kind. Observations on the possible function of such miniature pots in the context of the rituals performed at the temple have been made by Dr Henig (see chapter 6).

Table 5: The occurrence of miniature clay vessels by phase

Phase	*4b*	*5a–d*	*5e(i)*	*5e(ii)*	*5d–e*	*6b*	*7a*	*7 & 8*	*total*
Structure I	-	1	9	30	-	-	-	-	40
Structure II	-	-	-	-	3	-	-	-	3
Structure IV	9	2	-	-	-	3	-	-	14
Structure XIX	-	-	-	-	-	-	1	-	1
various	-	-	-	-	-	-	-	36	36
total	9	3	9	30	3	3	1	36	94

Phase 7 & 8 material is residual

The wide distribution of miniature pots in Roman Britain has been alluded to by Green (1976) and Henig (1984, 149) and their ritual connotation seems to be confirmed by finds on many temple sites. However, any detailed discussion of their form, variation and chronology is hampered by the lack of publication of many of the examples. Those illustrated by Green, from Verulamium and Island Thorns, Hampshire (Green 1976, pl xxviii, a and b) and some at least of the group from the triangular temple at Verulamium (Wheeler and Wheeler 1936, 191–2, pl lix, 2–4; Henig, 151, pl 72) seem to imitate standard pottery forms, and thus would equate to Class I at Uley. The larger assemblage from Coleshill, Warwickshire includes further true miniatures, but also simpler waisted and pedestal based forms, similar to the other classes found at Uley (Booth forthcoming). One of the simpler forms at Coleshill has been matched by Booth to a miniature cup from excavations at Mancetter (O'Neil 1928, no 38), and he suggests a local origin for the temple group.

Other baked clay vessels

The fragments described below form a distinctive group of material characterised by a fine, sandy, ox-

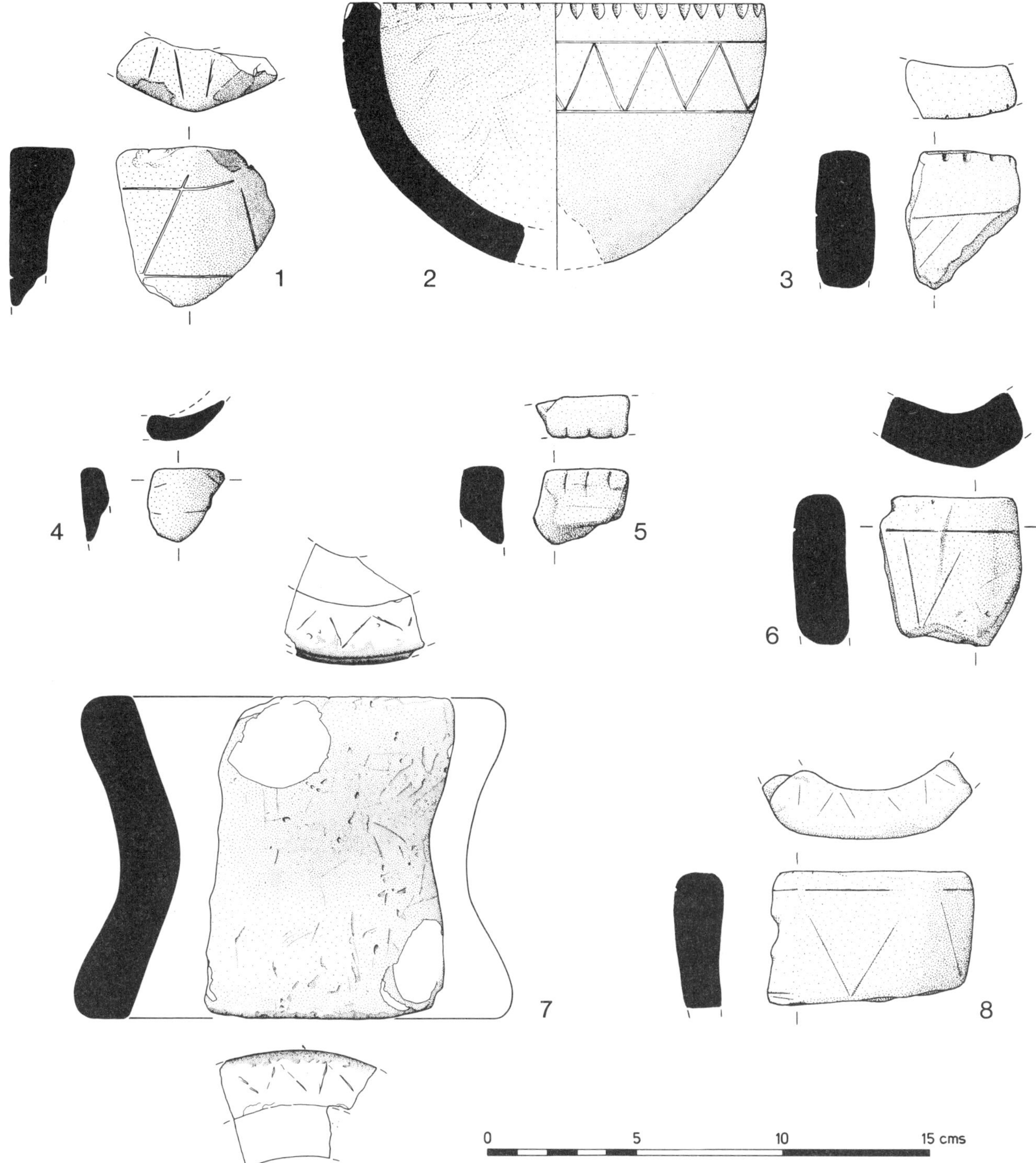

Fig 121 Other baked clay vessels, scale 1:2

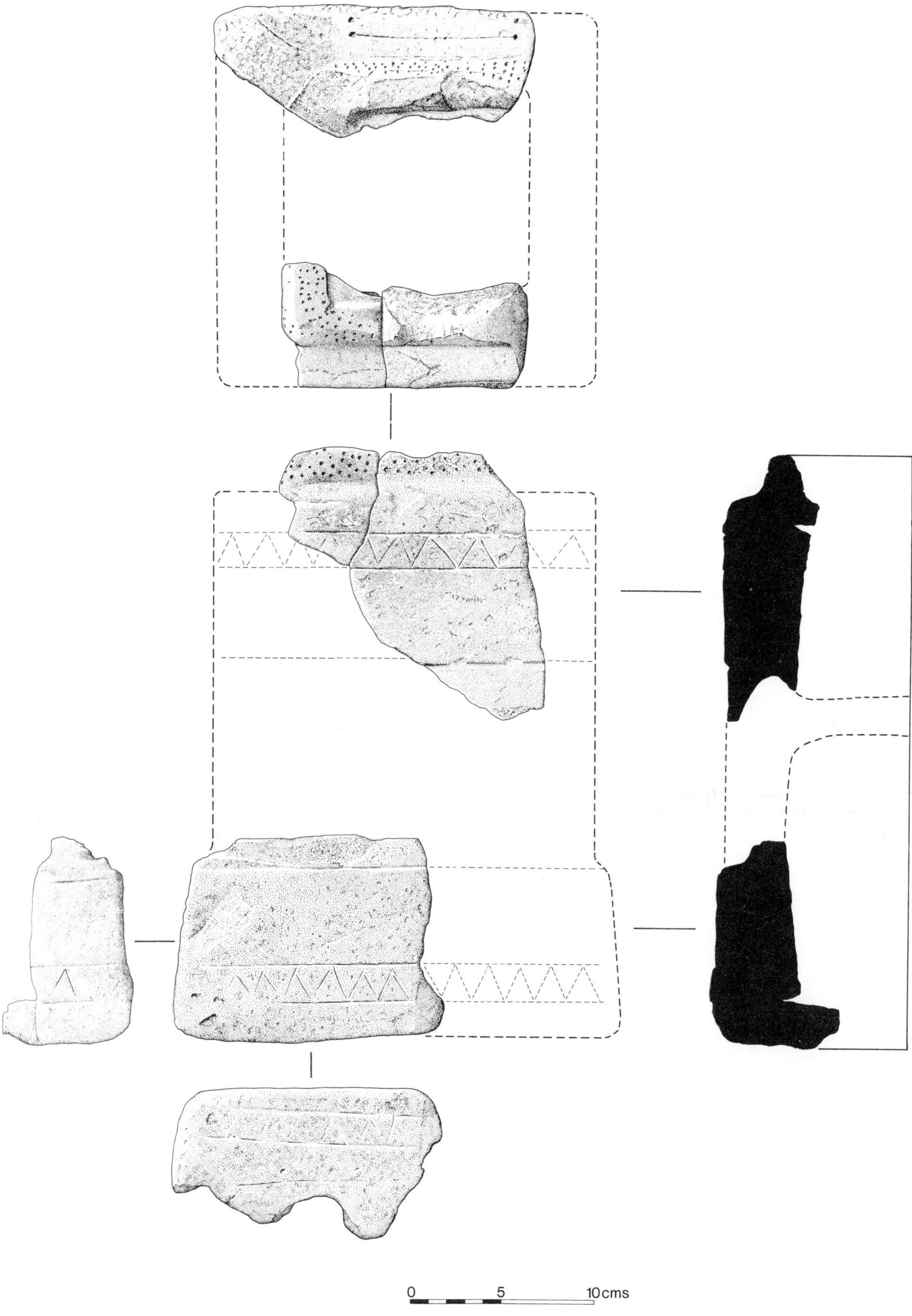

Fig 122 Ceramic 'altar' fragments: a reconstruction, scale 1:3

idised fabric similar to that employed in the manufacture of ceramic roof tiles. At least four vessels are represented, Find 5292 (Fig 121, no 2); Finds 4568, and 5194 (Fig 121, nos 3 and 5); Finds 8491, 5653, and 4489 (Fig 121, nos 1, 6 and 8); and Fig 121, no 7, from Context 300. The two reconstructed profiles (Fig 121, nos 2 and 7) provide evidence for a round based container and a hollow support that may have fitted together as a set. The fabric is similar to that of the incense burner or altar, Find 3687 (Fig 122) and a similar ritual function might be suggested for these smaller unusual vessels. This hypothesis is strengthened by comparing them to the terracotta objects found on the temple site at Nettleton, Wiltshire, which were similarly decorated with edge notching (Wedlake 1982, fig 59). These were described as a possible lamp and a series of flanges from lamp or incense burner chimneys by Professor Toynbee. However, the occurrence of items very similar to the Uley hollow support at the principally domestic sites of Kingscote (Swain 1977, 17, fig 12) and Frocester Court (Gracie 1970, 39, fig 6, 1 and 2), both situated very close to Uley, shows that their use was not restricted to the context of religious buildings.

Fig 121

1 Rim sherd from a polygonal vessel, decorated externally and on the top of the rim with incised lines, *Find 8491, context 1191, Structure XIV, Phase 7*

2 Almost complete circular round bottomed vessel, with decoration, comprising a single incised chevron between two incised lines, and with a row of nicks on the outer edge of the flat rim, *Find 5292, context 622, Structure IX, Phase 5c*

3 Flat rim sherd, worn, with nicks on the outer rim edge and incised geometric decoration below, *Find 4568, context 603, Structure XIX, Phase 7*

4 Very abraded rim fragment from a polygonal vessel, decorated on the exterior with incised diagonal lines, *Find 5077, context 1, Phase 8*

5 Flat rim sherd, with sharp incised nick decoration on the outer margin, *Find 5194, context 604, Structure XIX, Phase 7*

6 Rim sherd with a rough incised chevron below a horizontal line on the exterior, *Find 5653, context 602, Structure XIX, Phase 7*

7 Waisted hollow vessel fragment, with an incised chevron on the top of the rim, *Context 300, Structure IV, Phase 6b*

8 Flat rim from polygonal vessel with incised chevron on top of rim and another chevron below a horizontal line on the exterior *Find 4489, context 1, Phase 8*

Ceramic 'altar'

by Martin Henig

Fig 122

This object, approximately square in cross section, and made of a fine orange fired clay, is in the form of a miniature altar, reconstructed dimensions: height 305mm, length of side at base 250mm. On its upper face is a raised moulding also rectangular and demarcating the *focus*. Around the side at the top is a zigzag incision between parallel lines; below this is another single groove.

Towards the base the 'altar' is flared outwards and is again ornamented with a zigzag, as is the underside also, which must thus on some occasions have been visible (ie when the piece was picked up), *Find 3412, context 17, Structure II, Phase 6, and Find 3687, context 451, Structure VII, Phase 6–7a*

Parallels for this assuredly votive object may be sought amongst what are sometimes called 'miniature altars' (though note that these may sometimes have functioned other than as receptacles for libations: Green 1978, pl 124 (a little stone 'altar' from Piercebridge) looks like a candlestick. Low ceramic stands from Crookhorn, Hants (Henig 1989) and Colliton Park, Dorchester, Dorset (publication forthcoming) with multiple depressions in the upper face look like offering stands for first-fruits corresponding to the Greek *kernos*).

The closest parallels to this example, despite their much wider cup-like openings, are two fired clay incense burners dedicated to Coventina by Gabinius Saturninus and found in her sacred well at Carrawburgh (Allason-Jones and McKay 1985, 41–6, nos 142 and 143, Henig 1984; 149 and 152, pl 73).

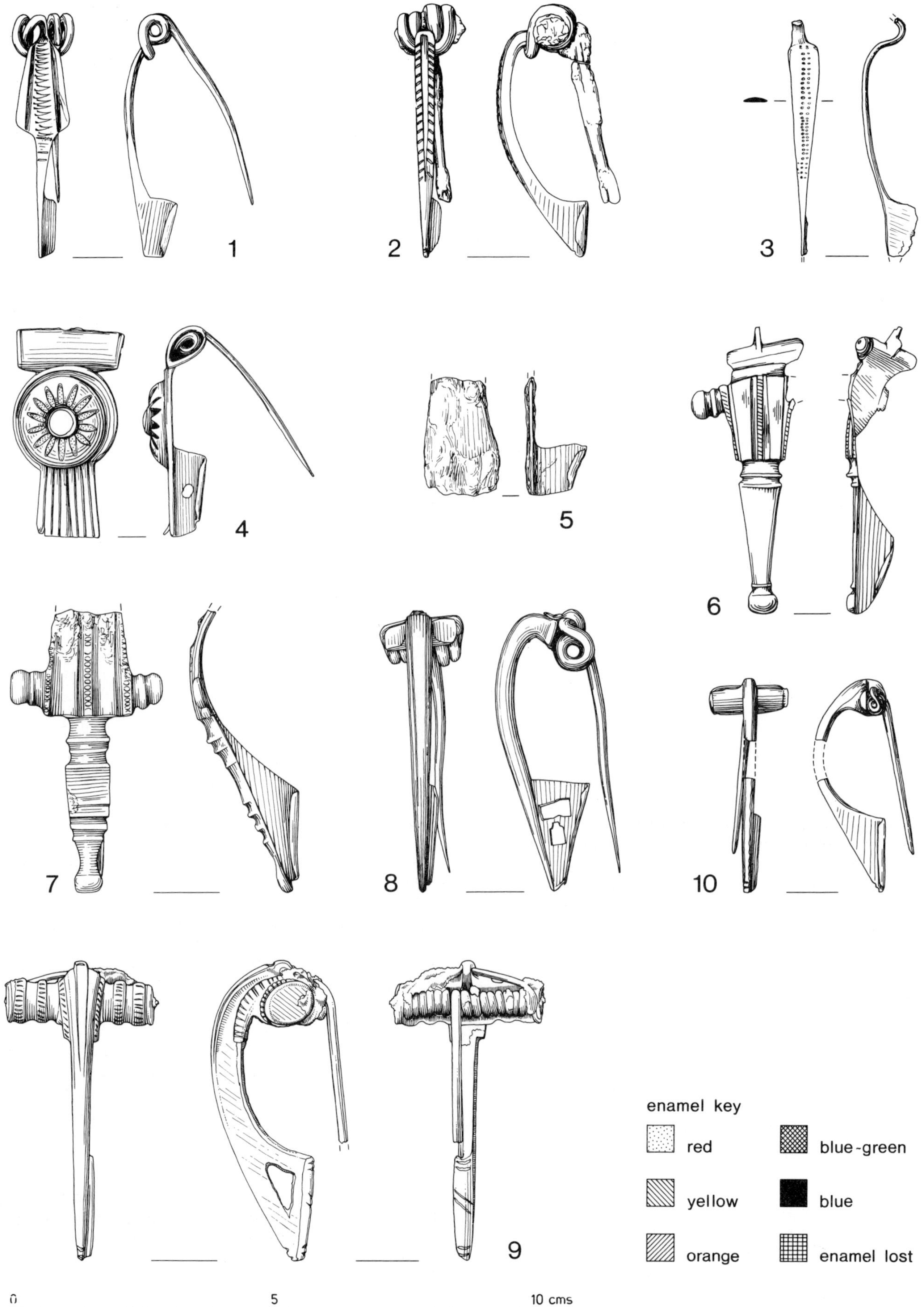

Fig 123 Brooches of copper alloy and enamel: first-century AD types, scale 1:1

9 Personal objects: jewellery and equipment

Brooches of copper alloy

by Sarnia Butcher

(descriptions of enamel and metal analysis by Justine Bayley)

Nauheim-derivative

The general type is common in the first century AD. It is most abundant in the southern part of Britain but a few have been found in the areas of the north reached by the Romans in the Flavian period, eg Aldborough, Yorkshire (in the site museum); Newstead (Curle 1911, 318, pl lxxxv, 1). So far no pattern can be discerned in the distribution: it occurs in both native settlements and Roman forts.

The type is found on sites occupied in the first half of the first century and not later (eg Hod Hill (Brailsford 1962, C16–26) but is also found in contexts of the period *c* AD 50–80, for example Verulamium, (Frere 1972, 114, no 2) and Fishbourne, (Cunliffe 1971, 100). These three examples are therefore most likely to date from *c* AD 40–80; they share the rather flat profile and solid catchplate which are thought to be later characteristics. Each has a different type of decoration, none of which is common but can be paralleled as follows: Find 3717 (Fig 123, no 1,) at Hayling Island, Hants, (Soffe forthcoming, no 2303); Find 6062 (Fig 123, no 3) at Hod Hill (Brailsford 1962, C22 and C25), and at Scole (Mackreth 1977, fig 54.6).

Fig 123

1 Bronze; finely-made and well preserved, spring of four turns, upper bow expands to broad plate bearing rocker-tracer decoration, catchplate plain, angular, *Find 3717, context 536, ditch F179, Phase 3b*

2 Brass; coarser details than no 1 above, spring of four turns, bow of sharply rectangular section with longitudinal central groove, cross-knurled, catchplate continuous with bow, *Find 3605, context 255, ditch F264, Phase 3a–5*

3 Bronze/gunmetal; spring missing, profile slightly recurved, two rows of punched dots on upper bow, *Find 6062, context 1, fieldwalking*

Rosette type

A few brooches of this type are known from Britain, chiefly from the south-eastern area associated with 'Belgic' contacts with the Romans. It is more common on the continent, *cf* Ettlinger 1973, 85 and Dollfuss 1973, nos 203–58.

The dating to the first half of the first century AD is clearly established by finds at Hod Hill (Brailsford 1962, C27), King Harry Lane St Albans (Stead and Rigby 1989, 94, fig 49, no G1), Camulodunum (Hawkes and Hull 1947, 316, no 81) and Sheepen (Niblett 1985, 116, no 22).

4 Brass; this is Camulodunum type XI (Hawkes and Hull 1947, 316) with flat plate-like 'bow' bearing a separate, riveted disc incorporating a small spot of red enamel, and with a cylindrical cover for the spring. None of the numerous examples from Normandy catalogued by Dollfuss (1973) has the same disc pattern as this example, but it is perhaps significant that he considers the type to be common on cult sites and in cremations, where, since they are unburnt, he suggests they were votive, *Find 5839, context 926, pit F251, Phase 2c*

Strip-bow

5 Bronze, tinned; the lower bow and catchplate only of a strip-bow brooch with a short catch, very corroded. The form of the bow (flat, broad, with traces of fluting) and the catchplate suggest that this was a brooch of a type found at several first-century sites in southern Britain eg Bagendon (Clifford 1961, 183, no 60a, fig 36, no 1)), Iwerne (Hawkes 1947, fig 9, no 4), and Hod Hill (Brailsford 1962, fig 7, C40–C42), *Find 5732, context 835, pit F836, Phase 2a–d*

Hod Hill type

Two Hod Hill brooches, with variants of the typical upper bow panel of decoration with side lugs. Although this is a common type it is very seldom that close parallels can be found for a particular combination of decorative details. Fairly similar brooches can be quoted as follows: Find 77 (Fig 123, no 6), Sheepen, Colchester, from period IV, AD 48–61 (Niblett 1985, no 36); Maiden Castle (Wheeler 1943, 262, no 28); Vindonissa (Ettlinger 1973, Taf 11.4); Find 5723 (Fig 123, no 7), Hod Hill (Brailsford 1962, C70, 9), Hùfingen (Rieckhoff 1975, Taf 4, 41).

The type as a whole is common in pre-Flavian contexts in Britain, Gaul and Germany.

6 Brass, tinned; bent but well preserved. The pin is hinged in a narrow (?cast) tube at the head. A broad panel on the upper bow has alternately broad and narrow longitudinal ribs; the central and outer ribs are engraved (probably cast) with fine cross hatching. There are two cross-mouldings at the waist and the lower bow is plain, tapering towards the foot, which is a broad flat moulding. The plain long catchplate is central, *Find 77, context 1, Phase 8*

7 Bronze, tinned; the head is missing leaving a broad panel on the upper bow which has longitudinal mouldings (ribs). The central and outer ones are beaded, and have projecting moulded lugs at the lower corners. On the lower part of the bow there are plain cross mouldings, flanking a plain square panel. The long triangular catchplate is central, and the back of the upper bow is flat. The brooch is large and well moulded but the surface is mostly covered with corrosion deposits. Shiny white metal shows through in places, *Find 5723, context 835, pit F836, Phase 2a–d*

Colchester type

At Camulodunum this type was found thoughout the occupation from *c* AD 10–65 (Hawkes and Hull 1947,

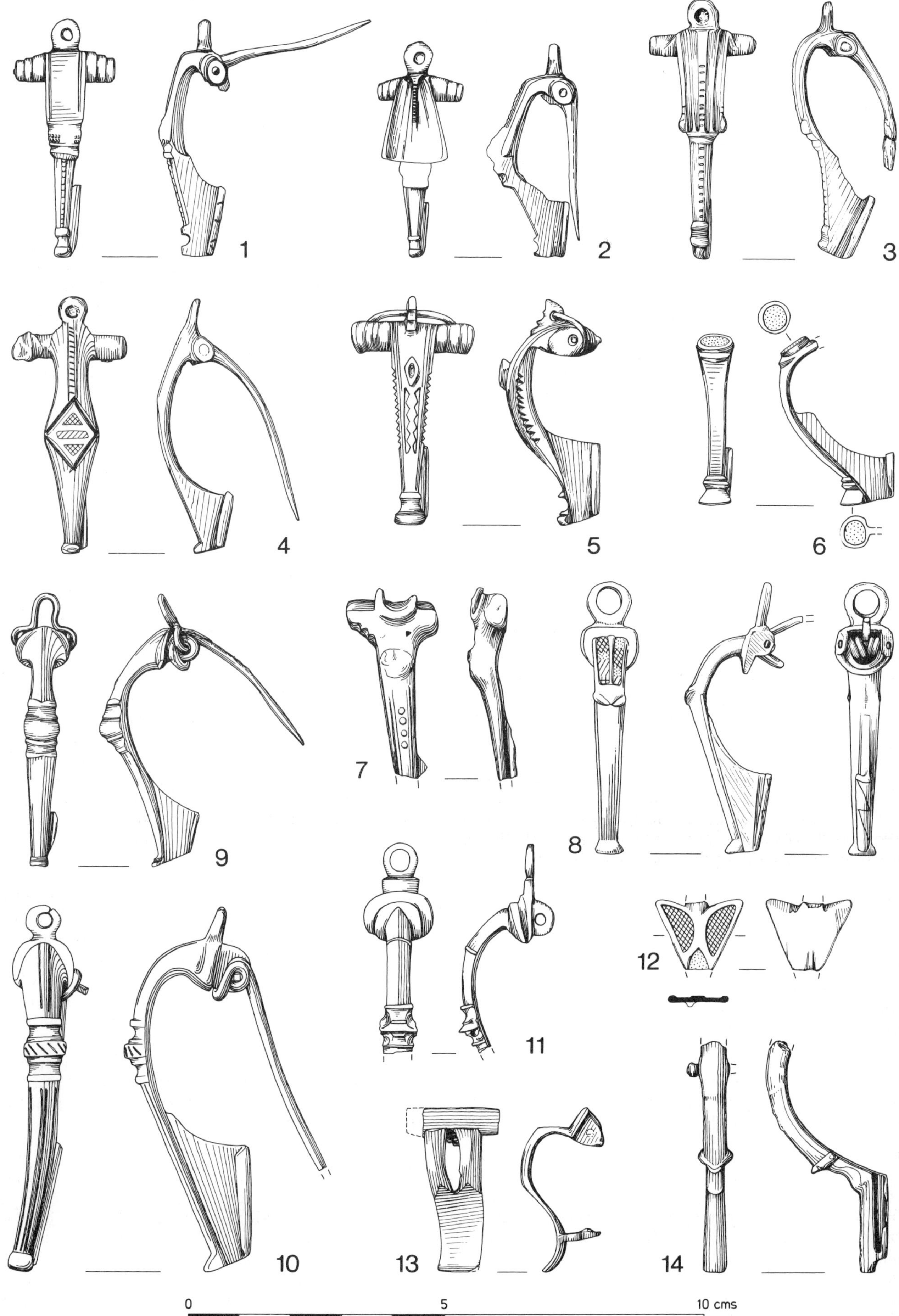

Fig 124 Brooches of copper alloy and enamel: mainly second-century AD types, scale 1:1

309). More recent excavations have supported this dating: the King Harry Lane cemetery at St Albans, which went out of use *c* AD 60, contained 70 examples (Stead and Rigby 1989). The 20-plus examples found at Richborough must have been in use in the post-conquest period, while two from Verulamium were in later first century contexts (Frere 1972, 114, nos 3 and 4).

Although very common in the primary Belgic areas of south-eastern Britain the type is also found further north; Lincolnshire and Yorkshire (Stead 1971b); and west, eg Lydney (Wheeler and Wheeler 1932, 76, fig 12, no 13), and Bagendon (Clifford 1961, 169).

8 Brass; standard Colchester one-piece brooch (Hawkes and Hull 1947, type III, 308 ff) with plain rounded bow, side wings covering the spring and fretted catchplate. The spring is of six turns and its chord is held by a rearward-facing hook. The catchplate decoration is very crudely cut, *Find 5824, context 594, ditch F584, Phase 3b*

Polden Hill type

9 Leaded bronze; an axis bar is anchored in discs at the end of the wings, and the chord is passed through a hole in a crest on the head, *Find 8222, context 959, Structure VIII exterior, Phase 6–7*

The type takes its name from an example in the Polden Hill hoard, (British Museum acc no 46.3-22.120) with the same spring construction. It is a development of the two-piece Colchester brooch of the mid-first century AD and various features of Find 8222, eg the shape of the lower bow and open catchplate, and the ribbed mouldings on the head, suggest that it should be dated within the later first century. There is a close parallel to this example from Charterhouse on Mendip (Bristol Museum F1877) and some of its features are present on brooches from the following sites: Exeter (Bidwell 1979, fig 72, no 3); Chew Valley Lake (Rahtz and Greenfield 1978, fig 114, no 6); Bagendon (Clifford 1961, no 26, 173); and Camerton (Wedlake 1958, fig 50, no 5). A south-western distribution is evident.

Various 'south-western' types

a) A derivative of the Colchester brooch, commonest in the area of Wiltshire, Oxfordshire and Gloucestershire, eg Woodeaton (Kirk 1949, 10, no 10), Wanborough (in prep). None is closely dated, but on typological grounds this group probably belongs to the later first century AD.

10 Leaded bronze; spring of eight turns, held by a lug at the rear of the head; plain narrow bow, *Find 2286, context 255, ditch F264, Phase 3a–5*

b) Hinged T-shaped brooches with rectangular panel on the upper bow. They probably owe this design to the Hod Hill series, *cf* especially the side knobs on Find 5683 (Fig 124, no 3), but they are also related to many brooches from south-western Britain. The nearest parallels usually have enamelled cells on the square panel, eg Charterhouse (two examples in Bristol Museum, acc nos F1903, F1911); Caerleon (unpublished); Caerwent (Nash-Williams 1930, 239–40, no 2); and Cirencester (unpublished). This general class of brooch is dated around AD 100 on typological grounds.

Fig 124

1 Leaded bronze; much obscured by corrosion, but examination in AM Laboratory shows that enamel was present. The fixed head-tab is perforated. The catchplate has diagonal grooves on the turn, *Find 2276, context 255, ditch F264, Phase 3a–5*

2 Leaded bronze; a finely moulded brooch, the surface tinned. The panel on the upper bow is triangular and has fluted mouldings with a central beaded rib. The head-tab is cut from both sides but not perforated, *Find 2339, context 350, Structure IV, Phase 6b*

3 Leaded bronze, tinned; a crudely moulded brooch. The rectangular panel on the upper bow has knobs at the lower corners. The central rib of the rectangular panel is roughly cross cut, as is the rib of the lower bow. The fixed head-tab is cut from either side but not perforated. The pin is hinged in a narrow head tube of triangular section, *Find 5683, context 824, pit F836, Phase 3c*

c) This is a very uniform type which was distinguished by M R Hull in the first Nornour report (Hull 1968, figs 13 and 35, nos 37–46). Since then further examples have appeared: Gadebridge, Herts, (Neal 1974, 125, no 18); Catsgore, Somerset (Leech 1982, 105, nos 7 and 8); Cattybrook, Avon (Bennet 1980, 181, fig 14.4); Carvossa, Cornwall (Carlyon 1987, 124, no 24); and a further example from Nornour (Butcher 1977, 59, no 22). Most of these are undated but one from Chew Valley (Rahtz and Greenfield 1978, 293, no 14, fig 114) was from a second-century context and this date would suit the typological development.

Several are from religious sites: Nornour (Butcher 1977, 44) (12 examples); Nettleton (Wedlake 1982, 127, no 55); and Woodeaton (Ashmolean Museum R47). Quite as many are from sites where no religious aspect has been proved, but all have a south-western distribution, Gadebridge (Neal 1974) being the furthest north-east. The largest single group is from the Mendip area but there is a scatter from Hampshire, Wiltshire, Oxfordshire and Gloucestershire,and also two from Caerwent.

4 Leaded bronze; hinged brooch with lozenge-shaped panel on the centre of the bow. The pin is hinged in a narrow crossbar and there is a projecting tab at the head which has rough sinkings on front and back but is not completely perforated. The upper bow has a central knurled longitudinal ridge. The lozenge panel is decorated with enamel in separate cells: the two triangles of translucent turquoise and the central rectangle of opaque red and orange. The lower bow is plain and ends in a small foot moulding. The back is flat and the catchplate springs from one side, *Find 5444, context 682, Structure X, Phase 4a*

d) Typologically this brooch appears to be close to the Colchester B brooch of the mid-first century: the crest holding the chord being a development from that type. However the moulded foot-knob and enamelled decoration represent a later development. Unfortunately there is no independent dating of the type, but it can be supposed to belong to the latter part of the first century. A number of similar brooches are known: the distribution is mainly in the south-west, but extends into Surrey, Farley Heath, (British Museum acc no 53.4-19.65); Hertfordshire, Gadebridge (Neal 1974, 125, no 15); Buckinghamshire, Magiovinium, (Neal forthcoming); South Wales, Caerleon (two examples, one in Wheeler 1928, fig 13, no 8); Caerwent, two examples (in Newport Museum); Liswerry (Nash-Williams 1924, 389, no 1); the furthest north is from Holt (Grimes 1930, fig 54, 5). The main group is from Somerset: Charterhouse (four examples in Bristol Museum); Shepton (Taunton Museum, A582); and Bath (Roman Baths Museum); Oxfordshire: Woodeaton (four examples, Ashmolean Museum acc nos R38, R39, 1946.188, 1921.120, Kirk 1949, pl H, B7); Gloucestershire: Cirencester (three examples, Corinium Museum, 1961.293, others no number recorded); Gloucester (City Museum); Wiltshire: Rushmore (Pitt Rivers 1887, pl 73, no 3); Rushall Down, (Devizes Museum acc no 319). Of these the examples from Farley Heath and Woodeaton are certainly from religious sites.

5 Leaded bronze; sprung brooch in which the chord is held by a crest on the head. The spring is of twelve turns. The bow bears a small raised lozenge-shaped cell and below this a panel of formerly enamelled decoration: two long empty cells flanking a bronze strip of running lozenge shapes; the sides here are toothed. The foot has a moulded terminal knob and the catchplate is solid. The brooch is well preserved except for the spring; it is a fine sharp casting and the surface shows marks of polishing or filing, *Find 2272, context 255, ditch F264, Phase 3a–5*

Headstud type

Although the head is absent this brooch has all the other features of the general type known as 'headstud'. The majority of these have decoration down the length of the bow, though a few plain ones occur. The lack of the head makes it impossible to classify closely (as in Painter and Sax 1970). The general type has been shown to exist before the end of the first century AD (Painter and Sax 1970, 173; Butcher 1977, 62–4) but it is frequently found in use well into the mid-second century.

6 Leaded bronze; a small brooch lacking the head. At the top of a narrow bow there is a raised stud containing red enamel. The foot is a moulded knob and on the underside this contains a cell of red enamel. The catchplate extends well up the centre of the back. Moulded details are sharp but the back is partly obscured by corrosion deposits. The red enamel has a rounded smoothed surface which suggests that it was applied as a cold 'button'. Both cells have irregular depressions in the centre of the enamel, *Find 2162, context 200, Structure II, Phase 6a*

7 Bronze; a badly damaged and corroded fragment. Only part of the head and bow survives, and this has been flattened and distorted. However it clearly belongs to the headstud type, although there is only a shapeless lump where the stud should be. The flattened head has a tube carrying the bar from a hinged pin, and part of a fixed head-loop. On the bow is a panel of decoration which appears to consist of reserved metal spots in a field which should contain enamel. Part of the catchplate is squashed against the back of the bow, *Find 2165, context 222, Structure XVI, Phase 2–3*

Too little remains for parallels to be quoted, but this belongs to the large class of headstud brooches for which references are given above. As with Find 2162 (Fig 124, no 6), the date should be within the range late first-century to mid-second-century.

For a further headstud brooch see Fig 160, no 4

Enamelled bow-brooch with fixed head-loop

This belongs to a group of brooches which show several variable features, each linking them with other major classes of brooch. The form of the enamel panel and the plastic decoration of leaves are south-western traits (*cf* Nornour, Hull 1968, fig 11 and 12, nos 11–21); the form of the head, without crossbar, links with the trumpet or Backworth type below. The link between these may be a type which has a similar D-shaped head plate, of which several occur at Wroxeter (none illustrated in publications. Shrewsbury Museum nos X24 and X26 are two examples). One from Wilderspool is illustrated in Thompson 1965, fig 20, no 3. Parallels for Find 7669 (Fig 124, no 8) occur at Manchester (Jones 1974, 121, no 7; fig 43), and Willoughby, Notts (Mackreth 1966, 9, fig 1). More elaborate versions have been found in the Chepstow hoard (British Museum acc no 91-3-27.15); at Woodeaton (Ashmolean Museum acc no R.33); Northchurch (British Museum 1958, 18, fig 10, no 21); Tarrant Hinton (British Museum acc no 92.9-1.1521); and Castle Martin (British Museum acc no 61.7-20.1).

The associations of the whole group are varied: a number came from military sites, but others from villages and towns. Only those from Woodeaton are certainly religious in context. The distribution is fairly general in Britain though with a preponderance in the Western Midlands.

8 Leaded bronze; the well-arched bow has a panel of enamel towards the head (two long cells with blocks of different coloured enamel, including opaque orange, opaque red and translucent turquoise, juxtaposed in each cell); two leaf-shaped mouldings in the centre, a plain lower bow and a foot-knob. At the head there is a projecting loop, cast in one with the bow. The spring of two turns is held on a pin between two projecting lugs at the back of the head. The turn of the harp-shaped catchplate has engraved zigzag lines, *Find 7669, context 1202, Structure XVI, Phase 5d*

Plain 'trumpet' brooches

9 Leaded bronze; there is a prominent moulding at the waist, flanked by two leaf-shaped mouldings (the back is flat). The plain bow expands towards the D-shaped head and tapers to a small moulding at the foot. The catchplate is offset. A spring of three turns is attached to a single lug behind the head by means of an axial tube, which also holds a wire head-loop, *Find 5327, context 647, Structure IX, Phase 5b*

Many similar brooches are known, eg Wroxeter (Bushe-Fox 1914, fig 10, no 5, Atkinson 1942, 206, late first or early second-century); Winchester (Cunliffe 1964, 88, fig 24, no 3, level III, AD 43–140) (but this has ribs on the head); Wanborough, Wilts (E Greenfield in prep, WANW 1); Chilgrove (Down 1979, 147, 6, fig 43);

Holt (Grimes 1930, fig 54, no 4); Whittington Court (O'Neil 1952, fig 12, no 1); Silchester (Boon 1969, 47, fig 6, no 7) with Hadrianic-Antonine pottery. One from Usk (Boon and Savory 1975, 54, no 9) appears to have all the characteristics of the type and was found with Neronian-Flavian material. Other examples have been found in second-century contexts (see above) and the type was widely distributed in Britain, though with a preponderance in the West Midlands (it was named the 'Chester type' by M R Hull in Dudley 1968, 42).

10 Leaded bronze, tinned; there is a prominent knurled moulding at the waist flanked by the plain mouldings; the back is flat. At the head the bow joins a flat D-shaped head with a cast head-loop; the spring of four turns is held by a rod which passes through a single projecting lug. The upper bow has a central ridge flanked by grooves, and the lower bow has similar grooves in the centre and at the sides. There is a plain projecting foot moulding. The bow is finely moulded and triangular in section; the harp-shaped catchplate springs from the centre of the flat back. The surface of the whole brooch (including back and catchplate) is tinned, *Find 3607, context 519, Structure I, Phase 5e (i)*

This type differs from Find 5327 (Fig 124, no 9 above) mainly in having the head-loop fixed. It is also quite common, especially in the west (several specimens from Caerleon, Chester and Wroxeter for example cp Hull 1968, 42, *sub* no 108). Some have been found in second-century contexts and it is likely to be of much the same date range as the preceding type, possibly starting later.

11 Leaded bronze; the upper part only survives. At the waist there is an 'acanthus' moulding, flat at the back. The head is a flat oval with a D-shaped plate where the bow joins it; above it a cast plate carries a loop. The spring is missing but was apparently housed in a hollow behind the head and held by a bar through two lugs at the sides. The upper bow was of triangular section and had two leaf-shaped mouldings halfway between waist and head. The surface shows white metal amongst the corrosion at both front and back, *Find 378, context 1, Phase 8*

A very similar brooch was found at Lydney (Wheeler and Wheeler 1932, 77, fig 12, no 18); another at Caerleon (Wheeler 1928, 164, fig 13, no 16; upper half only) was with pottery of *c*AD 130–60. Again the distribution is largely western but similar brooches have been found at Richborough (Cunliffe 1968, 82, no 33, pl xxix) and at Dover (Philp 1981, 151, fig 33, no 77, enamelled) where it was in the mid-second century occupation: this would seem likely to be the date of the type generally.

Brooch in the shape of a moth or fly

12 Leaded bronze, tinned; only a fragment survives: a flat plate expanding to a triangular shape with cells for enamel. Two semicircles on the 'wings' contain traces of translucent turquoise enamel and part of the upper body has traces of red enamel. The back is flat except for slight ridges at either end which are probably part of the pin attachment and catchplate, *Find 3880, context 1, Phase 8*

From parallels this fragment can be identified as a type of brooch which takes the shape of a moth or fly (*cf* Butcher 1977, 56, fig 7, no 13, and examples quoted there). To these examples can be added: one from Farley Heath in the British Museum (acc no 53.4-19.52); Kidlington (Hunter and Kirk 1954, 58, fig 26, no 7); Weston Turville (Waugh 1961, 109, fig 3, no 13 in burial *c*AD 190).

The indications are that this is a second-century type of British make.

Knee brooch

13 Leaded bronze; very plain and crudely made knee brooch, in which the upper bow is divided into two bars of triangular section. The head is a plain flat cross-bar with two lugs behind; the pin was hinged between these. The plain foot curves forward; behind it there is a transverse catchplate, *Find 4767, context 602, Structure XIX, Phase 7a*

Three similar brooches were found at Nornour (Hull 1968, fig 18, 113–15) but no others are known. A type with undivided bow, but generally very similar, is known from Lydney (Wheeler and Wheeler 1932, 77. no 21), Nornour (Hull 1968, fig 18, no 112) and Woodeaton (Kirk 1949, 12, no 22).

These must relate to the more common forms of knee brooch with cylindrical spring cover and transverse catchplate, which were described by Böhme (1972, 21–2) as common soldiers' brooches of the *Limes* in the second half of the second century AD. Several have been found in Britain, chiefly on military sites (though also at Woodeaton, Kirk 1949, 11, no 21). The distribution of the simplified versions, so far only from western religious sites, may be significant.

Sheath-footed brooches

14 Bronze, gilded and tinned; the head is missing, there are very small lateral knobs on the upper bow. The upper bow is faceted and the surface of the central facet is gilded; the rest of the brooch is tinned, *Find 4955, context 602, Structure XIX, Phase 7a*

This brooch had the shape of a type known from several sites: a P-shaped profile, a projecting moulding in the middle of the bow and a plain foot with a sheath for the pin behind. The upper part of this type has a cylindrical spring cover often with a knob or other decoration on it; alternatively the early form of cross-bow brooch had a similar lower part. Examples of the former type have been published from Housesteads (Charlton 1934, pl xxix 2, early third-century context) and from Woodeaton (Kirk 1949, 12, no 23) and the latter from Colchester (British Museum 1958, 20, fig 10, no 27) and Richborough (Bushe-Fox 1949, 119, no 55; earlier than AD 275–300).

The early crossbow brooches have a wide distribution in Britain and on the continent, where they are dated to the third century (*cf* Böhme 1972, 26–8 and Riha 1979, 166–7) and are mainly associated with the army. The other type, with shorter arms lacking end knobs, is also regarded as a 'soldier's brooch' and is dated to the second half of the second century.

Fig 125 Brooches of copper alloy and enamel: fourth-century AD types, (no 1–2), disc brooches (nos 3–7) and penannular brooches (nos 8–12), scale 1:1

Fig 125

1 Leaded bronze; a well preserved brooch of very typical form. The P-profiled bow is a sharp and heavy casting. The crossbar is voluted and contains the axis bar for a hinged pin. Each end of the crossbar bears a large knob, one of which appears to be pierced for the insertion of the axis bar; the other seems to be a solid casting. A third knob is riveted to the junction of crossbar and bow. The upper bow is plain, of rectangular section. The lower bow is broad and is decorated with two pairs of deeply incised ring and dot ornament. Behind this broad foot a flange is bent over to form the catchplate. There is an additional safety catch in the form of a pellet of metal loose within a recess in the casting, which falls forward (by gravity) to trap the pin. It must have been inserted before the catchplate was bent over, *Find 1219, context 82, Structure I, Phase 5e(i)*

This brooch belongs to a well known developed form of the crossbow type. Parallels can be quoted from many sites, including Richborough (Bushe-Fox 1949, 121, no 65, pl xxxii); Stowting, Kent (British Museum Catalogue 1958, 20, fig 10, no 29); South Shields (Allason-Jones and Miket 1984, 100, no 44); Lankhills (Clarke 1979, 260, no 74, from a grave dated AD 350–70). All the above have similar decoration. One from Lydney is of the same general type but with different decoration and foot shape (Wheeler and Wheeler 1932, 78, fig 13, no 26).

They are also common on the Continent: *cf* Riha 1979, Taf 52–4 for several from Augst quite close to this example. The general evidence points to a date not earlier than the mid-fourth century for the type.

These large and elaborate brooches have often been regarded as official insignia, but as Clarke (1979, 262) points out, this is by no means certain in view of the wide distribution and the local variations.

2 Brass; a very thin, small and light fragment; the head is missing and the foot is completely flat, with no trace of a catchplate. The strongly arched upper bow is very narrow and is decorated on the sides by stamped circle and dot ornament. Similar ornament appears on the flat lower bow. The edges of the whole bow are notched. The object is well preserved, showing sharp edges to the mouldings or stamps. The surface, of whitish metal, is heavily scored by a coarse file, *Find 1156, context 38, Structure I, Phase 5e(ii)*

Possibly this is only a plate for use in making up a complete brooch, or it may be an 'imitation' brooch. Alternatively it may be cut down from a whole brooch; the remains of the catchplate having been filed off. The top of the bow retains part of the socket for the knob. A brooch from Richborough (excavation no 5502, AM Lab no 7350970, unpublished) is similar in consisting of the bow without crossbar or catchplate; this suggests that crossbow brooches (which were frequently made up from a number of separate castings) tended to break up into their component parts. It is similar to a late development of the crossbow type in having a short, highly arched upper bow and long foot. This type dates to the later part of the fourth century.

Disc brooches

3 Brass, tinned; a flat circular plate, the design marked out by metal ridges. The central ring is now empty and may always have been; outside this is a zone containing metal spots in the points of a zigzag ring. The enamel here is black over red, the black probably a weathering product. The outer ring contained translucent blue/green enamel. The short spring is held on a bar between two lugs (several of the comparable brooches listed have a spring held on one lug), *Find 2046, context 216, Structure II, Phase 6a*

Several similar brooches are known, widely scattered in Britain: Nornour, Isles of Scilly (Hull 1968, 52, fig 21, no 191); Cold Kitchen Hill, Wilts (Devizes Museum 1934, pt ii, pl 34A.2); Richborough, Kent (Bushe-Fox 1949, 116, no 45); Rochester, Kent (Harrison 1973, 87, fig 20, no 8); Leicester Museum (acc no 554 1955); Rapsley, Surrey, (Guildford Museum); and Newstead (Curle 1911, pl 89, no 10). I know of none from the continent.

The examples from Nornour and Cold Kitchen are probably votive, the others apparently not. That from Newstead was described by Curle (*ibid*) as a stud, though Mr Hull's drawing shows a catchplate and pin. It was associated with the later occupation of AD 140–211. This is the only dating evidence for the type.

4 Leaded bronze; a flat disc bearing a design outlined by ridges of metal: a central circle surrounded by six smaller circles. The main field was enamelled translucent turquoise, the circles were opaque red (with central metal spot), the central ring was empty. The spring of four turns was held on a bar between two lugs at the back, *Find 1569, context 88, Structure II, Phase 6a*

A number of similar brooches are known. All those quoted are the same except for the enamel colours and very minor details, some have five circles in the fields instead of six; Gadebridge, Herts (Neal 1974, 128, no 28); Newstead (Curle 1911, 330, pl 89, 14); Zugmantel (Böhme 1972, Taf 26, 988); Köln (Exner 1939, 102, III, 21); Chepstow (from the hoard, in the British Museum). The following are from religious contexts: Woodeaton (Kirk 1949, 12, no 25); Hayling Island (Portsmouth Museum, kindly shown to me by Mr Graham Soffe); Hockwold, one (now in Norwich Museum), from Charles Green's excavation of the area where ritual crowns had been found (Gurney 1986, fig 40, no 7); two more also in Norwich Museum (one from the nearby Sawbench temple site); Carrawburgh, Coventina's Well, in Chesters Museum (Allason-Jones and Mackay 1985, 25, no 46).

Indications for a date in the late second or early third centuries from Newstead and Chepstow are borne out by the continental evidence (information kindly given by Dr P Spitaels) although the Hockwold brooch, like this example, was in a fourth-century context.

not illustrated not analysed, a flat circular plate with a single overall recess for enamel. Little of this now remains but the apparently burnt fragments show a uniform structure of very small square canes. The flat back has a small catchplate and single lug for the attachment of a (missing) spring, *Find 150, context I, Phase 8*

This brooch almost certainly contained an all-over pattern of millefiori chequers. If so it belongs to a well known type, found in Britain at Richborough (Bushe-Fox 1949, 117, no 47, pl xxix); Kidlington (Hunter and

Kirk 1954, 59, no 10); Corbridge (Corstopitum Museum acc no 75.471); Hockwold (Norwich Museum acc no 1966.72), from the field on Leylands Farm where the crowns were found; and Nornour (Hull 1968, 52, fig 21, nos 189 and 190, both very small). It is probably continental in origin (there is no evidence for millefiori chequers having been used by British manufacturers at this period) and many examples have been published, eg: from Pannonia by Sellye (1939, 55, pl xix, no 1, with bibliography) from the Rhineland by Exner (1939, 63–4, type III, 30). Both quote examples found in early third-century contexts, and this fits well with more recent finds.

Three other disc brooches of a strikingly distinct type were also found:

5 Bronze, gilded, *Find 5270, context 820, Structure X, Phase 4b*
6 Bronze, gilded, *Find 7810, context 1204, Structure IX, Phase 5c*
7 Brass/gunmetal, gilded, *Find 7814, context 1204, Structure IX, Phase 5c*

They have a conical glass paste setting in the centre, with one or more surrounding bands of finely engraved decoration, and are usually gilded. Some are round, as these three examples are, the others are oval, though otherwise similar.

Ever since Bushe-Fox published one from Wroxeter (1913, 23, fig 9, no 1) they have been considered as late, probably fourth century. The earliest dated example is from Zugmantel, abandoned *c* AD 260 (Böhme 1972, 43); one from Fishbourne (Cunliffe 1971, 106, 43) was in a late third to early fourth-century context. Although they have been found on the continent they are more numerous in Britain (See Böhme 1972, 42, and Riha 1979, 88), where the distribution is clearly regional. Most have been found in the south and east of the country, Gloucestershire forming the limit of the main distribution. There is also a cluster on the Tyne/Solway frontier, (Allason-Jones and Miket, 1984, 115–16) but none is known from Scotland. A number come from religious sites, including Thistleton (in prep); Lowbury (Atkinson 1916, 35, no 35); Hockwold (Gurney 1986, fig 40, no 9, in Norwich Museum); Farley Heath (British Museum acc no 83.4-19.72); Springhead (Penn 1959, 48, fig 9, no 1; Carrawburgh (Allason-Jones and Mackay, 1985, 23, no 41); Nettleton (Wedlake 1982, 148, no 7); Cold Kitchen Hill (Devizes Museum 1934, pl 34a, no 5); outlying examples from Nornour, (Hull 1968, 60, no 237) and New Grange (O'Kelly 1977, 53, pl viiA) were probably votive. However a greater number come from settlements.

Penannular brooches

8 Gunmetal; plain round wire ring with terminals rolled up into a spiral. The loose pin is formed of different metal and may be a replacement: it looks like part of a spring from a bow brooch rather than the bent-over pin usual on penannulars. *Find 5853, context 924, ditch F264, Phase 2c*

Similar brooches have been found in contexts of the first half of the first century: Maiden Castle (Wheeler 1943, 264, fig 86, no 6), Hod Hill (Brailsford 1962, 12, fig 11, E8).

9 Bronze; the ring is of plain round wire and the terminals are bent back over it and cross grooved; the pin is wrapped round the ring and has a crudely incised diagonal cross, *Find 3647, context 516, ditch terminal F538, Phase 3c*

10 Gunmetal, the ring is of plain round wire and the terminals are bent back over it and cross grooved; the pin is wrapped round the ring, *Find 5858, context 929, Structure VIII, Phase 6–7*

Although from deposits of very different date (Phase 3c and Phase 6–7 respectively) these are very similar brooches. The type is common in Britain and has been found on sites of the first half of the first century, eg Camulodunum (Hawkes and Hull 1947, 327, no 6); Hod Hill (Brailsford 1962, E11). Others are from later contexts: Camerton (Wedlake 1958, no 64); Verulamium (Wheeler and Wheeler 1936, 210, no 39). One from the Lamyatt Beacon temple site (Leech 1986, 316, no 5) had diagonal crosses on the terminals instead of, as here, the pin.

11 Brass; a small ring, cross-grooved to give a ribbed appearance. The terminals appear to be cast and have 'Celtic' style moulding. The pin is hooked round the ring and bears a diagonal cross. This belongs to a class of penannular brooches sometimes thought to have been the forerunners of the developed zoomorphic type but recently rejected as such by Kilbride-Jones (1980, 1), *Find 292, context 12, Structure II, Phase 6b*

There are no closely dated examples but in general they appear to belong to the third or fourth centuries. There are several from the Lydney temple site (Wheeler and Wheeler 1932, fig 14).

12 Brass; pin of a penannular brooch, showing characteristic curve, and the coil attachment to the ring of the brooch. It has a diagonal cross engraved near the centre (*cf* Finds 3647 and 292, above, where the cross is on the coiled end), *Find 5526, context 733, ditch F264, Phase 2d*

not illustrated
Brass; another pin with coiled end almost certainly belonging to a penannular brooch, although this has not got the characteristic profile, *Find 4662, context 602, Structure XIX, Phase 7a*
Silver; probably also the pin of a penannular brooch although the point is bent back. It has the coiled end for attachment, *Find 3945, context 600, above Structure XIX, Phase 8*

Unclassifiable fragments

not illustrated
Brass; the bow and catchplate of a brooch. It is plain and narrow and forms a continuous curve. This must be a first-century brooch from its form, *Find 5611, context 627, Structure IX, Phase 5a–c*
Bronze; pin and spring of eight turns with inferior chord and with axis rod threaded through the coils. Many brooches of the first century have this type of spring and attachment, *Find 1633, context 33, courtyard, Phase 4–6*

Discussion

The group of 36 brooches (plus fragments) recorded from all phases of the site includes a wide variety of types and dates and reflects the general range of Romano-British brooches rather than any strongly marked internal trends. Many of the types tend to have a western distribution, and several have been found at other religious sites. Only a few brooches appear in contemporary deposits;
Phases 2c–d: Find 5839 (Fig 123, no 4), Find 5732 (Fig 123, no 5), Find 5723 (Fig 123, no 7), Find 5853 (Fig 125, no 8).
Phase 5c: Find 7810 (Fig 125, no 7), Find 7814 (Fig 125, no 6)
Phase 5e: Find 1219 (Fig 125, no 1), Find 1156 (Fig 125, no 2)

While some of the second-century types which are not closely datable may not be far out of context, most are markedly so. This is not uncommon with brooches, which seem often to have been kept for long periods, but here this pattern presumably reflects their presence in redeposited soil. (It is noticeable that some, which were found in contexts hundreds of years later than their probable date of manufacture, were in good condition and still complete with pin).

Several of the brooches were found in votive deposits and it is likely that most had been used for this purpose. They are however types in general use, and have diverse origins and dates, so it is unlikely that they were made as votives, or at least not on this site. They were probably personal ornaments of visitors to the site. There are not enough of them to suggest that brooches were peculiarly associated with the cult, nor enough of any one type to suggest that it had particularly religious associations, such as the horse and rider brooches at Lamyatt Beacon (Leech 1986, 319). An exception to this might be the gilded disc type, of which there were three, Find 5270 (Fig 125, no 5); Find 7810 (Fig 125, no 6) and Find 7814 (Fig 125, no 7). Others of this type have come from votive contexts (see catalogue above), but many more are from apparently secular sites. It is impossible to guess at the motives of the donors: perhaps they were the most valuable object which a visitor could spare. Personal ornaments have been used as votives in many periods and cults.

The incised diagonal cross which occurs on the pins of three penannular brooches, Finds 3647, 292 and 5526 (Fig 125, nos 9, 11 and 12) probably has a religious significance. The motif appears on representations of Celtic deities (Green 1976, 111) and perhaps as a funerary symbol (Green 1977, 313). It also occurs on votive model axes and although in some instances this may merely represent a binding (eg Woodeaton, Kirk 1949, fig 8, no 3) its position on the blade of the Kirmington axe (Leahy 1980, 327) makes this unlikely.

About 50 brooches from Britain bearing a deliberate X-mark have so far been noted; on a few others the mark is present but may be part of the decoration. Of these, 20 are from religious contexts, including Lamyatt Beacon (Leech 1986, fig 34, no 5), Cold Kitchen Hill (Rodwell 1980, 335) and Nornour, Scilly, where the large group of brooches is now thought to be votive (Butcher 1978, 65). The marks occur on a range of types: penannular brooches, south-western bow brooches of mainly second-century date, headstud brooches and some crossbow brooches. The range of type and date is thus fairly wide, though geographically there is a bias towards those found and made in the south-west. Similar brooches occur without the mark, implying that it has some symbolic meaning, not closely associated with any one cult. Perhaps it was sometimes used in dedicating an otherwise secular object, much as a cross was scratched on some Christian possessions.

The brooches may give some indication of the origins of those who visited the shrine, though with the *caveat* that such portable objects are easily scattered, as gifts or by exchange or trade. A significant number (13 out of 36) are of types only found in the western counties of England and in south Wales, with a date range of perhaps late first to early third-century. A very few are of continental origin (scattered examples with dates of early first-century, late second-century, and fourth-century). A few more are of British origin with a fairly general distribution; these again have a wide range of dates (mid and late first, second and fourth centuries).

A review of brooches from other British temple sites, Table 6, confirms the impression given by this group: while brooches occur in considerable numbers at most temple sites, the types present are variable and not markedly different from those found at nonreligious sites in the same area. A few types do appear at several different shrines, and may eventually be proved to have a special significance.

Table 6: Brooches with parallels on other temple sites or in votive contexts

Bow-brooches		
Find 5839	Fig 123, no 4	Normandy: shrine & burials (cp Dollfuss 1973, 102)
Find 2272	Fig 124, no 5	Woodeaton; Farley Heath
Find 5444	Fig 124, no 4	Nornour (12); Cold Kitchen Hill; Nettleton
Find 7669	Fig 124, no 9	Woodeaton
Find 378	Fig 124, no 11	Lydney; Cold Kitchen Hill
Find 3880	Fig 124, no 12	Farley Heath
Find 4767	Fig 124, no 13	Nornour (3)
Find 4955	Fig 124, no 14	Woodeaton
Find 1219	Fig 125, no 1	Woodeaton; Lydney
Plate-brooches		
Find 2046	Fig 125, no 3	Cold Kitchen Hill; Nornour
Find 1569	Fig 125, no 4	Woodeaton; Carrawburgh (Coventina's Well); Hayling Island; Hockwold (3)
Find 150	not illus	Nornour; Hockwold
Find 5270	Fig 125, no 5	Lowbury Hill; Hockwold
Find 7810	Fig 125, no 6	Oval type: Carrawburgh; Thistleton; Lowbury; Hockwold
Find 7814	Fig 125, no 7	Cold Kitchen Hill; Nettleton; Springhead; (Farley Heath; Nornour)
Penannular		
Find 292	Fig 125, no 11	Lydney

Analysis of the brooches

by Justine Bayley

A total of 35 brooches and 5 fragments and brooch pins from the site were analysed qualitatively by energy dispersive X-ray fluorescence (XRF) and those which were sufficiently massive and well preserved were also sampled and analysed quantitatively by atomic absorption (AA) using the methods described by Hughes *et al* (1976). The AA results can be used to approximately calibrate the XRF results and so provide a better indication of the composition of all the brooches than would have been the case if only XRF analyses had been carried out. The results are given in Table 7.

Previous work has shown that Roman copper alloys contain deliberate additions of zinc, tin and/or lead, that individual brooch types have a preferred alloy composition or range of compositions, and that in some cases particular date ranges are associated with a specific alloy type (Bayley *et al* 1980, Bayley and Butcher 1981, Bayley 1990, Bayley and Butcher forthcoming). The individual analytical results for the Uley brooches are discussed below and compared with those of other brooches of similar types.

The specific compositions indicated by the AA analyses are given in Table 7, together with the alloy name which has been assigned to each object. These alloy names group similar compositions together, allowing an overall picture to emerge from the mass of data. Brasses are mainly copper and zinc though some may also contain up to a per cent or two of tin; zinc levels are typically 10–20% or a little more. Bronzes are copper and tin, and in some cases, a per cent or two of zinc, with tin levels mainly in the range 5–12%. Gunmetals contain more than a few per cent of both tin and zinc. Where more than one alloy name appears in Table 7 and the catalogue entries this is because the analysis indicates an intermediate composition. Many of the alloys also contain more than a few per cent of lead and are then described as 'leaded'.

Some brooch types, eg those that are cast, can be made in any of the available copper alloys, as the metal's properties are not critical. Other types, where the brooch is smithed (hammered) into shape or at least finished in this way, can only be made from low-lead or lead-free alloys as heavily leaded metal cracks when worked in this way. Leaded alloys also lack the necessary elasticity to make a satisfactory pin/spring assembly and so cannot be used to make one piece brooches.

Discussion

The group of three Nauheim derivative brooches, Finds 3717, 3605, and 6062 (Fig 123, nos 1–3) shows the range of compositions found in these types. Overall some 60% are bronzes, 25% brasses and the rest mainly gunmetals. As noted above, leaded alloys are not suitable for these brooches. On sites where there are larger numbers of these types there appears to be some correlation between composition and typological variation but the numbers here are far too low for any variations to be considered significant.

As over 90% of both rosette and one piece Colchester brooches from elsewhere are brasses, the results for these types from this site are as expected. Hod Hill brooches are another earlier first-century type that is also often made of brass (about 70% of the total) but the widespread use of tinning on them (as here) means that the use of varying alloys of differing colours below the tinning would go unnoticed.

The later first-century types, Colchester derivatives

Table 7: Analytical results for the brooches

type	*Cu %*	*Zn %*	*Sn %*	*Pb %*	*Ag %*	*Alloy*
Nauheim derivative						
Find 3717	-	-	-	-	-	bronze
Find 3605	-	-	-	-	-	brass
Find 6062	-	-	-	-	-	bronze/gunmetal
Rosette						
Find 5839	-	-	-	-	-	brass
Strip bow						
Find 5732	-	-	-	-	-	bronze
Hod Hill						
Find 077	-	-	-	-	-	brass
Find 5723	79.9	0.6	11.7	4.0	0.1	bronze
Colchester						
Find 5824	74.3	19.6	0.9	0.2	-	brass
Polden Hill						
Find 8222	70.5	-	9.4	19.5	-	leaded bronze
'South-western' types						
Find 2286	58.1	-	7.1	30.5	0.1	leaded bronze
Find 2276	61.5	1.4	9.9	18.3	1.0	leaded bronze
Find 2339	69.4	0.6	13.2	20.6	0.1	leaded bronze
Find 5683	78.6	1.2	5.8	13.3	0.1	leaded bronze
Find 5444	68.0	0.2	9.8	17.1	-	leaded bronze
Find 2272	66.9	0.2	11.2	13.0	0.1	leaded bronze
Headstud type						
Find 2162	-	-	-	-	-	leaded bronze
Find 2165	90.2	0.9	4.1	2.0	-	bronze
Bow-brooch						
Find 7669	73.5	-	6.6	16.3	0.1	leaded bronze
Trumpet						
Find 5327	71.7	0.1	8.4	11.3	0.1	leaded bronze
Find 3607	77.0	0.1	3.9	12.9	0.1	leaded bronze
Find 378	73.7	0.7	11.0	16.9	-	leaded bronze
Moth or fly						
Find 3880	-	-	-	-	-	leaded bronze
Knee						
Find 4767	-	-	-	-	-	leaded bronze
Sheath-footed						
Find 4955	80.5	1.3	5.7	0.4	0.1	bronze
Find 1219	75.2	0.6	4.9	13.2	0.1	leaded bronze
Find 1156	-	-	-	-	-	brass
Disc						
Find 2046	-	-	-	-	-	brass
Find 1569	-	-	-	-	-	leaded bronze
Find 5270	-	-	-	-	-	bronze
Find 7810	92.3	1.9	5.7	-	-	bronze
Find 7814	85.4	8.3	2.2	-	-	brass/gunmetal
Penannular						
Find 5853	-	-	-	-	-	gunmetal
Find 3647	-	-	-	-	-	bronze
Find 5858	-	-	-	-	-	gunmetal
Find 292	-	-	-	-	-	brass
Find 5526 (pin only)	-	-	-	-	-	brass
Find 4662 (pin only)	-	-	-	-	-	brass
Find 3945 (pin only)	-	-	-	-	-	silver
fragments						
Find 5611	-	-	-	-	-	brass
Find 1633	-	-	-	-	-	bronze
(pin only)						
Find 5787	-	-	-	-	-	
(pin only)	-	-	-	-	-	bronze/gunmetal
	Cu %	*Zn %*	*Sn %*	*Pb %*	*Ag %*	*Alloy*

Finds 1501, 305, 306 , and 3195 were not seen or analysed.

and Polden Hill brooches, are most often heavily leaded bronzes as is Find 8222 (Fig 123, no 9) here. Another group which are almost invariably leaded bronzes are the T-shaped brooches, represented here by the various south-western types and the head-loop and head stud brooches (*cf* Bayley and Butcher 1981, fig 7).

Trumpet brooches show a range of different compositions which correlate with typological differences. The types represented here are invariably made of leaded bronze as are Find 5327 (Fig 124, no 10), Find 3607 (Fig 124, no 9), and Find 378 (Fig 124, no 11). The moth brooch, Find 3880 (Fig 124, no 12) which is typologically related to trumpet brooches, is also leaded bronze, though two other brooches of this type from other sites are brass and gunmetal respectively. The knee brooch, Find 4767 (Fig 124, no 13) is a leaded bronze which is the alloy used for over two-thirds of these types. The minority alloys are concentrated in a narrow range of sub-types not represented here.

The final group of bow brooches represented among the Uley finds are the sheath-footed brooches. These are not common types so the number of sites producing examples with which they can be compared are limited. However the available data does suggest that those of light construction, *cf* Find 4955 (Fig 124, no 14), are usually bronzes while the heavier and more elaborate examples, *cf* Find 1219 (Fig 125, no 1), and Find 1156 (Fig 125, no 2) are divided between brasses and leaded bronzes so the compositions of this group are in agreement with those from other sites (Bayley forthcoming). Find 4955 is both tinned and mercury gilded. Many of the comparable brooches from other sites are also decorated in this way.

Plate brooches are less common finds than bow brooches, and they exist in a large number of typologically distinct forms, so there are no large numbers of either objects or associated analytical results from which the 'normal' composition for a particular type can be derived. The very distinctive type with a conical glass 'stone' is well represented here, two of the examples, Finds 5270 and 7810 (Fig 125, nos 5 and 6) are bronzes and one (which has now lost its 'stone'), Find 7814 (Fig 125, no 7) a brass/gunmetal. As expected, all three are gilded, two of them being mercury gilded, while the third (Find 5270) had no mercury detectable and was therefore most probably leaf gilded. Of the ten other brooches of this type that have been analysed (Bayley and Butcher forthcoming) seven are bronzes, two gunmetals and one a brass.

Most penannular brooches are wrought so leaded alloys are unusual. Bronzes, brasses, and gunmetals are all commonly found, as well as occasional ones made from silver or unalloyed copper. These penannular brooches show the usual range of composition; there is no apparent correlation between typological variation and alloy composition.

Most of this group of brooches show some signs of applied decoration, many being tinned and/or enamelled while some are gilded. This sort of decoration is not unexpected on these brooches, but it is less usual for these decorated brooches to form such a high proportion of the types present.

Miscellaneous enamelled objects

based on notes by Justine Bayley and Sarnia Butcher

Fig 126

1 Rectangular plate, leaded brass/gunmetal, with millefiori decoration. At one end a short rounded projection has a central hole; the other end is broken and turns upwards but seems to have been longer and to have had a hole roughly punched through, not in the centre.

One circular and two semicircular fields are separated from the background by annular fields. Each field is divided from its neighbours by narrow bands of reserved metal. The circular, semicircular and background fields are all filled with a regular array of millefiori with two patterns alternating. The first is red surrounding a 3×3 blue and white chequerboard with white at the corners. The second is a 5×5 blue and white chequerboard, again with white at the corners, encased in blue. These two are among the commonest millefiori patterns found (Bayley 1987). In a few places where the superimposition of a circle on the square background field produced a triangular space, this has been filled with a piece of a third millefiori pattern which is used in the annular rings. The third pattern is a 'fir tree' of blue on a white background. The spacing of these pattern elements in the annular bands is far from regular which suggests that the millefiori may, in places at least, be set in white enamel. This suggestion can be supported by the disruption of two individual pattern elements by plain white enamel. Judging by the pieces that appear in the background field, this millefiori block may have been triangular rather than the more normal square shape, *Find 5209, context 555, Structure XIX, Phase 7a*

Rectangular plates decorated with millefiori are usually buckle plates (several are illustrated in Henry 1933, fig 38) but the Uley object does not appear to have had the necessary attachments. Some illustrated by Sellye (1939, 87, pl xvi, nos 8 and 9) are described as panels from *pyxides*. The end pieces from the Uley example seem to exclude this interpretation but the decoration is very similar and they may well come from the same workshop. The off-centre hole surrounded by rust marks suggests that whatever its original use it was subsequently nailed up – probably as a votive offering.

The millefiori patterns are probably datable to *c* AD 200, see Find 305 (Fig 126, no 5).

2 This small flat enamelled leaded bronze disc, like Find 305 (Fig 126, no 5 below), has traces of solder on its back and was probably attached to another piece of metal. There is a small circular central field containing a piece of millefiori, a black circle on a white ground. The white outside the ring is not present all the way round as the field was not large enough. A ridge of reserved metal separates the central field from the outer annular field which contains turquoise enamel with 'black' spots. The spots were made by inserting rods into the matrix forming the background. These

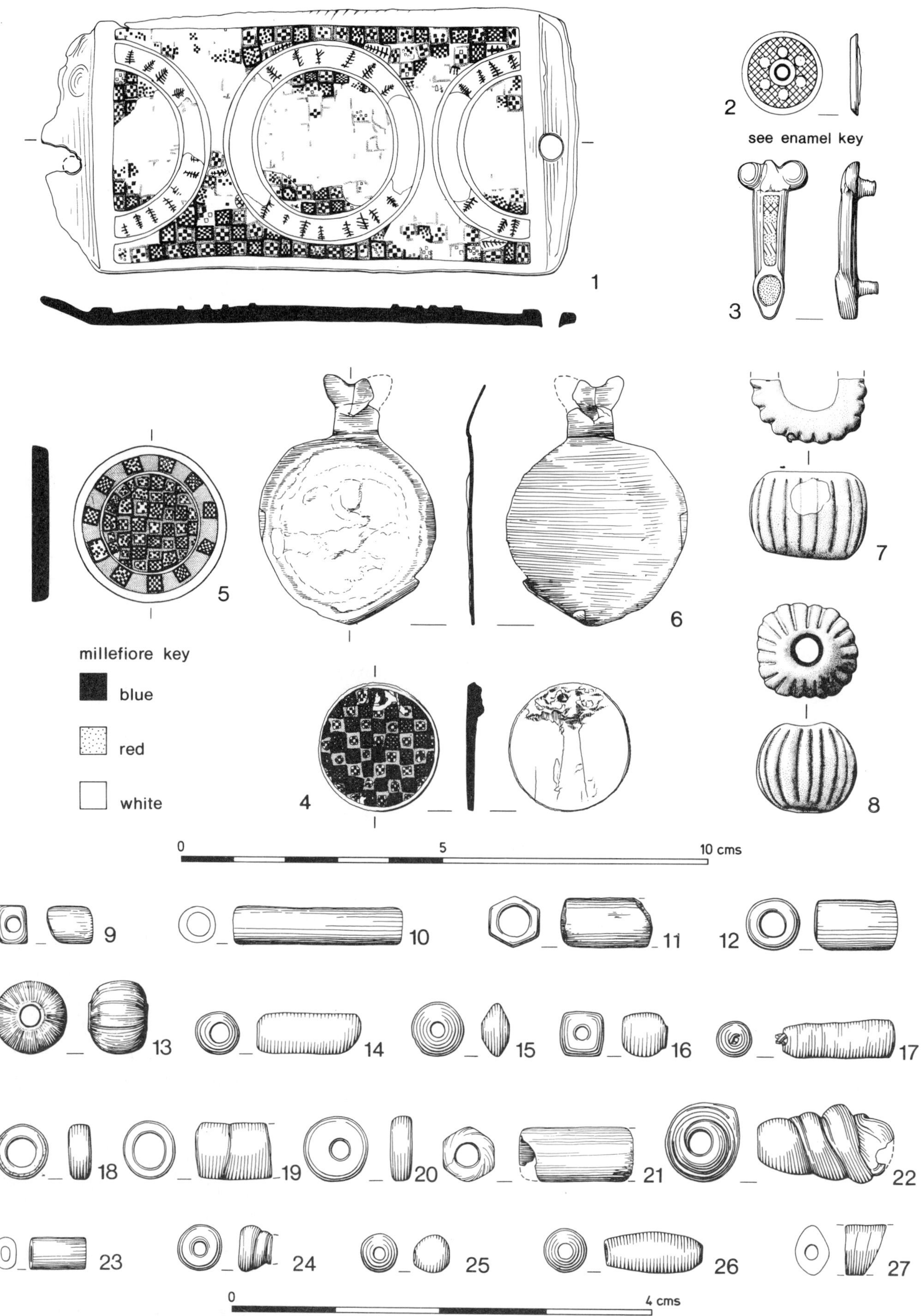

Fig 126 Enamelled objects, scale 1:1, and glass beads, scale 2:1

rods were of dark olive-green glass but the lack of light shining through them would have made them appear black. Five spots survive (out of six or seven) and they are not truly circular in shape, *Find 3195, context 237, Structure XVI, Phase 2–3*

This style of enamelling is often seen on studs and brooches: eg Nornour brooches 198 and 240 (Hull 1968, figs 22 and 24). A small brooch from Biesme (*Ann Soc Archaeol Namur* **55**, 1969, fig 28.8) with a similar colour scheme was from a grave dated to the early third century.

3 Small enamelled stud in phallic shape, length: 28mm. Two metal prongs at the back suggest that it was intended for attachment to leather. It has a field of red enamel at the tip and a rectangular field with seven adjacent blocks of enamel of equal size. The colours now appear (from the tip end) to be black, yellow, black, yellow, black, turquoise and black. The enamel that now looks black was probably originally red. The backing metal is leaded bronze, *Find 3875, context 1, Phase 8*

The style of enamel decoration represented on this piece is usually found in the second century AD. A very similar object from Chester is illustrated in Green 1978 (53, no 14, pl 143), where it is described as an amulet.

4 Leaded gunmetal disc set with millefiori decoration. The millefiori pattern is a very standard one with two blocks alternating. One is a 3×3 blue and white chequerboard (white at the corners), cased in red, and the other a 5×5 blue and white chequerboard (white at the corners) cased in blue as in the background field in Find 5209 (Fig 126, no 1, above). *Find 7688, context 1202, Structure XIV, Phase 5d*

The millefiori patterns also occur on Find 5209 and Find 306 (Fig 126, no 5); they are the most common of the limited number of Roman period millefiori patterns known (see references under Fig 126, nos 1 and 5). Numerous discs using these patterns have been found, both in Britain and on the continent, on brooches and on various other decorative discs. Find 7688 (Fig 126, no 4) lacks any attachments at the back and may have been soldered to another object as ornament; it is unlikely to have been a brooch since these usually retain part at least of the catch plate and pin attachment.

5 Leaded gunmetal disc of *c* 30mm diameter, set with millefiori decoration. Traces of tinning on its reverse side correspond with those on Find 306 (Fig 126, no 6, below) indicating that it was attached – probably soldered. There is no indication of its function. The front is decorated with an annular field of enamel, seperated from a central circular field by a narrow band of reserved metal. The central field is filled with the same two alternating millefiori patterns as the background of Find 5209, though the millefiori rods have been made with less care, so in places the pattern is less distinct. A smaller size of the second pattern has been used along one edge of the field, presumably because insufficient space remained to continue the regular arrangement. The annular field is red enamel in which millefiori blocks of the second pattern have been set. It is not (as is more common with this sort of design) alternating blocks of plain red and millefiori enamel, *Find 305, context 15, Structure II, Phase 6b*

6 A thin metal plate, roughly circular, with a projection on one side. There is no indication of its function, *Find 306, context 15, Structure II, Phase 6b*

The object cannot be part of a brooch and its attachment is unlike the usual studs, which have a central prong at the back. In view of the flimsy nature of the support it was possibly intended simply as a votive offering.

Beads

An assemblage of 89 Roman glass beads was recovered. Their distribution amongst the site phases is given in Table 8, from which it can be seen that no clear patterning or changes through time may be detected. A catalogue of unillustrated beads may be found in the fiche.

Table 8: The occurrence of glass beads by phase

Phase	*3*	*4*	*5*	*4–6*	*5–6*	*6*	*7*	*8*	*total*
Melon	1	-	1	-	-	-	-	-	2
Square sect	-	3	3	-	1	-	2	5	15
Cylinder	-	1	3	-	1	4	6	11	26
Hexagonal sect	-	-	1	1	-	-	2	-	4
Biconical	-	-	3	-	3	6	4	7	23
Globular	-	-	3	-	2	-	2	2	9
Segmented	-	-	-	-	1	-	2	1	4
Triangular sect	-	-	-	-	-	-	-	1	1
Fragments	-	-	1	-	2	-	-	2	5
total	1	4	15	1	10	10	18	29	89

Discussion

by Margaret Guido

Although the occupation of this site runs from the 1st century AD or even before, until possibly as late as the 7th century, it is noteworthy that there is no evidence either of any native pre-Roman beads from the site, or of any Teutonic post-Roman ones.

The earliest bead comes from Phase 3c (Find 5692; Fig 126, no 7) from the top of a votive pit, context 824. It is half a translucent blue melon bead of a type which is characteristic of Claudian and Antonine date. For this and almost all these beads, see Guido 1978.

Phase 4 (late second to early fourth century): This produced Finds 1930 and 2271, not illustrated, and Finds 2086 and 5686 (Fig 126, nos 9 and 10) none of which are exceptional in their context, Finds 1930 and 2086 being slightly squared in section and made of turquoise bluish-green opaque glass which is not common. Find 2271 is a chip of turquoise blue glass, and Find 5686 an unpolished light translucent green cylinder.

Phase 5 (fourth century): From this horizon came four short square sectioned beads, as well as five very small globular ones; six small biconical beads, three green and three blue; two hexagonal beads and four cylindrical ones; all typical fourth-century types. The only exception is Find 810 (Fig 126, no 13), an opaque, green globular bead with a brown ring around each perforation and spaced brown lines running between. As far as I know this bead is unique in Britain.

Phase 6 (late fourth to early fifth century): Characteristic small annular, cylinder, and biconical beads. Two less common ones are Find 1611 (Fig 126, no 16) and Find 2178, together possibly once part of a segmented bead in turquoise blue-green glass, apparently similar to Find 1602 (Fig 126, no 17), a cylinder still retaining a short length of wire.

Phases 7 and 8 (mid fifth to ?seventh century): These all appear to be fourth or fifth-century Roman beads, mostly almost certainly derived from earlier phases. An unusual occurrence is Find 3474 (Fig 126, no 22), a larger bead than usual, a broken twisted segmented bead of reused bottle glass, possibly made locally. Find 3971 (Fig 126, no 27) is a dark triangular sectioned bead and is also most unusual.

If the stratification on the site had been deeper it may have been helpful in enabling us to come to some conclusion about the length of time that late Roman or sub-Roman beads continued in use in areas of Britain outside those in which the Saxon presence was felt. But in the circumstances one must assume that all the beads from Phases 6, 7, and 8 belong to about the mid-fourth to mid-fifth centuries. Although a large number were recovered, these small beads may represent only a few necklaces, composed of 50 to 100 beads apiece. On the other hand they could represent individual offerings at the shrine (see Guido 1978, 38).

7 Half a translucent melon bead, *Find 5692, context 824, pit F836, Phase 3c*
8 Melon bead, *Find 7784, context 1208, Structure IX, Phase 5c*
9 Turquoise opaque bead of square section, broken, *Find 2086, context 320, Structure IV, Phase 4a*
10 Light translucent green cylinder bead; unpolished, *Find 5686, context 800, Structure X, Phase 4b*
11 Long green bead of hexagonal section; semi-translucent, *Find 2417, context 126, Structure I, Phase 5a–d*
12 Light translucent green cylinder bead, *Find 1175, context 45, Structure I, Phase 5e(i)*
13 Green globular bead with brown ring round each perforation and brown lines spaced around, a slight collar at one end suggests that it may have been originally segmented, but more probably it was knocked off the next bead and never perfected, *Find 810, context 38, Structure I, Phase 5e (ii)*
14 Light translucent green cylinder bead, *Find 1022, context 38, Structure I, Phase 5e (ii)*
15 Green biconical bead, *Find 1624, context 52, Structure II, Phase 6a*
16 Turquoise cylinder bead; slightly cube-shaped, *Find 1611, context 30, Structure III, Phase 6–7*
17 Turquoise (and white?) cylinder bead, still containing copper alloy wire, *Find 1602, context 301, over stucture IV, Phase 6b*
18 Translucent green biconical bead, *Find 1596, context 301, over Structure IV, Phase 6b*
19 Translucent bottle green cylinder bead with line (?accidental) around girth, *Find 4179, context 601, Structure XIX, Phase 7a*
20 Opaque emerald-green cylinder segment, *Find 4220, context 601, stucture XIX, Phase 7a*
21 Semi-translucent green bead of hexagonal section; unpolished. *Find 881, context 20, over Structure IX, Phase 7*
22 Broken segmented bead of twisted bottle glass, *Find 3474, context 433, over Structure VIII, Phase 7b*
23 Translucent green flattened cylinder bead, *Find 238, context I, Phase 8*
24 Part of a dark, opaque, round segmented bead, *Find 284, context I, Phase 8*
25 Bright translucent bottle green globular bead, *Find 674, context I, Phase 8*
26 Opaque blue long biconical bead, *Find 2559, context 277, Structures VII and XI, Phase 8*
27 Dark broken bead with triangular section, *Find 3971, context 600, above Structure XIX, Phase 8*

Jet and antler

Jet beads occur in small numbers on many Roman sites. In Gloucestershire it is noteworthy that they occur on the major temple site at Lydney (Wheeler and Wheeler 1932, 84 and fig 18, 76–80) although exact types cannot be matched. The bevelled and chamfered examples, Finds 2078 and 2737 (Fig 127, nos 3 and 5), may be paralleled at Silchester (Lawson 1976, fig 2, 15 and 16), while the large sub-rectangular bead, Find 3462 (Fig 127, no 2) resembles an item, albeit double perforated, from Colchester (Crummy 1983, fig 36, 1447).

all of jet except where stated

Fig 127
1 Spherical with single perforation, *Find 2715, context 160, Structure I, Phase 5a–d*
2 Sub-rectangular with rounded oval cross section and single perforation, *Find 3463, context 368, Structure IV, Phase 6b*
3 Rectangular with chamfered corners and double perforation, *Find 2078, context 309, Structure IV, Phase 4b*
4 Rectangular with faceted edges and double perforation, *Find 1537(b), context 17, Structure II, Phase 6*
5 Rectangular with bevelled pyramidal face and double perforation, *Find 6590, context 1100, above Structure XIV, Phase 7–8*

6 Bead, probably of deer antler, annular with central perforation, *Find 2737, context 162, fill of F158, above Structure I, Phase 5e(ii)*

Necklace fittings

all of copper alloy except where stated

7 Fragment of tapered spiral of wire, probably part of spacer from a necklace, *Find 2356, context 113, Structure I, Phase 5a–d*
8 Hook, the perforated end decorated with sinuous lines; necklace fastening, *Find 6951, context 1191, Structure XIV, Phase 5d–6b*
9 Hook, the perforated end decorated with rows of arc-shaped nicks; necklace fastening, *Find 8343, context 0410, Structure XIX, Phase 7*
10 Wire twisted to form a spiral link bearing an open ring at each end; necklace fastener, *Find 7936, context 0406, Structure XIX, Phase 7*
11 Silver hook of rectangular cross section and with ring terminal; probably a necklace fastener, *Find 3945, context 600, above Structure XIX, Phase 8*

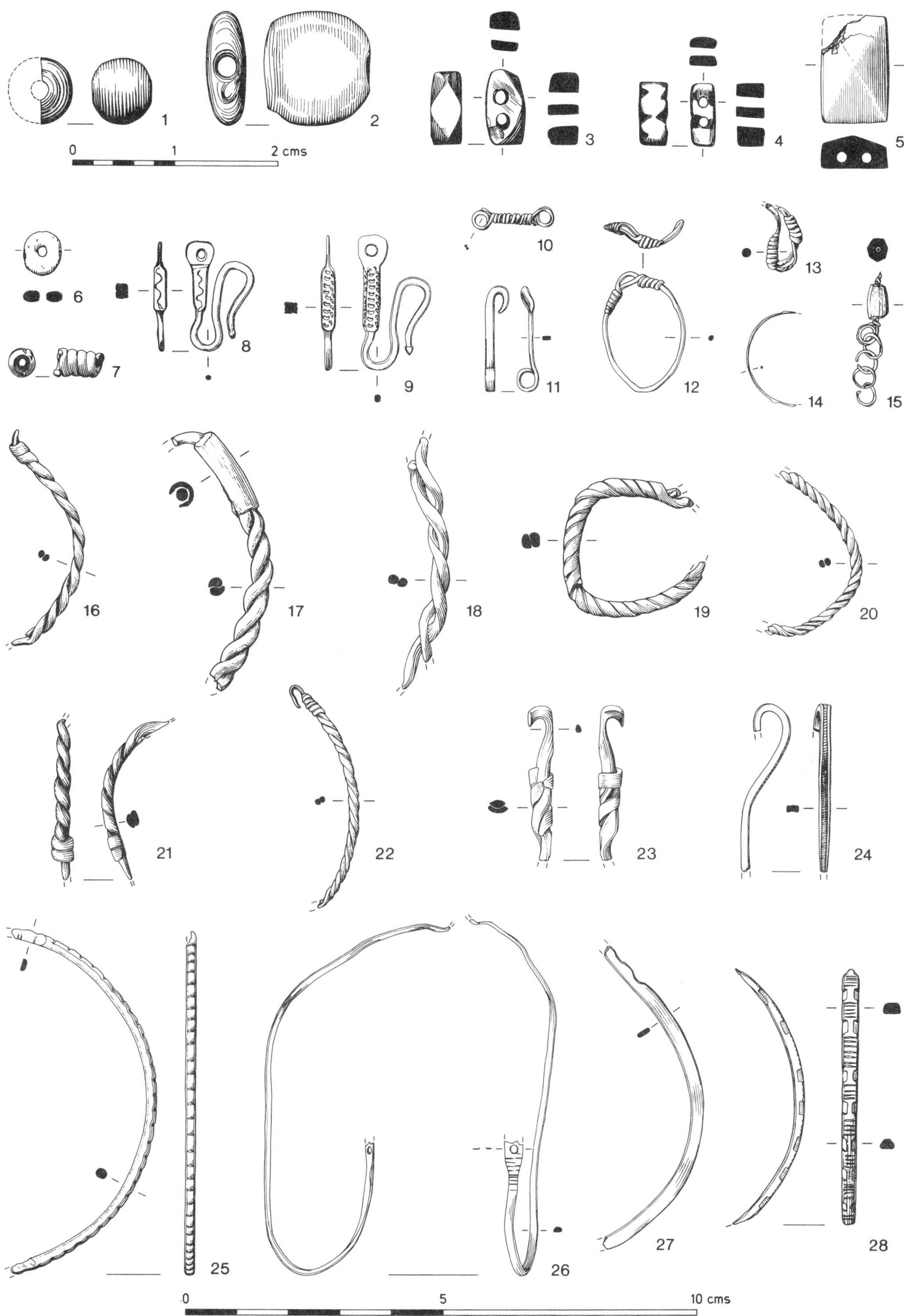

Fig 127 Beads of jet and antler, scale 2:1, necklace fittings, earrings, and bracelets of copper alloy, scale 1:1

see also Find 74 (Fig 133, no 10)

The necklace fittings include hook or eye components of hook and eye fastenings. At Lankhills (Clarke 1979, 297) similar simple examples were found eg Find 3945 (Fig 127, no 11) *cf ibid*, fig 69, grave 40, and the eye component Find 7936 (Fig 127, no 10) is similar to one from Lankhills, grave 326 (*ibid*, fig 87).

Earrings

all of copper alloy

12 Wire twisted together to form a ring with a small fastening loop, possibly for attachment to an earring, *Find 1902, context 302, Structure IV, Phase 4a*
13 Fragment of wire twisted in a similar manner to no 12, *Find 7912, context 1211, Structure IX, Phase 5b*
14 Fragmentary ring of very fine wire, *Find 4361, context 600, above Structure XIX, Phase 8*
15 Length of chain attached to a glass bead of sexagonal cross section; pendant from an earring or necklace fragment, *Find 223, unstratified*

Bracelets

A total of 43 copper alloy bracelets or fragments were recovered and these have been classified according to the system devised by Crummy (1983, 37–45) and listed below in decending order of occurrence.

Group 4: notched, toothed and crenellated forms
Finds 341 and 1912 (Fig 127, no 25)
Find 4146 (Fig 127, no 27),
Finds 1117, 951, 1468 and 2230 (Fig 128, nos 1–4),
Finds 1793, 2237 and 4524 (Fig 128, nos 6–8),
Find 4630 (Fig 128, no 11),
Find 2392, (Fig 128, no 15),
Find 3759,(Fig 128, no 16),
Finds 3762 and 4026 (Fig 128, no 18 and 19)
Finds 45 and 577 (Fig 129, nos 1–2);

Group 2: cable design
Finds 2062, 2318, 3314, 7000, 1622, 4742, 6531 and 6010 (Fig 127, nos 16–23);

Group 10: decorated with multiple motifs
Find 4884 (Fig 128, no 12),
Finds 224 and 705 (Fig 129, nos 3 and 4);

Group 5: with transverse groove decoration
Finds 243, 4146 and 779 (Fig 127, nos 24, 26 and 28)
Finds 4145, and 3741 (Fig 128, nos 10 and 17)

Also represented were:
Group 6: carrying diagonal grooves
Find 1793 (Fig 128, no 5)

Group 7: with punched or raised dot decoration
Find 6383 (Fig 128, no 14)

Group 8: with hatched lines
Find 4883 (Fig 128, no 13)

Group 9: bead imitative bracelets
Find 7254 (Fig 128, no 9)

Also represented, but not illustrated, were two examples of simple wire bracelets of group 1 and a plain hollow bracelet.

Analytical Results

by Justine Bayley

All the bracelets and bracelet fragments were analysed qualitatively by energy dispersive X-ray fluorescence (see brooch analysis above). Nearly 60% of all the pieces were brass, which is in some ways surprising as although this alloy was the normal one used for military fittings and for brooches in the mid first century AD, it was only used for about 10% of all other copper alloy metalwork in the later centuries of the Roman occupation of Britain (Bayley 1990). In the late Roman period bracelets rather than brooches were the common form of personal adornment and it may be that brass retained, or regained, its popularity for decorative metalwork, where its golden colour was appreciated.

Although the sample analysed was a relatively large one, there are not enough objects of individual types for it to be possible to say whether there is any statistical significance in the use of different alloys. The larger groups, eg the notched, toothed and crenellated bracelets, seem to be predominantly brass but the proportion is in fact little more than the overall average for all the bracelets. In the same way there is no obvious correlation between either composition or typology and phase. There are very few bracelets from pre-fourth-century contexts.

Individual analytical results have been incorporated in the catalogue

16 Brass bracelet fragment, two strand cable with stub of hook fastening, internal diameter 32mm, *Find 2062, context 302, Structure IV, Phase 4*
17 Brass bracelet fragment, two strand cable with sleeve adjacent to a broken hook fastening, internal diameter 64mm, *Find 2318, context 348, Structure IV, Phase 4b*
18 Brass bracelet fragment, two strand cable, *Find 3314, context 14, Structure II, Phase 6b*
19 Bronze bracelet fragment, two strand cable, *Find 7000, context 1191, Structure XIV, Phase 5d–6b*
20 Brass bracelet fragment, two strand cable, *Find 1622, context 300, Structure IV, Phase 6b*
21 Bronze bracelet fragment, two strand cable with stub of hook fastening, internal diameter 33mm, *Find 4742, context 602, Structure XIX, Phase 7*
22 Bronze/gunmetal bracelet fragment, two strand cable with hook fastener, internal diameter 56mm, *Find 6531, context 1100, above Structure XIV, Phase 7–8*
23 Bronze bracelet fragment, two strand cable with hook fastening, *Find 6010, context 0218, over Structure XIV, Phase 8*
24 Copper alloy bracelet fragment, transverse scoring between marginal grooves, *Find 243, unstratified*
25 Brass bracelet, joins Find 1912 (Fig 128, no 6); transverse notch decoration, internal diameter 64mm, *Finds 341 and 1912, context 14 and 206, Structure II, Phase 6b*
26 Bronze bracelet, plain except for transverse grooves on the expanded perforated terminal, *Find 4146, context 601, Structure XIX, Phase 7*

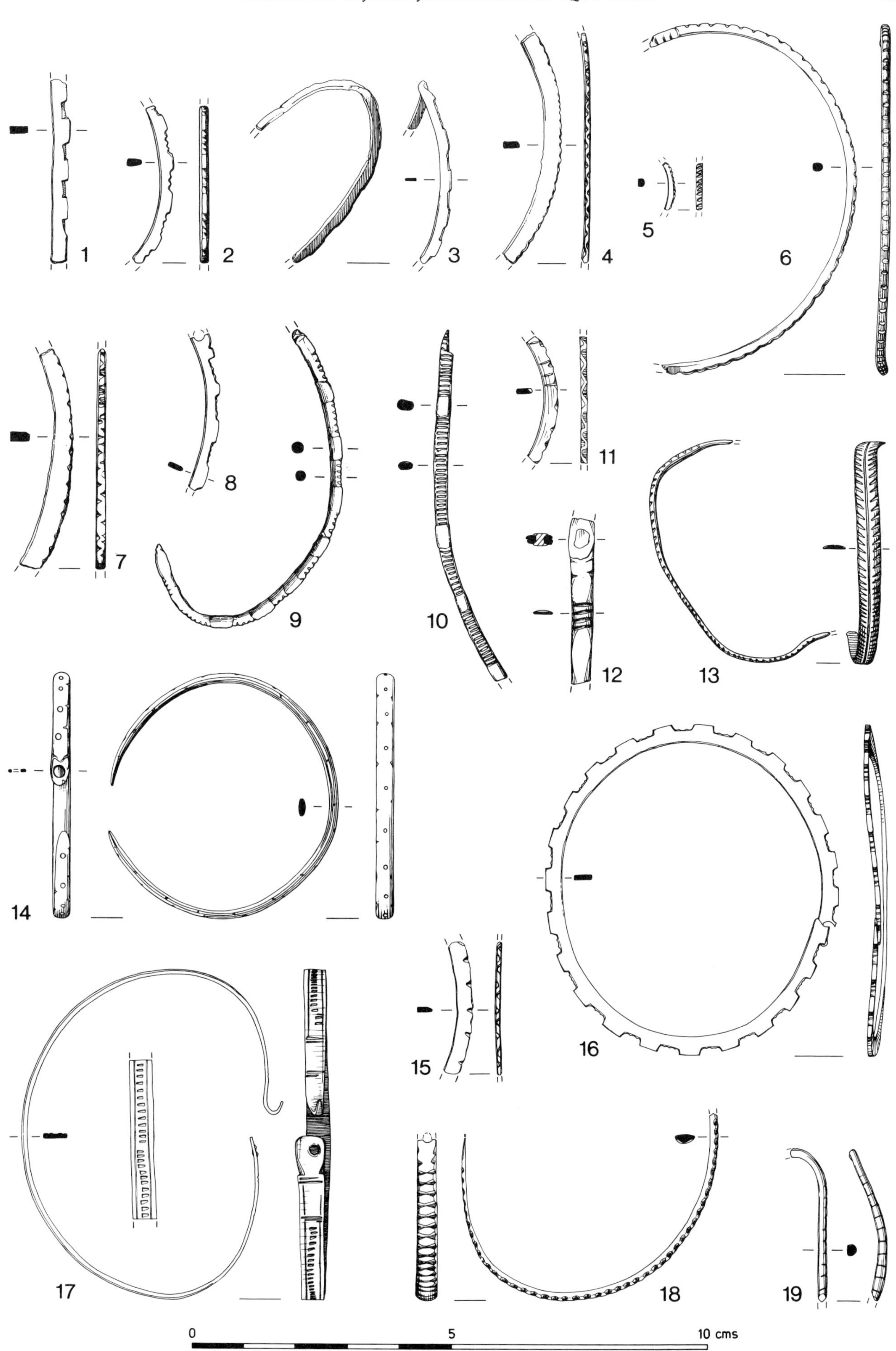

Fig 128 Bracelets of copper alloy, scale 1:1

27 Brass bracelet fragment with crenellated zone (two crenellations surviving), internal diameter 45mm, *Find 4094, context 601, Structure XIX, Phase 7*
28 Bronze bracelet fragment decorated with transverse grooves arranged in groups of four to seven grooves, separated by pairs of marginal notches, internal diameter 62mm, *Find 779, context 38, Structure I, Phase 5e(ii)*

Fig 128
1 Brass/gunmetal bracelet fragment with crenellations, *Find 1117, context 22, Structure I, Phase 5e(ii)*
2 Brass bracelet fragment with crenellations and toothing between the crenellations, Internal diameter 52mm, *Find 951, context 17, Structure II, Phase 6*
3 Brass bracelet fragment with crenellations, very distorted, *Find 1468, context 88, Structure II, Phase 6a*
4 Brass bracelet fragment with alternating notch decoration, internal diameter 70mm, *Find 2230, context 300, Structure II, Phase 6b*
5 Leaded bronze/gunmetal bracelet fragment with diagonal groove decoration, *Find 1793, context 300, Structure IV, Phase 6b*
6 Brass bracelet, joins Finds 341 and 1912 (Fig 127, no 25, above) *Find 1912, context 206, Structure II, Phase 6b*
7 Leaded gunmetal bracelet fragment decorated with alternating notches, internal diameter 92 mm, *Find 2237, context 331, Structure IV, Phase 6b*
8 Brass bracelet fragment with crenellations and toothing between them, internal diameter 65mm, *Find 4524, context 602, Structure XIX, Phase 7*
9 Leaded gunmetal bracelet decorated in imitation of beads, *Find 7254, context 0412, Structure XIX, Phase 7*
10 Bronze bracelet with transverse grooves arranged in groups, *Find 4145, context 511, Structure XIX, Phase 7*
11 Brass bracelet fragment with alternating notch decoration, internal diameter 40mm, *Find 4630, context 602, Structure XIX, Phase 7*
12 Brass bracelet fragment decorated with oval facets, groups of transverse grooves and ring motif, *Find 4884, context 602, Structure XIX, Phase 7*
13 Brass bracelet decorated with bands of opposed hatched grooves, *Find 4883, context 602, Structure XIX, Phase 7*
14 Bronze bracelet with hook and eye clasp decorated with spaced punched dots and marginal nicks, interior diameter 41mm, *Find 6383, context 1100, above Structure XIV, Phase 7–8*
15 Leaded gunmetal bracelet fragment with alternating notch decoration, internal diameter 67mm, *Find 2392, context 277, above Structure II, Phase 8*
16 Brass bracelet, crenellated with toothing between the crenellations and overlapping terminals, internal diameter 55mm, *Find 3759, ploughsoil*
17 Brass bracelet, decorated with transverse grooves between marginal lines and fastened by a hook and eye clasp, *Find 3741, ploughsoil*
18 Brass bracelet fragment decorated with opposed notching, part of eye clasp surviving, internal diameter 54mm, *Find 3762, ploughsoil*
19 Copper alloy bracelet fragment with notch decoration, *Find 4026, ploughsoil*

Fig 129
1 Brass bracelet decorated with alternating notches, internal diameter 40mm, *Find 45, ploughsoil*
2 Leaded bronze/gunmetal bracelet fragment decorated with diagonal grooving, *Find 577, ploughsoil*
3 Brass bracelet decorated with multiple motifs, transverse grooves, punched dots, ring and dot and marginal notching, *Find 224, context 2, Structure II, Phase 6b*
4 Brass bracelet fragments with opposed notching and a ring motif, *Finds 705 and 2426, contexts 12, Structure II, Phase 6b and ploughsoil, respectively*

Jet and shale

Jet and shale bracelets have been considered in detail by Lawson in connection with his analysis of the large assemblage from Silchester (Lawson 1976, 248). He was able to show that more than half of the bracelets there were plain, as in the preceding Iron Age, and that the simpler forms of decoration, comprising grooving and ribs, also reflected a pre-Roman background. New additions to the repertoire included the widespread employment of edge notching and carved versions such as the cable design. Crummy (1983, 36 and fig 38) has subdivided the notched category into four groups and defined three further categories: bracelets with ring and dot decoration, with transverse grooves, and an octagonal form.

Only the more common types have been found at Uley:
thirteen plain
shale: Finds 5843, 8532, 2288, 1886, 1184, 1560, 7663, 435, 480, 2248 (Fig 129, nos 5–14)
jet: Finds 2071, 670, and 1835 Fig 130, nos 7–9))
seven grooved
shale: Finds 1915, 1924, 7804, 67, 1908, 4618, 365, (Fig 129, nos 15–21))
six notched
shale: Finds 2038, 3125, 8282, 1527, 8260, 4794 (Fig 130, nos 1–6))
two of cable design
shale: Find 7766 (Fig 129, no 22), and Find 2139 (Fig 130, no 10)

Amongst the plain examples, the two from pre-Roman contexts, Finds 5843 and 8532 (Fig 129, nos 5 and 6) are of the massive type recognised as early by Lawson. Angularity of the inner face, resulting from the method of cutting from the core is present in several examples, eg Finds 1886, 1560, and 7663 (Fig 129, nos 8, 10 and 11), Finds 1527, 8260, 4794 (Fig 130, nos 4–6). The bracelets derive from contexts of all phases on the site except Phases 1 and 3, but a particular concentration (eight out of the twenty stratified examples) appear to have been associated with Structure IV of Phase 4.

all shale except where stated

5 Plain fragment with ovoid section, *Find 5843, context 928, ditch F264, Phase 2b*
6 Plain fragment, split, originally of ovoid section, *Find 8532, context 924, ditch F264, Phase 2c*
7 Plain fragment with ovoid section, *Find 2288, context 312, Structure IV, Phase 4*
8 Plain fragment of rounded section with angled inner face, *Find 1886, context 33, courtyard, Phase 4–6*
9 Plain fragment of D-shaped section, *Find 1184, context 68, Structure I, Phase 5e (i)*

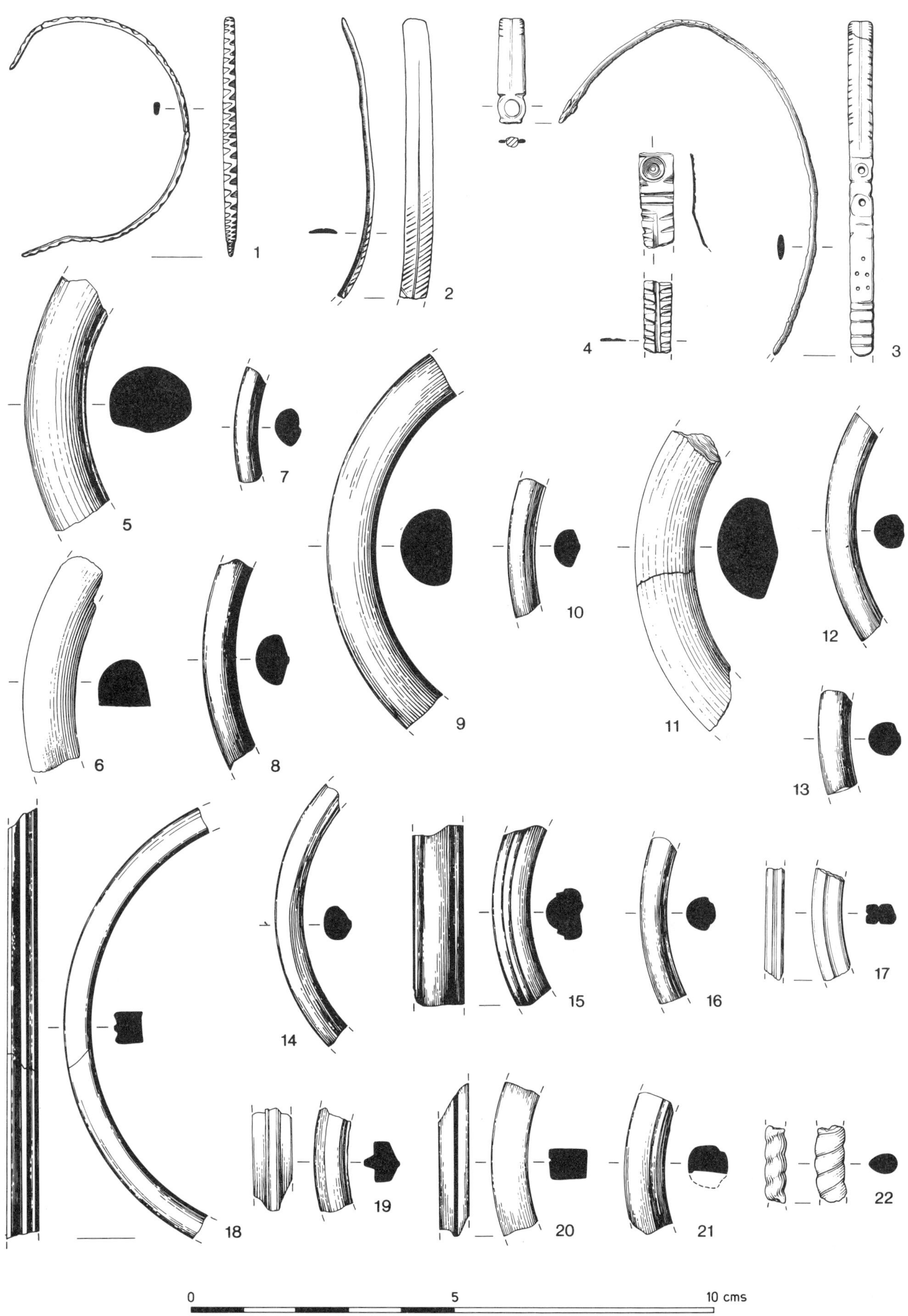

Fig 129 Bracelets of copper alloy (nos 1–4), and shale (nos 5–22), scale 1:1

10 Plain fragment of rounded section with angled inner face, *Find 1560, context 14, Structure II, Phase 6b*
11 Plain fragment of ovoid section with angled inner face, *Find 7663, context 1100, over Structure XIV, Phase 7–8*
12 Plain fragment of circular section with angled inner face, *Find 435, context 1, Phase 8*
13 Plain fragment of circular section with angled inner face, *Find 480, context 1, Phase 8*
14 Plain fragment of subrectangular section with angled inner face, *Find 2248, context 1, Phase 8*
15 Fragment with complex section and marginal groove decoration, *Find 1915, context 302, Structure IV, Phase 4a*
16 Fragment with marked internal grooves or steps, *Find 1924, context 302, Structure IV, Phase 4a*
17 Fragment of rectangular section, decorated with a single groove along each of the three exterior surfaces, *Find 7804, context 1204, Structure IX, Phase 5c*
18 Two joining fragments of square section with two longitudinal grooves on the outer face, *Finds 67 and 1908, contexts 67, Phase 8 and 302, Structure IV, Phase 4a*
19 Fragment of angled rectangular section with a longitudinal plain ridge on the outer face, *Find 4618, context 488, Structure II, Phase 6a*
20 Fragment of rectangular section with a single off-centre longitudinal groove on the outer face, *Find 365, context 1, Phase 8*
21 Fragment of subrectangular outline, now split, and with a marginal groove or step on the internal face, *Context 1, Phase 8*
22 Fragment of oval cross section carved in imitation of a metal cabled bracelet, *Find 7766, context 1203, Structure IX, Phase 5b*

Fig 130
1 Fragment of rectangular section decorated with sets of marginal opposed adjacent notches, *Find 2038, context 302, Structure IV, Phase 4a*
2 Fragments of rectangular section with a centrally placed longitudinal plain ridge and marginal alternating adjacent notches, *Find 3125, context 350, Structure IV, Phase 6b, and Find 3190, context 332, Structure IV, Phase 4b*
3 Fragment of square section with spaced notches on the upper face only, *Find 8282, context 1232, Structure X, Phase 5*
4 Fragment of angled square section decorated with marginal alternating adjacent triangular notches, *Find 1527, context 20, over Structure IX, Phase 7*
5 Fragment of angled rectangular section decorated with marginal small spaced notches, *Find 8260, context 0415, Structure XIX, Phase 7*
6 Fragment of angled rectangular section decorated with irregularly spaced marginal notches, *Find 4794, context 602, Structure XIX, Phase 7a*
7 Plain jet bracelet of circular section, *Find 2071, context 302, Structure IV, Phase 4a*
8 Plain jet bracelet fragment of D-shaped section, *Find 670, context 1, Phase 8*
9 Plain jet bracelet fragment of ovoid section, *Find 1835, context 1, Phase 8*
10 Jet bracelet fragment of D-shaped section carved in a cable design, *Find 2139, context 14, Structure II, Phase 6b*

Composite, antler and copper alloy

Composite bone or antler bracelets have been described by Clarke (1979, 313–4), who explains how the bone strips decay and straighten out after burial. At Lankhills in Hampshire, at least 42 such bracelets were found in late Roman grave groups. The bone or antler components were usually plain and were joined by copper alloy sleeves which sometimes were decorated with transverse grooving. All these features also occur among the Uley examples. Clarke argues that the type dates from the mid to late fourth century AD, with those incorporating ribbed sleeves possibly representing a later type than those with plain sleeves. The phasing of the three items here certainly conforms to this chronological patterning.
11 Worn fragment of ?deer antler of subrectangular section, one end still contained in part of a plain copper alloy sleeve of circular section, *Find 7105, context 1191, Structure XIV, Phase 5d–6b*
12 Three joining fragments of ?deer antler of rectangular section, one original end bearing two transverse grooves, *Find 4473, context 511, Structure XIX, Phase 7a*
13 Fragments of ?deer antler component of ovoid section, both original ends of the component are enclosed in copper alloy sleeves of ovoid section and decorated with transverse ribbing, *Find 7823, context 1206, Structure IX, Phase 5c*

Pins

all of copper alloy except where stated

Fig 131
1 Silver pin with flat circular head; the upper surface of the head decorated with a single ring and dot and marginal notches, *Find 2472, context 277, over Structure II, Phase 8*
2 Wire pin with point broken and bent; simple spiral head, *Find 5536, context 726, ditch F264, Phase 3a*
3 Pin with three grooves beneath a conical head; bent almost at right angles, *Find 5679, context 811, Structure IX, Phase 5a*
4 Pin with faceted cuboid head; bent near point, *Find 291, context 1, Phase 8*
5 Pin with a cuboid head , decorated with uneven geometric lines incorporating a circular setting, probably for a glass bead, *Find 5935, contex 0130, Phase 8*
6 Pin decorated with reel and cordon motifs below a spherical head, bent near point, *Find 6988, context 0415, Structure XIX, Phase 7*
7 Pin with flared cuboid head and inset blue-green glass bead, incised line spiralling round upper shaft, *Find 396, context 1, Phase 8*
8 Two joining pieces of a pin, point missing; elongated cone terminal with incised lattice decoration above cordon motifs, *Find 4532, context 1, Phase 8*
9 Jet pin, point missing, with faceted cuboid head, *Find 2156, context 302, Structure IV, Phase 4a*
10 Jet pin, point missing, with faceted cuboid head, *Find 401, context 1, Phase 8*
11 Jet pin, shaft and point, *Find 1916, context 302, Structure IV, Phase 4a*
12 jet pin shaft, *Find 2978, context 164, fill of F158, over Structure I, Phase 5e(ii)*

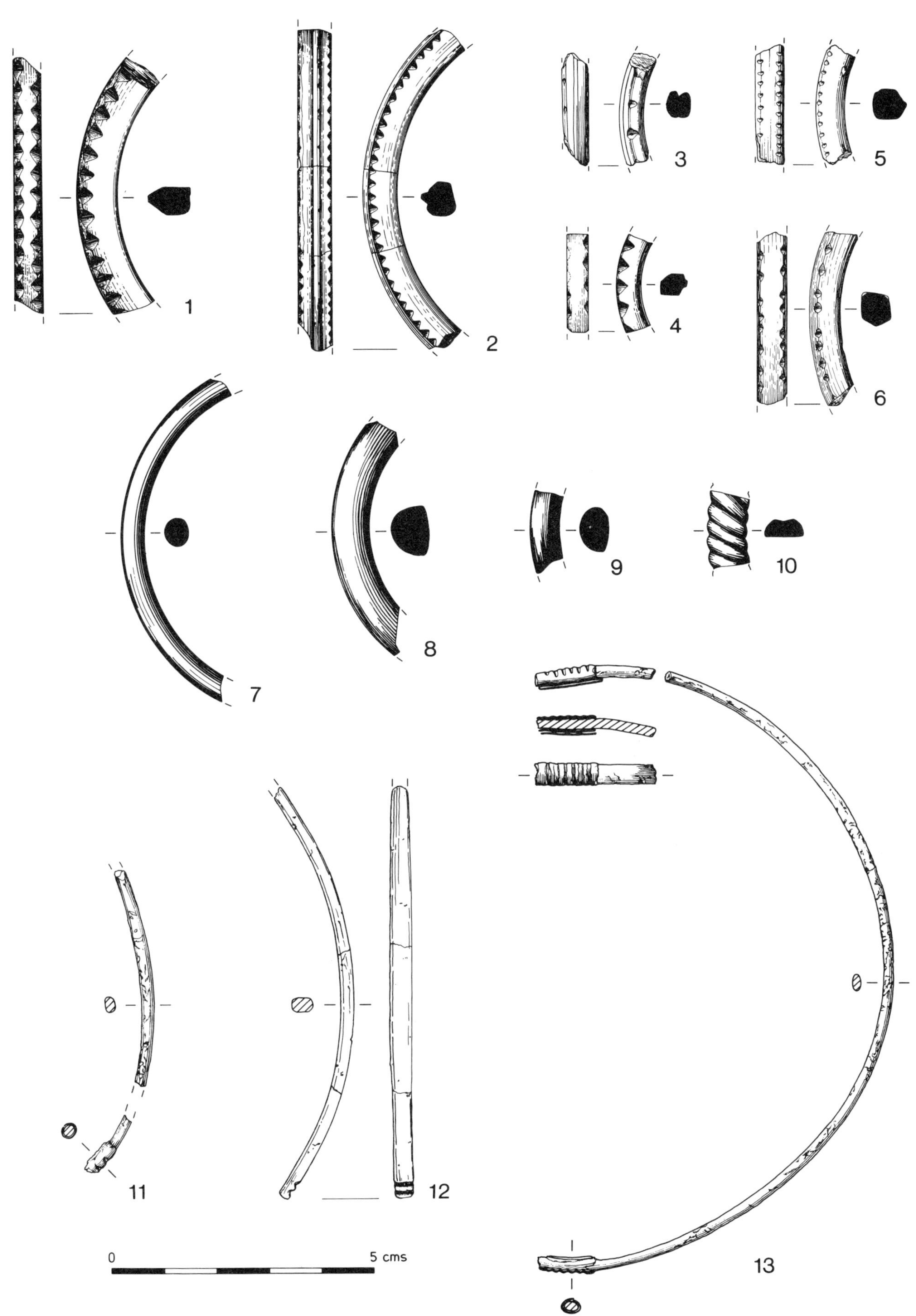

Fig 130 Bracelets of shale (nos 1–6), jet (nos 7–10), and composite antler and copper alloy (nos 11–13), scale 1:1

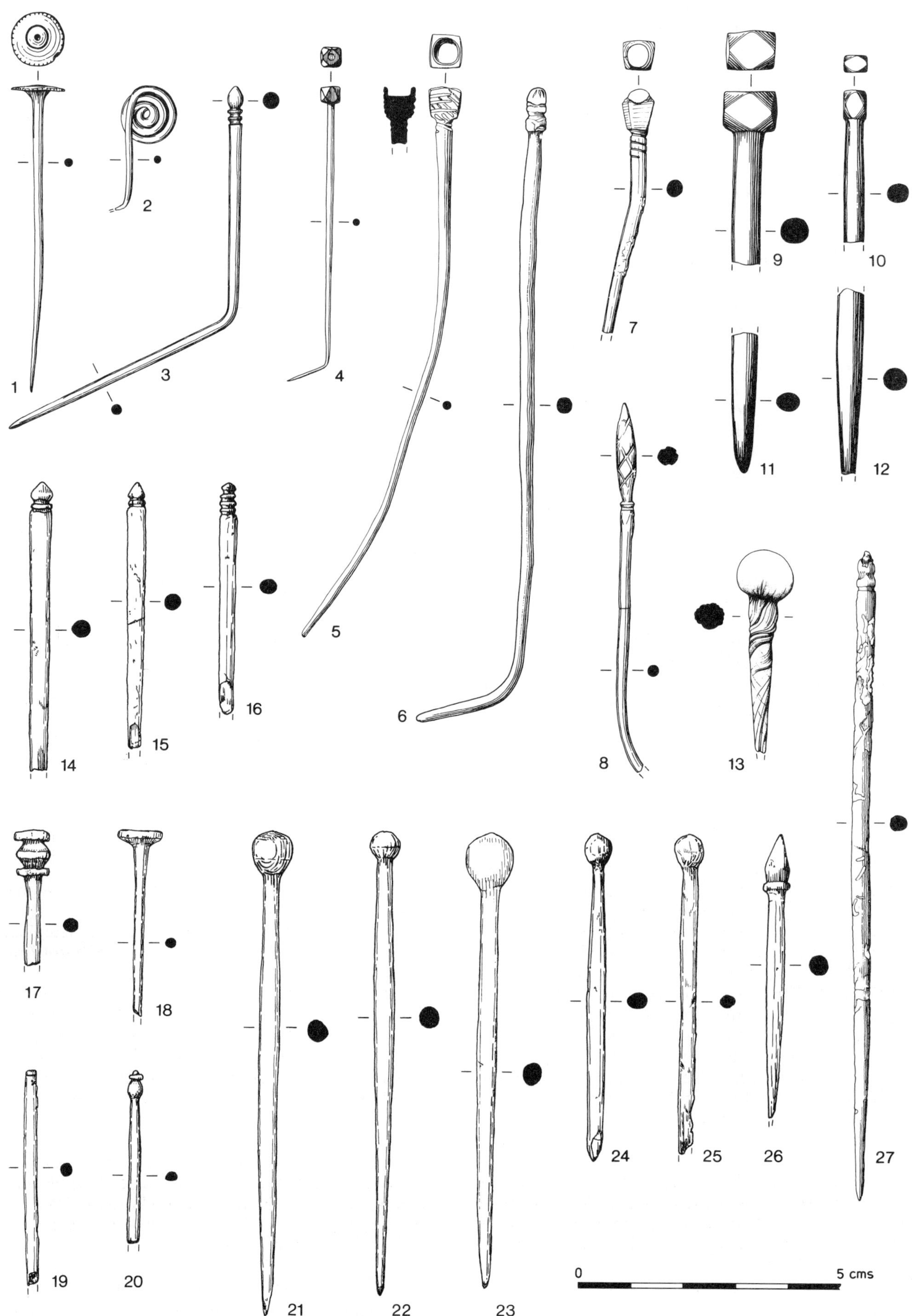

Fig 131 Pins of silver (no 1), copper alloy (nos 2–8), jet (nos 9–12), glass (no 13), and bone or antler (nos 14–27), scale 1:1

13 Glass hairpin, solid round head, Z-twisted stem tapering towards point (missing), pale-green coloured glass, present length 38 mm, *(J Price), Find 7554, context 1191, Structure XIV, Phase 5d–6b*
14 Bone pin with one groove beneath a conical head, *Find 2484, context 332, Structure IV, Phase 4b*
15 Bone pin with a single groove beneath a conical head, *Find 5878, context 901, Structure II exterior, fill above ditch F264, Phase 3b–5*
16 Bone pin decorated with three grooves beneath a conical head, *Find 5277, context 647, Structure IX, Phase 5b*
17 Bone pin with head comprising reel, cordoned bead, reel, *Find 1199, context 62, over Structure I, Phase 5e(ii)*
18 Bone pin with flat circular reel head, *Find 3484, context 368, Structure IV, Phase 6b*
19 Bone pin with a single groove below the head, *Find 3428, context 249, Structure VIII, Phase 6–7a*
20 Bone pin with head comprising bead, reel, bead, *Find 75, context 1, Phase 8*
21 Bone pin with slightly faceted spherical head, *Find 2179, context 302, Structure IV, Phase 4a*
22 Bone pin with spherical head, *Find 1894, context 68, Structure I, Phase 5e(i)*
23 Bone pin with spherical head, *Find 0103, context TF5, Phase 5*
24 Bone pin with spherical head, *Find 5720, context 820A, Structure X, Phase 4b*
25 Bone pin with spherical head, *Find 2734, context 162, fill of F158, over Structure I, Phase 5e(ii)*
26 Bone pin with a single reel below a conical head, *Find 4028, context 600, above Structure XIX, Phase 8*
27 Bone pin with two grooves beneath a damaged conical head, *Find 8170, context 1228, Structure IX, Phase 5a–b*

Bruce Levitan's analysis suggests that the 'bone' pins were most probably manufactured from deer antler.

The flat headed silver pin, Find 2472 (Fig 131, no 1) is a rare type; it probably derives from a late context over the temple and may be matched in the late Roman hoard of silver objects from Great Horwood, Bucks (Waugh 1966, 60–71, information from Elizabeth Fowler and Stephen Johnson). Amongst the copper alloy pins are represented Crummy's type 4: with faceted cuboid head (Crummy 1983); Find 291 (Fig 131, no 4); type 5: grooved below a spherical head; Find 6988 (Fig 131, no 6). The pin with a cone head, Find 4532 (Fig 131, no 8) may be compared with *ibid*, fig 31, no 504. The jet pins with faceted cuboid heads, Finds 2156 and 401 (Fig 131, nos 9–10) belong to Crummy's type 2 (*ibid*, 27–8) and equate with those described by Lawson as polyhedral (Lawson 1976, fig 7, 65a–d). They are a type belonging to the third or fourth centuries AD and were also found at Lydney (Wheeler and Wheeler 1932, fig 18, nos 70, 72 and 74).

The 'bone' pins include examples of Crummy type 2 dated to the later first and second centuries AD, Crummy type 3, of the third and fourth centuries and Crummy types 5 and 6, also late Roman in date (Crummy 1983, 19–25)
Crummy type 2: one to four grooves beneath a conical head
Finds 2484, 5878, and 5277 (Fig 131, nos 14–16) Finds 3428 and 8170 (Fig 131, nos 19 and 27)
Crummy type 3: more or less spherical head
Finds 2179, 1894, 0103, 5720 and 2734 (Fig 131, nos 21–5)
Crummy type 5: one to five reels below a conical or ovoid head
Find 4028 (Fig 131, no 26)
Crummy type 6: reel or bead and reel-shaped head
Finds 1199, 3484 and 75 (Fig 131, nos 17–18 and 20)

No pins occur in deposits prior to Phase 4 and most belong to Phase 4 or 5. The type 2 pins do not come from earlier contexts than the other types, but these particular items are all from destruction deposits so may be residual.

Finger rings

by Martin Henig

Rings with settings

all of copper alloy except where stated

Fig 132
1 Intaglio bezel of iron ring with nicolo glass intaglio of shape Henig F2 (Henig 1978, 35, fig 1), lower surface 9.5 by 8mm; 2mm thick; upper surface 6 by 5mm. The device is a Satyr prancing left (reversed in impression), *Find 6738, context 1100, Structure XIV, Phase 7–8*

For the type on cut gems compare Henig 1978, 207, no 172 (Castlesteads, Cumberland), no 175 (Colchester, Essex) and no 176 (Cappuck, Roxburghshire), pl vi

2 Circular bezel once filled with enamel, on each side of the shoulder is a moulding, most of the hoop is missing, *Find 5434, context 725, courtyard, Phase 4*
3 Flattened hoop with striations across shoulder, the bezel was enamelled, diameter 20mm, *Find 6950, context 1188, Structure XIV, XIV, Phase 5d–6b*
4 Flattened hoop, shoulder ornamented with two crossbars separated by notches, slight expansion towards attached bezel which is lost but was affixed by means of a small hole in the hoop at this point, diameter 20mm, *Find 1462, context 17, Structure 1, Phase 6*
5 Oval bezel with flattened hoop, incomplete, bezel contains a crazed glass setting. Length of bezel 7mm, *Find 6756, context 1114, Structure XIV, Phase 6*
6 Gilt copper alloy ring with octagonal bezel and expanded D-shaped shoulders. Apart from stubs, the lower part of the hoop is lost, diameter 19mm. The bezel contains a circular setting with a clear glass device, a raised cross. The type is related to the Romano-British imitation 'gems', compare Henig 1978, 257, no 582, pl xviii (Kent), *Find 379, context 12, Structure 11, Phase 6b*
7 Hoop expands towards bezel, and then narrows at shoulder. Raised bezel contains cabochon green glass setting, diameter 17mm. Compare Wedlake 1982, 148, no 8 (iii); fig 63, no 7, *Find 166, ploughsoil, Phase 8*
8 Simple ring expanding towards bezel. Inset green glass setting, *Find 6163, context 0257, ploughsoil, Phase 8*
9 Oval octagonal bezel, setting lost, moulding on shoulder at each side, diameter 21mm. Compare Kirk 1949, 22, no 4, fig 5, no 10; Wedlake 1982, 148, no 8, fig 63 (6), *Find 6540, ploughsoil, Phase 8*

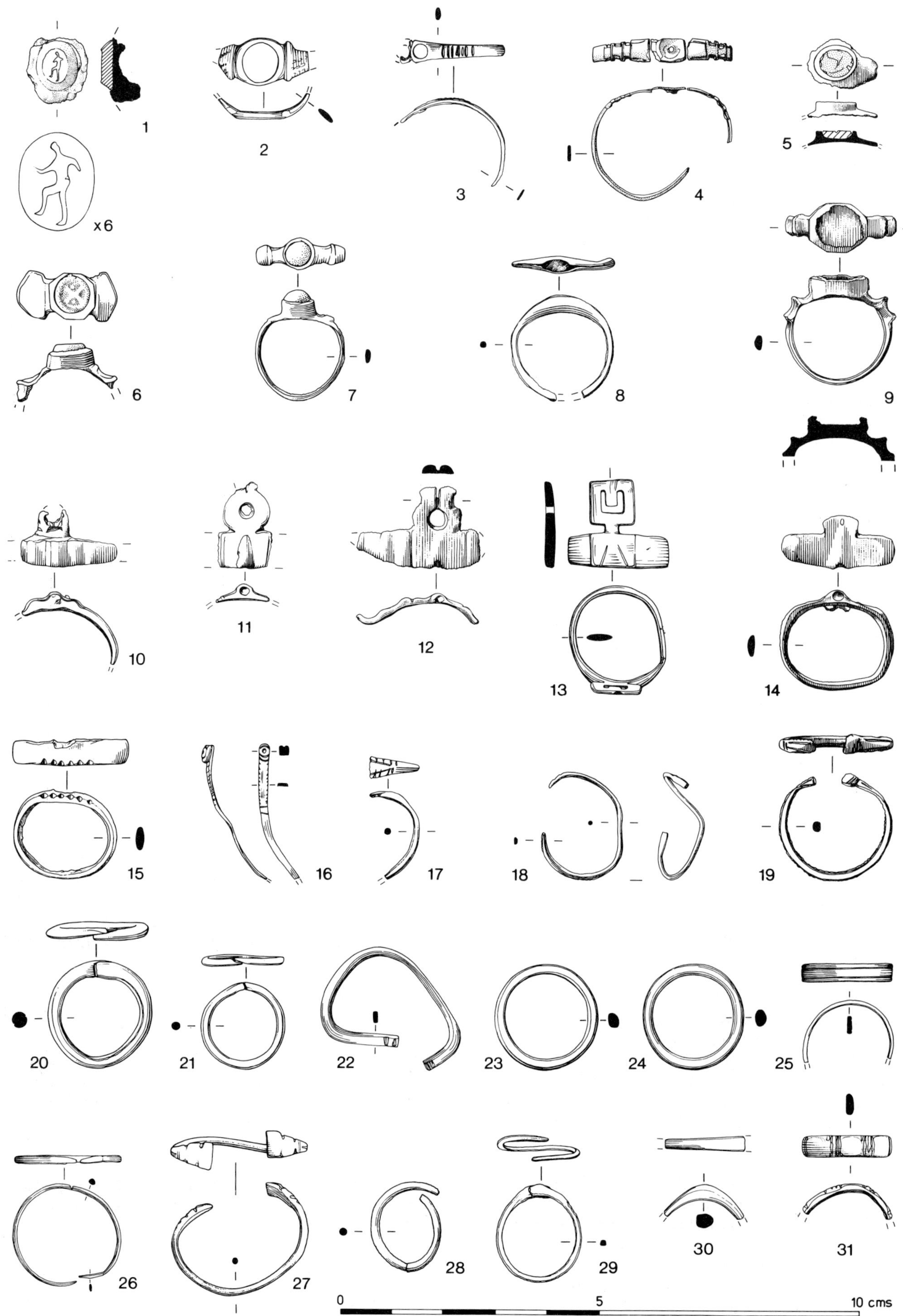

Fig 132 Finger rings of copper alloy, except nos 16, 23, and 24 of silver, scale 1:1

Key rings

10 Ring with circular pierced projection, at right angles to the hoop which is incomplete, *Find 2354, context 332, Structure IV, Phase 4b*
11 Ring with hollow triangular opening into bezel and circular pierced projection with 'ears', most of the hoop is missing, *Find 3009, context 160, Structure I, Phase 5a–d*
12 Similar to Find 3009 above, but the 'ears' on the projection are more prominent; much of the hoop is lost, *Find 1952, context 69, Structure I, Phase 5e (i)*
13 Flattened bezel, square projection with angular U-shaped opening, diameter 16mm, closely paralleled by Stead 1976, 202 and fig 105, no 51 from Old Winteringham, Lincs, *Find 5243, context 608, Structure XIII, Phase 5d–6a*
14 Silver ring, complete with hollow triangular opening into bezel and rectangular projection, diameter 22m, *Find 1640, context 300, Structure IV, Phase 6b*
15 Slightly flattened bezel, six notches down one edge, wards broken off, diameter 19mm, *Find 0102, pipe trench, Phase 8*

Finds 2354, 3009, 1952 and 1640 (Fig 132, nos 10–12 and 14) are a distinctive group and it is interesting that so many have been found at Uley. However, in view of the uncertainty as to whether they could have been functional, we can do no more than speculate on possible cult significance.

Boon (1979, 40–4, no 3) argues that such rings were probably not key rings and proposes a derivation from a type of decorative ring with confronted panthers and *cantharus* at right angles to the hoop, but the key-like appearance of the projections and the piercing do suggest that the type was based on the key ring. The close resemblance between the form of the projection on keys, Finds 3009 and 1952 (Fig 132, nos 11 and 12) in particular to a stylized *caduceus*, Find 6632 (Fig 89, no 5) may indicate that these rings likewise refer to Mercury. Also see Wedlake 1958, 252–3, no 12, fig 57,12R: third to fourth century AD.

Other rings

16 Silver ring, simple raised bezel, notches along shoulder, the other shoulder is missing, and the hoop has been straightened out, length 27mm, *Find 4546, context 602, Structure XIX, Phase 7a*
17 Ring with expanded triangular shoulders, notches cut into sides as decoration, diameter 16mm, incomplete; less than half of ring and only one shoulder remains, *Find 2264, context 320, Structure IV, Phase 4a*
18 Simple ring with open terminals but once hammered together, diameter *c* 19mm, *Find 7707, context 1202, Structure XIV, Phase 5d*
19 Simple ring with widened terminals, once hammered together *cf* Atkinson 1960, 40, no 10, pl xl, *Find 1345, context 17, Structure II, Phase 6*
20 Light ring, possibly hollow, with terminals hammered together from the side, diameter 20mm, *Find 360, context 12, Structure II, Phase 6b*
21 Simple ring with terminals hammered together from the side, diameter 16mm, *Find 368, context 12, Structure II, Phase 6b*
22 Flattened ring of rectangular section, the terminals seem to be hammered. Use as finger ring not certain, diameter *c* 23mm, *Find 5038, context 609, Structure IX, Phase 6b*
23 Simple silver ring, D-shaped section, diameter 19mm, *Find 5667, context 728, Structure VIII, Phase 7*
24 Simple silver ring, D-shaped section, diameter 19mm, *Find 5570, context 728, Structure VIII, Phase 7*
25 Silver ring, simple band with two grooves running around it – about half remains, width of hoop 4mm; diameter 17mm, *Find 4150, context 601, Structure XIX, Phase 7a*
26 Simple ring with open terminals, probably once hammered together, diameter 18mm, *Find 4590, context 603, Structure XIX, Phase 7a*
27 Ring which widens towards bezel ie a wedge or triangle on each side, with notched decoration. Open terminals, once hammered together, diameter *c* 25mm, *Find 6746, context 0409, over Structure XIX, Phase 7*
28 Simple ring, circular section; bent. Diameter 15mm, *Find 6448, context 1100, over Structure XIV, Phase 7–8*
29 Simple ring with terminals hammered together from the side, diameter 16mm, *Find 182, context 1, Phase 8*
30 Section of hoop of ring with marked carination at the base of the shoulder. A typical example of the third-century ring forms : Henig 1978, fig 1, type viii, *Find 3967, context 600, above Structure XIX, Phase 8*
31 Section of ring with flattened D-shaped section. Ornamented with regularly spaced triple bands of transverse grooving, *Find 6283, context 0227, Phase 8*

not illustrated

Fragment from hoop, diameter 15mm, *Find 1874, context 33, south courtyard, Phases 4–6*

Ring with simple moulding around it, diameter 27mm, *Find 3468, context 257, Structure II, Phases 4 and 5a–c*

Simple ring with very thin wire hoop, half remains, diameter 17mm, *Find 4361, context 600, above Structure XIX, Phase 8*

Scrap of wire from ring, *Find 4964, context 1, Phase 8*

Simple ring; about half remains, diameter 20mm, *Find 7108, context 1191, Structure XIV, Phase 5d–6b*

Simple hoop of flattened, ovoid section, diameter originally 15mm, *Find 7227, context 1191, Structure XIV, Phase 5d–6b* Simple ring, circular section, about half remains, diameter 22mm, *Find 8132, context 1229, Structure XIV, Phase 5b*

Jet rings

Fig 133

1 Fragment of a ring, flat plain bezel and stepped shoulder on one side only surviving, *Find 2227, context 331, Structure IV, Phase 6b*
2 Nearly half of a ring with plain flat oval bezel and stepped shoulder. *Find 73, context 1, Phase 8*
3 Fragment of a plain ring with slightly expanded bezel, no detailed treatment of shoulder, *Find 647, context 1, Phase 8*
4 Fragment of expanded shoulder with the remains of a step and an incised arc motif, *Find 6850, context 0230, Phase 8*
5 Half of a ring with flat rectangular section, decorated with two longitudinal grooves, *Find 2350, context 354, Structure IV, Phase 4b*

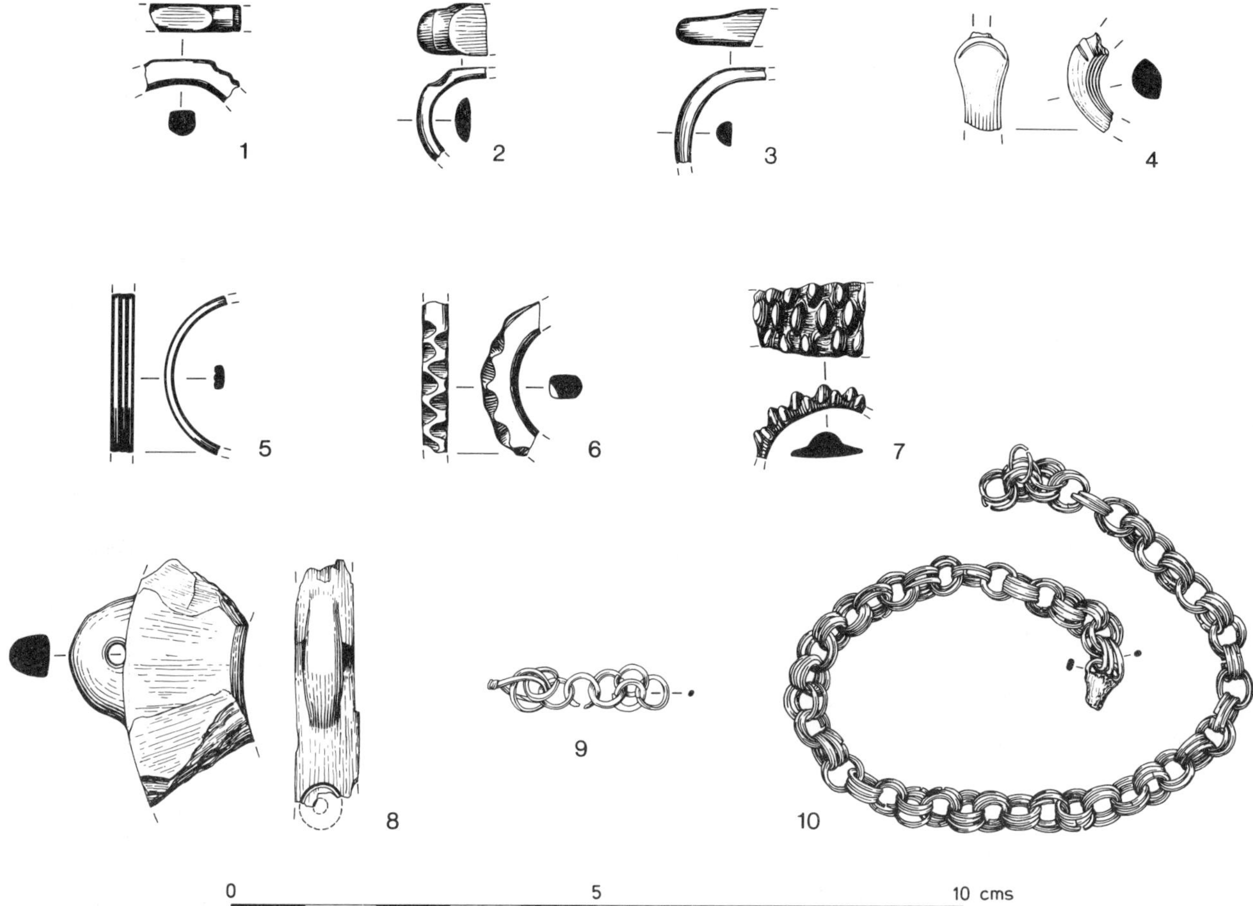

Fig 133 Finger rings of jet (nos 1–7), pendant of jet (no 8), and chains of copper alloy (nos 9–10), scale 1/1

6 Fragment of a ring with subrectangular section, decorated with interleaving notches along both outer margins, *Find 3138, context 171, below Structure I, Phase 4a*

7 Fragment of a wide ring with expansion, of flat cross section and decorated all over exterior surface with rounded oval projections, *Find 4148, context 600, above Structure XIX, Phase 8*

Discussion

The ring assemblage is not unusual for a native site save that the extreme flimsiness of some of the rings does suggest the trinket bought at the temenos shop, perhaps as an offering. It has been suggested above that a few rings have projections which suggest *caducei*, (see chapter 6, Fig 89) including one ring of silver, Find 1640 (Fig 132, no 14). It may be noted that Mercury wears a silver serpent ring around his neck on a bronze plaque from Caistor St Edmund, Norfolk (*Britannia* **2**, 1971, 270 and pl xxxvii B), while the King Harry Lane, Verulamium figurine of the same god sported an open ring or torque (*Britannia* **3**, 1972, 329–30 and pl xxv, B and C).

Although no gold ring was found, one is mentioned as a votive for the god on a *defixio* from the temple (Hassall in Ellison 1980, 327 and chapter 7, tablet 3 above). Normally, however Mercury was given rings of only token value and in this connection, Figs 114 and 115 in chapter 8 show flattened base metal rings probably produced on the site.

Pendant

8 Fragment of a plain, probably annular jet pendant with a perforated semicircular attachment loop and part of a countersunk perforation, *cf* Lawson 1976, 256 and fig 7, 61 and 62, *Find 5868, from fieldwalking, Phase 8*

Chains

all of copper alloy

9 Chain of fine circular section links, possibly a fragment from chain mesh, *Find 1817, context 61, Structure I, Phase 5e(i)*

10 Triple link units and remains of a fastening device at one end, possibly from a necklace, *Find 74, context 1, Phase 8*

see also necklace fittings above

'Mirror'

Fig 134

1 A fragment of copper alloy, with the upper face decorated with turned concentric circles, originally identified as from a mirror, the find has since been examined by Dr Glenys Lloyd-Morgan, who reports that the fragment is in fact probably the terminal disc of the handle of a large *patera* of the first or second century AD, the centre of the disc being pierced by either a crescentic or circular hole, cf, Boesterd 1956, 4–11, pl I nos 12, 13, 15, pl II, nos 22-24, 27, 28, pl XIII, no 12b, *Find 343, context 14, Structure II, Phase 6b*

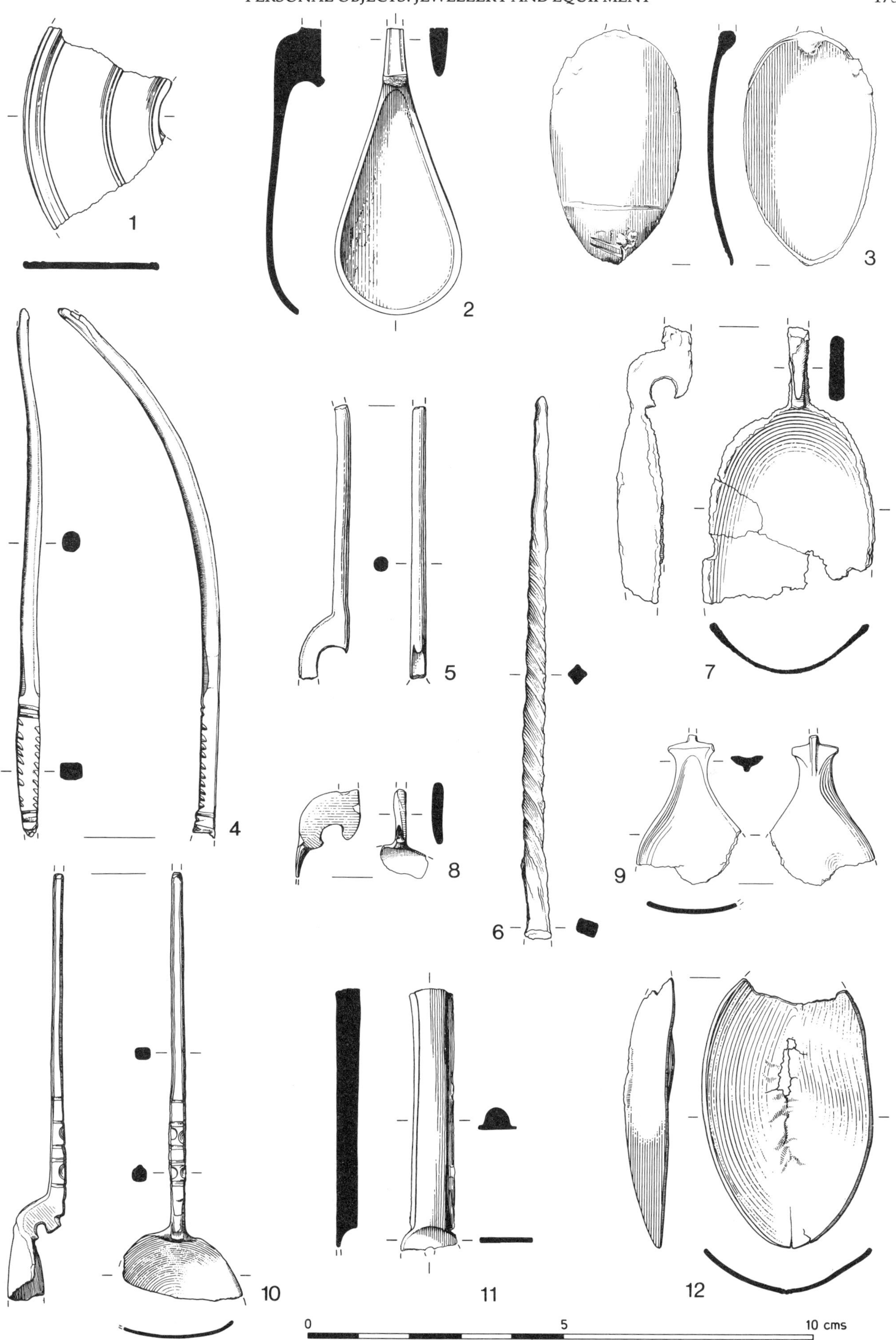

Fig 134 'Mirror' fragment (no 1), and copper alloy spoons, scale 1:1

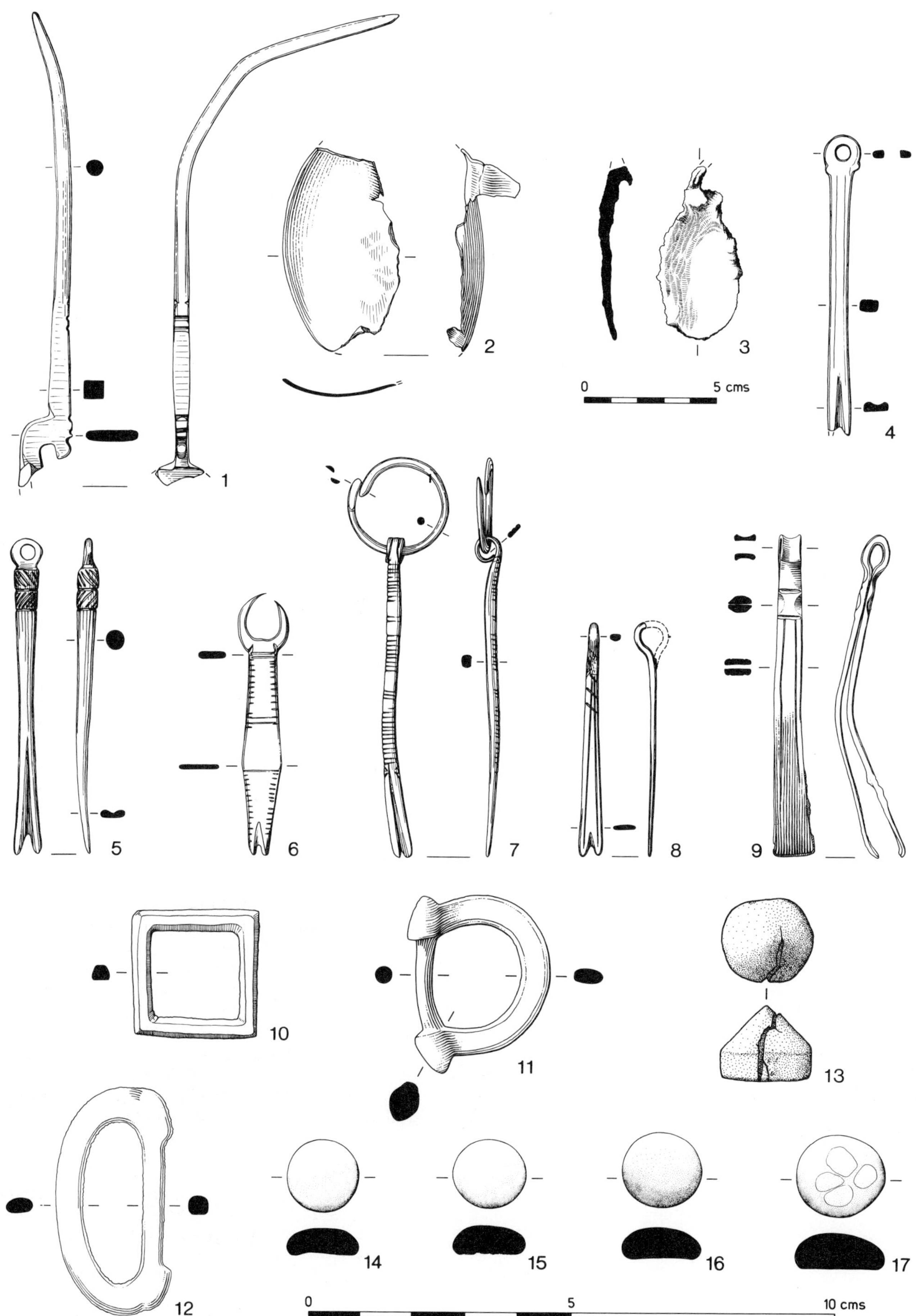

Fig 135 Copper alloy spoons (nos 2–12), toilet articles (nos 4–9), buckles (nos 10–12), gaming pieces of clay (no 13) and glass (nos 14–17), scale 1:1

Spoons

The spoons have been divided into three types according to the classification in Crummy 1983, 69. The early to mid-Roman type 1, with rounded bowl is not represented here, but there are four definite examples of the type 2 spoons with pear-shaped bowl, Finds 8331, 1757, and 245 (Fig 134, nos 3, 7, and 12) Find 771 (Fig 135, no 2). Two others belong to Crummy type 3, with a mandolin-shaped bowl, Finds 5447 and 414 (Fig 134, no 2 and no 9) Both of these types occur throughout the Roman period.

all of copper alloy except where stated

2 Spoon bowl, triangular in shape, *Find 5447, context 682, Structure X, Phase 4a*
3 Damaged spoon bowl, pear-shaped,*Find 8331, context 1241, Structure IX, Phase 5a*
4 Silver spoon handle, bent, decorated with tranverse grooves and marginal nicks near the position of the bowl, *Find 716, context 22, over Structure I, Phase 5e (ii)*
5 Handle and neck fragment from spoon, *Find 725, context 22, over Structure I, Phase 5e (ii)*
6 Twisted spoon handle, tinned, *Find 1754, context 38, over Structure I, Phase 5e (ii)*
7 Fragments of pear-shaped bowl and neck of spoon, *Find 1757, context 38, over Structure I, Phase 5e (ii)*
8 Neck and bowl fragment, *Find 5046, context 478, Structure XIX, Phase 7a*
9 Fragment of a spoon bowl, mandolin-shaped, *Find 414, context 1, Phase 8*
10 Tinned spoon, bowl and end of handle damaged, decorated with transverse grooves and circular hollows towards the neck, *Find 3429, context 301, Structure IV, Phase 6b*
11 Handle fragment with damaged, perforated terminal, possibly from a spoon, *Find 138, pipe trench, Phase 8* 12 Damaged silver spoon bowl, pear-shaped, *Find 245, context 1, Phase 8*

Fig 135
1 Handle and neck of spoon, decorated with transverse grooves and nicks, *Find 4537, context 13, Structure XIX, Phase 8*
2 Damaged spoon bowl, pear-shaped, *Find 771, context 1, Phase 8*
3 Iron spoon bowl, *Find 7776, context 1204, Structure IX Phase 5c*

Toilet articles

Crummy (1983, 57) type 1a of mid or late first-century to second-century date, Find 5393 (Fig 135, no 4); type 3 of the mid to late third century, Find 2187 (Fig 135, no 5) and type 4, belonging to the late third and fourth centuries, Find 6557 and 2130 (Fig 135, nos 6 and 7) all appear to be represented here.

all of copper alloy

4 Nail cleaner with straight, thick shaft of rectangular cross section, and suspension loop in the same plane as the blade, *Find 5393, context 634, above Structure X, Phase 5a–c*
5 Nail cleaner with shaft of circular cross section, suspension loop in same plane as the blade and decorated with two bands of diagonal lines below the loop, *Find 2187, context 45, Structure I, Phase 5e (i)*
6 Beaten out nail cleaner with flat, lozenge-shaped blade, decorated with marginal nicks, *Find 6557, context 1100, over Structure XIV, Phase 7–8*
7 Beaten out nail cleaner of square cross section, with the loop at right angles to the blade, and still attached to a simple ring; the blade is decorated with zones of transverse grooves, *Find 2130, context 2, Structure II, Phase 6b*
8 Nail cleaner with flat blade, suspension loop at right angles to the blade and decorated with three diagonal grooves below the top, *Find 5778, context 842, pit F836, Phase 2a–3b*
9 Tweezers, decorated with longitudinal lines on the blades, and cut mouldings below the loop, *Find 6336, pipe trench, Phase 8*

Buckles

all of copper alloy

10 Square cast buckle loop of trapezoidal section, *Find 1981, context 14, Structure II, Phase 6b*
11 D-shaped cast buckle loop of oval section, *Find 831, context 20, over Structure IX, Phase 7*
12 D-shaped cast buckle loop of oval section, *Find 8345, context 0410, Structure XIX, Phase 7*

Counters and gaming pieces

13 Conical gaming piece of very fine baked clay, *Find 5466, context 604, Structure XIX, Phase 7a*
14 Plano-convex glass disc with flat dimpled and uneven, dull, weathered surfaces, grey-white. Height 5.7mm, diameter 13,7mm, *(J Price), Find 8075, context 1200, Structure IX, Phase 5a*
15 Plano-convex glass disc, slightly oval, flat surface dimpled and uneven, dull, weathered surfaces; dark ground, probably yellow-brown, appearing black. Height 6mm, diameter 12.7 – 13.7mm, *(J Price), Find 7754, context 1204, Structure IX, Phase 5c*
16 Planoconvex glass disc, slightly oval, flat surface partly worn smooth, partly dimpled and uneven. Dull, weathered surfaces, dark ground, probably yellow-brown, appearing black. Height 6.5mm, diameter 14–15mm, *(J Price), Find 8116, context 1218, Structure XIV, Phase 5d*
17 Planoconvex glass disc, slightly oval, flat surface worn smooth. Dull, weathered; dark ground, appearing grey-black; four opaque blue insets with dark surrounds, appearing black, in convex surface. Height 6.5mm, diameter 15–16.8mm, *(J Price), Find 7572, context 1191, Structure XIV, Phase 5d–6b*

Fig 136
1 Trimmed circle of lead, *Find 1580, context 88, Structure II, Phase 6a*
2 Rectangular lead piece or offcut, *Find 4917, context 604, Structure XIX, Phase 7*
3 Trimmed circlet of lead, *Find 2820, context 400, over Structure II, Phase 8*
4 Baked clay counter, trimmed from a sherd, broken, *Find 5830, context 910, pit F251, Phase 3a*

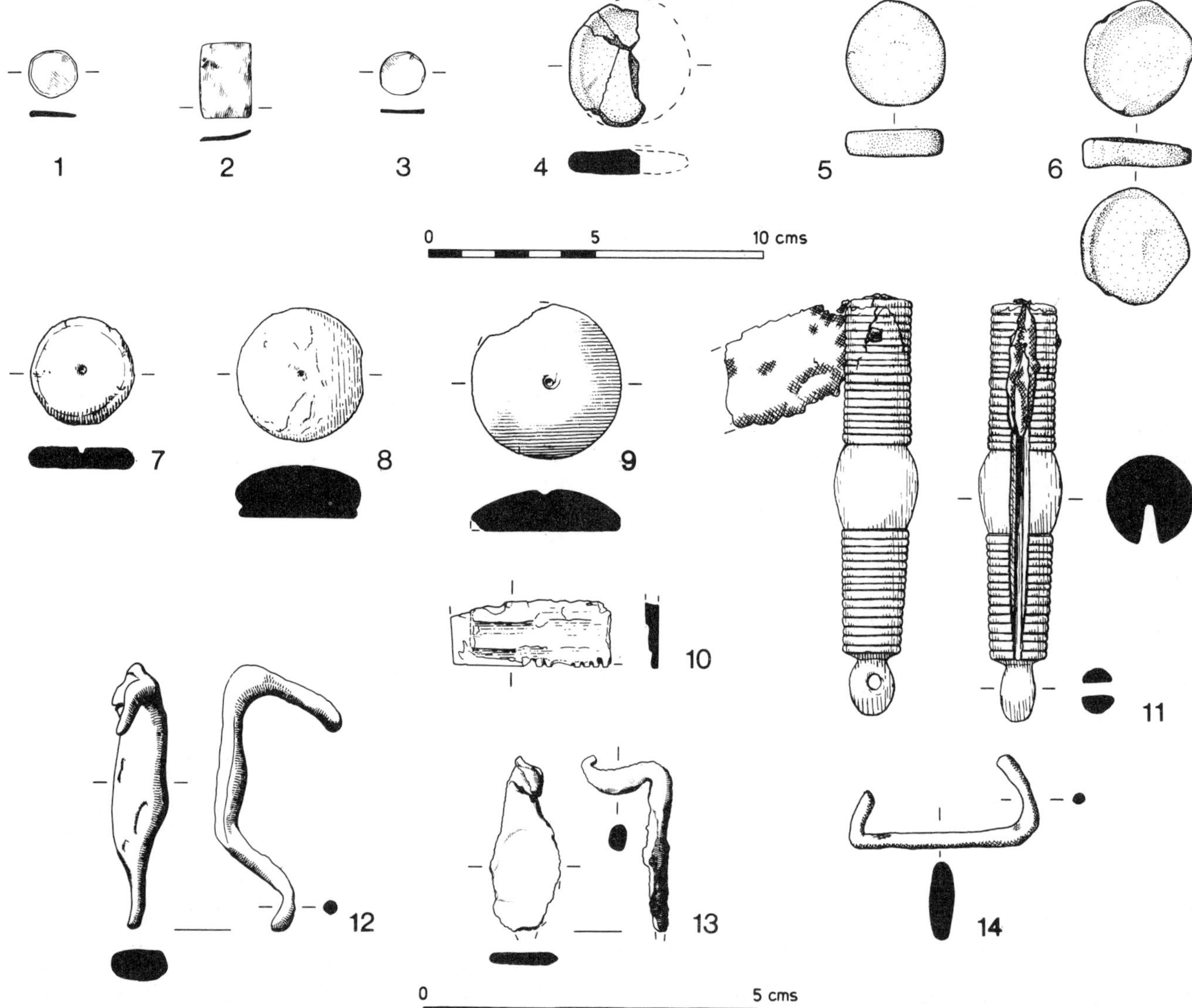

Fig 136 Gaming pieces of lead (nos 1–3), pottery (nos 4–6), and antler (nos 7–9), bone comb fragments (no 10), razor of iron and bone (no 11), scale 1:2, and shoe fittings of iron (nos 12–14), scale 1:1

5 Baked clay circular counter, trimmed from a sherd, *Find 5599, context 682, below Structure IX, Phase 4a*
6 Baked clay subcircular counter, trimmed from a sherd, *Find 5441, context 682, below Structure IX, Phase 4a*

nos 5 and 6 may be part of a set

7 Circular counter of ?deer antler, *Find 1857, context 33, courtyard, Phase 4–6*
8 Circular counter of ?deer antler, bun-shaped, *Find 5576, context 627, Structure IX, Phase 5a–c*
9 Circular counter of ?deer antler, low conical, *Find 6016, context 0226, Phase 8*

The 'bone' counters were lathe turned and retain the indentation of the lathe centre in each case

Comb

10 Fragment of bone comb with extant corner and stubs of six teeth, very eroded, *Find 1291, context 14, Structure II, Phase 6b*

Razor

11 Razor or clasp knife, with the stub of an iron blade pivoted on a single pin, cylindrical decorated bone handle, with a blade recess and a terminal suspension loop, *Find 2238, context 97, Structure I, Phase 5e(i)*

This can be paralleled from the sacred spring at Bath (Henig in Cunliffe ed 1988, 24, fig 13, no 58)

Shoe fittings

12 Iron cleat from a boot sole or heel, (Manning 1985, 131 and pl 61), *Find 3659, context 537, Structure F179, Phase 3b*
13 Iron cleat from a boot sole or heel. (Manning 1985, 131 and pl 61), *Find 4451, context 600, above Structure XIX, Phase 8*
14 Iron cleat from boot sole or heel. (Manning 1985, 131 and pl 61), *Find 1190, context 62, over Structure I, Phase 5e(i)*

see also chapter 10 for hobnails

10 Structural and functional materials: building components and fittings, tools, vessels, metalworking, and surface finds

Building components

Roofing

The Roman and some of the post-Roman buildings were substantial structures with all major components fabricated from stone. The walls were composed of roughly worked blocks and rubble of the local Inferior oolite with the frequent incorporation of reused materials, usually stone roofing tiles, from earlier building phases.

Roofing tiles were mainly of Pennant Sandstone although a few fragments of ceramic tegulae and imbrices were recovered. The sandstone roofing tiles were roughly hexagonal in shape and four near complete examples are illustrated.

Fig 137
1–4 Each tile possessed a single, off centre attachment hole and, in several cases, the original iron nails were preserved within these holes, *Context 97, Structure I, Phase 5e(i)*

not illustrated
One complete limestone block, with a shallow V-shaped indentation on one side, probably served as a section of roof ridge coping stone.

Flooring

Surviving floor levels were made up usually from closely set rounded pieces of the local limestone, as were the exterior courtyard surfaces. A large portion of plain buff tesselated flooring was excavated in the southern room (Room c) of Structure IX (see chapter 3 and Fig 48, F1216) and a total of 31 tesserae were recovered from layers above and adjacent to that floor. The tesserae in the surviving floor were all of a fine grained lias limestone but the loose examples included items of local coarse oolitic limestone, red ceramic tile and Old Red Sandstone as well as the buff lias limestone.

Carved masonry

Fig 138
1 Fragment of oolitic limestone column base, *Find 8330, context 1243, Structure IX, Phase 5b*

a selection of roofing tiles, the limestone coping stone and all the tesserae are housed in the British Museum

Structural fittings

all of iron

2 L-shaped wall hook, square sectioned hook and shank. *Find 5718, context 820A, Structure X, Phase 4b*
3 L-shaped wall hook, square sectioned hook and tapering shank, *Find 1389, context 52, Structure II, Phase 6a*
4 L-shaped wall hook, square sectioned hook and tapering shank, *Find 2848, context 48, Structure I, Phase 5a–d*
5 L-shaped wall hook, square sectioned hook and tapering hook, *Context 1, Phase 8*
6 Bolt, circular section, flattened head, *Context 1, Phase 8*
7 Bolt, square sectioned shank, flattened head of circular section, *Find 178, context 1, Phase 8*
8 Loop headed double spike, rectangular section, *Find 2149, context 200, Structure II, Phase 6a*
9 Loop headed ?double spike, sub-rectangular section, *Find 7395, context 1191, Structure XIV, Phase 5d–6b*
10 Loop headed double spike, lenticular section, *Find 251, context 1, Phase 8*
11 Loop headed spike or bolt, rectangular section, *Find 688, context 13, over Structure XIX, Phase 8*
12 Loop headed spike, rectangular section, *Find 2196, context 14, Structure II, Phase 6b*
13 Large loop headed spike or pin, sub-rectangular section, *Find 7958, context 0406, Structure XIX, Phase 7*
14 Small loop headed hook, circular section, *Find 1616, context 12, Structure II iii, Phase 6b*
15 Loop headed spike, circular section, *Find 6494, context 0401, Structure XIX, Phase 7*
16 Loop headed spike, sub-rectangular section, *Find 4583, context 12, Structure II iii, Phase 6b*
17 Double spiked loop, rectangular section, *Find 7615, context 0506, Structure XIX, Phase 7*
18 Holdfast with two fragmentary roves, circular section, *Find 1927, context 206, Structure II, Phase 6b*
19 Holdfast with mineralised wood fragment, circular section, *Find 2732, context 164, fill of F158, over Structure I, Phase 5e(ii)*
20 Joiner's dog or staple, *Find 679, context 18, over Structure XIX, Phase 8*

Keys, locks, and latch lifters

of iron except where stated

Fig 139
1 T-shaped lift-key, teeth missing (*cf* Manning 1985, 90 and pl 40), *Find 2114, context 322, F364, Structure IV, Phase 4a*
2 Simple lever-lock key, teeth corroded (*cf ibid*, 94 and pls 41 and 42), *Find 2814, context 332, Structure IV, Phase 4b*
3 Copper alloy lever-lock key with a three notched bit and hollow stem, top missing, *Find 5262, context 619, Structure IX, Phase 5c*
4 Barb-spring padlock key, bit missing (*cf ibid*, 96 and pl 43), *Find 18, context 1, Phase 8*
5 Barb spring padlock key, bit missing (*cf ibid*), *Find 1485, context 52, Structure IIiii, Phase 6a*
6 Corroded and damaged barb-spring padlock key bit, handle missing (*cf ibid*), *Find 2799, context 332, Structure IV, Phase 4b*
7 Barb-spring padlock mechanism, type 1 with a

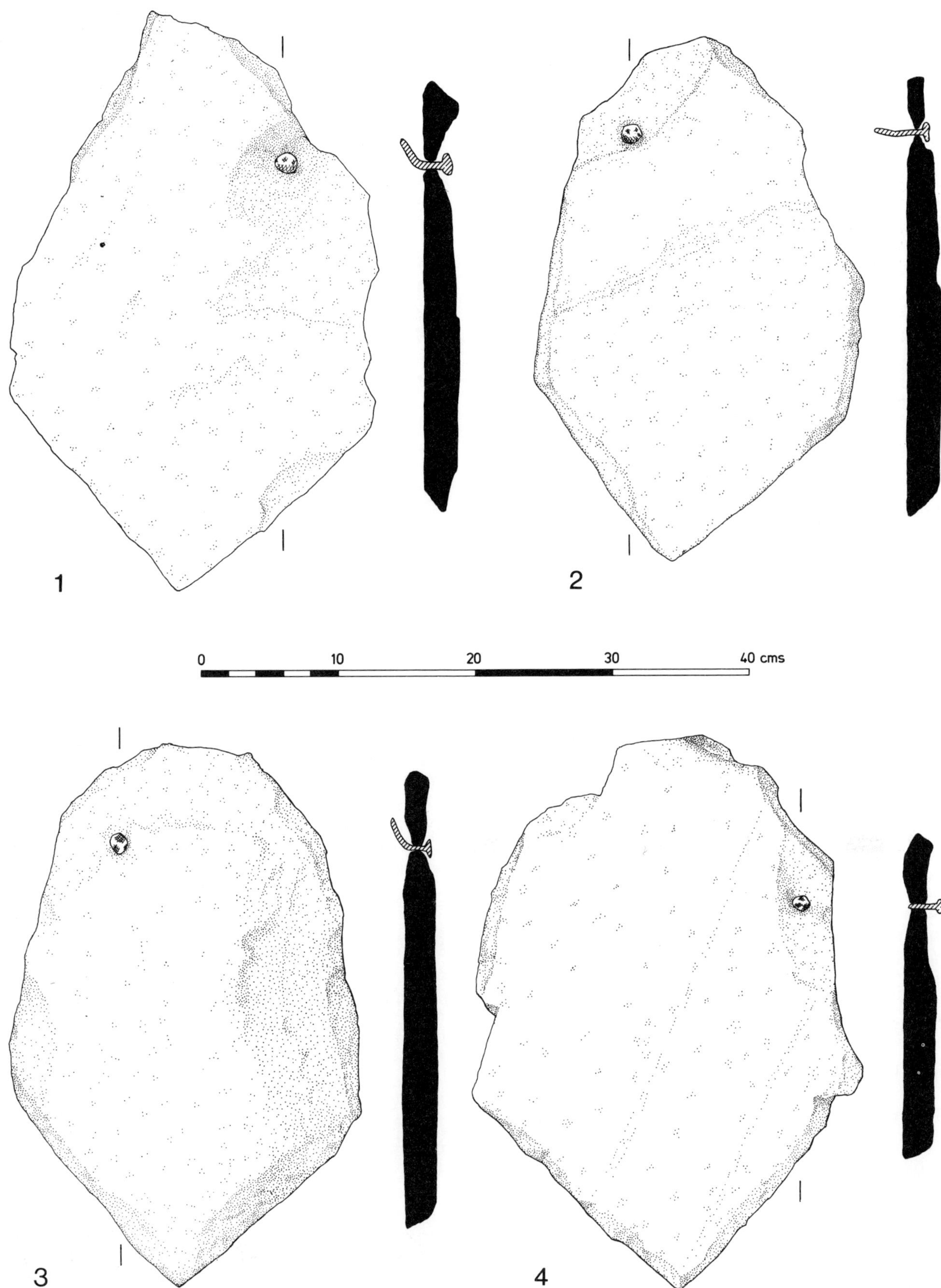

Fig 137 Stone roof tiles, scale 1:4
Fig 138 Limestone column base (no 1), and structural fittings of iron, scale 1:2 (opposite)

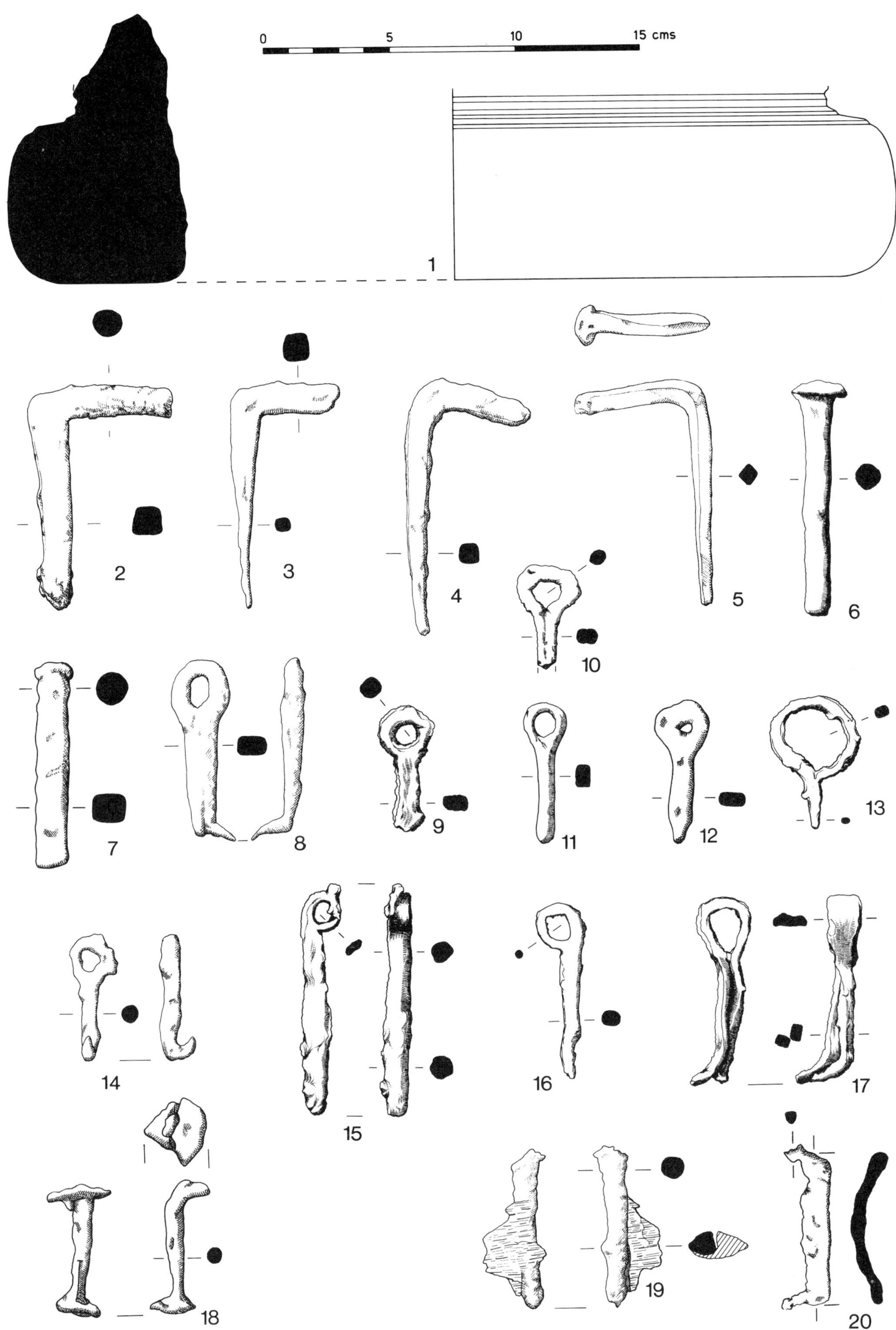
0
5
10
15 cms
1
2
3
4
5
6
7
8
9
10
11
12
13
14
15
16
17
18
19
20

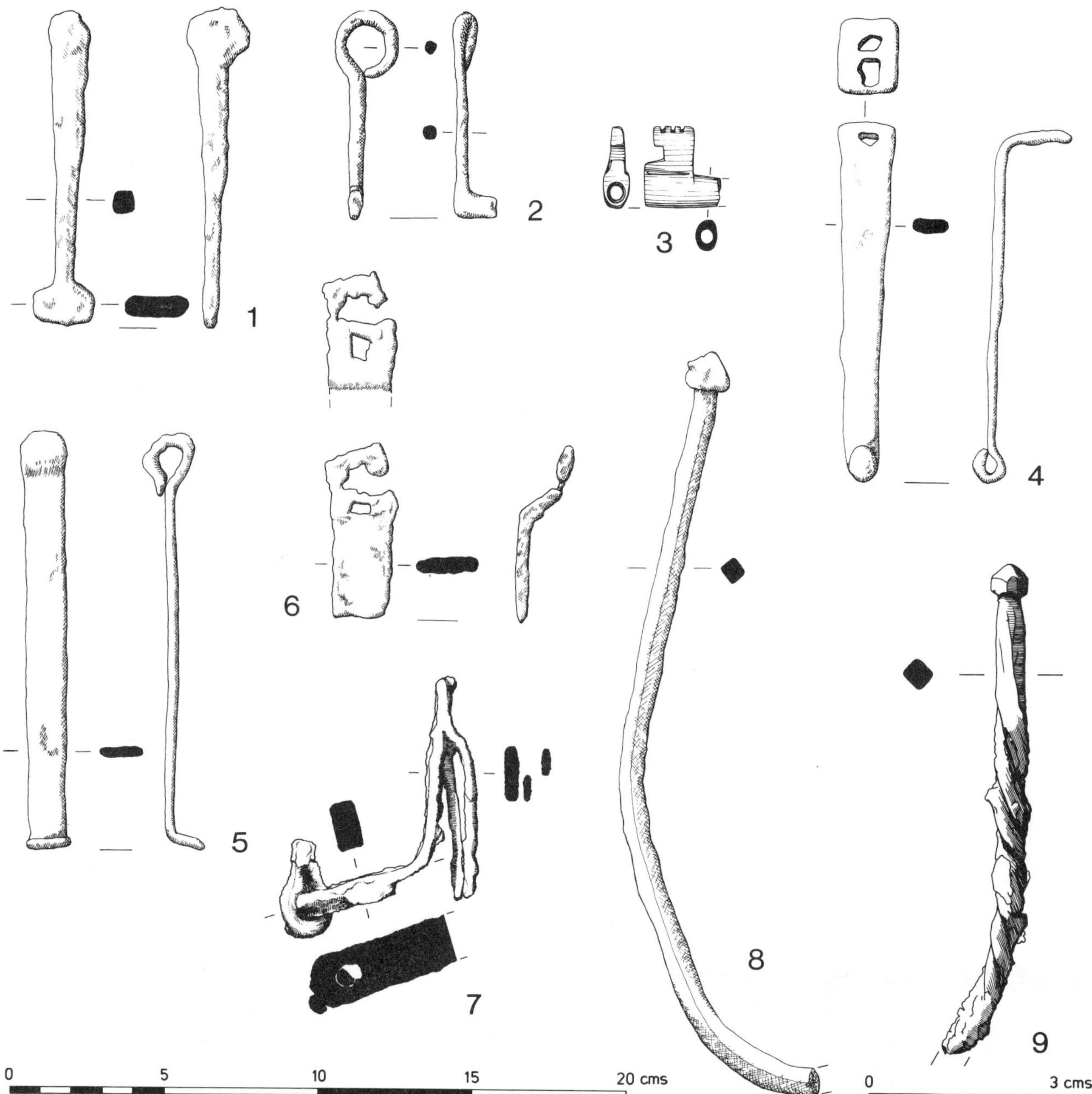

Fig 139 Iron keys (nos 1–6), lock fitting (no 7), scale 1:2, and latch lifters (nos 8 and 9), scale 1:1

forged loop attachment (*cf ibid*), *Find 6539, context 0402, Structure XIX, Phase 7*

8 Segment of a square sectioned curved bolt, with a domed head, probably a latch-lifter (*cf ibid*, 88–9 and pls 37–9), *Find 318, context 14, Structure II(iii), Phase 6b*

9 Part of a square sectioned, curved bolt with a twisted shank and square domed head, probably a latch-lifter handle, (*cf ibid*, 88–9 and pls 77–89), *Context 601, Structure XIX, Phase 7a*

Nails

Over 3,700 iron nails were recovered from the excavated areas, the bulk of which were not assigned individual find numbers. A classification system based upon physical characteristics was devised and the nail types were quantified by context and Structure. The following classification can be equated with one exception (Type B) to the system proposed by Manning (*ibid*, 134–5 and fig 32), based upon the British Museum Romano-British collections. A selection of the principal types here are illustrated.

Type A, large, square sectioned nail, tapering stem and rounded or rectangular head, originally conical or pyramidal but usually flattened or distorted by hammering. Length range 50–300mm (*ibid*, type 1a).

Fig 140

1 *Find 6958, context 1180, Structure XIV, Phase 5d–6b*

2 *Context 682, Structure X, Phase 4a*

3 *Find 6004, context 0211, Phase 8*

4 *Context 511, Structure XIX, Phase 7a*

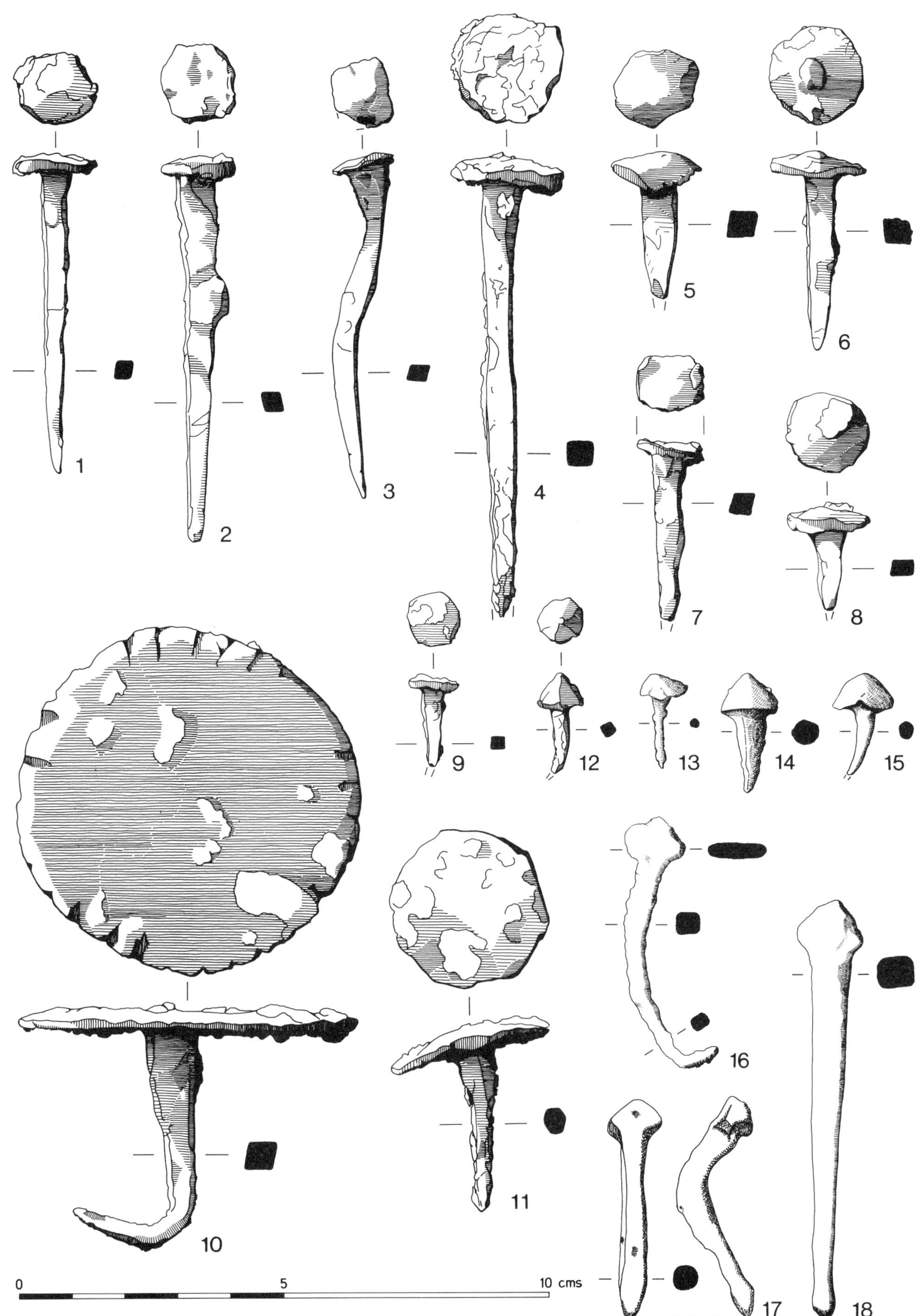

Fig 140 Iron nails and studs, scale 1:1

Type B headless nails. In reality nails whose heads have been lost subsequent to use and which could originally have belonged to any one of the several different classes.

not illustrated

Type C short, square sectioned nail, with tapering stem, usually with a flat sub-rectangular or rounded head, less than 50mm in length (*ibid*, type 1b).

5 *Context 609, Structure IX, Phase 6b*
6 *Context 484, Structure VII, Phase 7a*
7 *Find 8375, context 0115, Phase 8*
8 *Find 6142, context 0245, Phase 8*
9 *Find 724, 9 context 1191, Structure XIV, Phase 5d–6b*

Type D short, square sectioned nail, with tapering stem and wide discoidal head, usually termed tacks or studs (*ibid*, type 7).

10 *Find 6354, context 1, Phase 8*
11 *Find 7591, context 1191, Structure XIV, Phase 5d–6b*

Type E small nails or studs, with short stems and small domed or pyramidal heads, normally hobnails from boots or sandals (*ibid*, type 10) but some larger examples with hollow heads may be upholstery studs (*ibid*, type 8).

see chapter 9 above for other shoe fittings

12 *Context 33, courtyard, Phase 4–6*
13 *Find 4042, context 601, Structure XIX, Phase 7a*
14 *Find 4038, context 600, above Structure XIX, Phase 8*
15 *Find 4156, context 600, above Structure XIX, Phase 8*

Type F other miscellaneous types, primarily nails with flat rectangular sectioned tapering stems, and triangular heads of the same thickness as the stem (*ibid*, type 2).

16 *Find 707, context 22, over Structure I, Phase 5e(ii)*
17 *Find 1502, context 52, Structure II iii, Phase 6a*
18 *Find 1558, context 300, Structure IV, Phase 6b*

Type G exceptionally large shafts, some of which may not have been nails, the remainder would belong in Manning *ibid*, Type 1a.

not illustrated

The distribution of the various nail types amongst the major excavated structures is shown below. The ubiquitous long nails of Manning (*ibid*) type 1a occurred in all the main deposits of building debris, and may have been used to fix stone roofing tiles or in securing structural timbers. They were most common in the structures that are postulated as having been timber framed, namely Structure XIV and the bank, Structure XIX. Next most common were shorter tacks or studs of Manning (*ibid*) type D. These were more generally distributed, with slight concentrations in Structures IV and I, as well as in the bank material of Structure XIX. They may have been connected more therefore with internal fittings rather than basic structural timber framing. The distribution of nails within timber Structure XIV appeared to reflect the former possible positions of major roof timbers (see chapter 3 and Fig 53).

The occurrence of types in major structures

Types	*Phase*	*A, B G*	*C*	*D*	*F*	*total*
Structure II	4–5	3	-	10	-	13
Structure II	6	25	-	20	-	45
Structure IV	4a	24	-	33	7	64
Structure IV	4b	66	-	114	1	181
Structure I	5a–d	26	-	56	6	88
Structure I	5e(i)	13	-	66	3	82
Structure I	5e(ii)	16	2	95	-	113
Structure IX	5	107	9	11	4	131
Structure XIV	5d–6b	197	12	32	7	248
Structure VII/XI	7a	12	1	15	-	28
Structure VIII	7b	12	-	20	5	37
Structure XIX	7	355	26	91	6	478
total		856	50	563	39	1508

Totals for the whole site including ploughsoil

Uley	*Manning 1985*	*total*
Types A/B/G	type 1a	1709
Type C	type 1b	108
Type D	type 7	939
Type E	type 10	(min) 894
Type F	type 2	74
total		3724

The occurrence of hobnails across the site demonstrates major concentrations in two areas – the demolition deposits over timber Structure XIV and the bank material of Strucutre XIX. In the former case, the figures were distorted by the survival of at least one complete set of shoe nails *in situ*. The presence of so many hobnails in the bank material of Phase 7, along with a marked concentration of votive objects (see chapter 4), has raised the question of whether boots and shoes might have functioned as votive offerings in connection with the cult of Mercury in his guise of messenger and traveller.

The occurrence of hobnails (Type E) in major structures

context	*Phase*	*total*
Iron Age ditches	Phase 2–3	7
Structure II	Phase 4–6	9
Structure IV	Phase 4	1
Structure X	Phase 4	14
Structure I	Phase 5	1
Structure IX	Phase 5	39
Structure XIV	Phase 5d–6b	340
Structure XIII	Phase 5d–6b	1
Structure VII	Phase 7	4
Structure VIII	Phase 7	43
Structures XIX/XV	Phase 7	138

Painted wall plaster

by Elizabeth James and Ann Woodward

A total of 267 kilos of wall plaster were recovered during the excavations and, of this, 135 kilos was painted. Plaster fragments were distributed amongst the various structures as follows:

context	*Phase*	*weight*
Structure X	Phase 4	6.2kg
Structure IX	Phase 5	1.5kg
Structure IV	Phase 4–5	43.3kg
Structure I	Phase 4–5	46.1kg
Structure II	Phase 4–6a	40.0kg
Structure I	Phase 5e(ii)	35.8kg
above Structure IV	Phase 6b	74.6kg

Structure XIX (bank), Structure III, Structure VIII, XI, and courtyard, small residual collections

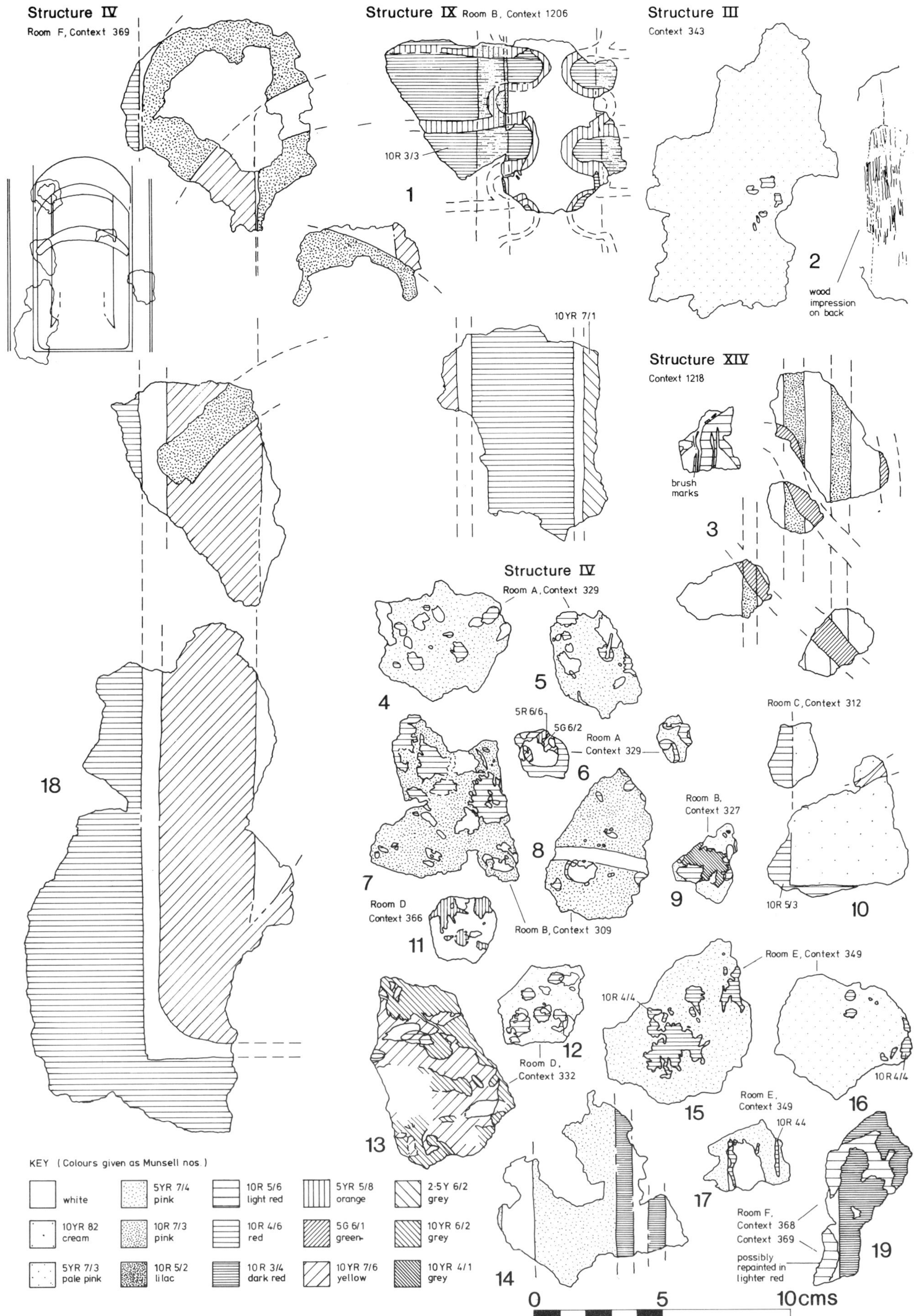

Fig 141 Painted wall plaster from Structures III, IV, IX, and XIV, scale 1:2

The painted wall plaster assemblage was studied initially by Elizabeth James who described the colours, motifs and combinations of patterns by context. The data was computerised by Charlotte Cane. Four fabrics were defined according to colour and inclusions:

Fabric 1, coarse cream mortar with frequent limestone inclusions of all sizes and sparse calcite.
Fabric 2, moderately coarse cream mortar with small, well sorted limestone inclusions, some calcite and occasional fired clay pellets.
Fabric 3, moderately coarse, usually hard, cream mortar with sparse small limestone inclusions.
Fabric 4, moderately coarse, cream-pink mortar with dense larger red pottery or clay pellets and rare limestone or calcite.

No patterns of fabric distribution could be discerned, but finds from Structure II, the temple, and layers derived there from, displayed the most variety. Fabrics 1 and 2 were very much more common than fabrics 3 and 4.

Although no very large fragments were recovered, different colours and motifs displayed very distinct spatial patterning and this has allowed the reconstruction of decorative schemes relating to the individual rooms of some of the buildings. A general summary of the colour combinations and designs which may be ascribed with confidence to particular rooms follows. Full descriptions and quantification may be found in the computer archive. Rooms not described below contained very little or no plaster: either none was present originally or almost all traces had been removed during demolition or structural modification. Selected border types, colour combinations and motifs are illustrated in Figures 141–42.

Structure X
not illustrated
The demolition deposits produced *c* 5.25 kilos of backing amongst the rubble; the few painted fragments indicated a decorative scheme of yellow and white geometric panels bordered in red, white and yellow stripes

Fig 141
Structure IX
Plaster from Room B indicated the former existence of red, grey and yellow panels and grey-green and grey stippling.
1 Two large fragments depicting dark red and orange tendrils or fragments of a vertical garland hinted at more elaborate motifs

Structure III
Residual plaster fragments from Phase 6–7 deposits included fragments stippled in red and white over a ground of pink.
2 One fragment, retaining the impression of wood on the reverse

Structure XIV
A large quantity of pink, white and grey or grey-green fragments, together with matching borders and further stripes in dark red and lilac were also recovered. One piece showed a brush marked pattern in red.
3 Pieces indicating a trellis pattern in pale green and lilac on white

This repertoire of colours is not matched closely by the range from underlying Structure IX, Room B (see above). Either the pieces relate to plaster decoration within the timber framed Structure XIV or they may derive from one of the other rooms of Structure IX, which must have been levelled in its entirety prior to the construction of Structure XIV.

Structure IV
Room A
4–6 A small quantity of plaster with red and white stippling on pink
Room B
7–9 A very large quantity of plaster indicating lilac panels stippled with red, white and grey, plain yellow panels, red/lilac and red/yellow borders, and edging provided by curved covings and/or skirtings in plain red
Room C
10 White panels, with some red and pink. Buff/yellow/pink/white stripes together with some red and buff patterns on white
Room D
11 Orange spattering on white
12 Red and white stippling on pink
13 brown/grey/white stippling on yellow
14 border stripes in pink/white/dark red

Nos 12–14 formed the majority of the pieces; a little of no 11 was also present. No 13 and many other similar pieces may represent depictions of vegetation in shades of grey and brown.
Room E
15–16 Red and white stippling on pink. These were associated with red/white or red/grey/pink borders
17 red and white stripes on pink free design
Room F
18–19 Geometric panels, probably white, framed by wide borders in red, white, and yellow, surmounted by a curvilinear motif in dark pink; no 19 shows evidence of repainting
Red stippling on pink, and orange on white, were also represented

Structure I
Room A
not illustrated
Plain yellow panels bordered in red; red/grey and white/red/ yellow stripes, together with dark grey stippling on grey

Fig 142
Room B
Yellow panels with red borders.
1–2 Dark grey stippling on grey, plus vegetative schemes in red/green (no 1) and brown/grey, (no 2)
3 White stripe on yellow
Room C
Yellow panels with red borders.
4 Yellow/grey/yellow/white, and yellow/white/grey stripes
not illustrated
Grey stippling on grey, and grey on yellow; white stippling on grey or pink. Some evidence of shaded grey stripes.
Room E
5 Pink panels stippled in red

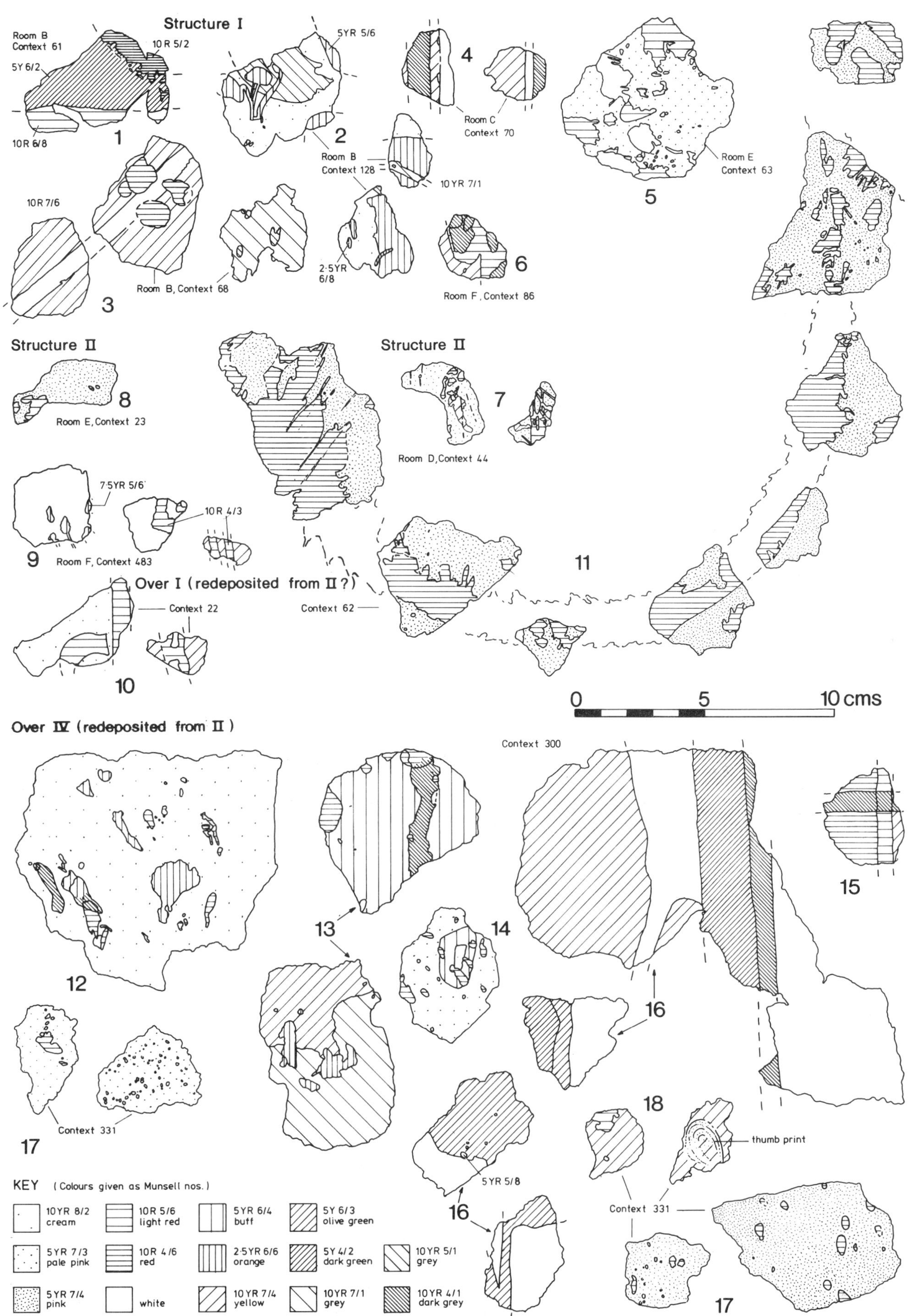

Fig 142 Painted wall plaster from the temple, Structure II, and over Structures I and IV, scale 1:2

not illustrated
Pink panels bordered with red/white/red/white stripes, some beige/brown stripes and plain yellow also
Room F
not illustrated
Yellow panels bordered in red. Some yellow/white stripes, dark grey stippling on grey
6 red and dark grey splotches on yellow

Structure II
Very little painted plaster was found *in situ* within the rooms of the temple. However, much evidence survived within the temple deposits which had been spread over Structures I and IV in Phases 5e (ii) and 6b respectively. The only major deposit from the temple itself was 39 kilos of plain coarse white plaster from the upper levels within Structure II, Room B. It is postulated that this derived from the linings and facings of the Phase 7 baptistery, Structure VII.

Room A
not illustrated
Plain pink, red, yellow; pink/red/yellow stripes
Room C
Plain yellow
Room D
Plain red; red/white stripes
7 Red and yellow pattern on pink
Room E (cella)
Plain pink, grey and red; red/white stripes
8 Red stippling on pink
Room F
not illustrated
Plain pink, red, yellow, white, and lilac; red/yellow/white stripes, white/dark red/red stripes, and red on white border angle
9 One piece painted white and bearing buds in yellow/buff, part of a vegetative design

Temple debris redeposited over Structure I, Phase 5e(ii)
A small proportion of the fragments bore colours and designs also found on plaster from the demolition deposits of Structure I but otherwise the plaster may be taken to derive from Structure II. Together with the material deposited over Structure IV, this considerably augments our knowledge of the decorative schemes belonging to the temple building.

Types also found in Structure I demolition deposits
not illustrated
plain yellow; red/white, yellow/grey, red/yellow/white, and red/yellow/grey borders; dark stippling on grey

Additional types
10 Pieces bearing red and yellow designs on a cream ground relate stylistically to the patterned pieces from Structure II, Room D, (Fig 142, no 7)
11 a vegetational design (garland) in red on pink
This may also be related to the pieces from Structure II, Room D
not illustrated
plain red (matches Structure II, Rooms A,D,E and F)
pink/red/yellow stripe (matches Structure II, Room A)
grey/white stripe; red/lilac stripe; red on pink stippling; yellow and orange stippling on white; red on white border corner (matches Structure II, Room E)

Temple debris redeposited over Structure IV, Phase 6b
Again, the material may be divided into a small group which may derive from disturbance of the underlying demolition layers (in this case of Structure IV) and a large assemblage of plaster, including complex designs and colour combinations, which most probably came from the temple immediately following its final demolition.

Types also found in Structure IV demolition deposits
not illustrated
plain white; pink/red/grey, red/white, pink/red and red/yellow/white stripes; pink on red stippling

Additional types
12 Yellow and orange stippling on white
13 Assorted fragments decorated in shades of grey/beige/brown/yellow
14 Yellow and orange stippling on white
15 Light red and grey crossing stripes on red and yellow
16 Dark green/grey/white stripes
17 Red, yellow and grey stippling on pink
18 Brown marbling on yellow
not illustrated
plain lilac (matches Structure II, Room F) red border angle on white

A very large proportion comprised fragments of pink stippled in red, whilst the shaded grey and beige pieces (Fig 142, no 13) appeared to derive from architectural designs, possibly incorporating columns. On the other hand, the dark green, grey and white pieces (Fig 142, no 16) may have come from vegetative patterns.

It should be noted that the designs and colours in these two separate late deposits of debris are different. Those from the layers over Structure I have more red and yellow elements and the main large scale design is the red garland on pink, possibly containing further vegetation depicted in yellow and light red. In contrast, the designs represented over Structure IV tend to be executed in more natural shades, with the two main sets of motifs comprising dark green or grey vegetation and the shaded grey or brown architectural features. It may well be that these sets of designs derived from different rooms or spaces within the temple. Thus the architectural scheme and green vegetation may have adorned the ambulatories, two of which (Rooms A and C) are postulated to have stood until the end of Phase 6, while the pink walls decorated with red garlands may have been designed for the interior of the cella and/or portico, both of which apparently fell prior to the deposition of the debris layers over Structure I in Phase 5e (ii).

Both types of decoration reconstructed as belonging to the temple are of a more complex nature than the schemes deduced for the other ranges of buildings. For instance, in Structures I and IV, most rooms were probably largely decorated with plain centre panels enclosed in striped borders, above a dado of further panels decorated with stippling in crude imitation of marble. In Structure I the main panels were usually yellow above grey 'marbling', whilst in Structure IV lilac or white panels were set off by 'marbling' in red and white on pink.

Plate I *Fragments of post-Roman window glass; left to right top row g, b, a, c; centre j, d; bottom row e, i, f, h (see page 189). (Photo: University of Leeds)*

Window glass

by Jennifer Price

Very little window glass has been recognised, and it seems probable that during most phases of occupation of the site the windows of the buildings were not glazed. The 23 small fragments recovered all come from blown panes which have been cylinder-blown, cut open and flattened, and they are unlikely to predate the third to fourth century. Thirteen of the fragments are probably from the green-colourless and blue-green panes which commonly occur at late Roman sites, and these have not been catalogued. The remaining ten are thin fragments in a shade of blue-green which is distinctly different in colour from most Romano-British window glass, and four have dark red streaks in the glass, for which there are apparently no parallels in Romano-British panes. Four pieces show slight signs of scoring or grosing, and one has a rounded edge from the side of the flattened cylinder-blown sheet.

It is likely that these ten fragments belong to the post-Roman period, and their contexts of discovery in the unsealed destruction levels over Structure XIV, and in the ploughsoil above, could be in accord with a date in the fifth century or beyond (Phases 6b to 7). A very few pieces of similar glass have been noted in late or unstratified contexts on other sites occupied during the Roman period, as at Silchester (J Price 1984, 116), Wroxeter (Cool and Price forthcoming b) and Atworth Roman villa (Cool and Price forthcoming c).

Most instances of this type of window glass have been recorded in association with Anglo-Saxon churches. Many fragments similar to these pieces, often from small triangular, square, or other shaped quarries, with grosed or rounded edges, have been found at the Anglo-Saxon monasteries of Jarrow and Monkwearmouth, and there is also a fragment from Whitby (Cramp 1970a and b, 1975). The occupation of these monasteries dates from the late 7th to the late 9th century AD. Fragments with dark red streaks have also been recorded in later Saxon contexts at several sites in Winchester and elsewhere (information from M Biddle and M Heyworth).

Catalogue of post-Roman window glass

Col Pl I

Blue-green with dark red streaks

a Fragment, bottom surface dull, small round bubbles, dimensions 13.4 by 16.3mm, thickness 2.25mm, *Find 6398, context 1100, over Structure XIV, Phase 8*

b Fragment, one edge grosed ?, bottom surface dull and pockmarked, small round bubbles, dimensions 20.8 by 21.3mm, thickness 2.25mm, *Find 6443, context 1100, over Structure XIV, Phase 8*

c Fragment, one edge scored ?, bottom surface dull, small round bubbles, dimensions 11.3 by 13.2mm, thickness 2.25mm, *Find 6455, context 1100, over Structure XIV, Phase 8*

d Fragment, bottom surface dull, small elongated and round bubbles, dimensions 18.8 by 7mm, thickness 1.6mm, *Find 7152, context 1191, Structure XIV, Phase 5d–6b*

Blue-green

e Triangular fragment, one edge rounded, one edge grosed. Depressions in top surface, bottom surface dull and pockmarked, small elongated and round bubbles, dimensions 24.5 by 16.5mm, thickness 2.5mm, *Find 6400, context 1100, over Structure XIV, Phase 8*

f Fragment, bottom surface dull and pockmarked, small elongated and round bubbles, dimensions 8.7 by 8.3mm, thickness 1.25mm, *Find 6412, context 1100, over Structure XIV, Phase 8*

g Fragment, small part of one edge grosed?, bottom surface dull and pockmarked, small elongated and round bubbles, dimensions 23.5 by 17.3mm, thickness 1.75mm, *Find 6622, context 1100, over Structure XIV, Phase 8*

h Fragment, bottom surface dull and pockmarked, small elongated and round bubbles, dimensions 11.5 by 10.5mm, thickness 2mm, *Find 7066, context 1191, Structure XIV, Phase 5d–6b*

i Fragment, bottom surface dull and pockmarked, small elongated and round bubbles, dimensions 6.8 by 19.5mm, thickness 1.5mm *Find 7218, context 1191, Structure XIV, Phase 5d–6b*

j Fragment, bottom surface dull and pockmarked, small round bubbles, dimensions 14 by 7.5mm, thickness 1.6mm, *Find 7344, context 1191, Structure XIV, Phase 5d–6b*

Analysis of the window glass

by Michael Heyworth

Analytical Method

The analyses were undertaken using inductively coupled plasma atomic emission spectrometry (ICPS) which gives compositional data for a wide range of elements at the major, minor and trace levels (Heyworth *et al* 1988, Thompson and Walsh 1983). This is especially important for the analysis of glass where major and minor elements determine the general type of glass and minor and trace elements have an important influence on its colour. Further details of the analytical method used can be found in AM Lab report 53/89 (Heyworth 1989).

Nineteen of the fragments of window glass from the site were analysed in the hope that this would confirm that the two groups were compositionally distinct, and provide further information on the nature of the glass in the two groups. The analytical results are reproduced in fiche.

Analytical results

All the glass is of the durable, soda-lime-silica type, though there are some variations in the levels of the main oxides which indicates differences in the raw materials used, or possibly even in the recipes used to make the glass.

The nine fragments of Roman date, which are a variety of lightly tinted translucent colours ranging from colourless to light blue-green, have a mixture of compositions. The three colourless fragments (Finds 6436, 6630 and 7583) have very similar compositions and may be part of the same pane. These glasses contain higher levels of antimony, about 0.07%, though at this level it is unlikely to have been effective as a decolourant and may be present in the glass due to the use of cullet (recycled glass). Three other fragments (Finds 3957, 6414, and 8125) contain no antimony but have particularly high manganese oxide levels, about 0.9%. The manganese level does not correlate with increased levels in other oxides/elements which may suggest that manganese was added separately, and deliberately, presumably to act as a decolouriser. Very few analyses of Romano-British window glass have been undertaken, however analysis of window glass from Roman Caerleon (Cole 1966) also showed the use of manganese as a decolouriser, though the glass was dated to the first/second century AD (Boon 1966), rather earlier than these examples.

The ten fragments of post-Roman date form a tight compositional group and probably all come from the same window pane. They can be distinguished from the Roman fragments on the basis of much higher iron oxide, potash, lead and copper contents. This suggests that different raw materials were used in the production of the post-Roman batch.

The red streaks in the post-Roman glass are likely to be the result of the presence of discrete coloured particles in the glass. These are probably crystals of cuprous oxide and/or metallic copper which are held in suspension in the glass. The crystals are present due to the precipitation of the copper out of solution when the glass melt has become supersaturated at the heat treatment temperature (Paul 1982). This type of coloured glass is known as copper ruby glass, in this case with a copper content of about 0.5%.

In the production of a copper ruby glass a batch containing copper together with a reducing agent, is melted in reducing conditions. The melt initially shows the blue colour characteristic of cupric (Cu^{++}) ions, but as the melting proceeds, and the furnace atmosphere becomes more reducing, the colour changes to become almost colourless (cuprous Cu^{+} ions). By subsequent heat treatment commonly known as 'striking', at a temperature somewhere between the annealing and the softening temperature, the ruby colour is developed (Paul 1982).

There has been much discussion over the state of the copper in a ruby glass but recent work (eg Debnath and Das 1986) has shown that it is likely to be in the form of metallic copper. In the Uley glass the presence of lead, at levels of about 0.8% may have facilitated the initial solution of the copper and the subsequent precipitation of the red crystals, by lowering the temperature necessary for the 'striking' (development of the colour) to take place (Guido *et al* 1984). The relatively high iron level of about 1.4% may have assisted in the process by acting as a reducing agent, though these levels are not sufficient on their own. Much has been made in the literature of the need to have tin in a copper ruby glass to act as the reducing agent (eg Duran *et al* 1984), however this does not necessarily seem to be correct (I Freestone personal comment). The ICPS analyses do not include a measurement of tin, but XRF analysis did not detect the presence of any tin in the Uley glass. The apparent lack of a suitable reducing agent in the glass composition is therefore significant and may indicate the use of carbon in the glass making process, probably as plant material.

It is unlikely that the ancient glass makers were attempting to produce a streaked glass, and the deliberate addition to the glass batch of copper probably indicates that they were attempting to produce a coloured glass. As copper ruby glasses are colourless when first made it is possible they were attempting to produce a colourless glass but it seems unlikely that they would add copper to a glass to achieve this. If they intended to produce a colourless glass then it is more likely that they would have added a decolouriser such as manganese to the base glass. Copper in glass is usually associated with a blue colour, though in the presence of lead it usually produces a turquoise-green colour, and it may be that this is what was intended, but the presence of higher than usual levels of lead and iron caused the glass to 'strike' unexpectedly, though this is unlikely to have occured without the presence of a stronger reducing agent. It is possible that they were attempting to produce a red glass, however modern experiments to produce an opaque red glass have shown it to be a difficult process. Attempts by Michael Cable often resulted in red streaks in the glass, which could develop either during initial cooling, or on reheating in an attempt to 'strike' the colour (Brighton and Newton 1986). It is possible that ancient glass makers reduced the level of copper to attempt to produce a paler red colour and got it to a level where it would 'strike' in some areas of the glass while adjacent areas would remain relatively colourless. However the lack of any known examples of pure (ie not streaked) red copper ruby glasses of similar date suggest this alternative may be unlikely.

To an extent, given their lack of understanding of the chemistry of the glass making process, ancient glass makers would have been at the mercy of the raw materials available to them and the impurities they contained (Newton 1978). However in the production of the post-Roman window glass from this site there was probably a deliberate attempt to produce a coloured glass by the addition to the glass batch of copper. The lead could have been added to make the glass colour a more turquoise-green. As the glass was to be coloured there would have been less worry about impurities in the raw materials and a lower grade sand may have been used which contained more iron. The attempt to produce a coloured glass would have relied on control over the thermodynamics of the redox system and in this case the control was not adequate to produce an evenly coloured glass.

Red streaking in glass is known from other early medieval sites such as Southampton, (Hunter and Heyworth forthcoming); Repton (unpublished) and Winchester (Biddle and Hunter 1990) and ICPS analyses of fragments from these sites have also shown relatively high levels of copper and lead in them. However further work will be needed to compare the compositions of these glasses before any generalisations can be made.

Summary

The two groups of window glass defined by visual inspection are compositionally distinct, though all the fragments are of the same basic type of glass. There was some variation in the composition of the Roman win-

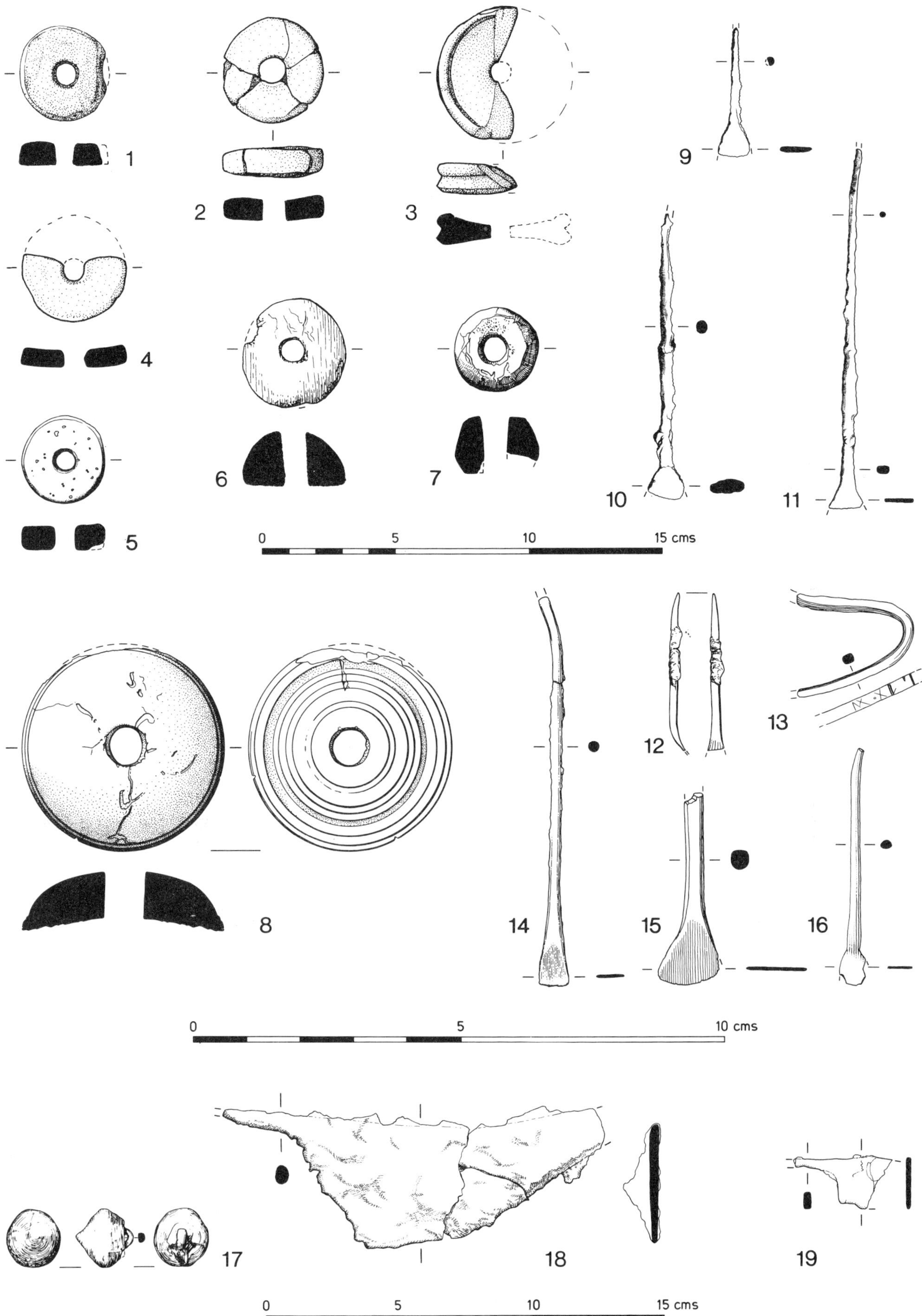

Fig 143 Spindle whorls of limestone (no 1), pottery (nos 2–5), and bone (nos 6–8); styli of iron (nos 9–11), scale 1:2, except no 8 scale 1:1; copper alloy (nos 12–16), scale 1:1, lead weight (no 17), and iron knives (nos 18 and 19), scale 1:2

dow glass fragments, with evidence for the use of manganese as a decolouriser in some fragments.

The post-Roman window fragments were all identical in composition and may originally have been part of the same window pane. The post-Roman window glass can be described as copper ruby glass, where the red streaks in the glass are probably caused by the precipitation of metallic copper out of solution, possibly facilitated by the presence of lead. The copper and lead were clearly added deliberately to the glass batch. It is likely that the ancient glassmakers were attempting to produce a coloured window glass, however they did not have sufficient control over the glassmaking process to achieve this end.

Spindle whorls

Finds 5818, 5827, 2382 and 5872 (Fig 143, nos 2, 3, 4 and 6) derive from votive deposits of Final Iron Age date

Fig 143
1 Oolitic limestone whorl with flat profile, *Find 5122, context 89, Structure II, Phase 4 or 5a–c*
2 Pottery whorl, slightly dished profile, *Find 5818, context 910, pit F251, Phase 3a*
3 Half of a pottery whorl with grooved edge and dished profile, *Find 5827, context 910, pit F251, Phase 3a*
4 Half of a pottery whorl, slightly dished profile, *Find 2382, context 334, ditch F382, Phase 3c*
5 Pottery whorl with flat profile, *Find 8328, context 1242, Structure IX, Phase 5b*
6 Conical bone whorl, made from femur caput of cattle, *Find 5872, context 726, ditch F264, Phase 3a*
7 Biconical bone whorl, damaged, *Find 3081, context 509, outside Structure III, Phase 6–7*
8 Sub-conical bone whorl (cattle femur) with lathe turned concentric groove decoration, *Find 1772, context 38, over Structure I, Phase 5e(ii)*

Styli

all of copper alloy except where stated

9 Iron stylus, tip missing, Type 1a (Manning 1985, 85 and pl 35), *Find 6185, context 0310, Structure XIX, Phase 7*
10 Iron stylus, complete, Type 1a (*ibid*), *Find 8272, context 1255, Structure IX, Phase 6*
11 Iron stylus, complete, Type 1a (*ibid*), *Find 6435, context 1100, Structure XIX, Phase 7–8*
12 Possible stylus, tip missing, *Find 5787, context 842, ditch F836, Phase 2a–d*
13 Possible shaft, decorated, *Find 4199, context 600, Structure XIX, Phase 8*
14 Stylus, *Find 1836, context 200, Structure II, Phase 6a*
15 Stylus, *Find 481, context 14, Structure II, Phase 6b*
16 Probable stylus, *Find 8131,context 1232, Structure IX, Phase 5a*

Weight

17 Drop-shaped lead weight with suspension loop, *Find 4822, context 602, Structure XIX, Phase 7*

Knives

all of iron

18 Knife, curved blade fragments with tang, Type 12 (*ibid*, 114), *Find 5814, context 864, Structure X, Phase 4b*
19 Knife, blade and tang fragment, Type 11? (*ibid*), *Find 5300, context 627, Structure IX, Phase 5a–c*

Fig 144
1 Knife, leaf-shaped blade and tang hafted upon remains of a mineralised wooden handle, Type 21 (*ibid*, 117), *Find 8290, context 1223, Structure IX, Phase 5c*
2 Knife, blade fragment, type indeterminate *Find 697, context 22, Structure I, Phase 5e(ii)*
3 Knife, blade fragment, type indeterminate, *Find 1075, context 15, Structure IIii, Phase 6b*
4 Knife, leaf-shaped blade and tang, Type 21 (*ibid*) *Find 735, context 32, Structure I, Phase 5e*
5 Knife, blade and tang fragment, Type 11? (*ibid*, 114), *Find 4322, context 603, Structure XIX, Phase 7a*
6 Knife, blade and tang fragment, Type 11 (*ibid*), *Find 118, context 1, Phase 8*
7 Knife, blade fragment with a looped tang, Type 11B (*ibid*), *Find 3830, context 1, Phase 8*

not illustrated
Knife, leaf-shaped blade, tang missing, Type 21 (*ibid*, 117), *Find 7922, context 0406, Structure XIX, Phase 7*

Handles

all of bone except where stated

8 Almost half of a handle decorated with groups of ribs and grooves, sheep/goat tibia shaft, *Find 8225, context 1242, Structure IX, Phase 5b*
9 Fragment of a handle decorated with at least two zones of three transverse grooves, sheep/goat tibia shaft, *Context 168, Structure I, Phase 5a–d*
10 Two fragments of a handle decorated with evenly spaced wide transvere grooves, sheep/goat tibia shaft,*Finds 7086 and 7267, context 0406, Structure XIX, Phase 7*
11 Two joining fragments of a handle, decorated with cross-hatched ornament and transverse grooved bands, probably deer antler, *Finds 6298 and 6305, context 0276, Phase 8*

Needles and points

all of ?deer antler except where stated

Fig 145
1 Peg, awl or unfinished needle, *Find 2280, context 33, southern courtyard, Phase 4–6*
2 Fragment of needle with rectangular eye in a flat spatulate head, *Find 2486, context 332, Structure IV, Phase 4b*
3 Fragment of a point, probably unfinished, *Find 2428, context 277, over Structure II, Phase 8*
4 Needle rectangular eye in a flat spatulate head, *Find 5955, context 0184, Phase 8*

Numbers 2 and 4 are of Crummy Type 2(a) (Crummy 1983, 65–6)

5 Copper alloy spatulate object with a sharp point of square cross-section and traces of one rivet or attachment hole, use unknown, *Find 1301, context 14, Structure II, Phase 6b*

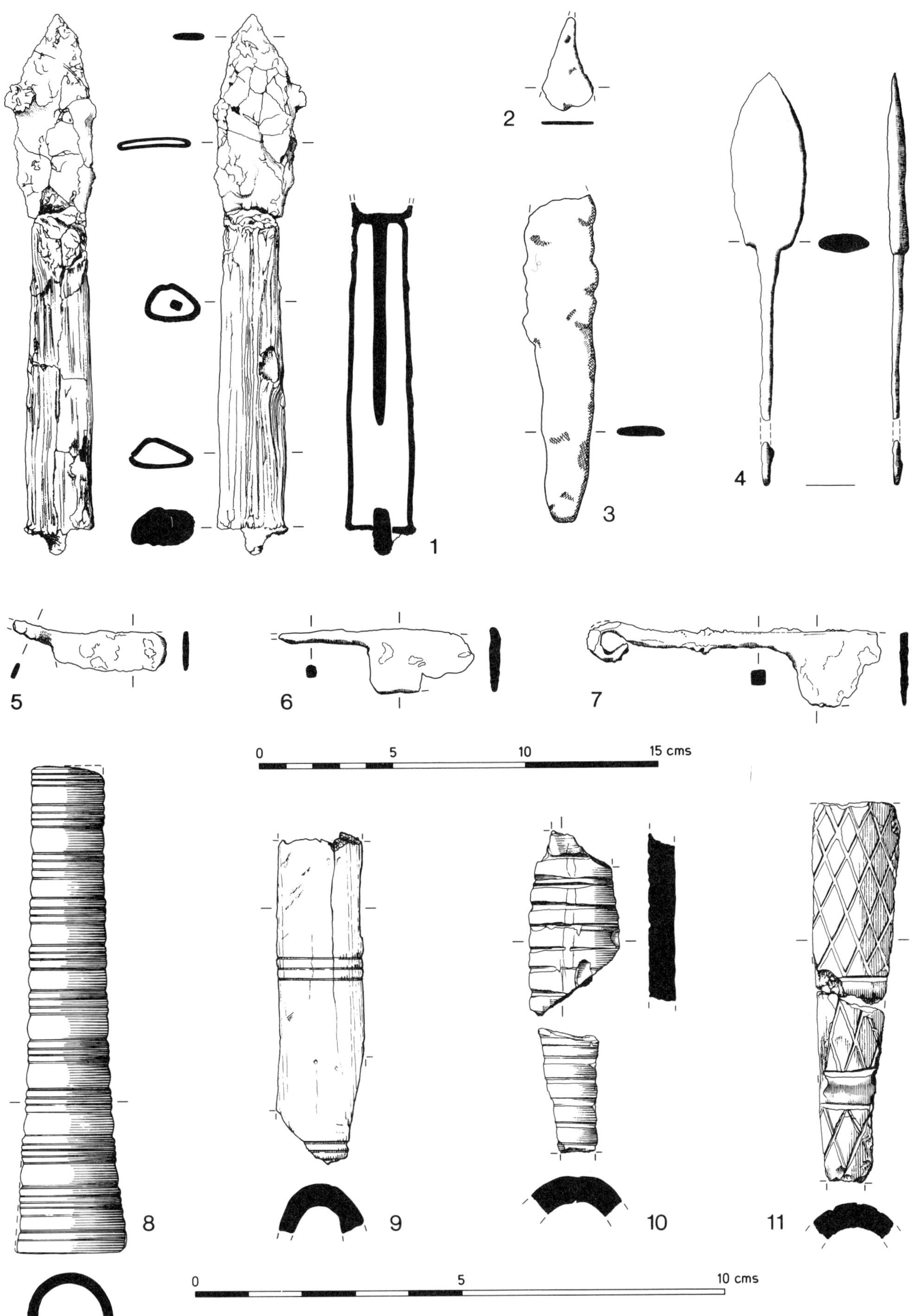

Fig 144 Iron knives, scale 1:2, and bone or antler handles, scale 1:1

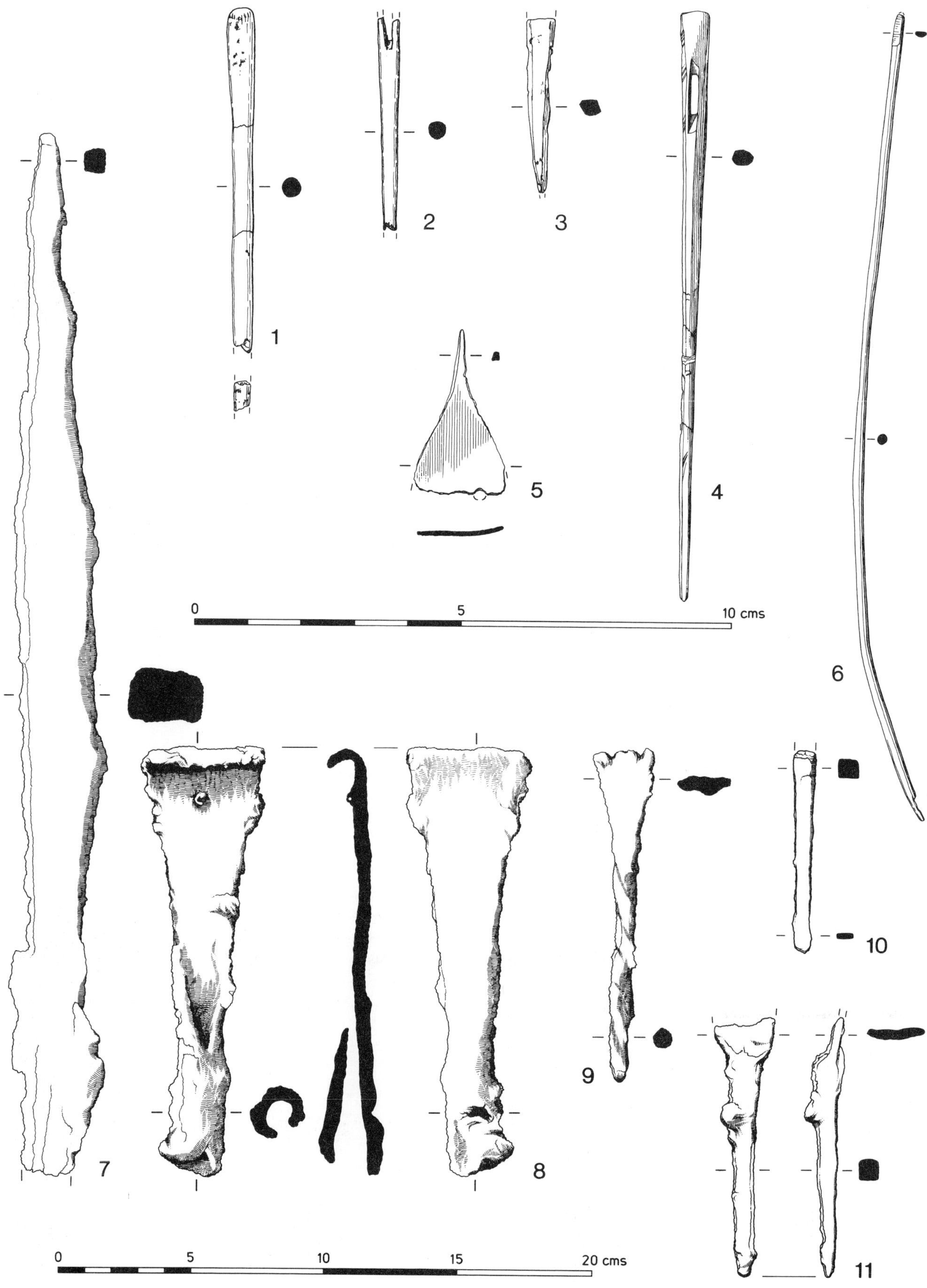

Fig 145 Antler needles (nos 1–4), copper alloy points (nos 5 and 6), and iron tools (nos 7–11), scale 1:1

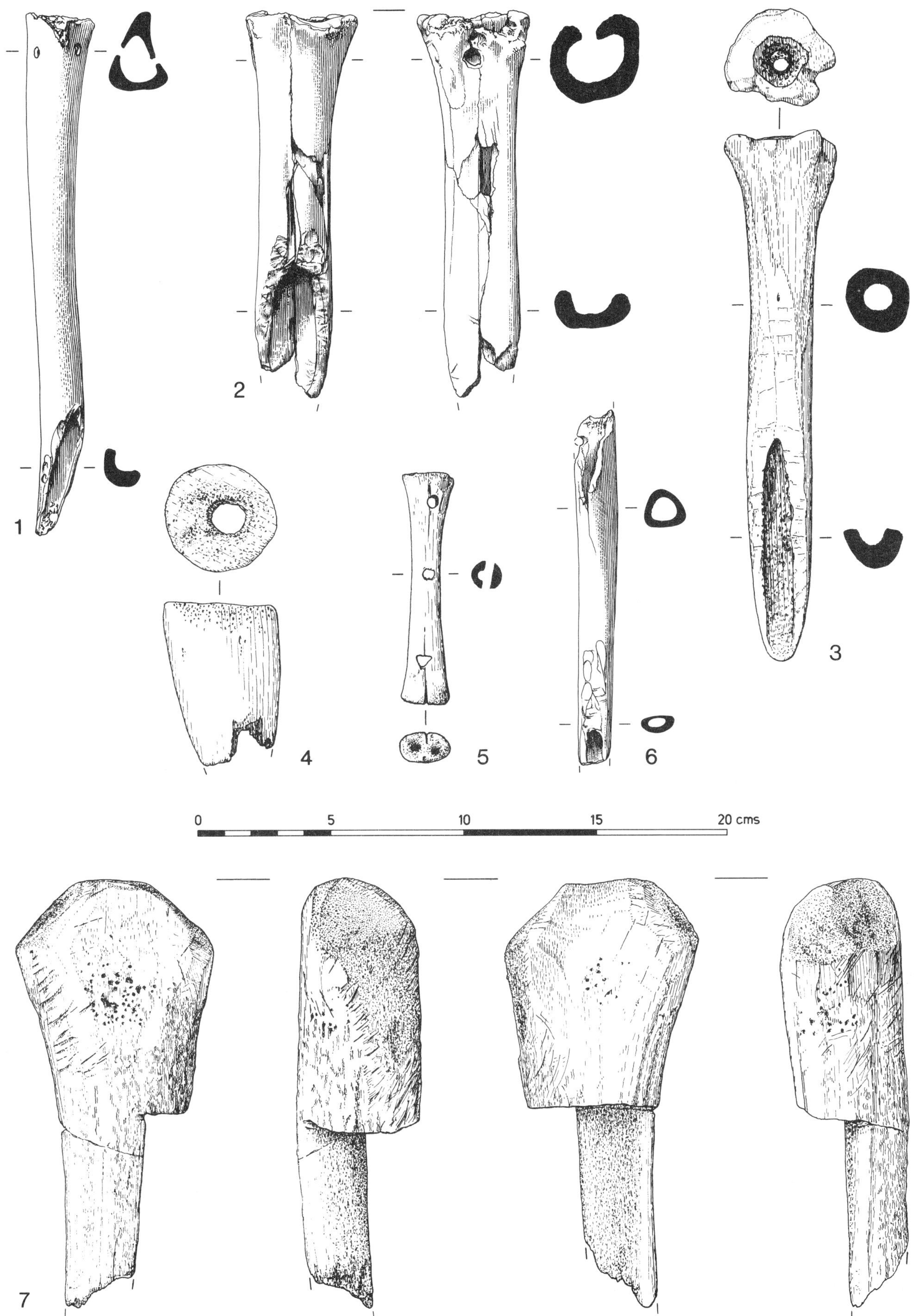

Fig 146 Tools of bone and antler from the Final Iron Age ditch, nos 1–6, scale 1:2, no 7, scale 1:1

6 Thin copper alloy rod of circular cross-section with rebates at each end, function unknown, *Find 4573, context 603, Structure XIX, Phase 7*

Tools

all of iron

7 Bar, rectangular cross-section, tapering to one end, a possible oven support, *Find 7976, context 1219, Structure IX (oven F1281b), Phase 5c*
8 Woodworking scraper or farrier's comb with a flanged socket, identity uncertain (see *ibid*, 21), *Find 7827, context 1206, Structure IX, Phase 5c*
9 Broad-bladed paring chisel with a twisted shank (*ibid*, 20–21), *Find 7689, context 1202, Structure XIX, Phase 5d*
10 Narrow-bladed paring chisel (*ibid*, 20–1), *Find 6285, context 0252, Structure IX, Phase 8*
11 Broad-bladed paring chisel, blade incomplete (*ibid*, 20–1), *Find 8238, context 1204, Structure IX, Phase 5c*

From the Final Iron Age ditch

all of bone or antler

Fig 146
1 Gouge, made from a sheep/goat tibia, two perforations at proximal end, *Find 2530, context 916, F264, Phase 2b*

not illustrated
Another gouge, also from F264, Phase 2b, is similar but with only one perforation.
2 Large gouge, made from a right metatarsal of cattle, single perforation at proximal end, *Find 8529, context 912, F264, Phase 2c*
3 Large gouge, made from a third right metatarsal of horse, *Find 5906, context 912, F264, Phase 2c*

not illustrated
Another tool, from the southern courtyard, is similar but with a single perforation at the proximal end.
4 Tapering tool with the functional end broken away, central hole, deer antler, *Find 5908, context 925, ditch F264, Phase 2b*
5 Sheep/goat metacarpal with three spaced perforations, *Find 5848, context 910, F251, Phase 3a*
6 Broken gouge, made from a right tibia of sheep/goat, *Find 8527, context 758, F264, Phase 2d*
7 Antler tool with an angled club-shaped head and deep rebate for hafting, red deer antler, *Find 5905, context 912, F264, Phase 2c*

This assemblage of bone tools, including gouges, points and bobbin, is typical for Iron Age sites in southern England and a full discussion of the types and their probable uses has been provided in analysis of the objects from Danebury (Cunliffe 1984, **2**). However there is so far no close parallel for the antler tool, Find 590, (Fig 146, no 7) above, which may have functioned as a mattock.

Flint Artefacts

by Alan Saville

A total of 110 pieces of humanly struck flint was recovered during the 1977–79 excavations. The typological composition of this collection is tabulated below.

The flint artefacts

type	*quantity*	*weight*
unretouched flakes	65	276.4g
cores	2	71.0g
core fragment	1	14.6g
scrapers	6	27.6g
piercer	1	4.8g
barbed and tanged arrowhead	1	2.0g
worn-edge flake	1	4.5g
edge-trimmed flakes	2	5.8g
gunflint	1	3.9g
misc retouched pieces	14	157.3g
unclassified burnt fragments	16	67.1g
total	110	635.0g

Most of the pieces of flint had densely discoloured (grey or white) exteriors resulting from cortication of the flaked surfaces. Two main types of raw material were represented in the collection, as indicated by the pieces retaining areas of cortex. Most common were nodules with an abraded cortex, red-brown to grey in colour, which probably originated in superficial chalkland deposits. The other type, represented only by two cortical flakes, was a pebble with a smooth, water-worn cortex, from an unknown, but definitely derived, source.

Apart from the gunflint (unstratified), a modern item of the 17th century or later, all the other flints could be presumed, on general typological grounds, to be the product of prehistoric knapping on or near to the site. The contextual provenance of the excavated flints was of little help in their dating. As shown, only three pieces came from the earliest phase. One of these was a small core of a type likely to be of Early Bronze Age or earlier date.

Summary of flints by phase

Phase	*period*	*total*
Phase 1	Bronze Age/ Early Iron age	3
Phase 2	Late Iron Age	34
Phase 3–6	early/latest Roman	36
Phase 7	post-Roman	13
Phase 8	ploughsoil	24
total		110

The collection contains few artefacts which are themselves typologically or morphologically distinctive enough to carry definite chronological implications. The main exception is the unstratified barbed and tanged arrowhead, (Fig 147, no 1), of unspecialized 'Sutton' type (Green 1984, 29–39), but nevertheless most likely to be of Early Bronze Age date.

Two of the scrapers, of the small 'thumb' variety, are also probably of Early Bronze Age date, while a larger one is of Neolithic or Bronze Age type. The core pieces are small and technologically simple, but help to provide a chronological starting point for the collection since they show no technologically Mesolithic traits.

This is true of the other implements and debitage, which lack any Mesolithic elements. Otherwise there is no particular indication of homogeneity about the collection, and a mixed Neolithic and Early Bronze Age origin is feasible.

The character of the collection as a whole suggests a casual accumulation of artefacts over time, rather than pointing to any focus of earlier prehistoric activity on the site in either time or place. Even in the earliest features the flint artefacts are likely to be residual, having been disturbed from the topsoil by later activity.

The collection of 94 flints from the excavation (of a much smaller area) at Uley Bury in 1976 (Saville and Ellison 1983, fiche B14–C2) was of the same general Neolithic/Early Bronze Age aspect as those from West Hill, and could be related to the dense scatter of flint surface finds known from the hillfort interior (*ibid*, 1). If the suggestion that the hilltop later occupied by the hillfort was an important Neolithic settlement (as indicated in particular by the number of polished flint and stone axehead fragments found on the surface) is correct, then it is of no surprise, and of no special significance, to encounter a low density of flint scatters across the surrounding fields.

Worked stone

by Fiona Roe

Whetstones

Twelve whetstones have been recorded, all from post-Iron Age contexts. Macroscopic examination suggested that they could be divided equally between two types of stone, a calcareous sandstone likely to be Kentish Rag, and a fine grained, micaceous sandstone likely to come from a Palaeozoic source. These two types of material can be correlated with two different shapes of tool. The Kentish Rag whetstones are now all broken, but they would originally have approximated to a cigar shape, with a cross-section that is either rectangular, Find 7729 (Fig 147, no 6) and Find 1203 (Fig 147, no 7), cylindrical, Find 1576 (Fig 147, no 10) and Find 1169 (Fig 147, no 11) or, (as Find 1550, Fig 147, no 9) half-way between the two.

By contrast, the Palaeozoic sandstone whetstones represent a stone that splits easily into slabs, while the morphology seems also to have been governed by the choice of waterworn pebbles. Two of these whetstones have been made from such slabs, Find 2121 (Fig 147, no 2) and Find 5595 (Fig 147, no 3), while the remainder suggest the utilisation of waterworn pebbles, Find 2048 (Fig 147, no 4), Find 5056 (Fig 147 no 5), Find 1598 (Fig 147 no 8), and Find 2328 (Fig 147, no 12).

Four whetstones were chosen for thin-sectioning in order to confirm the suggested materials. Only one made from Kentish Rag was sampled, Find 7729, an example from a Roman level, since both the shape and the calcareous nature of the stone were considered to be good diagnostic features. The thin section (thin section no R 186) showed that the main components were angular grains of quartz, set in a matrix of calcite, while the slide also contained abundant ostracod fragments, grains of glauconite, a little opaque iron, and occasional grains of chert, quartzite, chlorite, and muscovite. It can be compared with a sectioned whetstone from a Roman level at Beckford, Worcestershire (Roe 1987b, 16).

This is a material that appears to have been particularly favoured during the Roman period (Moore 1978, 69). It comes most probably from a Cretaceous source, the Lower Greensand Hythe Beds of Kent. Distance appears to have been no object in trading this material; a comprehensive list of sites where it has been recognised has yet to be compiled, but it occurs as far afield as Ilchester, Somerset (Moore 1982, 224); Scole, Norfolk (Moore 1978, 67, fig 3) and Droitwich, Worcestershire (Roe forthcoming a).

The three sandstone whetstones selected for thin sectioning, Find 5595 (Fig 147, no 3), Find 5056 (Fig 147, no 5), and Find 1598 (Fig 147, no 8) also come from Roman phases. For the thin section information see Roe 1988, AM Lab report 39/88. The study of these Palaeozoic whetstone materials is an ongoing project, so that revised views on the identification of the stone must remain a possibility. At present the closest comparisons that can be found for the Uley whetstones are mainly with Iron Age examples. The whetstones from Danebury, and those from the more recent excavations at Maiden Castle, were found closely to resemble one another. These were in turn traced to a probable source in the Lower Devonian Staddon Grit from near Plymouth (Roe, forthcoming b and d). The best parallels that can presently be found for the Uley whetstones are with such Iron Age finds, and though the affinities are less close than those between the Danebury and Maiden Castle whetstones themselves, the matter should repay further investigation. Another possibility would be in the Old Red Sandstone of Wales, this source being nearer to Gloucestershire. Further work is needed however, to check likely varieties of micaceous sandstone from this area. Again there are some similarities in thin section with the Pennant sandstone, a material already known to have been used for whetstones during the Roman period. The Uley finds appear however not to be made from this, but the problematic Coal Measures sandstones discussed by Moore (1978, 68) must remain a further possible source. Clues are now beginning to emerge about all these materials, but much research and fieldwork remains to be done.

At present a source in south Devon seems to be most likely for the Uley whetstones. Find no 1598 (Fig 147, no 8) can be compared with one of the Maiden Castle whetstones (Roe, forthcoming b, no 2543), while it is not unlike another from Danebury (Roe, forthcoming d, no 56). Find 5056 (Fig 147, no 5) compares best with an example from Maiden Castle (Roe, forthcoming b, no 7989) and a Roman find from Hengistbury Head (Roe 1987a, no 321). There is some variation between the Uley thin sections, and the third sample, Find 5595 (Fig 147, no 3) has to date been less easy to account for. It has a high content of quartz grains, mixed with a certain amount of iron, and seems likely to belong within the same range of sandstones as the other two thin sectioned examples.

The Kentish Rag and Palaeozoic sandstone are two apparently different rocks, and yet both may have been chosen to use for whetting and grinding because they share two basic characteristics. Both contain numerous angular grains of quartz, suitably sharp and hard for

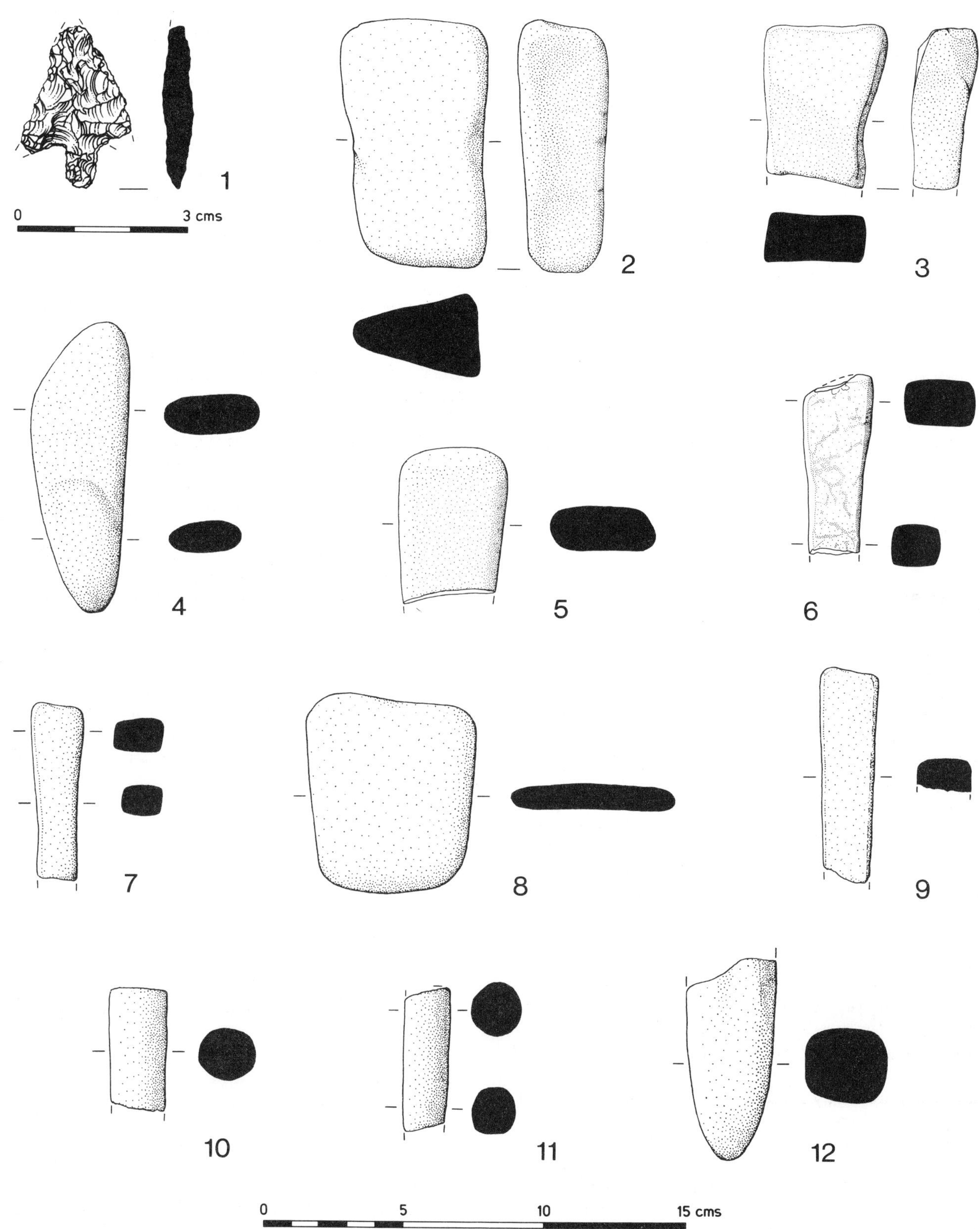

Fig 147 Flint arrowhead (no 1), scale 1:1, and whetstones (nos 2–12), scale 1:2

their intended purpose, and in both rocks the quartz grains are spaced out with other material, which should have had the effect of causing the stone to bite well. The Palaeozoic sandstone has a higher content of quartz grains, and the two stones therefore probably possess slightly different grinding properties. Whether they were used for identical or for complementary purposes remains a matter for speculation.

Catalogue of Whetstones

Fig 147
Roman

2 Slab of Palaeozoic sandstone, *Find 2121, context 320, Structure IVb, Phase 4a*

3 Slab of sandstone, thin section no R 187, *Find 5595, context 682, below Structure IXa, Phase 4a*

4 Pebble of Palaeozoic sandstone, *Find 2048, context 309, Structure IVb, Phase 4b*
5 Pebble of Palaeozoic sandstone, thin section no R 188, *Find 5056, context 89, Structure II(i)c ,Phase 4/5a–c*
6 Whetstone of Kentish Rag, thin section no R 186 *Find 7729, context 1204, Structure IX, demolition, Phase 5c*
7 Whetstone of Kentish Rag, *Find 1203, context 62, over Structure I, Phase 5e(ii)*
8 Pebble of Palaeozoic sandstone, thin section no R189, *Find 1598, context 22, over Structure I, Phase 5e (ii)*

Late Roman
9 Whetstone of Kentish Rag, *Find 1550, context 52, Structure II(iii)a, Phase 6a*
10 Whetstone of Kentish Rag, *Find 1576, context 88, Structure II (iii)c, Phase 6a*

Post-Roman
11 Whetstone of Kentish Rag, *Find 1169, context 20, over Structure IX, Phase 7*
12 Pebble of Palaeozoic sandstone, *Find 2328, context 207, Structure VII, (F275), Phase 7a*

not illustrated
Whetstone of Kentish Rag, *Find 5613, context 694, Structure X exterior, Phase 4b*

Querns

Thirteen broken pieces of quern have been examined and are listed in the catalogue. No complete querns were discovered, though two pieces fit together to form part of the upper stone of a rotary quern, Find 4738 (Fig 148, no 1). Some of the quern fragments have a tooled surface which has been worked into grooves: Finds 2713, 4936, and 5113 (Fig 148, nos 2, 3, and 5).

The stone used for querns was all imported to the site. It derives from the Devonian Upper Old Red Sandstone, and three varieties of this can be distinguished among the archaeological finds. One such variety is the quartz conglomerate, a distinctive rock containing pebbles of vein quartz together with some of jasper, chert, and decomposed igneous rocks, set in a sandstone matrix. This type of stone is already known as a quern material (Peacock 1980, 43), though little work has been done to compile records of finds from archaeological contexts or to identify a definite source. This quartz conglomerate occurs typically in bands about 20–50 feet thick (Welch and Trotter 1961, 50), and these bands may be separated by sandstone containing widely scattered pebbles. This pebbly sandstone accounts for the second variety of quern stone found here. Thirdly there are quern fragments made from sandstone that lacks pebbles but that otherwise resembles the pebbly variety. This sandstone is buff to pinkish in colour, fairly coarse, and consists mainly of quite well rounded grains of quartz, a few of which are stained pink, and scattered grains of feldspar.

Only one quern fragment, a late Iron Age piece, Find 5735, is made from quartz conglomerate, a near white version of this stone. There are three pieces of the sandstone with pebbles, all likely to be late or very late Roman in date. Two pieces of a reddish version, Find 4738, and the fragment from context 59 (both Fig 148, no 1) fit together as part of a rotary quern, while the third fragment, Find 7461, is more purplish in colour. The remaining quern fragments, Finds 2713, and 3481, (both Fig 148, no 2); Find 3440, (Fig 148, no 3), and Find 3437 (all possibly from the same quern); Find 4936 (Fig 148, no 4); and Finds 3482, 4574, 5113, and 5829 are all made from much the same kind of buff to pink sandstone, and these occurred mainly in post-Roman phases, though it seems a possibility that they may be residual, and should derive from earlier, probably Roman phases.

It has been possible to match all three varieties of stone used for the Uley querns, and though work is still progressing, and no thin sections have as yet been used to obtain more detailed comparisons, it is possible to suggest a likely source area. The Forest of Dean has sometimes been put forward as a locality likely to have been used as a source for obtaining quartz conglomerate (for example Rawes 1987, 90), and this stone can certainly be found in this general region, though the outcrops are mostly peripheral to the forest proper. More extensive outcrops are however to be found along the Wye valley, and it is to the west of the river Wye, in areas around Penallt and Trelleck, now in Gwent (Monmouthshire) that rock specimens have been collected that compare well with all the finds from Uley.

Quern fragments made from stone originating in the Upper Old Red Sandstone have been identified at other sites, most notably in the large collection from Beckford, Worcestershire (Roe 1987b), where this material appears to have been used extensively from the Late Iron Age onwards. Tooled pieces of quern, similar to those from Uley, occurred in Romano-British levels at Beckford. Upper Old Red Sandstone quern materials have also been seen amongst worked stone from two sites in Droitwich, The Old Bowling Green (Roe forthcoming a) and the Bay's Meadow Roman villa (Roe forthcoming c).

Catalogue of Querns

all of Upper Old Red Sandstone

Late Iron Age

not illustrated
Fragment of white quartz conglomerate, *Find 5735, context 750, F264, Phase 3a*
Fragment of buff sandstone, *Find 5829, context 910, F264, Phase 3a*

Fig 148
Late to very late Roman
1 Sandstone with pebbles, *Find 4738, context 482, Structure II (iii),Phase 6b*. Also sandstone with pebbles, joins Find 4738 above, *Context 59, Structure XI, Phase 7a*

not illustrated
Fragment of sandstone with pebbles, *Find 7461, context 1191, Structure XIV, Phase 5d-6b*
Grooved fragment of pink/buff sandstone, *Find 4574, context 487, Structure II (iii),Phase 6b*

Post-Roman
2 Grooved buff sandstone, *Find 2713, context 277, Structure XI,Phase 7a*. Also grooved buff sandstone, joins Find 2713,*Find 3481, context 428, Structure XI, Phase7a*

not illustrated
Grooved, buff sandstone *Find 3437, context 422, Structure XI, Phase 7a*

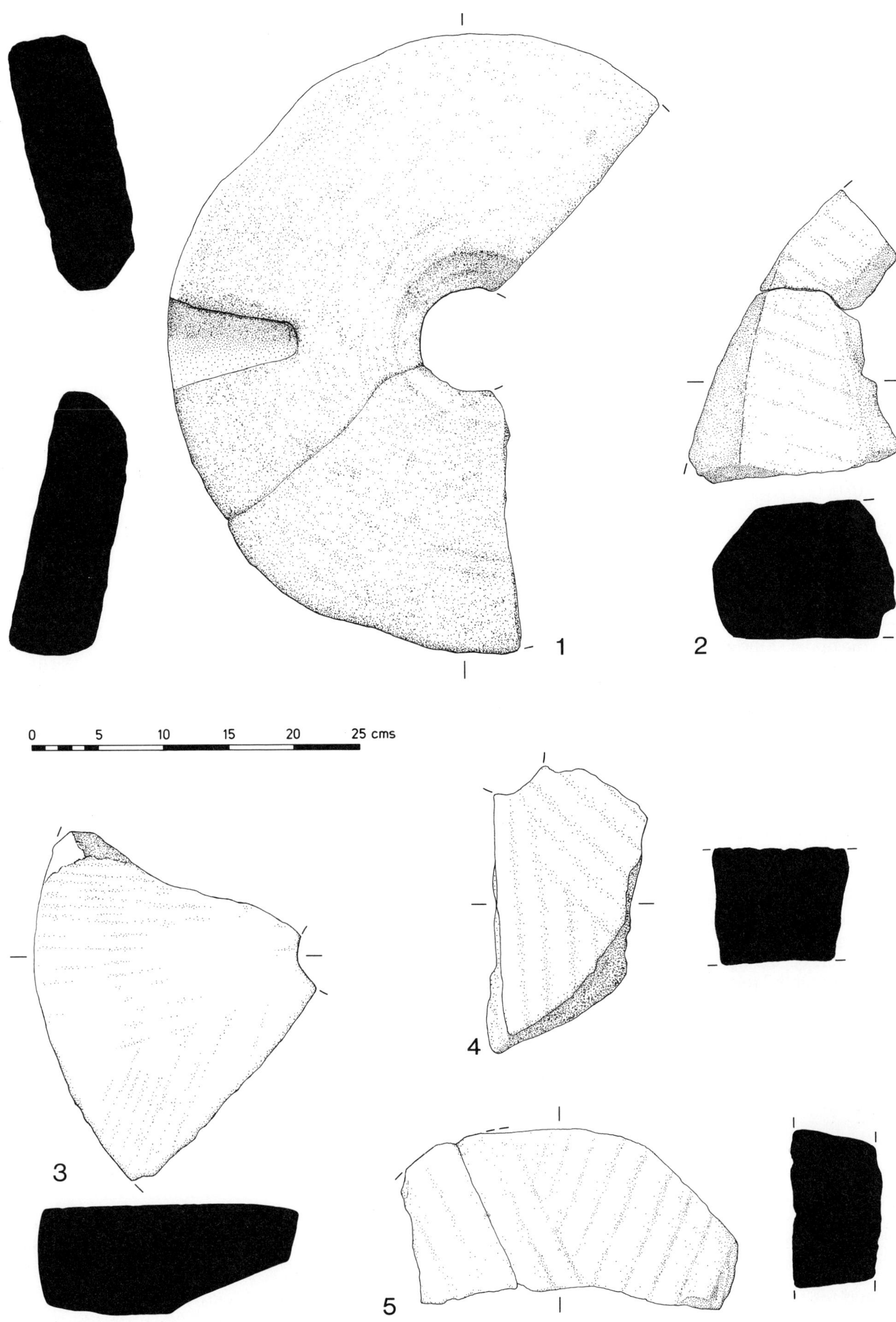

Fig 148 Querns, scale 1:4

3 Grooved, buff sandstone, *Find 3440, context 424, Structure XI, Phase 7a*

Finds 2713, 3437, 3440, and 3481 may all be the same quern

not illustrated
Grooved fragment of pink/buff sandstone, *Find 3482, context 428, Structure XI, Phase 7a*
4 Grooved fragment of pink/buff sandstone, *Find 4936, context 602, Structure XIX, Phase 7a*

Possibly modern
5 Two grooved pieces of pink/buff sandstone, *Find 5113, unstratified, Phase 8*

Comment

Attempts to find parallels for these querns and whetstones amongst Gloucestershire Roman sites have been less successful, since all too often stone objects of this sort appear to have been overlooked. In the past it seems that querns tended to go unnoticed, or were not collected, unless they happened to be complete, and two such querns made of Old Red Sandstone are known from Lydney (Wheeler and Wheeler 1932, 68). Similarly whetstones seem easily to have escaped notice unless made conspicuous by a perforation through one end as at Frocester Court (Gracie and Price 1979, 21) and also at Gloucester (Hurst 1986, 44). Some comparative material does exist, though a good deal more might have been expected from an area with a number of well known Roman sites. Finds from a well at Frocester included quern fragments of conglomerate likely to derive from the Old Red Sandstone (E G Price 1984, 60), and the Romano-British settlement at Haymes produced nine pieces of quern made from quartz conglomerate (Rawes 1987, 90). As for whetstones, one Pennant example is known from Gloucester (Hunter 1986, 71), while one of Kentish Rag seems a possibility from Frocester Court (E G Price 1984, 60). All in all the well documented assemblage of worked stone from West Hill assumes an unexpected importance in providing information to fill gaps in our knowledge about Gloucestershire archaeology.

Candlesticks

by Martin Henig

both of iron

Fig 149
1 Candlestick with socket for taper. The shank fits into a triangular plate with a leg at each corner and bisects another triangular plate with three prongs which probably all ended in volutes (one remaining). The latter is probably largely decorative although the plate would have served to catch drips from the candle, *Find 0134, context TF13–17, area of Structure IX/X in 1976 pipe trench*
2 Candlestick with three legs and socket for taper, *Find 7085, context 1191, Structure XIV, Phase 5d–6b*

see also Find 6978 (Fig 153, no 26)

A number of iron candlesticks have been found at shrines where they would have been used to lighten the gloom of the temple interiors and perhaps to provide receptacles for votive tapers, eg Lydney (Wheeler and Wheeler 1932, 93, fig 23, nos 191 and 192); Springhead (Penn 1962, 129, no 2, fig 6.2); Carrawburgh Mithraeum (Richmond and Gillam 1951, 84–5, no 3, pl xvb). Also *cf* an example from a secular context at Richborough (Cunliffe 1968, 109, no 271, pl liv).

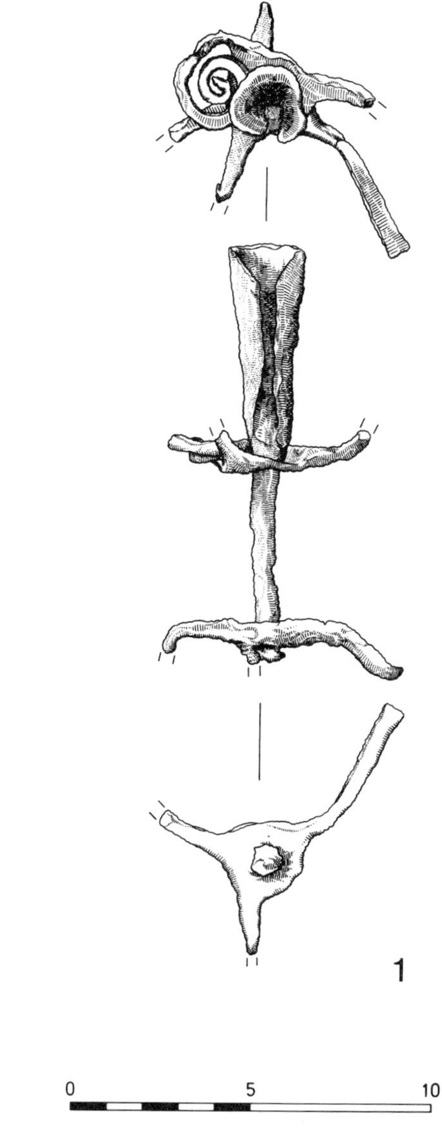

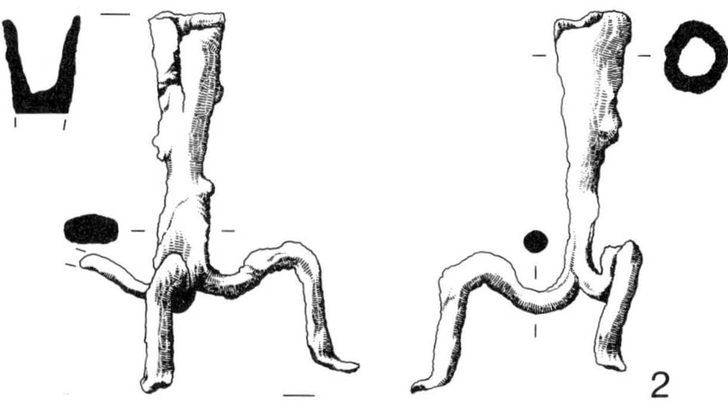

Fig 149 Candlesticks of iron, scale 1:2

Copper alloy candlesticks from temple sites include

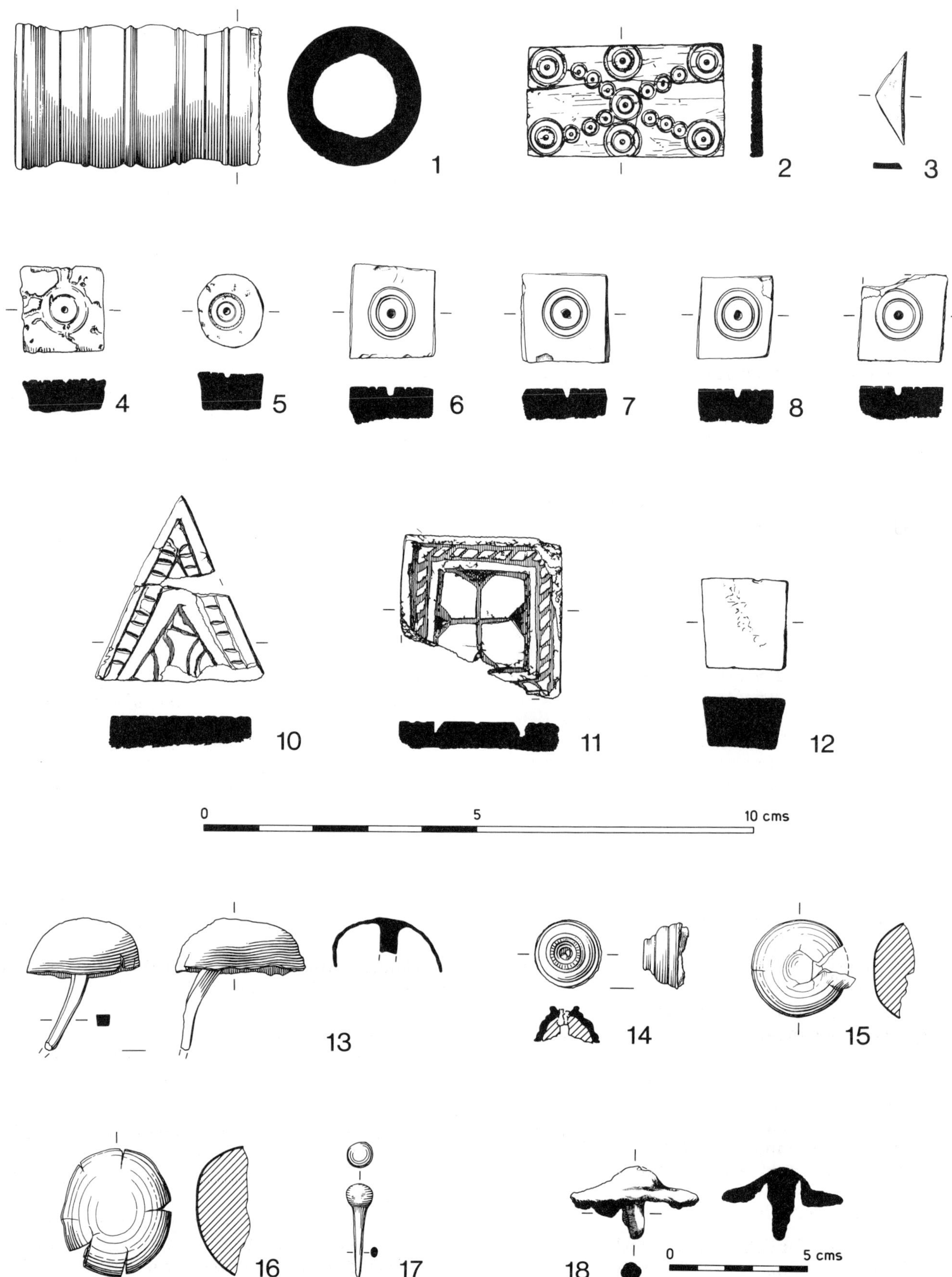

Fig 150 Fittings of bone and antler (nos 1–2), scale 1:4, and copper alloy studs (nos 13–18), scale 1:2

a rather grand one from Harlow, Essex (France and Gobel 1985, 86–7, fig 44, no 63) and those in the form of cockerels from Lydney (Wheeler and Wheeler 1932, 86 and fig 20, no 98) and from Nettleton (Toynbee in Wedlake 1982, 143, no 10 pl xxxia). A pewter candleholder in the form of a stag was found in the spring at Bath (Sunter and Brown in Cunliffe, ed 1988, ch 2, no 22). The provision of light to temples must have been a very important element in creating an effect.

Plaques and fittings

all objects are made from deer antler except Find 1124

Fig 150

1 Cylindrical sleeve, decorated with sets of transverse grooves, *Find 7640, context 1202, Structure XIV, Phase 5d*

2 Rectangular piece of inlay decorated with a cross motif composed of incised ring and dot elements of three sizes, *Find 5646, context 811, Structure IX, Phase 5a*

3 Plain triangular piece of inlay which may have been manufactured from a piece of rib, *Find 1124, context 22, over Structure I, Phase 5e (ii)*

4 Square piece of inlay (or possibly a counter), decorated with an incised ring and dot motif, *Find 1556, context 88, Structure II, Phase 6a*

5 Circular piece of inlay (or counter), decorated with incised ring and dot motif, *Find 1707, context 6, Structure II, Phase 6b*

Four similar square inlay elements (or counters), decorated with ring and dot motifs:

6 *Find 7926, context 0406, Structure XIX, Phase 7*

7 *Find 7957, context 0406, Structure XIX, Phase 7*

8 *Find 7967, context 0406, Structure XIX, Phase 7*

9 *Find 8342, context 0410, Structure XIX, Phase 7*

10 Triangular piece of inlay decorated with a curvilinear incised pattern within a lozenge, bounded by a geometric border, comprising vertical incised lines between two lines, following the margin of the piece, *Find 7968, context 0406, Structure XIX, Phase 7*

11 Square piece of inlay, one corner broken away, decorated with an incised cross motif bounded by a geometric border filled with diagonal incised lines, *Find 7274, context 0407, Structure XIX, Phase 7*

12 Plain square piece of inlay, *Find 4144, context 601, Structure XIX, Phase 7*

The plaques, Finds 1556, 1707, 7926, 7957, 7967, and 8342 (Fig 150 nos 4–9) can be paralleled at Lullingstone (Meates 1987, 144, fig 58, nos 395–97) where plaques of similar form were found in the temple-mausoleum, and were thought to derive from a bone inlaid box. Plaques similar to Finds 7968 and 7274, (Fig 150, nos 10 and 11) were also found there *ibid*, nos 399, 401) although the incised motifs are different.

Studs and rivets

Sheet metal covers for dome shaped studs were found in substantial numbers, especially in the area of the temple. They were usually formed over a matrix of solder. A representative selection are illustrated below:

all copper alloy

13 Hollow convex headed rivet, *Find 1089, context 32, over Structure I, Phase 5e(ii)*

14 Cast rivet head with decorated central disc and matrix of solder, *Find 828, context 36, over Structure VIII, Phase 7b*

15 Domed head of stud, solder matrix, *Find 3788, context 1, Phase 8*

16 Domed head of stud, solder matrix, *Find 3869, context 1, Phase 8*

17 Spherical headed upholstery nail, *Find 3838, context 1, Phase 8*

18 Flat headed rivet with domed centre, *Find 7045, context 1191, Structure XIV, Phase 5d–6b*

Fittings, mainly from boxes and furniture

all of copper alloy

Fig 151

1 Cast terminal plate with nicked outline, probably part of a lock plate (*M Henig*), *Find 3012, context 106, Structure I, Phase 5e(i)*

2 Part of a lozenge shaped plate with circular rivet holes, probably a box fitting (*M Henig*), *Find 4538, context 1, Phase 8*

3 Fragment of a pelta shaped object, possibly a box attachment (*M Henig*), *Find 6059, context 0248, Phase 8*

4 Circular stud with geometric floral motif, possibly from a military belt or apron, *Find 7515, context 1191, Structure XIV, Phase 5d–6b*

5 Sheet covering, square with repoussé star and dot decoration, *Find 6946, context 1167, Structure XIV, Phase 5d–6b*

6 Plate washer, *Find 5733, context 879, Structure X, Phase 4a*

7 Sheet furniture terminal filled with solder, *Find 699, context 22, over Structure I, Phase 5e(ii)*

8 Fragment of sheet furniture terminal, *Find 8001, context 0410, Structure XIX, Phase 7*

9 Oval plate with central perforation and incised linear decoration, *Find 8104, context 0406, Structure XIX, Phase 7*

10 Large dished sheet boss, the margin filled with solder, *Find 7258, context 1157, Structure XIV, Phase 5d–6b*

11 Conical furniture terminal, filled with solder, *Find 6633, context 0406, Structure XIX, Phase 7*

12 Sheet cover from furniture terminal, *Find 261, context 2, Structure II, Phase 6b*

13 Conical furniture terminal, filled with solder, *Find 1535, context 2, Structure II, Phase 6b*

Fig 152

1 Conical furniture terminal, filled with solder, *Find 3990, context 511, Structure XIX, Phase 7a*

2 Circular disc with twin rivets, *Find 1085, context 44, pit F57, Phase 7b*

3 Boss cover, with two possibly secondary perforations, *Find 5408, context 602, Structure XIX, Phase 7a*

4 Damaged boss with central projection, *Find 6542, context 1100, over Structure XIV, Phase 7–8*

5 Ovoid boss filled with solder, *Find 43, context 1, Phase 8*

6 Slightly domed disc with nicked margin, *Find 51, context 1, Phase 8*

7 Cast square stud, *Find 3814, context 1, Phase 8*

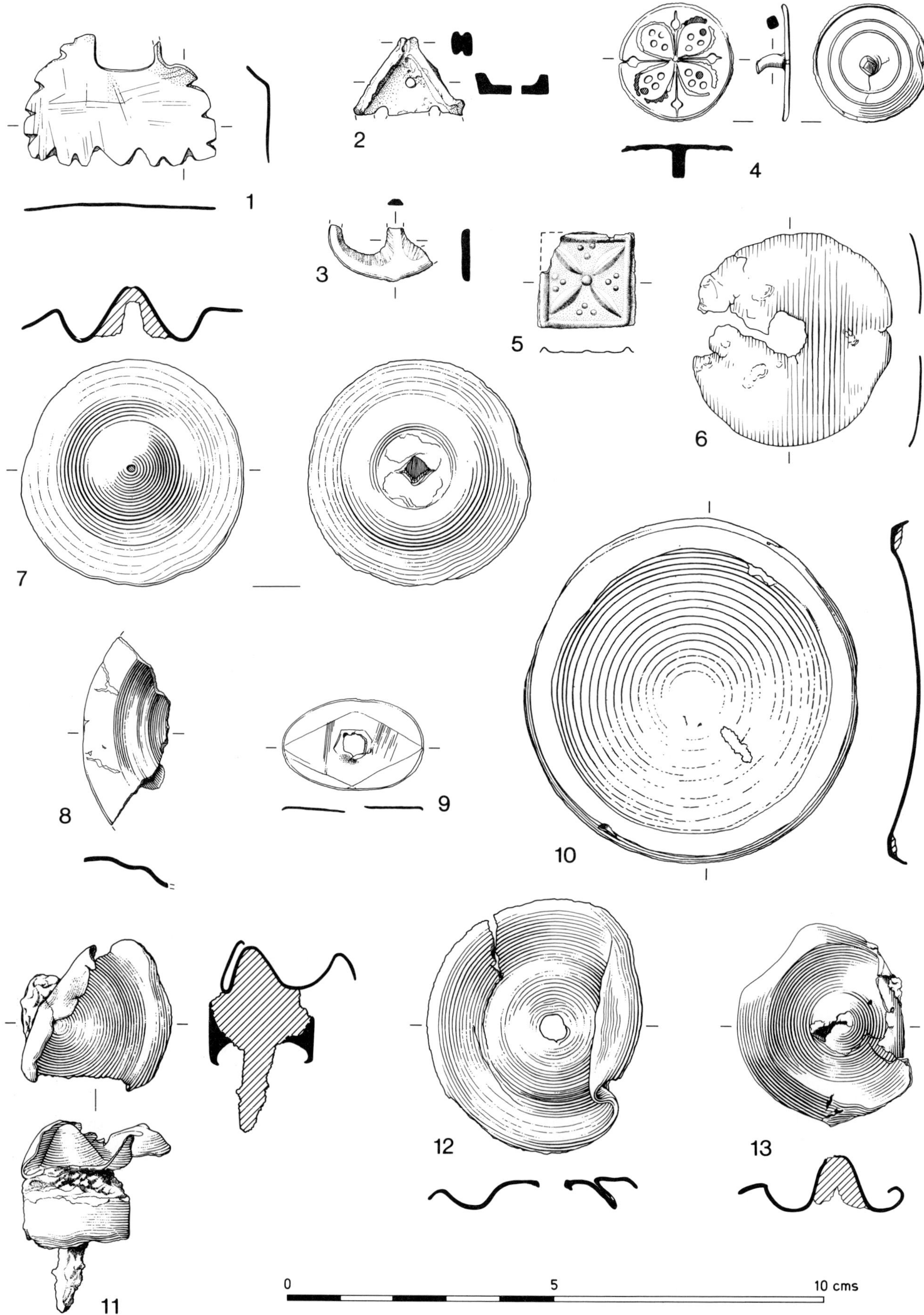

Fig 151 Fittings of copper alloy from boxes and furniture, scale 1:1

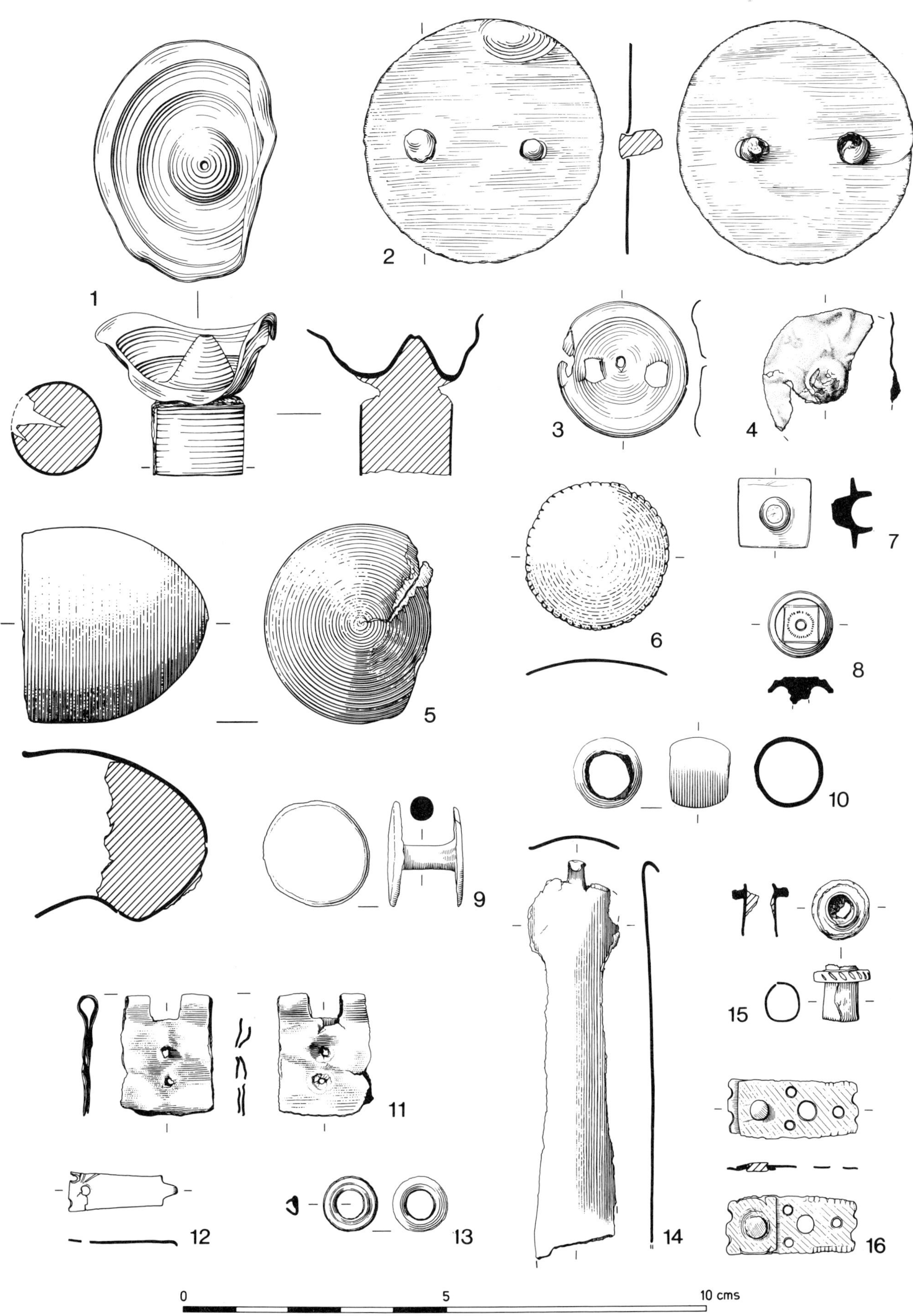

Fig 152 Fittings of copper alloy, scale 1:1

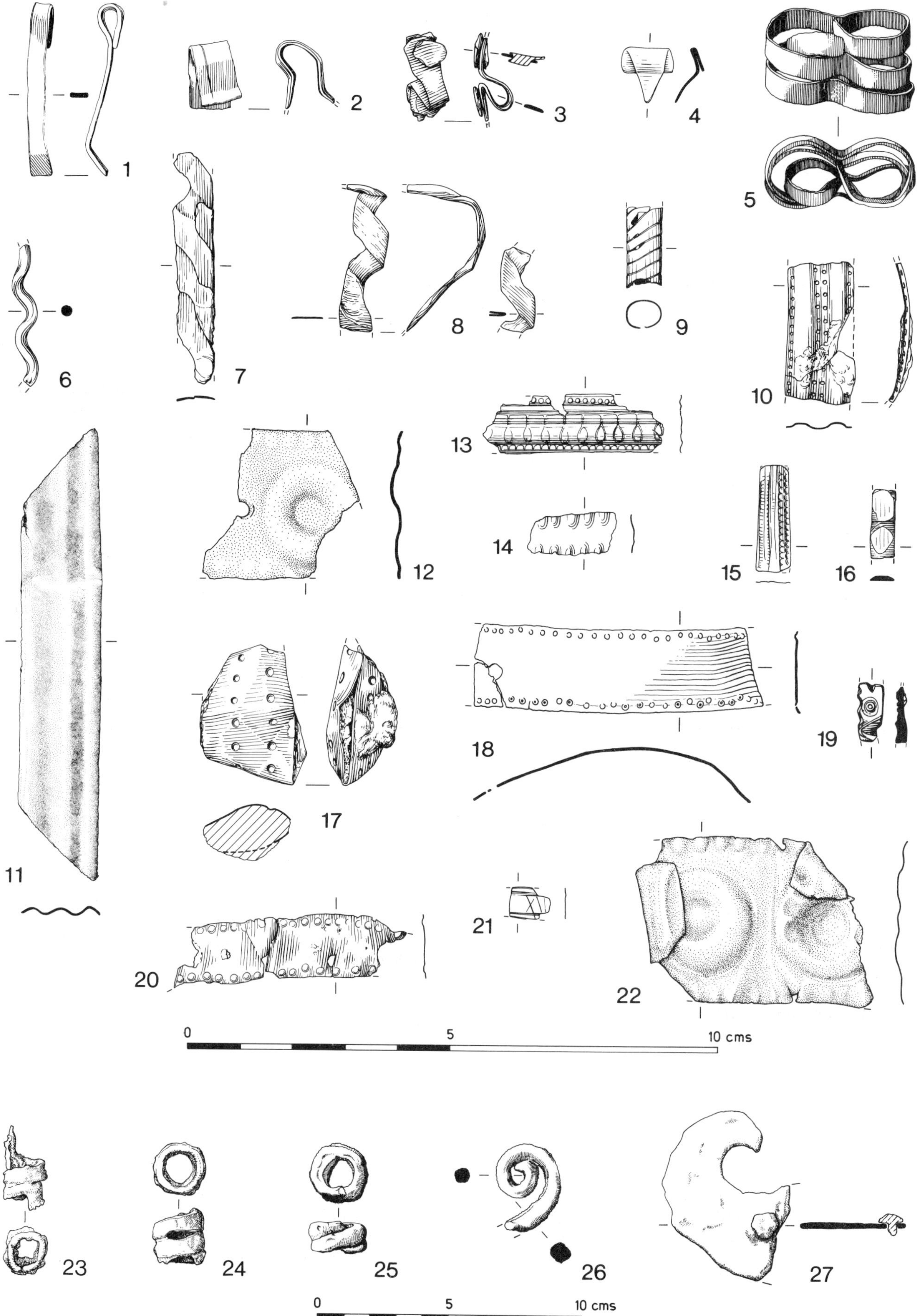

Fig 153 Decorative strips, spirals, and tubes of copper alloy and iron (nos 23–27), scale 1:2

8 Circular decorated stud, *Find 601, context 0230, Phase 8*
9 Large rivet, *Find 3014, context 360, Structure IV, Phase 4a*
10 Ovoid collar, *Find 2042, context 309, Structure IV, Phase 5b*
11 Strap plate, *Find 2281, context 33, courtyard, Phase 4–6*
12 Decorated plate with rivet holes and hook, *Find 256, context 1, Phase 8*
13 Binding or ringlet, *Find 8270, context 1255, Structure IX, Phase 6*
14 Curved plate with terminal hook, *Find 2207, context 14, Structure II, Phase 6*
15 Cylinder of sheet metal with protruding decorated collar, *Find 6498, context 0115, Phase 8*
16 Possible strap end with perforations and marginal nicked decoration, *Find 270, context 1, Phase 8*

Fig 153
1 Hook or catch, *Find 8122, context 1223, Structure IX, Phase 5c*

Sheet strips, spirals, and tubes

2 *Find 1198, context 62, over Structure I, Phase 5e(ii)*
3 *Find 4099, context 511, Structure XIX, Phase 7a*
4 *Find 4017, context 511, Structure XIX, Phase 7a*
5 *Find 1244, context 80, Structure I, Phase 5e(i)*
6 *Find 1090, context 22, over Structure I, Phase 5e(ii)*
7 *Find 4525, context 603, Structure XIX, Phase 7a*
8 *Find 4564, context 603, Structure XIX, Phase 7a*
9 *Find 3927, context 600, over Structure XIX, Phase 8*

Sheet strips from boxes or furniture, mainly decorated *en repoussé*

10 *Find 5707, context 824, over pit F836, Phase 3c*
11 *Find 1473, context 32, over Structure I, Phase 5e(ii)*
12 *Find 410, context 14, Structure II, Phase 6b*
13 *Find 4054, context 511, Structure XIX, Phase 7a*
14 *Find 4601, context 601, Structure XIX, Phase 7a*
15 *Find 4722, context 602, Structure XIX, Phase 7a*
16 *Find 4750, context 604, Structure XIX, Phase 7a*
17 *Find 4821, context 602, Structure XIX, Phase 7a*
18 *Find 314, context 13, over Structure XIX, Phase 8*
19 *Find 4987, context 602, Structure XIX, Phase 7a*
20 *Find 5064, context 602, Structure XIX, Phase 7a*
21 *Find 4326, context 600, over XIX, Phase 8*
22 *Find 4523, context 13, over XIX, Phase 8*

Ferrules and terminals

all of iron

23 Short spiral of a rod forming a ferrule with a projecting extention, probably an animal goad (*cf* Manning 1985, 140 and pl 67), *Find 5764, context 629, Structure X, Phase 4a*
24 Short spiral of a rod forming a circular ferrule (*cf ibid*), *Find 5647, context 823, Structure IX, Phase 4a*
25 Short compressed spiral rod forming a circular ferrule (*cf ibid*), *Find 6441, context 110, over Structure XIV, Phase 7–8*
26 Tightly coiled rod belonging to a spiral terminal, possibly from a candlestick (see Find 0134, Fig 149, no 1), *Find 6978, context 1180, Structure XIV, Phase 5d–6b*
27 Flat plate curved to form a tapering hooked ?terminal, one rivet central at the broader base, *Find 133, context 1, Phase 8*

Plates, washers, rings, and miscellaneous fittings

all of iron

Fig 154
1 Large double waisted flat plate or strap with triple fixing rivet holes, only the central rivet surviving, *Find 7808, context 1204, Structure IX, Phase 5c*
2 Segment of a flat band or plate (in two pieces), with three rivet holes, one surviving rivet with a decoratively forged quatrefoil head, *Find 6163, context 0245, Phase 8*
3 Rectangular plate or mounting, having a recessed panel with an inscribed circle as decoration, *Find 142, context 1, Phase 8*
4 Part of a curved plate with a single rectangular rivet hole through a cross shaped head, *Find 5143, context 617, Structure IX, Phase 5d–e*
5 Plain, flat circular washer with a central rivet hole, *Find 1158, context 22, over Structure I, Phase 5e(ii)*
6 Part of a ?circular rove or washer with a central raised, circular rivet hole, *Find 3934, context 511, Structure XIX, Phase 7a*
7 Square, slightly domed rove or washer with a central rivet hole, *Find 1504, context 52, Structure IIiii, Phase 6a*
8 Part of a plain, opened or D-shaped ring, circular cross section, *Find 5316, context 619, Structure IX, Phase 5c*
9 Complete plain circular ring, circular cross section, *Find 2000, context 313, Structure IV, Phase 4b*
10 Opened or corroded plain circular ring, circular cross section, *Find 1652, context 67, Structure I, Phase 5e(i)*
11 Opened plain oval ring, circular cross section, *Find 2028, context 14, Structure IIiii, Phase 6b*
12 Opened plain oval ring, circular cross section, *Find 5340, context 639, Structure IX, Phase 5b*
13 Complete plain circular ring, circular cross section, *Find 5395, context 624, Structure XIX, Phase 7a*
14 Part of a plate or mounting, the lower part curved to form a sheath or socket and pierced by a large nail, *Find 1062, context 20, over Structure IX, Phase 7*
15 Pair of flat, rectangular, hinged plates with no rivet holes, *Find 2151, context 201, Structure II(iii), Phase 6a*
16 Small, angled triangular plate with an expanded head pierced for a small central rivet, *Find 5169, context 478, Structure XIX, Phase 7a*
17 Rectangular plate or strap termination with one large and one small rivet hole, *Find 5165, context 545, Structure XV, Phase 7a*
18 Small hook and eye fitting, *Find 4772, context 602, Structure XIX, Phase 7a*
19 Solid, slightly tapering, circular cylinder, possibly a weight, *Find 111, context 1, Phase 8*

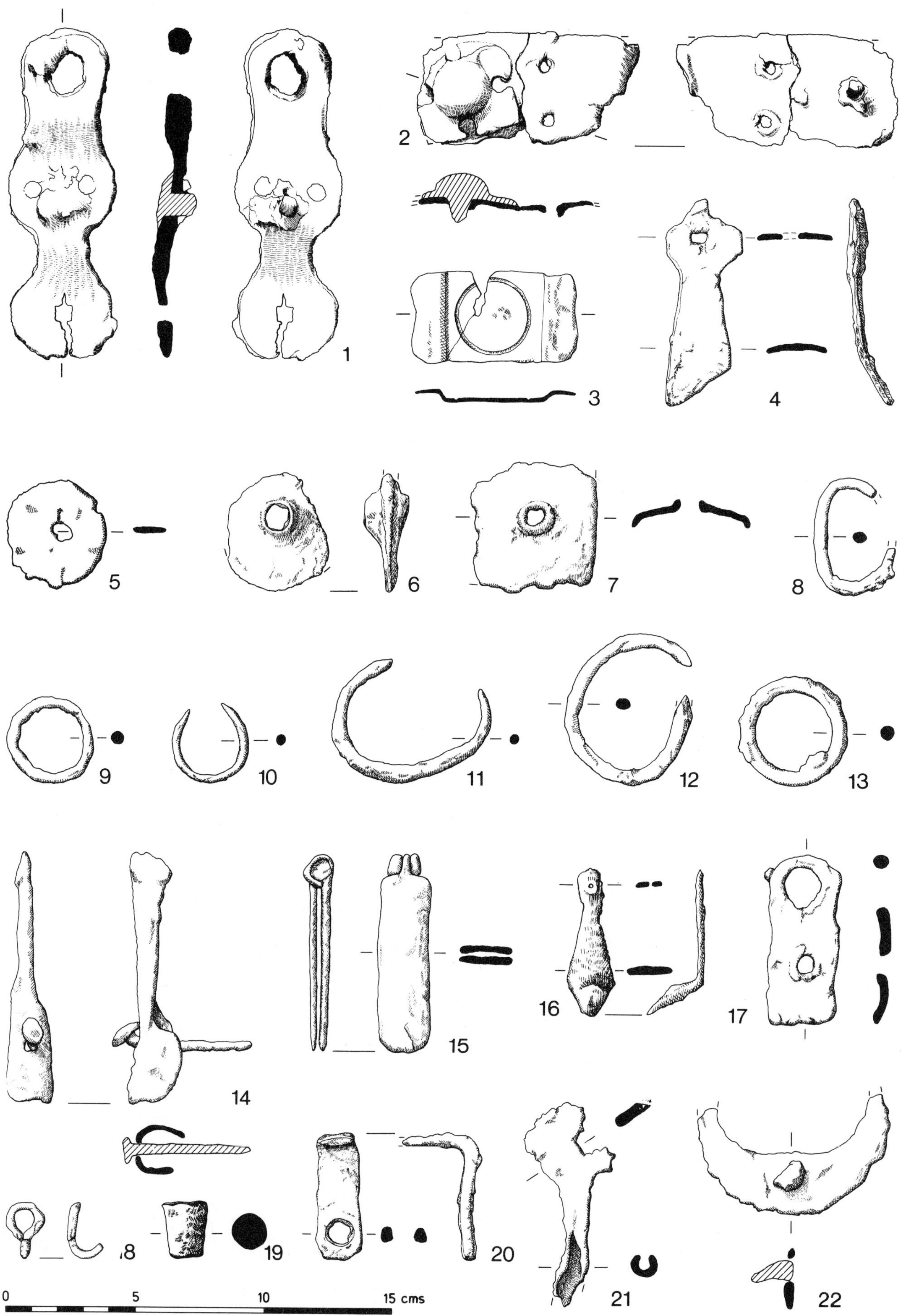

Fig 154 Plates, washers, rings, and other fittings of iron, scale 1:2

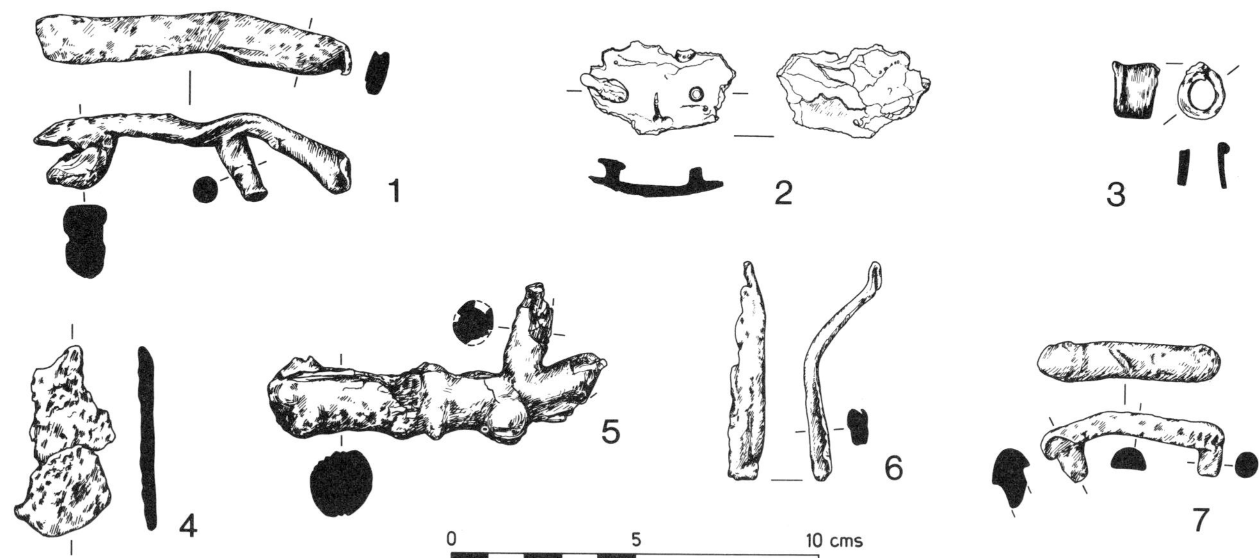

Fig 155 Fittings of lead, scale 1:2

20 Angle bracket plate with a single rivet hole, *Find 4915, context 1, Phase 8*
21 Part of a heavily corroded, socketed mounting or implement, *Find 89, context 1, Phase 8*
22 Crescent shaped plate with a single fixing rivet still in place, *Find 29, context 1, Phase 8*

Fig 155

all of lead

1 Strip with two projections of varying cross section, *Find 5775, context 901, Structure II exterior, fill above ditch F264, Phase 3b–5*
2 Portion of a flat plate with two projections, possibly a rivet, *Find 3515, context 201, Structure II, Phase 6a*
3 Fragment of small collar, *Find 4995, context 609, Structure IX, Phase 6b*
4 Two joining fragments of flat plate, *Find 4377, context 603, Structure XIX, Phase 7a*
5 Irregular bar of circular section with part of a projection, *Find 4706, context 604, Structure XIX, Phase 7a*
6 Tapering strip, *Find 3979, context 600, Phase 8*
7 Bar of semicircular section with two projections, possibly a rivet, *Find 5920, from fieldwalking*

Sealbox lid

by Sarnia Butcher

Fig 156
1 A copper alloy sealbox lid of leaf shape with enamel decoration. The whole of the flat top is divided by reserved metal ribs into fields for enamel; the main design repeats the leaf shape, with a central ring. Only a few traces of greenish-blue enamel remain, in the outer field, *Find 128, context 1, Phase 8*

Several other very similar sealbox lids are known: one from Verulamium (Wheeler and Wheeler 1936, 212, fig 54, no 53) was in a late third-century pit. Sellye (1939, pl xv 28 and p 85) lists several from Pannonia, and the Ashmolean Museum has one from Amiens. The leaf design often occurs on enamelled vessels. None of these objects is well dated but a second-century date seems most likely.

Vessels

all of copper alloy except where stated

2 Handle fitting, *Find 4712, context 484, Structure VII, Phase 7*
3 Handle fitting, *Find 5232, context 402, Structure VII, Phase 7* Nos 2 and 3 could derive from a single vessel.
4 Fragment from a decorated lid (*M Henig*),*Find 4976, context 602, Structure XIX, Phase 7a*
5 Rim fragment from bowl with out turned rim, *Find 5416, context 645, Structure IX, Phase 5b*
6 Rim fragment from plain small bowl, *Find 6239, context 0312, Structure XIX, Phase 7*
7 Portion of rim of plain bowl, much damaged and buckled, *Find 107, context 1, Phase 8*
8 Base angle portion from a sheet metal vessel with pressed decoration, *Find 335, context 13, over Structure XIX, Phase 8*
9 Circular hinged lid with central perforation and scratched motif (*M Henig*), *Find 2235, context 300, over Structure IV, Phase 6b*
10 Sheet binding, possibly from the rim of a vessel, *Find 6709, context 1100, over Structure XIV, Phase 7–8*

Fig 157
1 Buckled rim segment of lead or pewter plate or dish, *Find 141, context 1, Phase 8*
2 Rim fragment from lead or pewter bowl, *Find 6509, water pipe trench, Phase 8*
3 Base angle fragment from lead or pewter vessel, *Find 1260, context 68, Structure I, Phase 5e(i)*
4 Narrow circular base from a lead or pewter vessel, *Find 16, context 1, Phase 8*
5 Lead or pewter handle, D-sectioned, *Find 6032, context 0226, Phase 8*

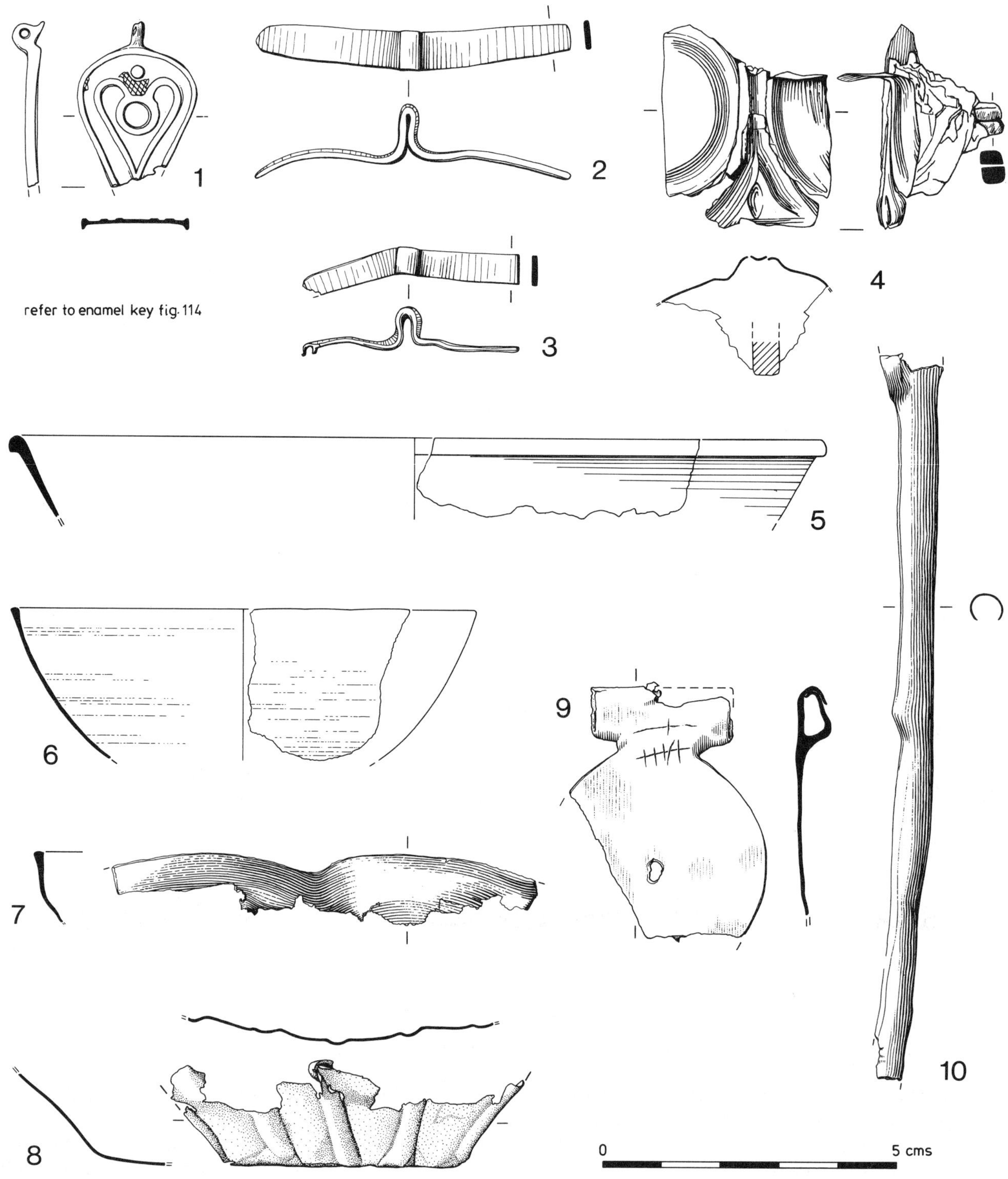

Fig 156 Seal-box lid and vessel fragments of copper alloy, nos 1–4 scale 1:1, nos 5–10 scale 1:2

6 Fragment of a plain iron bowl or cauldron with a beaded rim, *Find 1832, context 1, Phase 8*

7 Segment of a square sectioned iron bar with a forged loop, part of a handle, handle attachment for a vessel or, possibly, a hinge, *Find 6656, context 0402, Structure XIX, Phase 7*

8 Curved circular sectioned iron bar, possibly part of a handle or latch lifter, *Find 1017, context 32, over Structure I, Phase 5e(ii)*

See Fig 134, no 1, 'mirror' for another vessel fragment

Vessel glass

by Jennifer Price

A total of 959 fragments of Roman vessel glass were found during the excavations. The size of the fragments is generally very small indeed, which has inhibited the identification of the forms represented, but it is clear that very little glass was used on the site before the fourth century. All the vessels are types commonly found on domestic sites, and few are of more than ordinary quality. While there do not appear to be any

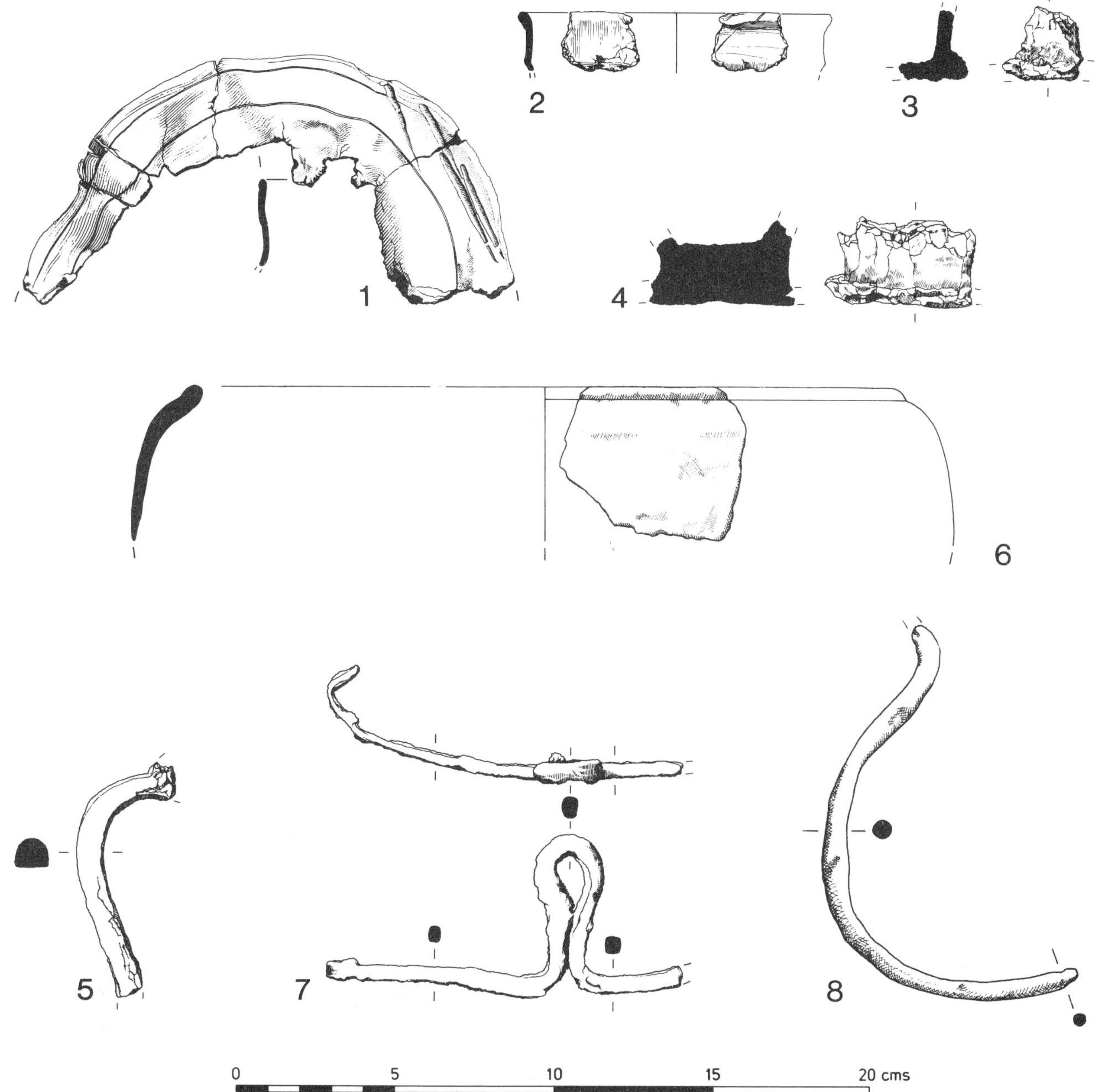

Fig 157 Vessel fragments of lead or pewter (nos 1–5), and iron (nos 6–8), scale 1:2

very unusual vessel forms the material is interesting and important because of the range of forms and number of vessels represented, and because of the nature of the site. The assemblage provides information not readily available elsewhere about the late Roman glass in use at a rural Romano-British temple.

A small quantity of first to early second-century, and of later second to third-century glass was found, though the vast majority of pieces come from fourth-century vessels. Among the early tablewares there is a ribbed conical jug with tall angular handle, Find 5712, (Fig 158, no 1 illustrates the handle), a form commonly found in Britain and the north-west provinces from *c* AD 65 to 125, and occasionally in mid second-century deposits (Isings 1957, form 55; Price 1987, 193–5), another jug or a globular jar (Isings 1957, form 67c) of similar date, Find 5796, (Fig 158, no 2) and at least three square bottles and one cylindrical one, Finds 7191, 7358, and 5628 (see Fig 158, nos 3–4) are represented among the first and second-century container fragments (Isings 1957, forms 50–1).

The facet and linear-cut hemispherical bowl, Finds 5076, 6052, 6372, 7657, (Fig 158, no 5), a good quality vessel produced in the second or third century, is comparable in form and design with others found in Britain, as at Verulamium (Charlesworth 1972, 208–10), fig 78, 48–51) and London (Wheeler 1930, 122 fig 42, 1–2), and the ribbed body fragment, Finds 7411 and 1195, (Fig 158, no 6) may come from a cup or from a jug, though the piece is too small for the vessel form to be identified. The other glass of this period is undecorated; pieces from two or three of the cylindrical cups with fire rounded rims in widespread use in Britain and the north-west provinces from the third quarter of the second to the middle of the third century (Isings 1957, form 85: Price 1987, 192–3), have been identified, Finds 8182, 5365, 5531, 5562, and 3148, (Fig 158, nos 7–9).

As stated above, the identifiable fourth-century glass

vessels at West Hill are forms in common use elsewhere in Britain and the north-west provinces, and none is of great luxury. The assemblage is quite similar to finds from numerous Romano-British domestic sites such as Portchester (Harden 1975), Frocester Court Roman villa (Price 1979), Barnsley Park Roman villa (Price 1982), and Towcester (Price and Cool 1983).

Drinking vessels, including hemispherical bowls and conical and footed drinking cups, form the largest group of vessels. Three small body fragments with coloured blobs or trails, and five mould-blown fragments with close set narrow diagonal ribbing or honeycomb patterns, Find 8321, (Fig 158, no 10) were found, but most pieces are free blown. Some have cracked-off rims and fine horizontal abraded bands, or no decoration at all, and simple concave bases, sometimes outlined by trails, Finds 8291, 6704, 5035, 4030, 6638, 2378, 7371, and 4741, (Fig 158, nos 11–19), or wide pushed in base-rings with tubular edges, Finds 6488 and 6707, (Fig 158, nos 20–1), and others have fire rounded rims and concave bases with pontil marks, Finds 6758, 4059, (Fig 158, nos 22–4).

All these drinking vessel types are found extremely frequently in the north-west provinces in fourth-century deposits (Isings 1957, forms 96, 106 and 109), and examples have often been recorded in Britain in funerary as well as domestic contexts. Conical cups with cracked-off rims occur in burials at Lankhills, Winchester (Harden 1979, class IIA), and fragments of bowls and conical cups with similar rims and a variety of bases have been noted at Portchester (Harden 1975, figs 197–8), Frocester Court (Price 1979, figs 16–17), Barnsley Park (Price 1982, fig 59) and Towcester (Price and Cool 1983, figs 46–7). Until recently cups with fire rounded rims have been thought to occur only in the very late fourth or early fifth century, but it seems likely, on the evidence of Towcester and elsewhere, that they were already in production by the middle of the fourth century, though they also continued in use for a long time afterwards.

Tubular-rimmed bowls, Finds 7771, 5687 and 4643, (Fig 158, no 25–7) are not very common in late Roman Britain. Most rim fragments retain little or nothing of the body below the rim so it is not possible to consider the body shape, but two substantially complete examples from Burgh Castle (Harden 1983, nos 81–2) and another which occurred as a Roman survival in grave 53 in the cemetery at Highdown, near Worthing (Harden 1956, type d ii) are similar to the fragmentary piece with a spiral trail on the upper body from West Hill, Find 7771, (Fig 158, no 25).

Nothing is known about the vessel forms of the small body fragments with applied self-coloured blobs and trails, Find 1174, (Fig 158, no 31, and nos 32–4), but similarly decorated pieces have been noted from many fourth-century sites.

The jugs represented by Finds 7920, 8003, 8067, and 5185 (Fig 159, nos 1–3) are common fourth-century forms (eg Isings 1957, forms 120–21, 124–5) in the north-west provinces. They are usually found in small fragments on British sites, though some complete examples are known from burials, as at Lankhills, Winchester (Harden 1979, class v), Butt Road, Colchester (Cool and Price forthcoming a) and elsewhere. The red streaks in the handle and trail of Finds 7920, 8003, 8067, (Fig 159, nos 1–2) are an unusual feature, and they suggest strongly that the two fragments come from the same vessel. The handle fragment, Find 8506 (Fig 159, no 4) may perhaps come from a small globular jug or flask similar to examples from late fourth-century contexts at Lankhills (Harden 1979, class vi), Burgh Castle (Harden 1983, nos 79–80), London (unpublished) and several other Romano-British sites.

The form of the flask, Find 7772 (Fig 159, no 5) is not identifiable from the surviving fragment, though the quality of the glass indicates that it is of late-Roman date. The reworking of the broken neck is a noteworthy feature.

Mould-blown cylindrical bottles with zones of horizontal corrugations at the top and bottom of the body, separated by a central undecorated zone, are represented by the fragments illustrated in Fig 159, nos 6–7. Complete vessels have one or two handles and often bear an abbreviated inscription such as 'F R O' on the base. Most of these vessels have been found in third and fourth-century contexts, though there is also evidence for production during the second century (Isings 1957, forms 89 and 128). They are common finds in northern and central Gaul and the middle and lower Rhineland, and fragments are quite frequently noted in Britain, as at Towcester (Price and Cool 1983) and Frocester Court (Price 1979), though only a few complete examples, as from the Butt Road cemetery, Colchester (Cool and Price forthcoming a) and London (unpublished), are known.

Catalogue of the illustrated fragments

Fig 158

Glass of the first and early second century AD

1 Fragment, tall angular handle with central rib, from a conical or globular jug. Bubbly, blue-green with some black specks and streaks, *Find 5712, context 824, infilling of F836, Phase 3c*

2 Fragment, wide lower body and open pushed in base-ring, from a jug or jar. Blue-green, bubbly, base diameter 76mm, *Find 5796, context 258, Structure XVIII, Phase 3a*

3 Two fragments, folded rim, neck and upper attachment of broad ribbon handle, from a bottle. Blue-green, rim diameter 40mm, *Finds 7191 and 7358, context 1191, Structure XIV, Phase 5d–6b*

4 Fragment, concave base with raised design, from a square bottle, small circle within square. Blue-green, *Find 5628, context 579, infilling of F584, Phase 3c*

Glass of the later second and third century AD

5 Five convex body fragments, from a hemispherical bowl with three horizontal bands of facet-cutting and two cut lines. Colourless, good quality, *Finds 5076, 6052, 6372, 7657, contexts 1, 1, 1100 and 1202, Structures IX/XIV, Phases 5d to 8*

6 Convex body fragment, from a cup or jug(?), with vertical raised ribs pinched to form spectacle trails(?). Colourless, some small bubbles, very weathered, *Finds 7411, context 1195, Structure XIV, Phase 5d–6b*

7 Rim fragment, edge fire rounded and thickened, from a cylindrical cup. Colourless, with weathered surfaces, rim diameter 120mm, *Find 8182, context 1231, Structure X, Phase 4b*

8 Four fragments, fire rounded rim and body, from a thin walled cylindrical cup. Colourless, small bub-

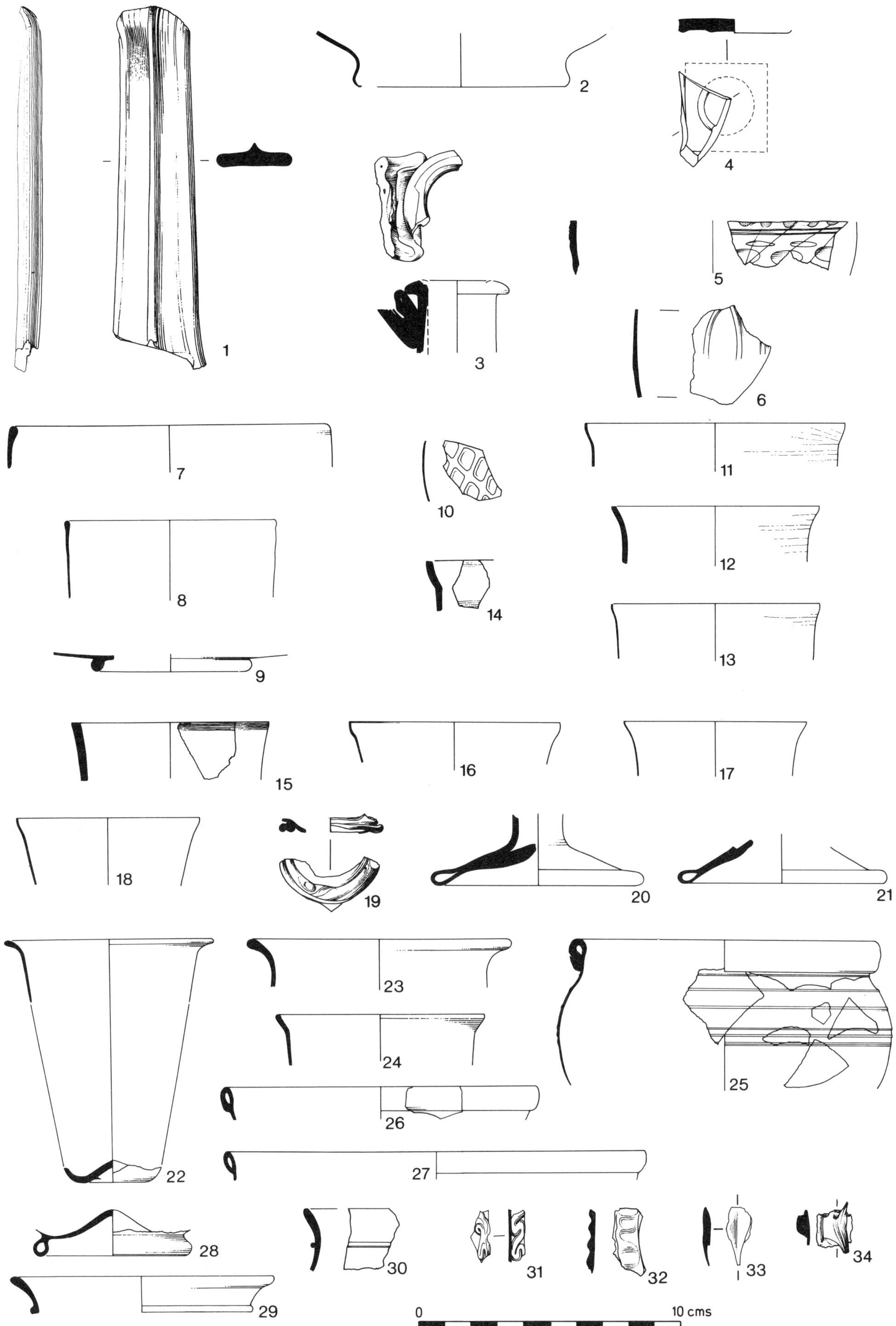

Fig 158 Vessel glass, scale 1:2

bles, very weathered, rim diameter 80mm, *Finds 5365, 5531 and 5562, contexts 660 and 682, over Structure XIV and Structure X, Phases 8 and 4a*

9 Fragment, wide lower body and tubular base-ring, from a cup(?). Colourless, good quality, base diameter 56mm, *Find 3148, context 127, infilling of F179, Phase 3c*

Glass of the fourth century AD

10 Convex body fragment with mould-blown decoration, cut(?), diamond lattice pattern in low relief. Colourless, bubbly, *Find 8321, context 1314, Structure X, Phase 4a*

11 Fragment, curved rim with cracked-off edge, from a cylindrical or hemispherical cup or bowl, decorated with a horizontal abraded band on the upper body. Colourless, bubbly, rim diameter 96mm, *Find 8291, context 1223, Structure IX, Phase 5c*

12 Fragment, curved rim with cracked-off edge, from a conical or cylindrical cup or bowl, with a horizonal abraded band on the upper body. Colourless, bubbly, rim diameter 80mm, *Find 6704, context 0416, Structure XIX, Phase 7*

13 Fragment, curved rim with cracked-off edge,from a thin walled conical or cylindrical cup or bowl, with a horizontal abraded band below the rim. Colourless, bubbly, rim diameter 80mm, *Find 5035, context 402, Structure VII, Phase 7a*

14 Fragment, curved rim with cracked-off edge, from a thick walled hemispherical cup(?), with a horizontal abraded band on the upper body. Yellow-green, *Find 4030, context 511, Structure XIX, Phase 7*

15 Fragment, slightly curved rim with cracked-off edge, from a thick walled hemispherical cup(?), with a horizontal abraded band on the rim. Yellow-green, *Context 14, Structure II, Phase 6b*

16 Fragment, curved rim with cracked-off edge, from a thin walled conical cup. Colourless, bubbly, rim diameter 80mm, *Find 6638, context 0406, Structure XIX, Phase 7*

17 Fragment, curved rim with cracked-off edge, from a thin walled conical cup. Colourless, bubbly, rim diameter 70mm, *Find 2378, context 332, Structure IV, Phase 4b*

18 Fragment, curved rim with cracked-off edge, from a thin walled conical cup. Colourless, bubbly, rim diameter 68 mm, *Find 7371, context 1191, Structure XIV, Phase 5d–6b*

19 Fragment, of base and trailed base-ring, from a cup or bowl, small concave base with a trail at the edge. Pale green, very bubbly, base-ring diameter 38mm, *Find 4741, context 602, Structure XIX, Phase 7*

20 Fragment, narrow cylindrical lower body and wide pushed-in base-ring with tubular edge,from a cup or jug. Yellow-green, bubbly, base diameter 80mm, *Find 6488, context 1100, Structure XIV, Phase 8*

21 Fragment, wide pushed-in base-ring with tubular edge, from a cup or jug. Pale green–colourless, base diameter 74mm, *Find 6707, context 1100, Structure XIV, Phase 8*

22 Three fragments, from a conical cup with everted fire rounded rim and small concave base with pontil scar. Pale green–colourless, bubbly, rim diameter 76mm, *Context 331, Structure IV, Phase 6b*

23 Fragment, from a conical(?) cup with everted fire rounded rim. Green–colourless, bubbly, rim diameter 100mm, *Find 6758, context 0410, Structure XIX, Phase 7*

24 Fragment, from a conical(?) cup with everted fire rounded rim. Yellow-green, bubbly, rim diameter 78mm, *Find 4059, context 600, over Structure XIX, Phase 8*

25 Five fragments, from a bowl, with a vertical tubular rim, edge rolled in, then bent out and down, convex body with spiral trail on upper part. Blue-green with many black specks, very bubbly, rim diameter 114mm, *Find 7771, context 1204, Structure IX, Phase 5c*

26 Fragment, vertical tubular rim bent out and down, from a bowl. Colourless, bubbly, *Find 5687, context 579, infilling of F584, Phase 3c*

27 Fragment, vertical tubular rim bent out and down, from a bowl. Pale green, bubbly, rim diameter approx 160mm, *Find 4643, context 482, Structure II, Phase 6b*

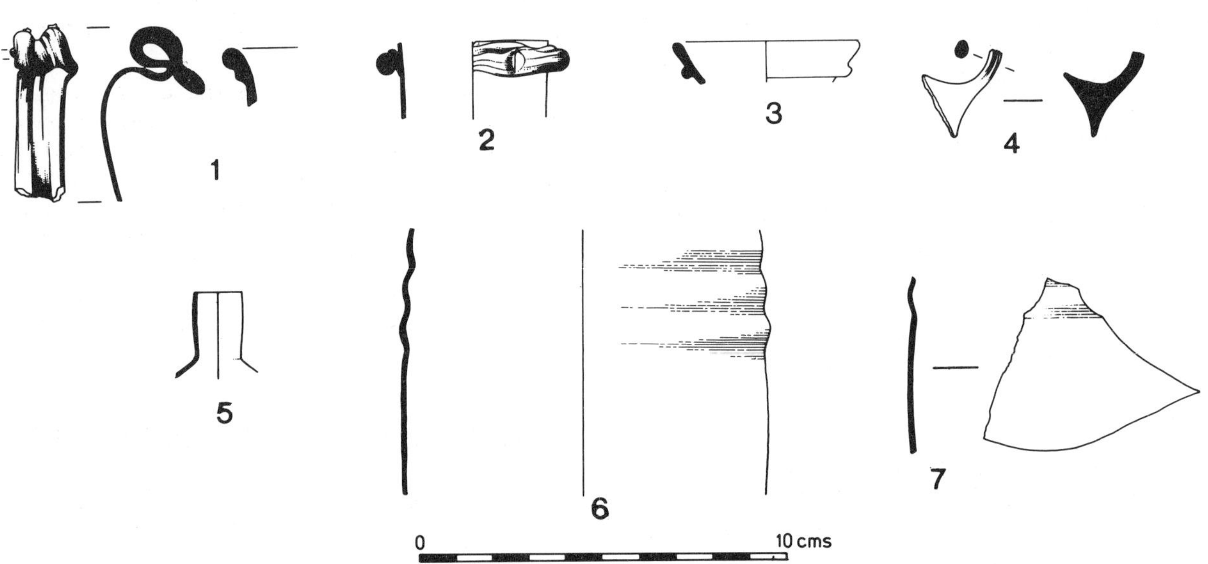

Fig 159 Vessel glass, scale 1:2

28 Five fragments, part of a tubular base-ring and concave base with central kick and pontil scar, from a bowl(?). Pale green, very weathered, bubbly, base-ring diameter 54mm, *Context 201, Structure II, Phase 6a*
29 Two fragments, from a bowl, everted rim with fire rounded edge, horizontal trail on upper body. Pale blue-green, bubbly, rim diameter 96mm, *Find 6159, context 0257, over Structure XIV, Phase 8*
30 Fragment,from a bowl, with everted rim with fire rounded edge, horizontal trail on upper body. Blue-green, bubbly, *Find 6990, context 1177, Structure XIV, Phase 5d–6b*
31 Small body fragment, fine vertical looped trail. Colourless, *Find 1174, context 36, Structure VIII, Phase 7b*
32 Small body fragment, wide vertical trail with horizontal scored ridges. Colourless, *Context 13, over Structure XIX, Phase 8*
33 Small body fragment, applied blob pulled into vertical trail. Colourless, *Context 22, Structure I, Phase 5e(ii)*
34 Small body fragment, applied blob pulled into vertical trail, distorted by heat. Colourless, very weathered, *Context 22, Structure I, Phase 5e(ii)*

Fig 159
1 Two fragments, from a jug with pouring spout?, fire rounded rim, distorted funnel mouth with trail outside, curved handle with two side ribs and looped thumb-rest. Yellow-green, bubbly, with red streaks in handle, *Finds 7920 and 8003, context 0406, Structure XIX, Phase 7*
2 Fragment, from the cylindrical neck of a jug(?), thick horizontal trail with vertical scored marks at intervals. Yellow-green, bubbly, with red streaks in the trail, *Find 8067, context 0406, Structure XIX, Phase 7*
3 Fragment, rounded rim and funnel mouth with horizontal trail outside, from a jug(?). Green–colourless, very weathered, bubbly, rim diameter 50mm, *Find 5185, context 545, Structure XIX, Phase 7*
4 Fragment, body and lower attachment of curved rod handle, from a jug, broken edges of body shaped to edges of handle. Green–colourless, bubbly, *Find 8506, context 88, Structure II, Phase 6a*
5 Fragment, short cylindrical neck and convex body, from a flask?, broken edge of neck roughly smoothed into secondary rim. Blue-green, bubbly, neck diameter 13.5mm, *Find 7772, context 1204, Structure IX, Phase 5c*
6 Twelve body fragments, from a mould-blown cylindrical bottle with zone of horizontal corrugations. Yellow-green, bubbly, body diameter *c* 100mm, *Context 52, Structure II, Phase 6a*
7 Body fragment, from a mould-blown cylindrical bottle, with a zone of horizontal corrugations. Yellow-green, bubbly, body diameter *c* 110mm, *Context 2, Structure II, Phase 6b*

The Metalworking evidence

by Justine Bayley

A small quantity of slag and other metalworking debris was found during the excavations, and more was collected during fieldwalking of adjacent unexcavated areas which geophysical survey (see chapter 1) had suggested might contain industrial features. The total weight of material was only about 1kg and over half of this came from the fieldwalking. There was evidence for a number of different industries but the quantities of material were in all cases very small so none are likely to have been carried out in the areas excavated, though they were probably going on nearby.

The ironworking slag contained both tap slag (which is a by-product of iron smelting) and smithing slag (which forms in a blacksmith's hearth) as well as a few pieces of intermediate structure. The small quantity of material suggests that it is just chance finds and that the workshops and furnaces must be at some distance from the areas excavated.

Copper alloy metalworking is indicated by a number of very small solidified blobs and dribbles of molten metal and a number of part-manufactured pieces, bars and rods of varying and uneven cross section as well as a number of clippings of sheet metal. There are also many undiagnostic sheet fragments which may be manufacturing waste but could also be parts of broken but once complete objects. In addition a baked clay fragment (Find 4587) could possibly be from the in-gate of a mould for casting metal objects, though neither form nor fabric are typical of those to be expected in Roman Britain. The distribution of the blobs and dribbles correlates with that of the votive rings and simple finger rings, which supports the idea that they may have been made on the site.

The finds included two pieces of lead-rich waste which were analysed qualitatively by energy dispersive X-ray fluorescence (XRF). Both were fragments of larger pieces which were probably originally roughly circular in plan and concavo-convex in section; Find 5161 would have been about 50mm in diameter and under 10mm thick while Find 850 was two or three times larger as well as being considerably thicker. The XRF results were similar for both pieces with lead and traces of copper being detected on the under (convex) surface while the upper surface gave strong signals for both lead and copper and weak signals for silver. The material is almost certainly litharge (lead oxide), similar to that from Doncaster described by Tylecote (1986) who notes that it is a by-product of the recovery of silver from lead by cupellation. He suggests that the copper content of the litharge indicates that it was debased silver, eg coins, that was being refined by 'lead soaking' rather than silver being extracted from newly smelted lead.

In addition to the specific evidence presented above there were a number of pieces of baked or overheated clay, some with a fuel-ash 'glaze' covering part or all of their surface, as well as a little fuel-ash slag. All this material indicates high temperature fires which are often, though not necessarily, associated with industrial processes such as metalworking (Bayley 1985). There is no way of associating them directly with any of the processes indicated above, though they are their most likely source.

Surface finds collected before 1976

Archaeological material has been collected from the surface of fields either side of the road since at least the 1940's. The main collector was a schoolboy, the late Ian Woodland, whose finds were donated to Stroud Museum. In addition to the items described below, there are flint flakes, animal bones, a considerable assem-

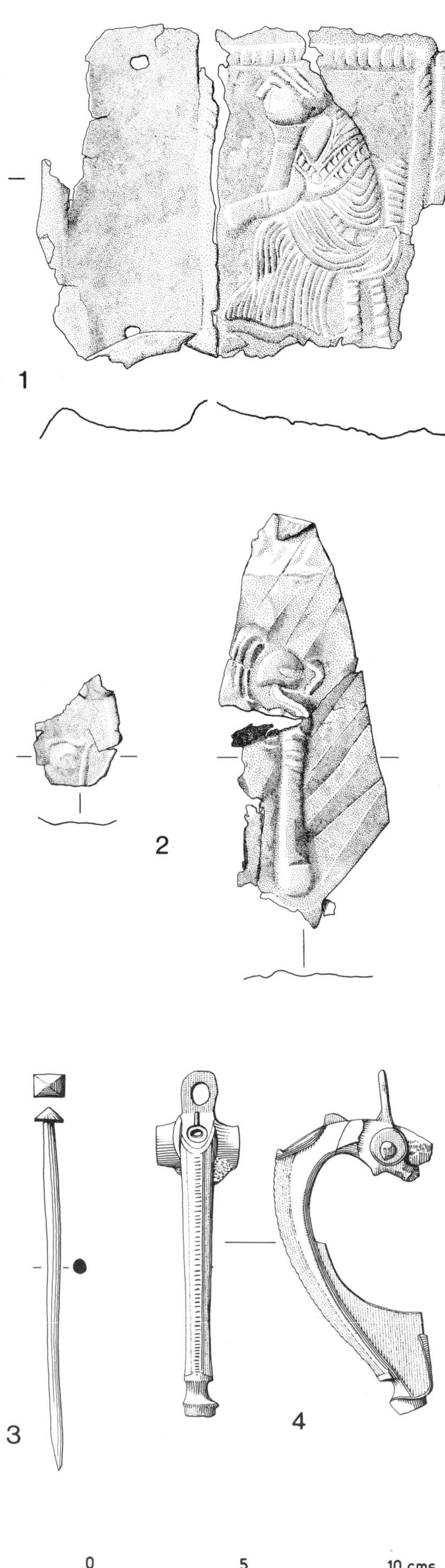

Fig 160 Surface finds of copper alloy, found prior to 1976, scale 1:2

blage of Roman pottery (samian, Oxford wares, local grey wares, and Black Burnished ware), pottery counters, a crucible fragment with slag adhering, a lead net sinker, and miscellaneous objects of iron. A piece of lead (P Griffin Collection) was examined by Dr Tomlin who found no visible inscription to confirm that it was a *defixio* tablet. A collection of 14 copper alloy coins includes issues of Victorinus, Helena, Constantine I, Constans, Constantius, Claudius II, Carausius, and Constantius II. They were identified by Mr Lionel Walrond and are listed in fiche.

Intaglios and other objects

by Martin Henig

Moulded intaglio of blue glass. 10 by 8 mm, Henig 1978, 256, no 553, pl xxvii, *Stroud Museum*
Gilded copper alloy ring (Type VIIIa with carinated hoop) containing moulded intaglio of blue glass. 10 by 8 mm, Henig 1978, 255, no 549, pl xvii, *Gloucester Museum*

These 'Romano-British imitation' intaglios seem to have been made in the second half of the third century. Their distribution is largely confined to southern Britain (Henig 1978, 132–3, fig 2), and a similar one was found at Kingscote (Henig 1972, 85).

all of copper alloy

Fig 160
1 Sheeting from casket, height 50 mm. Two panels, *Stroud Museum, acc no 61:64–65, Woodland Collection*

One is plain and pierced top and bottom by rivet holes; the other contains a figured device within a frame of cable design. A bend between these sections is probably ancient and represents a corner of the casket. The plain side may be part of the lock plate, though the opening for the key does not remain. The figure in the other panel, executed by beating the thin sheet into a mould, is a matron seated upon a chair in profile to the left. She wears a long flowing garment (*chiton*) down to her feet, and over this a mantle with a decorative neckline. There is a diadem around her brows. She rests her head on her right hand.

This is the type of the reflective or mourning woman, human or divine, such as Penelope longing for Ulysses, Demeter for Persephone, and Venus mourning Adonis (see references in Munby 1975, though Munby and I now both take the assumed jet figurine to be an eighteenth-century Wedgwood ceramic). In the absence of other figures on the sheet, it is not possible to be sure of the subject which might be any of these, or another female personage such as a muse. A garnet intaglio in Paris cut with a similar figure has been identified as a muse (perhaps Polyhymnia: Richter 1971, no 239) and muses are certainly shown on caskets though all those figured by Buschhausen (1971, 57–65 and 78–86 nos A25, A26, and A38 all from Hungary) are standing.

see also Find 477 (Figs 95 and 96 above)

2 Votive leaf, height 60mm, *Stroud Museum, acc no 61:66, Woodland Collection*

This is one of the usual type (Toynbee 1978). It is fragmentary and the two larger pieces probably show (against the regular transverse leaf-veining) the right hand column of an *aedicula*. This would have contained the image of a deity, perhaps Mercury (*cf* Toynbee 1978, 140–1, fig 7.1, no 27 from Barkway, Herts and especially, for the column form, Massy 1986, 304–5, fig 18 from Vic-sur-Seille, Lorraine). The column has a heavy rounded base and the shaft is embellished with cabling. Above this there appears to be freer vegetal ornament.

see also Fig 92 for other examples

3 Pin, height 56 mm. It has a shaft of circular section and low pyramidal head, similar to Bushe-Fox 1949, 146 and pl liii, no 200, *Stroud Museum, Coombes Collection*

Brooch

by Sarnia Butcher

4 Brooch of headstud type. (Described from a drawing, details verified by Ann Woodward), *Stroud Museum, acc no 61:63, Woodland Collection*

The pin is hinged and there is a headloop cast in one with the top of the bow. The flattened upper part of the bow carries a small central rib and a socket which may have held a separate stud; there is a knurled rib down the rest of the bow ending at the foot moulding.

It is unusual for the sub-type with hinged pin and fixed loop not to have enamel down the length of the bow, but there is one from Bollitree (Hereford and Worcs) in M R Hull's unpublished corpus and a brooch from Chepstow which is similar except that it is sprung (Painter and Sax 1970, 159, fig 4, no 6). As with the other headstud brooches the date range should be late first to mid-second century.

see Find 2162 (Fig 124, no 7) for another example

Finds from fieldwalking

The zone surrounding the excavated area, and the northern end of the field, were the subject of a programme of total surface collection, by 10m square, in late September, 1978. Finds were generally of low abundance owing to the fact that the shallow ploughing usually undertaken in the field hardly disturbs the layers of occupation and demolition debris which are protected to some extent by the surviving wall foundations. However, in some places large blocks of lime-

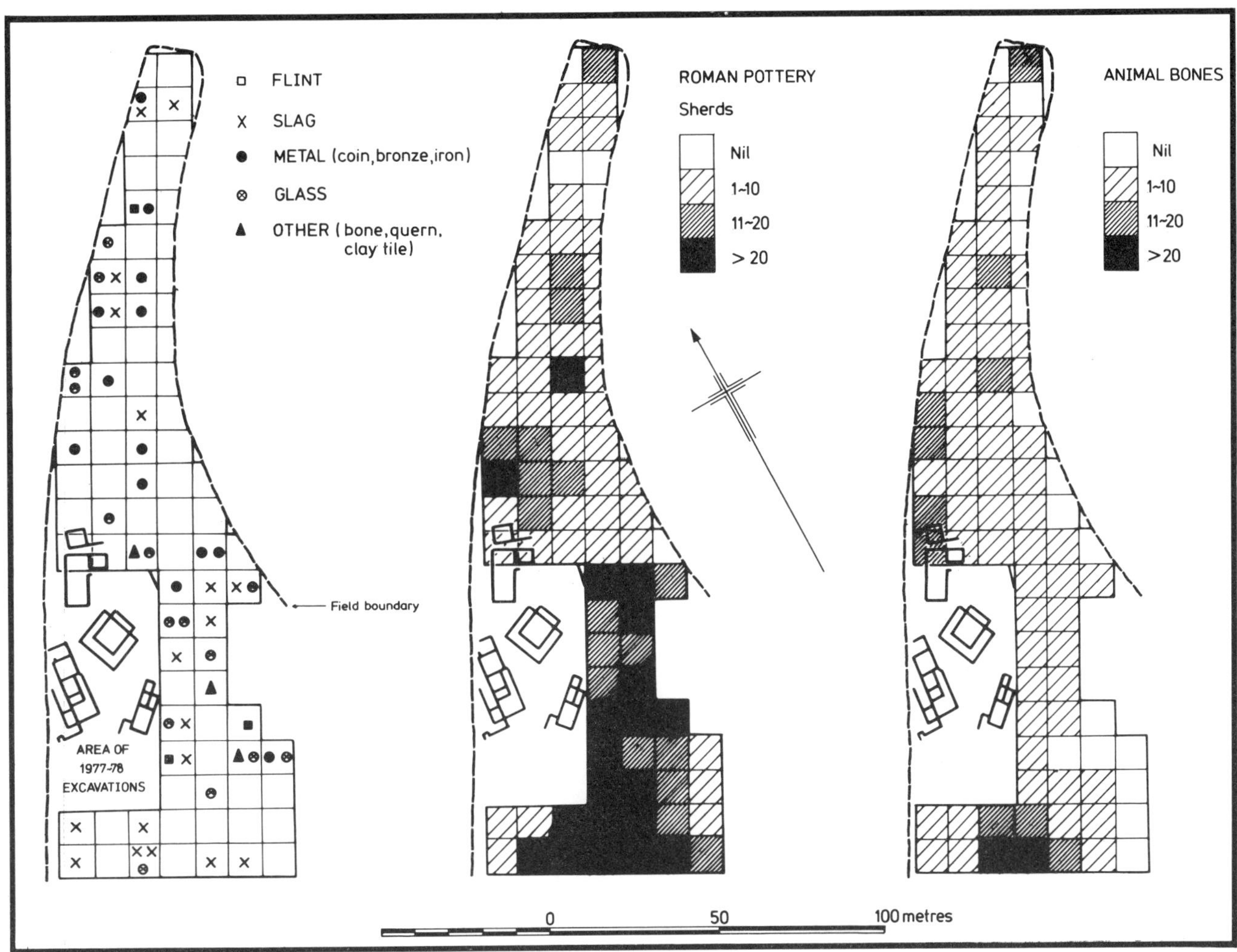

Fig 161 Distribution of finds from fieldwalking in 1978

stone from the walls themselves had been dislodged. For the distribution of finds recovered see Fig 161.

The distribution of pottery indicates that further buildings lie to the east and south of excavated area, as is also known from the partially recovered plans of Structures X and IV and the result of the geophysical survey (see chapter 1 and Fig 3). A second concentration lies north of Structure X, where further walls and a drain or culvert had been recorded in the waterpipe trench of 1976. The main animal bone concentration lies south of the excavated area and represents a continuation of the deposits of votive material spread over the demolished remains of Structure IV. Objects of metal, glass, bone, and stone were distributed fairly evenly over the area walked. The most common category of small find recorded was however slag. Most of the metalworking evidence from the site discussed above was in fact recovered during this fieldwalking exercise. Some derived from the northern end of the field where the results of the geophysical survey had indicated the former existence of industrial activity, but as much or more was found south and east of the excavated area, a zone where magnetic anomalies were low (see Fig 3). Items found during fieldwalking include a brooch, Find 6062 (Fig 123, no 3), one lead tablet (Tablet no 83, Find 5911), five fragments of Roman vessel glass (none illustrated), a jet pendant, Find 5868 (Fig 133, no 8), a jet finger ring fragment (not published), and part of a bone knife handle (not published). The slag comprised eleven pieces of smithing slag, three pieces of tap slag and two fragments of dense iron slag.

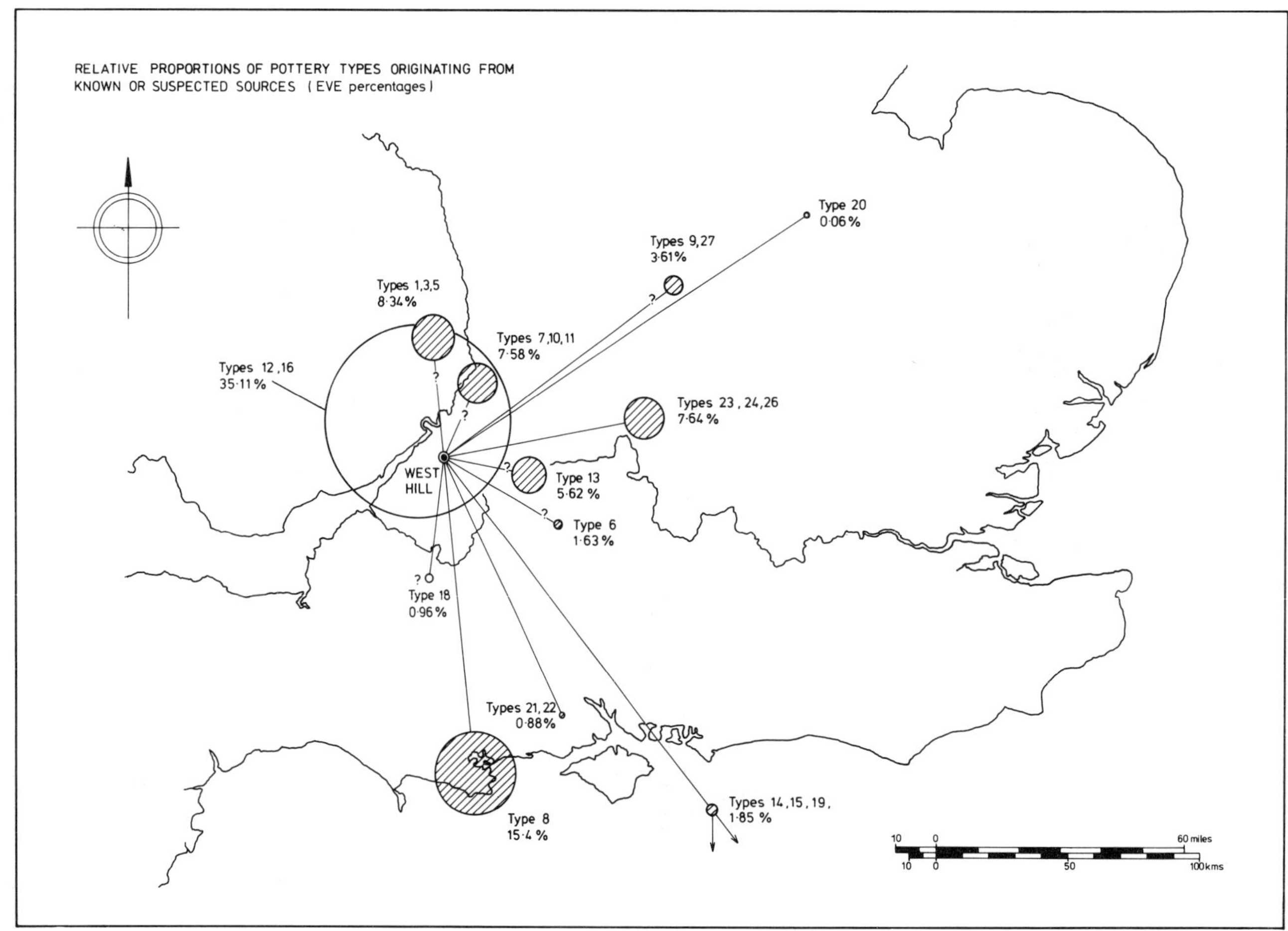

Fig 162 *Pottery sources, quantified relative proportions*

11 The pottery

by Peter Leach

Introduction

All the pottery recovered has been classified into a type series using fabric and form characteristics. This has provided the basis for quantification, which in turn permits an examination of the distribution of the assemblage in space and time. The type series of the fabrics and forms illustrated (Figs 164–71 and 174) aims to show a quantified chronological type series, to complement or support the site phasing (see chapters 2–4); and to present information which might make it possible to identify any social, economic, or cultural patterns discernible within the assemblage.

Over 67,000 sherds weighing almost 480kg were recovered in four seasons of work between 1976 and 1979; they probably represent a minimum of 395 individual vessels. The bulk of this material was moderately or heavily abraded, sometimes perhaps as a result of prolonged use, but to a greater extent through the functional and depositional characteristics of the site. The shallow and exceptionally stony archaeological deposits above a solid or fractured limestone bedrock are the most obvious explanation for the excessive wear encountered on the sherds.

Table 9: pottery phase totals (all fabrics)

Phase	*no*	%	*grams*	%	*EVE*	%
Phase 1	353	0.52	1.985	0.41	1.303	0.33
Phase 2	6451	9.58	54.724	11.42	32.703	8.27
Phase 3	8448	12.54	79.140	16.51	46.635	11.80
Phase 4	6492	9.64	42.811	8.93	39.074	9.89
Phase 5	10988	16.32	80.884	16.88	68.808	17.41
Phase 6	11119	16.51	69.191	14.44	62.358	16.28
Phase 7	11207	16.64	68.849	14.37	65.054	16.46
Phase 8	7472	11.10	44.760	9.34	43.401	10.98
U/S	4815	7.14	36.864	7.69	33.891	8.57
total	67345		479.208kg		93.227	

This is borne out by the fact that several groups of pottery from the earliest phases of the site, interpreted as 'votive/ritual' deposits, lie within relatively less stony and more deeply stratified soils in pits and ditches. These are almost invariably the best preserved and associated, as well as the least disturbed groups of material, in contrast to the severely abraded pottery, recovered from shallow contexts disturbed by the plough above the stony debris of destroyed buildings.

The influence of site function upon the pottery is considered more fully below.

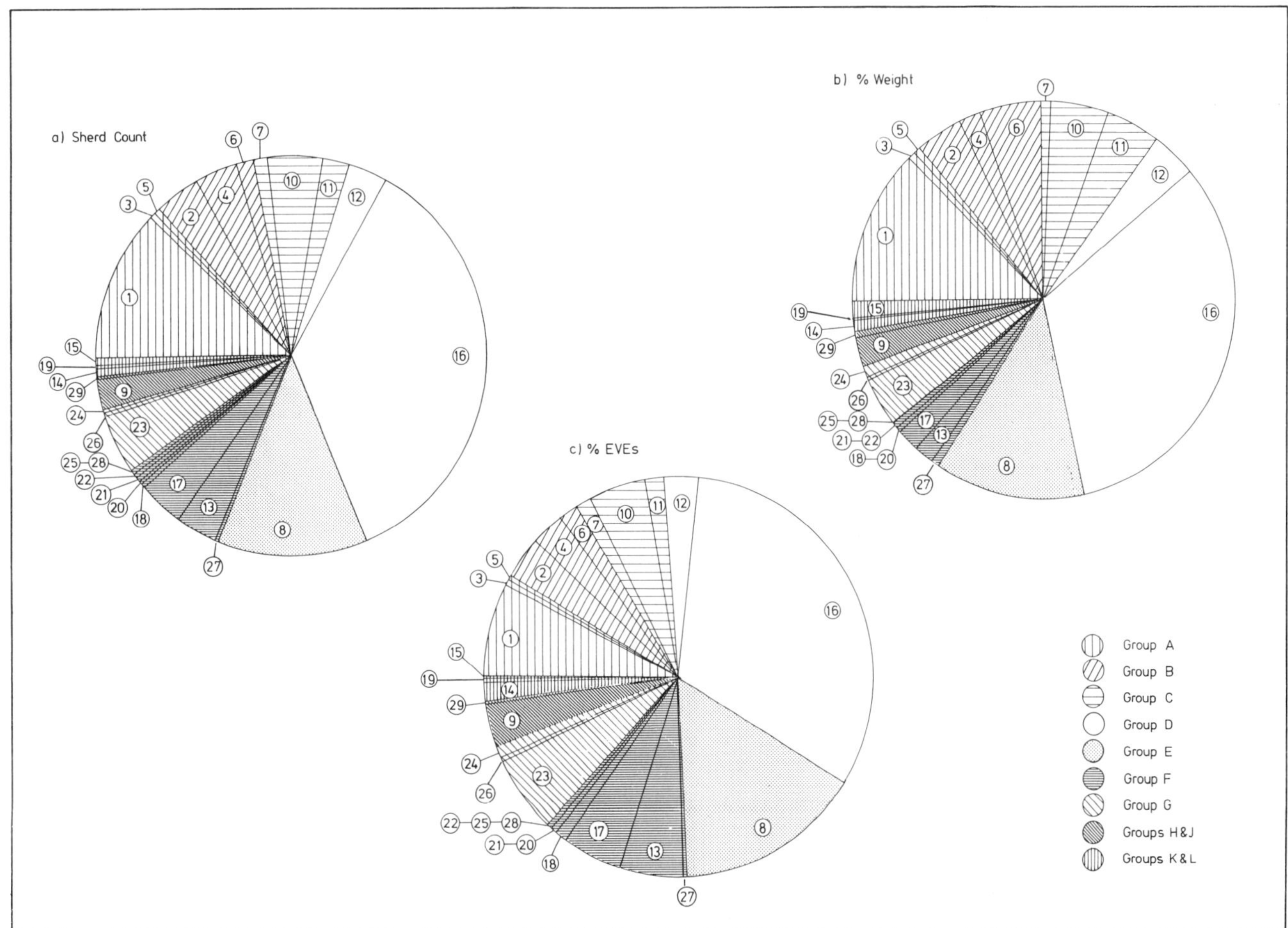

Fig 163 Total pottery assemblage by sherd count, weight, and estimated vessel equivalent (EVE) quantification

Despite the presence of extensive areas of relatively shallow stratigraphy, and excepting the zone of modern plough soil, the spatial distribution of the pottery as recovered is felt to correspond fairly well with events demonstrated in the site phasing. The interpretation is also supported by the distribution of other artefacts or groups of material, eg votive metalwork and animal bone. The virtual lack of obvious medieval or later disturbance to the site (ploughing excepted) limits the degree of residuality encountered within the assemblage. Areas where a succession of phases have incorporated debris containing earlier material are usually easy to distinguish. Thus for example a degree of residuality is very evident in the pottery associated with Structure VIII, which cuts into and overlies the components and deposits of several earlier phases (see chapter 4). Clearly the degree of residuality and contamination of the different deposits has had a variable, and not readily quantifiable, influence upon the reliability of the pottery evidence and its interpretation across the site. Nevertheless, general trends and changes of characteristics through time are apparent, and conclusions based upon a quantification of the whole, can, in view of the size of the assemblage, be justified.

Methods of study

To characterise and quantify the pottery assemblage a definitive type series was first established, as stated above, using fabric classification as well as characteristics such as form, finish, and decoration. Identification of types was by macroscopic examination of pottery fabric matrices, identifying their principal inclusions, textural attributes, firing and colour characteristics. Form and finish were generally considered as secondary elements, with a range corresponding to each fabric type. Exceptions to this rule include amphorae (fabric type 15) and samian wares (fabric type 14), groups where the significance of the forms within the assemblage takes precedence over their fabric sub-divisions or place of manufacture. On the other hand fabric variations within the local grey wares (fabric type 16) were encountered even on sherds from a single vessel, and here more reliance was placed on identifying vessel forms than on seriating all the fabric variants, even though this may have resulted in including fabrics from more than one source within a group, rather than risk spurious over division of fabric types.

Wherever possible types which can be identified as well known published varieties, such as the products of the Oxfordshire, the New Forest potteries, or the Dorset black burnished industry, are cross-referenced directly to those sources and classifications. Other types appear to belong to groups identified in assemblages elsewhere in the region or further afield, and where a reasonable correspondence of type can be established, reference is made to parallel published classifications. The pottery fabric types were first defined numerically in no particular order of significance, but have since been sorted into associated groups defined alphabetically. These groups show more effectively the main trends and significance of the individual ceramic types represented on the site. They, and their component fabric types, are set out below, with their relative proportions according to source areas summarised in Fig 162. The detailed fabric and form data are available in the site archive, where the ceramic content of each stratigraphically defined archaeological context is recorded by three quantification methods: weight, sherd count, and minimum vessel estimation. The latter was determined by the estimated vessel equivalent method (EVEs), (Orton 1975), the preferred method for the purpose of statistical spatial, typological and chronological analyses (Figs 163, and 177–80), although some comparisons with other quantification methods are also presented (Figs 163 and 172–3). No facilities for computerisation of the quantifiable data were available during its original collection or analysis. No attempt has been made to present a fully detailed range of form variation by fabric type, particularly in the case of well documented and defined groups, eg Oxfordshire wares or samian. Only the record of basic vessel form types (bowls, jars, beakers, flagons, etc) has been employed for the purposes of statistical form analyses (Figs 176–80).

The fabric type series

Group A

'Malvernian' limestone-tempered, pre-Roman Iron Age handmade wares (fabric types 1, 3, and 5)

Fabric type 1
Fabric: Coarse, moderately fired, reduced grey-black fabric, characterised by an abundant temper of large-medium grey and white palaeozoic limestone and calcite, and a sparse scatter of grog/clay and quartz. Exterior surfaces sometimes patchily oxidised cream-buff or brown; body and surfaces characteristically speckled with large, light-coloured angular inclusions.
Forms: A range of moderately thick-walled, uneven, handmade jar and bowl forms; the majority plain and globular with shallow out- turned rims and flat bases. Decoration uncommon but includes some finger nail or stamp ornamentation, and incised linear bands on upper shoulders (Fig 164, nos 16–18 and 20, and some with blunt-tooled vertical hatching over the body (Fig 174, nos 1–3); the latter also characterised by exterior surface burnishing.

Fig 164
13 Bowl, shouldered, *Context 758, ditch 264, Phase 2d*
14 Bowl, shouldered, *Context 758, ditch 264, Phase 2d*
15 Bowl, shouldered, *Context 835, pit F836, Phase 2a–d*
16 Bowl, shoulder stab decoration, *Context 912, ditch 264, Phase 2c*
17 Bowl, shoulder stab decoration, *Context 758, ditch 264, Phase 2d*
18 Bowl, linear incised decoration, *Context 889, Phase 1*
19 Bowl/jar, *Context 842, pit F836, Phase 2a–3b*
20 Bowl, linear incised decoration, *Context 928, ditch 264, Phase 2b*
21 Bowl, *Context 912, ditch 264, Phase 2c*
22 Bowl/jar, *Context 912, ditch 264, Phase 2c*
23 Bowl/jar, *Context 733, ditch 264, Phase 2d*
24 Bowl/jar, *Context 835, pit F836, Phase 2a–d*
25 Bowl/jar, *Context 262, Phase 2d–3a*
26 Jar, *Context 859, fill of F860, in pit F836, Phase 2a–d*

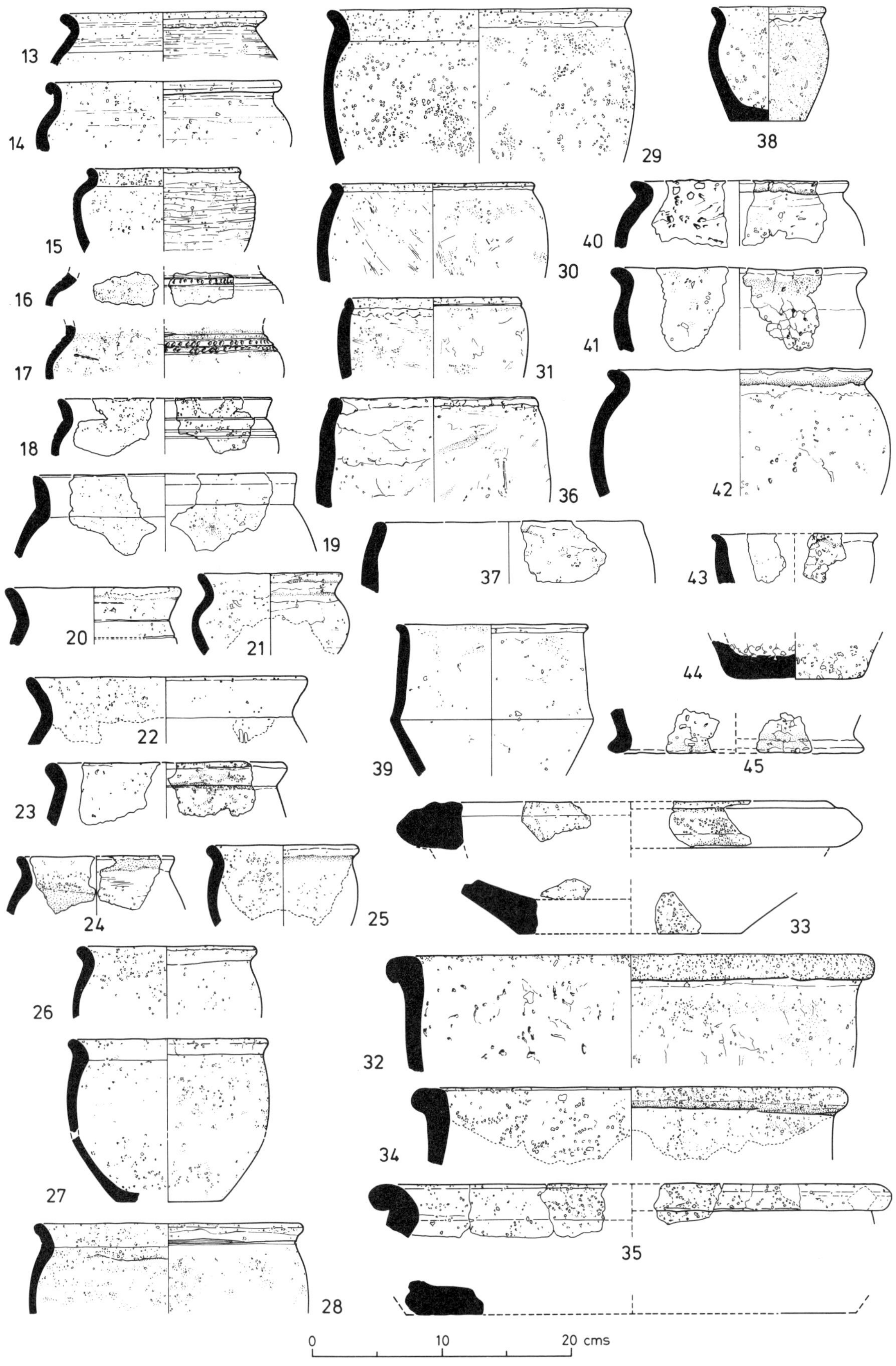

Fig 164 Pottery vessels, fabric types 1, 3, and 5

27 Jar, *Context 784, primary fill of F743, Phase 2–3*
28 Jar, *Context 928, ditch 264, Phase 2b*
29 Jar, *Context 910, pit F251, Phase 3a*
30 Jar, bead rim, *Context 758, ditch 264, Phase 2d*
31 Jar, bead rim, *Context 912, ditch 264, Phase 2c*
32 Storage jar, *Context 758, ditch 264, Phase 2d*
33 Bowl, flange rim, *Context 843, Phase 2a–d*
34 Storage jar, *Context 733, ditch 264, Phase 2d*
35 Storage jar, *Context 912, ditch 264, Phase 2c*
Fig 174, nos 1—3, *Pit group F251, Phase 2c*

Dating and parallels: The fabric and forms of this pottery type suggest that it belongs within the pre-Roman Iron Age ceramic traditions of the region; specifically those identified as originating in the vicinity of the Malvern Hills (Peacock 1968). The limestone temper characterises Peacock's group B1 (*ibid*) possibly being manufactured in the southern Marches from the second century BC. At West Hill, where it formed approximately 7.5% of the EVE total, it is difficult to isolate this group from its associations with group B wares, and it is thus uncertain if it appears here earlier than the beginning of the first century AD. Its relative scarcity at the neighbouring hillfort of Uley Bury (Saville and Ellison 1983) reinforce a suggestion that it only appears in this region as an ultimate pre-Roman Iron Age fabric. This seems also to be convincingly demonstrated at Bagendon, where similar forms and fabrics are associated with Belgic style wares and first-century AD Roman imports (Clifford 1961, 243–5).

Fabric type 3
Fabric: Coarse, moderately fired, reduced grey fabric, sometimes vesicular,tempered with a scatter of small to medium grey/white calcite and limestone, occasional larger fragments, and some fine quartz sand. Exteriors often unevenly speckled with inclusions.
Forms: Moderately thick-walled, uneven, handmade jars with plain or slightly everted rims, globular or carinated bodies, and flat bases. No surface treatment or decoration recorded.

36 Jar, bead rim, *Context 758, ditch 264, Phase 2d*
37 Jar, *Context 912, ditch 264, Phase 2c*
38 Small jar, *Context 262, Phase 2d–3a*
39 Bowl, carinated, *Context 830, fill of pit F839, Phase 2a–d*

Dating and parallels: A fabric closely allied to fabric type 1, forming less than 0.5% of the EVE total, and mainly distinguished by its much sparser temper. Palaeozoic limestone inclusions suggest a similar source in the southern Marches, and from its associations at West Hill, a first-century AD context. This is probably a variant within Peacock's group B1 (Peacock 1968),and can be distinguished within the Bagendon pottery assemblage (Clifford 1961, fig 68, no 165).

Fabric type 5
Fabric: Very coarse, poorly fired, reduced grey fabric, characterised by an abundant temper of very large and medium angular and sub-rounded grey and white shelly limestone and calcite. Surfaces sometimes an oxidised light buff-brown in patches, and often cracked and fissured around inclusions.
Forms: Crude handmade, thick-walled jars with shallow everted rims, globular bodies and flat bases. Plain untreated and undecorated surfaces.

40 Jar, *Context 758, ditch 264, Phase* 2d
41 Jar, *Context 758, ditch 264, Phase 2d*
42 Jar, *Context 912, ditch 264, Phase 2c*
43 Jar, *Context 757, ditch F264, Phase 2d*
44 Storage jar base, *Context 758, ditch 264, Phase 2d*
45 Storage jar base, *Context 733, ditch 264, Phase 2d*

Dating and parallels: Probably a variant of fabric type 1 forming less than 0.5% of the EVE total, and distinguished by its coarse heavy temper and cruder manufacture. Similar palaeozoic limestone inclusions suggest the same general source and period of manufacture, as a variant of Peacock's group B1 (Peacock 1968).

Group B

'Belgic' style pre-Roman Iron Age and early Roman wheel made coarse wares (fabric types 2, 4, and 6, Savernake ware)

Fabric type 2
Fabric: Soft corky, moderately-fired, reduced grey fabric, frequently vesicular but otherwise sparsely tempered with mica and clay metasediment or iron. Exteriors patchy with areas of buff-brown oxidisation, and often cracked and vesicular.
Forms: A range of short-necked, shouldered or carinated bowls (Fig 165, nos 46–53, and Fig 174, no 5), and an occasional flange rim (Fig 164, no 54) are the most common forms. High-shouldered globular jars with beaded or everted rims also occur (Fig 165, nos 55–8, and Fig 174, no 4), with flat bases or foot-rings common to both main forms. The majority are handmade but wheel-finished, evenly made vessels with wiped or burnished exteriors, plain or with shoulder cordons.

Fig 165
46 Bowl, shouldered, *Context 758, ditch 264, Phase 2d*
47 Bowl, shouldered, *Context 758, ditch 264, Phase 2d*
48 Bowl, shouldered, *Context 757, ditch F264, Phase 2d*
49 Bowl, shouldered, *Context 925, ditch F264, Phase 2b*
50 Bowl, shouldered, *Context 758, ditch 264, Phase 2d*
51 Bowl, shouldered, *Context 262, Phase 2d–3a*
52 Bowl, shouldered, *Context 733, ditch 264, Phase 2d*
53 Bowl, shouldered, *Context 912, ditch 264, Phase 2c*
54 Bowl, flange rim, *Context 755, fill of F756, ditch 264, Phase 3a*
55 Jar, *Context 817, Phase 3c*
56 Jar, *Context 758, ditch 264, Phase 2d*
57 Jar, *Context 758, ditch 264, Phase 2d*
58 Storage jar, *Context 906, Phase 3a*
Fig 174, nos 4 and 5, *Pit group F251, Phase 2c*

Dating and parallels: Both the fabric and forms of this type identify it as belonging to a group of predominantly 'Belgic' style wares which appear within the local Dobunnic cultural assemblage in the second half of the first century BC. This ware is common at Bagendon, the regional type site of this period (Clifford 1961, figs 52–4, 60, 65 and 66), and elsewhere in the upper Thames and south Cotswold area (Harding 1972). At West Hill, as at Bagendon, these types are often in association with early Roman post-conquest

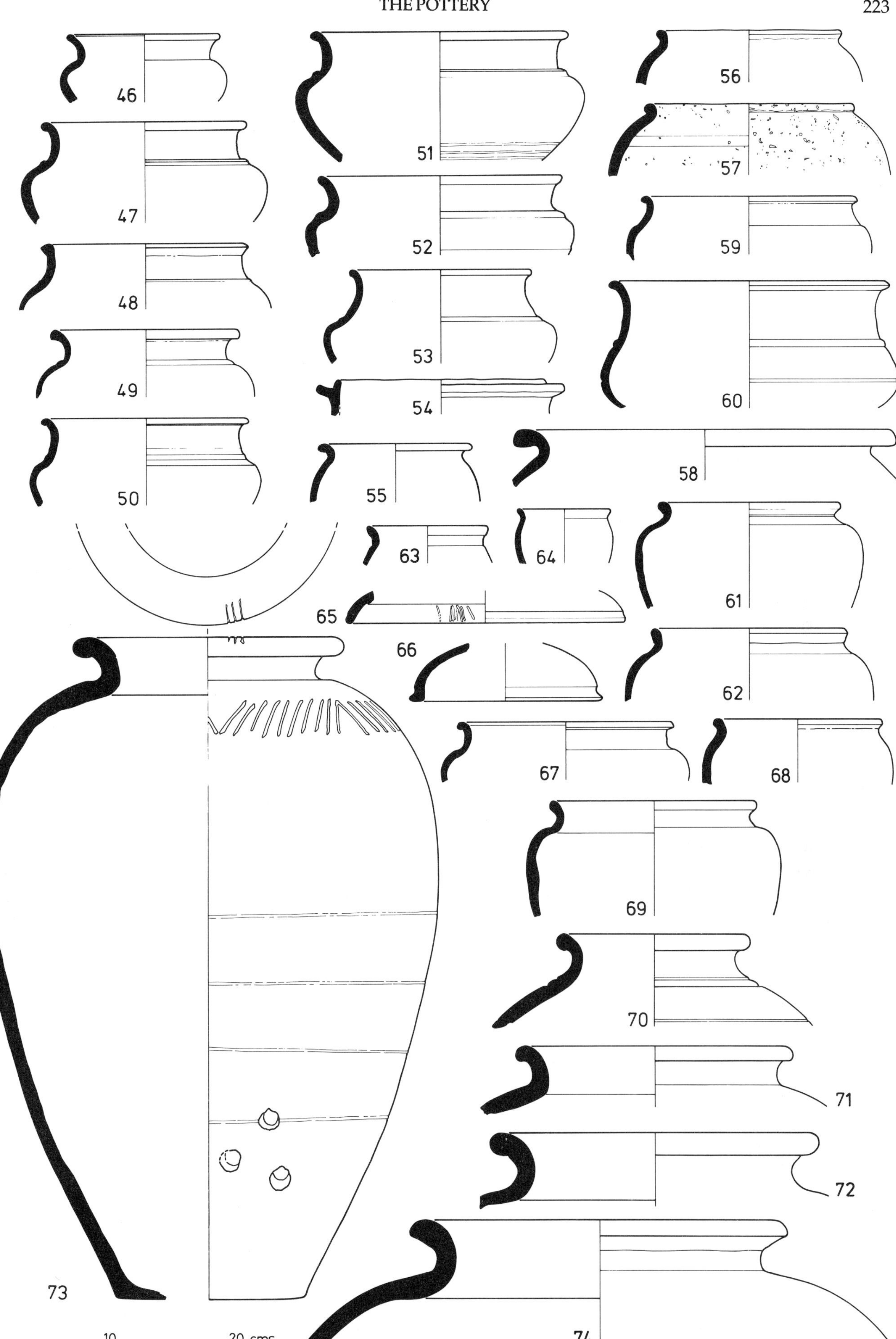

Fig 165 Pottery vessels, fabric types 2, 4, and 6

forms and fabrics, and they form nearly 3.5% of the EVE total. They may continue in currency if not production until well into the second century AD: see also at Cirencester, fabric 3 (J Keeley, personal comment); Lechlade, Rough Ground Farm, fabric 20 (Sarah Green, forthcoming); and at Frocester (E Price, personal comment). Roman forms in the West Hill assemblage (Fig 165, nos 54 and 58) reinforce the impression of post-conquest production for some of this ware.

Fabric type 4
Fabric: Moderately hard, sandy, dark grey reduced fabric, well tempered with small rounded quartz sand, some grog or clay, and occasional angular shelly limestone. Surfaces may be patchily oxidised buff/brown-red.
Forms: Most commonly wheel made or finished, shouldered or carinated necked-bowls (Fig 165, nos 59 and 60, Fig 174, no 6); globular jars or beakers with everted rims (nos 61–64); and occasional lids (nos 65 and 66). Surfaces wiped or burnished and frequently decorated with cordons or concentric, lightly incised rings.

59 Bowl, shouldered, *Context 258, ditch F264, Phase 3a*
60 Bowl, shouldered, *Context 757, ditch F264, Phase 2d*
61 Jar, shouldered, *Context 180, ditch F179, Phase 3b*
62 Jar, shouldered, *Context 912, ditch 264, Phase 2c*
63 Small jar/beaker, *Context 258, ditch F264, Phase 3a*
64 Small jar/beaker, *Context 726, ditch F264, Phase 3a*
65 Lid, with incised graffiti, *Context 258, ditch F264, Phase 3a*
66 Lid, *Context 333, Phase 3c*
Fig 174, no 6, *Pit group F251, Phase 2c*

Dating and parallels: Stylistically this type closely resembles fabric type 2, and belongs with the 'Belgic' and early Roman group B. At West Hill this formed over 2.7% of the EVE total, and similar fabrics in these forms are present at Bagendon (Clifford 1961, figs 52, 54 and 65); Cirencester, fabric type 5 (J Keeley, personal comment); Gloucester, fabric type 30 (Heighway 1983, appendix B1); Bath, fabric type 10.14 (S Green, personal comment); and at Lechlade, Rough Ground Farm fabric type 11.3 (S Green, forthcoming). Once again the presence of post-conquest romanised forms (eg Fig 165, nos 63–6), and their associations, suggest production and use of this type continuing at West Hill throughout the first, if not into the second century AD.

Fabric type 6
Fabric: Hard, rough, well fired, reduced fabric, well tempered with a prominent and coarse mixture of iron, flint, and some grog or clay. Normally a pale grey body, characteristically speckled with multicoloured inclusions, variable in density and proportion according to individual vessels. Surfaces generally similar, sometimes with buff or red-brown oxidisation patches, and pimply or mottled when worn or weathered.
Forms: Large, thick-walled, heavy wheel made or finished jars with narrow necks, everted rims, and plain flat bases (Fig 165, nos 70–4, and Fig 174, no 8), in which multicoloured inclusions are most prominent. A range of thinner-walled and smaller necked bowls and shouldered jars, with beaded or everted rims and plain, or foot-ring bases (Fig 165, nos 67–9, and Fig 174, nos 7, and 9–11), may characterise a slightly different fabric, in which the temper is sparser and less prominent. Some have wiped or burnished exteriors, occasionally decorated with cordons or lightly tooled bands of hatching (Fig 165, no 73, and Fig 174, no 7).

67 Bowl/jar, shouldered, *Context 910, F251, Phase 3a*
68 Jar, *Context 912, ditch 264, Phase 2c*
69 Jar, *Context 333, Phase 3c*
70 Storage jar, *Context 333, Phase 3c*
71 Storage jar, *Context 33, courtyard, Phase 4–6*
72 Storage jar, *Context 258, ditch F264, Phase 3a*
73 Storage jar, *Context 333, Phase 3c*
74 Storage jar, *Context 333, Phase 3c*
Fig 174, nos 7–11, *Pit group F251, Phase 2c*

Dating and parallels: The fabric and range of forms here compares closely with post-conquest first-century AD products of the Savernake kilns in Wiltshire (Swan 1975, fabric 1). This distinctive ware is widely distributed in southern Britain at this period, local occurrences being recorded at Bagendon (Clifford 1961, figs 52, 54, 56, 57, 59, 60, and 67–9); Cirencester, fabric 6 (J Keeley, personal comment); Gloucester, fabric 6 (Heighway 1983, appendix B1); Kingscote, fabric 12 (E Swain, personal comment); Bath, fabric 10.15 (S Green, personal comment); and Frocester (E Price, personal comment). The variation in fabric raises the possibility of an alternative, contemporary, source for some of the finer vessels; eg north Wiltshire kilns in the Swindon area (Anderson 1979). This fabric formed over 1.6% of the EVE total.

Group C

Oxidised Severn Valley wares (fabric types 7, 10, and 11)

Fabric type 7
Fabric: Soft, moderately fired, frequently laminated and oxidised fabric, moderately tempered with clay/grog, mica, occasional iron, and limestone or calcite. Buff-red-orange body, sometimes with a pale grey-buff core, lightly speckled with inclusions; surfaces even red-orange, similarly speckled.
Forms: Characteristic wheel made, carinated bowls with flared necks and foot-rings. Exteriors burnished but frequently weathered, and decorated with multiple grooves and cordons.

Fig 166
75 Bowl, carinated, *Context 784, Phase 2–3*
76 Bowl, carinated, *Context 910, pit F251, Phase 3a*
77 Bowl, carinated, *Context 258, ditch F264, Phase 3a*
78 Bowl/tankard, *Context 910, pit F251, Phase 3a*
Fig 174, no 12, *Pit group F251, Phase 2c*

Dating and parallels: A characteristic 'Belgic' style, early Severn Valley bowl type, possibly of pre-conquest origin, but current in the Severn and Cotswold region until at least the early second century. The type is distinguished from subsequent Severn Valley oxidised wares by its form and softer fabric. At West Hill, in association with wares of broadly contemporary groups A and B, it formed over 1.3% of the EVE total. Equivalent types are recorded at Bagendon (Clifford 1961, figs 59, 60 and 65); Gloucester, fabric 11 (Heighway 1983, appendix B1); Kingscote, fabric 3 (E

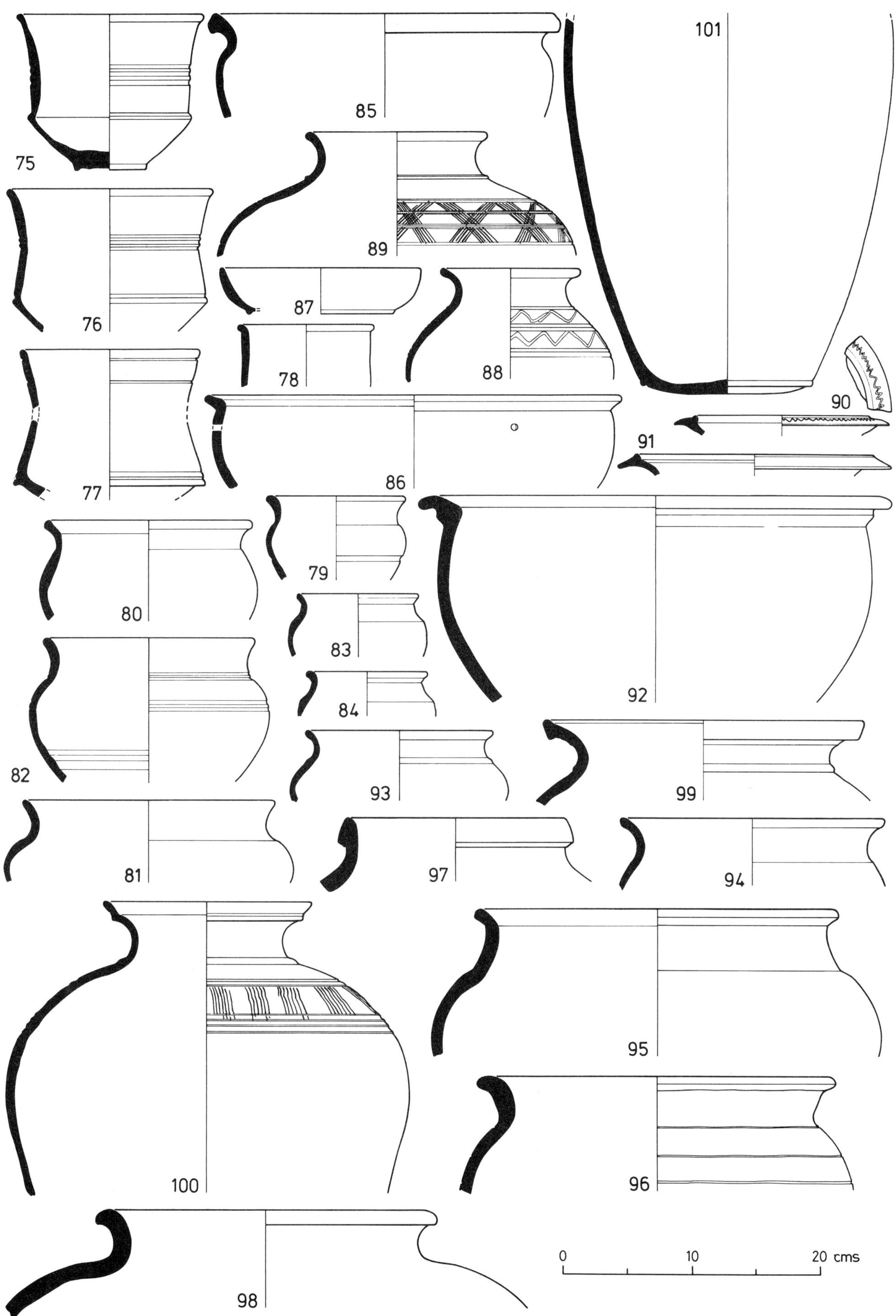

Fig 166 Pottery vessels, fabric types 7, 10, and 11

Swain, personal comment); and Frocester (E Price, personal comment).

Fabric type 10
Fabric: Medium soft, moderately fine fairly well fired oxidised fabric, lightly speckled with small sub-angular calcite/limestone, iron, grog, and some fine mica. Evenly fired orange-buff body and exteriors, occasionally with a buff-grey core.
Forms: A range of necked and globular bowls, some with shallow everted rims (Fig 166, nos 79–86), plain shallow bowls or dishes with foot-rings (Fig 166, no 87), and narrow-mouthed jars (Fig 166, nos 88 and 89); all regular wheel made forms. Exteriors smoothed and sometimes partly burnished; plain or with grooved and cordon decoration, and some lightly tooled hatched or linear decorative bands.

79 Bowl, shouldered, *Context 180, ditch F179, Phase 3b*
80 Bowl, shouldered, *Context 1318, ditch F816, Phase 2–3*
81 Bowl, shouldered, *Context 910, pit F251, Phase 3a*
82 Bowl, shouldered, ribbed band decoration, *Context 910, pit F251, Phase 3a*
83 Small bowl/beaker, *Context 278, Phase 8*
84 Small bowl/beaker, *Context 258, ditch F264, Phase 3a*
85 Bowl, everted rim, *Context 368, Structure IV, Phase 6b*
86 Bowl, everted rim, *Context 370, ditch F382, Phase 3b*
87 Dish, *Context 258, ditch F264, Phase 3a*
88 Jar, linear incised shoulder decoration, *Context 726, ditch F264, Phase 3a*
89 Jar, linear hatched shoulder decoration, *Context 333, Phase 3c*

Dating and parallels: An oxidised Severn Valley ware in more traditional romanised forms, although 'Belgic' style necked bowls continuing in modified forms. A similar though better fired variant of fabric type 7; possibly its successor as a product mainly of second-century manufacture, and forming over 4.7% of the EVE total. See also fabric type 11 a contemporary variety distinguishable mainly by forms and firing (Webster 1976). A widely distributed and common, mainly second-century product in the lower Severn Valley and Cotswold region, identified locally at Gloucester, fabric 11 (Heighway 1983, appendix B1); Cirencester, fabrics 106–10 (J Keeley, personal comment); Witcombe, fabric D1/4 (Leach forthcoming); Kingscote, fabric 3 (E Swain, personal comment); Bath, fabric 9.9 (S Green, personal comment); and Frocester (E Price, personal comment).

Fabric type 11
Fabric: Moderately hard and well fired reduced fabric, with a scatter of visible, sub-angular inclusions, including some iron, limestone/calcite, and fired clay/grog. Usually occurring with a light-medium or blue-grey body sandwiched by buff-orange oxidised surface skin, and speckled throughout with multicoloured temper. Weathered pimply surfaces, sometimes with voids.
Forms: Mainly wheel made, heavy globular and narrow-necked jars with everted rims (Fig 166, nos 97–101), but also some lighter, necked and flange-rim bowls, often with foot-rings (Fig 166, nos 90–92). Plain bodies, sometimes with traces of a cream-white colour wash, or with occasional cordons, grooves, and lightly tooled hatched or linear decorative bands.

90 Bowl, incised decorated flange rim, *Context 258, ditch F264, Phase 3a*
91 Bowl, flange rim, *Context 258, ditch F264, Phase 3a*
92 Large bowl, everted rim, *Context 639/681, Structure IX, Phase 4a and 5b*
93 Bowl, shouldered, *Context 334, ditch F 382, Phase 3c*
94 Jar, *Context 258, ditch F264, Phase 3a*
95 Storage jar, *Context 521, in ditch F179, Phase 2–3b*
96 Storage jar, grooved band decoration, *Context 901, Structure II exterior, fill above ditch F264, Phase 3b–5*
97 Storage jar, *Context 1191, Structure XIV, Phase 5d–6b*
98 Storage jar, *Context 33, courtyard, Phase 4–6*
99 Storage jar, *Context 258, ditch F264, Phase 3a*
100 Storage jar, incised and ribbed decoration, *Context 334, ditch F 382, Phase 3c*
101 Storage jar, base and body, *Context 755, fill of F756, ditch F 264, Phase 3a*

Dating and parallels: A fine, reduced, Severn Valley ware, probably a contemporary variant of fabric type 10 above, distinguishable mainly in forms and firing, and forming approximately 1.5% of the EVE total. A degree of overlap between fabric types 10 and 11 in both forms and firing, sometimes results in practical problems of identification (Webster 1976). Identified locally at Gloucester, fabric 23 (Heighway 1983, appendix B1); Witcombe, fabric D2 (Leach forthcoming); Kingscote, fabric 4 (E Swain, personal comment); and at Frocester (E Price, personal comment).

Group D

Reduced Severn Valley ware and local grey ware (fabric types 12, and 16)

Fabric type 12
Fabric: Soft, slightly granular, moderately well fired, reduced fabric, lightly tempered with small quartz sand and occasional iron. Body and surfaces an evenly fired pale or mid-grey colour.
Forms: A range of wheel made, flat and plain-rimmed bowls (Fig 167, nos 102 and 103); beakers and cups including butt beakers and necked forms (Fig 167, nos 104–8); and narrow-mouthed and everted-rim jars, including some with piecrust rim decoration (Fig 167, nos 109–12). Other decoration includes lightly tooled, hatched, or linear band designs, some cordons, and indentations. Some bands of exterior surface burnishing occur on unweathered vessels.

Fig 167
102 Bowl, everted rim, *Context 322, F364, Structure IV, Phase 4a*
103 Dish, *Context 603, Structure XIX, Phase 7a*
104 Cup/beaker, *Context 929, Structure VIII, Phase 6a*
105 Cup/beaker, *Context 255, ditch F264, Phase 3a*
106 Cup/beaker, *Context 255, ditch F264, Phase 3a*
107 Cup/beaker, *Context 834, Phase 3b*
108 Indented beaker, incised graffiti ...VS
109 Jar, *Context 1191, Structure XIV, Phase 5d–6b*
110 Storage jar, finger impressed rim and incised neck decoration, *Context 1100, Structure XIV, Phase 7-8*

111 Storage jar, finger impressed rim and incised neck decoration, *Context 0256, Phase 8*
112 Storage jar, cross-hatched, incised shoulder decoration, *Find 1310, context 8318, Phase 5a*
112a Jar body sherd, incised with graffiti leaf symbol, *Find 5226, context 619, Structure IX, Phase 5c*
112b Stamped recessed open cross within a roundel, worn base sherd or disc, *Find 4205, context 600, above Structure XIX, Phase 8*

Dating and parallels: A medium-fine grey ware, less familiar as a reduced Severn Valley fabric but broadly contemporary with fabric types 10 and 11. Some overlap with oxidised forms, but generally a characteristic group including finer enclosed vessels. Probably in production from the second century but may continue well into the third century and possibly later (Webster 1976). It formed approximately 3.0% of the EVE total.

Fabric type 16
Fabric: Moderately hard, rough, and frequently coarse textured fabric, occurring with variable proportions of temper; quartz and mica being most common. A reduced fabric of variable texture, occurring in a range of greys and buff-greys.
Forms: A wide range of plain and flange-rim bowls and dishes, the majority imitating Dorset black burnished ware forms. Jars with everted rims or narrow mouths, including some imitations of Dorset black burnished forms. Necked beakers, handled mugs and jugs or flagons less common. Decorative bands of lightly tooled linear or hatched decoration on some examples of all major forms, often combined with bands of burnishing.

Fig 168
113 Bowl, flange rim, *Context 22, over Structure I, Phase 5e*
114 Bowl, flange rim, *Context 13, over Structure XIX, Phase 8*
115 Bowl, flange rim, *Context 1100, Structure XIV, Phase 7–8*
116 Bowl, decorated flange rim, *Context 609, Structure IX, Phase 6b*
117 Bowl, decorated flange rim, *Context TF30 unstratified*
118 Bowl, decorated flange rim, *Context 1191, Structure XIV, Phase 5d–6b*
119 Bowl, flange rim, *Context 2a, Phase 6a*
120 Bowl, flange rim, curvilinear incised decoration, *Context 400, over Structure II, Phase 8*
121 Bowl, flange rim, curvilinear incised decoration, *Context 682, Structure X, Phase 4a*
122 Flanged bowl, *Context 0293, Phase 8*
123 Bowl, grooved band decoration, *Context 370, ditch F382, Phase 3b*
124 Bowl, inturned rim, *Context 579, infilling of F584, Phase 3c*
125 Dish, flange rim, decorated, *Context 38, over Structure I, Phase 5e(ii)*
126 Dish, *Context 602, Structure XIX, Phase 7a*
127 Dish, *Context 38, over Structure I, Phase 5e(ii)*

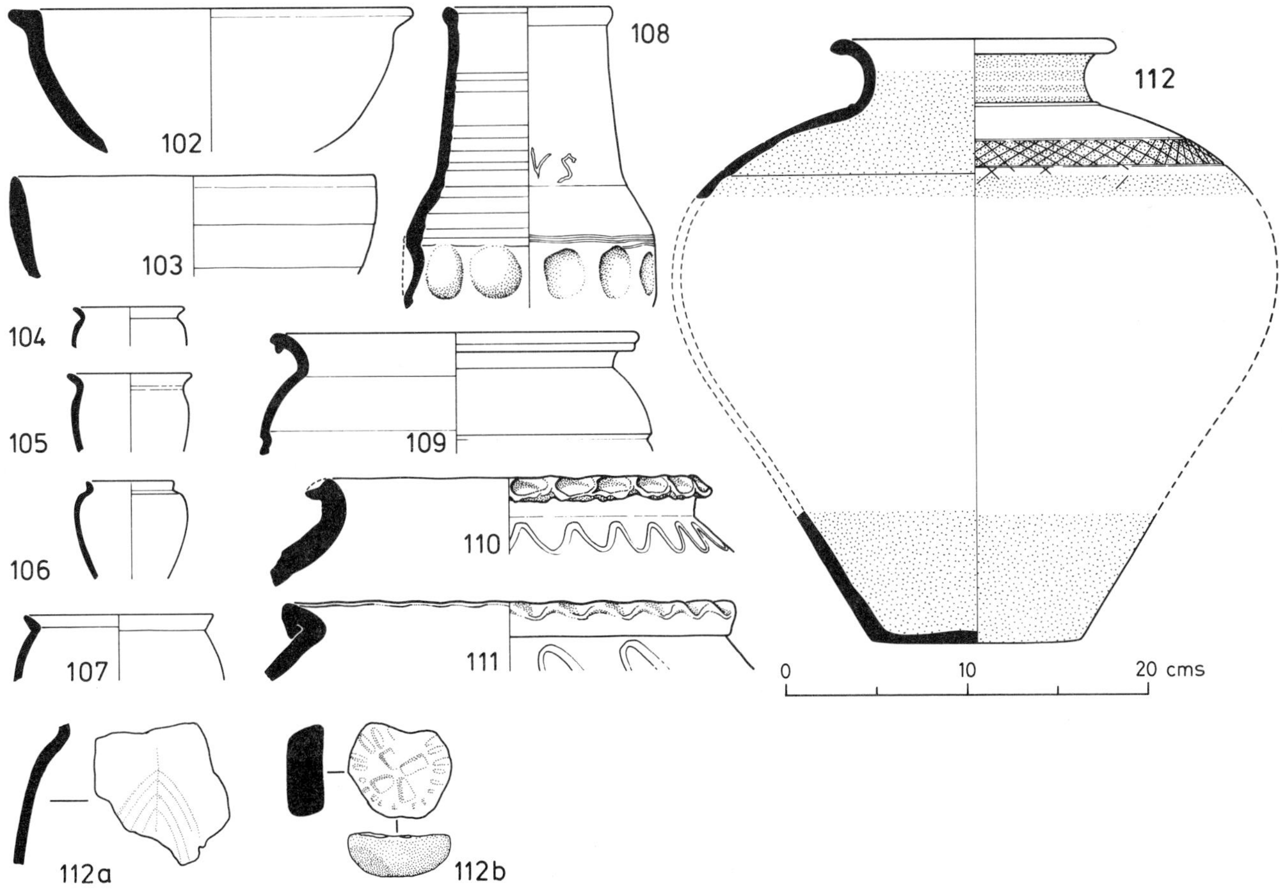

Fig 167 Pottery vessels, fabric type 12

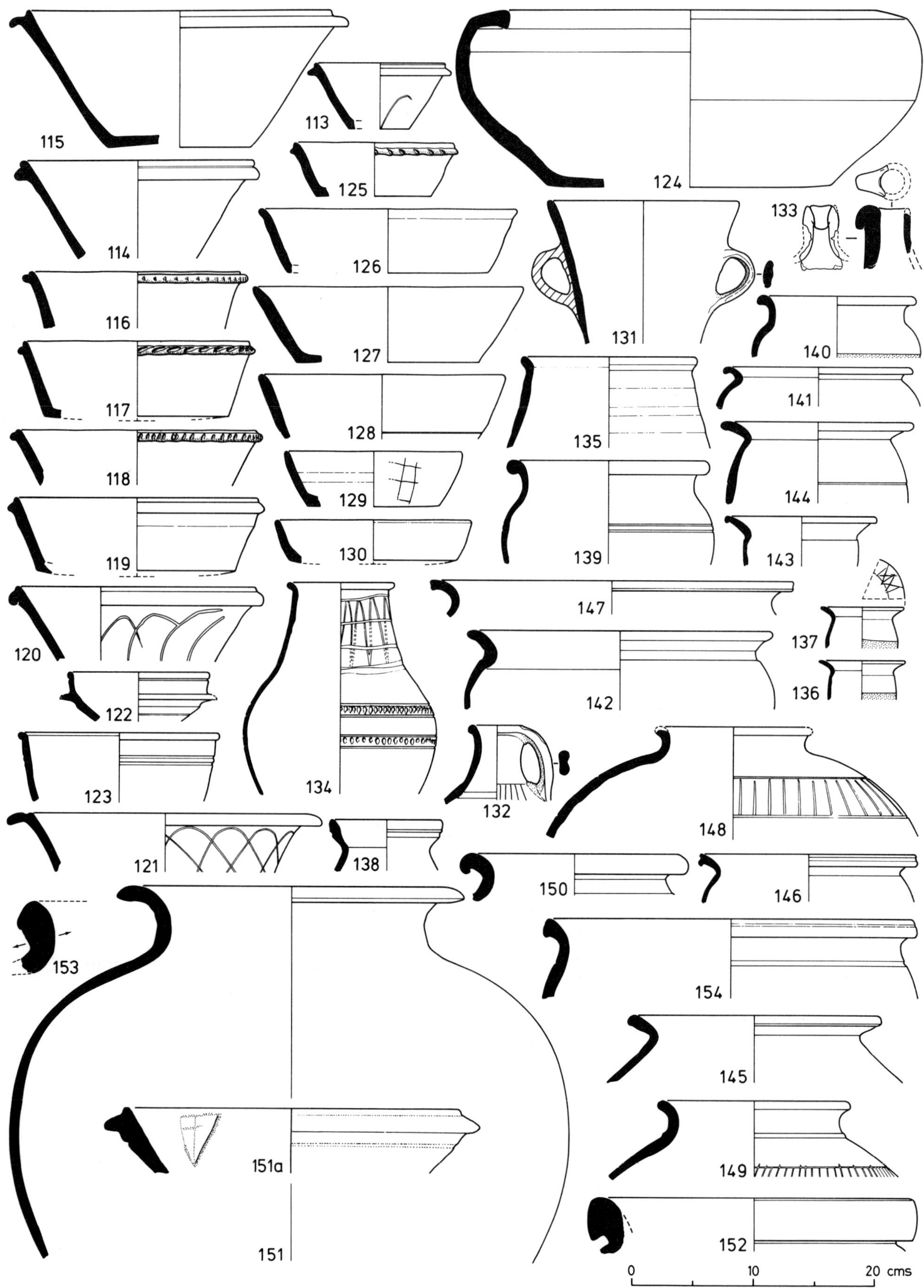

Fig 168 Pottery vessels, fabric types 16 and 17

128 Dish, *Context 602, Structure XIX, Phase 5e*
129 Dish, incised graffiti *Find 2925, context 14, Structure II, Phase 6b*
130 Dish, *Context 645, Structure IX, Phase 5b*
131 Mug, two handles, *Context 639, Structure IX, Phase 5b*
132 Flagon, one handle, *Context 80, Structure I, Phase 5e(i)*
133 Spout, flask or jug, *Context 255, ditch F264, Phase 3a*
134 Beaker, stabbed and linear incised decoration, *Context 38, over Structure I, Phase 5e(ii)*
135 Beaker, *Context 38, over Structure I, Phase 5e(ii)*
136 Cup/beaker, *Context 22, over Structure I, Phase 5e*
137 Cup/beaker, scratched graffiti on rim, *Find 3495, context 346, Structure IV, Phase 5d*
138 Flask/jar, *Context 38, over Structure I, Phase 5e(ii)*
139 Jar, *Context 216, Structure II, Phase 6a*
140 Jar, *Context 32, Structure II, Phase 5e(ii)*
141 Jar, *Context 903, foundation of F900, Structure II, Phase 5d–e*
142 Jar, *Context 61, over Structure I, Phase 5e(i)*
143 Jar, *Context 617, Structure IX, Phase 5d–e*
144 Jar, *Context 68, Structure I, Phase 5e(i)*
145 Jar, *Context 32, Structure II, Phase 5e(ii)*
146 Jar, *Context 604, Structure XIX, Phase 7a*
147 Jar, *Context 682, Structure X, Phase 4a*
148 Storage jar, incised shoulder decoration, *Context 20, over Structure IX, Phase 7*
149 Storage jar, incised shoulder decoration, *Context 369, Structure IV, Phase 4b*
150 Storage jar, *Context 2, Structure II, Phase 6b*
151 Storage jar, *Context 634, above Structure X, Phase 5a–c*
151a Bowl flange rim, interior body graffiti, heavily scored, *Find 176, unstratified 1977*

Dating and parallels: The forms, fabric, and occurrence of this type suggest relatively local manufacture, perhaps within the lower Severn Valley between the early second century and the later fourth century. Although variable in both firing and fabric, this type can be identified collectively as the dominant local coarse grey ware. Its occurrence in Severn Valley forms is augmented by a high proportion of forms derived from black burnished ware, suggesting both its primary sources of influence and its major competitor. Although distinct from the finer fabrics of classic Severn Valley types (Webster 1976), its ubiquitous occurrence on Romano-British sites (frequently as the most common type) in this South Cotswold/Lower Severn region, suggest its origin in the latter area and a relationship with the Severn Valley ceramic tradition. As the largest single group of fabrics, it comprises over 32% of the EVE total. Similar fabrics identified in the region include Gloucester, fabric 5 (Heighway 1983, appendix B1); Cirencester, fabric 133 (J Keeley, personal comment); Witcombe, fabrics 1A and B2 (Leach forthcoming); Kingscote, fabric 1 (E Swain, personal comment); and Frocester (E Price, personal comment).

Group E

Dorset black burnished Ware (BB1) (fabric type 8)

Fabric type 8

Fabric: Medium hard, granular, sandy, reduced fabric, well tempered with grey-white quartz sand, and occasional dark heavy minerals. The majority of vessels are fired dark-grey to black, and well speckled with light coloured sand temper, although firing variations sometimes produce cream-buff or orange-brown patches (Williams 1977).
Forms: Representatives of the more common forms in the Dorset black burnished repertoire were present. A selection of the principal jar, bowl, dish, and cup forms are illustrated. Vessels are characterised by highly burnished exteriors (and interiors on some shallow, open vessels), sometimes alternating with unburnished zones. Cross-hatched bands or lightly tooled curvilinear decorative motifs are relatively common.

Fig 169
155 Bowl, flange rim, curvilinear incised decoration, *Context 601, Phase 7a*
156 Bowl, flange rim, curvilinear incised decoration, *Context 639, Structure IX, Phase 5b*
157 Bowl, flange rim, curvilinear incised decoration, *Context 645, Structure IX, Phase 5b*
158 Bowl, *Context 38, over Structure I, Phase 5e(ii)*
159 Dish, curvilinear incised decoration, *Context 682, Structure X, Phase 4a*
160 Dish, curvilinear incised decoration, *Context 682, Structure X, Phase 4a*
161 Dish, curvilinear incised decoration, *Context 1219, Phase 5c*
162 Oval dish, incised base decoration, *Context 346, Structure IV, Phase 5d*
163 Oval dish, incised body decoration, *Context 126, Phase 5a–d*
164 Oval dish, incised base decoration, *Context 1204/1210, Phase 5b–c*
165 Cup, *Context 672, Phase 3c*
166 Cup, *Context 255, ditch F264, Phase 3a*
167 Cup, incised graffiti, *Context 38, over Structure I, Phase 5e(ii)*
168 Jar, double handled, *Context 537, Phase 3b*
169 Jar, incised lattice decoration, *Context 680, Phase 5b*
170 Jar, incised lattice decoration, *Context 682, Structure X, Phase 4a*
171 Jar, *Context 820b, Phase 4b*
172 Jar, incised lattice decoration and graffiti, *Context 160, Phase 5a–d*
173 Jar, incised lattice decoration, *Context 820a, Phase 4b*
174 Jar, incised lattice decoration, *Context 346, Structure IV, Phase 5d*
175 Jar, incised lattice decoration, *Context 135, Phase 5a–d*

Dating and parallels: Although of pre-Roman Durotrigian origin, Romano-British black burnished industry products are not widely distributed to civil sites outside the Durotrigian tribal region before the second century. This seems to conform with the situation here, where the majority of datable forms (third and fourth centuries) correlates with the periods of maximum loss. Representing well over 15% of the EVE total, black burnished ware was the second largest group present, and occurs widely on contemporary sites in the region.

Group F

Romano-British colour-coated, and mortaria fabrics from various sources; Cirencester/upper Thames Valley colour-coated ware (fabric type 13), colour-coated ware, source uncertain (fabric type 17), local colour-coated ware (fabric type 18), Nene Valley colour-coated ware (fabric type 20), New Forest colour-coated wares (fabric types 21 and 22), miscellaneous mortaria fabrics (fabric type 25), Pink grogged ware (fabric type 27)

Fabric type 13

Fabric: Medium-fine, hard, sandy, reduced fabric, mid-grey, with a thin buff-orange surface skin; well tempered with fine quartz sand.

Forms: A range of enclosed wheel made vessels, including flagons, bottles, and cups (Fig 170, nos 180–88). Interior surfaces are generally reduced and lack the characteristic oxidised exterior skin, which is frequently burnished or cream colour washed. A smaller group of mortaria and bowls (Fig 170, nos 176–79) in

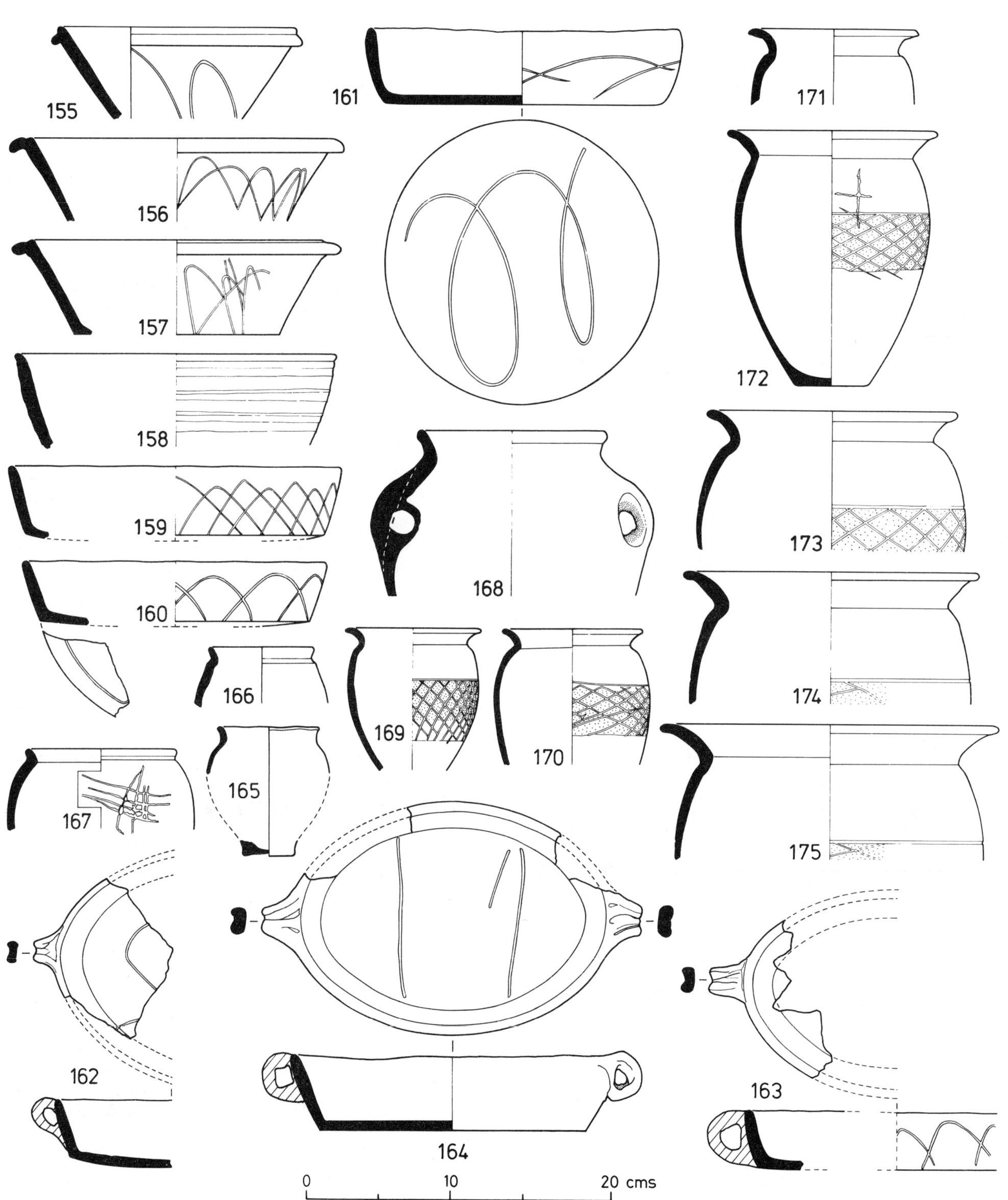

Fig 169 Pottery vessels, fabric type 8

the same fabric are thinly oxidised and cream colour washed on both surfaces; the mortaria have rounded coloured quartz trituration grits.

Fig 170
176 Bowl, cream colour-coat, *Context 255, ditch F264, Phase 3a*
177 Bowl, cream colour-coat, *Context 258, ditch F264, Phase 3a*
178 Mortaria, cream colour-coat, *Context 682, Structure X, Phase 4a*
179 Mortaria, cream colour-coat, *Context 332, Structure IV Phase 4b*
180 Cup, cream colour-coat, *Context 319, Phase 4a*
181 Cup, cream colour-coat, *Context TF31, Phase 4a*
182 Flagon, cream colour-coat, one handle *Context 645, Structure IX, Phase 5b*
183 Flagon, cream colour-coat, one handle, *Context 813, Structure X, Phase 4b*
184 Flagon, cream colour-coat, *Context 332, Structure IV Phase 4b*
185 Flagon, cream colour-coat, two handles, *Context 332, Structure IV Phase 4b*
186 Bottle, cream colour-coat, *Context 823, Structure IX, Phase 4a*
187 Bottle, cream colour-coat, *Context 1224/1231, Structure X, Phase 4b*
188a Spout from a ?puzzle jug, *Context 682, Structure X, Phase 4a*
188b Spout from a ?puzzle jug, *Context 682, Structure X, Phase 4a*

Dating and parallels: Probably of late second to fourth-century manufacture, this distinctive type is ubiquitous, in small proportions, on Romano-British sites over an extensive area in central southern and south west Britain. Its precise origin is unknown, but a source in the Cirencester/Upper Thames area is suspected (see also fabric type 18). The same fabric is identified elsewhere in the region at Gloucester, fabric 15 (Heighway 1983, appendix B1); Witcombe, fabric C5 (Leach forthcoming); Cirencester, fabric 88 (J Keeley, personal comment); Kingscote, fabric 5 (E Swain, personal comment); Lechlade, Rough Ground Farm, fabric 9.1 (S Green, forthcoming); Bath, fabric 6.10 (S Green, personal comment); and Ilchester, fabric CCv/Mi (Leach 1982, 139–40). It occurs at West Hill as over 5.6% of the EVE total.

Fabric type 17

Fabric: Medium-soft fabric; variably oxidised, or with a reduced core or body throughout; lightly tempered with small grog and quartz.

Forms: Enclosed, wheel made vessels, including bottles, flagons, and plain, globular, or indented, beakers. The majority are decorated with buff-red-brown or grey-black colour-coats; roulette stamps, cordoned zones, raised bosses, white slip, or barbotine decoration occur frequently in various combinations.

189 Beaker, *Context 617, Structure IX, Phase 5d–e*
190 Beaker, indented body, *Context 72, Phase 5e*
191 Flagon, one handle, *Context 1213, Phase 5c*
192 Bottle, *Context TF21/22, unstratified*
193 Bottle, *Context 70, Structure 1, Phase 5e*

Dating and parallels: A south-western British colour-coated ware group of uncertain and possibly diverse origins, but probably manufactured from the later second century into the third and possibly the fourth century. A somewhat loosely specified type in its apparent diversity, although widely identified on Romano-British sites in central/south western Britain; eg Cirencester, fabric 105 (J Keeley, personal com-

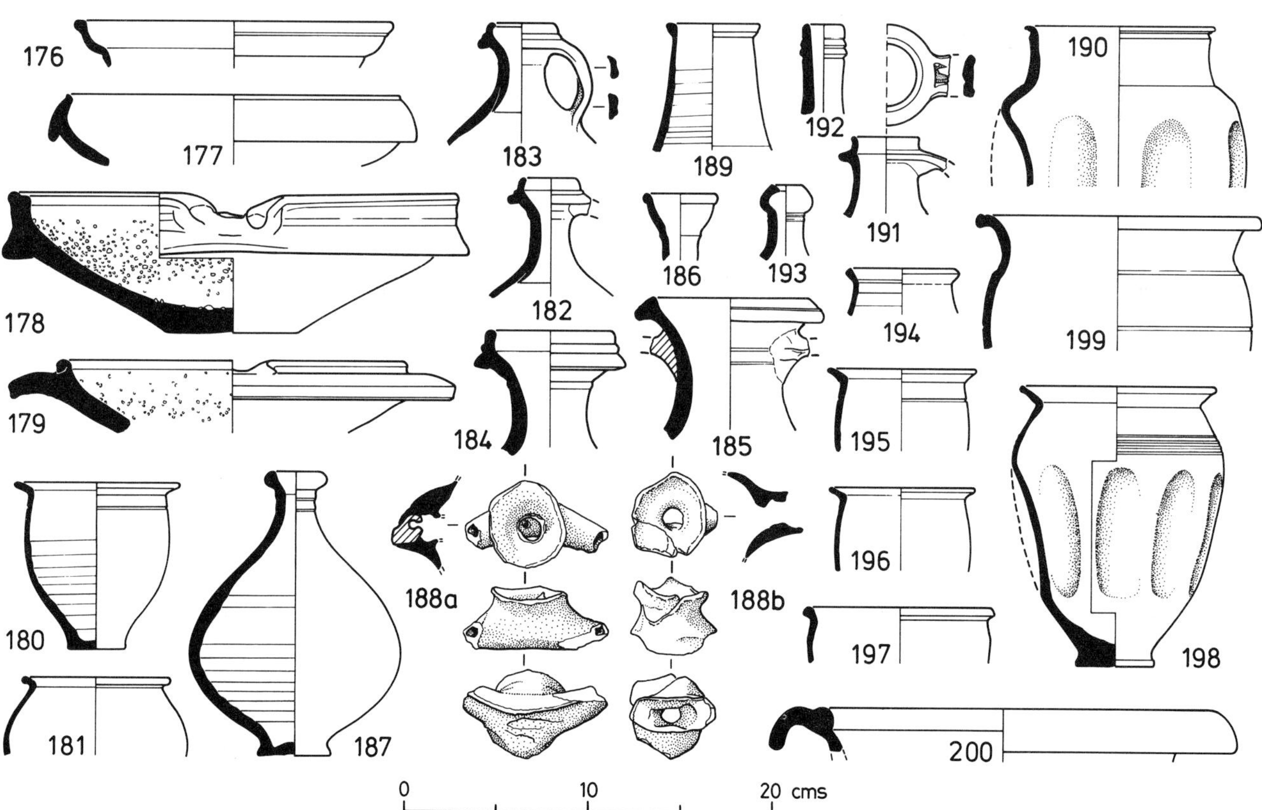

Fig 170 Pottery vessels, fabric types 13, 17, 18, and 23

ment); Kingscote, fabric 10 (E Swain, personal comment); Witcombe, fabrics C2/C6 (Leach forthcoming); and Ilchester, fabric CCii/iv (Leach 1982, 138–9). At West Hill this type comprised almost 5.0% of the EVE total.

Fabric type 18
Fabric: Moderately hard, sandy, reduced fabric, predominantly tempered with quartz sand, some grog, and iron. An even grey body within a thin oxidised surface skin, or possibly a thick colour-coat. Similar to and sometimes difficult to distinguish from fabric type 13.
Forms: Enclosed wheel thrown, thin-walled vessels, mainly plain globular or indented beakers and cups. Characterised by a thick buff-orange colour-coat, which may in part be an oxidised surface skin. Occasional barbotine or rouletted bands of decoration.

194 Cup, *Context 929, Structure VIII, Phase 6a*
195 Cup, *Context TF21 unstratified*
196 Cup, *Context 368, Structure IV, Phase 6b*
197 Cup, *Context 302, Structure IV, Phase 4a*
198 Beaker, indented body, *Context 126, Structure I, Phase 5a–d*
199 Jar/large beaker, *Context 21, Structure III, Phase 6–7*

Dating and parallels: Probably a second and third-century product, similar in character to fabric 13 and possibly also originating in the Cirencester/Upper Thames region. A closely comparable fabric (fabric CH) was probably manufactured at Combe Hay near Bath (Price and Watts 1980, MF 26) although only bowl and jar forms were recovered there. A similar fabric at Cirencester may be fabric 97/88 (J Keeley, personal comment). At West Hill this type comprised almost 1.0% of the EVE total.

Fabric type 20
Fabric: Medium hard, fine, cream or off-white fabric, sparsely tempered with iron.
Forms: Thin-walled, wheel thrown enclosed vessels; beakers and flagons, sometimes with rouletted bands, white slip and barbotine decoration on red-brown and grey-black, sometimes lustrous, colour-coated surfaces. Occasional bowl or mortaria forms with plain colour-coated finish.

200 Mortaria, Nene Valley fabric, *Context 42, Phase 6a*

Dating and parallels: Nene Valley colour-coated ware (Howe, *et al* 1980); later second to third-century types occurring as a rare import, less than 0.2% of the EVE total.

Fabric type 21
Fabric: Fine, well fired, medium hard, oxidised cream-buff to pink-brown fabric in a sparsely tempered iron-free clay. Equates with Fulford's New Forest fabric 1b, (Fulford 1975).
Forms: Wheel made bowl and mortaria forms with red-yellow or red-brown surface colour-coats; the mortaria characterised by grey-white angular flint trituration grits. Exterior surface designs include rouletted bands, stamps, and white slip decoration.

not illustrated

Dating and parallels: A later third and fourth-century oxidised colour-coated ware group manufactured in the New Forest kilns (Fulford *ibid*, 25). A rare late Roman import to West Hill, in direct competition with similar and more successfully marketed Oxfordshire kiln products (fabric 23). Comprises less than 0.1% of the EVE total.

Fabric type 22
Fabric: Fine, well fired, hard, stoneware fabric, usually reduced, sometimes partly oxidised. Indistinguishable in fabric from fabric type 21, but defined primarily by form and firing as Fulford (*ibid*) New Forest fabric 1a.
Forms: Enclosed, well made vessels, including a range of cups and beakers, flagons, bottles and jugs; the former types being the most common. Variable yellow-buff, red-brown, and lustrous purple exterior colour-coats; the latter being most characteristic and associated with the hardest fired stonewares. Rouletted, incised, barbotine, and white slip decoration, are all common, and can occur in combination.

not illustrated

Dating and parallels: A later third and fourth-century colour- coated group manufactured in the New Forest kilns (*ibid*, 24–5). A relatively uncommon late Roman import to West Hill, comprising less than 0.4% of the EVE total.

Fabric type 27
Fabric: Reduced, moderately hard fired fabric, somewhat variable in texture and composition; may be soapy or moderately rough, but with a sparse temper of large sub-angular limestone, clay/grog, and some small iron. A characteristically mid-grey body, speckled with inclusions, between thinly oxidised buff-orange surfaces.
Forms: A relatively restricted range of large, thick-walled storage jars, some with heavy rolled rims. Generally plain, sometimes with traces of a light cream-buff external colour wash.

Fig 168
152 Storage jar, *Context 20, over Structure IX, Phase 7*
153 Storage jar, *Context 300, over Structure IV, Phase 6b*
154 Storage jar, *Context 368, Structure IV, Phase 6b*

Dating and parallels: The almost exclusive occurrence of this type is in fourth-century or later contexts. It forms only a fractional percentage of the EVE total, which suggests both its period of production and its relative insignificance. Its origin of manufacture is uncertain, but it appears to equate with a fabric type known as pink grog-tempered ware, originating in the south east Midlands (Booth and Green, 1989). Locally the fabric is recorded at Gloucester, fabric 241 (Heighway 1983, appendix B1); Kingscote, fabric 9 (E Swain, personal comment); and at Frocester (E Price, personal comment).

Fabric type 25
Not strictly speaking a distinctly defined fabric type, but rather a small group of diverse fabrics, often represented by no more than one or two sherds. Their association is based purely upon form similarity, all being representatives of specific mortaria fabrics. They include material suspected to be from Mancetter/Hartshill, Colchester/Verulamium and one or two other pieces of uncertain origin. Together they com-

prise only a minute proportion (less than 0.1%) of the EVE total.

not illustrated

Group G

Oxfordshire wares; Red colour-coated ware (fabric type 23), White ware mortaria (fabric type 24), White ware (fabric type 26)

Fabric type 23
Fabric: Fine, moderately well fired, oxidised fabric, red-orange or buff-pink, sometimes with a buff or grey reduced core. Predominantly micaceous with some grog, iron, and occasional chalk and quartz temper. Corresponds to Young's oxidised red/brown colour-coated fabric C (Young 1977, 123–184).
Forms: Most common in a range of wheel made bowls and mortaria, many of the former imitating samian forms, while the latter are characterised by coloured and rounded quartz trituration grits. Enclosed vessels, including beakers and bottles, are characteristically red-orange or red-brown colour-coated wares, sometimes having a lustrous effect, and are often decorated with a variety of rouletted, stamped, incised, or white slip designs, often in combination.

Fig 171
201 Beaker, *Context 20, over Structure IX, Phase 7*
202 Bowl, roulette-stamped decoration, *Context 1100, Structure XIV, Phase 7–8*
203 Bowl, roulette-stamped decoration, *Context 1191, Structure XIV, Phase 5d–6b*
204 Bowl, roulette-stamped decoration, *Context 32, Structure II, Phase 5e(ii)*
205 Flanged bowl, *Context 62, Structure IL, Phase 5e*
206 Flanged bowl, inscribed graffiti, *Context 38, over Structure I, Phase 5e(ii)*
207 Bowl, *Context 325, Phase 4b*
208 Bowl/dish, *Context 149, Structure I, Phase 5a–d*
209 Bowl, flange rim, *Context 624, Structure XIX, Phase 7a*
210 Mortarium, roulette-stamp rim decoration, *Context 602, Structure XIX, Phase 7a*

Dating and Parallels: A later third and fourth-century oxidised colour-coated ware, manufactured at the Oxfordshire potteries and widely distributed throughout southern Britain (*ibid*). A well represented type, in particular the bowl and mortaria forms; it comprised almost 6.5% EVE total.

Fabric type 24
Fabric: A fairly hard, well fired, slightly sandy, oxidised fabric, lightly tempered with some grog, iron, mica, and above all, quartz sand. Usually occurs with a cream-white or pale buff to pink-orange body, sometimes with a grey core. Corresponds to Young's white ware mortaria fabric M (*ibid*, 156–79).
Forms: Occurs exclusively as mortaria here, with sub-rounded, coloured quartz trituration grits. A thin cream or buff-orange colour wash is sometimes applied, but other decoration is rare.

211 Mortarium, cream/buff colour-coat, *Context 619, Structure IX, Phase 5c*
212 Mortarium, cream/buff colour-coat, *Context 32, Structure II, Phase 5e(ii)*
213 Mortarium, cream/buff colour-coat, *Context 12, Structure II, Phase 6b*
214 Mortarium, cream/buff colour-coat, *Context 2, Structure II, Phase 6b*

Dating and parallels: A later third and fourth-century oxidised mortaria fabric, manufactured at the Oxfordshire potteries and widely distributed in southern Britain (*ibid*, 56–79). This type comprises over 1.0% of the EVE total.

Fabric type 26
Fabric: A hard, well fired, slightly sandy, cream-buff or pale grey oxidised fabric, moderately tempered with fine quartz sand and a little iron.
Forms: Thin-walled, wheel made, enclosed vessels, probably all flagons or bottles. Apparently undecorated, but possibly with a thin cream-white surface colour wash.

not illustrated

Dating and parallels: Primarily a third-century product of the Oxfordshire potteries. Rare here, comprising only a fraction of a per cent of the EVE total. Corresponds to Young's white ware fabric W (*ibid*, 93–112).

Group H

Late Romano-British shell-tempered ware (fabric type 9)

Fabric type 9
Fabric: Soft, moderately fired, reduced fabric, heavily tempered with abundant large plates and fragments of Jurassic fossil shell and limestone. Occurs with a medium-grey body speckled with the lighter coloured shell temper, and often with a thinly oxidised buff-brown surface skin.
Forms: A fairly restricted range of bowl and jar types, as represented by Fig 171, nos 215–20, handmade but wheel-finished. Normally undecorated, although fine concentric corrugation or rilling of exterior bodies is a frequent characteristic.

215 Bowl, flange rim, *Context 32, Structure II, Phase 5e(ii)*
216 Bowl, flange rim, *Context 602, Structure XIX, Phase* 7a
217 Jar, *Context 38, over Structure I, Phase 5e(ii)*
218 Jar, *Context 601, Phase 7a*
219 Jar, *Context 278, Phase 8*
220 Jar, *Context 301, over Structure IV, Phase 6b*

Dating and parallels: A late Roman reduced coarse ware type, widely distributed in midland and southern Britain, and probably originating somewhere in the south or east midlands Jurassic belt. This type barely appears before the mid-fourth century at West Hill, where it comprises over 3.5% of the EVE total. Local equivalent fabrics are identified at Gloucester, fabric 22 (Heighway 1983, appendix B1); Cirencester, fabric 115 (J Keeley, personal comment); Witcombe, fabric A5 (Leach forthcoming); Bath, fabric 17 (S. Green personal comment); Ilchester, fabric ST (Leach 1982, 143); Sea Mills, fabric E35 (Ellis 1987, 84); and Frocester (E Price, personal comment).

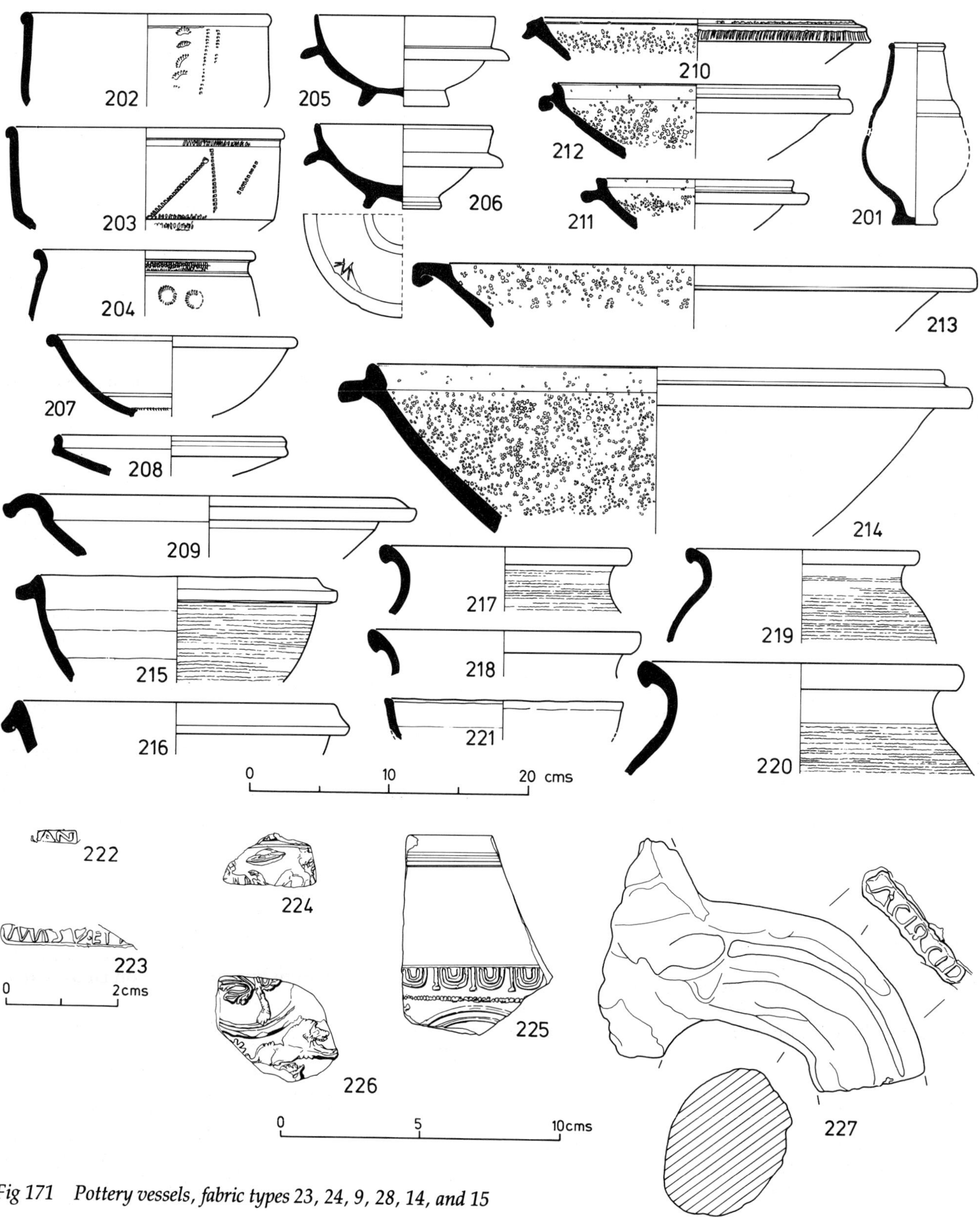

Fig 171 Pottery vessels, fabric types 23, 24, 9, 28, 14, and 15

Group J

Late/post-Roman handmade wares (fabric type 29)

Fabric type 29
Fabric and form: A somewhat loosely defined general group, whose common characteristics include poorly fired reduced fabrics, coarsely tempered, with mixtures of grog/clay, limestone, and sometimes organic inclusions. Crude handmade bowl or jar forms are identifiable, although only a very few vessels appear to be represented.

221 Bowl/dish, *Context 619, Structure IX, Phase 5c*

Dating and parallels: Although suspected of being of primarily late, or post-Roman local manufacture, some of this material may have been confused in identity with pre-Roman or other Romano-British coarse wares, particularly in the case of well-weathered sherds. Little of this material corresponds very closely with a more clearly defined equivalent group of handmade and grass tempered fabrics at nearby Frocester (Gracie 1970). At West Hill these fabrics were not recovered exclusively from post-Roman contexts, as they were also found associated with Romano-British wares, although they comprised less than 0.2% of the EVE total.

Group K

Imported Roman finewares; Rhenish (fabric type 19), and samian (fabric type 14)

Fabric type 19
Fabric: Very fine, moderately hard, well fired, oxidised fabric, generally with an even pink-orange body, sometimes alternating with a blue-grey core, and lacking visible inclusions.
Forms: Fine, thin-walled, moulded, or wheel made, enclosed vessels, primarily cups and beakers. Characteristic lustrous dark red-brown colour-coat on both surfaces, with rouletted bands, barbotine, and white slip external decoration frequent; often occurring in combination.

not illustrated

Dating and parallels: An uncommon, though widespread, later second and third-century import from Rhenish and east Gaulish factories, primarily Trier and Lezoux (Greene, 1978). Only a handful of beakers are represented here, comprising less than 0.2% of the EVE total.

Fabric type 14
by Catherine Johns

Taken as a whole, this is a small group of predominantly late second-century manufacture and even later deposition. Most of the sherds are quite small and worn, and there is a relatively high proportion of those too small for certain identification, though the majority of them will be from bowls of Dr 18/31 and 31. A full catalogue of identified pieces is in the site archive.

Decorated:
There are only fourteen sherds from decorated vessels, four of which are from the plain rims of Dr 37 bowls. Of the remaining ten decorated sherds three are illustrated. All the others are from Antonine central Gaulish Dr 37s, most of them too tiny for close identification. The exception is a minute and very worn sherd from context 532, which may be from a Flavian south Gaulish Dr 29.

224 A small fragment from the upper part of a central Gaulish Dechelette (1904) 64 in fine light orange ware with an orange-red slip. The decoration consists of two male figures with a 'flying saucer' motif between them. Too little remains for the identification of the figures, but the decorative detail is Rogers (1974) U 54, typical of Libertus. The decor, with a frieze of figures, the fabric, and the cup form also confirm this sherd as the work of Libertus. Trajanic, *Context TF21/22, unstratified*
225 Dr 37, central Gaulish. There is a squarish ovolo with a hammer tongue over a neat bead-row and part of a large plain double medallion. The ovolo is Rogers (1974) B 206, used by a large group of Antonine potters including Paternus II, Censorinus, Laxtucissa, Paullus and Quintilianus. Antonine, *Context 579, infilling of F584, Phase 3c*
226 Dr 37, central Gaulish. A plain double medallion contains a large leaf; beneath is a small boar running to the right above a small leaf. The leaves are Rogers (1974) H 15 and H 134 respectively, the boar 0.1642. All are used by Doeccus, the small leaf probably exclusively by him. The general style, with an animal below a medallion, also confirms the piece as Doeccus, cf Stanfield and Simpson, 1958, pl 148:13 amongst others. Late Antonine, *Context 656, Phase 5b*

Plain
The great majority of the sherds are from Antonine central Gaulish bowls of Dr 18/31 and 31 (including 31R). The other forms present confirm the generally late second-century focus: Dr 33, followed by Dr 45, Dr 36 and Dr 38. Specifically late forms represented include two examples of Walters 79 (1908) and one of the related form Ludowici (1929) Tg (here in a central Gaulish fabric). There are a few sherds of probably East Gaulish ware, and some half-dozen of late south Gaulish, mainly Dr 27, but with one example of Dr 24/25, and a basal fragment of a Dechelette (1904) 67.

Potter's stamps
by Brenda Dickinson

222 Stamp [SACERI·]MAN on bowl form 31. Sacerus ii of Gaul, presumably Lezoux, since most of the examples noted come from Britain. All are on Dr 31 and 33, and one is from Corbridge (unpublished). The fabric and glaze of this piece suggest an Antonine date, *Context 600, above Structure XIX, Phase 8*
223 Stamp MΛ.SV.ET[Ic] or [Ic] on bowl form 31. Mansuetus ii of Lezoux, where the die (2a') is known to have been used. The earliest impressions show a complete, small o at the end, but on others this appears as c, after the end of the die had been broken. A corresponding reduction in the beginning and depth of the frame, showing on this stamp, suggests that it comes from the later version of the die (2a'). Both versions seems to have been in use before *c* AD 160–65, since both appear on Dr 27, and the use of 2a on Walters (1908) form 80 suggests that the die was broken some time in the early 160s. The site record includes Chesterholm (2a) and Benwell, Halton Chesters and Malton (2a)(all unpublished). The overall range will be *c* AD 150–80, with 165–80 for 2a, *Context TF21/22, unstratified*

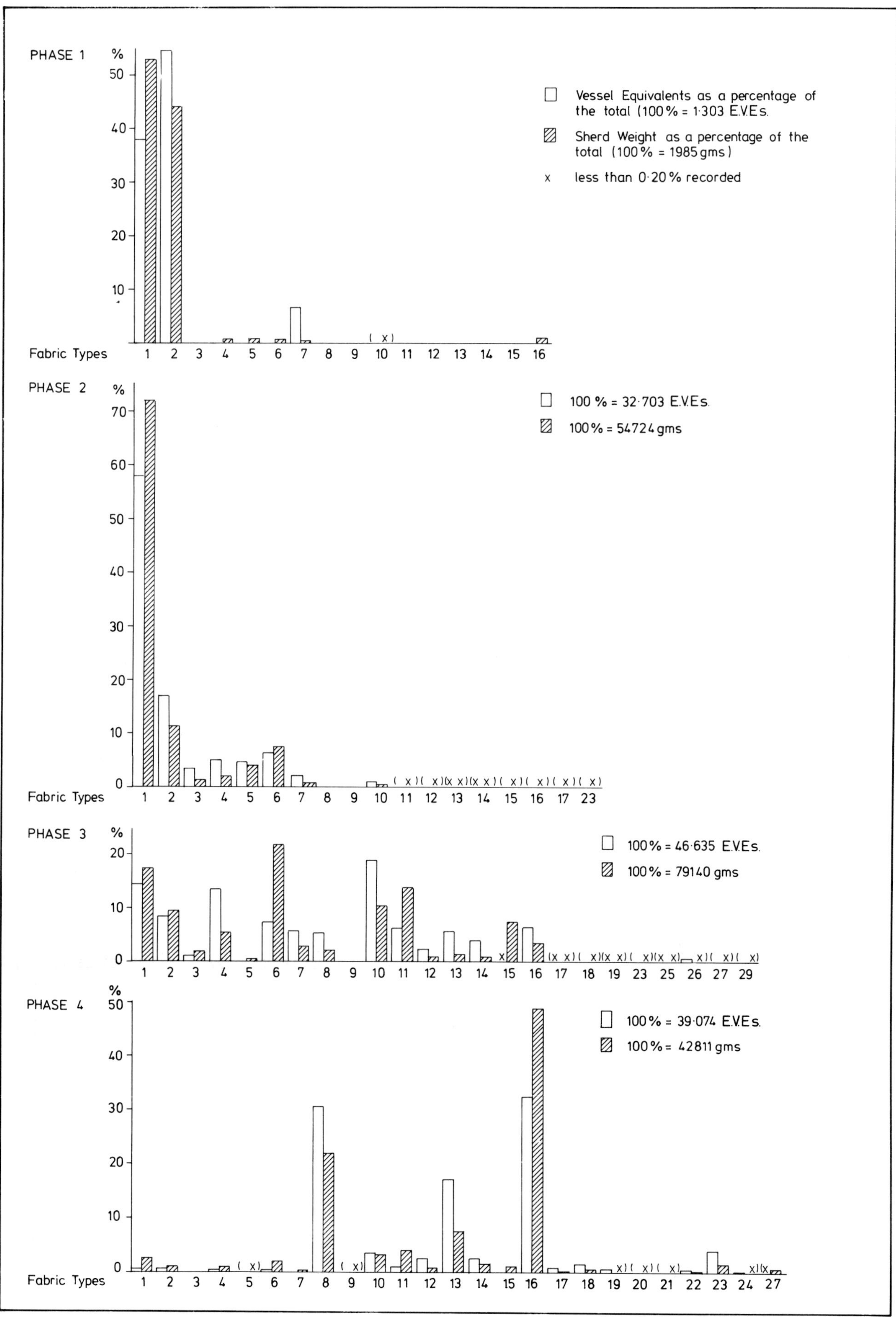

Fig 172 Pottery representation by phase, Phases 1–4

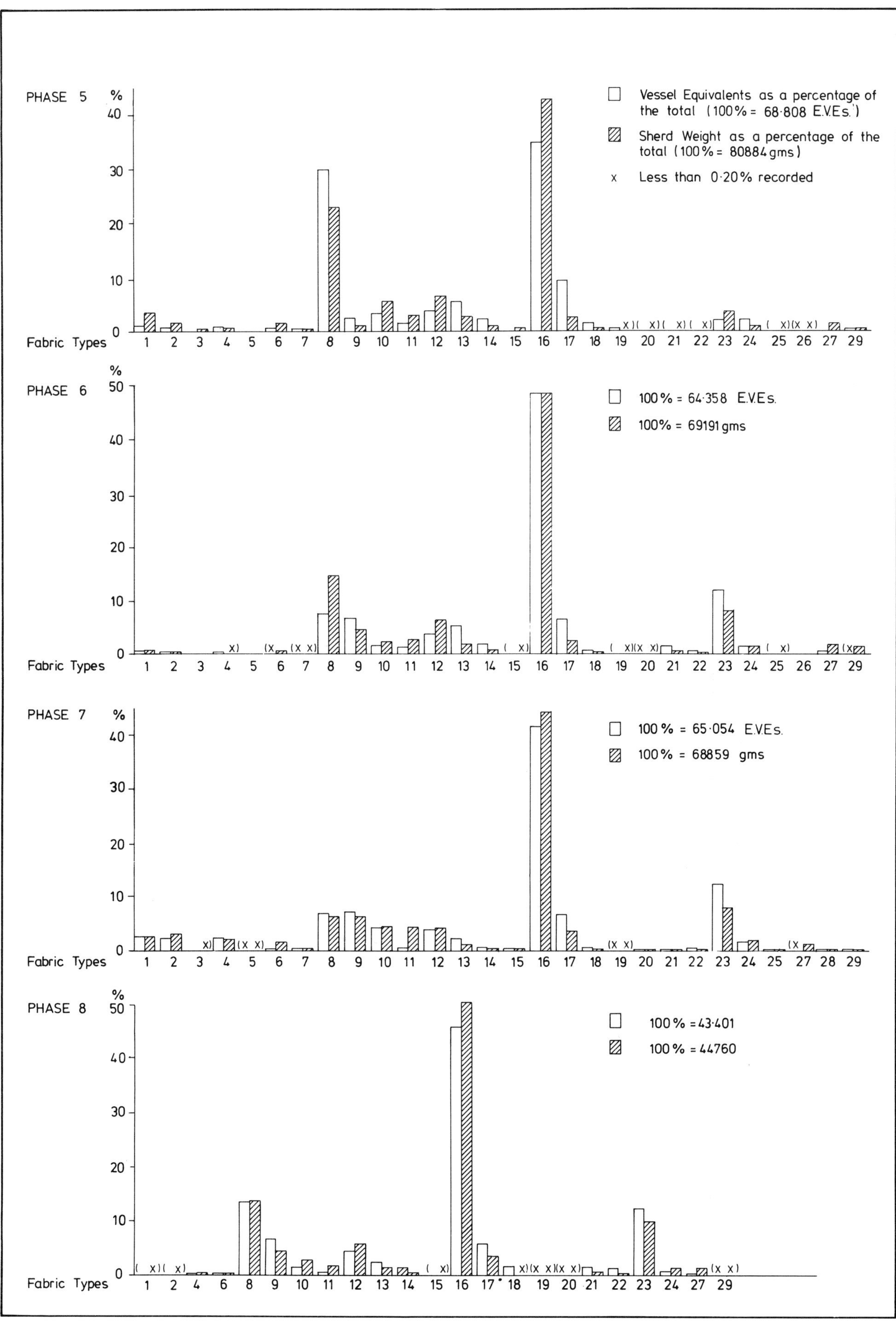

Fig 173 Pottery representation by phase, Phases 5–8

Group L

Amphoras (fabric type 15)

Fabric type 15
Specific fabrics have not been individually defined among this group of material, associated together by virtue of belonging to a distinctive, although uncommon form type. In practice, the majority of amphora sherds recovered appear to be of south Spanish origin, although other sources may be represented (Peacock and Williams 1987). Comprising but a fractional percentage of the total EVE assemblage, amphorae may well only have reached the site as broken fragments, or at best as containers employed in secondary roles.

227 Dressel 20 Amphora handle, stamped CIRCID, *Context 1224, Structure X, Phase 4b*

Chronology

Figures 172 and 173 show the occurrence by phase of the pottery fabric types present. It is hoped that the method of presentation will allow comparison with similar assemblages occurring on sites elsewhere in southern and south-west Britain. The suggested date ranges are in some cases supported by associated, independently dated artefacts, including samian.

It must however be emphasised that what is revealed in this analysis of the pottery types present are patterns of disposal or loss (as illustrated, Fig 175). The effects of contamination and residuality will tend to increase with time on a continuously occupied site, although the actual effect of this upon the occurrence patterns of particular fabric types or groups is difficult to estimate or compensate for.

Nevertheless an attempt has been made here to outline the overall ceramic trends, and relate them to the structural phases defined in chapters 2–4, the dates of which may also be suggested by other independent means.

Phase 1

The chronology of Phase 1 (see chapter 2) is perhaps the least exactly defined structural period. Ceramically there is less ambiguity. Phase 1 is dominated overwhelmingly by the pottery fabric types 1 and 2 of groups A and B, both of which represent an assemblage which should have accumulated from no earlier than the latter part of the first century BC (Fig 172). This impression is reinforced by small quantities of other wares, eg fabric types 4, 6 and 7, which could also be of this period, if not the result of later contamination of the groups in which they were found. Despite this relatively straight-forward picture, its statistical representation disguises a potentially more complex situation. Many of the Phase 1 contexts were in fact aceramic, or contained only pottery of fabric type 1. The bulk of this relatively small assemblage was recovered either from later fills or in contexts sometimes difficult to distinguish from Phase 2. Stylistically and materially, group A pottery belongs to a regional Iron Age pottery tradition with a pre-Belgic influence, which may originate in the second century BC (Peacock 1968). Whether or not the Phase 1 material is representative of activity this early, the fabric and style evidently survived well into the first century AD, during which time the bulk of it appears to have been lost on this site. It should also be noted that earlier Iron Age ceramics from excavated contexts at the neighbouring hillfort of Uley Bury, dating probably to the third or fourth centuries BC (Saville and Ellison 1983, 14–21), are not closely paralleled here.

Phase 2

In this phase (a more closely defined period which should equate approximately with the second half of the first century AD) the ceramic spectrum conforms more closely to expectations. Group A fabrics still predominate, but are everywhere associated with the Belgic-style fabrics of group B. A background of minor contamination is again discernible, but overall the assemblage typifies stylistically the later first century AD in this region (eg Bagendon, Clifford 1961). The virtual absence of Roman fabrics need occasion no surprise on a non-military rural site of this period, although the influence of the conquest is apparent in the appearance of Savernake ware (fabric type 6), and some contemporary metal finds. The deposit within the rock-cut pit, context F251, associated with a segment of the temenos ditch, F264, appears to represent in microcosm virtually the complete range of principal fabric and form types current at this time.

Pit group F251

Group A
Fabric type 1
Fig 174
1 Jar, decorated body, *Context 926, Phase 2c*
2 Jar, decorated body, *Contexts 924, 926–7, Phase 2c*
3 Jar, decorated body, pierced base, *Contexts 923–4, 931, Phase 2c*

Group B
Fabric type 2
4 Jar, *Contexts 923–4, and 931, Phase 2c*
5 Bowl, shouldered, *Context 924, Phase 2c*
Fabric type 4
6 Bowl, shouldered, *Contexts 924, 926, Phase 2c*
Fabric type 6
7 Jar, decorated shoulders, pierced base, *Contexts 923, 924, Phase 2c*
8 Jar, narrow necked, *Contexts 923–4, 926, Phase 2c*
9 Jar, pierced base, *Contexts 924,926, Phase 2c*
10 Jar, *Contexts 924, 926, Phase 2c* 11 Bowl, *Contexts 923, 926, Phase 2c*

Group C
Fabric type 7
12 Bowl, carinated, *Contexts 924, 931, Phase 2c*

Phase 3

The ceramic spectrum for the second century AD (Figs 172 and 175) illustrates a transition from the relatively restricted range of pottery in the earliest phases to a much broader assemblage receiving material from more diverse sources. The proportion of Iron Age and Belgic-style wares is markedly reduced, although still well represented, and indicates the continuing currency of group B fabrics in particular, well into the second century. The expansion of regional Romano-British industries, notably those of the Severn Valley, is apparent within the fabric and form representation. The oxidised wares of group C dominate here, reduced coarse wares of fabric types 12 and 16 (Figs 167–8) being in the minority, and perhaps in some competition with the continuing although progressively declining group A and B products. From other directions pottery products from kilns in the Cirencester/Upper Thames area (fabric type 13, Fig 170) began to reach West Hill, while from further afield came a small but significant group – Dorset black burnished Ware (fabric type 8, Fig 169).

Imports also make an appearance in this phase, notably samian (fabric type 14, Fig 171), little of which is stylistically of earlier than mid-second-century manufacture, and there is occasional representation of amphora (fabric type 15, Fig 171). Of the remaining fabrics some appear to reflect otherwise undetected later contamination, although small quantities of material from other sources were undoubtedly reaching the site.

Phases 4 to 6

From Phases 4–6 onwards the range of pottery present by phase takes on a similarity which identifies it as of later Romano- British accumulation. The contrast between Phases 3 and 4 is almost as great at that between Phase 3 and its predecessors. In addition it corresponds to a major building expansion and change of layout of the temple, Structure II and its precinct (see chapter 3). These events heighten the probability of contamination

Fig 174 Pottery vessel group from pit F251

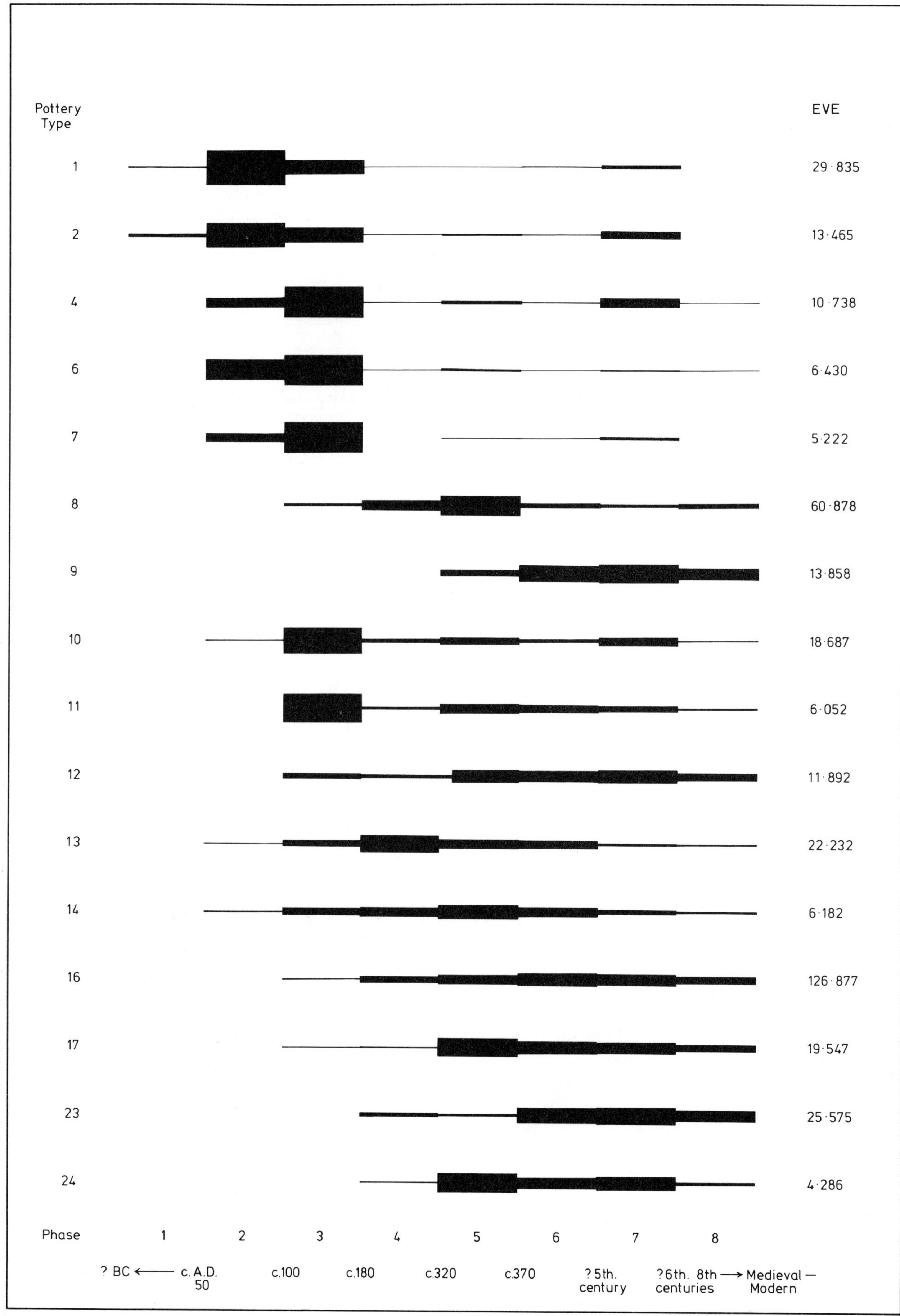

Fig 175 Chronological patterns of ceramic deposition

from the disturbance of earlier deposits, although the degree of contamination may, to some extent, be assessed by the occurrence of pottery of groups A and B. It may reasonably be assumed that by the third century these groups were no longer in production and that few vessels in these fabrics would remain in circulation. Thus the much reduced presence of these types should reflect a real replacement by other groups, virtually all that occurred being redeposited material.

Oxidised Severn Valley wares (fabric types 7, 10 and 11) evidently decreased in importance during these phases, and on stylistic and other external dating criteria, do not appear to have been supplied to the site beyond the third century. Their continuing presence may, in part, reflect the higher survival rate of these vessels, relative to other coarser fabrics, and thus an extended life in circulation. In contrast, the reduced Severn Valley and related wares, notably fabric type 16, dominate the coarse ware assemblage of this phase, and overall form by far the largest fabric group on the site. This is paralleled to a lesser extent by a corresponding increase in black burnished ware imports (fabric type 8), although these appear to decline by the later fourth century in Phase 6. The appearance of characteristic south Midland shell-tempered ware (fabric type 9) during the fourth century may to some extent have countered the decreased availability of black burnished ware.

Of the remaining pottery types the great majority are colour-coated wares from a variety of sources. Fabric type 13 along with related fabric type 18, of local origin, appear to dominate in Phase 4, but give ground during the fourth century to fabric type 17, a colour-coated ware of uncertain origin, widely distributed in south-west Britain. The third major group, comprising both oxidised colour-coated vessels and mortaria from the Oxfordshire kilns (fabric types 23, 24, and 26), were evidently making an impact by the later third century, and were dominant by the fourth century. This late Roman dominance of the fineware sector of the market by Oxfordshire products is a trend recognised widely in southern Britain whenever quantitative analyses of site assemblages have been undertaken. No other colour-coated ware approaches the amount of Oxfordshire ware represented, although the characteristic purple colour-coated stoneware beakers and flagons of the New Forest kilns (fabric types 21 and 22), Nene Valley products (fabric type 20), and possibly wares from other sources are present. Both Rhenish ware (fabric type 19) and samian imports (fabric type 14) continue to occur, although the durability of these wares, ensuring above average survival in use, and/or redeposition in later archaeological contexts, may explain their presence.

Phases 7 and 8

Beyond Phase 6 and the fourth century the chronological controls provided by coin loss or other datable finds are no longer applicable. Residuality and survival are clearly the dominant factors to be taken into consideration when assessing the ceramic assemblage in a period when pottery manufacture had all but ceased in this region. The incorporation of material current towards the end of the fourth century within fifth-century or later contexts of Phases 7 and 8 will inevitably result in an echo of the earlier pattern (Figs 173 and 175). While this may be largely true, closer examination reveals other trends, some of which have a bearing upon the survival of Roman pottery in essentially post-Roman contexts (see also chapter 5).

It is hardly surprising that there should be a decrease in the quantity of pottery recovered, given the assumed decline of pottery production during these phases. Despite this the proportion of principally late fourth-century fabrics represented in Phase 7 compares well with that of the preceding phase. In certain instances an increase in the recovery of this material, peaking in Phase 7, suggests maximum discard in the fifth century, if not later. This pattern is best exemplified by the Midland shell tempered ware (fabric type 9) and Oxford red colour-coated ware (fabric type 23), the latter in particular, a relatively fine and durable ware, whose retention and use might be expected to continue well beyond the period of current production. Thus a high residuality factor may influence the post-Roman representation of Oxfordshire wares, in much the same way that the deposition of 'antique' samian affects the occurrence of that type, both here and upon virtually every other contemporary Romano-British site.

One other factor which should be noted is the effect of Phase 7 activity in disturbing earlier deposits. This is demonstrated most dramatically by a small upsurge in the presence of pottery of groups A and B.

Function and form

As the areas excavated are interpreted as lying within a religious precinct throughout most, if not the entire period of pottery deposition, it is reasonable to ask whether this is reflected in the ceramic assemblage. One immediate problem in attempting to assess this is the scarcity of comparable site and period pottery analyses. This difficulty may be resolved in the future but in the meantime this analysis is a contribution to an ever-expanding data base. It provides a characterisation of the site through its pottery record, offers suggestions as to its local and regional significance, and makes it possible to construct hypotheses to account for chronological, morphological, or spatial variations.

One functionally comparable site assemblage in the region, that from Henley Wood (Watts and Leach forthcoming) was available in advance of publication and some attempt at ceramic comparison is made below.

An analysis which quantifies by vessel equivalent percentages (EVEs) the occurrence of basic vessel types, ie jars, bowls/mortaria, dishes, cups/beakers, and flagons/bottles/amphorae, is presented in Fig 176a. No attempt was made to analyse the form and size variations within each major group, although the data is available in archive, and computer processing would doubtless have facilitated this. The overall pattern of forms present provides a crude picture of the dominance of jar and bowl types, the absence of other forms before Phase 3, and a fourth-century climax of occurrence and loss for many groups. The latter is probably a reflection of the concentration of activity centred upon the temple and its precinct in that century, as is emphasised by other artefactual evidence, although material resulting from the disturbance of deposits from all the earlier periods is also present.

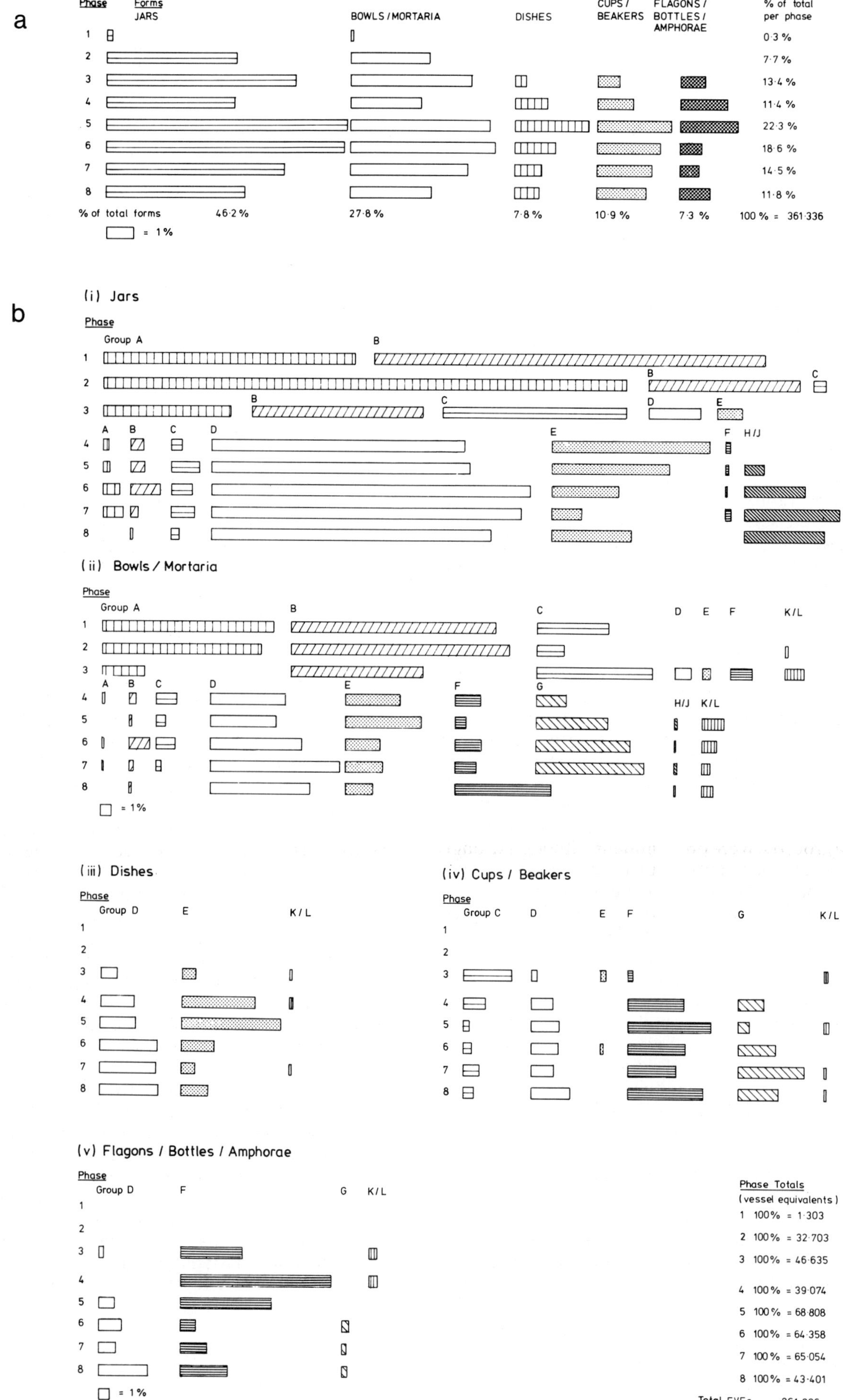
a
Phase
Forms
JARS
BOWLS / MORTARIA
DISHES
CUPS / BEAKERS
FLAGONS / BOTTLES / AMPHORAE
% of total per phase
0·3 %
7·7 %
13·4 %
11·4 %
22·3 %
18·6 %
14·5 %
11·8 %
% of total forms
46·2 %
27·8 %
7·8 %
10·9 %
7·3 %
100 % = 361·336
= 1%
b
(i) Jars
(ii) Bowls / Mortaria
(iii) Dishes
(iv) Cups / Beakers
(v) Flagons / Bottles / Amphorae
Phase Totals (vessel equivalents)
1 100% = 1·303
2 100% = 32·703
3 100% = 46·635
4 100% = 39·074
5 100% = 68·808
6 100% = 64·358
7 100% = 65·054
8 100% = 43·401
Total EVEs 361·336

More informative is a chronological analysis of the form types relative to the principal fabric groups (Fig 176b). Once again the contrast between pottery assemblages of Phases 1 and 2 and the later phases is most marked, with Phase 3 pottery transitional between the two. This is well illustrated by the dominance of jar and bowl forms in a restricted range of fabrics during Phases 1 and 2. This gives way progressively to a wider spectrum of forms and fabrics from Phase 3 onwards, undoubtedly as a reflection of the integration of the site into the cultural fabric of Roman Britain. It is possible however to see additional functional influences operating. For example in the early phases the structural and perhaps organisational emphasis seems to be upon the ritual aspects of the site, and it may be the case that many of the bowls and jars occurring in contexts of these phases performed a specific function in relation to these suspected religious activities. A high proportion of the material was recovered from contexts which contained almost complete, if not complete vessels, and in circumstances where deliberate deposition, with religious connotations, appears likely (eg the contents of pit F251, Fig 174). Moreover a significant proportion of the vessels bear indications of secondary adaption, best illustrated by the drilling of holes, often in threes, in the base or lower sides of certain vessels (Fig 174, nos 2, 7, and 9; and Fig 165, no 73). There is no indication other than this that the vessels were not within the normal range of domestic pottery and no other specially made or exceptional types were recognised in the assemblage, nor was anything comparable to the ceramic material discussed in chapter 8 (Figs 117–19, and Fig 121) related to this early period.

From Phase 3 the form and fabric repertoire expands to include dishes, and a range of enclosed vessels, the bulk of which could be interpreted as tablewares. Jars and bowls are still dominant, maintaining roughly equivalent proportions to each other throughout. Jars formed the largest single group, among which the local fabrics (group D) were predominant, although strongly challenged by Dorset black burnished wares (group E). A similar pattern is manifest in the occurrence of bowls, although in both instances black burnished ware occurs less frequently in deposits formed toward the end of the fourth century, perhaps reflecting a decline in the availability of products of that industry. To some extent this is countered by the increased presence of substitutes, although the quantity of local wares also increases. Shell-tempered ware (group H) helps to maintain jar quantities overall, while Oxfordshire red colour- coated bowls and mortaria (group G) become the principal rivals to the local products.

The appearance of tableware from the second century onwards represents a more widely recognised phenomenon, involving social changes in cooking and eating habits in Roman Britain (Fulford 1971, 250). In this respect the occurrence of tablewares on the site conforms to the pattern, but the wider trend may mask changes characterised in the other evidence regarding the nature of the site and its environs. The development of the precinct from at least Phase 4 involved not only the temple, but a range of ancillary buildings. Some of these contained evidence of domestic or industrial use, and their presence doubtless influenced both the character and magnitude of the later assemblages. Indeed it is debatable whether it is possible to recover evidence that pottery played any direct role in ritual or votive activity associated with the temple. Miniature clay vessels are the only obvious exception, considered separately (chapter 8 and Figs 117–19). Otherwise the later Romano-British assemblage, particularly from Phase 4 onwards, resembles that which might be anticipated at other contemporary rural or suburban domestic occupation sites in the locality. Major groups of material at Frocester and Kingscote for example are currently undergoing comparable analyses (J Timby and E Swain, personal comment) and suggest similar patterns.

Inter-site comparisons

Despite the relative frequency of extensively excavated rural temple sites in the Severn Estuary/South Cotswold region, only one other pottery assemblage, that from Henley Wood, Avon, has been analysed in such a way as to permit meaningful comparisons to be made with West Hill (Watts and Leach forthcoming). Since this comparison is to some extent explored in that volume it is necessary to reiterate only the main points here.

Henley Wood, Yatton, in Avon (formerly north Somerset) was the site of a succession of Romano-Celtic temples, occupying an outlying hilltop overlooking the north Somerset Levels and lower Severn Estuary. Ceramic comparisons have been restricted to the later phases of pagan religious activity on both sites, arguably the time of maximum prosperity, through much of the fourth century. Specifically, comparisons are made between assemblages associated with religious buildings themselves or thought to derive from them, and deposited towards the end of that century. Both sites were on shallow limestone soils with generally shallow, poorly defined stratigraphy. A further dimension to the Henley Wood analysis was provided by a comparative study of local 'secular' assemblages, notably that from Gatcombe (Branigan 1977). This type of data is still not at present available for Gloucestershire, although work at both Kingscote and Frocester nearby is in progress.

Both the size and range of the late Roman ceramic assemblage at Uley exceeds that of Henley Wood. Sample size and site origins are factors to be taken into account here, although West Hill does appear to have been the more extensive and flourishing religious precinct of the two. Among the coarse ware the dominance of a range of grey wares (fabric type 16) could argue for a very local source, as can be demonstrated more securely at Henley Wood (type fabrics A1–3 and B2). In practice the West Hill grey wares may be of more

Fig 176 Occurrence of basic vessel forms by phase
a: by percentage estimated vessel equivalent (EVE) for all fabric groups, (excluding unstratified material)
b: by fabric group as an estimated vessel equivalent (EVE) percentage for each phase

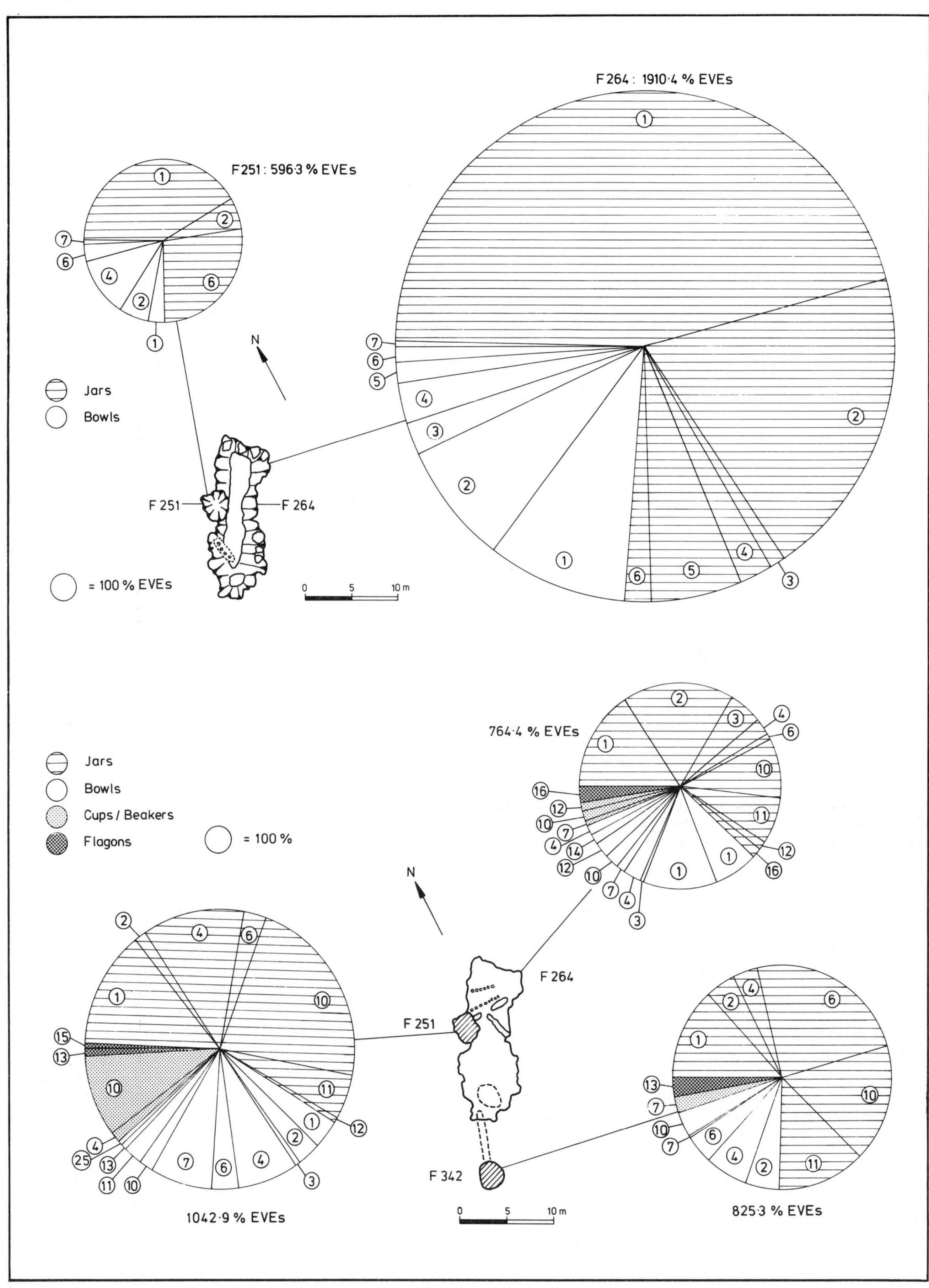

Fig 177 Pottery forms and fabrics from ditch F264 and pit F251 as estimated vessel equivalent (EVE) percentages

diverse character although relatively local sources are still suspected.

The greater range and proportionally higher representation of finewares and imports at West Hill, 24.2% compared with 7.3% at Henley Wood is another factor favouring the former's interpretation as a 'superior' site. The balancing factor emphasising how little we know about cross-site comparison was the character and representation of samian assemblages at both locations. As might be expected the samian, incorporated with late-Roman material, and wholly residual by the fourth century, was predominantly late Antonine in style with some third-century types; it was generally undistinguished in character, and heavily abraded on both sites. In contrast the proportion it represents of the pottery at each site gives a rather different picture. At Henley Wood samian comprised over 3% of the total ceramic assemblage (the largest fine ware group), while it formed less than 1% of the West Hill material overall.

To put this divergence in perspective it is necessary to examine the proportional representation of another fabric type, Oxfordshire red colour-coated ware (fabric type 23), arguably to be regarded as a substitute for samian, both functionally and aesthetically. Less than 2% of the Henley Wood pottery corpus was identified as this fabric (Henley Wood type fabric C1), in contrast to 15.5% present at West Hill. This may have reflected the higher status or prosperity for the shrine at West Hill, a greater requirement or preference for pottery of this type here, or perhaps the increasing availability of such ware towards the end of the fourth century (by which time Henley Wood may have been in decline or out of commission). West Hill is anyway closer to the Oxfordshire production sources.

Functional comparison between the assemblages suggests a greater emphasis upon table wares at West Hill, and it is tempting to see some link here with the considerable evidence for animal (and fowl) sacrifice and perhaps consumption of offerings, (see chapter 12). Such observations are considered to reflect the nature of rituals and practices specific to individual cults or shrines throughout the Roman world, here specifically to the god Mercury.

They barely hint at some of the questions to be addressed through inter-site comparative studies of ceramic assemblages. To advance these many more compatible analyses are required, both from contemporary religious and secular sites of the period.

Spatial patterning

The prime objective of the analysis of the pottery was to attempt to understand any functional patterning which could be perceived in the assemblages, as an aid to the interpretation of the structures or areas of occupation. Groups from completely excavated buildings (or parts thereof) of differing chronological periods were selected for this analysis. The availability of a sufficiently large pottery sample was also a factor in selection. Basic form types within each fabric are presented through pie diagrams, but attempts to provide more detailed analyses through vessel form and size variations were statistically invalidated by insufficient sample sizes (Figs 173 and 175–6).

As has been previously demonstrated, the greatest contrast exists between the assemblages from Phases 1–3 and those from Phase 4 onwards. This is in part due to external changes in the range of forms and fabrics available at different periods, but may also be a reflection of site function. The suggestion has already been made that presumed religious activity may have involved the use and deposition of considerable quantities of what appears to be pottery of primarily domestic function in the first three major phases of the site's use. This is demonstrated specifically by the contents of features associated with the temenos ditch segment F264 (Fig 177). Jars dominate bowls – the only other form present in the Phase 2 assemblages by approximately 3:1. All the fabrics and principal form types of this phase were present here, notably within the pit F251 (Fig 174 above).

Phase 3 assemblages from the same area reflect fairly closely the overall range of forms and fabrics for this period. The greater diversity of fabric types is well represented, and although jar forms still dominate, followed by bowls, other forms also appear, notably beakers and cups. The deliberate depositional character of the deposits is however maintained and presumably embraces all the forms present (Fig 177).

The depositional history of contexts containing pottery from buildings of the later phases contrasts with those analysed for Phases 2 and 3 above. All of the former were contained within the rooms of stone buildings, and as such were interpreted as residual deposits relating either to occupation or destruction of those structures. While some correlation between content and function of rooms or buildings as a whole is to be anticipated, what remains to be recovered archaeologically will only be a residual remnant, which will probably also have been subject to subsequent contamination. Thus the reliability of these samples will not only be much lower than the Phase 2 and 3 assemblages, but also of different origin. A further problem relates to the sample size, which in many instances is barely sufficient per room for reliable comparisons to be made. This is particularly apparent for Structures I and IV (Fig 178), where there appear to be mixtures of fabric and form representative of their respective phases, but quantities are relatively small. This may have more to do with the fate of the buildings after abandonment than with their function while occupied. Both structures were deliberately demolished, and relatively little of their associated ceramic content (if this existed) remained behind.

This is in marked contrast to Structure IX and its successor Structure XIV (Fig 179) which appears to have been destroyed by fire. Its contents were apparently left *in situ* and the material recovered might thus reasonably be considered as that contained by, and in use within, the building at the time of destruction. Structure IX was deliberately demolished and the demolition debris in part retained as a foundation for Structure XIV. It is possible therefore that material recovered from this structure may in part be derived from the demolition phase. The difference in the pottery forms present in the two buildings does not appear to be significant, and perhaps reflects the similar domestic and industrial interpretation for the function of both. More apparent are changes in the pottery fabrics present, which reflect the changes already recognised

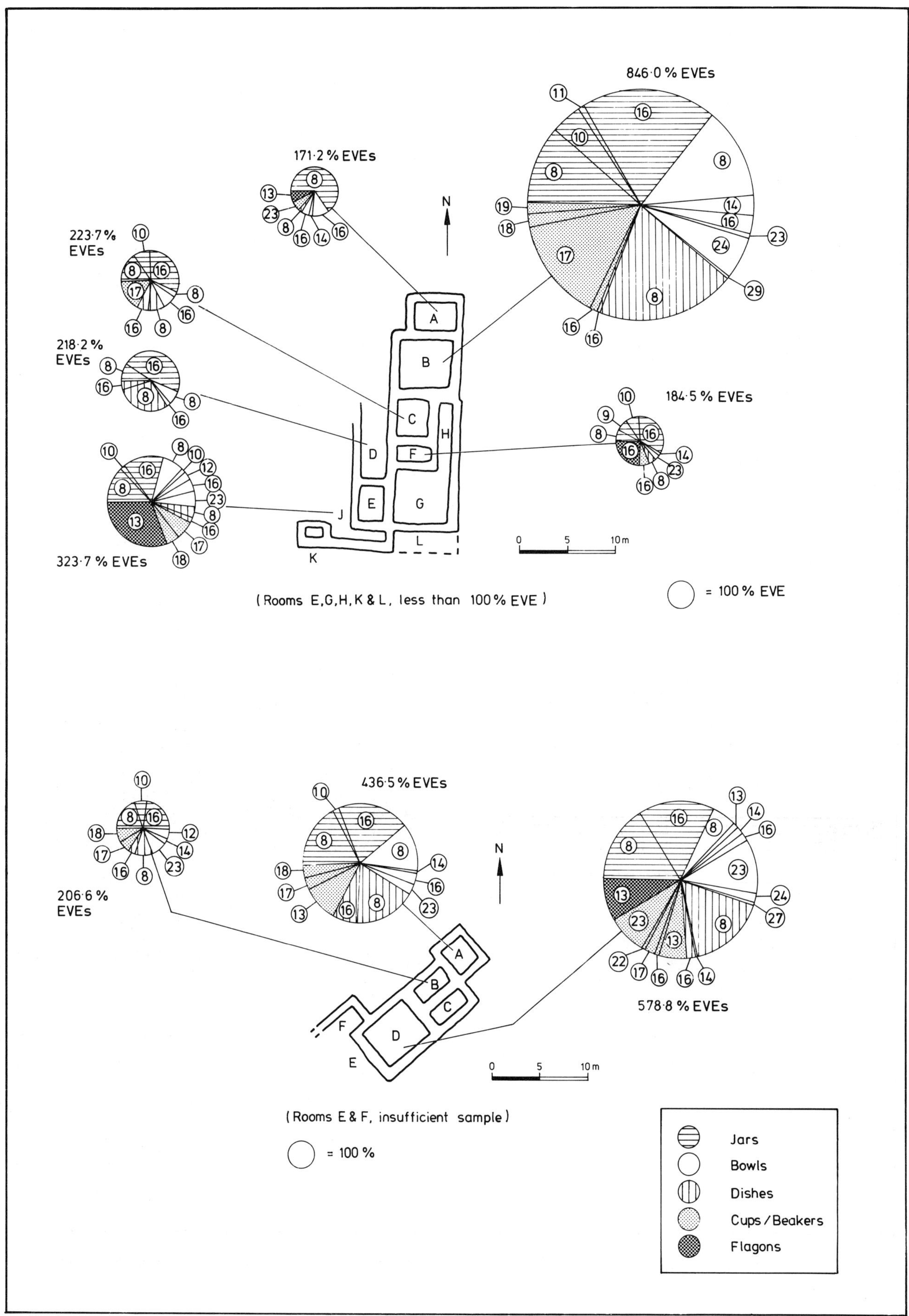

Fig 178 Pottery forms and fabrics, Structure IX, Phases 5a–c, and Structure XIV, Phase 4 as estimated vessel equivalent (EVE) percentages

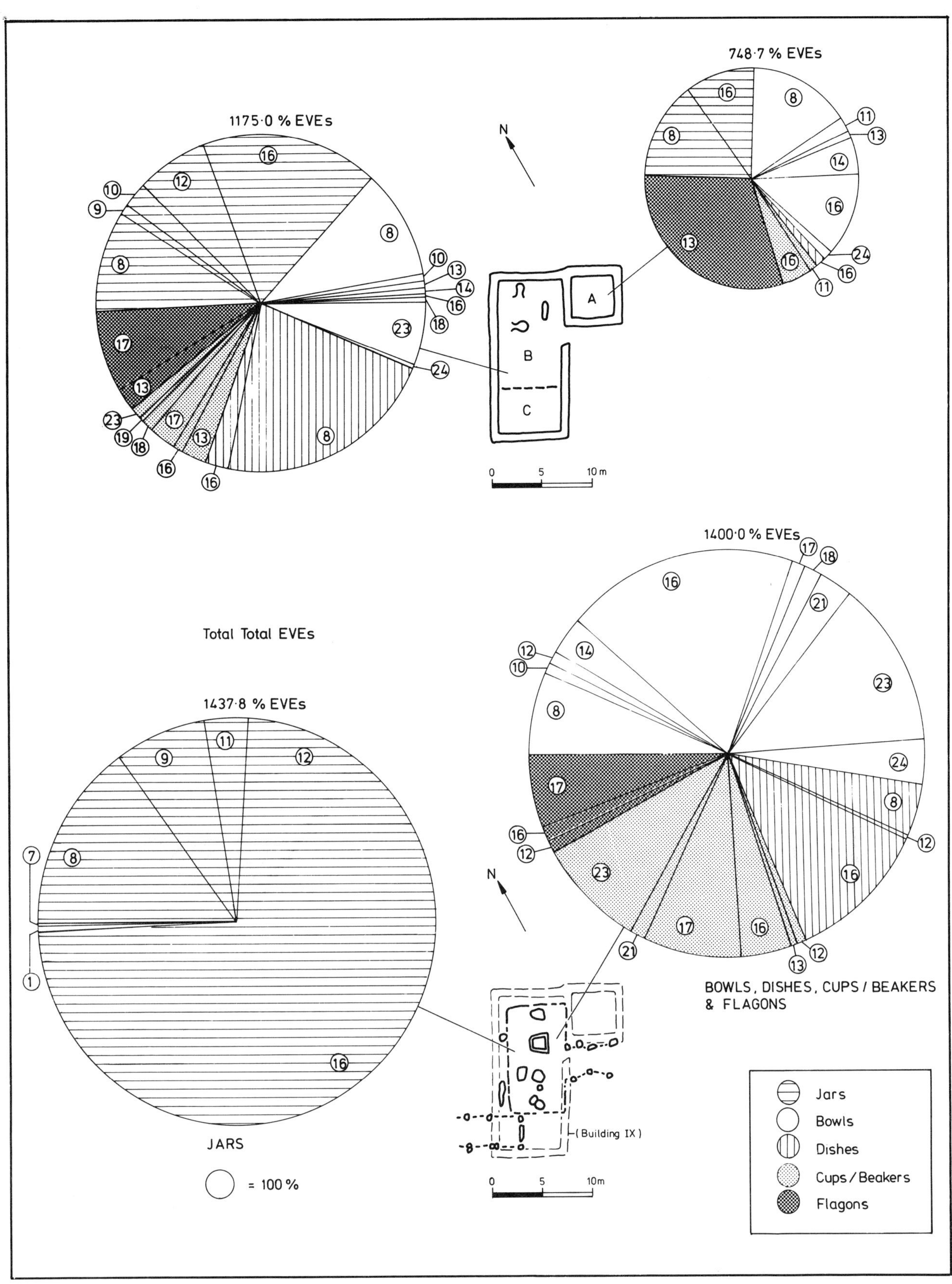

Fig 179 Pottery forms and fabrics, Structure IX, Phases 5a–c, and Structure XIV, Phases 5d–?6 as estimated vessel equivalent (EVE) percentages

as occurring in the overall chronological quantification of fabric types (see Phases 4–6 above).

All the analyses of pottery from these ancillary buildings in the temple precinct reflect very mixed assemblages of essentially domestic content. Variations within the pottery groups may reflect differing activities within the various rooms, but unless these activities have a demonstrable and exclusive relationship with the use of certain vessel types, interpretation of function within specific areas of the site is not likely to be achieved. This is difficult even for areas where there is an accumulation of structural and other artefactual evidence. Where contrasts are most evident, and samples are of a sufficiently large size, eg between Room A and Rooms B and C in Structure IX, the underlying reasons for the contrast may not be explicable, or if reasons can be suggested, need not relate to apparently comparable circumstances elsewhere on the site.

Finally, the pottery from the Romano-Celtic temple, Structure II and its environs, were analysed (Fig 180). The results here are perhaps the least satisfactory in terms of functional indications. Only by combining the material from all the rooms and for an extended period, could a sufficiently large sample be obtained. The consequent diagram closely resembles those obtained for the ancillary buildings, and suggests no different pattern which might suggest a religious function. It is difficult to assess whether otherwise domestic vessels might have been employed or deposited within the temple in a ritual or religious context as there are few features of the pottery which would make it possible to distinguish domestic from ritual use. Two further deposits, interpreted as successive clearances of the contents and fabric of Structure II, were also available for analysis. Assuming that the interpretation is correct, both deposits could be assumed to represent the ceramics present at two separate and late phases of the temple's life.

In terms of content neither group appears to be particularly distinctive, and reflects reasonably well the overall assemblage of forms and fabrics within their respective phases. Despite differences in detail, contrasts between these groups and the content of other pottery groups from buildings in the precinct, notably the temple, are not outstanding. Quantitative comparisons between the two deposits may reflect changes in the availability of pottery by the end of the fourth century, given the much smaller assemblage from a much larger volume of material in Phase 6b. This could also be accounted for if the pottery had accumulated within a shorter period following the Phase 5e clearance, or if it was derived from a different portion of the building which had not been cleared in the earlier phase.

Clearly there are too many variables and uncertainties, not least in our understanding of the role of pottery in a late Roman pagan religious precinct, to be able to draw many fundamental conclusions from this study. The most important aspect is the evidence for pottery surviving in currency, albeit in a religious, (and therefore possibly ultra conservative), context, well into the fifth century.

This report has sought to identify and characterise the West Hill ceramic assemblage, to attempt to highlight functional, spatial and chronological trends, and to suggest something of its cultural context. It is hoped that its value will be enhanced by future study and publication of other contemporary or complementary pottery collections from sites both within and beyond the region, as well as by the application of similar basic quantitative and analytical techniques.

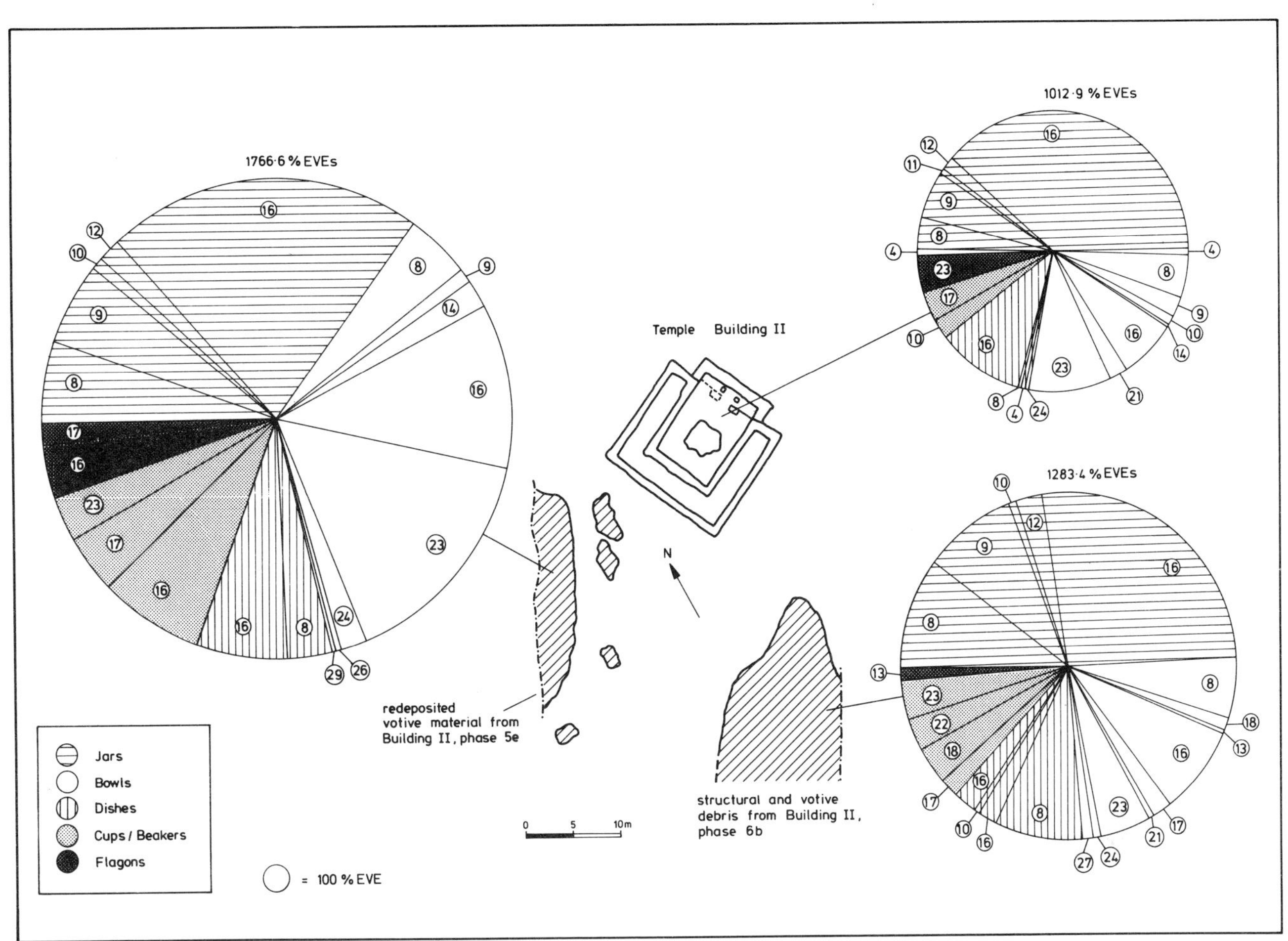

Fig 180 Pottery forms and fabrics, Structure II, Phases 5–6b as estimated vessel equivalent (EVE) percentages

12 Biological and environmental analysis

Plant macrofossils, arthropods and charcoal

by the late Maureen Girling and Vanessa Straker

Introduction

A small number of samples was collected during the excavation and processed later in the laboratory to extract macroscopic plant and animal remains. Sub-samples from the following contexts were examined:

Sub-sample 142, 500gm, *Context 842, fill of ritual pit F836, Phase 2*
Sub-sample 143, 500gm, *Context 885, ground surface associated with Context F836, Phase 2*
Sub-sample 83, 250gm, *Context 924, pit F251, burnt fill in pit F257, Phase 2c*
Samples II–VI, each 2kg, *Context 188b, fill of latrine pit, Structure I, Room K, Phase 5a–d*
Sub-sample 190, 500gm, *Context 22, over Structure I, clear-out from Temple, Phase 5eii*

The samples were wet sieved to a minimum mesh size of 250 microns and sorted using a binocular microscope. With the exception of the late-Roman latrine pit, context 188b, the samples contained only occasional small bones or bone fragments and molluscs. No plant remains were preserved and no further sub-samples were processed.

The situation was different with the late-Roman latrine pit, context 188b, excavated within Room K of Structure I. This contained mineralised fragments of arthropods, mineralised seeds, small bones, occasional molluscs and concretions. The last are described by Bell (1981, AM Lab report 3389) who concluded that they were probably fossil faecal material. Some definite coprolites were also preserved and some of these are probably of goat and rat. These have not been examined further.

Further sub-samples (to a total of 2kg each) were wet sieved, flotation or wash-over techniques being inappropriate for the extraction of mineralised material which does not float. All the material coarser than 500 microns was examined, as well as a proportion of the finer fraction, which was found to contain virtually no plant or animal remains. Nomenclature is according to Clapham *et al*, 1962.

Mineralisation

The process of mineralisation and its effects upon seeds and arthropods has been described by Green (1979), Girling (1979) and Carruthers (forthcoming).

It is probable that the chemical conditions required for mineral replacement of plant and animal tissue were available as a result of the quantities of excreta and animal bone in context 188b, the latrine pit, and possibly also because of the calcareous substrate.

The brown limestone soils are well drained and plant remains would not survive in such soils unless carbonised or, as in this case, mineralised. Little is known about the precise conditions and timescale required for mineral replacement to occur, but it has now been observed on a variety of soils with differing drainage properties. It is usually assumed that calcium, phosphate, and semi-liquid conditions are required for this replacement to occur. Such conditions occur in garderobes and cess pits and thus mineralised plant remains are usually found on sites of medieval date, although finds have been made on Late Iron Age, Roman, and Saxon sites, as well as in the Bronze Age midden at Potterne (Green 1979; Carruthers forthcoming).

Carruthers (*ibid*) has noted that certain seeds have a predisposition to mineralisation, while others, cereal grains and seeds of leguminous plants for example, may be under represented. Green (1979) noted that it is often only the softer tissues of the seed which become mineralised. The fact that the seed coat or testa is often missing hinders identification. It is normally the characteristic sculpturing of the outer surface of the seed coat, associated with other aspects of seed morphology, which allows accurate identification to be made.

Plant and animal macrofossils

The plant remains are listed in Table 10. Examination of the habitats in which these plants are usually found, and the uses they can be put to by man, suggests that grassland, food, and cultivated or waste ground plants are represented, and these three groupings can be recognised in each of the levels looked at, sample II being the uppermost fill which was examined. (*See also* Girling and Straker, 1989, AM Lab report 45/89)

Grassland plants

As Table 10 shows, a number of taxa are usually associated with grassland communities. These communities are complex and their particular characteristics, which might be detectable in the archaeological record, are affected by a number of factors including soil type, underlying geology, flooding and management. Tansley (1939) regards grasslands as natural communities which have been extended and exploited by man. He points out that the broad classification of grasslands according to their use: notably meadows, which are usually mown for hay; and pastures, which are grazed, is of the utmost importance ecologically as these different uses can result in the development of very different plant communities. In practice, most meadows which are cut for hay are also grazed for limited periods, such as the MG4 and MG5 meadows described by Rodwell (1992) where grazing of the aftermath is permitted.

The only unimproved grassland which survives on the Cotswolds today is the Association Cirsio-Brometum which has developed over Inferior Oolite, the older formation of the Oolite series. This ungrazed or lightly grazed grassland is most common on the steep north and west facing scarp slopes (Shimwell 1971b). Unfortunately no descriptions are available for unimproved hay meadows on limestone in southern England. Such a community would probably be somewhere between the Cirsio-Brometum described by Shimwell (1971b) and the Centaureo-Cynosuretum

Table 10: Mineralised plant remains from context 188b, latrine pit

FAMILY / *Taxon* (common name)	*habitat/use*	*Samples* II	III	IV	V	VI
POLYPODIACEAE						
Pteridium aquilinium (L) Kuhn pinnules (Bracken)	scrub, heaths	15	24	15	1	-
CRUCIFERAE						
gen et sp. indet		-	2	-	-	2
HYPERICACEAE						
Hypericum sp. (St John's Wort)	varied	-	-	1	-	-
CARYOPYLLACEAE						
cf Silene sp. (Campion)	varied	1	-	-	-	-
Stellaria media agg. (Stitchwort)	cultivated land, woods	-	-	1	-	-
CHENOPODIACEAE						
Chenopodium/Atriplex spp.		1	2	-	-	-
CHENOPODIACEAE/CARYOPHYLLACEAE						
gen et sp. indet		-	-	1	-	-
LEGUMINOSAE						
gen et sp. indet		-	1	-	-	-
cf Lotus corniculatus L. (Birdsfoot-trefoil)	grassland, hay meadow	-	2	-	-	-
Trifolium cf pratense L.(pod) (Clover)	grassland, hay meadow	-	1	-	-	-
ROSEACEAE						
Malus/Pyrus sp. (Apple/Pear)	scrub (edible)	2	6	-	-	1
Rubus fruticosus L. (Blackberry)	scrub (edible)	5	12	16	-	3
R. fruticosus/idaeus (Blackberry/Raspberry)	scrub (edible)	-	2	-	-	-
Malus sylvestris Mill. (Apple)	scrub (edible)	7	12	2	-	2
UMBELLIFERAE						
Apium graveolens L. (Wild celery)	damp ground, brackish water (edible)	-	1	-	-	-
POLYGONACEAE						
Polygonum aviculare group (Knotgrass)	cultivated land, woods, esp light soils	2	11	7	-	2
P. *cf persicaria* L. (Persicaria)	cultivated land, woods	-	-	1	-	-
Rumex sp. (Sorrel)	varied	-	2	1	-	-
URTICACEAE						
Urtica dioica L. (Stinging nettle)	varied, esp phosphorous enriched	-	1	-	-	-
Urtica urens L. (Small nettle)	cultivated land, woods	-	-	2	-	1
MORCAEAE						
Morus nigra L. (Mulberry)	cultivated (edible)	-	1	3	-	-
SCROPHULARIACEAE						
Rhinanthus cf minor L. (Yellow rattle)	grassland, hay meadow	-	8	-	-	-
LABIATAE						
Prunella vulgaris L. (Self Heal)	grassland, hay meadow	-	-	1	-	-
gen et sp. indet		-	-	-	-	1
CAPRIFOLIACEAE						
Sambucus nigra L. (Elder)	woods (edible)	-	-	1	-	-
COMPOSITAE						
Centaurea cf. nigra (Lesser knapweed)	grassland, hay meadow	-	3	1	-	-
cf Centaurea sp. (*cf* Knapweed)	varied, grassland, hay meadow	-	1	-	-	-
GRAMINEAE						
gen et sp. indet (spikelet fork)	varied, grassland	2	2	-	1	-
gen et sp. indet (caryopsis)	varied, grassland	1	14	1	-	2
gen et sp. indet (portion of ear)	varied, grassland	2	2	-	-	-
Cereals						
Avena sp. (Oats, spikelets)	wild or cultivated	-	-	-	-	2
Triticum sp. (Wheat, glume base)	cultivated	1	-	-	-	-
gen et sp. indet (straw fragments)			-	2	-	-
Other mineralised items						
gen et sp. indet (bran fragment)		+	+	+	-	-
unidentified seeds, general		17	40	54	-	4
bud, unidentified		1	-	-	-	-
stem fragments		+	+	+	+	+
arthropod fragments		+	+	+	-	+
worm eggs		+	+	+	+	+
total		57	152	108	2	20

+ = present
All plant macrofossils, unless otherwise stated are 'seeds'

cristati described as MG5 (Rodwell 1992). It is therefore difficult to interpret this assemblage with the confidence that is possible with, for example, grassland assemblages on the Thames floodplain (Lambrick and Robinson 1988).

The particular problems and potential of interpreting archaeobotanical grassland assemblages and their use for indicating the management of grasslands have been described in detail by Greig 1984 and Lambrick and Robinson (*ibid*).

It is dificult to argue for a particular biotype from the absence of certain species when working with archaeological deposits, because of taphonomic processes and, in the case of mineralised seeds, as the susceptibility of particular seeds to mineralisation is not fully understood. The following suggestions are therefore tentative. It is possible that the grassland plants were brought to the site as hay for animal fodder. *Centaurea nigra* (Lesser Knapweed) and *Rhinanthus* sp. (Yellow Rattle) will grow in pasture but are not common, whereas they are particularly characteristic of hay meadows. Calcicoles such as *Poterium sanguisorba* (Salad Burnet) and *Scabiosa columbaria* (Scabious), which are characteristic of Mesobromion grassland (Shimwell 1971), were not identified. Bracken was present in the assemblage and probably grew on more acid drift deposits further away from the limestone scarp. It may have been used for animal (or human) bedding. Had the hay also been cut from grassland growing on acid soil, other acid ground species such as *Potentilla erecta* (Tormentil) would also be expected. It is also unlikely that the hay came from a flood meadow as the only plant characteristic of at least a seasonally waterlogged habitat is *Apium graveolens* (Celery) and this was probably a food plant.

Bearing these points in mind, and the fact that we cannot assume that the composition of grasslands was in the past the same as for modern day survivors, the most likely phytosocological association which can be suggested using present day observations is the Centaureo-Cynosuretum cristati (Braun *et al* 1952), an unimproved hay meadow on circumneutral brown soils, which is usually grazed after the hay is mown in June until April, when the fields are shut up and, traditionally, lightly dressed with farmyard manure (Rodwell, 1992). This is the typical grassland of grazed hay meadows common on the brown soils of lowland Britain. The flora of this grassland includes several taxa which occur in the Uley asemblage:

Lotus corniculatus (bird's foot trefoil)
Prunella vulgaris (self-heal) *Centaurea* sp. (probably *nigra* lesser knapweed)
Rumex sp. (sorrel) *Rhinanthus* sp. (yellow rattle)
Trifolium sp. (probably *pratense*, red clover)

The remains of hay used for fodder in Roman Britain have been noted before by Greig (1984) and Wilson (1979). Wilson (*ibid*) identified seeds of grassland taxa among an assemblage preserved in horse dung from a well in second-century Lancaster. She also quotes classical sources who describe how Roman horses were fed; their diet included barley, spelt, oats, grass, and hay.

Many goat bones were also recovered from the excavation (*Levitan below*). The presence of hay in the plant record has given rise to the suggestion that these animals were stalled on the site and given hay as fodder while there. This suggestion is further supported by the presence of mineralised coprolites in the latrine pit, some of which are comparable with the description of goat droppings by Bang and Dahlstrom (1972). The presence of the coprolites and hay remains in combination suggests that sweepings from stalls may have been thrown into the latrine pit. On sites with other differing types of occupation such waste might well have been used as manure and thus not have been recovered.

Food plants

The edible plants present in context 188b, the latrine pit, are all previously known from Roman Britain, though usually such evidence has been recovered as a result of preservation in waterlogged conditions. Apples, blackberries, and elder, plants of hedges, woods, scrub, and waste ground, would all have been easy to obtain locally. Seeds of wild celery (*Apium graveolens*) are indistinguishable from those of the cultivated plant. Celery seeds were a spice favoured by the Romans (Apicius; Greig 1983) and as wild celery is a plant of brackish water it is unlikely that it had been growing locally and must have been transported or traded as a food seasoning. Celery seeds were also present in quantity from Roman deposits at Mount Farm, Oxfordshire (M Robinson, personal comment). Celery can of course also be used as a vegetable, but the stems would usually be cut for this purpose before the seeds had set.

The mulberry (*Morus nigra*) is not native to Britain but has previously been recorded in Roman deposits such as those in London (Willcox 1977). Mulberries could therefore have been imported, either dried, or in the form of preserves, but equally plants could have been introduced and grown in Britain (Greig 1983).

The cereals: a glume base of hulled wheat, an oat floret and cereal bran, and also the other plants, could have been consumed either by humans or animals.

Plants of cultivated and waste ground

The final group of plants present in the context 188b latrine pit are associated with disturbed ground or waste places and include:

Stellaria media group (stitchwort)
Polygonum aviculare group (knotgrass)
P. persicaria (persicaria)
Urtica dioica and *U. urens* (stinging nettle and small nettle)

Stinging nettle is especially characteristic of phosphorus enriched soils (Piggot and Taylor 1964) and the small nettle has a preference for light soils (Clapham, Tutin and Warburg 1962). Although some of the plants in this group could have been associated with the cereals in the deposit, they could equally well have grown around the temple area which may have provided those areas of disturbed ground and nitrogen enriched soils which are common in and around areas of human activity. Elder, a useful food plant, is also particularly characteristic of disturbed base and nitrogen rich soils.

Arthropods

As mentioned above, mineralised remains of arthropods were extracted from all levels within the context 188b latrine pit. Those from a 200gm sub-sample from the basal fill of the latrine pit were examined by Dr M Girling. She identified the following:

Insecta
Coleoptera (beetles)
  Staphylinidae: indeterminate – abdominal segments
  Carabidae/staphylinida: indeterminate – larval head
Hymenoptera (ants, bees, wasps, sawflies)
  Parasitica indeterminate
Diptera (flies)
  Indeterminate – larval and pupal remains
Myriapoda (centipedes and millipedes) – indeterminate
Isopoda (woodlice) Porcellionidae:
  Porcellio sp.
  Porcellio sp. juvenile specimen

The following notes are taken from Dr Girling's report (Girling 1981, AM Lab report 3377). The insect and woodlice remains were partially replaced and in the context 188b latrine pit it is probable that the phosphates and other organic compounds were complexed with the calcium carbonate in the replaced skeletons of the arthropods. The fauna is dominated by puparia and larvae of flies (Diptera) suggesting that they were breeding in the pit. Woodlice, the other main element in the sample, are general scavengers and are common in damp conditions with mould and decaying animal or vegetable debris. Their exoskeleton contains calcium carbonate and so they are very susceptible to calcium phosphate replacement.

A similar range of replaced arthropods was identified by Maureen Girling at Potterne, Wiltshire (Carruthers forthcoming) and it was observed that the adult cuticle is usually not replaced, whereas the tissues of the juvenile stages appear to mineralise readily.

Conclusion

The groups of plant and animal remains studied from the context 188b latrine pit suggest, as might be anticipated, that human excrement was present, and that there was much rotting organic material on which colonies of flies lived and bred. Perhaps more interesting is the evidence for animal fodder in the form of hay cut from a managed grassland, probably not dissimilar to the relicts of a type of unimproved hay meadow which still survives in some areas of lowland Britain today. It is probable that this represents the remains of hay fed to the goats which are suggested to have been kept in the vicinity of the temple.

Charcoal

The samples were collected from a wide variety of contexts, most of which are interpreted as of ritual significance. It was hoped that exotic, possibly imported wood might be present in the assemblage, but this proved not to be the case. The results of the identification are given below:

Taxon
Fraxinus excelsior L Ash, *Context 262, F264, Phase 2d–3a*
Salix sp. or *Populus* sp., Willow or Poplar, *Context 255, pre Structure VIII, Phase 3–5*

Fraxinus excelsior L, *Context 422, Structure VII, Phase 3b*
Cf *Carpinus betulus* L, Hornbeam, *Context 383, F382, Phase 3b*
Acer campestre L, Field Maple, *Context 127, F179, Phase 3c*
Quercus sp., Oak, *Context 520, F179, Phase 3c*
Corylus avellana L or *Alnus glutinosa* (L) Gaertn, Hazel or Alder, *Context 520, F179, Phase 3c*
Quercus sp., *Context 520, F179, Phase 3c*
Corylus avellana L, *Context 520, F179, Phase 3c*
Alnus glutinosa (L) Gaertn, *Context 520, F179, Phase 3c*
Corylus avellana/Alnus glutinosa (L) Gaertn, *Context 520, F179, Phase 3c*
Quercus sp., Oak, *Context 33, Structure ? Courtyard, Phase 4–6*
Quercus sp., twig, 5 years old, *Context 171, below Structure I, Phase 4a*
Quercus sp., *Context 351, Structure IV, Phase 4a*
Cf Pomoideae, Hawthorn, Apple, etc, *Context 369, Structure IV, Phase 4b*
Quercus sp., *Context 369, Structure IV, Phase 4b*
Corylus avellana L, *Context 451, pre Structure VIII, Phase 4–5*
Quercus sp., *Context 512, pre Structure I, Phase 4a*
Fraxinus excelsior L, *Context 63, Structure I, Phase 5e(i)*
Pomoideae, *Context 67, Structure I, Phase 5e(i)*
Pomoideae, *Context 184, Structure I, Phase 5a–d*
Quercus sp., *Context 187, Structure I, Phase 5e(ii)*
Quercus sp., *Context 208, Structure II, Phase 5d–6*
Acer campestre L, *Context 208, Structure II, Phase 5d–6*
Quercus sp., *Context 346, Structure IV, Phase 5d*
Corylus avellana L, *Context 519, Structure I, Phase 5e(i)*
Corylus avellana L, *Context 95, Structure II, Phase 6a*
Quercus sp., *Context 204, Structure II, Phase 6a*
Corylus avellana L or *Alnus glutinosa* (L) Gaertn sp, *Context 204, Structure II, Phase 6a*
Quercus sp., *Context 224, Structure II, Phase 6a*
Quercus sp., *Context 462, Structure II, Phase 6a*
Pomoideae, *Context 462, Structure II, Phase 6a*
Alnus glutinosa (L) Gaertn, *Context 206, Structure II, Phase 6b*
Pomoideae, *Context 424, Structure VII, Phase 7*
Quercus sp.,*Context 426, Structure VII, Phase 7*
Fraxinus excelsior L, *Context 426, Structure VII, Phase 7*
Fraxinus excelsior L, *Context 426, Structure VII, Phase 7*
Fraxinus excelsior L, *Context 428, Structure VII, Phase 7*
Quercus sp.,*Context 430, Structure VII, Phase 7*

Taxon	*common name*	*context*
Quercus sp.	Oak	15
Fraxinus excelsior	Ash	6
Pomoideae	Hawthorn etc	6
Corylus avellana	Hazel	4
Corylus/Alnus	Hazel/Alder	3
Acer campestre	Field Maple	2
Alnus sp.	Alder	2
cf *Carpinus betulus*	Hornbeam	1
Salix sp./*Populus* sp.	Willow/Poplar	1

The charcoal was not quantified by weight because of lack of information about how it was collected. The relative abundance of the taxa, in terms of the number of contexts in which they were recorded, seemed a more appropriate basis for comparison. Oak and ash and Pomoideae (Hawthorn etc) were the most abundant. This group includes hawthorn, apple, pear, rowan, and whitebeam, which cannot be reliably differentiated on the basis of wood anatomy. All the trees are native to the British Isles, would have been well established in Roman Britain, and easily obtainable locally. Most of the species are woodland or hedgerow trees, though hazel and Pomoideae are also characteristic of scrub or secondary woodland vegetation. The willow or poplar probably came from farthest afield as these trees prefer damper conditions than the other species present. The hornbeam is not a definite identification as the sample is poorly preserved. Hornbeam is confined generally to areas of southern and eastern England and only small areas are said to occur farther west (Rackham 1980), and so if this identification is correct, it is interesting to record an occurrence in this area.

With the exception of one oak twig, all the charcoal appears to derive from mature wood.

Land mollusca

by Beverley Meddens

During the 1978 excavations 158 samples were taken for mollusc analysis. Methods described by Evans 1972 were used for extraction and identification. Despite excellent preservation of the shells the numbers extracted were disappointingly low. The samples were taken from stratified deposits which span the whole occupation of the site from the pre-Roman Iron Age to the post-Roman phases. It was hoped that the results would reflect any changes in the immediate environment that had occurred in and around the site during these periods. Unfortunately palaeosoils were not generally present on the site and therefore samples were mostly taken from ditches. The major disadvantage of samples from ditches is that the fauna recovered may reflect the micro-environment of the ditch rather than the surrounding areas. However, as large numbers of samples were taken, it was hoped that if results consistent across the site within each phase were obtained, then the possibility of an interesting outcome would be greater, despite the nature of the deposits. Due to pressure of time, alternate samples only were analysed throughout most of the columns. The more productive columns are discussed below: the remainder are shown in MF Fig 2.

Figure 181 shows the positions of the published sample columns and the analyses are presented in a series of abundance diagrams in Figure 182.

Results

Ditch F816

Section 99 (Figs 181 and 182, *see also Fig 18*) cut through the shallow flat-bottomed enclosure ditch F816 of Iron Age date. Sample 220/19, from context 849, the primary fill, Phase 2, contained a woodland fauna with typical components such as *Discus rotundatus* and *Acicula fusca*. Sample 222/3, from context 803, the later fill, Phase 3 (late first to early second century AD), shows an increase in *Vallonia costata* and *Vallonia excentrica* combined with a decrease in shade-loving species. This could indicate a response by an 'open country' fauna to a newly created more open habitat around the enclosure.

Section 13 (Figs 181 and 182, *see also Fig 49*) was sampled by means of two columns located to cut the two palisade trenches visible in this section of ditch 816.

Column I cut the palisade trench F845. Sample 192, from the primary fill, contained very few mollusca. The presence here of *Helicella itala*, an obligatory heliophile, conflicts with the overall shade-loving fauna. Samples 193–6, from the upper palisade fills of Phases 2 to 3a show a substantial increase in *Vallonia* species. Again this could represent the response of the molluscs to clearance.

In column II sample 198, from context 849, the primary fill, although low in numbers, does contain a woodland fauna similar to that in section 99. These samples could be interpreted as indicating a woodland environment in the area, around the time the ditches were dug. Sample 201, from F853, the upper palisade ditch fill of Phases 2 to 3 (first century AD), again shows an increase in open country species. The continued presence of *Discus rotundatus* could suggest that shady woodland habitats were close by during this period.

Ditch segment F264

Section 54 (Figs 181 and 182, *see also Fig 21*) crossed the deep ditch constructed and modified through Phases 1 to 4. Three columns were cut through the fills in this feature.

Columns I and IV sampled the same layers except the top layer. They should therefore be considered together. In both columns there is one sample that contains substantially more snails than the other samples. In both it seems that the interface between contexts 733 and 758 might be of particular interest, with samples 59 and 123/4 containing a dry grassland fauna. Although the numbers are small in the later samples both columns show an overall decrease in open country species.

Interestingly column III, cut mainly through context 755, the Roman palisade ditch fill of Phase 3, contained open woodland fauna. These samples contained many more shade-loving species, and more catholic species, than those contained in columns I and IV, and fewer open country species, perhaps suggesting a little more vegetative cover.

Structure XIX, bank

Late Roman soils from section 106 (Figs 181 and 182), samples 225 and 227, related to the late Roman courtyard and contained few open country species. The presence of *Discus rotundatus* could imply more vegetation cover, but this soon gave way to open country once more in the post-Roman period (Layer 602) and on into the medieval and modern ploughsoils.

Conclusions

The numbers of snails recovered were generally low and this has made interpretation difficult because it is all the more possible that the population is not representative of the surrounding environment. Also it is difficult to determine whether ditch deposits might have supported a live snail population or were dumped material. A third factor which is important is that many of the recovered faunas were of a mixed nature. How-

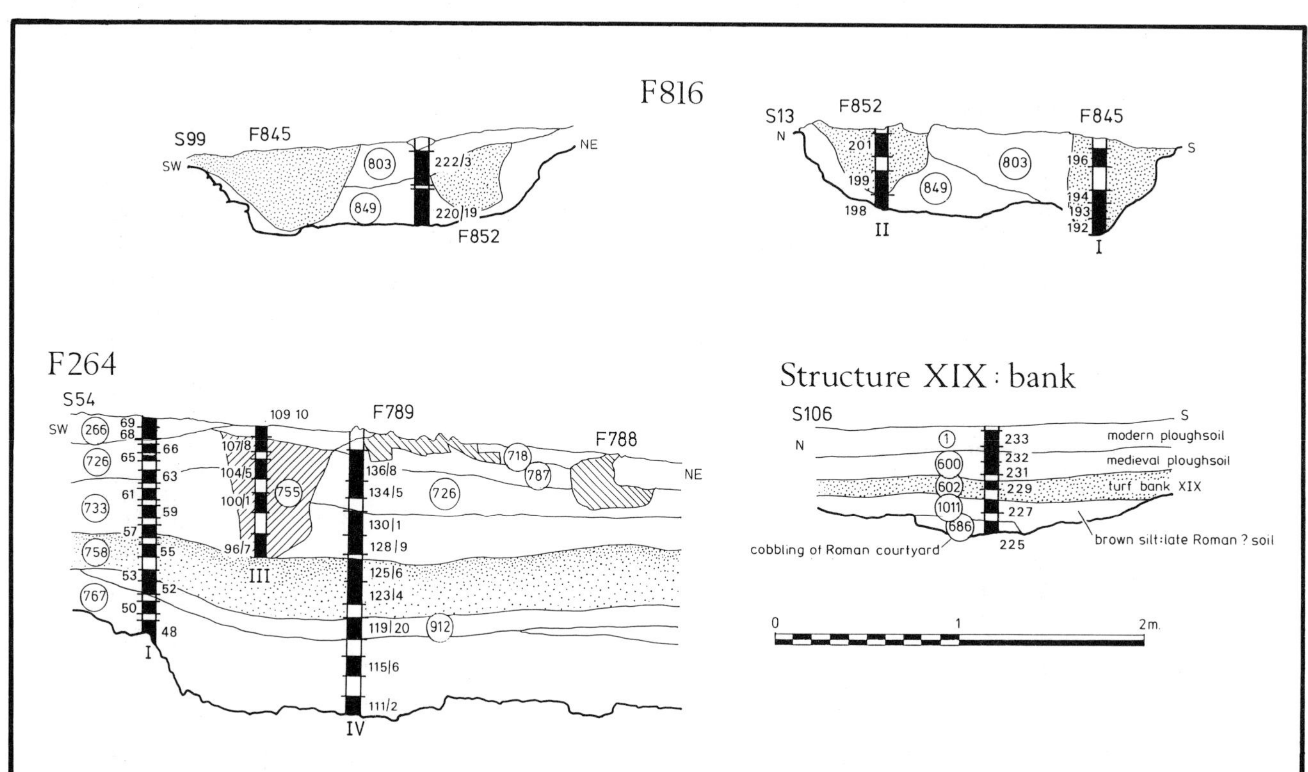

Fig 181 Land mollusca: location of sample columns

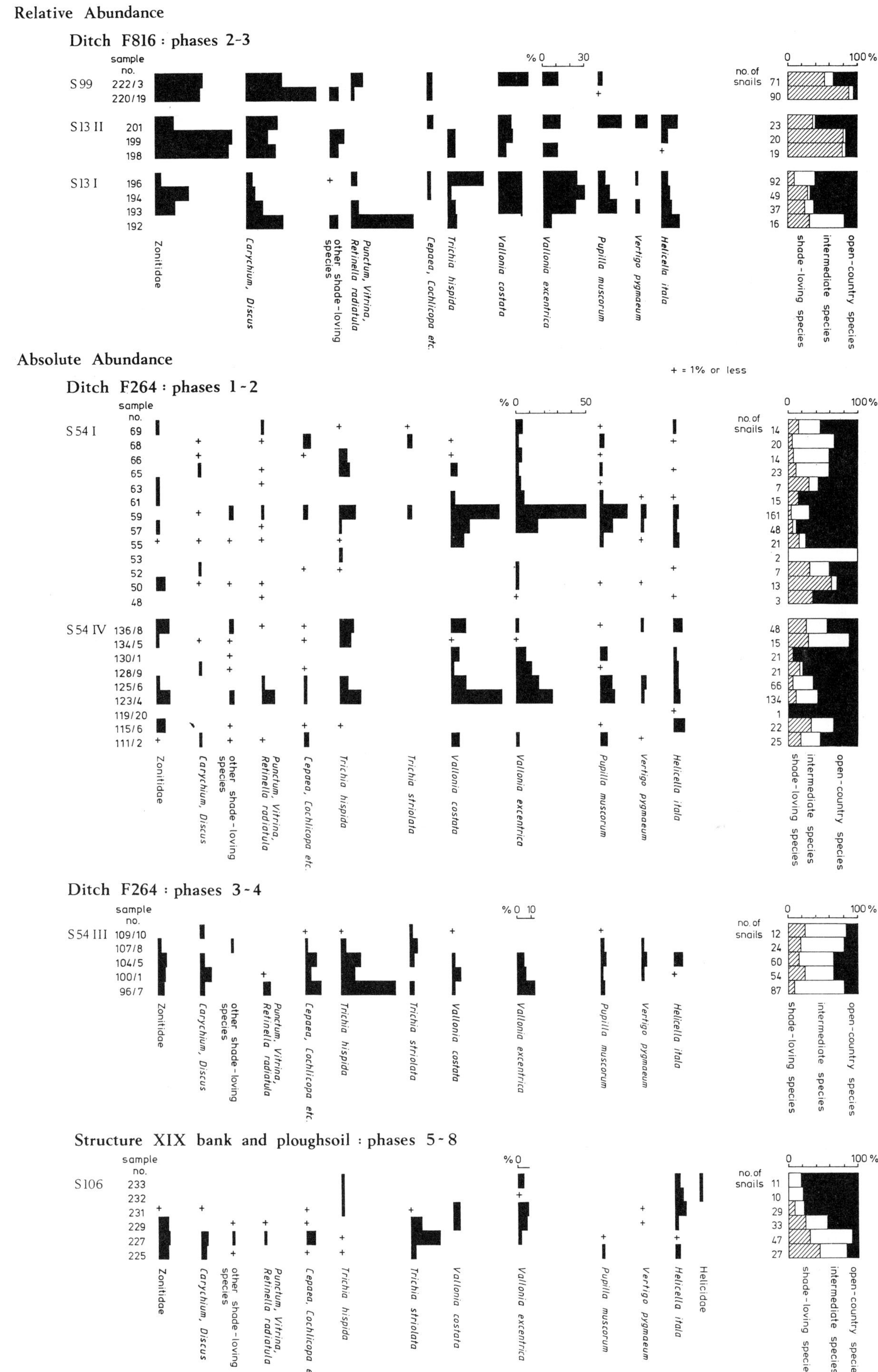

Fig 182 Land mollusca: abundance diagrams

ever it is possible to make some statements with a little caution.

Initially when the Late Iron Age ditches were dug the environment was one of woodland, as shown in the primary fills of sections 99 and 13 but not in section 96. Relatively quickly the proportion of species preferring open country habitats increased and throughout the first centuries BC and AD, with the building of more palisades, the environment became more open. By the mid-first century AD when the large ditch segment F264 was partly filled, the immediate environment of the site was quite open. During the periods of construction and use of the temple and courtyard, there is very little molluscan evidence, but high numbers of *Trichia striolata*, a synanthropic species in sample 227, section 106 may indicate the proximity of hedgerows and gardens. Finally the 'open woodland' of the immediate post-Roman period (Phase 7) gave way to arable farming by the medieval period.

Human remains

by Lynne Bell and Juliet Rogers

Bones from at least eight individuals – three adult, one immature, and four infants – were received for examination. They date largely from the Late Iron Age and Roman periods, although some disarticulated frag-

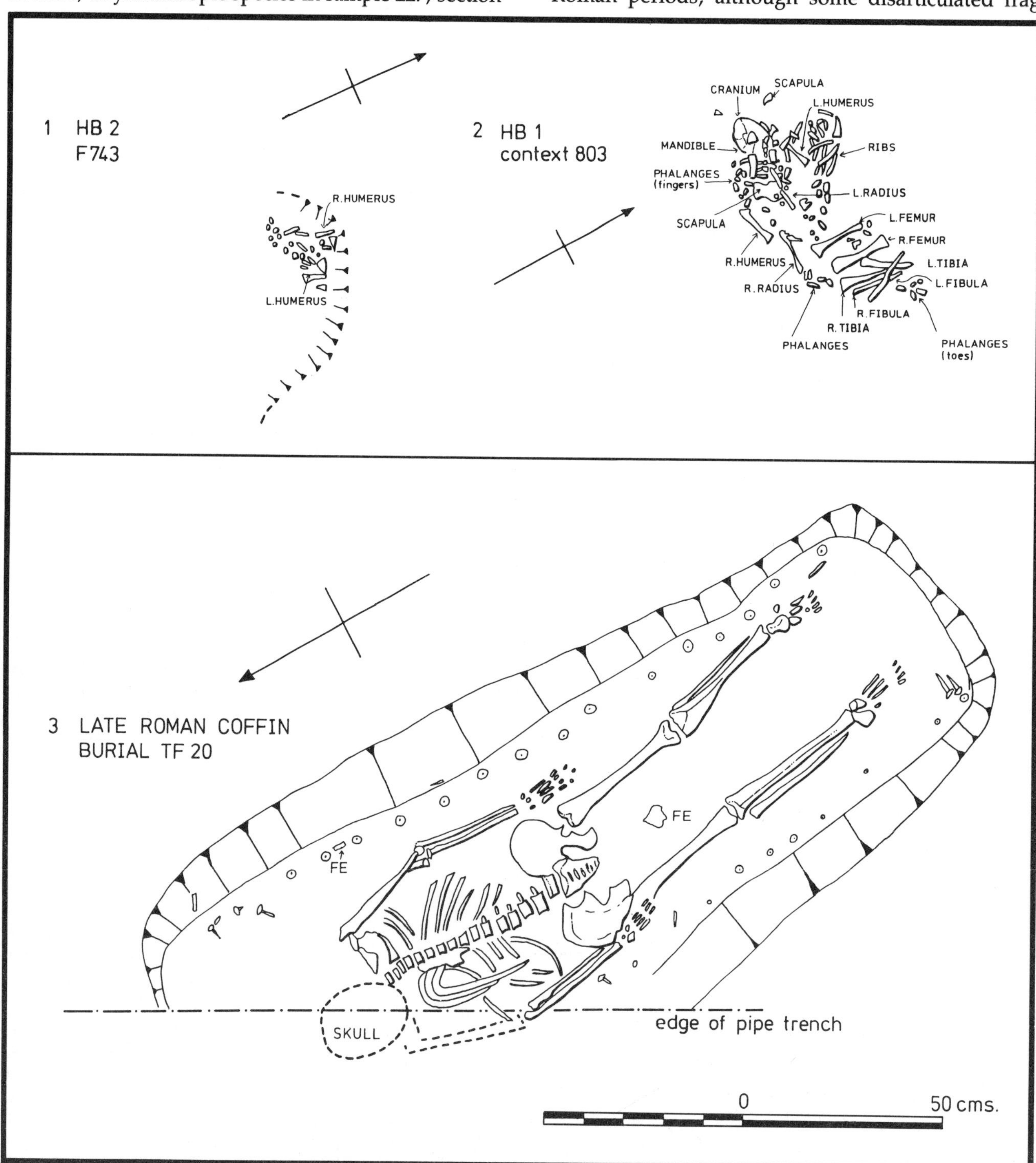

Fig 183 Plans of human burials

ments from later contexts are present. All the skeletons were in either a fragmented or disarticulated condition, and some reconstruction work had to be undertaken before the study could be completed. Each skeleton was then examined and biometric measurements taken wherever possible.

The sex of adults was deduced from the relevant features of the skull and pelvic bones. The age was estimated from the degree of epiphyseal fusion and the state of tooth eruption and wear (Brothwell 1972). Information on the dentition is given by the dental formula based on Brothwell's system (*ibid*, 47)

Articulated bone

Pre-Roman Iron Age

Fig 183
1 HB2: a child skeleton of indeterminate sex. The age is considered to be approximately seven to nine months, as indicated by teeth having not erupted, and also there is no fusion of the epiphyses. The skeleton was 80% present, *Find no 784, Structure XVI, Phase 3a*

Later first century AD

2 HB1: another child skeleton of indeterminate sex; 80–90% of the skeleton was present in a fragmented state; the skull and palate were partially present, as was the entire unfused vertebral column. Age is considered to be approximately twelve months, since the teeth had partially erupted and there was no fusion of the epiphyses.

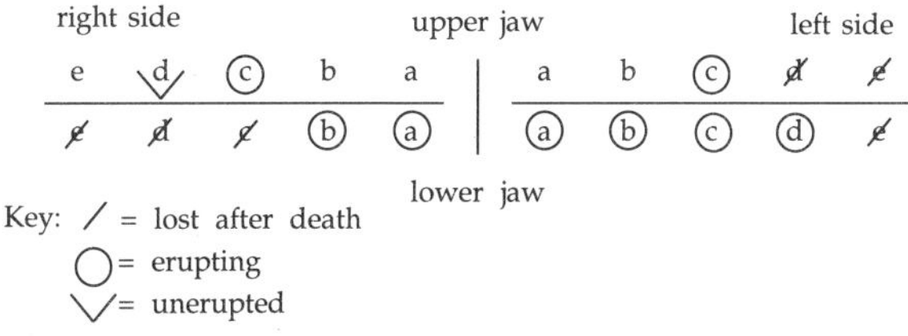

Extra teeth (unerupted) were one crown and one incisor, *Find 5670, context 803, Structure XVII, Phase 3a*

not illustrated
A further child skeleton of indeterminate sex. The skeleton was only 25% present and in a very fragmented state. The age is considered to be approximately nine to twelve months, *Find 5698, context F838, Structure XVII, Phase 3a*

Late Roman

3 A male skeleton aged between 25–35 years according to the dentition, 90% of the skeleton was present, although the skull, which lay within the pipe trench, was too fragmented to rebuild.

right side							upper jaw								left side
8̸	7	6	5	4	3̸	2̸	1̸	1̸	2	3	4	5	6	7	8
8	7	6	5	4	3̸	2̸	1̸	1	2	3	4	5	6	7	8
							lower jaw								

Pathology: Schmorl's node present on thoracic vertebrae at T10/T11 and T8/T9. Osteophytosis present on distal part of left and right femur,and also on three medial rib joints, *TF20, pipe trench, 1976*

Disarticulated bone

Iron Age

not illustrated
The shaft of the left femur and one adult molar, of which attrition gives an age of 45+ years, *Context 912, palisade packing in F264, Phase 2c*
One molar with caries and attrition which indicates an age of 25–35 years, *Context 750, fill of F751 in F264, Phase 3a*

Early Roman

not illustrated
One vertebral arch, one rib, one epiphysis, and one phalange (all unfused). The age is considered to be approximately nine months, *Context 157, fill of ditch F584, Phase 3c*
The proximal end of a damaged radius and also the distal end of the right third metatarsal. The bones appear adult as they are fused, *Context 357, floor of Room E, Structure IV, Phase 4a*

Late Roman

not illustrated
Left ilium which appears to belong to a nine-month-old baby, *Context 1220, Structure IXi, Room C, floor foundation for context 1216, Phase 5a*
One crown of a molar with no wear; therefore the age is considered to be below 17 years, *Context 67, fill of robber trench F64, Structure I, Phase 5e(i)*
One deciduous canine which therefore belongs to a child, *Context 1208, destruction over hearth F1284, Structure IX, Phase 5c*

Late Roman or later

not illustrated
A few skull fragments; the sutures present are fused, therefore the skull is adult, *Context 1191, general destruction over Structure XIV, Phase 5d–6b*
A few skull fragments (partial frontal and base) with fused sutures. These fragments are of adult age, *Context 1100, sub- ploughsoil over Structure XIV, Phase 7–8*
Two bone fragments, one of which is an adult rib, *Context 02, ploughsoil, Phase 8*

Vertebrate remains

by Bruce Levitan

The assemblage, totalling 232,322 fragments, was collected from a watching brief in 1976, during the three seasons of excavation between 1977 and 1979, and from fieldwalking in 1978.

Apart from its size, which is unusual for a rural site, there are a number of other aspects of this assemblage which make it unique and important. Firstly the bones are dominated by sheep/goat to an extent that is so far unprecedented from any other site in the country, with sheep/goat proportions as high as 90% or more in some periods. Secondly the sheep/goat bones that were identified to species level are mainly goats, this being the converse of the situation found at other sites in the country. Other factors include patterns of butchery on the sheep/goat bones and higher than usual proportions of domestic fowl bones. These aspects, together with other classes of site evidence, form a consistent pattern, which appears to relate to ritual practices, and the bulk of the bone assemblage appears to be related to ritual activities.

Tables, figures, and other supporting matter additional to the text below, are reproduced in fiche (and prefixed MF where referred to). The written archive is housed by the Environmental Archaeology Unit, University Museum, Oxford, and will eventually be transferred to the British Museum where the bones are housed.

Provenance and methods of recovery

Bones were recovered from all areas of the site, and all periods are represented. Lateral variation is considered an important factor since deposits from different areas of a site may reflect different activities. Thus, the location of the bone assemblages has been considered wherever relevant.

The recovery methods used were trowelling, use of mattock/pick/fork, with only a rapid sort through of the sediments, and on-site wet sieving of 'spoil' (only used in the 1979 season, Levitan 1982a, 30–32). Finally, some bones were recovered from laboratory samples (see Girling and Straker above).

Treatment and archive

The sample was so large it was necessary to use subsampling techniques as discussed in Levitan (1983b). A total of 108,997 fragments were examined, of which 77,878 (71.4%) were identified (Table 11). The following abbreviations are used throughout:

for quantification
NIF number of identified fragments
NIB number of identified bones (based on non-repeatable characteristics)
MNI minimum number of individuals
NFI number of fragments per individual (NIF divided by MNI)
NBI number of bones per individual (NIB divided by MNI)
SGF sheep/goat/fowl

for anatomical analysis
Group A axial bones excluding cervical vertebrae
Group B skull, cervical vertebrae, limb extremities
Group C girdles and upper limbs

The greatest problem in presenting bone identification analyses is the definition of identified. As far as possible every fragment was identified to the level of anatomy and taxon. Ribs and vertebrae were recorded as cattle or sheep/goat unless obviously of another species. Some of the cattle ribs may be of horse or other similar animals, and some sheep/goat may be roe deer or pig. However the majority of large-size mammals are cattle, and medium size ones sheep/goat, so the number of wrongly assigned ribs and vertebrae should be very small.

A problem with NIF counts is that highly fragmented bones may be over-represented relative to more complete ones (ie a fragmented bone may be counted more than once). Various methods have been employed to combat this kind of bias, eg epiphyses only counts (Grant 1975, 379) and minimum number of individuals estimates (Chaplin 1971, 69–75). Such methods do have the advantage of reducing the bias described above, but can introduce other kinds of bias, and they reduce sample size (see Uerpmann 1973, O'Connor 1985, for discussion of quantification methods). The method used here was based on the epiphyses only counts of Grant (1975, 379) and recorded non-repeatable characteristics for other skeletal parts as follows: vertebrae – anterior and posterior faces of centrum present; ribs – caput present; pelvis – acetabulum comprises at least two elements (eg ilium/pubis, ischium/ilium, etc); small bones such as carpals, tarsals, and phalanges where half or more of the bone was present; horncores – half or more of the core present (including cranial end); skull – at least frontals, parietal, and occipitals present. These figures are 'identified bones' (NIB).

Minimum numbers (MNI) were based on the method of Chaplin (1971, 69–75) but used the modifications described by Bourdillon and Coy (1980, 83) and took ageing evidence into account (eg if MNI of 12 obtained from mandibles, of which 7 have deciduous dentition, and MNI of 9 obtained from calcanei of which all have fused tubercles, then the final count would be 16: 9 adults plus 7 juveniles. In calculating MNI the unit of analysis was taken into account, and MNI estimates for rooms, for example, were not simply added to get MNI for a structure, but recalculated at each level (for a full discussion of the problem see Watson 1979, 127–8 and 137).

A good, simple method of estimating the amount of material lost and of variability between skeletal elements is the index of bones per individual (by element and by species totals) (Noddle 1977, 201). This average has been calculated using both fragments per individual (NFI) and identified bones per individual (NBI).

Anatomical representation gives detailed consideration to the individual elements, shown as triangular plots based on economic criteria (Halstead *et al* 1978, 121–4) drawn with the skeletal elements divided into three groups:
Group A axial bones excluding cervical vertebrae (thoracic, lumbar, and caudal vertebrae, sacrum and ribs),
Group B skull, mandibles, cervical vertebrae, and limb extremities (carpals, tarsals, metapodials, and phalanges),
Group C scapulae, pelves, and upper limb bones.

Bar graphs are used where samples are large enough, to compare individual context groups with phase (or sub-phase) totals, or to assess lateral variation (eg room floor deposits).

Ageing mainly used dental criteria (Grant 1975, and Payne 1973), but also epiphysial fusion where dental data were lacking. The work was done before Grant 1982 was published, but it was not thought necessary to modify the results to take account of it.

The criteria of Boessneck *et al* 1964 were used for separation of sheep and goat, but many problems were encountered due to the presence of many possibly sheep-like goats. In most assemblages sheep/goat bones may be confidently treated as sheep since goats are generally uncommon, but here goats can be shown to outnumber sheep and it is unwise to make this assumption. The terms 'sheep' or 'goat' are therefore here used only where identification is possible, otherwise the term sheep/goat is applied.

Machine-based methods of recording and analysis were not available for the analysis of this material, which was as a result carried out manually using record cards and record sheets. Because of this the collating and counting was exceptionally tedious and time consuming. To try to reduce calculation errors, routine checks were made, but error tracing was only employed where a second count showed a greater than 1% difference. It is probable therefore that not all calculation errors have been detected. Further errors may have been introduced where a context has been later reinterpreted as from a different sub-phase. Some attempt was made to accommodate such changes, but if the number of bones involved seemed too small to affect interpretation they were ignored. This will have lead to small inaccuracies, and as a result some summary tabulations do not correspond exactly with the tables and archive.

Where sample size was sufficient, analysis of sheep/goat anatomical representation included consideration of bones identified to species. The sheep and goat identifications were compared to assess the validity of analysis of sheep/goat bones as a single group. Large differences between the two species could be a source of bias in the analysis of both species together. It was found however that one species was often predominant and where one species did outnumber the other by a large margin, the biasing effect of combining them was considerably reduced. It was necessary to combine samples which were too small using species only, and also excluded parts of the anatomy not easily identified to species level (eg tibia).

Condition of the assemblage

Although the larger bones were often fragmentary, there is little evidence of weathering, chewing, or trampling, suggesting that the bones were not left open to the surface; exceptions to this are in small groups of bones from contexts in courtyard areas or bank deposits. Little evidence for burning is present, fresh breakage was more common, but generally the bones had been handled well. The bone analyst was present on site and supervised processing during all three seasons.

Analysis

The assemblage is considered as two distinct groups: the votive and the non-votive assemblage. The non-votive assemblage comprises remains of animals consumed, site scavengers (eg dogs, birds), and wild animals (including fish) and forms less than 12% of the bones. The votive bone, goat, sheep, and domestic fowl, comprised the major part of the assemblage. This is so far unique in Britain; no other known assemblage has such a large concentration of bones of these few selected species. The ritual nature of the bones is best demonstrated in Phase 5 contexts where the samples are largest; in particular the accumulations over Structure I where there was a dense concentration of bone from context 136 (see chapter 3). At the edge of the field where there had been no plough damage these bones formed a layer 0.50–0.75m thick, with practically no soil matrix, and few other finds. The ploughed areas of the context may have been originally of a similar nature. The context was not fully excavated, but even so over 35,000 fragments were recovered, of which over 90% are sheep/goat.

Table 11 provides a general summary of NIF and MNI for the site. It shows that the assemblage is totally dominated by sheep, goats, and domestic fowl.

The aims of the analysis were initially to describe and interpret the nature of the votive assemblage, to investigate the evidence for on-site activities, and examine any detectable changes in them through time.

During the first two seasons of excavation it became clear that a number of problems existed relating to the distribution of the bones over the site, and subsequently a number of ancillary aims were developed. These were to investigate lateral variation across the site, to analyse the sheep/goat assemblage for the conformation of the animals, to separate the species on the basis of morphological and metrical characteristics, to compare the assemblage with other votive and non-votive assemblages, and to attempt to identify the original location(s) of the votive assemblage. There was insufficient evidence to trace these original locations, which may well have lain outside the excavated areas, so this last aim was not achieved.

Definition of votive assemblage

It is not possible in reality to attempt to identify individual bone fragments as deriving from votive or non-votive activity or deposition but it is possible in general terms to identify species which were probably votive, on grounds of predominance and observable patterns which differ from those related to domestic activities. For example the sheep and goat bones are characterised by very low proportions of butchery marks, often less than 2% of the bones. Additionally, the butchery that is present is commonly on skulls and horncores, a pattern not normally found on Roman sites. Although this cannot be said to be intrinsically indicative of ritual use, the archaeological evidence from the site backs up this deduction. In essence three species: sheep, goat, and domestic fowl, are treated in this analysis as votive animals.

It is emphasised however, that not all the sheep, goat, and domestic fowl were necessarily of votive origin. Other Romano-British sites are characterised by fairly high proportions of sheep/goat, and the surveys by King (1978, 1984) may be used as a convenient means of comparison with other Roman sites. These surveys are summarised here for comparison (Fig 184, MF Tables 39 and 40) showing the West Hill data in relation to those from other sites. A proportion of the sheep/goat from the site seems likely to have been used for domestic purposes. Conversely there is evidence that, on particular occasions, other species were also

Table 11: Site summary (MF Table 1)

Species		Phase 1 no	%	Phase 2 no	%	Phase 3 no	%	Phase 4 no	%	Phase 5 no	%	Phase 6 no	%	Phase 7 no	%	site total no	%
Mammals																	
Sheep/Goat	NIF	554	68.2	2261	72.0	2951	79.2	6798	86.7	26806	93.3	10432	91.7	9409	83.1	65809	88.3
Ovis/Capra	MNI	32	65.3	174	79.8	171	72.8	209	74.9	742	81.6	319	80.6	234	65.7	2214	79.6
Cattle	NIF	217	26.7	746	23.7	564	15.1	772	9.9	1158	4.0	615	5.4	1405	12.4	6164	8.3
Bos taurus L.	MNI	7	14.3	23	10.6	28	11.9	23	8.2	44	4.8	28	7.0	37	10.4	190	6.8
Pig	NIF	14	1.7	63	2.0	113	3.0	192	2.4	459	1.6	224	2.0	349	3.1	1647	2.2
Sus Domesticus Erxleben	MNI	4	8.2	11	5.0	13	5.5	26	9.3	73	8.0	26	6.6	35	9.8	188	6.8
Horse	NIF	12	1.5	47	1.5	6	0.2	5	<0.1	7	<0.1	2	<0.1	57	0.5	153	0.2
Equus caballus L.	MNI	2	4.1	4	1.8	2	0.8	2	0.7	4	0.4	2	0.5	18	5.1	34	1.2
Dog	NIF	11	1.4	19	0.6	62	1.7	47	0.6	216	0.8	35	0.3	38	0.3	459	0.6
Canis domesticus L.	MNI	2	4.1	3	1.4	4	1.7	12	4.3	20	2.2	5	1.3	6	1.7	52	1.9
Other mammal	NIF	4	0.5	-	-	15	0.4	18	0.2	51	0.2	33	0.3	37	0.3	199	0.3
	MNI	2	4.1	-	-	8	3.4	4	1.4	15	1.7	2	0.5	12	3.4	49	1.8
Small mammal	NIF	-	-	6	0.2	14	0.4	5	<0.1	28	0.1	35	0.3	22	0.2	110	0.1
see Table 12	MNI	-	-	3	1.4	9	3.8	3	1.0	11	1.2	14	3.5	14	3.9	54	1.9
total	NIF	812	99.0	3142	99.7	3725	98.5	7837	92.4	28725	96.7	11376	94.6	11317	96.1	74541	95.7
	MNI	49	89.1	218	96.0	235	87.7	279	66.9	909	80.4	396	70.0	356	73.9	2781	78.0
Birds																	
Domestic fowl	NIF	7	87.5	8	66.7	40	93.0	604	97.6	877	96.1	477	95.6	398	97.1	2939	96.8
	MNI	5	83.3	5	55.6	23	92.0	109	90.1	171	91.0	101	92.7	89	89.9	552	90.4
Other bird	NIF	1	12.5	4	33.3	3	7.0	15	2.4	36	3.9	22	4.4	12	2.9	96	3.2
see table 13	MNI	1	16.7	4	44.4	2	8.0	12	9.9	17	9.0	8	7.3	10	10.1	56	9.6
total	NIF	8	1.0	12	0.4	43	1.1	619	7.3	913	3.1	499	4.2	410	3.5	3035	3.9
	MNI	6	10.9	9	4.0	25	9.3	121	29.0	188	16.6	109	19.3	99	20.5	608	17.5
Fish	NIF	-	-	-	-	6	0.2	27	0.3	47	0.2	118	1.0	47	0.4	258	0.3
see table 14	MNI	-	-	-	-	6	2.2	17	4.1	30	2.7	51	9.0	24	5.0	137	4.0
Amphibian	NIF	-	-	-	-	7	0.2	-	-	6	-	27	0.2	4	-	44	<01
	MNI	-	-	-	-	2	0.7	-	-	3	0.3	10	1.8	3	0.6	18	0.5
total	NIF	-	-	-	-	14	4.6	27	8.9	53	17.5	145	48.0	51	16.9	302	
	MNI	-	-	-	-	8	5.2	17	11.1	33	21.6	61	40.0	27	17.6	153	
site total	NIF	820	1.1	3154	4.0	3781	4.9	8483	10.9	29691	38.1	12020	15.4	11778	15.1	77878	
	MNI	55	1.6	227	6.6	268	7.7	417	12.0	1130	32.6	566	16.3	482	13.9	3463	

Notes: Site total column includes Phase 8 (unstratified) bones
Unidentified fragments (cattle-size and sheep-size) and unidentified small mammals not included
Contexts from Phases 4-6 have been sub-sampled where original context totals more than 3000 fragments

utilised for ritual, although generally they provide patterns which are similar to the domestic exploitation seen on many other sites. While it is therefore not possible to identify, bone for bone, which sheep and goat are votive and which are domestic, the votive nature of most of the sheep and goat bone is undoubted, and all the sheep and goat have been treated as votive (Fig 185, MF Table 41). This is a reasonable assumption for the goat in particular, since a typical Roman site might be expected to produce less than 10% goat, whereas here goats are often 60% or more of the bones (by extrapolation from the identified sheep/goat). An attempt has been made to assess how much of the sheep and goat may have been votive and how much domestic in the analysis below.

Similarly, the larger mammals: cattle, pig, horse, dog, and wild mammals (excluding deer antler) are treated as non-votive as the bias of including a few votive bones in this part of the assemblage is assumed to be minimal.

The non-votive assemblage

This includes all animals other than sheep, goat, and domestic fowl. Detailed reports on the birds and fish here summarised are included in fiche. A report on the amphibians is incorporated with that on the small mammals.

Larger mammals

These include domestic animals probably exploited as part of the site economy, rather than having a defined ritual function, ie cattle and pigs as food animals, or pets/scavengers, eg dogs. Other mammals, such as voles and shrews may have been present at the time or could be modern intrusions. They would not in any case have formed part of the site economy (the same is true of some of the birds).

Cattle

Cattle bones are present in each phase in small numbers, rising above 1000 only in Phases 5 and 7 (Table 11). The complexity of the phases, and the high degree of fragmentation renders detailed analysis difficult. Certain trends can be identified however, and although samples from individual features and phases are small, the consistency of these trends lends credence to the interpretation of the results.

A comparison of cattle with sheep/goat indicates that the importance of cattle decreases through time from proportions of 28% in Phase 1 to 4% in Phase 5, though thereafter recovering to 13% in Phase 7 (Table 11). This however may not be a true reflection of the importance of cattle since the sheep/goat proportions are considered votive rather than non-votive. The cattle:pig ratios may be a more reliable indicator. Remarkably, the same pattern occurs: cattle proportions fall consistently from Phase 1 to Phase 5, then recover.

	cattle	*pig*
Phase 1	94%	6%
Phase 2	92%	8%
Phase 3	83%	17%
Phase 4	80%	20%
Phase 5	72%	28%
Phase 6	75%	25%
Phase 7	80%	20%

There is no question that cattle were always more important than pig, but the pattern does strongly imply that cattle became a less important factor in the diet on the site from the first to the fourth centuries AD, and that although the incidence increased afterwards, it never again reached its early levels.

There are differences in cattle proportions within the phases which might be ascribed to function, those features/structures with higher proportions of cattle being considered more domestic in nature. This point is discussed in more detail later, but is summarised briefly below.

In Phase 1–2 (prehistoric–first century AD) cattle are a more important component of the bone assemblages in ditches F584 (33%) and F816 (34%) than in ditch F382 (22%) (Fig 186i, MF Table 2). The implication is that F584 and F816 may have contained dumps from domestic activities.

In Phase 4 (second–third centuries) cattle are both more abundant and in higher proportions from Structure X than Structure IV (Fig 188i, Table 15), and by this reasoning, Structure X has a more domestic character. It is possibly significant that within Structure IV cattle are most abundant in Room B (MF Table 10), which is adjacent to Room A, which contained a hearth and might have been a kitchen. The implication is that the function of Room B might also relate to this, and therefore possibly contain a more domestic deposit.

For Phase 5 (mid-fourth century) cattle are more important from Structure IX (8–15%) than from Structure I (2–6%) (Fig 195i) though it should be noted that cattle frequencies even in Structure IX are very low (Table 16).

Butchery marks on cattle bones are generally infrequent, about 10–15% of bones on average, though there are exceptions (for example 65% from pit F264, of Phase 2), but the patterns are similar from all phases, indicating that butchery methods did not change. The summary diagram (Fig 207ii) illustrates common locations of butchery marks. There are clear concentrations at the joints, along the fore and hindlimbs, and particularly at the limb/girdle articulations. Vertebrae were chopped laterally, indicating that the cattle were butchered on the ground. The head was removed at the skull/atlas, atlas/axis, or axis/third cervical joints. Cuts on the skull and mandibles are similar to those found at other sites, and consistent with removal of jaw muscles, tongue, and jaw bones. Some horn cores were removed, presumably for the horns. Cuts on the distal metapodials and phalanges probably relate to skinning.

Generally the cattle bones are a mixture of all parts of the anatomy, indicating a mixture of levels of butchery, from the primary stage (when skulls and limb extremities are removed), to the table waste stage (eg ribs, upper limb fragments). Figure 196iv is fairly typical of the cattle remains, although it is the only instance of a large enough sample to be worth illustrating. There is a greater emphasis on Group A bones than the other bones, but Groups B and C are still quite well represented.

Age structures are difficult to reconstruct because of small samples. Most cattle were sub-adult and adult in all phases, with the emphasis sometimes on younger animals (Phases 2, 3, and 4) and sometimes on older ones (Phases 5, 6, and 7).

The cattle bones are mostly highly fragmented, and this can be seen by comparing the NFI and NBI. For example, taking Structure IX (Table 16) where samples are fairly high, the NFI counts range from 18–48 but NBI are 3–7 (ie there are much smaller numbers of bones in the NIB category). Few measurements were taken because of the degree of fragmentation, but comparisons with other Roman sites indicate that these cattle were similar to cattle from other sites of this period.

The pathological anomalies recorded are few, implying that only healthy individuals were consumed. Most pathological conditions were related to joint stress such as eburnation and grooving on the acetabulum of a pelvis, and eburnation and exostosis on a calcaneum. Such anomalies can be age and work related, and are fairly common on draught animals.

These bones are typical of cattle remains from other Roman sites both in terms of economy (fairly late kill-off, implying uses other than rearing for meat) and butchery patterns. Additionally, the cattle were of a similar stature to other Romano-British cattle.

Pigs

There are only 1411 pig bones in the identified assemblage from Phases 1–7, a total too small to allow detailed analysis. The following therefore, are general and subjective observations.

Cattle and pig proportions compared above show that pig proportions rose from Phases 1 to 5, and then fell. A similar, though less consistent trend is seen when pigs are compared with all the other mammals (Table 11). Pigs, however, cannot have been very important in the site economy, since even in comparison with cattle only, their proportions are generally 20% or less.

There is limited evidence for butchery on pig bones from most phases and features. This is consistent enough to indicate that pigs were regularly butchered in patterns that conform to typical domestic sites, but too limited to allow detailed analysis (Fig 207iii).

Ageing evidence is very limited and the following comments are based on overall impression rather than detailed analysis. In Phase 2 juveniles and infants account for about half the ageable pig bones, and in Phase 3 this proportion decreases, with higher survival of sub-adults. Phase 4 is similar to Phase 3, though there is a lot of variation between the structures and sub-phases. This variation is also seen in Phase 5, and here there are cases of high proportions of infant and peri-natal deaths, and also of adult deaths, as well as the patterns described above. Similar variation is seen in Phase 6. The general impression is that kill-off of pigs was focused upon juveniles and sub-adults. Pigs cannot therefore be said to have played a very important role in the diet, though they were eaten during all phases on the site. Ageing and butchery patterns are essentially similar to those found on other Romano-British sites.

Other mammals

These are principally horse and dog, each forming less than 1% of the total bones. The other mammals are red and roe deer and a number of perinatal bones not easily ascribed to species, but perhaps sheep/goat or pig, which also amount to less than 1% of the site total (Table 11). None of these species was common enough to have been economically important. This is also true of the phase totals, although there is some fluctuation, eg horse ranges from 1.5–>0.1%, dog from 1.7–0.3%, but even at their highest frequencies, the species were not important.

Dog bones included some partial skeletons, eg four articulated thoracic vertebrae from Phase 3b (no butchery evidence), ten articulated vertebrae (thoracic and lumbar) from Structure X, Phase 4a, and from Structure IV, Phase 4b, a mature individual comprising skull, atlas, axis, two lumbar vertebrae, two caudal vertebrae, left scapula, both humeri, right pelvis, and both tibia. The most complete skeleton came from robbing in Structure I, Phase 5e, and consisted of 119 fragments from a mature individual of small size (MF Table 38) which may possibly have been a pet buried in robbing backfill (context 72, fill of F71, see chapter 3).

The deer bones are roe deer from Structure IX, Phase 5, and red deer antler from Structure XI, Phase 7. Finally, an intriguing find was that of three dolphin teeth (*Delphinus delphis*), one from palisade destruction and infill in Phase 3c, two from Structure I, occupation, Phase 5.

The small mammals

The small mammal and amphibian bones are summarised in Table 12; both groups were identified with the help of R Jones then of AM Lab. Most bones are from Structures IX and XIV (excavated in 1979 and sieved, Levitan 1982a). All the species present (except house mouse) can be found at or near the site in the present day. Thus, the bones might all easily be modern and intrusive (in fact several active burrows were excavated). Some of the bone may have been archaeologically contemporary, in which case they may reflect similar types of habitat at (or close to) the site. Although there was no evidence for lagomorphs living on the site in the present, it is likely that they, too, are modern intrusions, although the house mouse (*Mus musculus*) is possibly archaeologically contemporary. The small mammals generally represent habitats that are in keeping with the environmental data provided by the mollusca report (*Meddens above*). Finally the weasel (*Mustela nivalis*) may also be of Roman date, but the two bones recovered can have little significance.

Amphibians

There are 44 bones of frog/toad (Table 12). It is possible that these are modern intrusions, and not contemporary with the site. If they were contemporary the remains need not represent permanent water on site, especially in the case of toads. A water container like a pool or the rainwater tanks associated with Structure II (see chapter 3) would have been an ideal habitat.

Table 12: Summary of small mammal, dolphin, and amphibian bones (MF Table 16)

	Phase 1–2	*Phase* <---2--->		*Phase* <-----3----->			*Phase* <--4-->		*Phase* <5>	*Phase* <-------6------->				*Phase* <----------7---------->					*totals*	
Feature/Structure		*F264*[a]	*other*	*XVII*	*XVIII*	*other*	*IV*	*X*	*I*	*IX*	*II*[b]	*XIV*	*F1255*[c]	*VII*	*VIII*	*XI*	*XV*[d]	*Post-XIV*	*no*	*%*
Species																				
Rabbit *oryctolagus cuniculus* L.	-	-	-	-	-	-	-	-	-	2	1	1	-	-	-	-	-	-	4	3.7
Hare *Lepus* sp.	-	-	-	-	-	2	-	-	-	7	-	-	-	-	-	-	-	-	10	9.3
Mole *Talpa europaea* L.	-	-	-	-	-	2	-	-	1	-	-	1	-	-	-	-	-	-	3	2.8
House mouse *Mus musculus* L.	-	-	-	-	-	3	-	1	2	-	-	3	-	-	-	-	-	-	9	8.3
Wood mouse *Apodemus cf sylvaticus* (L.) Hinton	-	-	-	-	-	1	-	-	-	-	-	1	-	-	-	-	-	-	2	1.9
Mouse indet *Apodemus* S.	-	-	-	-	1	1	-	2	-	6	-	3	-	-	-	-	1	-	14	13.0
Common shrew *Sorex araneus* L.	-	-	-	-	-	1	-	-	-	-	-	-	-	-	-	-	-	-	1	0.9
Pygmy shrew *S. minutus* L.	-	-	-	-	-	-	-	-	-	2	-	2	-	-	1	-	-	1	6	5.6
Short-tailed vole *Microtus agrestis* (L.) Miller	-	4	1	-	-	2	2	-	2	1	1	16	-	-	2	-	2	15	48	42.6
Bank vole *Clethrionomys glareolus* Schreber	-	-	-	-	-	1	-	-	-	3	-	-	-	-	-	-	-	-	4	3.7
Water vole *Arvicola terresttris* L.	-	1	-	-	-	-	-	-	1	-	1	4	-	-	-	-	-	-	7	6.5
Weasel *Mustela nivalis* L.	-	-	-	-	-	-	-	-	1	-	-	-	1	-	-	-	-	-	2	1.9
total	-	5	1	-	1	13	2	3	7	21	3	31	1	-	3	-	3	16	110	100.0
Small mammal indet.	12	83	2	14	53	225	2	99	48	308	7	229	-	2	9	2	43	114	1252	
Frog/toad	-	-	-	1	-	6	-	-	-	6	-	27	-	-	1	-	1	2	44	
Dolphin[e]	-	-	-	-	-	1	-	-	2	-	-	-	-	-	-	-	-	-	3	
Total	12	88	3	15	54	244	4	102	55	335	10	287	1	2	13	2	47	132	1406	

Notes: [a] includes Phase 3a; [b] includes Phase 5d; [c] Phases 5–6; [d] mostly residual; [e] teeth only, not included in total

Table 13: Summary of bird bones excluding domestic fowl (MF Table 17)
compiled by B Levitan from data supplied by G Cowles

	Phase 1–2	*Phase* <- - - - - 2 - - - - ->			*Phase 3*	*Phase* <- - - - -4 - - - - ->			*Phase* <- - - - -5 - - - - ->			*Phase* <- - 6 - ->		*Phase* <- - - - 7 - - - - ->			*Phase 8*	*total*	
Feature/Structure		[illegible]	*F264*	*other*	*pre-X*	*IV*	*X*	*other*	*I*	*IX*	*other*	*II*	*XIV*	*VIII*	*XV*	*XI*		*no*	*%*
Species																			
Goose *Anser sp.* (domestic)	-	-	-	-	-	-	1	-	-	-	-	-	-	-	-	-	-	1	1.0
Teal *Anas crecca* L.	-	1	-	-	1	-	3	-	-	6	-	-	7	-	1	1	-	21	21.9
Wigeon *A. penelope* L.	-	-	-	-	-	-	-	-	-	-	-	-	-	-	1	-	-	2	2.1
Mallard *Anser sp.* (*cf* domestic)	-	-	-	-	-	-	1	-	-	2	-	-	-	-	1	-	-	4	4.2
W-tailed sea eagle *Haliaeetus albicilla* L.	-	-	-	-	2	-	-	-	-	-	-	-	-	-	-	-	-	2	2.1
Golden plover *Plivialis apricaria* L.	-	-	-	-	-	1	1	-	-	1	-	-	-	-	-	-	-	3	3.1
Grey plover *P. squatarola* L.	-	-	-	-	-	-	-	-	-	1	1	-	-	-	-	-	-	2	2.1
Woodcock *Scolopax rusticola* L	-	-	-	-	-	2	-	-	-	14	-	1[a]	11	-	3	1	2	34	35.4
Snipe *Gallinago gallinago* L.	-	-	-	-	-	-	-	-	-	1	-	-	-	-	-	-	-	1	1.0
Domestic rock dove? *Cf Columba livia* Gmelin	-	-	1	-	-	-	-	1	-	2	-	-	-	-	-	-	-	4	4.2
Skylark *Alauda arvensis* L.	1	-	-	-	-	-	-	-	-	-	-	-	-	-	-	-	-	1	1.0
Redwing *T. iliacus* L.	-	-	-	-	-	-	-	-	1	-	-	-	-	-	-	-	-	1	1.0
Blackbird *T, merula* L.	-	-	-	-	-	-	-	-	-	3	-	-	1	-	1	-	-	5	5.2
Thrush family *Turdus* sp.	-	-	-	-	-	-	-	-	-	1	-	-	-	1[b]	1	-	-	3	3.1
Starling *Sturnus vulgaris* L.	-	-	-	-	-	-	-	-	-	-	-	-	1	-	-	-	-	1	1.0
Yellowhammer *Emberiza citrinella* L.	-	-	-	-	-	-	-	-	-	1[c]	-	-	-	-	-	-	-	1	1.0
House sparrow *Passer domesticus* L.	-	1	-	-	-	-	1	-	-	-	-	-	-	-	-	-	-	2	2.1
Small passerine	-	-	-	1	-	-	1	-	-	-	-	-	-	1	-	-	-	3	3.1
Magpie *Pica pica* L.	-	-	-	-	-	-	-	-	1	-	-	-	-	-	-	-	-	1	1.0
Jackdaw *C. monedula* L.	-	-	-	-	-	1	-	-	1	-	-	-	-	-	-	-	-	2	2.1
Raven *Corvis corax* L.	-	-	-	-	-	2	-	-	-	-	-	-	-	-	-	-	-	2	2.1
total no	1	2	1	1	3	6	8	1	3	32	1	2	20	2	8	2	3	96	99.8
%	1.0	2.1	1.0	1.0	3.1	6.3	8.3	1.0	3.1	33.3	1.0	2.1	20.8	2.1	8.3	2.1	3.1		99.8

Notes: [a] Phase 5d; [b] Phase 7a; [c] includes one sieved bone

Birds

by Graham Cowles

Twenty wild living species and two or possibly three domesticated species have been identified. The domestic fowl are discussed separately and relative proportions mentioned below exclude fowl bones. Bones of woodcock (*Scolopax rusticola*) and teal (*Anas crecca*) were those most commonly recovered from the site. Almost 40% of the wild species found are associated with water, marshes and other wet ground areas. The three species of duck (Table 13) are all surface feeders, frequenting shallow lakes and rivers. The snipe (*Gallinago gallinago*) is typical of the marshes, water meadows, bogs and wet ground at the edges of rivers. The grey plover (*Pluvialis squatarola*) is a winter visitor to Britain and during these months would be found on the marshes and coastal or estuarine mud-flats. In winter, too, it is likely that the golden plover (*Pluvialis apricaria*) would be seen feeding on the shore or mud-flats.

Although the woodcock is predominantly a woodland bird, favouring, in the south, oak or other broad-leaved woods, it feeds at dusk on nearby marshes and boggy ground. In severe winters it may search for food along rocky shores. Woodland is also the habitat for blackbird (*Turdus merula*) and redwing (*T. iliacus*), the latter species being present as a winter visitor. Similar woodland habitat is also suitable for yellowhammer (*Emberiza citrinella*) and magpie (*Pica pica*) where they may inhabit the edges of woodland areas.

Jackdaw (*Corvus monedula*), raven (*C. corax*) and magpie (*Pica pica*) would, in Roman Britain, probably be in the close vicinity of man, his buildings and refuse. These birds may have been killed because of their nuisance as scavengers. Starlings (*Sturnus vulgaris*) and house sparrows (*Passer domesticus*) would also be attracted to the site of human occupation.

Two domestic species, fowl (*Gallus sp* domestic) and goose (*Anser sp* domestic) are represented. A possible third is the domesticated rock dove (*Columba livia*). It is difficult from this bone material (humerus, coracoids and tarsometatarsus) to differentiate between the rock dove and the stock dove (*C. oenas*), which would have been a wild living bird of the open woodland.

With the exception of the white-tailed sea eagle (*Haliaeetus albicilla*) all the birds listed could have been killed and eaten. It is interesting that some species could have been taken quite locally, others required a journey to wetter areas, perhaps in the winter months. The white-tailed sea eagle is not an uncommon find at Roman sites, but was probably not taken for food. Before it became extinct in Britain it was found around the coast and inland, close to lakes and rivers where it could obtain a diet of fish and waterfowl.

The phases and features from which the bird bones were recovered are summarised in Table 13. Most bones came from Phase 5 (37.5%), and most species were also present from this phase (12 of the 20 species). Sieving had little impact on the bird bone quantifications, but the yellowhammer was not represented in manually recovered samples. Only 2% of the sieved bird bones however were easily identified. The work involved in identifying them to family or genus would not repay the time and effort required in new information, particularly as the sieved portion of the site was very small, only about 5% of the layers that were sampled, and therefore less than 0.1% of the site as a whole.

The fish

by Alwyne Wheeler

As is usual with fish skeletal material much of it is too fragmentary or lacking in distinctive features to be identified. A summary of identified bones is given in Table 14 (which includes a salmonid scale from Structure VII, Phase 7). The comparison between sieved and unsieved samples is striking and is best shown in Structure XIV, Phase 6. In the unsieved portion of Structure XIV there were nine identified bones representing two fish taxa (45 bones). By comparison the sieved sample yielded four fish taxa (213 bones). As might be expected the sieved remains were from much smaller fishes than those from the unsieved remains, the range in length being 0.35–1m in hand samples versus 0.12–0.75m in sieved samples. Sieving thus considerably increases the yield of information on fish remains in comparison with hand recovery.

Table 14: Summary of fish (MF Table 18)
compiled by B Levitan from data supplied by A Wheeler

Identification	*no*	*MNI*	*size range (mm)*	*sieved*
Phase 3c				
pre Structure X				
Flatfish, Pleuronectidae	2	2	small	S
Salmon/trout, *Salmo* sp.	3	3	300 - 700	S
Eel, *Angilla anguilla* L.	1	1	-	S
Phase 4a				
Structure IV				
Flounder, *Platichthyd flesus* L.	1	1	-	-
Structure X				
Salmon/trout, *Salmo* sp.	11	4	200 - 950	S
Flatfish, Pleuronectidae	2	2	small	S
Eel, *Angilla anguilla* L.	4	1	small	S
Bass, *Dicentrarchus labrax* L.	1	1	300	S
Flounder, *Platichthys flesus* L.	1	1	330	-
Phase 4b				
Structure IV				
Salmon/trout, *Salmo* sp.	1	1	-	-
Structure X				
Flounder, *Platichthys flesus* L.	1	1	350	-
Flatfish, Pleuronectidae	2	2	150 - 330	-
Perch family, Percidae	1	1	-	-
Bass, *Dicentrarchus labrax* L.	1	1	small	S
Salmon/trout, *Salmo* sp.	1	1	800	-
Phase 5a, b				
Structure I(i,ii)				
Red sea-bream, *Pagellus bogaraveo* L.	8	2	small - large	-
Salmon/trout, *Salmo* sp.	1	1	-	-
Phase 5a				
Structure IX				
Salmon/trout, *Salmo* sp.	2	2	small - 850	S
Flatfish, Pleuronectidae	9	4	150 - 200	S
Perch family, Percidae (?Mugilidae)	2	2	-	S
Flounder, *Platichthys flesus* L.	1	1	250	S
Salmon/trout, *Salmo* sp.	1	1	200	S
Phase 5b				
Structure IX				
Flounder, *Platichthys flesus* L.	1	1	330	S
Phase 5c				
Structure IX				
Flatfish, Pleuronectidae	16	12	150 - 400	S
Salmon/trout, *Salmo* sp.	1	1	-	
Eel, *Angilla anguilla* L.	2	1	small	
Phase 5e				
Structure I(iv,v)				
Red sea- bream, *Pagellus bogaraveo* L.?	1	1	-	-
Salmon family, Salmonidae	2	1	-	-
Phase 6a				
Structure XIII				
Salmon/trout, *Salmo* sp.	1	1	650	-
Structure XIV				
Salmon, salmonidae	1	1	950	-
Flatfish, Pleuronectidae	6	2	250	S
Eel, *Angilla anguilla* L.	3	3	small - 600	S
Phase 6b				
Structure XIV				
Flatfish, Pleuronectidae	78	22	150 - 450	S
Salmon/trout, *Salmo* sp.	11	7	120 - 750	S
Flounder, *Platichthys flesus* L.	2	2	250	S
Eel, *Angilla anguilla* L.	10	8	small - 250	S
Salmon, salmonidae	1	1	large	S
Grey mullet, Mugilidae	2	1	200	S
Salmon, salmonidae	3	3	800 - 1000	-
Phase 7a				
Post-Structure XIV				
Flatfish, Pleuronectidae	27	9	200 - 350	S
Salmon/trout, *Salmo* sp.	8	7	200 - 900	S
Eel, *Angilla anguilla* L.	2	2	small	S
Phase 7b				
Structure VII				
Salmon/trout, *Salmo* sp. (scale)	1	1	-	S
Structure XV				
Flatfish, Pleuronectidae	6	2	200 - 250	S
Salmon/trout, *Salmo* sp.	1	1	200	S
Eel, *Angilla anguilla* L.	1	1	small	S
Unstratified				
Context 0100				
Flatfish, Pleuronectidae	6	3	200 - 300	S
Salmon/trout, *Salmo* sp.	3	2	200	S
Context 0200				
Flatfish, Pleuronectidae	2	2	200 - 300	S
Salmon/trout, *Salmo* sp.	1	1	small	S
Eel, *Angilla anguilla* L.	1	1	small	S
total	257	136		

The fishes represented in all phases are with one exception similar. Flatfishes (of which only flounder (*Platichthys flesus*) was positively identified) are present in all phases except for Phases 5 and 6. Members of the salmon family are present in all phases, and the fresh-water eel (*Anguilla anguilla*), in all except Phases 4, 5, and 6. The remaining species, bass (*Dicentrarchus labrax*), grey mullet (Mugilid), and red sea-bream (*Pagellus bogaraveo*), occurred in one or two of the buildings and were thus relatively infrequent. Both the grey mullet and the bass are found in estuaries and show a certain affinity for low salinity situations. Their occurrence is thus in keeping with the other, more abundant species. All these fishes could be caught locally, probably in the River Frome close to the site, or possibly further away in the Severn. It seems unlikely that bass or grey mullet would be attracted to so small a river as the Frome, and the presence of these species argues for a fishery on the larger River Severn.

The occurrence of red sea-bream in Phase 5 is in contrast to the other fish remains. It is most unlikely to be caught as a large fish in estuarine conditions. It can only indicate trade with some area towards the open sea, and the import of the fish, possibly salted, from a considerable distance away. It is an excellent food fish with, at this size, a good quantity of rich, fatty meat. Its gastronomic quality places it with the salmon as far superior to the flounder, eel, and grey mullet which dominate the fish remains. It is out of keeping with the remainder of the fish fauna, though it has occurred on other Roman sites.

The bird and fish bones; summary

These small assemblages provide much useful information about the site economy and activities. The fish remains have obviously benefited from the sieving programme, the bird bones to a lesser extent with yellowhammer found only in the sieving: a species not previously recovered from a Romano-British site (Parker 1988, table 1).

The majority of the wild birds exploited represent wet habitats with an emphasis on just those environments represented by the fish, so there is a possibility that both activities were carried out together. There is also a hint of seasonal exploitation since some winter migrants are present in the bird fauna. Rooks and ravens, and white-tailed sea eagles sometimes, feed on carrion. It could well be that these birds were taking

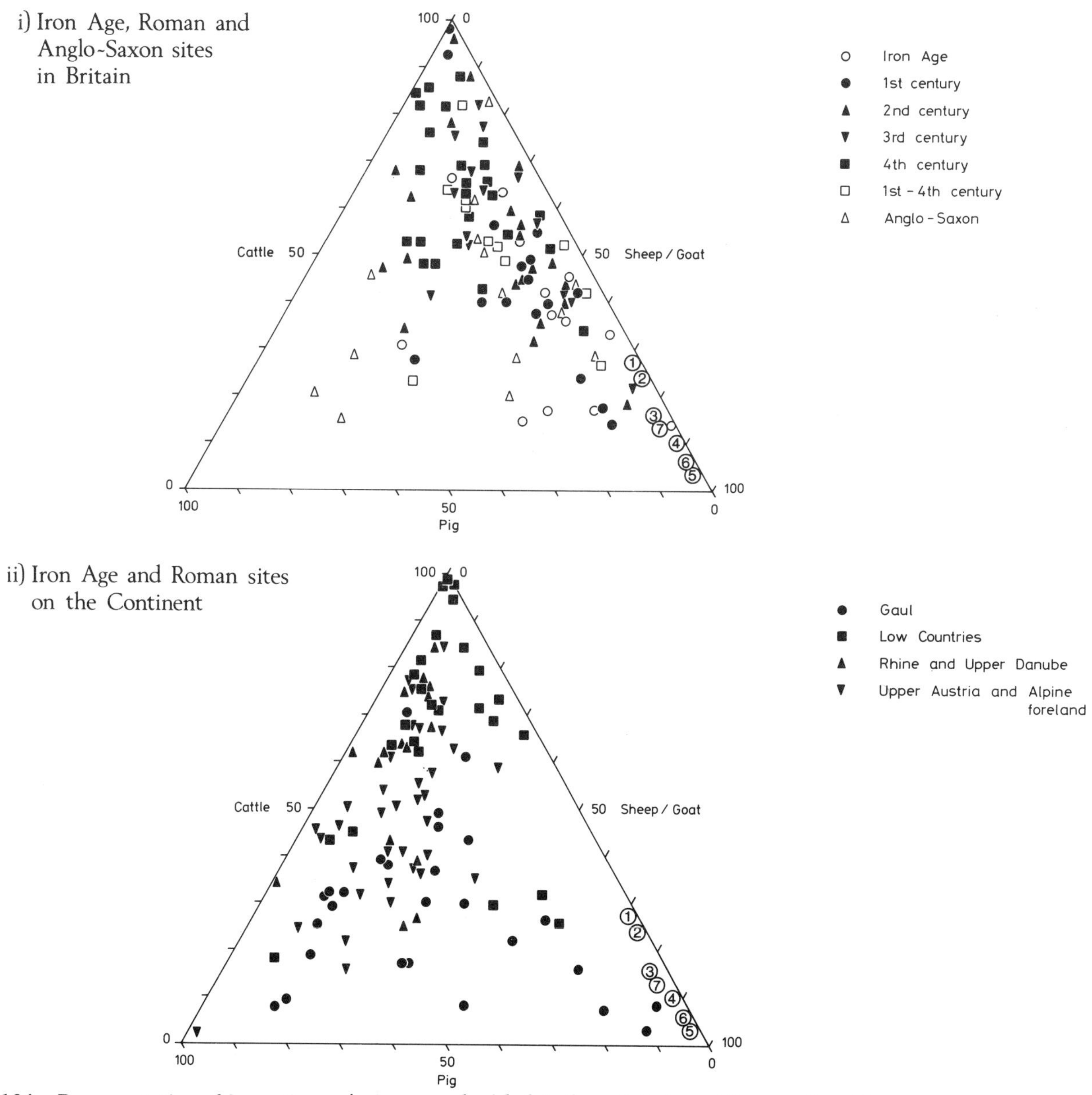

Fig 184 Representation of domestic species compared with data from Britain and Europe (from King 1978 and 1984), numbered circles denote Phase 1–7 sheep/goat representation at Uley

advantage of humanly generated carrion at the site. The presence of such birds would possibly not be welcome, which might explain their being killed.

The rarity of domestic birds other than fowl may well attest to the non-domestic nature of the site, birds such as geese and ducks were apparently not being reared at the site, though the odd goose was eaten. Such a lack of other domestic birds serves to underline the importance of the domestic fowl which account for 96.4% of the bird bones (Table 11).

There are four components to the bird assemblage: birds killed for food, the domestic and standard game species; commensuals, eg sparrow and starling; nuisances, eg white-tailed eagle, corvids; and finally the votive component, the majority of the domestic fowl (although, like the sheep/goat, some of the fowl were probably non-votive).

The fish which were consumed at the site were mainly quite small; with the exception of the large red sea-bream, they could all have been caught either in the Frome or the Severn, and thus they probably represent a local trade, dominated by relatively inexpensive fish exploited throughout the period of occupation. The red sea-bream represents trade over a long distance, and probably a very expensive meal. Its occurrence, in Structure I, might reflect on the status of that building, both as a place for the consumption of food generally, and in terms of the quality and price of food obtained there.

The votive assemblage

Several points already briefly mentioned are further considered here. The analysis of the votive assemblage is divided into a comparison of the votive and non-votive assemblages and a detailed analysis of the votive assemblage. It is first necessary to define and separate the votive and non-votive elements.

Determination of the votive assemblage

The unusual nature of this assemblage: ie the unprecedented domination of sheep/goat, most of which are goat, has already been referred to. Comparison with other Romano-British sites (Fig 184, MF Table 40) shows that these assemblages are uniquely high in their proportions of sheep/goat. Some other sites do have quite high proportions of sheep/goat however, and it cannot be assumed that all the sheep/goat here derives from activities different from those on other contemporary sites. It is probable that some of the sheep/goat bones are part of a 'normal' site economy based upon cattle, sheep, and pig husbandry.

It is the number of goats, sheep, and domestic fowl present which makes the assemblage unique (MF Table 39). The relationship between this and the ritual nature of the site is undoubted; eg the cult figure of Mercury with goat and cockerel (Fig 76), the altar stones depicting Mercury flanked by a sheep or goat and a cockerel (Figs 78 and 79), and the copper alloy figurines of a sheep or goat and a cockerel (Fig 88, nos 3 and 4). The main problem in dealing with these remains is the difficulty of differentiating those bones derived from ritual and those derived from non-ritual activity. Similarly, there is a problem in separating the bones of other species which may be votive from the non-votive majority.

Despite the possible inaccuracy of lumping all the sheep/goat together as 'votive' and all the cattle and pig as 'non-votive' this does provide a framework for further assessment, making it possible to look for anomalies in each component group. For example, cattle bones found in a pit containing purely votive artefacts are unlikely to be simple domestic rubbish (eg F251, Phase 2, where a cache of iron projectile heads and other finds are associated with the articulated hindlimb of a cow and a human femur, see chapter 2).

In an attempt to identify material which can be separated the proportions of sheep/goat/domestic fowl were compared with cattle/pig. Where the SGF occur in high proportions, the deposit might be mainly votive. Where SGF occur in smaller proportions the non-votive component may be more important. Patterns of exploitation were also considered relevant, for example, analysis of body part distributions may show differing components which could be related to votive or non-votive accumulations.

Votive/non-votive comparison

The sheep/goat/fowl and cattle/pig elements can be reduced to simple proportions indices. Indices in the range 0.70–1.00 are considered to indicate votive material. They are calculated, using identified NIF, as the total of sheep/goat/domestic fowl divided by total bones excluding small mammals, wild birds, and fish (referred to as SGF proportions). Another method of comparing the bones is using triangular graphs of sheep/goat plotted against cattle and pig. Plots where sheep/goat form 70% or more of the material are interpreted as mainly votive. These graphs may be directly compared with the data plotted by King (1978, 1984, and Fig 184). The use of 70% to indicate mainly votive material is not completely arbitrary since it will be seen from King's data that the vast majority of sites plotted have less than 70% SGF.

The SGF indices increase from 66% (0.66) in Phase 1 to 94% (0.94) in Phase 5, and then decrease to 84% (0.84) in Phase 7 (MF Tables 19 and 41). Only in Phase 1 are the proportions below 70%, so the interpretation is that the other phase totals all comprise mainly votive material. Phases 5 and 6 with proportions above 90% represent the extreme of this result. There is quite a lot of variation within the phases, particularly where the archaeology is complex, eg Phase 5. Such variation is difficult to assess from tabular data (MF Table 19) but is clearer in MF Table 41, where a weighting procedure has been employed, and in Figure 185.

Figure 185i shows that the increase in votive content from Phase 1 to Phase 5, is followed by a decrease to the levels of Phase 4. The variation is shown by comparing individual bar heights with the phase mean. The structure variation is also shown; for example, the high variation for Phase 7 results from the variability within the temporal divisions, (i) to (iv), of Structure VIII. If the phase mean is a crude indicator of the mixture of votive and non-votive deposits, then higher proportions might represent votive material, with the lower proportions more domestic in nature, but showing the influ-

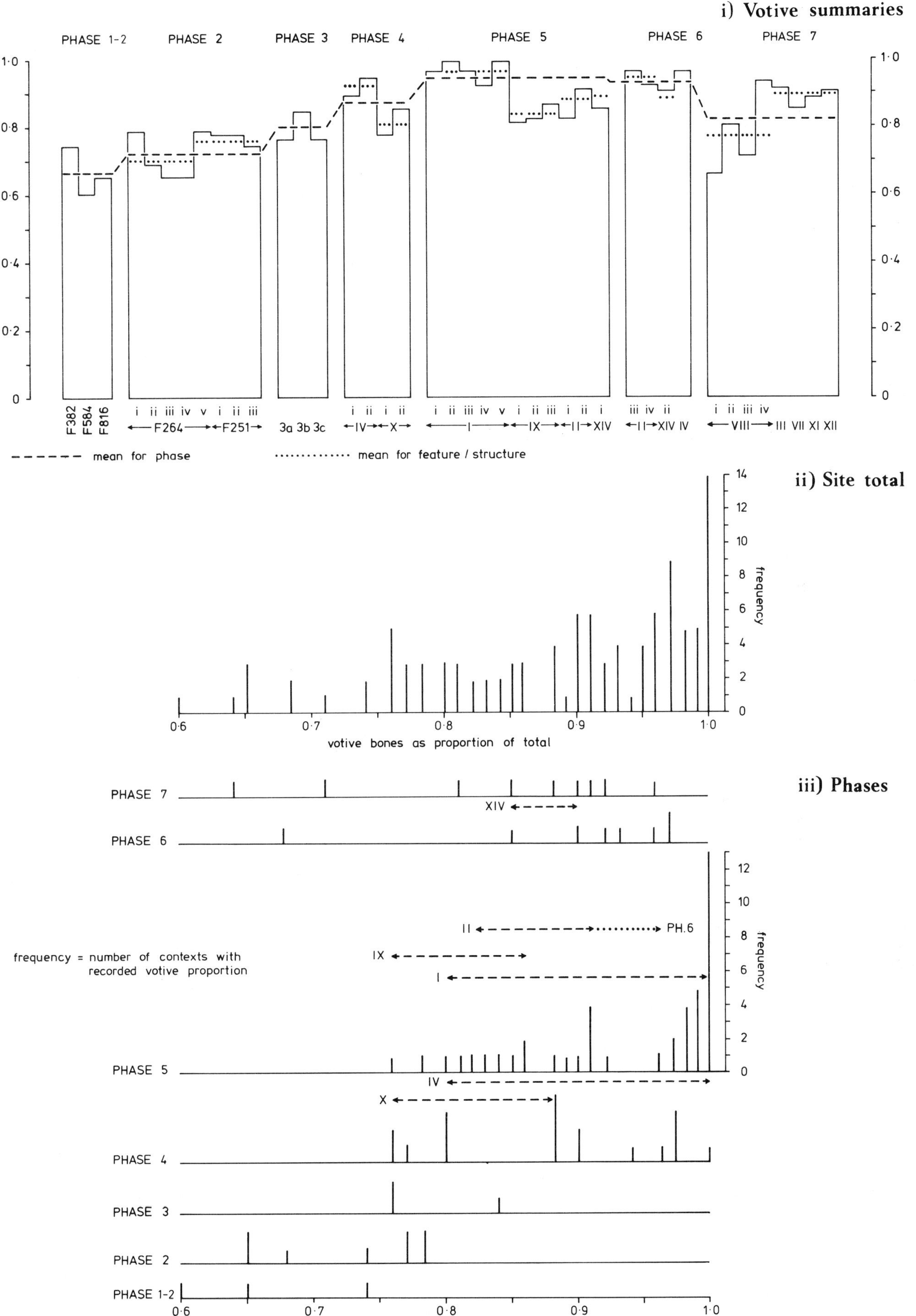

Fig 185 Proportions of votive species present

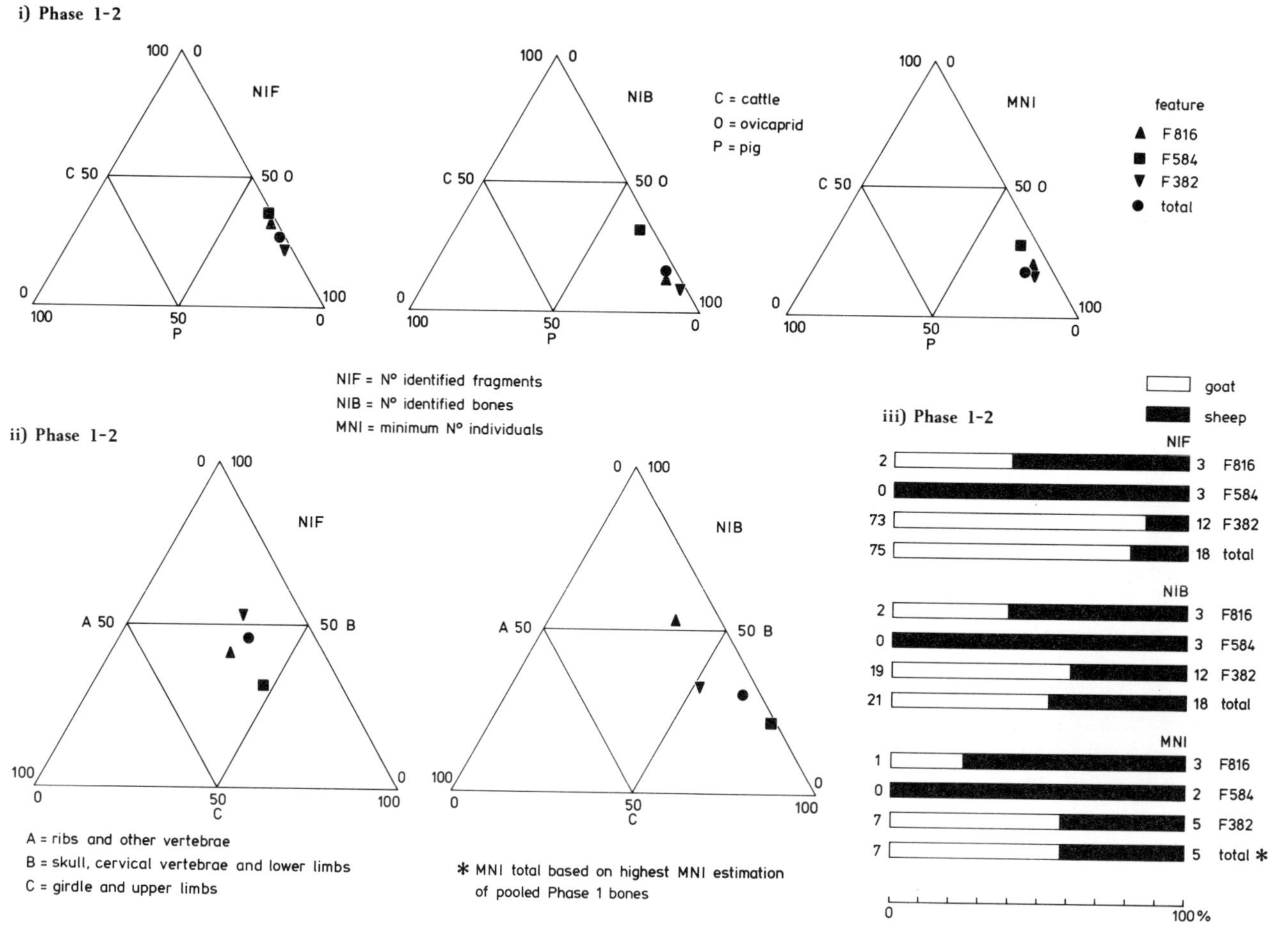

i) Phase 1-2

NIF NIB MNI

C = cattle
O = ovicaprid
P = pig

feature
▲ F816
■ F584
▼ F382
● total

NIF = N° identified fragments
NIB = N° identified bones
MNI = minimum N° individuals

ii) Phase 1-2

A = ribs and other vertebrae
B = skull, cervical vertebrae and lower limbs
C = girdle and upper limbs

* MNI total based on highest MNI estimation of pooled Phase 1 bones

iii) Phase 1-2

goat sheep

	goat	sheep	feature
NIF			
	2	3	F816
	0	3	F584
	73	12	F382
	75	18	total
NIB			
	2	3	F816
	0	3	F584
	19	12	F382
	21	18	total
MNI			
	1	3	F816
	0	2	F584
	7	5	F382
	7	5	total *

0 100%

Fig 186 i) Representation of cattle, sheep/goat, and pig, ii) Sheep/goat anatomical representation, iii) Sheep – goat ratios

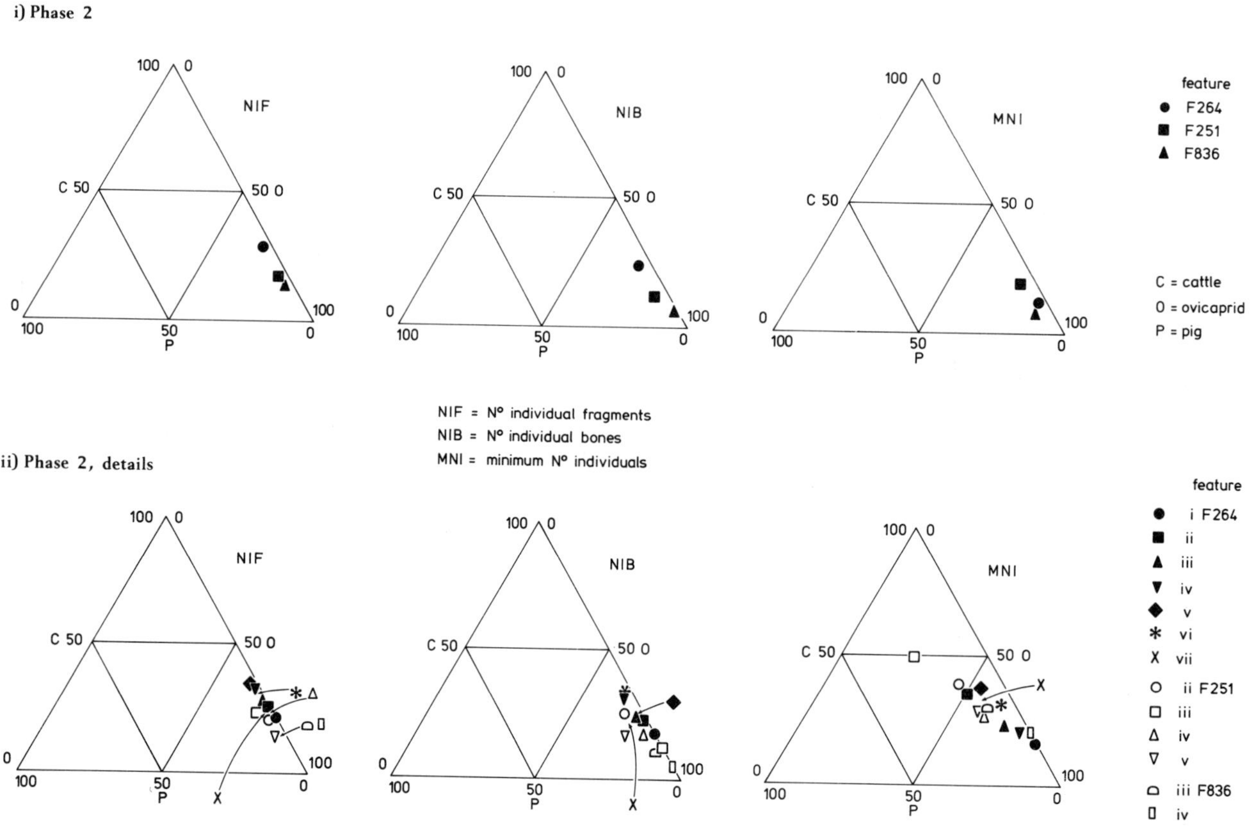

Fig 187 Representation of cattle, sheep/goat, and pig

ence of the votive 'background noise'. This assumption, although it cannot be supported by independent data, provides a starting point for the interpretation.

Phase 1–2

In this phase ditch F382 has a proportion higher than the mean, and is the only ditch with SGF above 70% (Fig 186i). Thus F584 and ditch F816 potentially contain non-votive material, the other features apparently reflecting a high votive focus. Perhaps the ditches to the east of the enclosure were singled out for dumping votive material, whilst those to the north (F816) and west (F584 and F179, the latter with no bones) were not considered so 'special'. This takes on further significance as there were no goat bones from ditch F584, though sheep were present, sheep outnumbered goat in ditch F816, and in ditch F382 goat far outnumbered sheep (Fig 186iii, MF Tables 2 and 20).

Phase 2

The principal features from this phase are compared in Figure 187i). Ditch F264 has indices below 70% in all but the earliest and the latest levels. In contrast pit F251 has indices above 70% throughout. On this basis pit F251 is interpreted as being of ritual use, whereas ditch F264, which started life with a ritual purpose was later used for mixed votive and non-votive dumps. Pit F251 can also be seen to be ritual from its artefacts (see chapter 2) and it contained the articulated rear limb of a cow, and an adult human femur, which are of a probable votive nature.

F836, a large, circular pit, seems to have the highest proportion of votive material of all the features in this phase (Fig 187i) and, interestingly, it contained the highest proportion of goat bones (MF Fig 3). It was 2m in diameter and 1.7m deep, but contained no intact primary deposits. About a third of its depth from the top, there was a layer which contained fragments of two cattle skulls, and no other bones. These, perhaps, were related to ritual activity, and the pit may be a possible parallel for pit F251.

Phase 3

The bones from Phase 3a come from several features and structures, but the samples are small, so no attempt has been made to compare them. The SGF proportion in Phase 3a is 0.76, it is higher during Phase 3b (0.84), but down to 0.76 again in Phase 3c (Fig 185, MF Fig 5, MF Table 19). It is difficult to interpret this material, but generally the impression is of votive deposits. This is supported, for Phase 3a and 3b at least, by the sheep:goat ratios, with goat predominant (MF Fig 6iii–v), and by the close correspondence of sheep/goat proportions for the different deposits (MF Fig 5ii, iii, MF Table 4).

Phase 4

Structures IV and X, multi-roomed masonry buildings, existed during this phase. Construction and occupation deposits relate to Phase 4a, and demolition to Phase 4b (later deposits spread over the area of Structure IV, are in Phase 6 below). The six rooms from Structure IV were revealed in excavation, but not all were completely excavated. Only the edges of the very large Structure X, first identified as a cropmark, were excavated, the north, north-east, north-west rooms, and the north extension. The phase mean is well above the 70% level (Fig 185i), influenced by high proportions of SGF from Structure IV since all phases of Structure X lie below the phase mean. It is possible to interpret Structure IV as having a rather more ritual association than Structure X which may have been more domestic in function, even though it is above the 70% level (Table 16). Figure 188i confirms this pattern.

On a room-by-room basis there is a fairly wide spread from 0.80 to 1.00 (Fig 185iii), however, this spread is in the form of a tight group of deposits for Phase 4a (Fig 188ii). In Phase 4b the spread of deposits is even more restricted (Fig 189i).

Taken as a whole, the Structure X proportions overlap with those of Structure IV (Fig 185iii), but it is notable that Structures X(i) and IV(i) (Phase 4a) do not overlap, and neither do Structures X(ii) and IV(ii) in Phase 4b (Fig 188i). Thus, although SGF proportions increase in Structure X, they do not reach the levels of Structure IV (Figs 185ii and 188iii). As with Structure IV, the frequencies indicate that the spread of proportions is fairly even. The Phase 4 pattern is thus one of increasing SGF proportions from Phase 4a to 4b, with Structure IV possibly relating directly to ritual, and Structure X more domestic, at least in those areas excavated.

Phase 5

The peak in votive proportions, is reached in Phase 5 (Fig 185i). The SGF proportions are dominated by Structure I; Structures II and XIV, and Structure IX all have proportions below the phase mean. These structures all have SGF proportions above the 70% level and Structures I and IX may be compared with the earlier pair, Structures IV and X. Both these pairs follow the same general trends and have remarkably similar patterns of spread and temporal change (Fig 185iii). There is also a similarity of plan in Structures I and IV (although Structures IX and X are not similar) (Figs 191, 194, 198). Perhaps one can assume that Structures I and IV were primarily concerned with ritual activities, and that Structures IX and X more domestic.

Structure II, the temple, ironically contains a lesser SGF proportion than Structure I (Fig 185i, iii, Table 16), but these proportions are well above the 70% level, and range above the highest proportions for Structure IX (Fig 185iii). The smaller SGF proportions, and the small sample size, in comparison with Structure I may reflect clearances of material from the temple, and/or the possibility that animal votive material was not actually kept in the temple at all.

Structure XIV replaces Structure IX and lasts into Phase 6. Simpler in plan, and more modest in size, it falls neatly into the Structure IX – X pattern of SGF proportions rather than that reflected by Structures IV – I, so Structures X, IX, and XIV might be seen as a three phase continuity of purpose. Certainly this must be the case for Structures IX and XIV at least, since they are so very similar in plan, and occupied the same location.

Structure I contained ten rooms, and an exterior area. There is a spread during the construction phase, Structure I(i), falling into two groups, one of proportions between 0.86 and 0.93 (five deposits) and one at 1.00

(five deposits). The occupation deposits are more clearly divided into two groups with proportions clustered around 0.95–0.96 and at 1.00. The demolition deposits are more diffusely spread between 0.91 and 0.99, but the majority lie in the range 0.98–0.99 (six out of ten groups); there may be three groups (Fig 195ii, iii and MF Table 19). The robbing deposits of Structure I(iv) have two clear groups: one with proportions at 0.88–0.91 and one at 0.97–1.00. Finally, the votive material spread over Structure I(iv) has the widest spread (0.80–1.00), but if the obvious outlier, 0.80 is excluded, the spread is much less (0.97–1.00), and the co-efficient of variation is reduced from 6.8% to 1.4%.

These patterns from Structure I are somewhat varied, but two general points are fairly clear: most deposits are clustered around proportions of 0.95 and higher (only 11 of the 46 deposits are less than 0.95), and many of the structure's phases are characterised by a minor group of lower proportions. A third point to note is the outlier of the final phase of Structure I (spatial group a) which clearly represents a different deposit to the other groups from this phase.

i) Structures IV & X, phases 4a & 4b

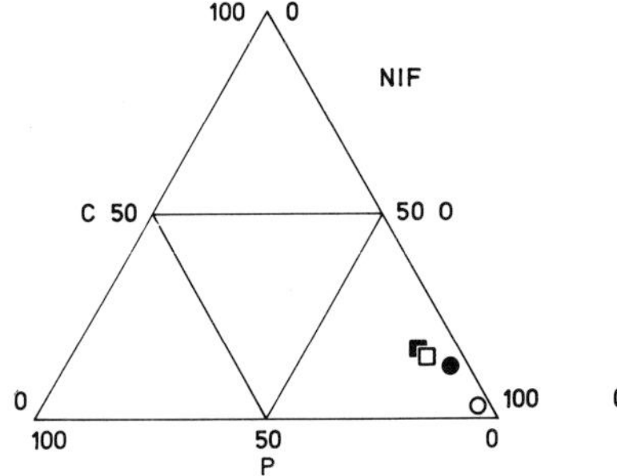

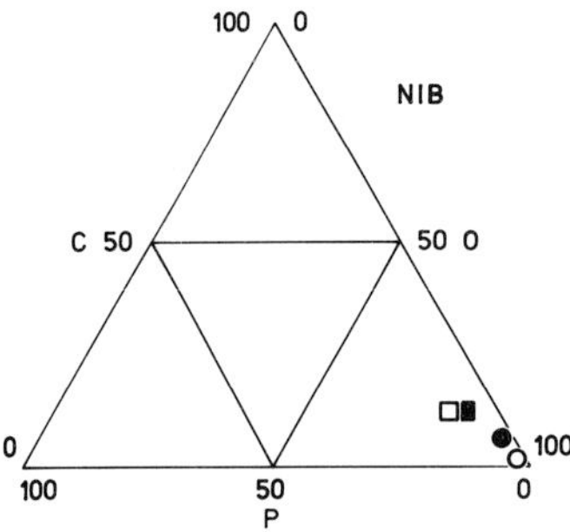

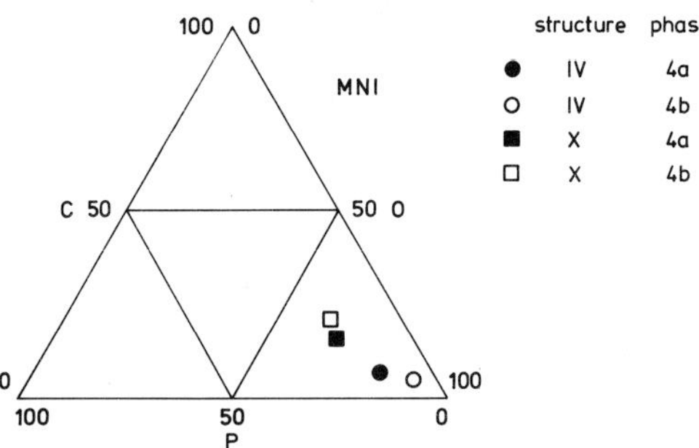

C = cattle
O = ovicaprid
P = pig

ii) Structure IV, phase 4a

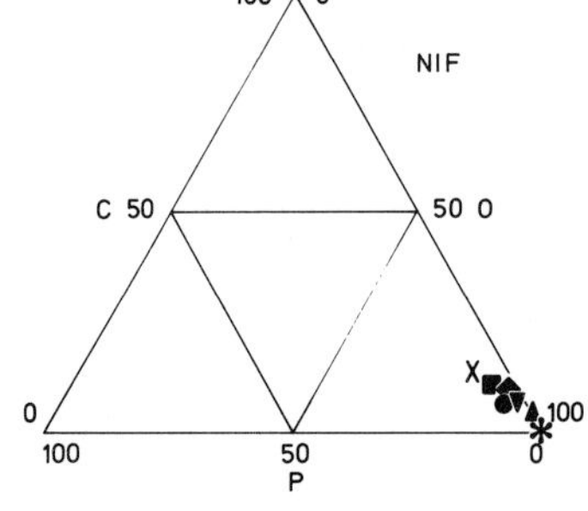

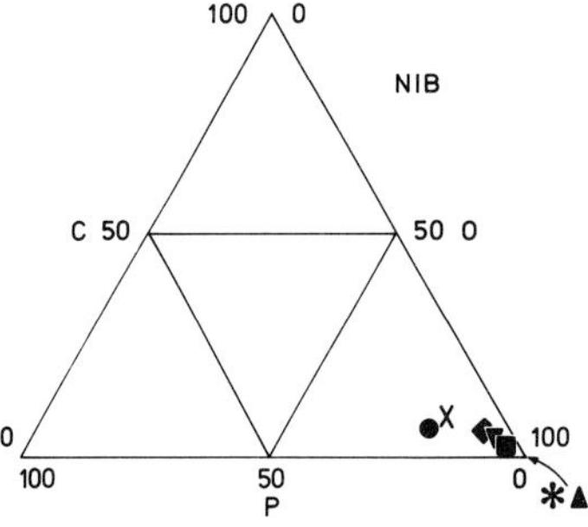

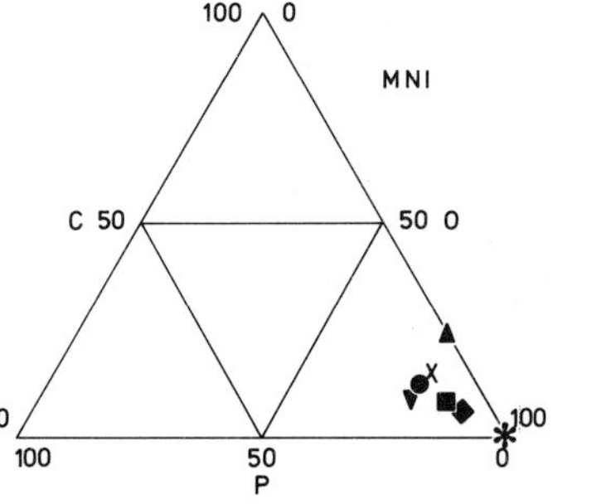

room
● A
■ B
▲ C
▼ D
◆ E
✱ F
X exterior

NIF = N° identified fragments
NIB = N° identified bones
MNI = minimum N° individuals

iii) Structure X, phase 4a

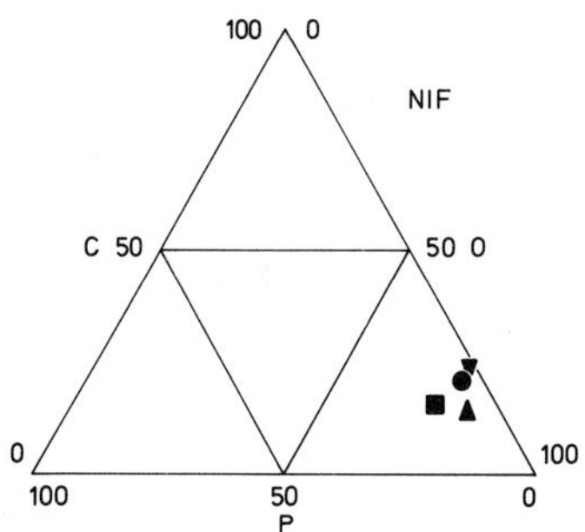

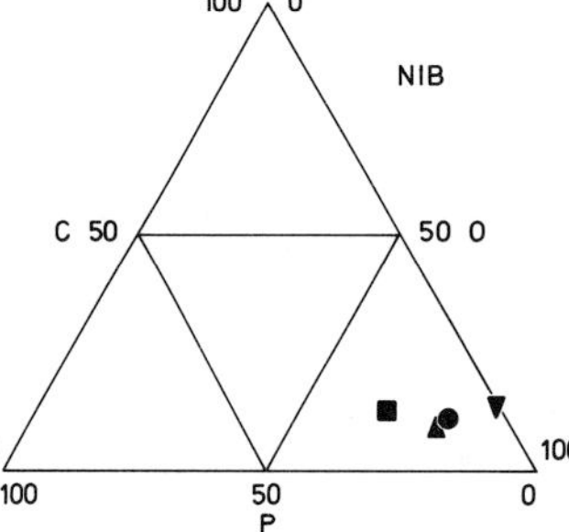

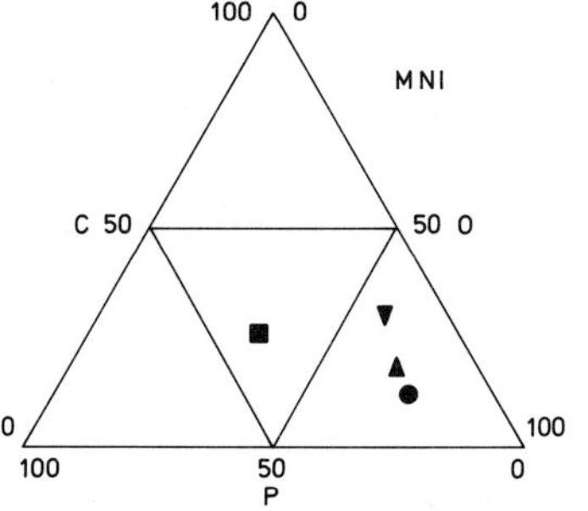

room
● NE
■ N
▲ N extension
▼ NW

Fig 188 Representation of cattle, sheep/goat, and pig

The rooms with the highest SGF goat proportions (Rooms C, E, F, H, J, and L) have the lowest concentrations of bone (Fig 194i); this is paralleled (in sample size) in Structure II. Similarly, the deposits with lowest SGF proportions over Structure I, Phase 5e, group a, also have the smallest sample size. This pattern is the reverse of the one noted for the occupation deposits, but if most of the votive deposits were cleared away from the temple and associated buildings and then dumped over Structure I, this contrast does not appear to be anomalous.

There is apparently very little variation in the deposits from Structure IX, temporally (Fig 200i) or laterally (Fig 200ii–iv) with a small and gradual increase in votive proportions. Initially the greatest concentration of bones is also the most domestic in nature (Room C: Figs 198ii and 200), but in the later period of use, Room A has the lowest SGF proportions.

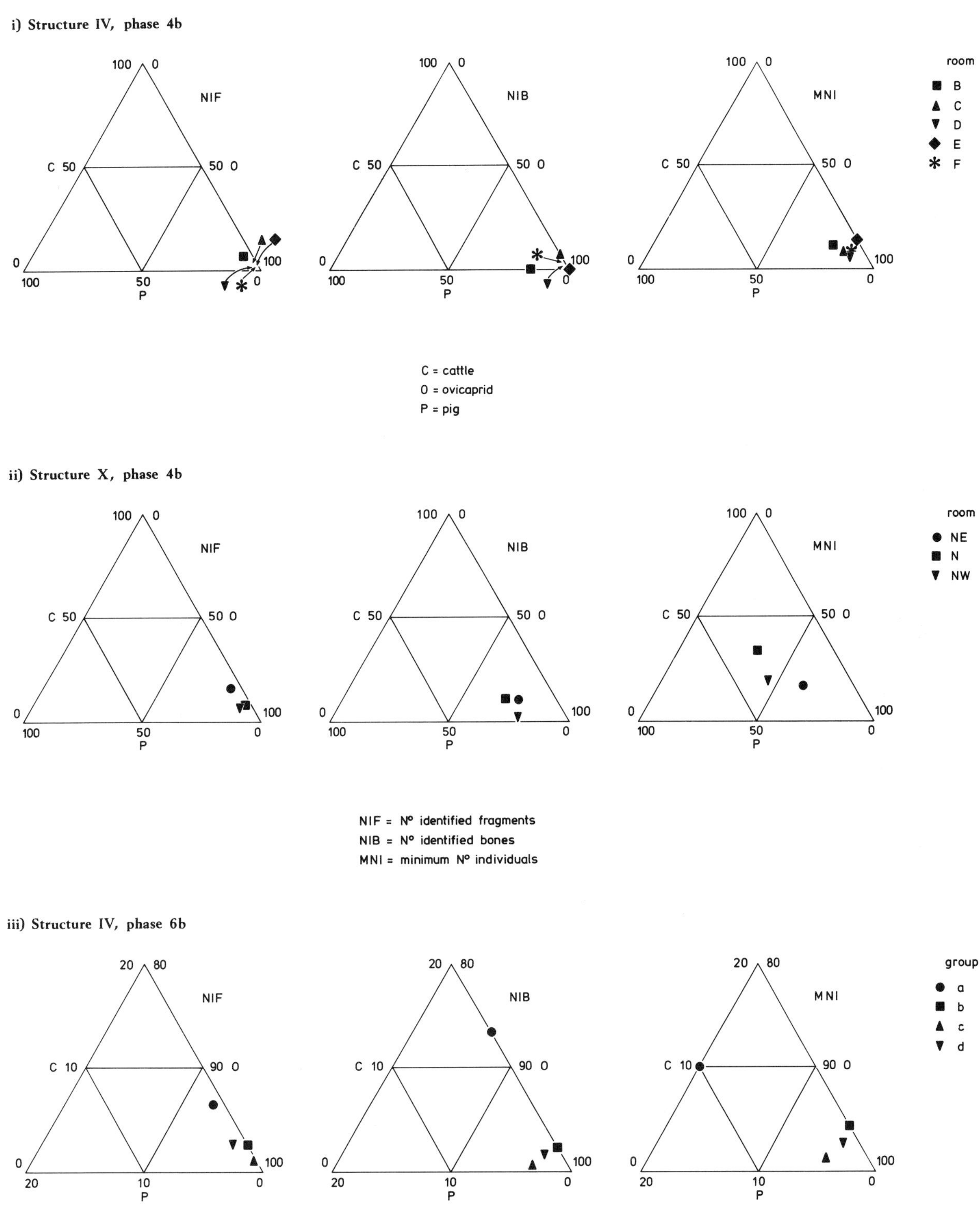

Fig 189 Representation of cattle, sheep/goat, and pig

Phase 6

Deposits from Structure II and over Structure IV have the highest votive proportions (Fig 185i). The SGF content of Structure II rises over that of earlier phases (Structure II(i) and II(ii) from Phase 5, MF Table 19). The paucity of votive material from Structure II may possibly result from the small samples, which, in turn, may represent deliberate clearance of the building. In Phase 6, however, it is notable that Structure II samples are larger, especially those of Structure II(iii) (Table 17). Thus, the apparent change from Phase 5 to Phase 6 is paralleled by an increase in sample size.

Structure XIV can be seen as a continuation of Structure IX in terms of bone proportions, and the occupation and demolition deposits are both fairly similar (Figs 185iii and 201ii).

The votive deposits over Structure IV have been noted above. They are broadly similar to those of Phase 5 over Structure I, and are concentrated in the south area of the former building (Fig 191iii). The similarity between the Structure I and Structure IV deposits is striking: there is even an outlier, with smaller proportions of votive material, to the north of the main concentration over Structure IV, as for Structure I (Fig 194iii and MF Table 19), and this group (group a), like Structure I, was the most diffuse in terms of volume. These structures can be seen therefore as equivalents.

Phase 7

In this phase the mean SGF proportion has decreased, but still remains over 70%, although one has to consider that these percentages are affected by residual material, and the true SGF proportion may be smaller. All the structures have proportions above 70% (Fig 185i), though Structure VIII has 71% SGF in Phase 7a (MF Table 19). This structure has proportions which are very much in contrast to Structure II since they range so widely, and do not overlap with the later Structure II proportions (Table 18, MF Table 19). The contrast between the two buildings is shown in Fig 201i; the only overlap between the structures is the Structure VIII demolition.

Summary

The SGF proportions for all structures and features show clearly the strong cluster of values close to 1.00 (and 1.00 itself is the most common value, Fig 185ii, MF Table 41). Of the 106 values plotted, the range is 0.60–1.00, but 43 of them (40.6%) fall within the range 0.95–1.00 (12.5% of the range), and over half fall within 0.90–1.00 (25% of the range). Thus the great majority of the values are very close to pure SGF deposit values. The overall grouping is unimodal, though it could be that there is a second group in the range 0.60–0.86.

Figure 185i shows the temporal changes in the SGF proportions, and the extent to which individual structures and features can be said to be votive or non-votive in nature. In each phase there are features or structures which can be associated with both functions, and from Phases 4–6 there is a notable consistency for Structures IV and I, and X, IX, and XIV (Fig 185iii). On this basis structures and features have been assigned a votive or non-votive link, and the nature of the votive material present in each of these features and structures is discussed in detail.

	Votive	*non-votive*
Phase 1	F382	F584, F816
Phase 2	F251, F264(i), (v)	F264(ii)–(iv)
Phase 3	Structures XVI, XVII, XVIII*	uncertain
Phase 4	Structure IV	Structure X
Phase 5	Structures I and II*	Structures IX and XIV
Phase 6	Structures II and IV	Structure XIV*
Phase 7	Structures III, VII, XI, and XII*	Structure VIII

* indicates status uncertain

Nature of the votive assemblage

Deposits from the structures and features discussed above form the basis for this analysis. Other deposits, where bones samples were too small, were not considered. The aspects examined here are the nature of the votive bones (SGF), and whether this can be related to the associations suggested above, taking into consideration anatomical representation, sheep:goat ratios, age structures, butchery evidence, metrical data, and pathology. Sheep:goat ratios are based upon bones identified to species level, and include horncores. Sheep may be under-represented because of this as horncores occur more frequently for goat than for sheep. This is not considered a problem as generally goat bones are more common than sheep.

The domestic fowl bones are being analysed by Don Brothwell, but his report is not yet complete. The fowl bones have been considered within the context of subsampling, below, and as a whole, without subsampling. A summary report on the 2939 fowl bones is in fiche.

Phase 1–2 (Prehistoric)

Bones were present in the boundary ditches, in quantities ranging from over 400 bones from ditch F382 (MF Table 2) to none in ditch F179. The abundances appear to be related to the relative frequency of cattle and pig compared with sheep/goat, the smaller samples having higher cattle and pig proportions. In contrast the largest sample (from ditch F382) has higher sheep/goat proportions of which the majority are goats (Fig 186i, iii). The grouping together of sheep and goat (Fig 186ii) may obscure the possibility of different sets of skeletal elements being present for sheep and goat, so the results may not be representative. A comparison for ditch F382 was made using NIB. Although only a small sample, 12 sheep and 19 goats, it was concluded that the anatomical patterns were similar. The majority of the goat fragments were however horncores, NIF 75.3%, and only one of these qualified as NIB. Comparisons of identifiable elements for the other features in this phase was not possible owing to small sample size (MF Table 2). Pooling the two species gives a larger sample and makes it possible to compare features. For NIF the three features cluster fairly closely about the phase total, perhaps indicating a general similarity (MF Fig 3), which is less obvious using NIB. The ditch F382 result is distorted by the high incidence of goat horncores too fragmented to be included in NIB. This reinforces the difference between F382 and the other features, and shows that goat horncores are an important aspect in the votive deposits. Only 13 bones (2.4%) have evidence of butchery; F382 (0.9%), F584 (11.8%),

F816 (0.8%). Fragmentation patterns may be important (Maltby 1979, Wilson 1978a), and this assemblage is characterised by a high proportion of fragmentation. Ageing evidence from tooth eruption and wear with 13 mandibles providing data (12 using Grant 1982) showed that 56.5% of mandibles are in age stage C, and 28.2% in stage D (Payne 1973). No mandibles of stages later than G are present. Using Grant's method, 66.7% have values between 7 and 11 (peaking at 9: 25.0%), the remainder lie between values 30 and 40. The sample is too small to divide the data usefully among the features.

Only seven bones of domestic fowl are present (Table 11), the single additional bone being skylark (Table 13). The bones are from ditches F382 (two bones) and F584, three from adults, one a sub-adult, and two immature. Ditch F382 stands out from the other features, with high proportions of SGF, larger sample size, and dominance of goats, probably the most important characteristic (MF Table 20). On this basis F382 is interpreted as containing mainly votive bone, whilst the other ditches seem to contain non-votive bones.

These results may be compared with those from Uley Bury hillfort, only a mile away (Saville and Ellison 1983), where there were 11 goat and 33 sheep bones from the Middle Iron Age period. This gives species rankings of cattle/sheep/goat; different to any of the patterns for this phase at West Hill (MF Table 20). Period 3 from Uley Bury, Later Iron Age, is more comparable temporally. The sheep/goat bones could not be identified to species level, but sheep/goat are 54.3%, followed by cattle at 36.2%. At West Hill the proportions are generally higher for sheep/goat (MF Table 2). There was little evidence of butchery at Uley Bury, a similar result to West Hill, but the anatomical proportions and fragmentation patterns appear to represent a more domestic economy (ie the animals reared for consumption) (Levitan 1983a). Ditches F584 and F816 are similar to the Uley Bury results, with F584 perhaps the most directly comparable (*cf* species proportions, MF Table 2).

Phase 2 (Early first century)

In order to assess whether there was any variation within the features a fine tuning of the phasing was introduced. This is chronological, with divisions indicated by lower case roman numerals. Division i in each feature is the earliest deposit, but these divisions do not correlate between features and are separate from the structural phasing used elsewhere in this report.

Ditch F264 has a close correspondence of NIF and NIB for sheep:goat proportions (MF Fig 3i). Except in division i, sheep predominate, and there is a steady rise in proportions from division i–iv, followed by a fall in divisions v and vi to about the level of division iii. An apparent break is represented by division vii with a higher proportion of sheep, but this sealing, weathering layer (Phase 3a) is possibly residual.

To test the effect of pooling sheep and goat bones for anatomical analysis, a comparison of the elements identifiable to species has been made. For divisions v–vii the evidence is very similar for each species, less so for divisions ii–iii and very different for division iv. Thus pooling of bones in divisions ii–iv may be more suspect (MF Fig 4i), but sample size could be a factor, with larger samples less variable. A Spearman Rank-Correlation test indicates that there is no correlation between NIF/NIB difference and sample size at the 5% and 1% levels. This makes the changes between divisions difficult to assess except in general terms. Using NIF, all the divisions are fairly similar, with Group A bones 40–50%, Group B 40–50% and Group C 10–20%. All the divisions are characterised by low proportions of Group C bones (maxima are 30% NIF and 20% NIB), and a predominance of Group B bones (minima 30% NIF, 45% NIB).

Bone disposal evidence is often clarified by comparing anatomical information and butchery, but here only 40 fragments are affected (2.3%).

The mandibles were aged using the methods of Payne (1973) and Grant (1975), though the latter cuts down the sample from 79 to 49 by requiring the presence of all three molars. The method of Payne (1973) shows a clear peak in stages C and D which Payne equates with ages (in modern Turkish sheep) of 6–12 and 12–24 months old (Fig 190), with a second, minor peak at stage F (3–4 years old). In the earlier divisions of the feature the main peak is stage C with a second peak centred on stage G (4–6 years), for later divisions (Phase 2d–3a) the main peak is at stage D with a second peak at stage F. Grant's method (1975) has peaks which agree with the above (at stages 8–9 and 34–35, Fig 190), but with a much smaller first peak.

There are only seven bones of fowl from ditch F264,

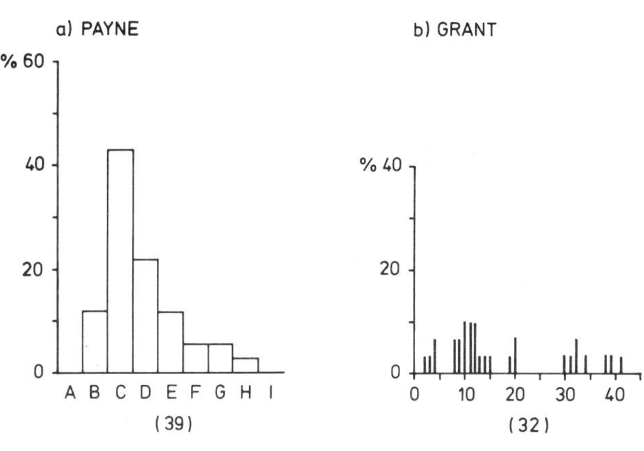

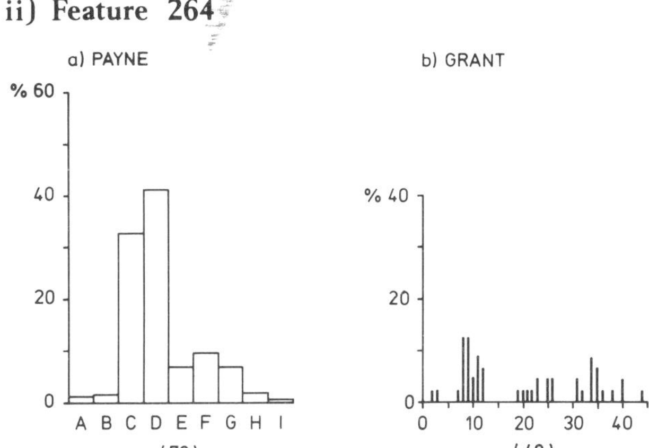

Fig 190 Tooth ageing results

one each from Phases 2c and 2d and five from Phase 3a. Of these two (a radius and an ulna) are immature, the other five are from adult birds.

Pit F251 has sheep predominant, and NIF/NIB results agree for sheep:goat proportions (MF Fig 3ii). Sheep are more common here than in ditch F264, and except for division v, there is little difference temporally within the feature. There was also little difference in anatomical proportions temporally, especially in terms of NIF, and the pattern is of a general mixture of the three anatomy groups (MF Fig 4iii). As for F264, butchery evidence is scarce, with only 1.4% (13 bones, 8 of them ribs) having any. Of three sheep pelves one is male and two female. The ageing evidence (Fig 190i) shows convincingly that most deaths were of juveniles (stage C of Payne 1973; 10–13 of Grant 1975), though the result using Grant's method has a smaller peak.

F836 was a deep, nearly circular pit filled with large limestone blocks in a silty matrix with large voids. Bones were mainly included in the upper third of the feature which included two complete, but fragmented, cattle skulls in contexts 847 and 842 (divisions iiid and e), and a partially complete cattle skull in context 848 (division iiib). Only two of the four temporal divisions contained bones, and these were concentrated in the upper zone. Division iii is a mixed group of votive and other deposits combining six layers (a–e), but only layers b and e have more than 50 bones. Few of these are identifiable to species, and this may account for the apparent variation in sheep:goat proportions (MF Fig 3iii). It is difficult to assess this as the feature total has nearly equal proportions. The anatomical representation is very similar to pit F251, and there is little difference between the divisions (MF Fig 4iv). It was possible to age nine mandibles, six at Payne's stage C (Grant 1982, 8–15), one at D (18), one at E (28) and one at G (40).

F860 a small pit, context 859, which contained 78 teeth, was sealed by context 830, which in contrast had only 10 bones. This difference between the layers does not appear to be significant, however, and the teeth appear to be important for their anatomy rather than their species (sheep, goat, cattle, pig, horse, and dog are represented). In addition to the teeth, 166 fossils were present, all apparently derived from the site bedrock, the Upper Inferior Oolite. Such fossils turned up in small numbers right across the site, but never in such a large concentration; 41 are from context 830 (10 of which are burnt) and 125 from context 859.

In addition to the domestic fowl from F264, the only other fowl bones from Phase 2 (six bones) are from palisade and related contexts; two are from immature birds (tarsometatarsus and ulna), the rest are from adults.

Discussion: Studies such as those of Halstead *et al* 1978, and Wilson 1978b illustrate that intra-site variation is common on prehistoric and rural sites. Maltby has been able to demonstrate that preservation and deposition patterns vary according to feature type (Maltby 1982, 81–8). The variation within and between the four features discussed above is, therefore, hardly surprising. Pit F860 is clearly a special deposit and cannot be readily related to a domestic function, and again for pit F836 some kind of ritual function is indicated.

Pit F251 is also clearly a ritual feature as shown by the material recovered, including iron arrowheads, partly complete Dobunnic fineware vessels, the articulated remains of the hindlimb of a cow, and a human femur (*see chapter* 2). The bones were dominated by sheep, mainly slaughtered between about one and two years old. In Phase 1–2 the dominance of goats was interpreted as indicating votive material, and this seems true for the site generally. It is surprising therefore that sheep are more common in pit F251. As SGF proportions are all in excess of 70%, it seems that in this instance sheep rather than goat were important.

Ditch F264 is the largest and most complex of the Phase 2 features, and was possibly a key element of the temenos ditch system. Interestingly, the sheep/goat proportions are the smallest (MF Fig 3) and correspond most closely to the proportions from other sites plotted by King (1978, 1984) (Fig 184); it also contained the highest proportions of goat bones.

None of these features is typical of domestic deposits, either in anatomical representation or butchery evidence (the latter being scarce). Goats are common, but generally outnumbered by sheep in all the features. Nevertheless, goats are more common than on contemporary sites elsewhere, and it would appear that their importance had increased over the Phase 1–2 proportions. Domestic fowl bones are rare, with only eight from Phase 2 as a whole (a further five, from F264, are of Phase 3a).

Phase 3 (Late first century)

The bones from Phase 3a relate to Structures XVI, XVII and XVIII, and pit F342. The small samples from these structures, and the ephemeral nature of the features, makes temporal or spatial division inadvisable. The larger sample, deposits overlying the boundary ditches, F179, F584 and F816 from infilling of the ditches after removal of the palisades in Phase 3b, may well be residual. The smaller number of bones from Phase 3c is also possibly largely residual.

Phase 3a shows little apparent variation between the pit F342 and the three structures in species representation (MF Fig 5ii). The structures all also contained bones of foetal animals (pigs or sheep/goats). The smallest sample comes from the largest structure, XVI, which occupied a fairly central location within the enclosure (Figs 15 and 22). The others were on the north (Structure XVII) and the east (Structure XVIII) margins of the enclosure. Sheep predominated in all the deposits (MF Fig 6iv), ranging from all sheep in Structure XVI to *c* 60% in pit F342, though the quantity of identified bone is small. Body part representation shows that the four deposits are all similar, and comprise generally mixed anatomies, though with Group B predominant (MF Fig 6i). There was no evidence for any butchery. Ageing was possible for only 14 mandibles, so the results (MF Fig 5iv) may not be representative. They indicate that most of the sheep/goat were juvenile (certainly in the case of Structure XVII and F342), with some adults also present (in Structure XVIII). Apart from domestic fowl bones in the upper fill of F264, there is only one further fowl bone, from pit F342 in Phase 3a.

Phase 3b bones, possibly largely residual, have been divided into three spatial units: those overlying ditches F179 (1053 NIF), F584 (591 NIF), and F816 (85 NIF) respectively. Like Phase 3a, there is apparently little variation in species representation between the groups, though the F179 group may be an outlier (MF Fig 6iii). A notable difference from the earlier phases is the sheep:goat ratios, with goat now predominant (MF Fig 6iii, v). F816 has all sheep, but there are only two identified bones, so the F179 and F584 results are more credible. Using NIF the anatomical representation indicates that the three groups are quite similar, and very close to the pattern for Phase 3a (MF Fig 5i, iv), not unreasonable if the Phase 3b deposits are residual. Using NIB, however, the three groups are very different, only F179 echoing the NIF result. There is a correlation here between sample size and degree of difference between NIF and NIB results, with the largest sample least different and the smallest sample most different. To some extent, therefore, the results from NIB may be unrepresentative, but the wide divergence does give concern in grouping of sheep/goat anatomies. Taking the F179 and F584 sheep and goat identifications, the goat cranial group comprises 52% (F179) and 6% (F584). For sheep the cranial group comprises 20% (F179) and 44% (F584) respectively. In both groups, sheep and goat also differ markedly for the other anatomical elements. Only eight bones have butchery (including three goat horncores), 0.2% NIF for F179 and 1.3% NIF for F584. Sexing of bones from F584 indicates three females and three males, all goats. From F179, 22 bones were sexed, male:female ratios are – goat 6:5, sheep 4:3, sheep/goat 3:1. 18 mandibles were aged, 14 from F179, of these 43% are juveniles, stages

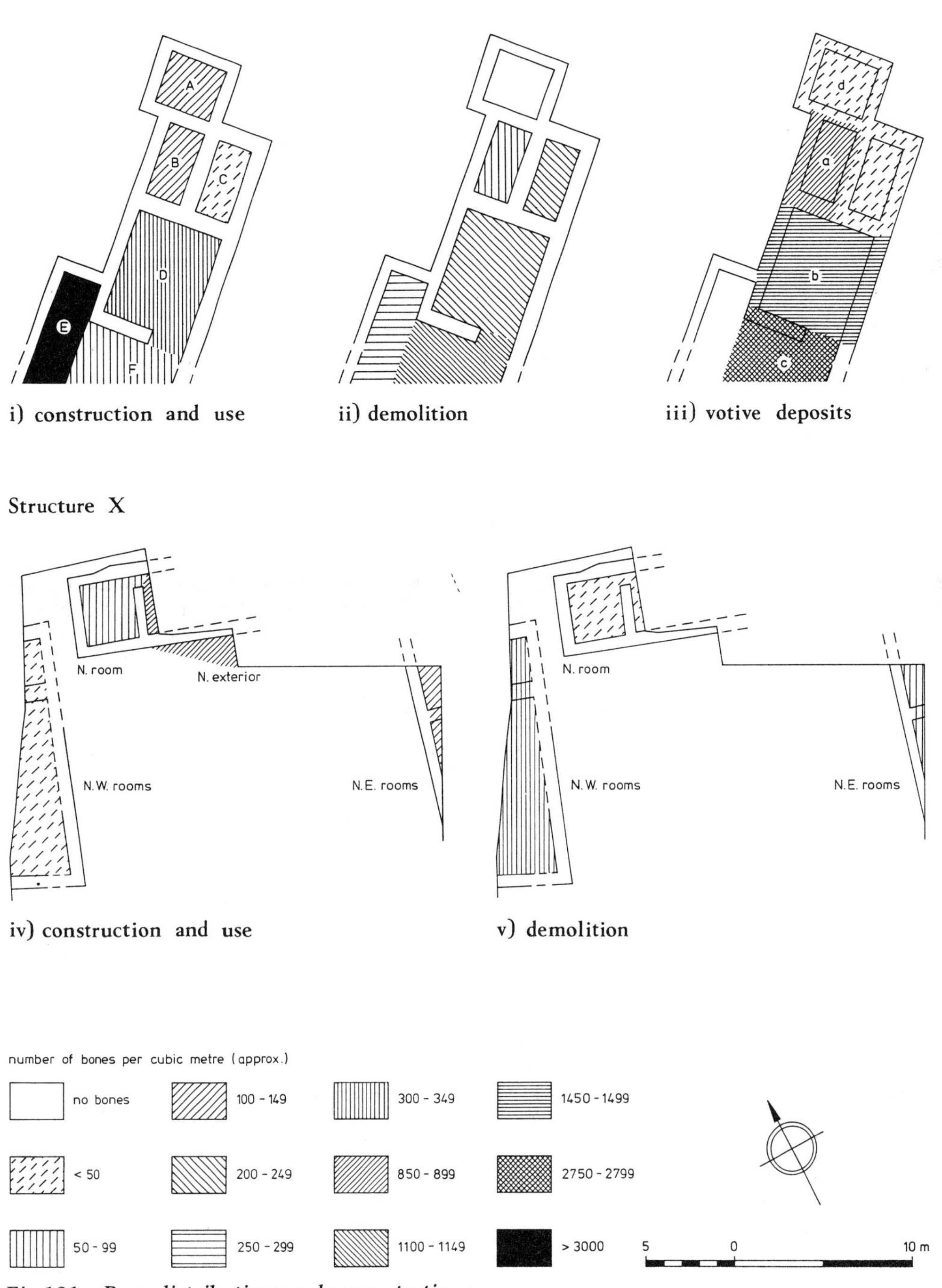

Fig 191 Bone distributions and concentrations

C and D of Payne (1973) (4–22 of Grant 1982) and 36% young adults stage E (30–32) with none being older than stage G (43). There are six domestic fowl bones from Phase 3b, three from F179, two from F584 and one from F816; two (coracoid and humerus) are immature, one sub-adult (ulna) from F179, the remainder are adults. This is 0.3% of the bones from Phase 3b, compared with 0.1% from Phase 3a (excluding upper fills of F264) – slender evidence for an increase in the importance of fowl.

Phase 3c bones relate to palisade removals, with most bones, as in Phase 3b, centred on the F179 area, so detailed analysis was not attempted, but sheep are more common than in Phase 3b, with goats only just more frequent using NIF and NIB. These deposits are therefore intermediate between Phases 3a and 3b, which supports the view that the bones are residual. In contrast, domestic fowl bones are most common during this phase; 18 of the 27 bones, 5 of which are from immature birds, come from pre- Structure X layers (MF Table 4).

Discussion: Phase 3a must be seen as a continuation of activities from Phase 2 in features F251, F264, and F836, though there are no bones of Phase 3a for F836. This is reflected in the species representation (Fig 187 and MF Fig 5), and sheep:goat ratios, with sheep predominant (MF Fig 3 and MF Fig 6). It may also be significant that the bones are deposited mainly in peripheral features (except Structure XVI) although it is uncertain whether this reflects different sets of activities in the enclosure and on its margins, or simply the dumping of bones in the pits and ditches. The latter seems most logical (eg Wilson 1978a, 1985); certainly there is no marked difference between deposits from Structure XVI and the marginal deposits.

It is suggested above that ditch F264 and pits F251 and F836 served ritual functions. Bone deposits of a similar nature occur in Structures XVI, XVII, and XVIII implying that these structures had similar ritual functions (underlined by the infant human burials related to Structure XVII and Structure XVI, *see Bell and Rogers above*). The sheep/goat bones cannot be related easily to domestic activities, because of the virtual absence of butchery, and the species representation which is unlike that from other contemporary sites (Fig 184 and MF Fig 5).

The bones change character in Phase 3b, with goats becoming predominant. The previously high proportions of goat, though smaller than sheep, were unusual; the predominance of goat in this sub-phase underlines and increases the difference of this assemblage from those of other sites. The deposits are difficult to relate to structural units, but lateral variation between the deposits is apparent. The anatomical representation for the goats is also unusual, with deposits from F179 dominated by horncores (the cranial elements from F584 are all horncores, although the cranial proportion is smaller).

Phase 3c is, in some ways, intermediate between Phase 3a and 3b, supporting the hypothesis that the bones are from largely residual deposits. The domestic fowl bones, however, belie this because they are here at their highest proportions for the phase. The overall picture from Phase 3 is firstly, a continuation of the patterns from earlier periods, followed by an increase in goat as an important votive element. Fowl are also becoming more important, though their increase in Phase 3c is a problem.

Phase 4 (second–third centuries)

Structure IV bones were recovered from all parts of the building for Phase 4a, but not from Room A in Phase 4b (Fig 191). The main concentrations of bones were in Phase 4a mainly in Room E, and in Phase 4b mainly in Room D. The deposits all had remarkably similar species representation, with proportions of sheep/goat, much higher than other sites in the country (Figs 184, 188ii, 189i, Table 15, and MF Fig 9i), though perhaps Room A, a later addition, and the deposits to the exterior of the building are a little different (using NIB Fig 188ii). Sheep:goat ratios show that, except for the exterior and Room F (with too small samples), goats greatly predominate, being 70% or more for NIF, around 70%

Table 15: Summary of bones from Structures IV AND X, Phase 4 (MF Table 5)

Species	*NIF*		*NIB*		*MIN*		*NFI*	*NBI*	*NIF*		*NIB*		*MNI*		*NFI*	*NBI*
	no	*%*	*no*	*%*	*no*	*%*			*no*	*%*	*no*	*%*	*no*	*%*		
Structure IV			*Phase 4a*								*Phase 4b*					
Sheep/goat	1408	87.9	382	91.4	73	83.9	19	5	2560	95.9	578	94.8	72	83.7	36	8
Cattle	136	8.5	14	3.4	3	3.5	45	5	65	2.4	8	1.3	3	3.5	22	3
Pig	50	3.1	16	3.8	9	10.3	6	2	18	0.7	8	1.3	5	5.8	4	2
Horse	-	-	-	-	-	-	-	-	-	-	-	-	-	-	-	-
Dog	8	0.5	6	1.4	2	2.3	4	3	26	1.0	16	2.6	6	7.0	4	3
Other mammal	-	-	-	-	-	-	-	-	-	-	-	-	-	-	-	-
Total	1602	85.8	418	63.9	87	59.1	-	-	2669	96.6	610	87.6	86	81.1	-	-
Domestic fowl	266	14.2	236	36.1	60	40.8	4	4	94	3.4	86	12.4	20	18.9	5	4
Structure X			*Phase 4a*								*Phase 4b*					
Sheep/goat	1511	76.0	407	75.4	41	53.2	37	10	1319	79.6	323	76.7	24	50.0	55	14
Cattle	332	16.7	57	10.6	13	16.9	26	4	239	14.4	46	10.9	8	16.7	30	6
Pig	124	6.2	64	11.9	17	22.1	7	4	85	5.1	39	9.3	10	20.8	9	4
Horse	2	0.1	1	0.2	2	2.6	1	1	3	0.2	2	0.5	2	4.2	2	1
Dog	12	0.6	11	2.0	3	3.9	4	4	1	0.1	1	0.2	1	2.1	1	1
Other mammal	7	0.4	-	-	1	1.3	-	-	11	0.7	10	2.4	3	6.3	-	-
Total	1988	93.1	540	79.5	77	68.8	-	-	1658	91.2	421	75.9	48	62.3	-	-
Domestic fowl	148	6.9	139	20.5	35	31.2	4	4	159	8.8	134	24.1	29	37.7	5	5

Sheep/goat identifications:		*NIF*	*NIB*	*MNI*			*NIF*	*NIB*	*MNI*
Structure IV	Phase 4a:	45:108	45:88	8:25	***Structure X,***	Phase 4a:	38:33	37:33	9:9
	Phase 4b:	56:143	50:116	20:24	,	Phase 4b:	24:21	22:21	7:6

for NIB and 50% or more for MNI during Phase 4a. In Phase 4b, the Room E–F deposits comprise smallest goat proportions, but here goats predominate in all rooms (MF Fig 7i, ii).

The samples are large enough to allow more detailed resolution of anatomical representation (Fig 192i, iii, MF Fig 8i, iii for sheep and goat identifications, and MF Fig 9iii for sheep/goat, Phase 4a and b). There is no apparent consistency between the rooms or between NIF and NIB results. The NIF results place the rooms in a broad group of mixed body parts, with a larger spread in Phase 4b than Phase 4a. Comparison of sheep and goat results shows that in some rooms there is a general similarity between the species, but in others there is not (MF Fig 8i, iii). The possible biases of grouping sheep and goat together have already been discussed. In this case the samples are very small, especially for sheep, so too much emphasis cannot be placed upon the results. It seems that there probably are different body-part distributions for the two species, so here grouping them may introduce bias. Goats are generally predominant, however, so this may not be serious, although the different, but much smaller sheep bone sample may be cancelled out as a result. There is a fairly good correspondence in anatomical distribution between Phase 4a and 4b for each room using NIF, although there are some differences (MF Fig 9). For example in Phase 4a Room C has greater proportions of mandibles, vertebrae, metapodia, and phalanges, while in Phase 4b Room B has higher incidences of scapula and metapodia. The correspondence is least good for Room F. Using NIB, there is very little correspondence, but this may be because of the much smaller sample sizes involved (see MF Table 10 which also shows the differences between the rooms). Using NIF Room A is predominated by cranial and axial bones. In Room B there is a high proportion of cranial bones, axial bones are rare, but girdles and limbs are well represented. This is a pattern which changes little from Phase 4a to 4b, indicating that demolition here did not cause mixing of the deposits. NIB results are more erratic, but generally support the NIF ones. Room C appears to change little from Phase 4a to 4b, although Phase 4b has more ribs than Phase 4a. Room D, aside from the large proportion of ribs (NIF), resembles Room B, and thus has elements of similarity to Rooms B and C. The lack of ribs (NIB) exaggerates the other elements, but the patterns are fairly similar, and there is no great change between sub-phases. In Room E cranial bones, ribs, and scapulae are common in Phase 4a, Phase 4b is similar, but with hind limbs also well represented. Room F has the only marked contrast between occupation and demolition deposits. In Phase 4a, extremity bones are well represented (and very common using NIB), but in Phase 4b these elements are in a minority, with ribs very well represented. This indicates a possible mixing of demolition deposits, though other areas of the building do not appear to have suffered this to any extent. The exterior deposits (Phase 4a only) have cranial bones and ribs in the majority, with lesser peaks for upper limbs.

There is apparently little correspondence between the rooms, but there are some groupings using NIF. In Phase 4a Rooms B, E, F, and the extension have higher proportions of Group A and B bones than Rooms A, C, and D (Group A 15–25% compared with about 30–40%, Group B 40–50% compared with around 15–25%). In Phase 4b Rooms B, D, and E have Group B bones at 35–50% and Group A bones at 20–35%. Rooms C and F differ with Group B bones at 10–20% and Group A bones 60–75% respectively (Fig 192i and iii). Taking NIB there does not seem to be a consistent relationship between Phase 4a and 4b, and the room-groups are different. In Phase 4a Rooms A, C, F, and the extension (with high proportions of Group B bones, 50–70%, and low proportions of Group C bones, 25–50%) compare with Rooms B, D, and E (Group B bones 35–40% and Group C bones 50–60%). In Phase 4b, however, there does not seem to be any true grouping of rooms at all.

Ageing evidence from mandibles shows that in Phase 4a Rooms A–E all have main peaks in the juvenile to sub-adult age range, stages D of Payne (1973), 20 of Grant (1975) (MF Fig 10i, ii). The exterior also peaks at this age, but there is a second peak at stage G (39), an age stage that only occurs here and in Room F (one mandible). In Phase 4b the outstanding sample is from Room D where 228 mandibles were aged using Payne's method (143 using Grant 1975). In all rooms most deaths occurred in stages C and D (Payne 1973) (8–35 of Grant 1975), juvenile to sub-adult. In Room D mandibles of stages B–H (6–46) are present indicating a wide age-range which is perhaps representative of the structures demolition deposits as a whole. The results using Grant's method give three peaks, each with a gradual build-up, followed by a sharp decrease. They centre on stages 9, 21, and 31, the main peak being the last one (in Payne's method the main peak is at stage D). These might represent deaths at the same time of the year, once a year (ie at *c* 6 months old, at 18 months, and at 30 months). If one assumes spring births, this represents seasonal kill-off in August/September.

Butchery is rare as in previous phases, with only 14 bones (1.0%) from Phase 4a and 16 bones (0.6%) from Phase 4b. Most parts of the anatomy are represented: cranial bones, cervical vertebrae, ribs, girdle, upper limb, and extremity. Sexing of bones provided the following male:female ratios, Phase 4a, from 18 designations: goat 9:5, sheep 3:1, Phase 4b, from 33 designations: goat 17:8, sheep 5:3. Thus, males dominated in both sexes, but since this small sample cannot be divided into age groups, it cannot be taken as representative.

Both in sample size and proportions domestic fowl rise over previous periods (Table 15). In both Phase 4a and 4b the representation is variable. In Phase 4a this ranges from none (Room E and exterior) to 12% (Room A), and in Phase 4b from 0.9% (Room B) to 5.1% (Room D). The proportions are not related to sample size (ie smallest samples do not equate with least representation) (MF Table 10). The largest number of bones from Phase 4a comes from Room B, but from a sub-sampled context (Levitan 1983b). The anatomical analysis is based upon the total domestic fowl assemblage, not upon the sub-sample (which is used for species representation only in the case of fowl). The fowl body parts are divided into four groups: head, neck, and extremities (leg phalanges); body (includes sternum, ribs, and vertebrae other than cervical); wing (includes furcula, coracoid, scapula and the other bones of the wing); and leg (lumbrosacrale, femur, tibiotarsus and tarsometa-

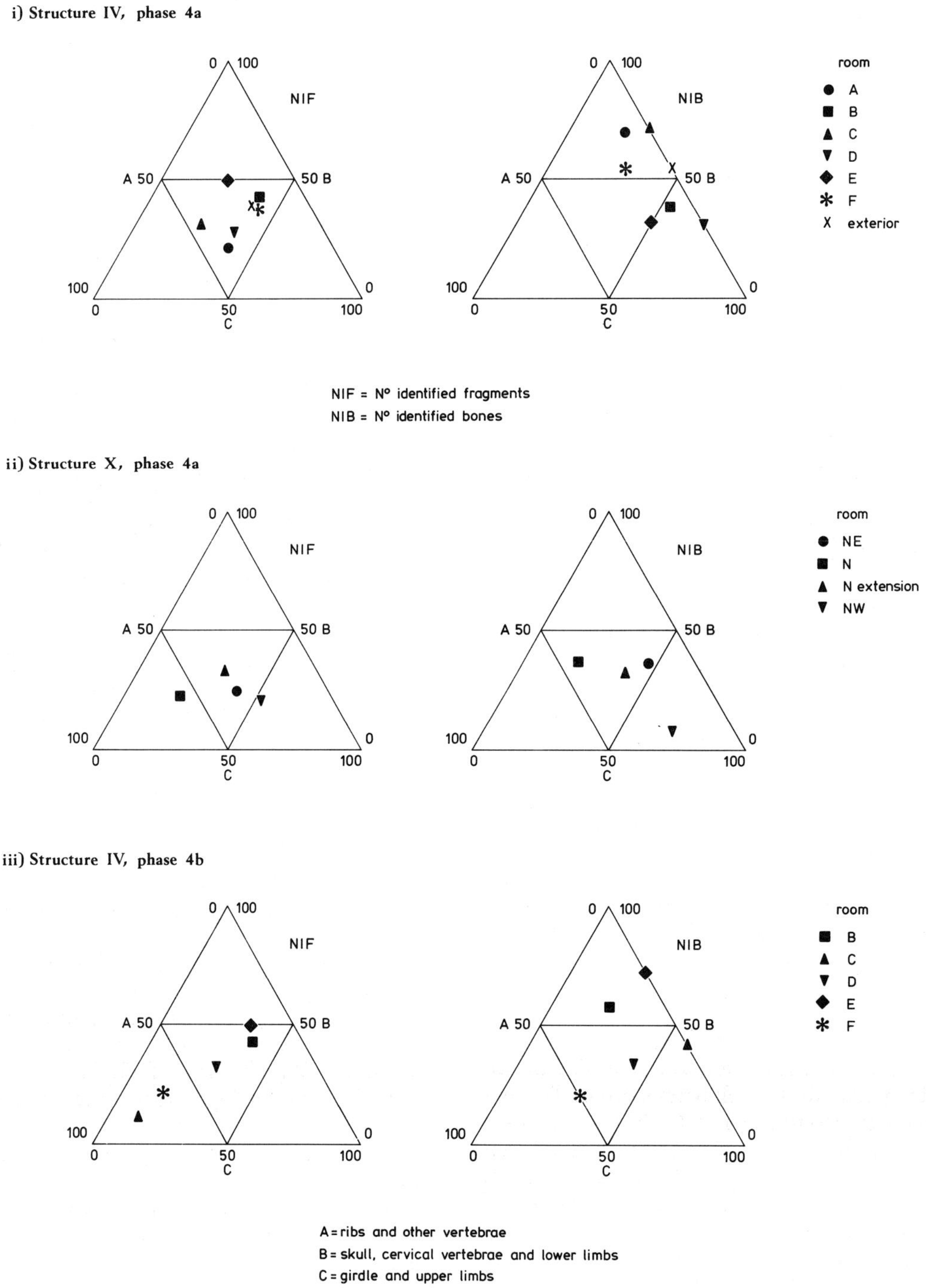
i) Structure IV, phase 4a
NIF
NIB
room
A
B
C
D
E
F
exterior
NIF = N° identified fragments
NIB = N° identified bones
ii) Structure X, phase 4a
NIF
NIB
room
NE
N
N extension
NW
iii) Structure IV, phase 4b
NIF
NIB
room
B
C
D
E
F
A = ribs and other vertebrae
B = skull, cervical vertebrae and lower limbs
C = girdle and upper limbs

Fig 192 Sheep/goat anatomical representation

tarsus) (Fig 197). The first group may be under-represented because it includes very small bones (phalanges and vertebrae) and fragile skull bones, and this was one of the deposits which was not sieved. The wings and legs are clearly in the majority, but since these are paired bones (furcula excluded: lumbrosacrale was generally recorded in right and left halves separately), they are over-represented. The various skeletal groups are possibly much more equally represented, though probably wings and legs are still predominant. No attempt to divide the data among the rooms has been made since samples are too small. The fowl bones comprise juveniles and adults (based on fusion status of the bones); 57 bones from Phase 4a (54.8%) are adults and 47 (45.2%) juveniles, while 22 bones from Phase 4b (50.0%) are adult and 22 (50.0%) juvenile. The room results vary, possibly because of small samples. Larger samples are consistent with the summary results. In both sub-phases there are approximately equal proportions of juveniles and adults. Tarsometatarsi, if spurred, are generally males, though unspurred specimens are not invariably females. From Phase 4a out of eleven bones, seven are spurred, and from Phase 4b all three are spurred (adult bones only are involved). Males, are therefore in the majority.

Structure X bone sample was smaller overall than that from Structure IV (Table 15), but the concentration of bones per unit volume of soil was similar (Fig 191ii, v). The excavated portion of the building was small, three sections, the north-west rooms, north rooms, and north-east rooms. The area exterior to the north rooms contained the main concentration of bone in Phase 4a, but the demolition deposits of Phase 4b had the greatest concentration over the north-west rooms. Species representation (Figs 185iii and 189ii) is similar for the room groups using NIF, but less so using NIB and MNI. The sheep:goat ratios are varied, ranging in Phase 4a from no goat in the north-west rooms, to 70% goat in the north-east rooms and, in Phase 4b from no goat in the north rooms, to 60% goat in the north-east rooms (the north-east rooms are most consistent) (MF Fig 7iv, v). The smallest goat proportions are in the smallest samples, although the largest samples do not necessarily contain most goats.

When sheep and goat anatomical proportions are compared it is evident that there is little correspondence between the species, although small samples preclude detailed analysis (MF Fig 8ii, iv). The validity of treating the sheep/goat bones as a single group again arises, but is necessary in order to boost sample sizes. The bias introduced may be greater in Structure X than Structure IV since here no one species is predominant.

The north-east and north rooms show least contrast between Phase 4a and 4b, possibly indicating little disturbance of deposits during demolition (MF Fig 9iv). The two room ranges are also similar to each other in comparison with the rest. In the north-east rooms ribs are predominant, followed by forelimb and hindlimb bones (NIF), although for NIB the ribs are less common. The north rooms have a greater predominance of ribs in Phase 4a (NIF), but in Phase 4b ribs are predominant using NIB. Limb extremities are fairly well represented using NIF, but are very common using NIB, in contrast to the north-east rooms. Body parts are quite strongly contrasted temporally for the north-west rooms (especially using NIB) with predominant ribs the only common factor. In Phase 4a the emphasis is on scapulae and forelimbs, with fairly good representation of hind limbs and metapodia. Phase 4b has vertebrae and ribs particularly well represented. There is also a contrast between the rooms. In the exterior area, cranial bones and ribs are dominant (using NIF), differing from the other groups. The NIB results are similar to the north-east rooms, but with fragmented skull and ribs less well represented.

This variation, both spatially and temporally, is underlined in Figs 192ii and 193i. In Phase 4a, sheep:goat ratios indicate that the north-east and north rooms are goat-predominant, and the north-west rooms and exterior sheep-predominant (MF Fig 7iv). When broken down into anatomical groupings there is no clear association, but the north-east rooms may form a group with the north-west rooms and exterior, leaving the north rooms as an outlier (using NIF); alternatively (using NIB), the outlier is the north-west rooms (Fig 192ii). In Phase 4b the sheep:goat ratios indicate that the north rooms may be an outlier, and this is supported by the NIB results (Fig 193i), though not by NIF. The temporal contrasts are also underlined (Figs 192ii and 193i).

Ageing evidence for Phase 4a is based upon 17 mandibles (9 using Grant 1982), and for Phase 4b on 11 mandibles. In Phase 4a main deaths were in stages D–E (Payne 1973) (22–9, Grant) (the exterior sample is based on only three specimens, but the death peak is stages 7–10). The oldest animals, from the exterior deposits, survived to stage G (37). In Phase 4b the north-west rooms have a convincing peak at stage D (20), but the north-east rooms have two peaks, at stages B (11–15) and E (37–40) ie about one and three years old. Butchery evidence is present on 5.6% of the sheep/goat bones in Phase 4a and on 11.1% in Phase 4b. The butchery patterns are fairly typical of processing for consumption. Very few bones were sexed: from Phase 4a there were one male goat, one female goat, and two female sheep. In Phase 4b there were one male goat, one male sheep, four male sheep/goat, and only one female sheep/goat.

Domestic fowl proportions are around 8% (Table 15), but variation between the rooms ranges from 3.8% (north-west rooms) to 13.4% (north rooms) in Phase 4a, and from 6.9% (north-west rooms) to 14.9% (north rooms) in Phase 4b; thus showing some consistency (Table 11). Wing bones appear to be in the majority, followed by leg bones with temporal variations in relative proportions of body bones and head/etc (heads are more common in Phase 4a) (Fig 197i). Adults are in the majority, in Phase 4a 67.1% (57 bones) adult, 32.9% (28 bones) juvenile, and in Phase 4b 71.2% (79 bones) adult and 28.8% (32 bones) juvenile. Where samples are large enough, the individual rooms agree well with the sub-phase totals. There are four out of seven tarsometatarsi that are spurred (male) in Phase 4a, and one spurred specimen from Phase 4b.

Structures IV and X

These contrast as follows:

1) Structure IV has higher proportions of sheep/goat (Fig 189)

2) Bones from Structure IV were more abundant (Table 15) and more densely deposited (Fig 191)

3) Sheep were more common in Structure X; sheep:goat ratios are 6:5 for Structure X and 1:3 for Structure IV (Table 15, MF Fig 7)

4) The types of deposit are quite different: anatomical representation patterns hardly overlap (Fig 193iii, iv) while similar differences occur for domestic fowl (Fig 197i)

5) There is a greater frequency of butchery on bones from Structure X (6–10% compared with 1% or less on those from Structure IV)

Similarities also occur:

1) Sheep/goat kill-off peaks are in August/September (MF Fig 10)

2) There is similarity within each structure between occupation and demolition deposits, indicating little disturbance of deposits

Discussion: Structure IV contains deposits which have extremely high proportions of sheep/goat (with goat predominant). The sheep/goat were apparently mostly males, and butchery evidence was almost non-existent. These are patterns completely atypical of domestic deposition on comparative sites, and seem likely to be derived from ritual activity. In contrast, Structure X contains more elements of domestic patterning, such as increased butchery, superimposed upon the predominantly ritual character of the assem-

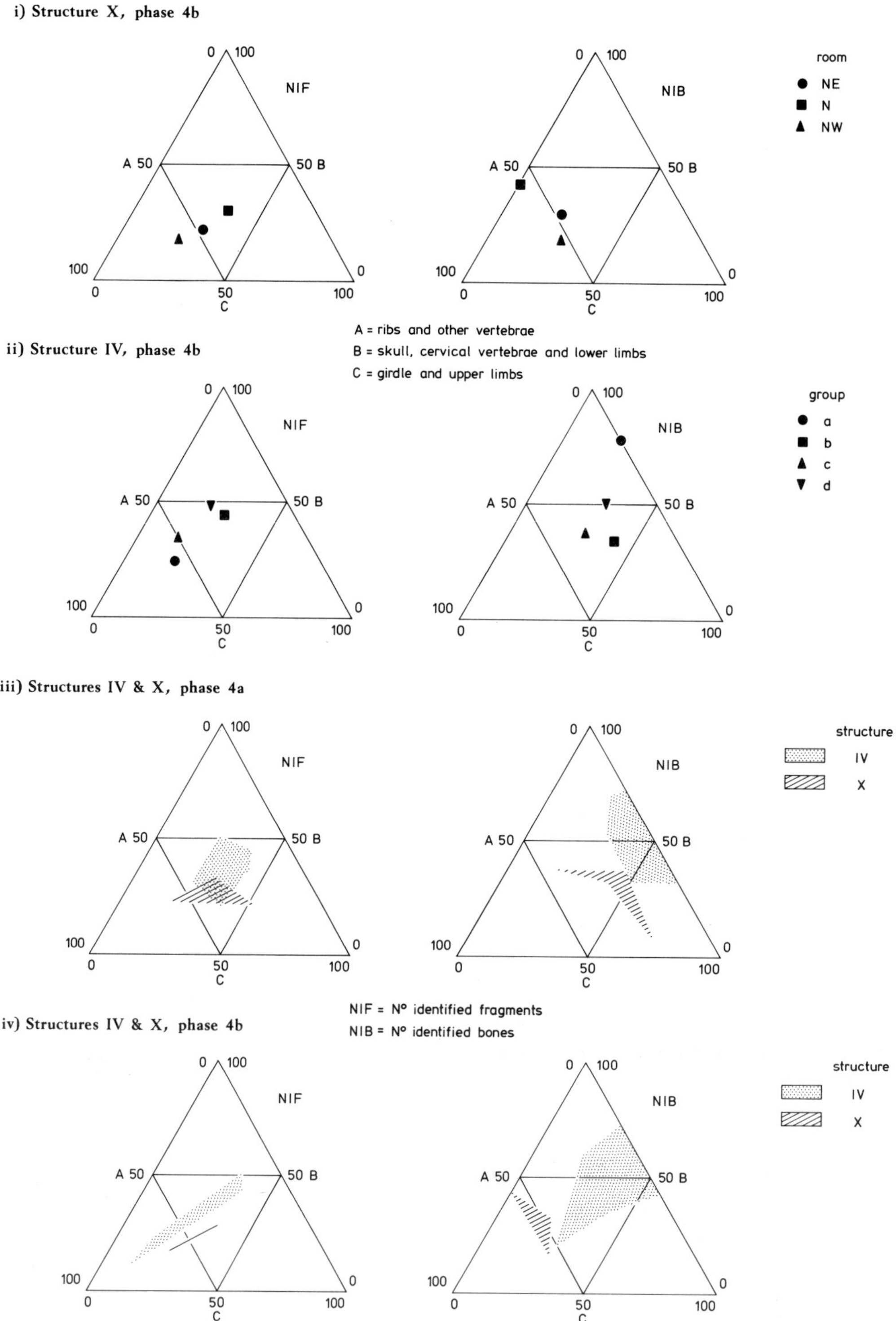

Fig 193 Sheep/goat anatomical representation

blages. Possibly Structure X can be interpreted as a building having a more domestic function within a ritual context, eg a guest house. In this case, some of the ritually slaughtered animals may have been eaten, with the more common sheep perhaps having a lesser ritual status which made it possible to eat them. In contrast the large numbers of goats, mainly unbutchered, from Structure IV may indicate that these individuals were not eaten, or not cut up before cooking. Structure IV cannot be considered to have a domestic function on the evidence of these bones. This picture of ritual animals, some being eaten and others perhaps not, is enhanced by the presence of domestic fowl, which become more common during this phase. In Structure IV, characterised by approximately equal proportions of adults and juveniles, most of the adults appear to be male, while in Structure X there are higher proportions of adults, though males still predominate.

The kill-off peaks indicate that the main rites using animals were probably centred on August/September. Perhaps the smaller number of deaths during the rest of the year represent a non-votive or only partially votive element, with animals killed mainly for consumption.

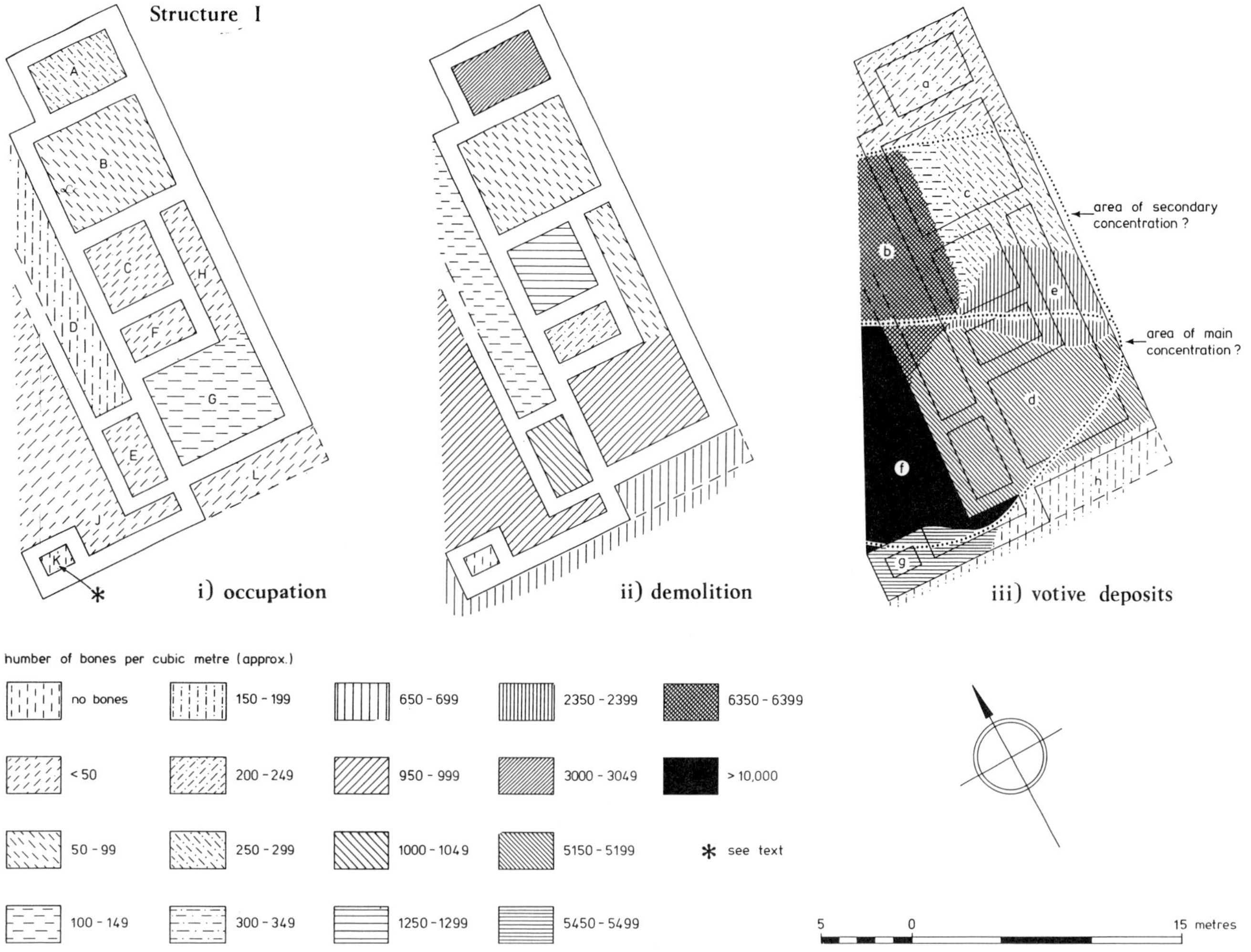

Fig 194 Bone distributions and concentrations

Phase 5 (Mid-fourth century)
Structure IV was joined by Structure I during this phase and Structure X was succeeded by a similar range of buildings, Structure IX. Structure II was also in use. Species representation identifies Structure I deposits as mainly ritual, and those from Structure IX as more domestic; similar to Structures IV and X in Phase 4. Although Structures XIII and XIV originate in Phase 5, they continue into Phase 6, as does Structure II, and for convenience they will be discussed here.

Structure I has sheep/goat proportions which can be paralleled in Structure IV, but Structure I proportions are higher. Using NIF these are never below 90%, with three exceptions in Phase 5e (Fig 195, MF Table 19). The increase in proportions of goat over other species in Phase 4 peaks in Phase 5 (MF Fig 12). With very few exceptions, goat proportions are above 70% for all areas of Structure I during this whole phase. Figure 194 illustrates the bone distributions and concentrations for the structure, and underlines the density of the bone concentrations, especially in Phase 5e (MF Fig 12i, MF Table 12).

When occupation deposits are compared for sheep and goat there is a clear contrast between the species. Sheep are represented by only two body-part groups, goat by all but one, with a high proportion of goat horncores, which were not present at all for sheep. Rooms with larger samples emphasise this difference.

Demolition deposits, in contrast, are similar for the two species (MF Fig 12ii). There are peaks in cranial bones, girdles, and extremities for both species, though for goat (NIF) the emphasis is on cranial bones and for sheep on girdles. The cranial bones of both species are dominated by horncores. All areas except Room H have goat horncores present, in most cases as a major or even dominant body-part. The goat bones are dominated by cranial elements (mainly horncores), with girdles also important. The robbing deposit (MF Fig 12iii) again shows a contrast between sheep and goat. Both species have horncores present, but goats are again represented predominantly by cranial elements, while sheep are still dominated by girdles.

Finally, the structure total for votive deposits is practically identical to that for the demolition deposit (MF Fig 12iv). This is important because it suggests that the deposits from Structure I itself correspond with the votive deposit which post-dates the demolition of the structure. As with the demolition deposit, there is little similarity between sheep and goat, either by area or for the structure as a whole.

The dissimilarity of sheep and goat anatomical representation again questions the validity of amalgamation of sheep/goat bones. Goat so greatly outnumber sheep however that any species bias is possibly swamped by the goat data (MF Fig 11, MF Tables 12 and

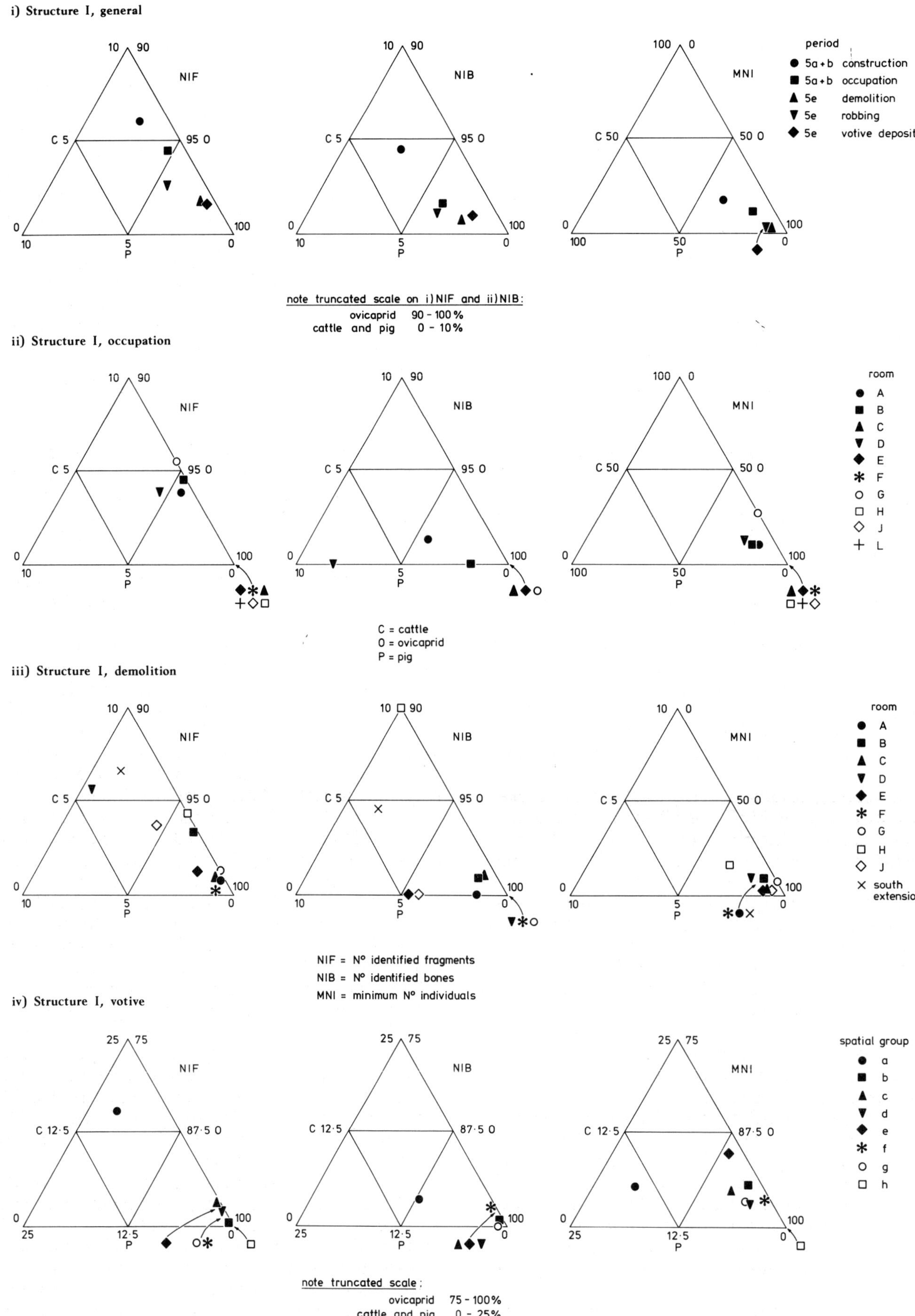

Fig 195 Representation of cattle, sheep/goat, and pig

13). Thus the results can probably be taken to represent goats (MF Fig 13).

The most striking factor for the occupation deposit is the very high proportion of ribs, even using NIB where heads only are counted. Rooms A, B, and G correspond quite closely with the structure total (MF Fig 13i), particularly for NIF. Room D has a similar pattern, but with cranial and limb bones better represented. Where there are larger samples there appears to be relatively little variation from room to room. The remaining rooms do not give very useful results as the samples are small (MF Table 12). They do seem to form a different group, but the samples are too small to be sure this is the case.

Ribs dominate in the demolition deposits also, the NIF results are very similar to the occupation result (MF Fig 13ii). The correspondence holds for Rooms A, B, and G, but is much less clear for Room D. Such results imply that demolition deposits echo the occupation, but this is somewhat belied by the samples per room which vary quite widely. A Spearman's Rank Correlation test on these deposits gives a result of −0.11, which indicates that the correlation is not at all good. Thus sample sizes and densities do not correspond well (Fig 194). This may indicate input from other sources during demolition, or that some rooms had been cleared before demolition. The rooms exhibit a range of patterns. Room A has very high proportions of ribs which swamp all other body-parts. Rooms B and G also have very high proportions of ribs, but with cranial and extremity bones better represented. This trend of increased presence of cranial bones and extremities is continued in Rooms C and E, where the emphasis is on cranial elements. Room D has ribs and cranial bones about equal, and limbs (but not extremities) well represented. Room J and the south extension have cranial bones most common, ribs next, and limbs in third place. Room F has vertebrae predominant, followed by limbs, while Room H has high proportions of ribs, but more extremities.

The robbing results (MF Fig 13iii) are not broken down by area (as in MF Table 12) as the material may be residual, from disturbed deposits, or introduced by backfilling after robbing. The rather different results reflect a mixture of influences: ribs are most common, but much less so than previously, cranial bones are well represented, followed by vertebrae, hindlimb, and forelimb.

The correspondence between ritual and earlier deposits seen for goat bones (MF Fig 12), does not hold up for sheep/goat bones as well (MF Fig 13iv). Ribs are predominant, but cranial bones are also well represented. The structure total for robbing is intermediate between the ritual and the occupation/demolition deposit, lending credence to the hypothesis that the robbing represents mixed deposits. In the ritual deposit, upper limb bones are next most common, after ribs, for sheep/goat, followed by girdles, vertebrae, and extremities. Spatial groups b, d, e, f, and g are fairly similar to the total, leaving a, c, and h, all of which are small samples compared with the other deposits (MF Table 13). Groups c and h have high proportions of cranial bones, and smaller proportions of ribs, group a the reverse.

Using anatomical representation triangular plots the occupation NIF falls into three groups (Fig 196i), Rooms A, B, and G; Rooms C, D, H, and L, and Rooms E, F, and J. The Room A, B, G group, (identified above, MF Fig 13) also shows that Room D was closest to this group (Fig 196i). Using NIB, the Room A, B, G group is rather looser, and includes Room D. The Room E, F, J group has no ribs and vertebrae, but is otherwise disparate.

The demolition deposits result (NIF) supports this, with Rooms A, B, and G similar, and includes Rooms C, E, and perhaps F (Fig 196ii). The NIB result however separates Rooms A, B, and G from these others, which all group together quite closely, although the group formed by Rooms A, B, and G is looser. Rooms D, H, J, and the south extension form a second, tight group.

The votive deposit histograms indicated that groups a, c, and h are outliers, and this is certainly the case for a and h (MF Fig 13). Figure 196iii however shows group c as very close to the others. The NIB results are rather different, with all groups forming a tight-knit group of mixed body-parts. The triangular plots (Fig 196) bring out the increase in importance of cranial elements for sheep/goat, in contrast to the cattle and pigs.

Samples for the pre-votive deposits are too small for spatial analysis, but they provide 726 aged mandibles (366 using Grant's method) (MF Fig 14). The main peak of kill-off is stages D–E (Payne 1973) (around 20–30 with Grant 1975). A feature of the construction period sample is a high incidence of infants at stage B (Payne 1973, 3–9, Grant 1975) and a pattern of three peaks, at stages B, D, and G. This implies kill-off at ages of about 6 months, 18 months, and 30 months old, ie in the same season of the year, around August/September. Thus, the same kill-off peaks as for Phase 4 are present.

The occupation deposits have a clear single peak in stage E (Payne 1973) with no infants or older adults present at all. Grant's method gives two peaks, at stages 14 (about 6–8 months) and 30–34 (30 months), similar, but slightly later in the year, and with the emphasis on first and third year individuals.

The demolition deposits also have a single peak (Payne 1973) at stages D–E, but a wider age range is represented: from stage B to stage I (stages 7–44, Grant 1975). The Grant results give three peaks: at stages 8–9 (about 6 months), 20–22 (about 18 months), and 30–34 (about 30 months), ie the same pattern as the construction and occupation deposits (although the occupation deposits do not have second year individuals).

This pattern is repeated in the robbing deposits, and is best shown by the votive deposits (groups b and f, MF Fig 14ii). The other groups give patchier, more extreme results which surely must result from smaller samples (particularly groups a and c). The major peak is in the 18 month old animals, but 6 month old and 30 month old animals are also clearly used, and notably, also animals in the stage F–I (37–48) range: animals of about three to eight years old.

Butchered bones are present in all sub-phases of the building, with 2.7% of sheep/goat bones from construction (MF Table 42). The incidence after that is always below 1%, ranging from 0.2–0.8%. Although post-cranial bones have butchery in all periods, one important element is its incidence on horncores from the occupation deposits onwards. In all cases the

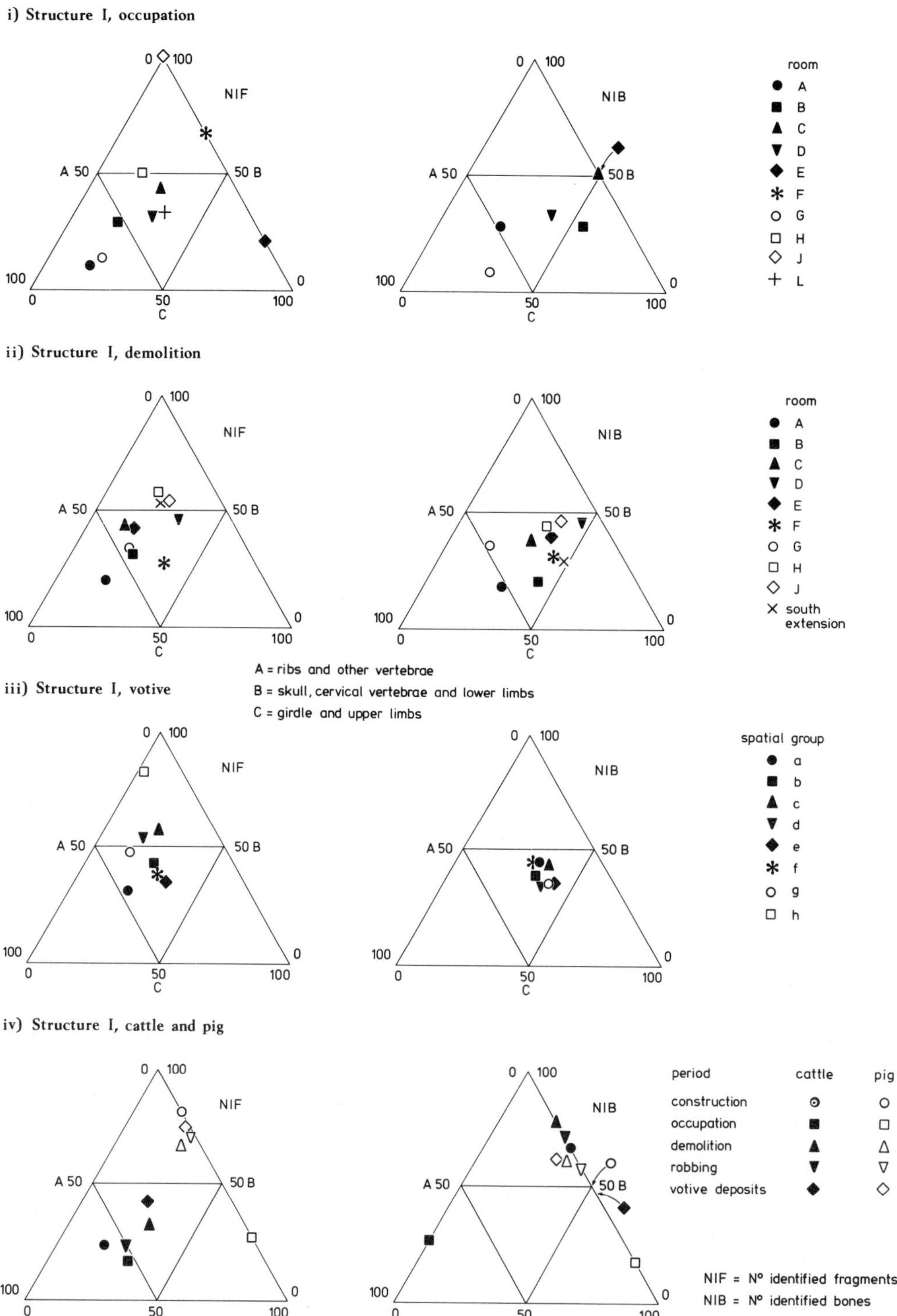

Fig 196 Sheep/goat anatomical representation

butchery of horncores is the predominant pattern (Fig 208). This is based upon proportions of the element total with butchery higher for horncores than for any other element. This and the extremely low incidence of butchery, make the evidence for sheep/goat contrast with that from cattle, where incidence is higher overall (ranging from 12% in demolition and votive deposits to over 50% in construction deposits), and where there is no evidence of butchery on horncores.

For sex ratios for the demolition and votive deposits see MF Fig 15. Ratios for male:female goats for the other periods are: construction 3:3, occupation 2:2, robbing 38:7, and for sheep; occupation 1:0, robbing 18:7. Thus males predominate, at over 70%, except in the earlier periods; this holds true for the spatial divisions of the deposits. Sexing is based upon morphological features of eg pelves and astragali, so cannot be easily related to the age structure of the sheep/goat population. A subjective impression, however, is that males predominate at all ages.

Numbers of bones and proportions of domestic fowl (Table 16) show that fowl proportions gradually fall from the construction phase (4.5%) to the demolition phase (1.6%), thereafter remaining reasonably constant. There is much variation in the fowl proportions for the spatial units of the structure, with some areas

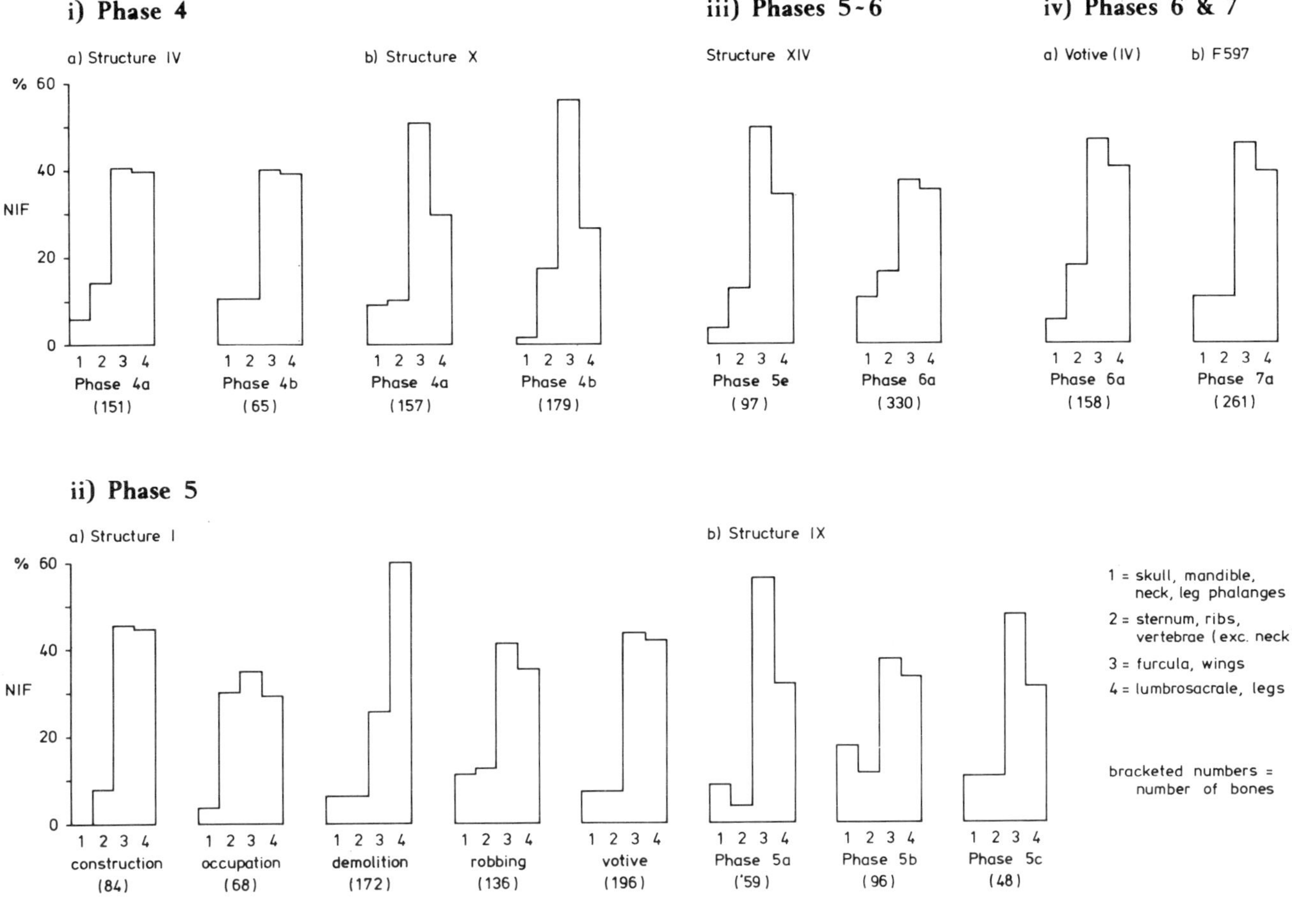

Fig 197 Domestic fowl anatomical representation

having no fowl bones, and others having proportions over 10% (MF Tables 12 and 13). Small sample size makes it difficult to make sense of the variation spatially or temporally as the fowl proportions do not correlate at all.

Anatomical representation shows a changeable pattern, with head and body bones much less common than limb bones, based upon the total fowl sample (Fig 197). The sub-samples which are used for species representation contain much smaller numbers of fowl bones. Head/neck/leg extremity bones are consistently less common than other body-part groups, but the body bones range from equal lowest representation to second highest. Similarly, wing bones are generally the best represented, but in the demolition period the leg bones are commonest. Ageing indicates that adults are most common, with a range from 51.4% (36 bones) in the construction phase, to 82.9% (29 bones) in the immediately following occupation phase. Proportions of adult bones then fall to 65.3% (81 bones), followed by 72.2% (70 bones), and 61.4% (94 bones), a rather variable pattern. Of the few tarsometatarsi complete enough to record presence of spurs, 7 out of 18 are spurred.

Structure IX is less complex than Structure I, and three rooms can be identified (Fig 198). Room A is an annexe in use during Phase 5b, but not represented in the demolition deposits of Phase 5c. Structures I and IX are contemporary, but Structure I exists until Phase 5e. Sheep/goat dominate, rising from about 80% in Phase 5a–b to nearly 90% in Phase 5c (Fig 200, Table 16). Room B has the highest and most consistent proportions while Room C has rising proportions in contrast to Room A where proportions fall (Fig 200ii–iv).

In Phase 5a the main bone concentration is in Room C, in Phase 5b it is in Room B, a pattern reflected in the demolition deposits (Fig 198i–iii). These patterns are underlined by the sample sizes (MF Table 14). Sheep dominate, at 70% or more, throughout the history of the building. Room A has the highest proportions in Phase 5b, followed by Room B (Phases 5a and 5b), with proportions in Room C of around 65–70% (lowest in Phase 5b). Proportions are very high in the Room B area in Phase 5c, and lower for Room C (MF Fig 17iv).

The samples of sheep and goat bones are small, and comparison a problem because there is little similarity between the sheep and goat. Where larger samples occur however, there is better correspondence between the species, eg in Rooms A and B in Phase 5b (the largest sample). The structure total shows a fairly close similarity between the species.

Plots of the sheep/goat bones are confined to Phase 5c (MF Fig 16iv). The deposits overlying Rooms B and C, with high proportions of metapodials, are intermediate in pattern to the bones found in the rooms, which had high proportions of ribs and forelimbs (common to all the deposits), but low proportions of metapodials. Proportions of skull, vertebrae, ribs, and girdles increase north to south. Conversely, proportions of upper forelimb and upper hindlimb decrease north to south.

Figure 199iii, which illustrates this, also shows that similar patterns are not seen in the earlier phases.

Phase 5a is characterised by a similarity between Rooms B and C, with Room A very much an outlier. In Phase 5b, Room A relates more closely to Rooms B and C (but using NIB, Room B is an outlier). Room C shows little change from Phase 5a to 5c, but Room B displays increasing change, beginning as very similar to Room C in Phase 5a, and ending in Phase 5c. Room C is characterised by high proportions of ribs, skull, and upper forelimb (in that order). Room B changes from a pattern similar to Room C to a differing one, with upper forelimb, upper hindlimb, then ribs. In Phase 5a Room A has high proportions of girdles and upper limbs, which greatly decrease in relation to the other groups which both increase by similar proportions.

In Phase 5a there is one female sheep from Room C, in Phase 5b, one male goat, two male and one female sheep, and in Phase 5c two male and one female sheep.

The summary ageing data using mandibles shows a peak in stage D (Payne 1973, 21 using Grant 1975), with lesser peaks in stages E and F (24–31) (MF Fig 18ii). This is seen in the results from Phase 5b–c, and the single mandible from Phase 5a is also from stage D (21). The evidence from epiphysial fusion was also used because the mandible samples were so small (MF Fig 18i). In Phase 5a there is one female sheep from Room C, in Phase 5b one male goat, two male and one female sheep, and in Phase 5c two male and one female sheep.

Butchery occurs on about 2–4% of bones (MF Table

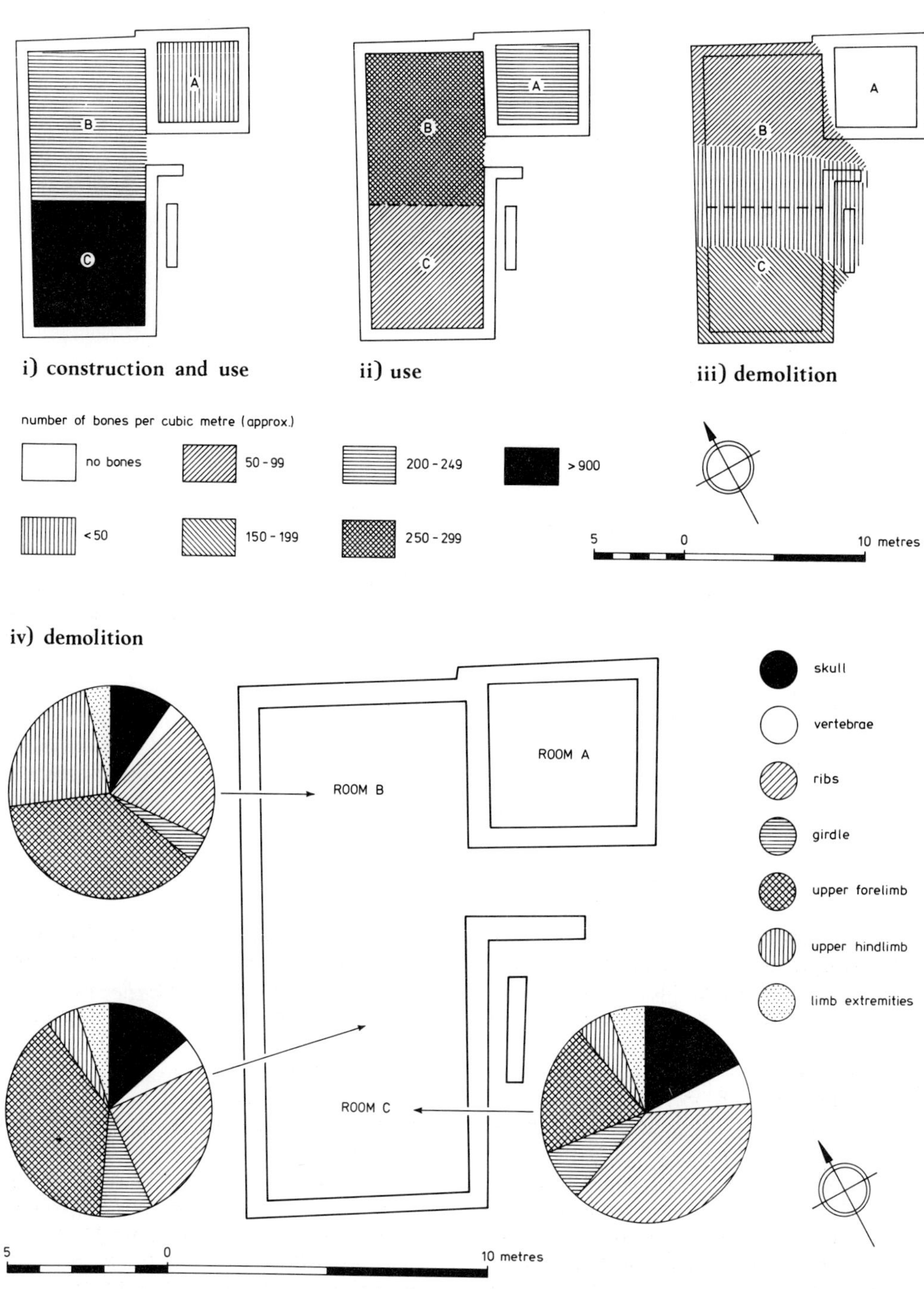

Fig 198 Bone distributions and concentrations, Phase 5

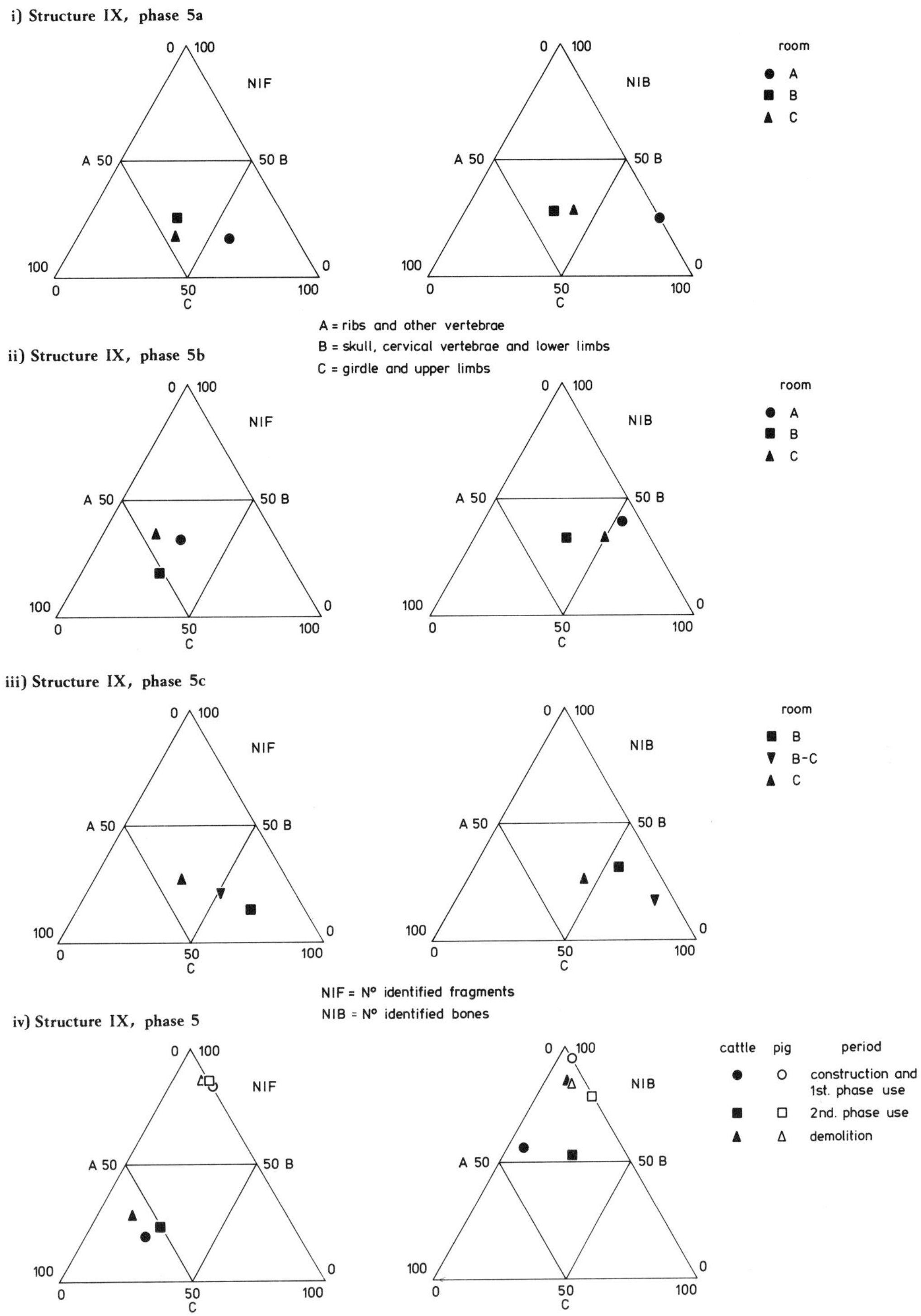

Fig 199 Sheep/goat anatomical representation

43). Butchery is concentrated on the ribs (56 of the 88 have butchery marks), In contrast to Structure I where butchery is mainly on horncores. Most parts of the skeleton show evidence of butchery, particularly upper limbs and girdles.

Although proportions of domestic fowl decrease from Phase 5a (8.6%) to Phase 5c (5.9%) the numbers of bones rises from 60 to 88 (Table 16). The largest samples are from Room B: in Phase 5a 7.7%, in Phase 5b 5.2%, and in Phase 5c 5.8%. In Room A, a larger sample (MF Table 14), the proportions rise from 5.9% in Phase 5a to 6.3% in Phase 5c, and in Room C proportions fall from 9.3% in Phase 5a to 6.1% in Phase 5c. These contrasts may not be important, as the total range in proportions here is 4.1%. Anatomy patterns are similar for each period, with wing bones most common, followed by legs, head, and body (Fig 197). There are differences in the proportion of each group. In Phase 5a, for example, wings, at 56%, are 23% higher than legs, but in Phase 5b it is only 4%, while in Phase 5c the difference is 12%. Similarly, body bones are equal to head bones in Phase 5c, but in Phase 5a there is a 5% difference and in Phase 5b a 6% difference. Adults are in the majority, proportions being 61.5% (39 bones) in Phase 5a, 50.0% (58 bones) in Phase 5b, and 73.9% (23 bones) in Phase 5c. Of the six adult tarsometatarsi complete enough to determine presence of spurs four are spurred.

Table 16: Summary of bones from Structures I, II, and IX, Phase 5 (MF Table 6)

	NIF		NIB		MNI		NFI	NBI	NIF		NIB		MNI		NFI	NBI
Species	no	%	no	%	no	%			no	%	no	%	no	%		
Structure I	<------------- *Phase 5a*							------------->	<-------------*Phase 5b*							------------->
Sheep/goat	334	92.5	64	92.8	7	63.6	48	9	973	94.6	247	96.1	29	80.6	34	9
Cattle	22	6.1	3	4.4	2	18.2	11	2	48	4.7	4	1.6	4	11.1	4	1
Pig	5	1.4	2	2.9	2	18.2	3	1	7	0.7	6	2.3	3	8.3	2	2
Horse	-	-	-	-	-	-	-	-	-	-	-	-	-	-	-	-
Dog	-	-	-	-	-	-	-	-	-	-	-	-	-	-	-	-
Other mammal	-	-	-	-	-	-	-	-	-	-	-	-	-	-	-	-
Total	361	95.5	69	85.2	11	55.0	-	-	1028	96.0	257	86.5	36	72.0	-	-
Domestic fowl	17	4.5	12	14.8	9	45.0	2	1	43	4.0	40	13.5	14	28.0	3	3

	NIF		NIB		MNI		NFI	NBI	NIF		NIB		MNI		NFI	NBI
	no	%	no	%	no	%			no	%	no	%	no	%		
Structure II	<-------------*Phase 5a*							------------->	<------------- *Phase 5d*							------------->
Sheep/goat	161	81.3	15	88.2	10	71.4	16	2	85	91.4	13	81.3	6	60.0	14	2
Cattle	31	15.7	-	-	2	14.3	16	-	4	4.3	-	-	1	10.0	4	-
Pig	5	2.5	1	5.9	1	7.1	5	1	2	2.2	1	6.3	1	10.0	2	1
Horse	-	-	-	-	-	-	-	-	-	-	-	-	-	-	-	-
Dog	1	0.5	1	5.9	1	7.1	1	1	2	2.2	2	12.5	2	20.0	1	1
Other mammal	-	-	-	-	-	-	-	-	-	-	-	-	-	-	-	-
Total	198	97.5	17	85.0	14	82.4	-	-	93	98.9	16	94.1	10	90.9		
Domestic fowl	5	2.5	3	15.0	3	17.6	1	1	1	1.1	1	5.9	1	9.1	1	1

	NIF		NIB		MNI		NFI	NBI	NIF		NIB		MNI		NFI	NBI	NIF		NIB		MNI		NFI	NBI
	no	%	no	%	no	%			no	%	no	%	no	%			no	%	no	%	no	%		
Structure IX	<-------------*Phase 5a*-							------------->	<------------- *Phase 5b*							------------->	<--------------- *Phase 5c*							--------------->
Sheep/goat	505	78.9	88	67.1	9	36.0	63	10	1100	80.3	209	74.6	20	57.1	55	11	1215	87.3	128	74.4	19	51.4	64	7
Cattle	82	12.8	16	12.2	2	8.0	41	8	208	15.2	39	13.9	6	17.1	35	7	110	7.9	19	11.0	6	16.2	18	3
Pig	41	6.4	23	17.6	10	40.0	4	2	61	4.5	32	11.4	8	22.9	8	4	59	4.2	20	11.6	7	18.9	8	3
Horse	-	-	-	-	-	-	-	-	-	-	-	-	-	-	-	-	1	0.1	1	0.6	1	2.7	1	1
Dog	-	-	-	-	-	-	-	-	-	-	-	-	-	-	-	-	-	-	-	-	-	-	-	-
Other mammal	12	1.9	4	3.1	4	16.0	-	-	1	0.1	-	-	1	2.9	-	-	7	0.5	4	2.3	4	10.8	-	-
Total	640	91.4	131	72.8	25	58.1	-	-	1370	94.1	280	80.5	35	57.4	-	-	1392	94.1	172	72.0	37	68.5	-	-
Domestic fowl	60	8.6	49	27.2	18	41.9	3	3	86	5.9	68	19.5	26	42.6	3	3	88	5.9	67	28.0	17	31.5	5	4

	NIF		NIB		MNI		NFI	NBI	NIF		NIB		MNI		NFI	NBI	NIF		NIB		MNI		NFI	NBI
	no	%	no	%	no	%			no	%	no	%	no	%			no	%	no	%	no	%		
													Phase 5e											
Structure I	<------------- demolition							------------->	<------------- *robbing*							------------->	<--------------- *votive*							--------------->
Sheep/goat	6142	97.0	1429	97.3	200	92.6	31	7	3745	92.0	1415	93.0	189	87.5	20	8	10399	97.5	2512	96.9	322	93.1	32	8
Cattle	116	1.8	9	0.6	4	1.9	29	2	100	2.5	16	1.1	3	1.4	33	5	176	1.6	22	0.8	8	2.3	22	3
Pig	46	0.7	27	1.8	10	4.6	5	3	75	1.8	42	2.8	15	6.9	5	3	62	0.6	31	1.2	10	2.9	6	3
Horse	2	<0.1	1	<0.1	1	0.5	2	1	1	<0.1	1	<0.1	1	0.5	1	1	3	<0.1	3	0.1	1	0.3	3	3
Dog	23	0.4	2	0.1	1	0.5	23	2	150	3.7	48	3.2	8	3.7	19	6	16	0.1	12	0.5	2	0.6	8	6
Other mammal	-	-	-	-	-	-	-	-	-	-	-	-	-	-	-	-	13	0.1	13	0.5	3	0.9	-	-
Total	6329	98.4	1468	95.2	216	90.8	-	-	4071	98.2	1522	95.5	216	93.5	-	-	10669	98.7	2593	96.3	346	92.0	-	-
Domestic fowl	100	1.6	74	4.8	22	9.2	4	3	74	1.8	71	4.5	15	6.5	5	4	140	1.3	99	3.6	30	8.0	5	3

Sheep/goat identifications

		NIF	*NIB*	*MNI*
Structure I				
	Phase 5a*	7:20	2:16	2:5
	Phase 5b*	8:59	7:44	2:11
demolition,	Phase 5e	96:424	90:342	34:52
robbing,	Phase 5e	57:454	57:403	20:59
votive,	Phase 5e	91:765	90:559	37:93
Structure II				
	Phase 5a	1:2	1:2	1:1
	Phase 5d	3:1	2:1	1:1
Structure IX				
	Phase 5a	21:4	16:3	3:2
	Phase 5b	55:22	52:22	7:6
	Phase 5c	31:8	31:7	13:3

*Phase 5a and Phase 5b = Phase 5a+b

Structures I and IX: The temporal change in species proportions peaks in Phase 5, with highest proportions of sheep/goat (Table 11). The analysis of the spatial elements shows the need to consider lateral variation as well as temporal sequences. Structures I and IX were broadly contemporary (Structure IX was demolished first), yet there are many differences between them.

Structure I contained over 90% sheep/goat (NIF) in most cases, Structure IX had lower (though still very high) proportions (Figs 185, 195, and 200, Table 16, MF Tables 12, 13, and 14). Structure I has goat:sheep ratios of 3:1 or greater, while Structure IX has goat:sheep ratios of 1:3 to 1:5 (MF Fig 11 and MF Fig 17). The occupation deposits of Structure I had a lower concentration of bones than Structure IX, while the demolition deposits from Structure I contained more bones than those from Structure IX (Figs 194 and 198). This may imply that bones were cleared out of Structure I before demolition, while those from Structure IX were not.

Although evidence for butchery is rare for sheep/goat from both structures, it is slightly higher for Structure IX. Butchery of horncores, a characteristic of the Structure I assemblage (Fig 208), is absent from Structure IX. In addition the goat bone from Structure I has a high proportions of horncores (MF Fig 12), but these are rare in the Structure IX assemblage (MF Fig 16). The NFI and NBI results show that bones from Structure I are more fragmented than those from Structure IX (Table 16, MF Tables 12, 13, and 14). The site of Structure I, after its demolition, had a complicated series of votive deposits spread over it, and no further structures were built there (Fig 194). In contrast, there were no votive deposits over Structure IX, which was succeeded by Structure XIV before the end of Phase 5. In addition proportions of domestic fowl are generally higher in Structure IX (Table 16, MF Tables 12, 13, and 14).

Similarities between Structures I and IV, and Structures IX and X indicate continuity of activities in Phases 4 and 5. It is striking that like Structure I, there was no further building on the location of Structure IV, and that a votive deposit (later than that over Structure I) was also spread over the demolished Structure IV (see Phase 6).

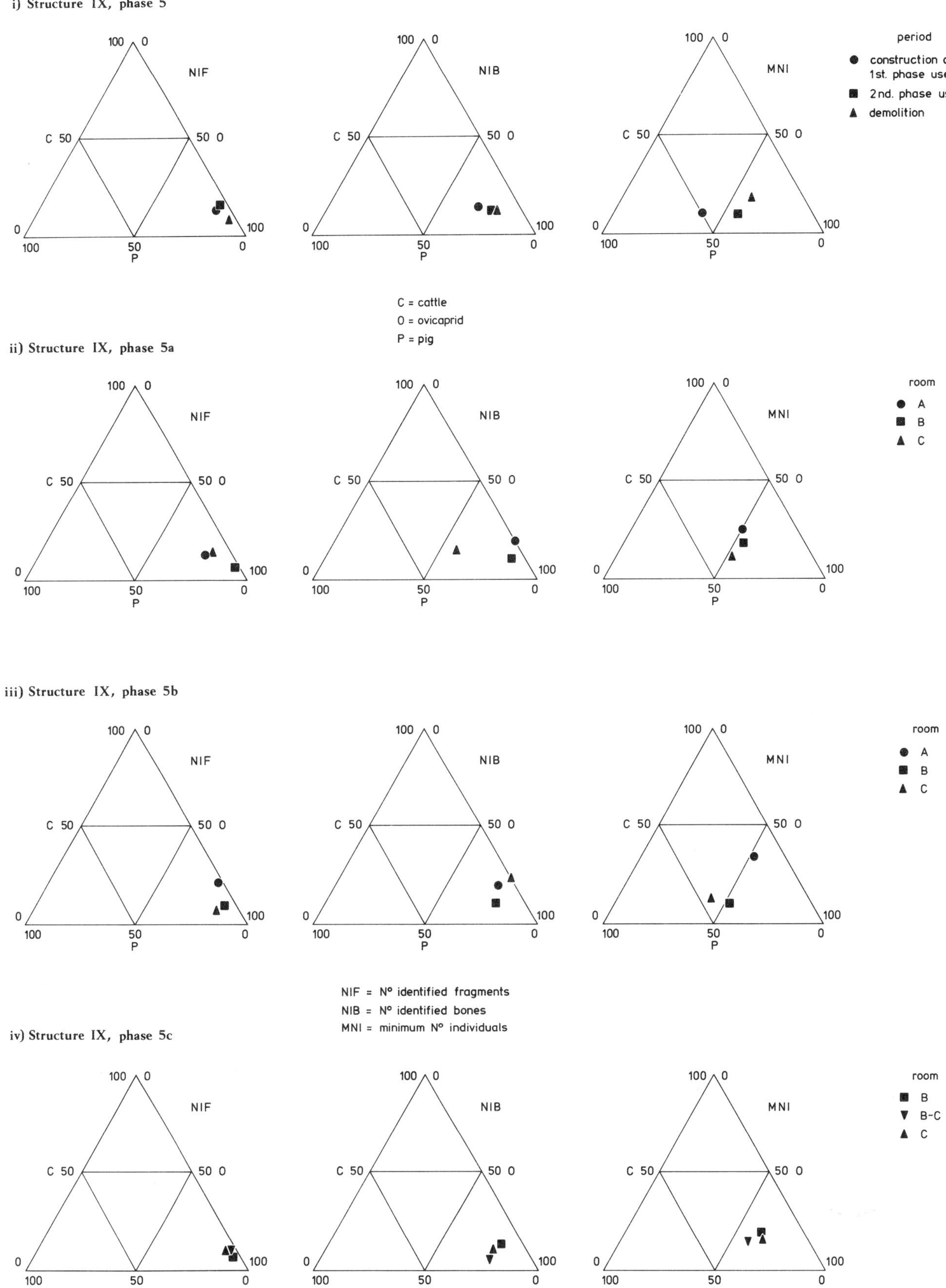

Fig 200 Representation of cattle, sheep/goat and pig

Structure II, like Structure I, originated in Phase 4, going through a large number of modifications in Phases 4 to 6. The deposits relating to Phase 5 are very small samples (Table 16), those from Phase 6 larger (Table 17).

Proportions of sheep/goat are high in all periods and increase from Phase 5a to Phase 6a (occupation deposits), but are slightly lower in Phase 6b (demolition) (Fig 201i, Tables 16 and 17). The relatively long life of the building means that other buildings from Phase 5 were contemporary during different activity periods. The first period of surviving deposits (Phase 5a) coincides with the use of Structures I and IX. In Phase 5c Structure IX was replaced by Structure XIV, and Structure XIII was erected. In Phase 5d–e Structure II was partially demolished and remodelled, and votive deposits comprising vast quantities of bone were spread over the demolished remains of Structure I. In Phase 6a, a third phase of remodelling occurred and the structure was finally demolished in Phase 6b, when a second series of votive deposits were spread (over Structure IV).

It is not certain that bone deposits from all activity phases are represented. The small samples in Phase 5a and 5d could either be remains from a clear-out of the temple, or deliberate selective deposition. The deposits from Phase 6a are possibly too large to represent remains after clear-out. High proportions of goat probably relate the material to ritual activity. Only a small number of bones are identifiable to species, except for the Phase 6a material. Goat proportions are very high in Phase 6a and 6b, quite high in Phase 5a, but low (around 30%) in Phase 5b. (The Phase 5a and 5b results, however, are based upon only three and four bones respectively.) The two deposits from Phase 6 are, perhaps, more representative, and here the goat proportions imply a ritual nature (MF Fig 19i). Anatomical representation indicates little temporal difference in NIF (Fig 202i), though the Phase 5 material comprises higher proportions of Group C bones and lower proportions of Group A bones than the Phase 6 material. Structure VIII which was constructed in Phase 7 is very close to the Phase 5 results of Structure II. There are 26 horncores present from Phase 6a, and 5 from Phase 6b, all from goats. The Phase 6 results most closely resemble the pattern of the Structure I votive deposit with high proportions of group B bones (Fig 196iii). There are only five ageable mandibles from Structure II, from Phase 6a at stages E, F, and G, and from Phase 6b, at stages C and E. Epiphysial fusion data are also limited (28 bones). The data provides no clear pattern, but some perinatal/infant deaths are represented, as well as all the other age groups. Sex determinations are possible on six bones, all goats: Phase 5a one male; Phase 6a two of each sex; Phase 6b one male.

Domestic fowl increase in proportions from around 1–3% in Phases 5a–6a) to *c* 7% in Phase 6b (Tables 16 and 17). This does not appear to be related to sample size since the largest sample is from Phase 6a, the increase is even larger using NIB or MNI. The samples are rather small to assess anatomical representation, but Phases 5a, 6a, and 6b, are not dissimilar, with 7.1% each for head and body, 39.3% for leg bones, and 46.4% for wings. In Phase 5 the ageable bones are dominated by juveniles 60% (10 bones), but in Phase 6 the proportions of adults are 66.7% (15 bones)in Phase 6a and 70.6% (34 bones) in Phase 6b. The only two adult tarsometatarsi are unspurred.

Structure XIV replaces Structure IX and coincides with the second period of activity in Structure II (the temple). Bones come from occupation (Phase 5e) and demolition (Phase 6a). Samples recovered were fairly large, particularly for Phase 6a, enhanced by the sieving of selected samples from context 1191 (Levitan 1982a).

Table 17 : Summary of bones from Structure II and over Structure IV, Phase 6, (MF Table 7)

Structure II

	NIF		*NIB*		*MNI*		*NFI*	*NBI*
	no	*%*	*no*	*%*	*no*	*%*		
Species	<- - - - - - - -		- - - - - - - *Phase 6a*		- - - - - - - -			- - - - ->
Sheep/goat	1376	95.7	172	91.5	49	89.1	28	4
Cattle	46	3.2	11	5.9	3	5.5	15	4
Pig	15	1.0	4	2.1	2	3.6	8	2
Horse	-	-	-	-	-	-	-	-
Dog	1	0.1	1	0.5	1	1.8	1	1
Other mammal	-	-	-	-	-	-	-	-
total	1438	96.9	188	83.2	55	87.3	-	-
Domestic fowl	46	3.1	38	16.8	8	12.7	6	6
	<- - - - - - - -		- - - - - - - *Phase 6b*		- - - - - - - -			- - - - ->
Sheep/goat	310	87.8	42	93.3	12	75.0	26	4
Cattle	36	10.2	-	-	1	6.3	36	-
Pig	6	1.7	3	6.7	2	12.5	3	2
Horse	1	0.3	-	-	1	6.3	1	-
Dog	-	-	-	-	-	-	-	-
Other mammal	-	-	-	-	-	-	-	-
total	353	93.4	45	68.2	16	76.2	-	-
Domestic fowl	25	6.6	21	31.8	5	23.8	5	4
Over Structure IV								
	<- - - - - - - -		- - - - - - - *Phase 6b*		- - - - - - - -			- - - - ->
Sheep/goat	3707	96.9	844	95.7	201	93.5	18	4
Cattle	73	1.9	9	1.0	6	2.8	12	2
Pig	21	0.5	13	1.5	5	2.3	4	3
Horse	1		1	0.1	1	0.5	1	1
Dog	25	0.6	15	1.7	2	0.9	13	8
Other mammal	-	-	-	-	-	-	-	-
total	3827	95.8	882	86.0	215	86.3	-	-
Domestic fowl	168	4.2	144	14.0	34	13.7	5	4

Sheep/goat identifications

		NIF	*NIB*	*MNI*
Stucture II:	Phase 6a	0:50	0:24	0:5
	Phase 6b	3:17	3:13	2:6
Structure IV:	Phase 6b	72:193	61:153	19:49

Proportions of species, may be compared with Structure II (Fig 201) and Structure IX (Fig 200i). Occupation and demolition deposits are very similar to Structure II, though with slightly lower sheep/goat proportions (Tables 17 and 18). In common with Structure II, sheep/goat proportions are higher in Phase 6a than in Phases 5d and 5e. Occupation and demolition deposits are also remarkably similar to the second period occupation and demolition of Structure IX (Structure XIII, however, is rather different).

Sheep and goat proportions are practically identical in the occupation and demolition deposits (about 30% goat). This is low compared with Structure II (MF Fig 19), but is similar to Structure IX (MF Fig 17i). Comparison of sheep and goat body parts indicates differences in cranial elements, goats having higher proportions than sheep, and the cranial elements of goat comprising entirely horncores (with no sheep horncores present) (MF Fig 19v). Proportions of girdles, are higher in goats but limb bones and extremities are in similar proportions.

Anatomical representation underlines the temporal similarity seen in species proportions and sheep:goat ratios (in both NIF and NIB, Fig 202ii). Body parts are dominated by Group A (ribs and non-cervical vertebrae), with approximately equal proportions (around 25%) of Groups B and C (using NIF). Contemporary deposits from Structure II have higher proportions of Group C bones in Phase 5d–e and higher proportions of Group B bones in Phase 6a. Structure IX is similar to

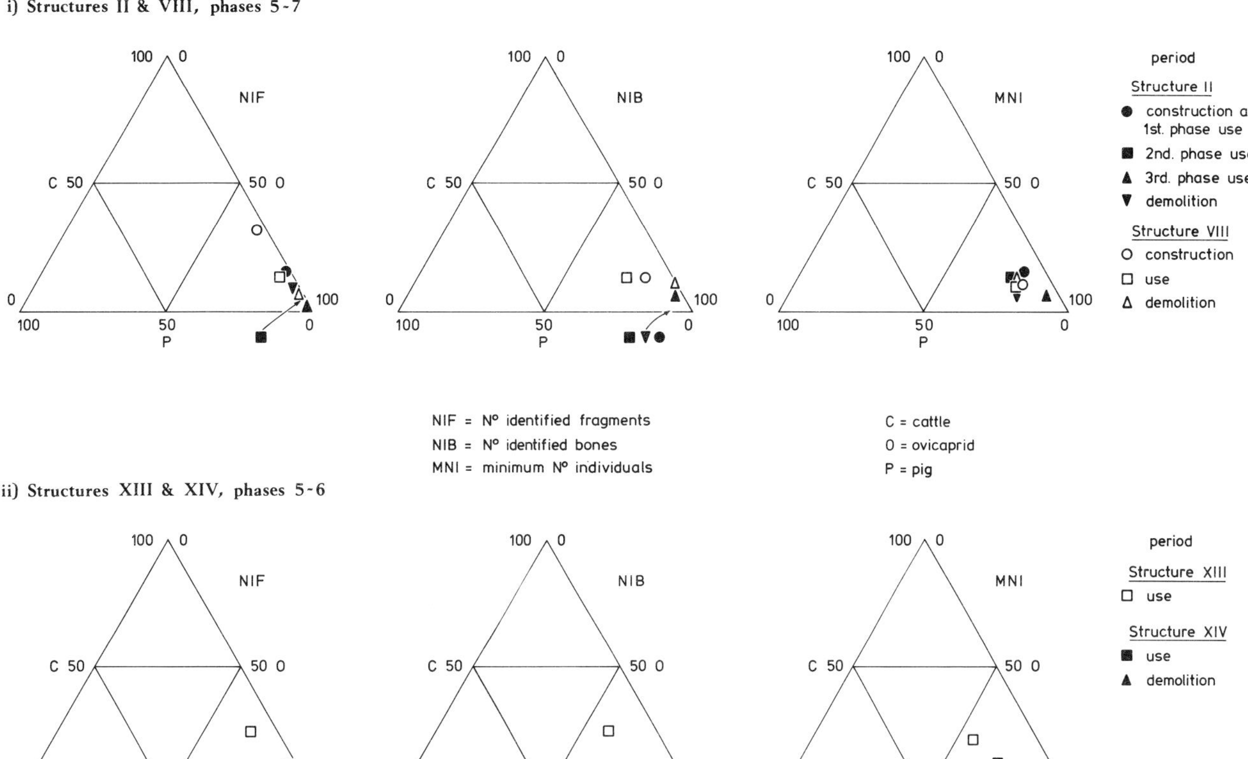

Fig 201 Representation of cattle, sheep/goat and pig

Structure XIV for Rooms B and C in Phase 5a and Room B in Phase 5b, but generally only Room C is similar for the structure total (Fig 199). The body part pattern here is intermediate between Structure IX (where goat horncores are absent) and Structure II, which is more votive in nature. Ageing results indicate kill-off peaks in stage D (Payne 1973) in Phase 5e, and stages C and E in Phase 6a. The earlier sample is small, so is, perhaps, less reliable. The range in age stages represented is very similar however, with mandibles of stages B–E and G–I present; there are none at stage F in either period of the building. Possibly the larger, later, sample can be taken as representative of the structure as a whole. There are three clear periods of kill-off, centred on stages C, E, and G–I. Using Grant (1982) each has wider limits, stages 7–14 (6–12 months, centred on about 10 months), 20–32 (24–38 months, centred on 26 months), and 37–45 (3–8 years, centred on 6 years) respectively. There is also a small group at stages 2 and 4 (less than 6 months). Accepting these age estimates and a spring birth regime, this represents kill-off at several different times of the year: around May–July for the infants, December–January for the next oldest group, May–July for the two-year-olds, and uncertain for the older adults. Sexing results are: occupation, two male and two female sheep; demolition, one male and one female goat, three male and six female sheep. Overall proportions of butchery are very low, at about 1.5% (compared with about 8% in cattle). Most butchered bones are ribs, but highest frequencies are on vertebrae and ribs equally (about 2.5–3.0%). Other butchered bones are upper forelimb and girdles (around 1%).

The similarity between phases is echoed by domestic fowl proportions: 2.2% and 2.9% NIF (less similar using NIB or MNI, Table 18). This does not apply for anatomical representation, however, with higher head and body proportions in the demolition deposits, and much lower wing proportions (Fig 197). The general pattern is very much as expected if all body parts are present, with head and neck bones least common because there are fewest parts of anatomy in this group, followed by body bones, leg bones, and wing bones. The influence of sieving here is apparent in the greater representation of smaller bones such as leg and wing phalanges, although these are still rather under-represented. Ageing results are 66.7% adults in both occupation and demolition deposits. Adult tarsometatarsi are dominated by spurred bones in both phases: occupation, 75% (3:1); demolition, 60% (9:6).

Structure XIII also crosses the Phase 5–6 boundary, constructed in Phase 5d and demolished in Phase 6b. Only bones from the Phase 5e–6a occupation are represented. This was possibly a wagon stance, and structural details are tenuous. Sheep/goat account for about 65% of the bones, so proportions are lower than from other contemporary structures, and below the 70% level used to denote votive material (Fig 201). Only two bones are identifiable to species, one each of sheep and goat (Table 17). Anatomical representation (Fig 202ii) indicates that Group A and B bones predominate (40%). Ageing, using epiphysial fusion, indicates that the majority are juvenile/infant, with no evidence of adults.

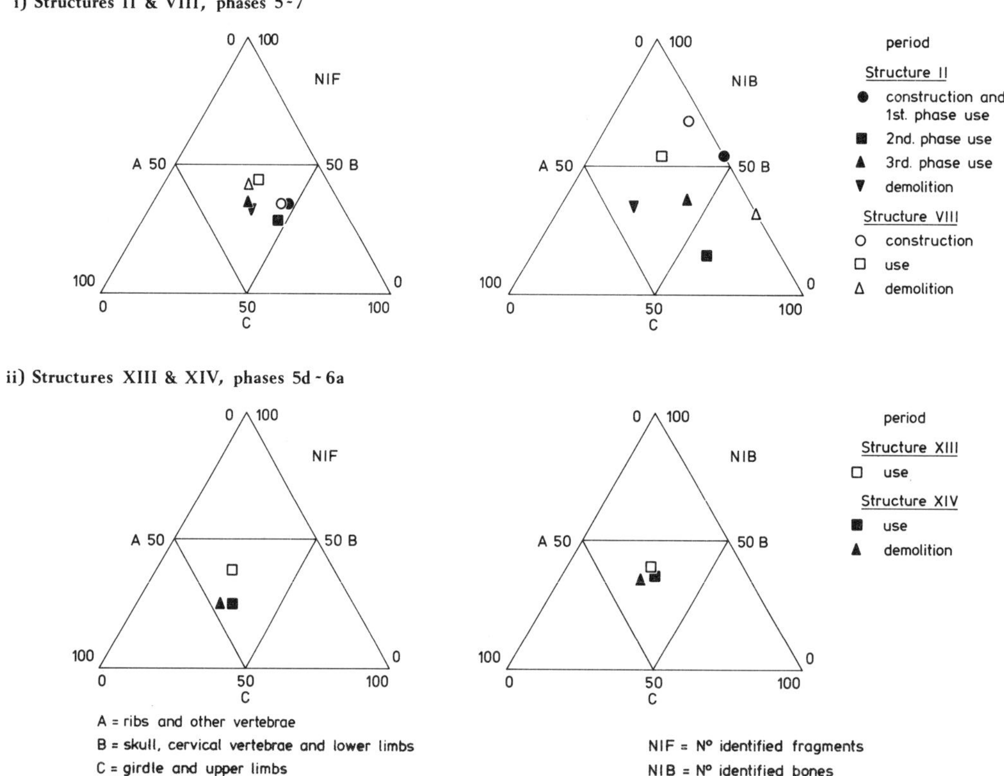

Fig 202 Sheep/goat anatomical representation

Discussion: Phase 5 represents the peak of the trend of increasing importance of sheep/goat, with a growing emphasis on goat. The site as a whole is characterised by higher than usual proportions of sheep/goat, but in Phase 5 these rise to over 90%. Within the overall proportion there is much variation, in a complicated temporal sequence involving the several structures above. These structures all related to the Structure II temple, in use throughout Phase 5, and continuing into Phase 6. It is difficult to try to interpret these relationship in terms of the bones present. Comparison of the assemblages from Structures I and IX shows that the deposits separate into votive (from and over Structure I) and non-votive (but still overshadowed by the votive material). There is not enough variation within the structures to warrant votive/non-votive internal divisions with the exception of the votive material over Structure I. Here group a is clearly different from the rest of the material, and may represent debris from sources of a more domestic nature, perhaps demolition of Structure IX.

Structure XIV bone deposits are essentially similar to those from Structure IX, and may be a continuation of the same kind of activities. The paucity of remains in the early occupation deposits of Structure II may reflect clear-out of material from and associated with remodelling the temple. One such clear-out may have been the source of the votive deposits over Structure I, while a later one can be identified in material over Structure IV. These bones may represent deliberate selection of material to be deposited, though this seems less likely in view of the actual bones involved. Ageing results imply that mainly young goats were killed, whereas domestic fowl were mostly adults. The results from Structure I indicate kill-off in August/September, perhaps reflecting a concentration of ritual activities at harvest time. There is enough mandible ageing data to indicate some year-round killing as well, when older goats may have been used. It is unclear if ritual or domestic patterns are being reflected by this. Sexing shows that males were preferred for sheep, goat, and fowl. Butchery evidence is very limited but the removal of goat horncores is characteristic. The small amount of butchery could imply either that sacrificed carcasses were not butchered for consumption, or that they were cooked whole, thus minimising the amount of butchery that occurred. The removal of horncores may have been part of the ritual, the horns forming some kind of sacred trophy.

Phase 6

Votive deposits over Structure IV date from Phase 6b, and presumably relate to the final remodelling or even the demolition of the temple. Like the deposits over Structure I, these are characterised by large samples which required sub-sampling (Table 17 and MF Table 15). They were, however, less extensive and comprised lesser concentrations of bones (*cf* Figs 191iii and 194iii), and the overall sample is smaller (*c* 10,000 compared with *c* 53,000). The smaller samples may relate to preservation since a substantial portion of the Structure I deposits were protected by the field boundary, whereas those over Structure IV suffered plough damage and were not fully excavated. The deposit can be divided into four clear groups with increased concentration of bones from north to south (Fig 191iii and MF Table 15). The deposits comprise extremely high proportions of sheep/goat, over 90% for all groups. Group a however, is an outlier with about 92% (NIF, supported by results using NIB and MNI) compared with about 98–9% for the other groups (Fig 189iii).

Group a here (unlike group a of Structure I) does not stand out from the other groups in other respects, Group c, coincidentally, the largest sample from the deposit (MF Table 15), is the outlier, with goat proportions of 60%, compared with over 70% in the other groups (MF Fig 7iii). In contrast with Structure I, this deposit has similar body-part representations for sheep and goat (*cf* MF Figs 8v and 12iv) and there are high proportions of both goat and sheep horncores; however this similarity is only seen in group c,(MF Fig 8v). The sample from group a is small, but samples from the other groups are more useful, though possibly only groups c and d are good samples of sheep as well as goat; group d is also similar for the two species, with the exception of sheep mandibles. Grouping sheep and goat bones is, therefore, in this instance possibly non-biasing.

The anatomical make-up of groups a and c, and groups b and d form associated patterns using NIF (MF Fig 9v). In groups a and c ribs are predominant, with cranial bones second in importance, though the differences are more extreme in group a than in group c. Groups b and d have more or less equal representation of skulls, mandibles, and ribs, while other body-parts are generally more common than in groups a and c. If NIB are used, the results are different. Group a becomes too small to be useful, group b has high proportions of hind limbs, with other body-parts all quite well represented, group c is still dominated by ribs, with cranial and other axial bones also important, while group d has peaks in mandibles and upper limb bones. It is difficult to assess if either of these results (NIF or NIB) are representative but there are distinct groupings within the deposit, suggesting more than one dump (and more than one origin?). Such patterns also emerged in the Structure I deposits. NIB supports and emphasises the a–c, b–d groups, and shows the difference between NIF and NIB results; they indicate however that groups b, c, and d might be related, whilst group a becomes a clear outlier (Fig 193ii). Ageing results show that the three groups have similar overall

Table 18 : Summary of bones from Structures VIII, XIII, and XIV, Phases 5–7 (MF Table 9)

	NIF		*NIB*		*MNI*		*NFI*	*NBI*	*NIF*		*NIB*		*MNI*		*NFI*	*NBI*
	no	*%*	*no*	*%*	*no*	*%*			*no*	*%*	*no*	*%*	*no*	*%*		
Structure XIII																
Species	<- - - - - *Phase 5d–e* - - - - ->															
Sheep/goat	145	64.2	28	65.1	7	58.3	21	4								
Cattle	74	32.7	12	27.9	3	25.0	25	4								
Pig	7	3.1	3	7.0	2	16.7	4	2								
Horse	-	-	-	-	-	-	-	-								
Dog	-	-	-	-	-	-	-	-								
Other mammal	-	-	-	-	-	-	-	-								
total	226	89.3	43	66.1	12	46.1	-	-								
Domestic fowl	27	10.7	22	33.9	14	53.9	2	2								
Structure XIV	<- - - - - *Phase 5d–e* - - - - ->								<- - - - - *Phase 6a* - - - - ->							
Sheep/goat	1076	84.3	150	72.1	16	55.2	67	9	4042	89.2	549	80.5	50	70.4	81	11
Cattle	131	10.3	15	7.2	3	10.3	44	5	315	7.0	42	6.2	5	7.0	63	8
Pig	53	4.2	30	14.4	4	13.8	13	8	135	3.0	58	8.5	13	18.3	10	5
Horse	-	-	-	-	-	-	-	-	-	-	-	-	-	-	-	-
Dog	9	0.7	7	3.4	2	6.9	5	4	3	<0.1	1	0.1	1	1.4	3	1
Other mammal	8	0.6	6	2.9	4	13.8	-	-	36	0.8	32	4.7	2	2.8	-	-
total	1277	97.8	208	92.9	29	82.9	-	-	4531	97.2	682	87.8	71	79.8	-	-
Domestic fowl	29	2.2	16	7.1	6	17.1	5	3	132	2.8	95	12.2	18	20.2	7	5
									Phase 7							
Structure VIII	<- - - - - (i) - - - - ->								<- - - - - (ii) - - - - ->							
Sheep/goat	79	64.2	18	75.0	6	66.7	13	3	379	80.5	46	70.8	16	72.7	24	3
Cattle	39	31.7	3	12.5	1	11.1	39	3	69	14.6	8	12.3	2	9.1	35	4
Pig	4	3.3	1	4.2		11.1	4	2	16	3.4	7	10.8	2	9.1	8	4
Horse	-	-	-	-	-	-	-	-	-	-	-	-	-	-	-	-
Dog	-	-	-	-	-	-	-	-	3	0.6	2	3.1	1	4.6	3	2
Other mammal	1	0.8	1	4.2	1	11.1	-	-	4	0.9	2	3.1	1	4.6	-	-
total	123	100.0	23	100.0	9	100.0	-	-	471	97.9	65	91.5	22	84.6	-	-
Domestic fowl	-	-	-	-	-	-	-	-	10	2.1	6	8.5	4	15.4	3	2
	<- - - - - (iii) - - - - ->								<- - - - - (iv) - - - - ->							
Sheep/goat	329	71.2	43	63.2	19	76.0	17	2	165	92.7	10	90.9	6	75.0	28	2
Cattle	112	24.2	12	17.7	3	12.0	37	4	11	6.2	1	9.1	1	12.5	11	1
Pig	18	3.9	11	16.2	2	8.0	9	6	2	1.1	-	-	1	12.5	2	-
Horse	3	0.7	2	2.9	1	4.0	3	2	-	-	-	-	-	-	-	-
Dog	-	-	-	-	-	-	-	-	-	-	-	-	-	-	-	-
Other mammal	-	-	-	-	-	-	-	-	-	-	-	-	-	-	-	-
total	462	99.6	68	98.6	25	92.6	-	-	178	90.4	11	40.7	8	61.5	-	-
Domestic fowl	2	0.4	1	1.4	2	7.4	1	1	19	9.6	16	59.3	5	38.5	4	3

Sheep/goat identifications

		NIF	*NIB*	*MNI*
Structure XIII	Phase 5e–6a	1:1	1:1	1:1
Structure XIV	Phase 5d	33:14	31:9	5:2
	Phase 6a	114:47	107:43	22:10
Structure VIII	Phase 7(i)	4:1	4:1	3:1
	Phase 7(ii)	10:12	10:9	4:3
	Phase 7(iii)	8:7	6:7	1:2
	Phase 7(iv)	0:2	0:2	0:2

Note: Structure XIII Phase 5d-e = Phase 5e–6a

peaks in kill-off: at stages D–E (Payne 1973). Using Grant (1975) they have three peaks, at stages 8–9, 19–21, and 30–32 (MF Fig 10iii). The similarity with Structure I (where peaks are at 8–9, 20–22, and 30–34) is striking; an August/September peak is again indicated (MF Fig 14). Males predominate for both goat and sheep, though some individual groups differ (eg female goats predominate in group c, and sexes are equal for sheep in groups a and c). There are 40.5% (15) female and 59.5% (22) male goats, and 33.3% (3) female and 66,7% (6) male sheep. Group c is the only one with evidence of butchery, five bones representing 0.2% of the bones from the group.

Domestic fowl bones range in proportions from 0.8% in group b to 3.6% in group d (MF Table 15). Group b is the only group sub-sampled, fowl bones are thus a little under-represented in this group, the real proportion being about 1.1%. As with other sub-sampled groups, the fowl sub-sample is used only in species comparisons, the anatomical and other analyses are based upon the whole sample. Anatomical representation is similar in pattern to Structure I, though torso elements are more frequent here, and leg bones less so (Fig 197). Groups b–d are all very similar to this pattern, with no more than 2% different for any body-part group. The same correspondence is seen in ageing (where samples are greater than ten: groups a and c are below this). The deposit total is 73.9% adult (group b at 72.9% and group d at 76.2% respectively are very close). Adult tarsometatarsi are present only in group b, where there are three spurred and five unspurred specimens.

Discussion: The similarities between the votive deposits from over Structures I and IV clearly imply that the activities which led to their accumulation were similar. Assuming that the Structure I deposits refer to the earlier part of Phase 5 (5a–d), and that the Structure IV deposits relate to Phases 5e–6a, they infer that these ritual activities lasted throughout the period 310–420 AD.

Phase 7

Structure III produced a very small sample (MF Table 8), and hardly warrants detailed analysis. In terms of species proportions it is very similar to other contemporary features (Fig 203 ii), but the anatomical representation is unlike the other structures, having higher proportions of group B bones than other structures (Fig 203i). It seems likely that many of the bones from this structure are merely fragments of residual material which was accidentally accumulated here (in nooks and crannies of courtyards, etc).

Structure XI, the basilica: here species proportions are virtually identical to Structure VII using NIF, though less similar for NIB and MNI (Fig 203ii), and the anatomical representation is also remarkably close (Fig 203i). A further parallel is the association of red deer antler with this structure. Even the sample sizes of the two structures is similar, and the only real contrast is in the presence of domestic fowl, which are apparently absent from Structure VII (MF Table 8).

Structure VII, the baptistery: this sample is again small, so little detail can be extracted from it (MF Table 8). Sheep/goat predominate, as in the other Phase 7 structures (Fig 203ii). Most of the bones from this struc-

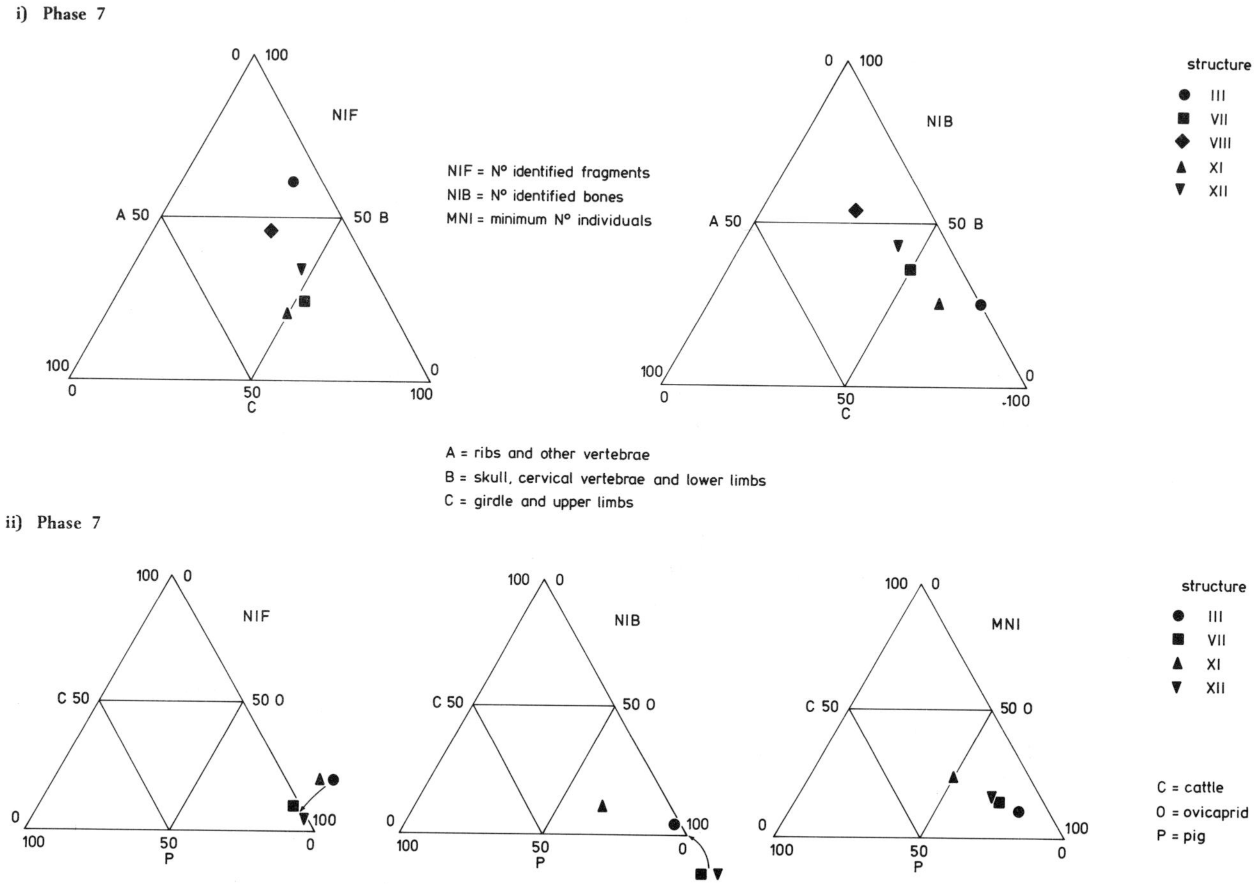

Fig 203 i) Sheep/goat anatomical representation, ii) Representation of cattle, sheep/goat, and pig

ture are from postholes or post pits, so may represent similar kinds of accumulations to those of Structure III, though the deposits do not resemble these in anatomical proportions. This structure comprises mainly Group C bones and much lower proportions of Group B bones than Structure VIII (Fig 203i). Perhaps the most interesting bones from this structure are the four antler fragments of red deer. Structure XII species proportions are very similar to those in Structure III (Fig 203ii), as is sample size (MF Table 8), although anatomical representation is rather different. The similarity of the bones from the two structures possibly does not reflect on their function, but rather the nature of the accidentally accumulated largely residual material.

Structure VIII, a small rectangular building, postdated Structure XI. The foundations contained fragments of the cult statue of Mercury (Fig 76), and its head had been placed in a pit dug beneath them. Although sheep/goat proportions are very high (Table 18), they are lower than those from the temple (Fig 202i). Structure VIII was considered non-votive on the basis of the species proportions, but this is perhaps inappropriate in view of the inclusion of the fragments of the Mercury cult-figure in the foundations. The goat:sheep ratios, like the sheep/goat proportions, increase through time, ranging from about 20% goat to 100%, in contrast with Structure II. Sheep and goat anatomical representation indicates little similarity between the species but samples are small (Table 18, MF Fig 19iv). Structure VIII generally comprised higher proportions of Group B bones than the temple (Fig 202i), with construction deposits most like those from the temple (NIF). The use and demolition of Structure

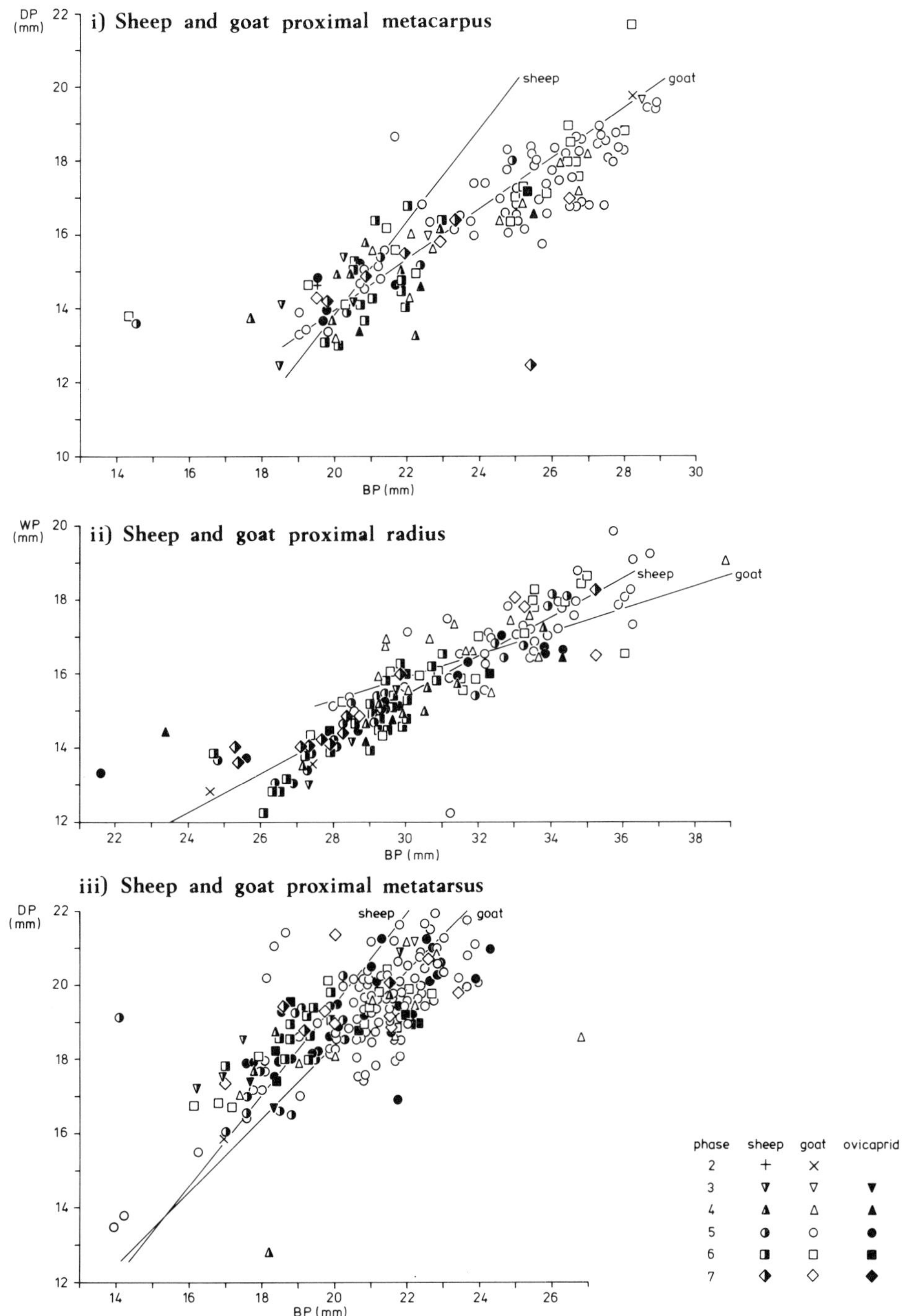

Fig 204 Goat and sheep metacarpus, radius, and metatarsus dimensions

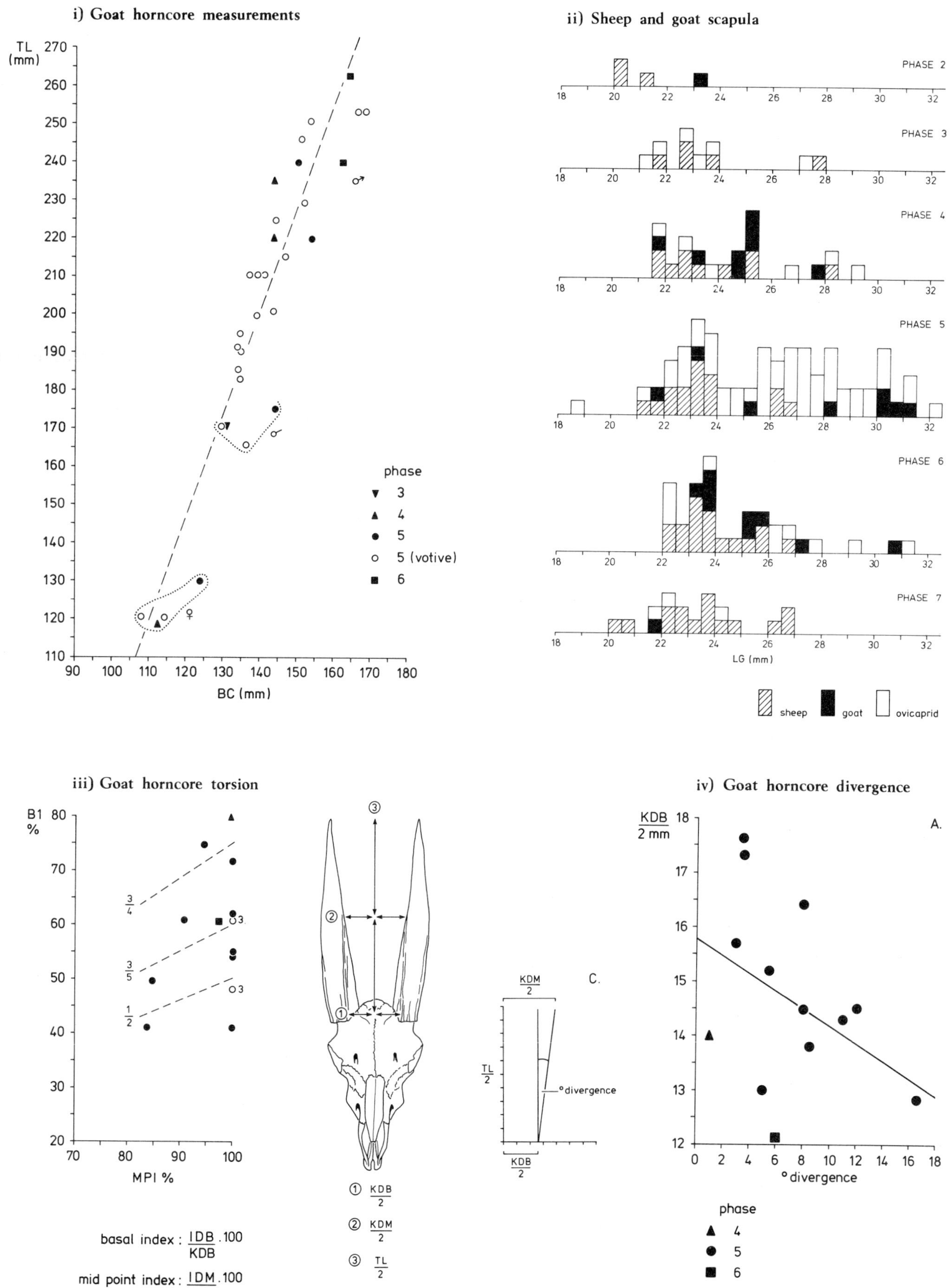

Fig 205 Goat horncore dimensions

VIII form a clear group using NIF, with Group B around 45%, Group A about 35% and Group C about 20%. In contrast construction deposits have lower proportions of Group B and correspondingly higher proportions of Group C. These relationships do not occur using NIB. Ageing results from occupation deposits give two mandibles at stage D, one at stage E, one at stage F, and two at stage G (Payne 1972; only four are ageable using Grant 1975, at stages 23, 31, 34, and 39). The demolition deposits have one at stage D–E, and one at stage F (34). Epiphysial fusion, also limited, indicates mostly juveniles. Only four bones from the occupation deposits could be sexed: one female sheep, two female and one male goats. Butchery is again rare with only three bones (0.2%) from occupation and two (0.6%) from demolition showing evidence of butchery. With the exception of demolition deposits, domestic fowl bones are uncommon in Structure VIII (Table 18), and proportions fluctuate, rising, falling, then rising again. The majority of ageable fowl bones are adults (63.2%), and three out of four tarsometatarsi are spurred.

Discussion: Phases 5–7 are represented in the fourth to the seventh centuries by ritual activities involving the sacrifice of goats, rams, and cockerels. There was a change in emphasis at the end of Phase 6 (*c* 420 AD), with goats and sheep less important than in the earlier period. Furthermore, if some of the bones are residual, sheep/goat proportions may actually be smaller still. On the evidence of the bones, a non-votive interpretation seems realistic (MF Table 8). This does not imply that these structures had a domestic use however. One scenario could be a cessation of animal sacrifice, but a continuation of ritual practices with a shifted emphasis.

Metrical analysis

The detailed metrical analysis is reproduced in fiche. The main aims were to investigate sheep/goat differences, sex determination and species conformation.

Species distinction was found to be less clear than expected, possibly with larger and more 'goat-like' sheep obscuring the distinctions (Fig 204). Sex determination was also rather unclear, but wherever bimodal distributions did clearly occur, males predominated, agreeing with the morphological evidence described above (eg Fig 205ii, MF Table 28). Size changes in goat occur, with an apparent increase from Phases 1–5, followed by a decrease in size in Phase 7 (Fig 205ii). There are no obvious or consistent changes seen in sheep. Some clues about conformation can be gained. Goats are more variable than sheep, consistently showing the greatest range in sizes (possibly reflecting greater sexual dimorphism). Long-bones are generally shorter for goats than for sheep indicating a stockier build. Goat horncores are not very curved, but do display torsion and divergence (Fig 205iii).

Mandible ageing methodology

A fuller report in the fiche can be consulted for detailed discussion of the following points. Ageing estimates based on cheek teeth wear patterns are more reliable than incisor wear states. Variations in wear states occur: the patterns from Uley were compared with data from Turkey (Payne 1987) (MF Fig 20i, Table 37). The Uley sequence has many variants from the 'normal' pattern defined by Payne, but most of them were predicted as possible variants by him (*ibid*).

A comparison of the correlation between Payne and Grant age stage sequences at Uley and at Porchester Castle (MF Fig 20ii) showed that there is a different relationship at the two sites. This calls into question the efficacy of such ageing schemes, since one of their main aims is to provide cross-site consistency. However it may be that the differences seen here are taxonomic (Uley representing goat and Porchester sheep) rather than actual wear variations.

Pathology

The presence of such a large sample, particularly of mandibles, presented a rare opportunity for pathological analysis, even though pathology, especially non-mandibular pathology, is very infrequent, reflecting a high standard of health in the animals (possibly a selection criteria for votive use). Some extremely unusual items were present (eg Brothwell 1979). Sheep/goat oral pathology and non-mandibular pathology were studied in detail, and the report of this analysis is reproduced in fiche.

One of the commonest infections in mandibles was periodontal disruption (gingivitis, periodontal disease etc). It was most severe in permanent dentition, particularly fourth premolar (MF Fig 31). This can be correlated with ante-mortem tooth loss (Fig 206) which indicates that the premolar/molar interface was the most vulnerable. This is hardly surprising as the loss of deciduous fourth premolar and eruption of its permanent replacement could cause severe disruptions. An

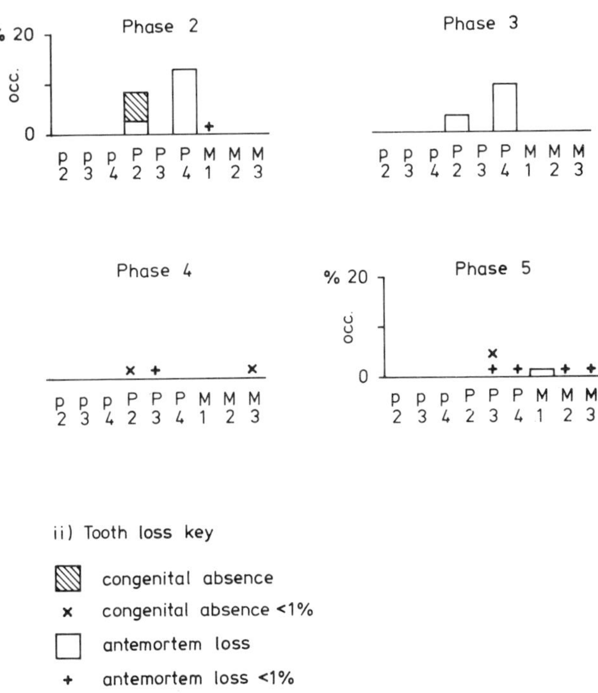

Fig 206 Periodontal disease

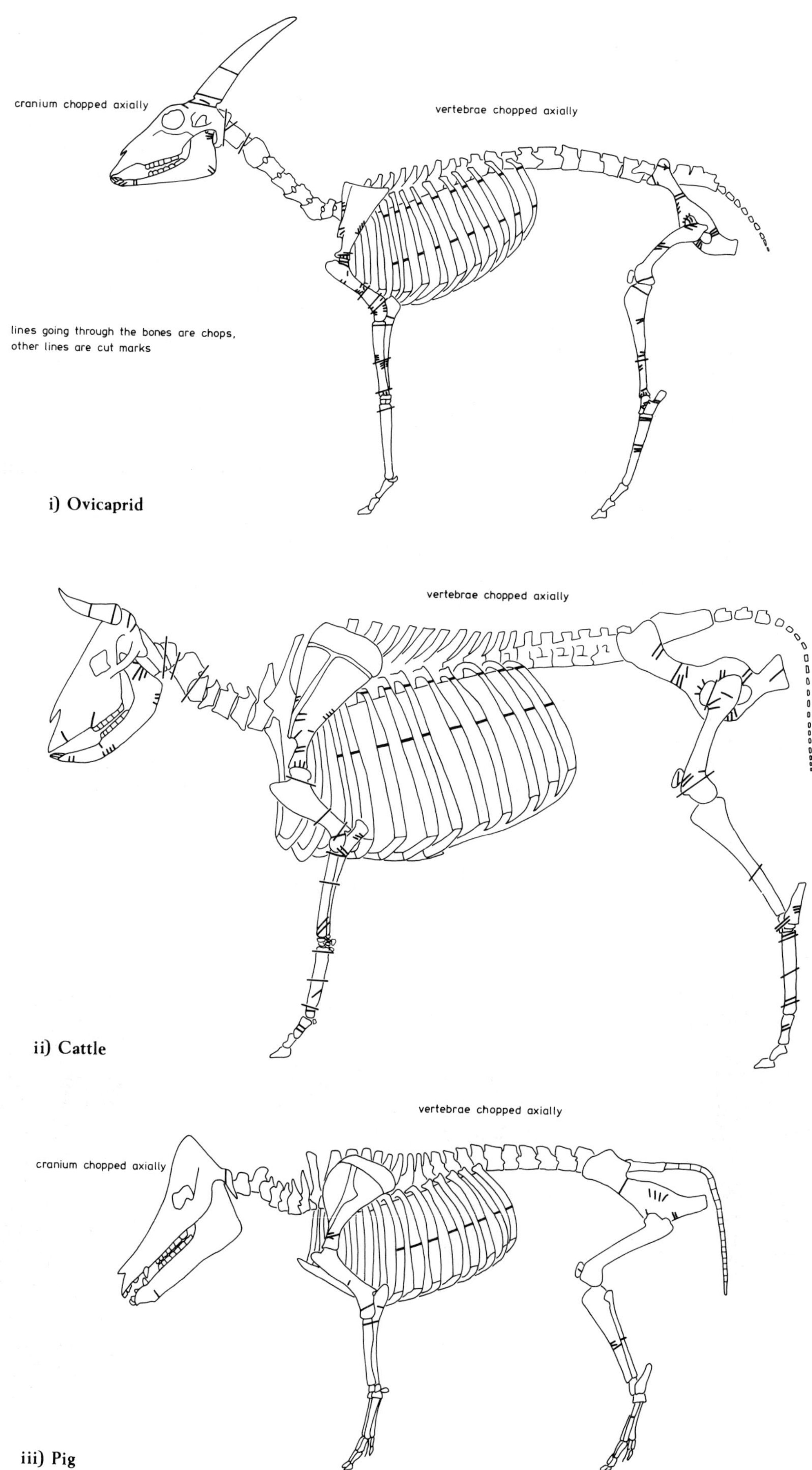

Fig 207 Butchery summary diagrams

extremely common phenomenon on these mandibles is the occurrence of extra numerary nutrient foramina (*c* 45%). It is potentially a useful measure of variation if it can be related to other differences, eg in race, type or conformation. In this respect it is intriguing to note that there are different patterns in extra foramen occurrence for Structure IV (votive) and Structure I (non-votive), perhaps a hint of 'type' selection for votive purposes.

Butchery

The sheep/goat bones show clear zones of butchery on the limbs: at the girdle/limb joint, at the elbow, knee, midshaft in the radius and tibia, and at the wrist and ankle (Fig 207i). There are also butchery zones on the girdle concerned with filleting on the scapula, and with detaching the pelvis from the sacrum. Ribs have butchery at the caput and on the blade, and vertebrae are chopped axially, both in the midline and laterally. The removal of rib capita is related to the lateral trimming of vertebrae. Skulls were detached either at the atlas/occipital condyle joint, or between the atlas and axis. Mandibles have cuts and chops at the symphysis and diastema (to separate the mandibles) and at the articular condyle (to detach the mandible). Horncores were detached mainly close to the skull, but sometimes also further up the horncore (Fig 208). Finally, a few skulls were chopped open axially, presumably to remove the brains.

The very low incidence of butchery overall, already mentioned, is worth re-emphasising. Most sheep/goat butchery occurs on less than 2% of bones, with incidence and frequency varying according to skeletal element. Thus, whilst the patterns encountered are in keeping with those usually found on other Roman sites, the most frequent occurrence, on horncores, puts the emphasis on elements commonly associated with non-consumption. The presence of meat bearing elements however, and the patterns of butchery on them (although low) lead to the conclusion that some sheep/goat were being butchered for consumption. Whether this very small proportion of butchery indicates that consumption was the exception is uncertain. Cooking of the carcass whole would result in very little butchery, and roasting of young animals whole was not uncommon (Frayn 1984, 4), so this is a possible explanation. Certainly the immense wastage of resources in not eating the sacrifices would be very illogical. Ageing data above show August/September peaks in kill-off with a background of year-round killing, possibly representing sheep/goat which were not part of the votive assemblage. The removal of horncores may represent use of horns as ritual trophies particularly as many splendid specimens are present. Frayn comments 'it should be noted that sacrifices ... by individuals at shrines often consisted of a goat rather than a sheep for reasons of economy ... Rams were offered to male deities and ewes to female.' (Frayn 1984, 39).

Votive bone of other species

Although the focus of the ritual activities was undoubtedly upon goats, sheep, and domestic fowl, other bones of a possibly ritual nature were recovered. These include cattle, red deer antler, dolphin, and human bones. From Phase 2 an articulated cattle hindlimb was recovered from F251 in association with a human femur, as well as worked bone and artefacts. F836 also

Fig 208 Goat skull and horncores illustrating characteristic butchery. (Photo: Bruce Levitan)

contained cattle bones including some complete skulls which may well have been related to a ritual function. In Phase 3 there is the association of infant human burials with structure foundations, which has parallels on other ritual Iron Age sites, as do the votive pits described above (Ellison 1980, 309). The red deer bones, all antler and antler fragments, from Phase 7 appear to have a ritual association. In particular there is the antler from pit F57. This, the only object in the pit, had had tines removed by cutting and sawing, and a number of depressions in the beam had been made by a pointed object. Finally, although dolphin bones are not unique to this site, they are rare enough elsewhere for their presence here (teeth, from Structure I, Phase 5) to be notable, and perhaps also associated with the ritual nature of the site.

Summary and conclusions

This bone assemblage is unique and of major importance. Most significant is the unparalleled dominance of sheep/goat (and primarily goat) bones, in comparison with contemporary sites in Britain and on the Continent (Fig 184, King 1978 and 1984). This difference is interpreted as reflecting exploitation mainly for ritual purposes – the majority of the bones being derived from animals used for sacrifice. This interpretation is supported by the details of the analysis: the dominance of goat; the unusually high percentage of domestic fowl bones; the high proportion of male goat, sheep, and domestic fowl; the seasonal peak in kill-off of sheep/goat; and butchery patterns which reveal concentration on removal of horncores (Fig 208).

The comparanda (Fig 184) reveal that the majority of sites have sheep/goat in the range 0–70%; whereas here the range is 71–94%, with a site average of 84% (Table 11). King (1978 and 1984) surveyed 119 Late Iron Age and Romano British sites, and the West Hill data are illustrated alongside these in Fig 184i. Only five of King's sites have sheep/goat (SG) percentages in excess of 70%: Hod Hill Iron Age (n=151); Hod Hill Roman (n=494); Newham's Pit, first century AD (n=242); Brixworth, second century AD (n=123); and Lincoln, third century AD (n=56). Only one of these sites exceeds 80% SG (Hod Hill Iron Age). The Continental sites reveal a similar picture (Fig 184ii). None of the German sites have SG over 70%. Two out of 25 Gaulish sites have SG percentages above 70% (Calissane II (n=181) at 85%; Marseille (n=1205) at 86%). One out of 27 Italian sites has SG above 70% (Pizzica (n=87) at 81%). The above data also underline the uncommonly high numbers of bones at West Hill: few of the surveyed assemblages have totals above 1000 bones, and most of those that do are urban sites.

Not only are the high proportions of SG significant, but the fact that most of these are goats makes the assemblage truly unique. Goats occur in proportions of up to 77% of the major mammals total (Phase 5), yet they are not a commonly identified constituent of Roman assemblages. Maltby (1981, 160) noted that while goats were more common in Roman than in Iron Age assemblages, they were still only rarely present: yet at West Hill goats outnumber sheep in the order of 4:1. Maltby (1981) gives little quantified information to support his comments on the rarity of goats in Roman Britain. Nor does King (1978, 1984) assess the relative importance of the two species, but implies, in his 1978 paper at least, that sheep were predominant. Luff comments (1982, 261) that goats are present on some sites, but that goats are generally rare. The major problem, in attempting to assess the relative importance of sheep and goat from published sources, is that often there is no separation into species, or, only the goat identifications are quantified. Usually the number of goats identified is so small that it is concluded that they were unimportant. There is no good basis, therefore, for comparison of the West Hill results.

The closest parallel for this assemblage seems to be the Romano-British temple at Harlow, Essex. A total of 3631 bones from Belgic and Roman periods were analysed, and sheep/goat bones accounted for over 80% of the mammalian bones in all but the disturbed layers (Legge and Dorrington 1985, 123). The largest single sample (1777 bones) came from the Belgic period, and this corresponded with the highest sheep/goat proportions (87.9%). In this respect, the results from Harlow differ from West Hill, where the highest proportions are late Roman rather than Iron Age and the largest samples are also late Roman, but the generally high sheep/goat proportions are remarkably similar. A major difference, however, is seen in the sheep:goat proportions: at Harlow, Legge and Dorrington (*ibid*, 124) concluded 'that virtually all of the sheep-goat group are, in fact, sheep'. The analysis of the sheep age structure at Harlow revealed that over 80% of the ageable mandibles are from Payne's age stage C (three to nine months old), and this is another difference from the West Hill pattern, although one point of similarity from the ageing results is that the Harlow sheep were slaughtered in the autumn (*ibid*, 132). Thus, although the evidence from Harlow is superficially very close to that from West Hill, there are enough differences to indicate a different (though still markedly ritual) regime.

The large number of domestic fowl bones occur in greater quantity and proportion (compared with identified bone totals and with bird bone totals) than at other Roman sites; and like sheep/goat, male birds appear to predominate.

Confining the discussion to Phase 5 MNI counts, Table 11 gives a figure of around 1100 goat and sheep sacrificed over a 50 year period, that is 22 per year. There is no doubt that this is an extremely conservative estimate: the NFI determinations reveal an average of around 40 bones per individual. representing a 'loss' of about 75%. Taphonomic factors can easily account for even greater losses of bone after deposition. and a more reasonable estimate of the number of animals sacrificed is 9300, or 186 per year (this assumes a bone loss factor of 75% on top of the above). The ageing results clearly imply an autumn peak in kill-off. Assuming 80% of sacrifices occurred during the autumn, we have about 150 goats and sheep being killed over a two to three month period, every year for 50 years, with a smaller rate of sacrifice occurring throughout the rest of the year. These figures are highly speculative, but they do provide a reasonable guide to the scale of the operation, and reflect upon the wealth of the region in being able to sustain this sort of practise (see Noddle 1987).

The other phases do not indicate anything like this intensity of activity, but the ritual nature of the remaining assemblage is equally undoubted: see Noddle's comparison of sites in the region (*ibid*, tables 3 and 5). The climax of activities may have occurred in Phase 5, but it should be noted that not all of the site was excavated, and other phases may have had bone dumps in other locations. The results from fieldwalking in 1978 indicate other possible bone concentrations (Fig 161).

The SG bone measurements have highlighted the difficulties of separating the two species at this site, where their similarity appears to be greater than at other sites (eg Fig 204). Possibly this reflects the selection criteria of animals for sacrifice which may have included factors such as size and horn growth, larger individuals being preferred. Thus we may have a biased picture of sheep (and possibly goat) size and conformation, which is nevertheless informative.

Study of pathological anomalies indicated that the animals were, in general, fit and healthy, with just a few individuals whose health or fitness may have been below par. This impression is gained from the mandibles, where although a wide range of anomalies is present, these are seldom severe or frequent. This is supported by Frayn's view (1984, 39) that the Romans did not generally choose diseased animals for sacrifice.

The analysis of intra-site variation illustrated deposits of greater and lesser bone concentration and ritual content. In some cases it was possible to see distinctions between rooms within a single building (eg Structures I and IV), and in most cases it was possible to roughly define the nature of the deposit on a structure by structure basis. Most notably, it was possible to trace a continuity from Phase 4 to Phase 6: Structure X (Phase 4) correlating with Structures IX (Phase 5) and XIV (Phase 6) as non-ritual; and Structure IV (Phase 4) correlating with Structure I (Phase 5) as ritual. Furthermore there is the coincidence of dumps of votive material over both the latter structures, though the dumps were not contemporaneous.

The predominance of sheep in the generally available zooarchaeological evidence conflicts with that from classical writers, who apparently held goats in higher regard than sheep. The evidence presented here, suggests there may be a case for a reassessment of the evidence for goat husbandry in the Roman period.

A great deal has been written by classical authors about Roman agriculture, but little relates directly to Britain; and to what extent the existing accounts can be extrapolated to Britain is a moot point. The price-fixing edict of Diocletian referring to the *birrus Britannicus* is frequently taken to be an allusion to the presence of goat in Britain, as it is reputedly a goat hair cloak (Rivet 1964, 123). Despite the scarcity of references, Roman commentaries do provide an invaluable source of evidence not available by other means. For example some details about animals offered up for sacrifice can be gained from the classical sources. Both Frayn (1984) and Luff (1982) quote a passage from Varro which describes qualities to be sought in sacrificial animals. Varro is talking about cattle (*Res Rusticae*, 2:5), and Luff uses the passage to conclude that it was common practice to use weak and sickly animals, but Frayn feels that the reference is ambiguous, quoting also the passage at 2:3,5 to suggest that it is diseases such as fever that are alluded to, and not the general physique of the animals. Frayn also comments

> 'although the animals used for sacrifice were a small proportion of the total, each farmer had to produce at least one per annum, and those who provided animals for use in the great religious centres, such as Rome, would be parting with many more in this way. One thinks for example of the *ovis Idulis* sacrificed in Rome on the Ides of every month.' (Frayn, 1984, 39).

The zooarchaeological literature gives no clear impression of the status of goats from the general reviews. Modern comparative data shows that goats yield nearly three times as much milk in proportion to body weight as cattle, and four times as much as sheep (MacKenzie 1980, 346–7), though goat milk has a relatively lower fat content. Cheese was also an acknowledged favourite of the Romans (White 1970, 315). This importance seems to have been recognised in Roman Britain as well as in Rome (Liversidge 1968, 225–6). In fact goats and sheep were reared mainly for their milk since antiquity in the Mediterranean according to Ryder (1983, 68–70), and something of this bias may have been carried into Britain.

The impression that goats were an important stock animal (Wacher 1980, 109) is not so clear from the bone evidence. Maltby in a review of bone reports (1981, 159–61) concluded; 'The archaeological evidence suggests that goats were ... of little importance in Roman Britain. They certainly provided very little of the meat diet' (*ibid*, 160) and 'it would be misleading to regard the goat as a principal stock animal' (*ibid*, 161). However Cram and Fulford (1979, 205) found, from foot mark impressions in tiles from Silchester, that of 22 individuals, seven were definitely sheep and five definitely goat. One reason for the fact that so little goat is reported in bone analyses might be that goat was generally eaten as young kid, so that adult goat bones are rare. Payne has found a fair number of very juvenile goat mandibles at Castle Copse, a late Roman villa complex near Marlborough, but very few adult goat bones as yet (Payne, personal comment).

This unique assemblage has provided a rare opportunity to view Roman ritual practices through the evidence from the animals sacrificed. Not only does it provide us with information about the ritual practices, but it gives us a glimpse of the wealth and sophistication of a region able to sustain this kind of site.

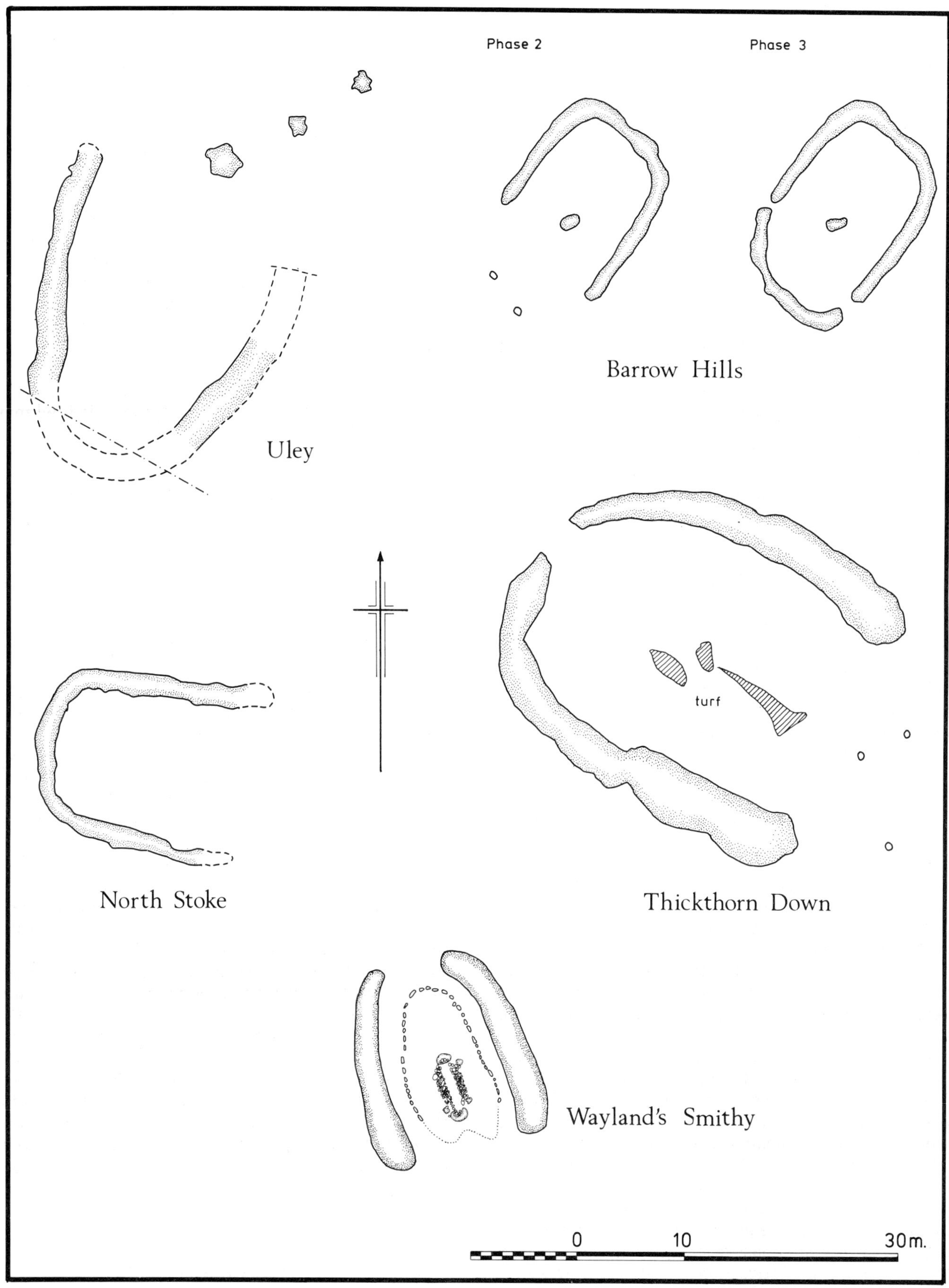

Fig 209 Neolithic long barrows and enclosures

13 Synthesis

The sacred place

From a study of field and place names, and in particular from the etymology of the name of the village situated nearest to West Hill, we may learn that this inconspicuous hilltop, lying in the lee of the massive hillfort of Uley Bury, was the site for a *nemeton* or Celtic sacred place of extreme importance. Firstly , the nineteenth-century field name Money Quarries may refer to the finding of Roman coins immediately north of the temple site. More significantly, the ancient field names recorded for the locality suggest that there may have been an area of common land, shared by three parishes, which was not enclosed until the seventeenth century or later (see Drinkwater, Appendix B). This area may have reflected the folk memory of a shared and hallowed focal place. Of the three parishes concerned, the one containing the nearest Domesday settlement to the site of the shrines on West Hill was Nympsfield. Also the name West Hill would relate more logically to Nympsfield village, lying just to the north-east, rather than to Uley, which lies due south of the temple site (*ibid*). Furthermore the name Nympsfield means 'the tract of open country belonging to a place called Nymed', where *nymed* is the Celtic word for a shrine, a sacred grove or holy place (Smith 1965, 2 244). The actual name of the place, and that of the Celtic deity there venerated, are enshrined within the inscriptions on at least seven of the lead tablets, although a reading of these names, and their etymology, requires further study. A ditched enclosure, which may have had its origins in a Neolithic monument of the third millennium BC, occupied a clearing within the virgin forest, and may itself have contained one or more sacred trees, posts, or standing stones. Towards the end of the Iron Age the enclosure was extended to enclose a sequence of timber shrines, and the site of the central building was subsequently used for the construction of a Romano-Celtic temple in stone. Finally, the site was used for the establishment of a series of buildings in timber and stone, which can best be interpreted as successive Christian churches. In the Iron Age and Roman periods at least, we know, from the results of fieldwalking and geophysical survey, that the shrines formed the focus for major settlement areas.

A generalised outline of the environmental history of the site has been obtained from analyses of land molluscan assemblages. The dense woodland of the prehistoric era gave way to more open conditions as land was cleared to extend the ritual enclosure in the first century AD. A little regeneration of scrub and woodland may have occurred around AD 100, and, from very limited evidence, it appears that trees existed nearby throughout the life of the Roman temple. During the post-Roman phase of site use clearance appears to have commenced once more, leading to the creation of the open arable landscape of the medieval period. From a study of the charcoals deriving from constructional timbers or fuel, we have found that the woodland comprised common native species such as oak, ash and hawthorn, while more damp-loving varieties such as willow or poplar must have been brought in from further afield. A late Roman latrine shaft (F188b, see chapter 12) contained the mineralised remains of plants and animals, included in fossil faecal material and the coprolites of goat and rat. Among these remains were indicators of food plants, managed grassland in the form of hay meadows, and of waste ground: nettles, which would have thrived on the disturbed nitrogen-enriched soils around the temple buildings.

The animal bone assemblage was dominated by large numbers of bones from animals which had been sacrificed in ritual contexts. This aspect will be further discussed below, but it is also important to recognise that domestic assemblages were present in many of the buildings. Amongst this domestic evidence, the occurrences of different species were similar to those represented on other Roman sites. An unknown proportion of the sacrificial sheep, goats and domestic fowl may have been domestic, but the next most common species found was cattle. These fell in relative importance through the Roman phases and then increased from the later fourth century. This is at variance with the evidence from other Roman sites, where the relative importance of cattle to other domestic animals increases throughout the Roman period. However, cattle were still always more numerous than pigs, the proportion of which rose through the Roman phases and then decreased. The pathological conditions recognised on the cattle bones can be work-related, and may suggest that draught animals were involved. Species occurring in minor proportions included horse, dog, and roe deer, while in addition to the domestic fowl, water birds, domestic goose, and scavengers such as rooks and magpies have been identified. Fish remains mainly comprised bones from species that could have been taken from local rivers or the Severn, although at least one deep-sea specimen, of red sea-bream, was represented also.

The only evidence for plant foods recovered from the excavation consisted of fragments contained within the fossil faeces from the late Roman latrine shaft referred to above. Cereals, wild celery, and various wild fruits of wood and hedgerow were identified, along with examples of the more exotic mulberry. This deposit, infested with fly larvae and woodlice, provides an unusual gloss to the more clinical impressions of the environs of ancient shrines conveyed by many conjectural architectural reconstruction drawings. The perspective views presented below (Figs 212, 213, and 217) are populated by men, women, and children, goats, chickens, draught animals, trees, and bushes; in addition one must imagine the nettle patches and magpie-ridden middens hidden behind some of the buildings, often among the ruins or levelled sites of their predecessors.

The pre-Roman monument

The earliest features excavated were the ditches F179 and F382, running below the Roman building ranges of Structures I and IV, and a series of pits located further to the north. These structural elements have been ascribed to Phase 1 (Fig 11). With the exception of one shallow pit, none of the primary fillings within any of these features produced any finds beyond a small handful of worked flints. No pre-Iron Age pottery has been recovered from the site and no charcoal deposits suitable for dating were located. The two early ditches F199 and F382 have been separated chronologically from those in the northern sector of the site on the grounds of morphology, and the general distribution of flint artefacts. Both ditches exhibited wide rounded profiles and, according to the evidence from the transects excavated, varied in depth. The sides and edges of the cuts were weathered considerably. In contrast, the ditches to the north were sharply cut, flat based, and relatively unweathered; furthermore they were evenly cut with little variation in depth along their lines. Parts of the two-phase Phase 1 ditches and some of the pits were characterised by a well consolidated, reddish stony clay filling which was devoid of any finds, and contrasted quite distinctly with the deposits encountered within later features on the site. Whilst traces of contemporary bank material were found outside the Iron Age ditches to the north, no such traces were located either inside or outside the Phase 1 ditches. This suggests that any upstanding monumental element that may have been associated with them had been destroyed at an earlier period.

Although only three of the flint artefacts recovered during the excavation were found in unassailably Phase 1 contexts (see chapter 10) a consideration of the general distribution of flint across the site is pertinent to the attempt to define features of potential Neolithic or Early Bronze Age date. Most of the flint items were residual in contexts of Iron Age and Roman date, It is likely that the flints will have become incorporated in these deposits as a result of the disturbance of underlying soils and fills during the sequential processes of construction and demolition. Thus the occurrence of flints in the Iron Age and Roman layers may well reflect the distribution of pre-Iron Age features below. It is interesting therefore to note that two thirds of the flints from Iron Age and Roman contexts derived from the southern portion of the site, above and between the ditches F179 and F382, whilst only one third derived from deposits above the ditches in the northern sector. This contrast might be seen to be even more marked when it is recalled that more sensitive recovery techniques were developed during the excavation campaign, and that these became more rigorous in the northern sector, excavated in 1978 and 1979 than those employed in the area of the postulated early ditches excavated in 1977. Alan Saville has shown (chapter 10) that the flint assemblage was of mixed Neolithic and Early Bronze Age origin and that any Mesolithic elements were absent. He also highlighted a probable connection with a substantial Neolithic settlement which is suspected to lie beneath the Iron Age hillfort of Uley Bury (Saville and Ellison 1983, 1). Surface finds from within the hillfort have included scrapers, flakes from polished axes, a grooved polished stone implement, and 'sling-stones', now housed in Gloucester and Stroud Museums, and a large collection of over 2000 flints: arrowheads, scrapers, knapping debris, and more fragments from polished implements, curated at Cheltenham Museum.

The two Phase 1 ditches exhibit similar dimensions and profiles. Neither was excavated totally and the variations in depth suggest that the ditches were unevenly constructed, or may have been built by gangs, and thus were discontinuous. Their lines converge towards the south-west but continue beyond the confines of the excavated area. Whether each ditch terminated in a similar manner as on the north, or whether they joined to form a U-shaped enclosure could not be determined, but the angles and configuration of the ditches in plan suggests that the latter was the case (see Fig 209). Morphologically, the dimensions, shape and disposition of the earlier ditches best match two groups of monuments belonging to the early Neolithic period: the quarry ditches of earthen long barrows, and long mortuary enclosures. The locally represented class of long barrow is the Severn-Cotswold type which is not renowned for the existence of linear quarry ditches (Darvill 1982). Indeed quarries have been encountered very rarely, largely due to the confined extent of the recorded barrow excavations, and those excavated recently at Hazleton North appear to be of uneven plan and extent (Saville 1984, fig 1, and 1990). However, further south and east, on the chalklands of Wessex, one may find long barrow quarry ditches which are remarkably similar in configuration to those here. Two examples are illustrated in juxtaposition with the Uley plan in Figure 209. The unchambered barrow at Wayland's Smithy I, Oxon (Atkinson 1965) possessed flanking ditches similar in width to those here, and a further close parallel is provided by the barrow at Thickthorn Down, Dorset (Drew and Piggott 1936, 81), defined by Ashbee (1970, 42–3) as one of a group of earthen long barrows enclosed by U-shaped ditches. At Thickthorn the ditches were of uneven depth as here, with the deepest sectors occurring at the terminals.

A series of ditched oval enclosures in the upper Thames valley which may represent the remains of ploughed-out long barrows or Neolithic mortuary enclosures has been discussed by Bradley (in Bradley and Holgate 1984, 116–18 and fig 5). In plan and morphology, these resemble the layout of ditches and pits associated with the well known earthen long barrow at Nutbane, Hants (Morgan 1959). At Barrow Hills, Radley, Oxon (Bradley and Holgate 1984, 116–18, and fig 5) a multi-phased barrow enclosed by U-shaped ditches was dated by pottery to the mid-third millennium BC. The two latest phase plans are shown in Figure 209, as is the plan of a ditched earthwork which was joined to the south end of a bank barrow at North Stoke, Oxon (*ibid*). If the monument excavated at Uley had been succeeded by a larger Severn-Cotswold tomb, as at Wayland's Smithy (Atkinson 1965), all evidence of any quarries would lie outside the limits of excavation. Multi-phased long barrows are known elsewhere on the Cotswolds, and if such a monument existed on West Hill it may have formed a pair with Hetty Pegler's Tump which lies in the adjacent field. However, they would not have been as closely spaced as the other pairs of Severn-Cotswold tombs, such as those known at Hazleton, Eyford Hill, or Ascott-under-Wychwood, Oxon (Darvill 1982, 95).

At Uley, no mound material survives between the ditches. This area, however occupied the highest and most eroded point of the rounded hilltop, and any traces of internal structures such as post or stone holes would have been ploughed away. Slightly further north, where the land dips slightly, traces of shallow and deeper pits and postholes did survive. Holes, intended to hold major posts or stones, and pits or hearths for ritual feasting, occur in the forecourts of tombs and within the entrances of mortuary enclosures. Pits F1002 and F790 are in alignment with the central pit F19, located within the cella of the Roman temple, and it is likely that this irregular and multiphased feature had been in existence since Phase 1. These holes may have held large posts or standing stones, while the portions of ditch and shallow pits excavated towards the northern limit of the site may represent an associated activity area. It was one of these features, F855, which produced the only closed group of flints from the site, comprising two scrapers, a core, a broken piercer and eighteen flakes, associated with an assemblage of fossils. The positioning of the major long barrow, Hetty Pegler's Tump, and the newly postulated barrow or mortuary enclosure on West Hill, just outside the major Neolithic centre that is thought to lie beneath the Uley Bury hillfort (Saville and Ellison 1983, 1) can be paralleled further south, where major causewayed enclosures occur in close proximity to long barrows, as at Abingdon, Oxon (Bradley and Holgate 1984, 115–16), or on Hambledon Hill in Dorset (Mercer 1980).

The discovery of the remains of a possible Neolithic monument beneath the Iron Age shrine and Roman temple on West Hill is of considerable importance to studies of the reuse of *loci* set apart for ritual activities. The possibly deliberate siting of Roman temples on, or near to, prehistoric barrows is known elsewhere in Britain, and a few examples will be cited below. In a more local context it is of interest to note that the Severn-Cotswold barrows of Gloucestershire appear to have been of particular significance to the Romano-British populace. Professor Piggott was one of the first to discuss the possible meaning of Roman finds in prehistoric barrows, because he found six Roman coins in the facade area of the West Kennet long barrow (Piggott 1962, 55). Many such finds relate to inserted inhumations of Romano-British date, but almost as many seem to have been deposited as a result of robbing or hoarding. In Gloucestershire, Roman burials have been recovered from Hetty Pegler's Tump itself (Clifford 1966) and from round barrows at King's Stanley, Minchinhampton, and Withington (O'Neil and Grinsell 1960, 22). Long barrows disturbed in other ways include Wayland's Smithy, Oxon (Atkinson 1965), where the monument was modified by the digging of two Roman ditches, one of which ran in front of the Neolithic facade, and which contained a deliberate deposit of sarsen boulders and fragmentary human bone. At Adlestrop (Donovan 1938, 161–2), the missing orthostats from the chamber were probably removed in the Romano-British period, and at Sale's Lot, Withington (O'Neil 1966, 28) Roman sherds and tile fragments were found above the forecourt area which had been disturbed considerably. Roman coins or pottery have also been recovered from the long barrows at Bown Hill, Randwick, Rodmarton, and the Hoar Stone, Enstone (Crawford 1925, 17). Perhaps the most dramatic evidence for the veneration or reuse of barrows by Roman worshippers is provided by the finding of deliberately placed Roman altars, one within a barrow at Tidenham, and a hoard of no less than six in a round barrow at Bisley (Clifford 1939). It seems that a tradition of appropriation of ancient monuments for religious sanctification and veneration was particularly prevalent in Roman Gloucestershire, and in this context the siting of an Iron Age and Romano-British religious complex above the decaying remains of an earlier prehistoric monument is very fitting.

The juxtaposition or superimposition of barrows and temples is however by no means unique. At Mutlow Hill, Cambridgeshire (Neville 1852) a circular temple was located next to a barrow and a series of Bronze Age urned cremations. In the same county, at Haddenham, octagonal and square shrines were superimposed upon the remains of a Bronze Age round barrow (Hodder, personal comment). The Brean Down temple in Somerset (ApSimon 1965, fig 41) was sited immediately north of an unexcavated round barrow, the most easterly of a row of three along the brow of the peninsula. Beneath the Iron Age and Roman shrines at Harlow, Essex (France and Gobel 1985, 21, figs 5 and 54) were five Bronze Age pits, three of which contained fragments of Collared Urns. An assemblage of Neolithic to Early Bronze Age flints was also present (*ibid*, fig 51) and it can be postulated that these may have derived from an old ground surface sealed beneath a destroyed barrow, to which the urned burials might have been related. The configuration of features shown in the plan (*ibid*, fig 5) further suggests that the large pit dated to the Early Iron Age by the excavators (F–G on fig 5) would have been situated at the centre of such a barrow, and thus could represent robbing or reuse of the barrow centre in that period. Lastly, it should not be forgotten that the postulated Iron Age shrine on site L at Maiden Castle, Dorset, and the Romano-Celtic temple of site B (Wheeler 1943, pls i and iii) were located over, and immediately north of, the focal eastern end of one of the longest Neolithic barrows in Britain.

The Final Iron Age and early Roman enclosure

Later Iron Age features associated with Roman temple sites usually comprise postholes or beamslots of timber buildings located beneath stone Roman temple structures (Drury 1980). The discovery and definition of such a building here, in association with a large ditched enclosure, a smaller trapezoidal timber structure, votive pits, and human infant burials, provides a notable contribution to studies of such structures. In a local context, it also serves to throw some light on the religious traditions of the Dobunni, previously glimpsed only fleetingly by Wheeler's discovery of a handful of postholes, and a displaced door pivot-stone, below the cella of the temple at Lydney (Wheeler and Wheeler 1932, fig 2).

By the late Iron Age the prehistoric ditches of Phase 1 had silted but must have been visible still as hollows. Their alignments were reused for the cutting of slots for substantial timber palisades, although the evidence for this was clearer in ditch F179 than in ditch F382. Dating evidence for the destruction of the palisades, in the form of brooches dated to the early first century AD, implies that these structural modifications probably occurred in the first, or possibly second centuries BC.

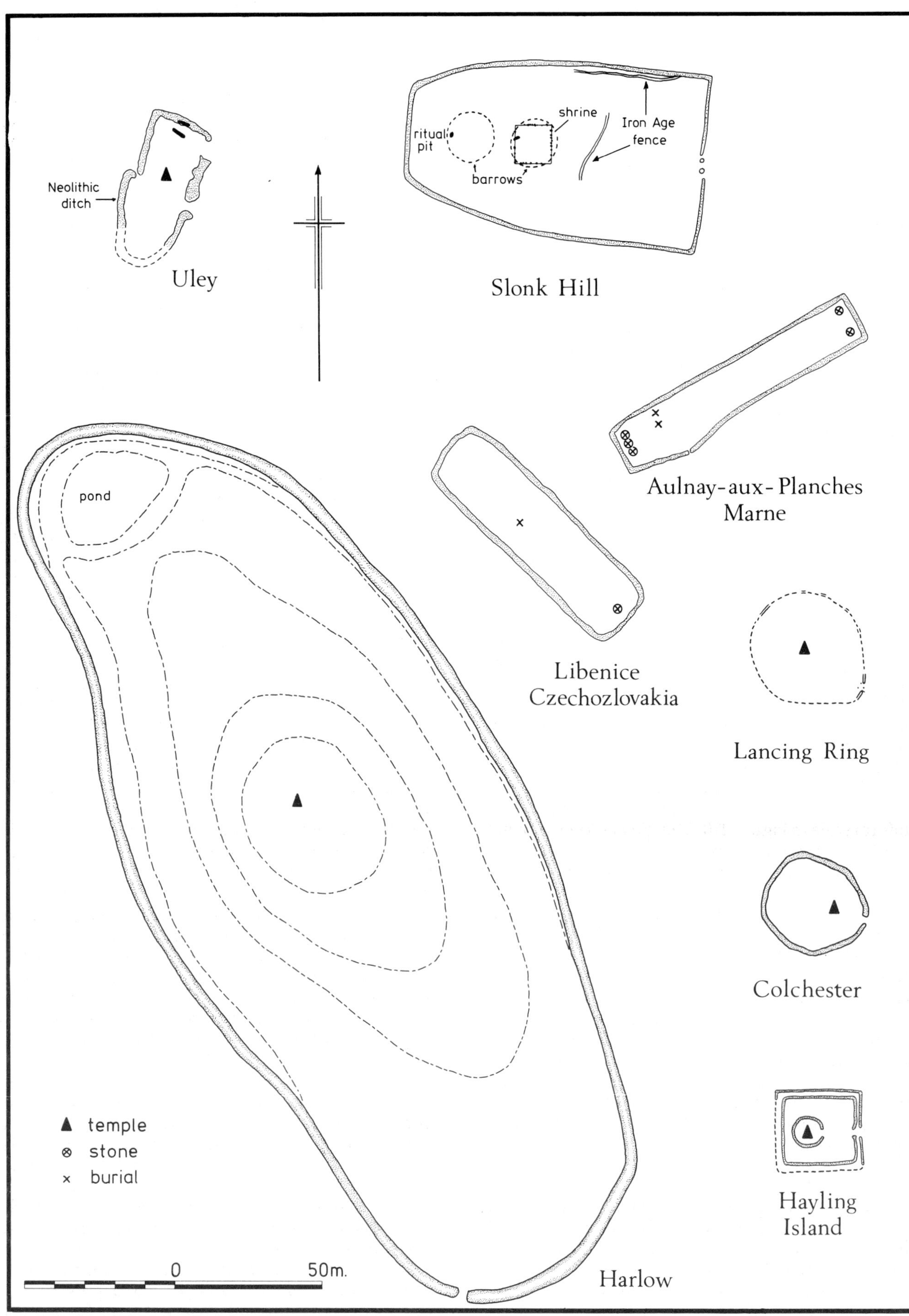

Fig 210 Iron Age ritual enclosures

During Phase 2, probably in the early part of the first century AD, the enclosure was extended, and almost doubled in size, by the addition of two square cut ditches, F594 and F816, which contained a single timber palisade on the west and a double palisade to the north (Fig 15). On the eastern side, a separate and very much deeper segment of ditch F264, contained significant deposits of Iron Age Malvernian pottery (fabric group A), which were not mixed with 'Belgic' types, and it may be that this particular segment of ditch was constructed first, during the last centuries BC. Also in contrast to the palisade ditches, the deeper ditch F264 contained a series of deposits of votive material. The truncated remains of bank material were recognised immediately east of ditch F264, west of ditch F594, and north of ditch F816, indicating that the northern part of the Phase 2 enclosure at least, was delineated by a discontinuous ditch, lengths of palisade, and an external bank. The Phase 2 extended enclosure appears to have been designed to surround a square timber building, Structure XVI, which probably functioned during Phases 2 and 3. Towards the end of Phase 2, a circular pit, F251, was cut into the central margin of ditch F264 and immediately north-east of Structure XVI; this pit was used for the deposition of votive offerings in Phases 2 and 3. A further similar pit, F836, was found outside the northern palisaded ditch but this contained little in the way of primary deposits. Two further pits F56 and F158 also cut into earlier enclosure ditches in this period, the former a focus for subsequent votive deposit of Phase 3 (ditch F342). In Phase 3, only the western palisade survived (Fig 22). A second timber building, Structure XVII, was built over part of the infilled northern ditch (F816) and a series of slots and pits were constructed within the hollow that survived above the largely silted ditch F264.

The enclosure belongs to a group of ritual centres which have been defined in Britain and on the continent. A selection of relevant site plans is shown at a uniform scale in Figure 210. The ditches long known to exist beneath the Roman *temenoi* at Harlow and Colchester, Essex (Lewis 1966, figs 111 and 113) are both curvilinear although substantially disparate in size. More detail of construction has been obtained from Lancing, Sussex (Bedwin 1980, figs 2–3) and Hayling Island, Hants. (Downey *et al* 1980, fig 14.1); at Lancing there was evidence of palisade posts, and at Hayling Island the excavators have suggested that the enclosure limit was defined by a hedge supplemented by timber fencing (*ibid*, 290). However, the best parallels for the Uley enclosure are provided by the long ditched enclosures of continental Europe. These are exemplified by the tenth-century BC enclosure of Aulnay-aux-Planches (Piggott 1965, 232, 234, fig 132, and references there cited) with its ditch, which may have contained a palisade, and terminal stone monuments, and the Czechoslovakian site of Libeniçe where an area of intersecting pits formed a sunken sanctuary where libations were poured (Piggott 1968, 57–9 and pl 16 and 17). The pit area at Libeniçe bears a striking formal and functional similarity to the complex of pits and offerings excavated within the ditch segment F264.

The finding of deliberate deposits of votive objects within earth or rock cut pits conforms to the known Iron Age activity of placing ritual deposits in pits, shafts and wells (Ross 1968). However, usually such shafts or pits have been recovered on domestic or military sites, and not in close association with contemporary enclosures of shrines. The earliest such deposits were contained in the deep ditch F264, where apparently votive assemblages of Phases 2b and 2c included antler tools, iron projectile heads, animal bones, large pottery fragments and two Dobunnic coins. Similar groupings of objects, but associated with a copper alloy spiral headed pin and an early Roman coin, were recovered from Phase 3a contexts. Pit F836, roughly 2m in diameter and 1.80m deep, contained ash and charcoal, but no artefacts in the primary deposits. On the other hand, the Phase 2c votive pit, F251, which was 2.85m in diameter and 1.80m deep, was found to contain many original and primary deposits. These dark layers contained iron bolt heads, brooches, and half-complete pots, while contexts of Phase 3a contained further projectiles, pottery, a quern fragment, and a whetstone. The bones found within this pit included the articulated hind limb of a cow, a human femur, and one human molar.

Ritual deposition within pits and shafts of Iron Age and Romano-British date has been reconsidered by Wait (1985, ch 3), who has refined the definitive characteristics of such sites initially isolated by Ross (1968). He has compared the Iron Age examples with those of Roman date and studied the geographical distribution of the various traits. For the Iron Age, he was able to define two spatial groups, one in Kent and Surrey, with frequent deposits of bird and dog bones, and the other including the other southern British sites, which displayed more deliberately layered deposits and the inclusion of horse bones. All the Iron Age pits tended to contain pottery and ash along with the bones of cattle or humans. Wait (*ibid*) suggested a minimum depth for such sites as 2.5m. The Uley pits are shallower than this, but the deposits do seem to bear comparison with those contained within the deeper shafts and wells. Wait (*ibid*) notes however that by the Roman period, the shafts did tend to be shallower. Also new categories of votive offering were now common; these tended to be objects more representative of personal wealth and individuality: tools, explicitly votive objects, coins, and (mainly in military contexts) querns, weapons, and armour. At Uley the deposits of tools, weapons, coins, pottery, and bones appear to fit the model well. Votive pits are generally rare in the west and none are known from Gloucestershire. In final Iron Age contexts the best comparable assemblage derives not from a pit, but from the courtyard of the Iron Age enclosure at Hayling Island (Downey *et al* 1980, 293–4). Votive finds there included horse and vehicle equipment, seventeen socketed spearheads, scabbard binding and sword chapes, brooches, coins, currency bars, and bones of sheep and pig. In the Roman west, the 12m deep well at the Brislington villa, Avon (Ross 1968, 262) contained a deposit of animal bones, human skulls, and complete ceramic and metal vessels, while two Roman temples possessed ritual shafts or wells. At Jordan Hill, Dorset (*ibid*, 267–8) a shaft 4m deep contained sixteen bird burials associated with coins, and two separate stone cists had been built for the deposition of pots, swords, and spearheads. The well west of the late Roman temple at Pagan's Hill, Somerset (Rahtz and Harris 1957, 105–12; Rahtz and Watts, forthcoming) was found to contain animal bones, fifteen coins, branches of oak, and potsherds. In addition, it remained in use as a repository for votive offerings far into the post-Roman period. However, care must be taken in the definition of votive deposits in such wells. At Chew Park, Avon (Rahtz and Greenfield 1977, 56–65, table i, pls xxvi–xxviii) the well contained bucket fittings, rope fragments, metal jugs, wooden tools, various personal items, wooden writing tablets, leather shoes, 1104 animal bones, and 1669 sherds from 40 or 50 vessels. This well was interpreted as domestic by the excavators and is not included in Wait's gazetteer (Wait 1985). The list of contents is not dissimilar to that noted for the Brislington well (Ross 1968, 262) or indeed for the one on Pagan's Hill (Rahtz and Harris 1957, 105–12). It is the later deposits in the Pagan's Hill well, the sculpture fragment and post-Roman glass jar, which indicate its ritual function, not the Roman contents listed above. In this case the ritual function of the well in relation to the temple is in little doubt, but the status of the villa wells is less certain. For a domestic well-assemblage located close to Uley we may cite the groups of early Roman finds from the well belonging to the Frocester Court villa (Price 1984).

Two timber structures excavated within the late Iron Age enclosure at Uley were of unusual square and trapezoidal plan, quite unlike the local examples of Iron Age houses such as the round hut at Frocester (Price 1983, 140). The central structure possessed postholes which were found to contain iron projectile heads and a complete pot, and both buildings were associated with the remains of human infants, which may have been deposited at the time of construction. From the square Structure XVI the bones of a seven to nine-months-old baby were recovered (HB2) while the bodies of two slightly older infants had been buried under posts of Structure XVII to the north (HB1 and HB3) (see chapter 12). Other human remains from the site included fragments from the skeleton of a nine-months-old baby found in the enclosure ditch F584, the shaft of a femur and one adult molar from the votive pit F251, and a further molar from a slightly younger individual, within the ditch deposits of F264. In an interim report (Ellison 1980, 309) the infant burials were cited as further evidence for the presence of a religious site and were compared to finds from Frilford site A, Oxon (Harding 1972, pl 33) and Maiden Castle, Dorset (Wheeler 1943, pl xx). However, Harding has now reinterpreted the circular timber building at Frilford in a domestic context (Harding 1987, 16) and Wait's analysis of the finds of human remains on recently excavated Iron Age settlements (Wait 1985, appendix iv) has shown that neonatal and infant burials are very commonly found in pits. They also occur in the posthole fillings of domestic structures at Old Down Farm and Winnall Down, Hants (*ibid*).

The square timber Structure XVI comprised a simple arrangement of separate postholes forming an 8.20m square. No evidence can be adduced to indicate whether the posts supported a roofed building or the fence for an open enclosure. Centrally within the square lay pit F19 which probably existed earlier in Phase 1. If this contained a standing stone, timber post, or living tree, then the structure may have been open rather than roofed; certainly it appears to have been constructed around this focal feature. Further north, and constructed slightly later, Structure XVII was 3.80m wide at the west, 4.60m wide at the east, and 5.20m long. There were no associated finds apart from the infant burials. In contrast to the post construction of the square structure, this building was supported by closely spaced circular posts held in continuous bedding trenches.

The last twenty years of excavation has revolutionised our knowledge of Iron Age ritual structures, and a selection of rectangular shrines are shown in Figure 211 alongside, and at the same scale as, the two Uley buildings. The trapezoidal building, Structure XVII, cannot be paralleled easily, although a similar building plan was recovered from the mainly domestic site at Marshfield, Avon (Blockley 1985, 36, R2). Its building trench construction can be matched in ritual buildings at Danebury (Cunliffe 1984, 81–7) and South Cadbury (Alcock 1972). The square building, Structure XVI, is of similar size to the shrines at Heathrow, Middlesex (Grimes 1961, fig 7) and Danebury, Hants (RS1) (Cunliffe 1984, 83, fig 4.32). Whilst the building at Heathrow could be of two phases, or have functioned as a small trench built shrine within a post built fenced enclosure, at Danebury structure RS1 appears to have been free standing. The interior is relatively undisturbed by pits, and traces of any interior sub-structure were not present. However, at Uley the interior of the square enclosure defined by posts was heavily disturbed by Roman and post-Roman features, and the possibility of the former existence of a subsidiary structure around the focal pit cannot be ruled out. Although this shrine was of similar dimensions to RS1 at Danebury (*ibid*, 86–7), all the rectangular shrines there were supported in bedding trenches, and some were possibly built of planks. At South Cadbury, Somerset (Alcock 1972, fig 10) two of the rectangular shrines were supported by posts and one had a bedding trench; a further post structure, apparently possessing an internal enclosure, has been suggested at Chelmsford, Essex (Drury 1980, 54).

At South Cadbury, the shrines were associated with animal burials and a metal pendant with duck's head ornament (Alcock 1972, 153–5). At Danebury, South Cadbury, Heathrow, and Little Waltham, Essex, the shrines occupied central positions within major domestic or proto-urban settlements (Drury 1980, fig 3.4). When the main occupation ceased at Danebury and South Cadbury, the shrines seem to have survived in use into the final Iron Age period. The same may have been the case at Maiden Castle, where Wheeler's 'Belgic hut' can be viewed as a circular shrine (eg Cunliffe 1974, fig 15.4). It lies adjacent to a fourth-century Romano-Celtic temple and directly beneath a post-Roman structure that can be interpreted as a shrine in the fifth century AD (Rahtz and Watts 1979). In this respect it provides a close parallel for the situation at Uley, and reconstruction of the finds lists relating to layers associated with the latest pre-Roman Iron Age shrine at Maiden Castle (compiled from Wheeler 1943) emphasises that the range of votive material was broadly similar. The main groups of finds from Belgic levels near the shrine included fine Belgic pottery, fifteen brooches of pre-Conquest or first-century AD type, pony bones with harness fittings, iron weapons, and six British coins, in addition to several crouched infant burials. Wait (1985, 171) has pointed out that 70% of known ritual structures in the Iron Age are square or

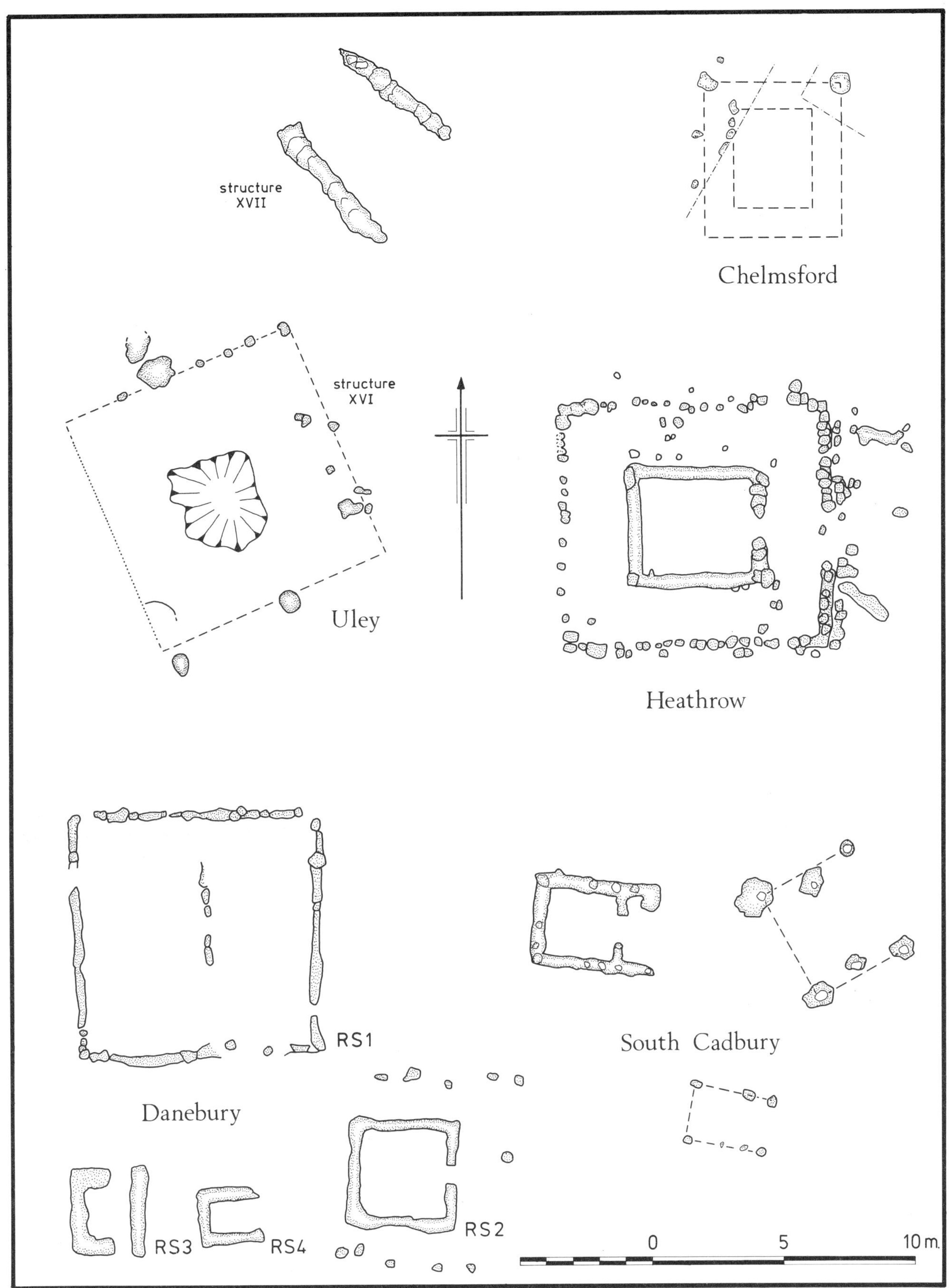

Fig 211 Iron Age shrines

rectangular in shape; and eastern entrances predominate. They usually occur in open areas set aside for ceremonial use and are spatially separated from domestic buildings. Analysis of building sizes has shown that they tend to be small and probably were not intended to hold large congregations of worshippers. At Uley, the results of the geophysical survey have suggested the presence of a major Iron Age settlement south and east of the excavated area. The shrine was separated from the presumed domestic and industrial areas by one of the most long-lived and complex ritual enclosures that has ever been investigated in Britain.

The Roman temple

Probably in the early second century AD the focal timber shrine was replaced, on exactly the same alignment by a square stone structure, which conforms in plan to those of a sub-type of Romano-Celtic temple occurring in Britain and continental Europe. The foundations were fragmentary, razed to ground level, much disturbed by modifications executed in later periods, and then further damaged by many centuries of arable agriculture. The plan (Fig 29) could be resolved into two major building phases. The first of these involved a slightly rectangular cella surrounded on three sides only by an ambulatory of even width. The main entrance was located on the north-east side and comprised, probably, an applied doorcase supported in two major postholes attached to a screen wall, all foundations of which had been destroyed except for two stone plinths. Reconstruction of the temple floor level suggests that two steps would have been necessary to allow access to the courtyard in front of the temple (Fig 30). No original floor levels survived and the only internal features that could have related to the temple as it was primarily conceived, were the central pit, which may have contained a lead tank or other water container, and a mortar base centrally positioned in the south-western ambulatory. This base may have been the remnant of a foundation for a plinth intended to support the major cult statue. In a later phase the temple was extended and aggrandised by the addition of a rectangular projecting foundation, which could have supported an open portico, raised well above the level of the main courtyard and approached by a flight of four steps. The primary screen wall was remodelled, probably at this time, but no definite traces of foundation had survived.

In interim reports (Ellison 1977, 1980) it was suggested that the extremely unusual temple plan might best be explained in terms of a roofed and totally enclosed ambulatory surrounding an open courtyard and dominated by a focal tree, post, or menhir surviving from the prehistoric phases. Such a reconstruction would have related to the class III temple plans defined by Lewis (1966). However, detailed post-excavation analysis has shown that the layers and distributional information, upon which the case for a courtyard interpretation had been built, related not to the periods of construction and use of the stone temple, but to com-

Fig 212 Perspective view: Phase 4. (Drawn by Joanna Richards)

plex modifications to the structure, which followed towards the end of the fourth century AD. Rodwell was able to discuss the Uley plan in relation to new comparative data and, in particular, to a new interpretation of the Titelberg relief (Rodwell 1980, 230). He has argued convincingly for the former existence of an enclosed tower cella at Uley. The Titelberg relief shows a temple with a tall central cella, but no front ambulatory, and thus may be equated with the primary plan at Uley. The side ambulatories are shown to be gabled, rather than possessing the pent roof more commonly associated with temple ambulatories, and drainage would have been achieved by means of a valley gutter between the inner slope of the ambulatory roof and the upper cella wall. This gutter could have disgorged at the front into two tanks and by this means the sacred water, falling on the roofs above the venerated cult image, could have been conserved and used, maybe, as a source for the filling of tanks or pools associated with the temple ritual (*ibid*, 231). The Titelberg relief also appears to show a temple embellished by a classical doorcase, and overall, the resemblances between this depiction and a possible reconstruction for the temple at Uley are most striking.

A series of reconstruction drawings, devised to show various phases and alternatives, are presented in Figures 212–14. The figures show the primary and secondary temple phases associated with contemporary buildings. The general proportions and style of these conjectural reconstructions owe much to the reconstruction of the Romano-Celtic temple on Brean Down, Somerset (ApSimon 1965, fig 51). Walling would have been of roughly squared oolitic limestone, and the roof would have been built with timber and polygonal red sandstone tiles. The exterior wall surfaces may have been coated with pale-coloured plaster or stucco from the beginning, and would certainly have been so treated by the later more classical phases. By then, the elevations may also have been embellished by moulded pilasters rising from a plinth, although the only surviving evidence for pilasters was a projection from the foundations at the south-west corner of the building. The roofs of the ambulatories, doorcase and portico are shown to be gabled, as in the Titelberg relief (Rodwell 1980, 230–1). In the main reconstruction drawings, the cella is surmounted by a regular pyramidal roof and the ends of the ambulatory roofs are hipped, but an alternative pair of reconstructions (Fig 214) shows a more classical scheme whereby the cella is provided with a gabled elevation from conception, and this is matched by gables at the front ends of each ambulatory. All these gables could have been embellished with classical ornament. The more formal scheme of these alternative reconstructions (Fig 214) was suggested by Warwick Rodwell who has pointed out that temples of this kind would have possessed rather shorter towers, in order that the slopes of the cella roof would be more or less in line with the outer slopes of the ambulatory roof. In the simpler reconstruction drawings (Figs 212 and 213) fenestration comprises rows of small square or round-headed windows, set high up in both cella and ambulatory walls. The

Fig 213 Perspective view: Phase 5d–e. (Drawn by Joanna Richards)

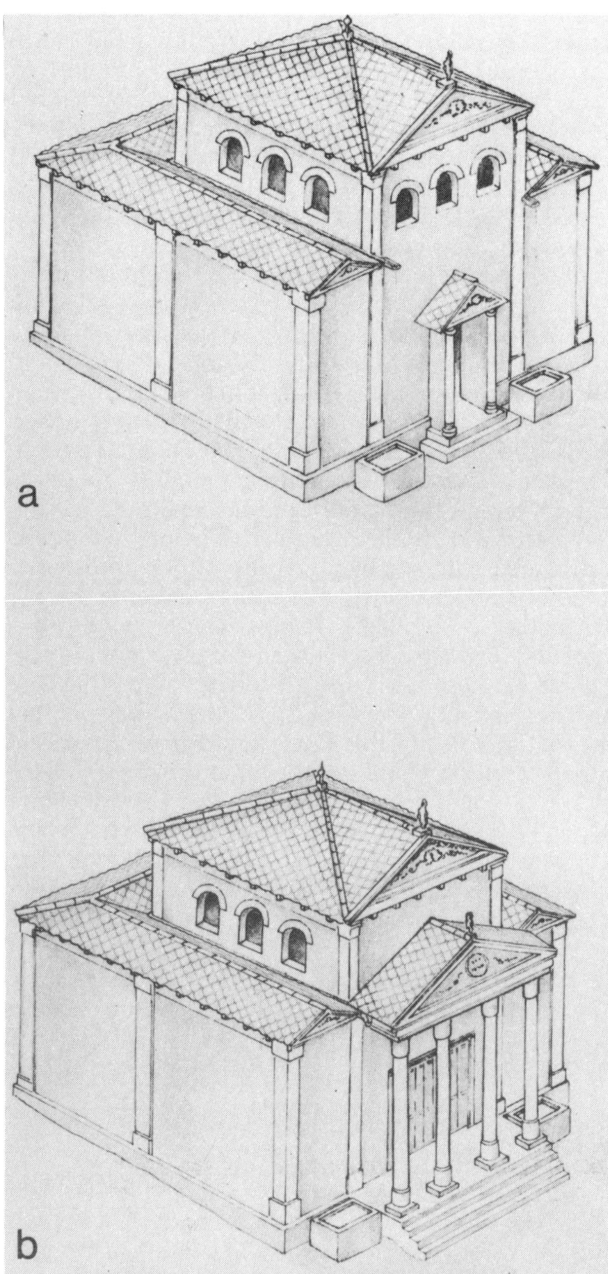

Fig 214 Alternative temple reconstructions, Phase 5. (Drawn by Joanna Richards)

more classical buildings, with their elegant pilastered elevations, would more probably have been windowless, with the exception of a row of small openings in the upper cella wall which would have been largely hidden from view by the ambulatory roof (Fig 214). In all cases the valley gutter, which was probably of stone, would have debouched into cisterns located on either side of the temple steps. These cisterns have been depicted in the reconstructions as stone, but equally they might have been made of lead. The proportions deduced in the drawing of the portico were influenced by the axonometric reconstructions of the temple of Sulis Minerva at Bath (Cunliffe and Davenport 1985, fig 110), and it may be that the original portico was constructed by individuals who were familiar with that very building.

The watercolour reconstruction of an interior view of the temple (Colour Plate II) shows the inside of the tower cella and suggests that there could have been fenestration within both cella and ambulatory. The cult statue occupies a *suggestus* in the position of the mortar foundation, illuminated by candles held in candlesticks within niches, and by other hidden lighting. The colours and motifs displayed on the plastered walls are those represented in the fragments of painted plaster recovered during the excavation (see chapter 10). Centrally placed within the cella is a square lead-lined water tank, separated from the cult statue by a plain mosaic floor panel. The priests are officiating at altars set against the cella wall and votive offerings are stored within a cupboard or leant up against the *suggestus* of the cult image. The public are shown to have access only as far as the pool within this temple. Although the plan is strictly Romano-Celtic, this direct access from main entrance to cella suggests a more classical pattern of liturgical use (Henig, personal comment). In most Romano-Celtic temples the cella would have been strictly reserved for the cult figure and attendant priests.

This leads on to a discussion of parallels for the temple plan. These may be found most easily amongst a group of temples that show evidence for porches and antechambers. These would have allowed direct access, or a direct view into the central cella, but not into the rear and side ambulatories, which appear to have been reserved for the priests, or for the secure storage of votive offerings. A selection of such plans, shown at the same scale as plans of the two major phases at Uley, are provided in Figure 215. In the Altbachtal at Trier, the plan of temple 2 (Wilson 1975, fig 85) shows a portico with direct access to the cella and restricted doorways leading to the enclosed ambulatories; a very similar pattern is displayed at Caerwent (Caerwent 1, Lewis 1966, fig 3). Also in continental Europe, three-sided ambulatories are known at Mont Beuvray (Fig 215, after Horne and King 1980, fig 17.10.2), Trier temple H (*ibid*, fig 17.6.6) and Eu temple B (*ibid*, fig 17.19.1). A similar separation of the ambulatory space is seen at Brean Down, Somerset (after ApSimon 1965, fig 50) and Lamyatt Beacon, Somerset (after Leech 1986, fig 3), although in the case of Brean Down, the forechamber extends right across the front of the building. In this respect further continental parallels may be invoked, including the plan of the temple at Hochscheid (after Horne and King 1980, fig 17.9.6). Finally it is illuminating to consider the disposition of space within the great temple of Nodens at Lydney. Here the original temple plan Lydney (i) (Fig 215, after Wheeler and Wheeler 1932, fig 2) would have supported 'a unique, quasi-basilican building which defies classification' (Rodwell 1980, 572). However, following an almost immediate collapse, as one of the major piers fell into the earlier iron mine below, the temple was rebuilt with an enclosed cella, Lydney (ii) (Fig 215, after Wheeler and Wheeler 1932, fig 3). Further, the ambulatories were cut off from the entrance area by new partition walls, so that the worshippers would have obtained a direct, but limited, view of the triple sanctuary occupying the far end of the cella. Yet again, as at Uley, the ambulatories seem to have been designed for secret priestly activities and not for public access.

It has seldom been possible to record internal features and structures during the excavation of temple sites in Britain, but those investigated on the continent have sometimes produced more useful evidence. Centrally placed pits or wells are known from eight of the

Plate II The temple interior; a reconstruction: c200 AD. (Drawing: Joanna Richards) *(see page 312)*

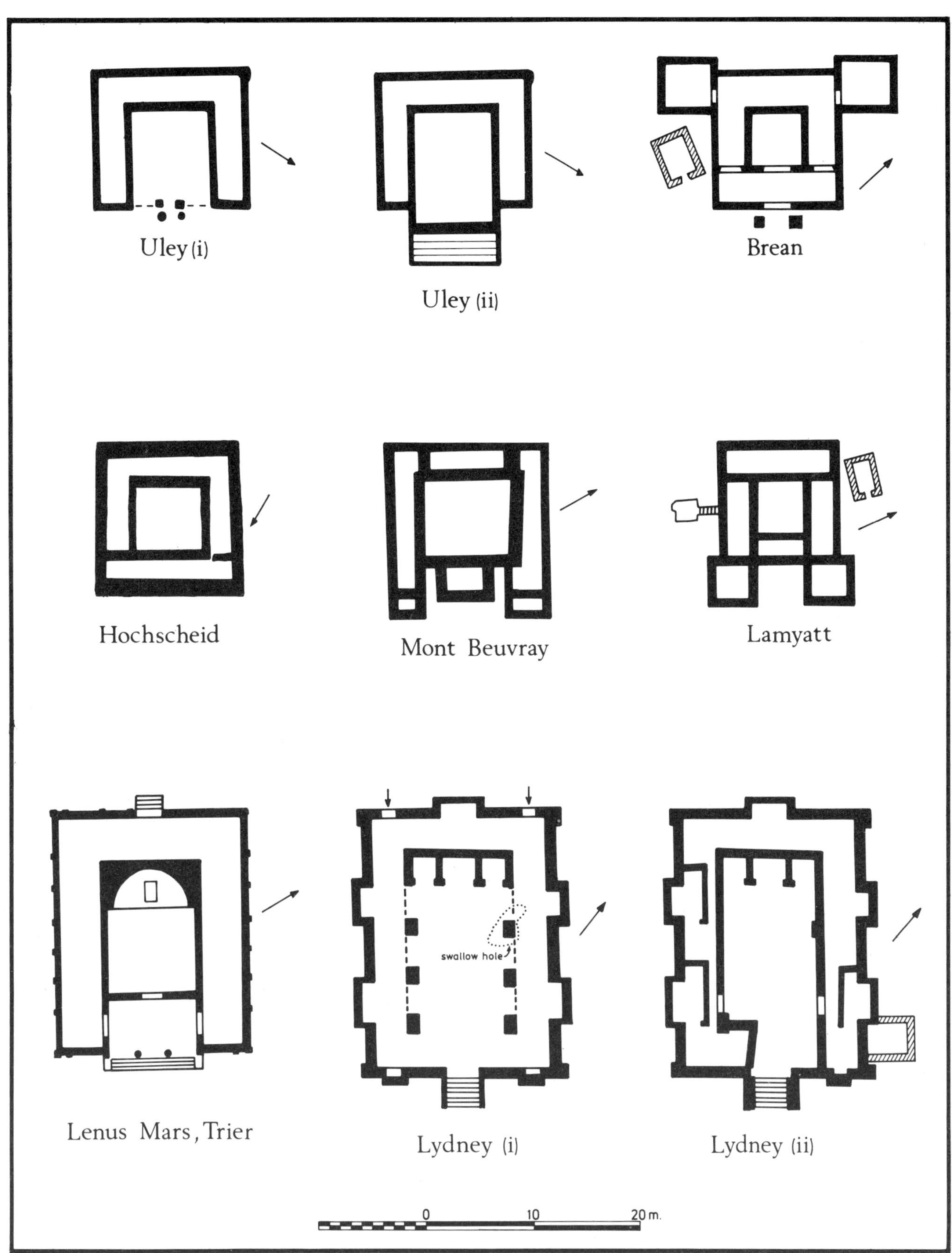

Fig 215 Roman temples

temples listed by Horne and King (1980), including those at Chassenon, Colombières-sur-Orb, Epiais-Rhus, Regensburg, St Margarethen (Austria) and Vielle-Toulouse. At Alésia a central pit predated one of the temples, but continued in use (*ibid*, 373) as we have suggested at Uley, while at Friesen the centre of a temple was occupied by a deep well (*ibid*, 411). Central water containers were found at a further two sites; at Hochscheid (Fig 215) the centre of the cella was occupied by a basin into which a spring rose, and at Montbuoy a centrally located piscina was fed from a spring which lay in a nearby enclosure (*ibid*, 419 and 434). Similarly, the positions of cult images or altars have not been deduced for many temples in this country, while in Europe foundations for plinths or bases are widespread. From the useful gazetteer of continental Romano-Celtic temples compiled by Horne and King (*ibid*) it is possible to extract at least 25 examples of such statue or altar bases, 11 of them centrally located in the cella and the rest occupying the margin of the cella, most often on the western side. Thus the postulated positioning of the Uley cult image within the ambulatory remains anomalous and not certain. Although there are records of the finding of statues themselves in ambulatory locations, these may not have been in primary contexts. At Avallon, a whole series of figures, of life size or larger, were found in the ambulatories (*ibid*, 381) and at Bierbacher Klosterwald the torso of a statue of Mercury was found outside the northern wall of the cella. Whether this statue had been housed there previously, or had stood upon a base found just inside the cella, cannot be determined.

Precinct buildings

The stone temple, Structure II, lay at the centre of a large settlement. It is known from the results of the geophysical survey that stone buildings and industrial activity extended well north and east of the excavated area. Preliminary assessment, but not collection, of surface finds from the field west of the modern road, indicated that stone buildings extended for at least 120m towards the Neolithic barrow Hetty Pegler's Tump. Only the ranges of buildings nearest to the temple were investigated during the excavation campaign. Their nature and extent is best shown in Figure 9 where the phases of extension, contraction and reuse of each structure are summarised. The detailed accounts in chapter 3 have provided the evidence for the distribution of hearths, ovens, possible kilns, and various flooring types. The distribution of finds categories amongst the individual rooms and buildings is considered below. The stone structures had substantial foundations, with wall bases rather thicker than those of the temple itself, some of them may have been two storied, and all were roofed with red sandstone tiles. By the later fourth century newly built ancillary buildings were timber framed while remnants of some of the earlier stone structures were repaired and modified for reuse.

Reconstruction drawings of the excavated buildings are provided in Figures 212 and 213; Structures I, IV, and X in the earlier phase and Structures XIII, XIV, and a modified Structure I in the later phase associated with the extended temple. The courtyard is occupied by

Fig 216 A view west from West Hill across the Severn to Wales and the Forest of Dean. (Photo: Sebastian Rahtz)

temporary booths and stalls set up for the selling of votive offerings to the pilgrims, and in the background grazing goats occupy the pasture in front of the still venerated Hetty Pegler's Tump. Beyond, across the Severn estuary, the site of the Lydney temple might have been glimpsed (Fig 216). The reconstruction drawings have been based upon the excavated evidence for plan and building materials, with some influence from the town scenes of Alan Sorrell (Sorrell 1981) and reconstructions of similar buildings excavated at Cirencester (McWhirr 1981, 53 and 56) and Frocester Court (Price 1984, 87).

Structure X was a major building of maximum dimensions 38m × 23m and probably of two storeys, with two wings projecting southwards. A verandah surrounded the courtyard between them, and a focal room projected northwards from the far elevation. Some elements of the plan are known only from the aerial photographs (Figs 5 and 42). Structure I started its life as a simple rectangular suite of rooms measuring 14m × 7m and was extended several times until it reached a length of 27m and a width of at least 17m. Structure IV was the corner of another large and multi-phased rectangular range of rooms, of unknown total dimensions. In comparison, Structure IX was a much more modest building, measuring only 16m × 8m, although this too was rebuilt and extended during its lifetime. Structures XIII and XIV were of timber construction, Structure XIII probably having been a wagon shed supported on sill beams, and Structure XIV a domestic structure with a hearth and porch also of timber framed construction. The dimensions of these buildings were 11m × 5m, for Structure XIV excluding its porch and possible south wing, and for the wagon shed, Structure XIII, 6.2m by 4m.

Most precinct buildings described in the literature have been associated with isolated rural temples. At Colchester, Essex, the temenos of temple 6 included a second building which Hull interpreted as an assembly hall (Crummy 1980, 258–9), and at Pagan's Hill, Somerset, ranges of large rooms with long corridors or verandahs in front were laid out with a high degree of architectural sophistication (Rodwell 1980, fig 10.5 after Rahtz and Harris 1951). No specific functions could be ascribed to these buildings, but at Lydney Wheeler was able to define a major bath complex, associated with the healing cult of Nodens, a guesthouse or inn, and a long building or '*abaton*'. The guesthouse presented a 'concise and co-ordinated plan' with three ranges of small rooms opening, through a verandah, onto a central courtyard, and a forebuilding facing the temple itself. The small rooms were arranged in pairs, and projecting from the centre of the middle range was a larger focal room (Wheeler and Wheeler 1932, 44–9). With the exception of the forebuilding, the plan of this structure echoes that of Structure X at Uley, even to the presence of the focal projecting room, and it is suggested therefore that Structure X at Uley may well also have functioned as a guesthouse and hostelry for visiting pilgrims. The Wheelers' long building at Lydney comprised a range of eleven or more rooms, arranged in groups of three, opening onto a verandah behind the temple building. Mosaics were present throughout, and there was evidence for three or four phases of repair and modification, the latest of which may have taken place in the post-Roman period (*ibid*, 49–52). The building may have functioned as a row of shops selling votive offerings, or served as a house of incubation for worshippers submitting themselves to sacred slumber, a necessary adjunct of cults primarily concerned with healing (*ibid* 51–2). Thus at Lydney all three ancillary structures were interpreted as possessing very specialised functions.

Where temples were situated in more constricted situations in the midst of major rural settlements, the possibility of making distinctions between specialised and domestic buildings is much more limited. In Gloucestershire, a better parallel than Lydney is provided by the site at Wycomb, excavated during the nineteenth century by Lawrence (McWhirr 1981, 72–3). Here a major settlement included a temple, and nearby, a row of simple one or two-roomed rectangular buildings which may have been shops. But finally our attention must turn to the major complex at Nettleton, Wilts, excavated over many years and recently published by Wedlake (1982). Here a major series of precinct structures have been assigned to three main phases of temple use and two phases of post-temple occupation. The exposition of evidence for the phasing is not always clear, and it is difficult to check relationships, as the published finds reports do not contain detailed contextual information. However, the general scheme suggests a plausible division into one minor and two major building phases, even though the details of sub-phasing and stratification between buildings cannot be deduced from the report. The phasing, sizes, and interpretation of most structures can be summarised as follows:

Early phase (contemporary with the circular shrine)
Building 11 22 sq m, with marginal corridor; 'first hostelry' (Wedlake 1982, 17)
Building 13 31 × 4m, one room plus extensions; superior domestic plus latrine or stable (*ibid*)

Middle phase (contemporary with the octagonal podium)
Building 9 8 × ?m, three rooms; 'priest's house', then industrial (furnace) (*ibid*, 27)
Building 10 22 × 9m, one room; 'precinct shop' (*ibid*, 30)
Building 12 34 × 11m, ?no of rooms; 'second hostelry' (*ibid*, 31)
Building 14 12 × 7m, one room; unknown function (*ibid*, 32)
Building 16 14 × 8m, one room; 'west lodge', then industrial (*ibid*, 34)
Building 17 23 × 9m, one room; domestic (*ibid*, 34)
Building 26 8 × 9m, one room; 'iron forge or foundry' (*ibid*, 35)

Later phase (contemporary with the octagonal temple)
Building 10 (see above); extended (*ibid*, 30)
Building 14 (see above); rebuilt (*ibid*, 32)
Building 15 20×16m, three to four rooms; domestic (above building 14) (*ibid*, 58)
Building 19 11+ × 8m; 'east lodge' (*ibid*, 59)
Building 20 17 × 8m; domestic (*ibid*, 59)
Building 25 17 × 15m, two rooms; domestic (*ibid*, 60)
Building 30 8 × 15m, one room; unknown function (*ibid*, 60)
Building 21 *c*11 × 4m, industrial: pewter (above building 20; *ibid*, 68)

The structures ascribed an industrial function contained evidence for iron or pewter working. Otherwise identifications have been based on relative positions within the settlement; 'lodges' next to the precinct gates, and a 'priest's house' adjacent to the temple itself; or on plan type. Thus the large square building (building 11, replaced by 12) has been interpreted as a hostelry or guesthouse, and the long narrow structure (building 10) near the temple has become the 'precinct shop'. In plan, most of the buildings at Nettleton are reminiscent of the local form of farmhouse or barn typical of roadside settlements, as at Catsgore (Leech 1982), Bradley Hill (Leech 1981) and Camerton (Wedlake 1958), all in Somerset. In the absence of specific functionally related finds from individual buildings it is difficult therefore to confidently ascribe any particular labels to the rectangular buildings at Nettleton. However this need not preclude some of the interpretations proposed by Wedlake.

Sadly, the same argument must apply at Uley, although a few clues may be supplied by the finds distributions (Figs 223–27 below). With the exception of Structure X, all other ancillary structures may be domestic in character, especially those which lie behind the temple itself. Indeed there may be a further specialised building, but if so, it lies immediately east of the excavated area, on the open side of the courtyard. The multi-phased rectangular buildings are best paralleled by local domestic and farm buildings, such as those excavated at Frocester Court (Gracie and Price 1980) and Barnsley Park (Webster 1967), rather than with anything so exotic as the *'abaton'* at Lydney. However, this should not be surprising, for it is only the elaboration of ritual associated with major healing cults that requires the provision of several suites of buildings of special plan. At this site the only large building needed may have been the guesthouse, for within a flourishing large rural settlement the commercial and marketing networks may well have encompassed quite effortlessly the profitable trade in votive offerings, and the necessary movement of sacred goats from their grazing fields to the temple forecourt.

The converted temple ruin

Towards the end of the fourth century, the front of the aggrandised stone temple fell, or had to be demolished. Possibly subsidence above the fillings of the deep early Roman ditch (F264) and votive pit (F251) caused the foundations of the north- eastern corner of the temple to give way eventually. When this happened the portico would have collapsed, and along with it the main superstructure of the cella, which appears to have been reduced to a heap of rubble and fallen roof tiles. Only the north-western and south-western ambulatories survived. Apparently the late Roman worshippers did not possess the means or motivation to reconstruct the edifice to its former glory, for almost immediately, the rubble was cleared away, some of it being spread over the remains of Structure I to the south-west, where spreads of rubble, and dark soil containing votive debris, survived in hollows above the fillings of the robber trenches. The surviving ambulatories were restored, modified, and extended to provide a unique L-shaped building which possessed at least four rooms (Fig 56). The two former ambulatories were divided from each other by a blocking wall, the south-eastern end of the south-west ambulatory was converted into a small square room, and a rectangular timber framed annexe was built over a former opening from the ambulatory, and upon part of the former floor area of the fallen cella. Evidence of hearth positions, and deposits containing votive objects in quantity, indicate a continuing religious function.

A tentative reconstruction of this enigmatic building is offered in Figure 217. The surviving ambulatories have been re-roofed and some of the former arches between them and the fallen cella blocked. The timber framed annexe is shown faced in reused stone blocks from the temple, but equally the walls could have been of wattle and daub; no firm evidence had survived. The traces of the other temple walls were probably still visible, and it is here suggested that some of these may have been used to support a low wall, defining a courtyard or garden area, in front of the newly built annexe. Such an extraordinary and makeshift structure could have been built with great speed, and probably for a very specific and pressing purpose; perhaps the furtherance of the flourishing, and economically beneficial, cult of Mercury, or to provide safe and appropriate shelter for the stone cult statue. It is suggested that offerings continued to be made in the north-western ambulatory and the adjacent timber framed annexe, whilst the statue may have survived in its former position, or have been re-erected within the new annexe, or the safe confines and darkness of the newly constructed square room at the end of the former south-western ambulatory. We have little knowledge of the associated structures of this period, although the timber framed buildings to the north may have been still in use. If so this would have provided shelter and services for the visiting pilgrims. Thus the cult of Mercury continued, and on the evidence of the Theodosian coinage, the cult image was carefully curated and venerated within its asymmetrical makeshift shrine for another generation.

Fig 217 Perspective view: Structure II, Phase 6. (Drawn by Joanna Richards)

Examples of converted temple ruins do not abound in the literature on Roman temples in Britain. However the processes of extension, modification, demolition, and reconstruction that may be demonstrated for English churches between the eleventh and sixteenth centuries may provide a useful parallel to the processes operating in Roman temples between the first and fifth centuries. The reasons for the lack of recognition of such processes are twofold. Firstly, there are few detailed temple excavations adequately recorded and published in the latter part of this century (see Rodwell 1980, 211), and secondly, temple chronologies have been compressed all too often, due to misinterpretations of coin evidence (Rahtz and Watts 1979, 183–7). Thus, in order to find parallels for the situation here we must look perforce to the continent, where traces of blocking walls within temple ambulatories and late conversions have been noted more often (eg Horne and King 1980, 398, 407, 454, and 466). In particular, at Civaux, Vienne (Eygun 1968) the temple possessed blocking walls within the ambulatory and, presumably subsequently, an early Christian church was constructed alongside its south side. This sequence echoes that recovered now at Uley. With all these points in mind it is worth reconsidering evidence from some of the more detailed and extensive excavations that have taken place on Romano-Celtic temple sites in Britain. Consideration has first been given to the identification of examples of late fourth or early fifth-century conversions or modifications, probably executed in a continuing pagan context. The analysis of coincident structures built *de novo* in the post- Roman period is considered in detail later in the discussion.

At Bath, Avon, the inner precinct of the great temple of Sulis Minerva was resurfaced many times and continued in use well into the fifth century, if not beyond into the early sixth (Cunliffe and Davenport 1985, 74). Detailed evidence for any late modifications to the temple itself is not available, but the recent excavations within the inner precinct demonstrated the existence of a small room converted from part of the portico to the sacred reservoir. This building measured 6.8m × 5.5m and incorporated reused column drums at its corners and entrance (*ibid*, 66 and fig 42). This structure dated probably from the late fourth century; in two subsequent phases, probably extending well into the fifth century, timber structures were present within the precinct and built against the walls of the portico (*ibid*, 68–70 and figs 43 and 45). By this time the temple itself was in a dilapidated state, but the upper part of the Roman reservoir building was not demolished until the sixth century or even a little later. Cunliffe has suggested that the room, converted from part of the reservoir portico, may have functioned as a small shrine.

From a modern, impeccably recorded excavation, we now turn to the less recent but brilliantly executed programme of research mounted at Lydney Park (Wheeler and Wheeler 1932). The importance of the post-Roman earthwork at Lydney has been noted and reconsidered by Rahtz and Watts (1979, especially appendix I), but remarkably little attention has been paid to the construction sequence displayed by the temple plan itself. A complex and extraordinary building history was conflated by the Wheelers to a system of three main periods spanning only 40 years in all (*ibid*, 23–33). A more expansive interpretation of the coin evidence than that embraced by the Wheelers (Casey 1980) would suggest not only that the first temple may have originated well before their promoted date of AD 364, but also that the building remained in use, albeit in a modified form, further into the fifth century than they had envisaged. The main basis for this new argument lies in reinterpretation of the coin lists which, for instance, include 40 coins of Theodosian date (Wheeler and Wheeler 1932, 110). The plans of the period I 'Classical' temple and the reconstructed more Romano-Celtic version of the Wheelers' period II have been illustrated above (Fig 215). The second temple there probably does date to the later fourth century, and the plan shows that the ambulatory was divided from the entrance area by a peculiar system of blocking walls, which may have belonged to more than one phase of conversion. The cella floor was relaid to include a fine fish mosaic and the votive funnel. At around the same time, three L-shaped screen walls were erected within the ambulatory to form the Wheelers' 'side-chapels'. In an even later phase of refurbishment, period III, also dated by them to the fourth century, new mosaics were laid in two of the chapels and the whole ambulatory floor was raised by more than a foot. This phase must belong to the fifth century AD, and the small rectangular room projecting eastwards from the entrance facade of the temple, which produced no dating evidence, may well belong to this last (or an even later) phase, rather than to period II as they suggested. The short chronology invoked by them was influenced probably by the general pattern of the 1928–9 coin list. However, they were able to point to some earlier discoveries of significance, such as the 531 coins found by Bathurst and King (1879) between the cella and the floor of the triple sanctuary. These included 22 Theodosian issues and a coin of Honorius from the assemblage contained within the votive funnel. Although the Wheelers had termed the subdivisions within the ambulatory 'chapels', they did not view them in any way as evidence for Christianisation (*ibid*, 43). They felt that their purpose may have been that of subsidiary shrines, areas set aside for different categories amongst the worshipping population, or cubicles provided to accommodate ritual dreamers. Whatever their specific purpose, the process of increasing compartmentalisation can be seen to echo the situation at Uley, although at Lydney in a temple that had not yet finally collapsed.

At Maiden Castle, Dorset (Wheeler 1943), his 'primitive oval hut', located south of the Romano-Celtic temple, has been reinterpreted as a post-Roman shrine by Rahtz and Watts (1979, fig 12). In addition, as at Lydney, it is instructive to peruse the records of the temple building itself (Wheeler 1943, 131–5 and pl xxii). The latest repair of the temple floor incorporated reused roofing slabs and sealed coins, which included Theodosian issues. Further such coins where found, amongst others, upon this floor and nearby. As at Lydney, the implication must be that the temple continued in use well into the fifth century. No evidence of blocking walls was recovered, but further 'compartments' were provided firstly by the oval shrine, which may have been at least in part contemporary with the continuing use of the temple, and secondly possibly by the so called 'priest's house', which contained no dating evidence and, according to the plans, was of two phases. The primary room, measuring 5.5m × 4.5m, was of similar size to the portico shrine at Bath and to the late projecting eastern room at Lydney. Indeed, as a separate structure it also recalls the late rectangular buildings located outside the temples at Brean Down (Apsimon 1965) and Lamyatt Beacon, Somerset (Leech 1986), which are considered below.

Another temple which underwent a remarkable sequence of modification and compartmentalisation in its later phases is the shrine of Apollo at Nettleton, Wiltshire (Wedlake 1982). The enlarged octagonal temple, with its colonnaded ambulatory, was modified probably in the early to mid-fourth century by the insertion of a series of blocking walls. These were built across alternate outer chambers of the octagonal cella structure such that a new central space of cruciform plan was formed. This space was refloored but there was no evidence for any continuing access to the sealed chambers (Wedlake 1982, 61 and fig 35). Largely on the basis of this cruciform plan, Wedlake argued that the temple had been converted to provide a Christian church. Subsequently, following a partial collapse of the cella vault, an improvised room, incorporating reused column bases and voussoirs, was constructed across the north-western portion of the former cella (*ibid*, 79–82 and fig 43). Evidence provided by a single coin suggests that this room was constructed after AD 360 and finds from its floor indicated a continuing religious, indeed pagan, use. Wedlake's adjacent 'Post-Shrine Homestead', occupying the other half of the former cella and some of the outer chambers, was assigned by him to a later phase, but on the evidence of the published sections there seems no reason why both groups of occupation materials should not have been contemporary. The 'Homestead' layers produced coins of the late fourth century and Theodosian issues. As Wedlake points out – 'A striking feature of the Nettleton excavation has been the unusually large number of coins that cover the period from AD 330 to 402' (*ibid*, 108) and there can be no doubt that the whole complex continued to flourish well into the fifth century, and possibly longer still. The case for the existence of a mid-fourth-century cruciform church remains unproven, but the process of compartmentalisation, and the provision of 'secret' rooms, can now be seen to have occurred elsewhere – at Bath, and at Lydney, as discussed above, as well as at Uley, usually it seems in a continuing pagan context. Finally, no discussion of modified temples can be complete without reference to the octagonal example on Pagan's Hill, Somerset (Rahtz 1951), where a three sided substructure or screen was reconstituted or inserted in the later fourth century or later, and religious observance can be attested in the earlier Anglo-Saxon period. The ruined building was in use still during the medieval period, and there may have been some continuing memory of its former character even in modern times.

The timber basilica

The large post pits and beam slot cut through the demolished remains of the stone temple were very conspicuous features; they were recognised at the time of excavation to have been associated as remains of the footings for timber buildings. It was apparent also that they were cut from a level which matched that of the roughly apsidal floor surviving above the wall foundations of the north-western temple ambulatory. Originally these features were resolved to suggest the former presence of a Christian building aligned north-west to south-east and the resulting plan was published (Ellison 1980, fig 15.4). However, it was always clear that the 'apse' was not in correct alignment with the major post pits and the well-defined beam slot was assigned perforce to a later timber building which possessed no convincing evidence for wall supports on the other three sides. Subsequent post-excavation analysis has suggested an explanation which is both more economical and intelligible, and the arguments for the former existence of a single timber building have been expounded above (chapter 4).

The preferred reinterpretation of these features is for a double-aisled structure, with its support lines provided by the north-west cella wall foundation, three rows of major posts, the south-east cella wall footing, and a line of timbers held in slot and pits constructed over, and in exact alignment with, the demolished temple remains (Fig 61). One post pit and an associated levelling layer contained fragments from the cult statue and a second, smaller, figure. The south-western end wall was supported on the footings of the outer ambulatory wall and traces of dry stone footings in front of the major post pits could have supported the facade. In front of a central doorway was an area of stone paving, approached by a step over the robbed foundations of the Roman portico wall. This step had been made using a segment of a large Roman altar, depicting the god Mercury, but placed face downwards (Fig 62). Two joining fragments of the top of the same altar (Figs 79 and 80), and a second complete altar which also bore a sculptured figure of Mercury (Fig 78), had been placed in inverted positions within the paving of the apsidal feature, which lay over the remains of the south-western ambulatory. The remains of dry stone footings around part of this floor matched those of the facade described above and could have supported a timber apse or polygonal extension to the main building.

The best parallels for such a building plan in the late fourth or fifth centuries AD lie among the group of late Roman basilican churches from southern Britain. If the Uley building was a Christian church, then the linear setting of stone slabs centrally positioned at the south-western end could have supported an altar, and behind this, there may have been a small apse. However no evidence for this putative apse was found and if it had existed, any traces in this zone of the site would have been destroyed by ploughing. Were such an apse present this would reinforce Warwick Rodwell's interpretation of the building as representing a classical basilica (see below). The timber basilica was constructed probably during the fifth century and may have survived into the sixth century AD. A tentative reconstruction of the building is offered in Figure 218, which shows an aisled timber structure with simple window openings at clerestory level. The roof is covered by wooden shingles and the gables are embellished with crossed finials. Beyond the central entrance, the side of the polygonal extension may be seen. Sources used during compilation of this drawing were the reconstruction of

Fig 218 Perspective view: Phase 7a. (Drawn by Joanna Richards)

the late Roman church at Silchester, devised by Sorrell (1981, 81), and in marked contrast, drawings of post-Roman timber halls such as those at Cowdery's Down, Hants (Millet and James 1983, fig 71). An asymmetrical extension of the type deduced for this building is, in a Christian context, most likely to have functioned as a baptistery. Indeed, Warwick Rodwell has viewed the building as a truly classical fourth or fifth-century double-aisled basilica with a western sanctuary. As we shall see the basilica can be paralleled in Britain, but the attached baptistery cannot. Several examples of separate baptisteries occur in close association with such churches, but attached baptisteries are known at present only from southern Europe (Rodwell, personal communication). The church at Uley was surrounded by a timber-revetted bank with tower entrances. These perimeter features will be further discussed below.

Late-Roman churches have been the subject of much recent discussion (eg Morris 1983, Rodwell in Rodwell and Bentley 1984), and the evidence has been sifted in exemplary fashion by Thomas (1981). Rodwell has divided the known examples usefully into four groups: large urban basilicas, smaller urban churches, rural churches and house churches (Rodwell and Bentley 1984). The structure at Uley fits best into his group of smaller urban churches, rather than with the rural examples. A selection of late Roman church plans are shown in Figure 219 where it can be seen readily that the Uley church lies more comfortably with the smaller urban basilicas than with the very much smaller, rural example from Icklingham, Suffolk (after Thomas 1981, fig 33). In terms of size, the Uley building (*c*11m × 9.2m) fits very neatly into Charles Thomas's graph showing the dimensions of congregational areas for Romano-British churches (Thomas 1981, fig 30); indeed, it falls just below the mean there defined. The alignment is best paralleled in the building found in the south- east quarter of Verulamium (Wheeler and Wheeler 1936, 123 and pl xxxv). This possessed a western square protuberance and an eastern porch; it was identified quite plausibly as 'small Christian church' (*ibid*). The Silchester church is closest to the Uley building in size, but was of more substantial fabric, and was subdivided to provide side chambers or a *porticus* and a *narthex* in addition to the western apse (Frere 1975). The base for a baptistery lay immediately east of its entrance. The rather larger church at Richborough also possessed a separate baptistery, in this case on the north-eastern side (Brown 1971, fig 1). There probably was an eastern apse, and a timber superstructure has been postulated. At Canterbury (Jenkins 1976), the large eastern apse of St Pancras phase I was actually polygonal; at Icklingham the rectangular building is known from foundation trenches only, and the eastern apse is conjectural (Thomas 1981, fig 33). An apsidal baptistery was located 10m to the east. The large urban basilicas are best represented by the examples from Lincoln and Colchester. In the Butt Road cemetery, Colchester (Crummy 1980, 264–6 and figs 11, 16 and 17) a building 20.5m long and 5m wide was of four or six bays, with a small eastern apse. A ritual pit near the eastern end is known now to have been associated with

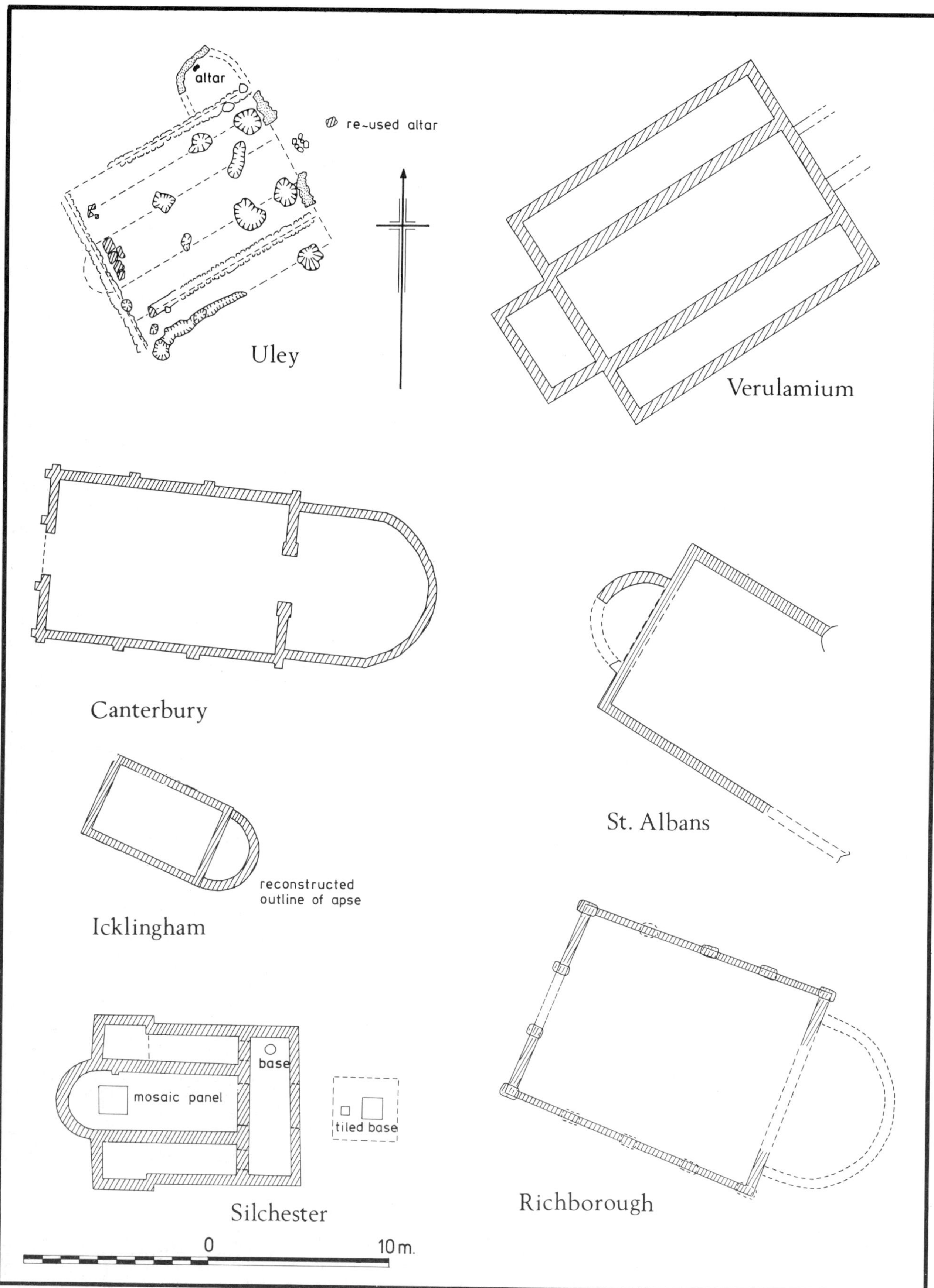

Fig 219 Early churches

a primary grave, while outside the western end lay a 'rectangular post-built structure containing a tile hearth' (*ibid*, 266). It seems not impossible that this 'tile hearth' might have supported another separate baptismal tank. At Flaxengate, Lincoln (Colyer and Jones 1979, fig 2) the five bay basilica with *narthex* and eastern apse was extremely large (see Thomas 1981, fig 37 for a hypothetical reconstruction) and possessed a small *porticus* or aisle on the northern side only. At the time of writing this asymmetrical room is the sole parallel for the attached baptistery postulated at Uley, although it is not a close one. Full publication of the Lincoln data, and of details for all the larger urban basilicas should clarify this issue.

The inclusion of reused fragments of statues, and defaced Roman altars from the temple, in the fabric of the timber basilica is of particular interest. The processes of mutilation and redeposition suggest the performance of acts of ritual cleansing and rededication. This subject has been explored at length by Merrifield (1987, 96–106). An instance comparable to those at Uley is that of the Walbrook Mithraeum, where in the mid-fourth century the pagan sculptures were removed, larger pieces were dismembered, and then the pieces were buried in groups at salient points in the building. The structure may have been converted thus to function as a Christian church (Rodwell and Bentley 1984, 19). The church construction levels at Icklingham sealed a pit which contained items possibly deriving from a dismantled pagan shrine: decorated roof tiles and a limestone pillar, along with human skulls and bones (West and Plouviez 1976). As already stated above, some of the dismembered portions of statue at Uley may have been stored, or hidden, above ground, for a further phase of ritual cleansing apparently occurred when the smaller stone church was constructed.

Perimeter bank and burials

During the late fifth or sixth century, and probably contemporary with the construction and use of the timber basilican church, a perimeter bank was built around the focal area of the site. The core of the bank comprised a dark, fine soil, possibly the remains of turves, and was revetted with timbers which may have supported a continuous fence (Fig 61). The line of the bank was traced north and west of the basilica, but to the south its foundations had been destroyed by ploughing. In two places there were rectangular foundations of dry stone footings and adjacent post-holes, indicating the positions of complex entrances (Structures VI and XV). In the reconstruction drawing (Fig 218) these are shown as timber towers with gabled shingled roofs, and the line of the enclosure has been projected in a curve to form a roughly oval precinct. It is impossible to tell whether any further buildings occupied the southern and eastern sectors of this enclosure because of the severity of the plough damage on the crest of the hill. The turves in the bank material must have been gathered from the near vicinity, as they contained large numbers of votive objects, mainly in small fragments, as well as Theodosian coins. This assemblage matches that found in the ritual deposits associated with the converted temple ruin.

Enclosure banks of this type and of early post-Roman date can be matched at some other temple sites in the south-west, and may also define early Christian monastic sites in northern and western Britain. At Lydney, the rampart of the Iron Age promontory fort, within which the Roman temple precinct had been set, was doubled in height and an outer bank was added on the north side (Wheeler and Wheeler 1932, 63–5). The make-up material contained demolition rubble from the temple settlement and was ascribed by Wheeler to 'some period of recrudescent barbarism after the beginning of the fifth century' (*ibid*, 64). As Rahtz and Watts have pointed out

> "such an attitude to our post-Roman 'natives' is hardly acceptable today from ethical, political or historical standpoints; nor is the easy acceptance of a military explanation for the latest phases of the Lydney enclosure. We can at least suggest the possibility that somewhere on the promontory, perhaps in the northern open area which Wheeler did not explore very much, will be found structures or evidence of a religious character which succeeded the destruction of the Romanised buildings, which could not adequately be maintained; and that the earthwork additions are the equivalent of the earlier temenos; or, if we invoke a new religion, that they are the *vallum monasterii* of a Christian site"
>
> (Rahtz and Watts 1979, 192)

In the light of the evidence recovered at Uley, it might be suggested further that the slight and elusive remains of any timber church that might had been erected over the remains of the temple at Lydney would have been disturbed and destroyed irrevocably by the 1805 excavations of Bathurst and King (1879). At Nettleton, Wedlake's 'Wick Valley bank', running south and west of the building complex, was ascribed by him to the medieval period or later (Wedlake 1982, 94). However, Richard Kemp has been able to argue that this bank, with its collapsed dry stone wall of oolitic limestone and exterior ditch, may belong to an earlier post-Roman period (Kemp, unpublished typescript). Similarly, at Lamyatt Beacon the boundary bank and ditch which Leech felt to be of Saxon date (Leech 1986, 270 and 274) might have been earlier; the bank sealed three burials which were dated by radiocarbon to between the fourth and tenth centuries AD (on two standard deviations). On the other hand curvilinear enclosure banks of earthen construction are also a characteristic of early Christian sites in Ireland and the western extremities of Britain, eg Iona, Applecross (Wester Ross) and St Helens, Isles of Scilly (Thomas 1971, figs 8, 15 and 16). On excavation, these seldom produced any dating evidence, but at Ardwall Island the dry stone bank was thought to be original, and contemporary with the early chapels and cemeteries of sixth to seventh-century date (Thomas 1967, 143).

The evidence for Roman or post-Roman human burials from the main excavation area at Uley is slight, comprising fragments of bone or teeth from contexts in buildings south and north of the temple, together with skull and other fragments from the ploughsoil. They may be the clue to the location of a burial ground or cemeteries on the site, for, if the fragments have been dragged by the plough from shallow inhumation burials, as seems likely, then a cemetery may lie unexcavated not too far beyond the confines of the area excavated between 1977 and 1979. The only complete Roman or post-Roman burial found was that disturbed by the pipe trench in 1976. This was located *c* 60m north of the main excavated area, and was an adult male, laid without grave goods, in a nailed coffin. The grave was orientated north–south, with the head at the north end. Unless the late shrines and churches had become the focus for a very large cemetery, then it seems that we are dealing here with at least two burial grounds, possibly of differing date.

The existence of such a cemetery or cemeteries is to be expected on analogy with many other late Roman and post-Roman religious sites, several of which have already figured prominently in our discussion. The sixteen west–east findless graves north of the temple on Lamyatt Beacon included eleven females and one male. Two yielded radiocarbon dates of AD 559 ±90 and AD 782 ±90 (Leech 1986, 268–70 and figs 3 and 10). At Maiden Castle, several east–west findless burials may have been contemporary with the latest use of the temple and construction of the oval shrine, or may have been later; they may be components of a larger cemetery (Rahtz and Watts 1979, 194 and fig 12), while at Henley Wood, Avon, fifty west–east graves were located mainly east of the site of the temple (Watts and Leach, forthcoming), many of them cutting the filling of a temenos ditch. A few of the burials may have been interred within an ambulatory that survived the general phase of temple demolition. A series of fourteen radiocarbon dates suggests that the central period of cemetery use embraced the fifth to seventh centuries, and more probably the fifth to sixth centuries AD (*ibid*). Just east of the temple site on Brean Down lies a major cemetery of similar graves which has suffered erosion by sea (ApSimon, *et al* 1961; Bell 1990), and at Nettleton part of a cemetery of west–east graves, lying east of the temple complex, was dated to the late-fourth century and later, and was associated with a stone building which may have functioned as a chapel or mausoleum (Wedlake 1982, 90–92: cemetery A). None of these cemeteries can be ascribed a Christian context on the basis of grave orientation or other attributes. However, cemeteries do occur in early Christian contexts further west. These have been described and discussed by Thomas (1971, 48–90). With reference to Uley it is most important to note that many of these early Christian cemeteries were associated intimately with oratories or chapels which are some of the closest parallels for the stone church which is postulated to have succeeded our timber basilica some time in the sixth century.

The baptisteries

It has been suggested above that the apsidal stone-paved extension attached to the northern corner of the timber basilican church may have functioned as a baptistery. In a later phase, following the demise of the basilica, this portion of the building was the only area remodelled. A new perimeter wall was constructed, impinging slightly upon the paved floor of the former apse but also reusing it. This wall was of dry stone construction and incorporated fragments of reused painted wall plaster and mortar. The walls were of unknown height but were lined and faced most probably with a thick layer of white plaster. The remnants of these plaster facings were found spread southwards above the remains of the north-western temple ambulatory, and the survival of this debris indicates that the remodelled plaster-covered structure may have been one of the latest to have been used on the site. The most economical hypothesis would be that the remodelled apse replaced the attached baptistery in terms of location and function, but that it now served as a free-standing structure, a detached baptistery for the stone churches of Phase 6b (see Figs 29 and 220). The configuration of the remaining wall fragments, and the outline of the floor, suggest that the modified baptistery may have been octagonal in shape. Associated with the structure were three postholes, two of which may have been employed in the support of timbers designed to hold a temporary covering of cloth or leather or, indeed, a flimsy but more permanent cover building constructed of timber and wattle.

A series of detached baptisteries of fourth and fifth-century date have been recognised recently in southern Britain and the plans of some of these are given in Figure 220 in relation to a reconstructed octagonal plan for the Uley Structure VII. The rite and context of late Roman baptism has been discussed in a full and stimulating manner by Thomas (1981, ch 8). He describes the evidence for detached baptismal tanks or fonts, as well as the probable existence of insubstantial or temporary shelters for them, and had deduced that the most probable ritual executed in practice would have been affusion. The act of affusion involves the pouring of water over the head and allowing it to dribble down the body; certainly such baptisms would have been more appropriate to the virtually outdoor ceremonies, which more often than not would have taken place in periods of inclement weather, than a rite of total immersion.

The existence of detached baptisteries in Britain was expounded first by Brown (1971) who was able to reidentify sets of pillar bases and a tank excavated at Richborough, Kent as the remains of a late Roman basilican church and free-standing baptistery, by referring to several examples then known from the Rhine–Danube frontier. The font or baptismal cistern at Richborough was hexagonal in shape, constructed of tiles and mortar, and with six incurved faces, two of which had been blocked perhaps for the provision of steps. The exterior was faced with pink plaster and the inside of the basin had been plastered also (Fig 220, after Brown 1971, pl xxx). Thomas has been able to argue convincingly that the setting of tiles, 3.2m square, placed upon a flint plinth just east of the entrance to the late Roman church at Silchester, may have supported a similar detached tank or font (Thomas 1981, 214–6 and fig 40). A soakaway was located immediately to the west and the whole may have been covered by a light wooden enclosing structure. A further detached baptismal tank has been excavated at Icklingham, Suffolk (West and Plouviez 1976; Thomas 1981, fig 40). This was apsidal in shape and provided with an internal step and an interior lining of white plaster. Immediately north of the baptistery a lead tank was found containing a group of iron objects: hinges, hinge-pins, nails and saw blades that 'could point to the dismantlement of a light wooden shed or some-

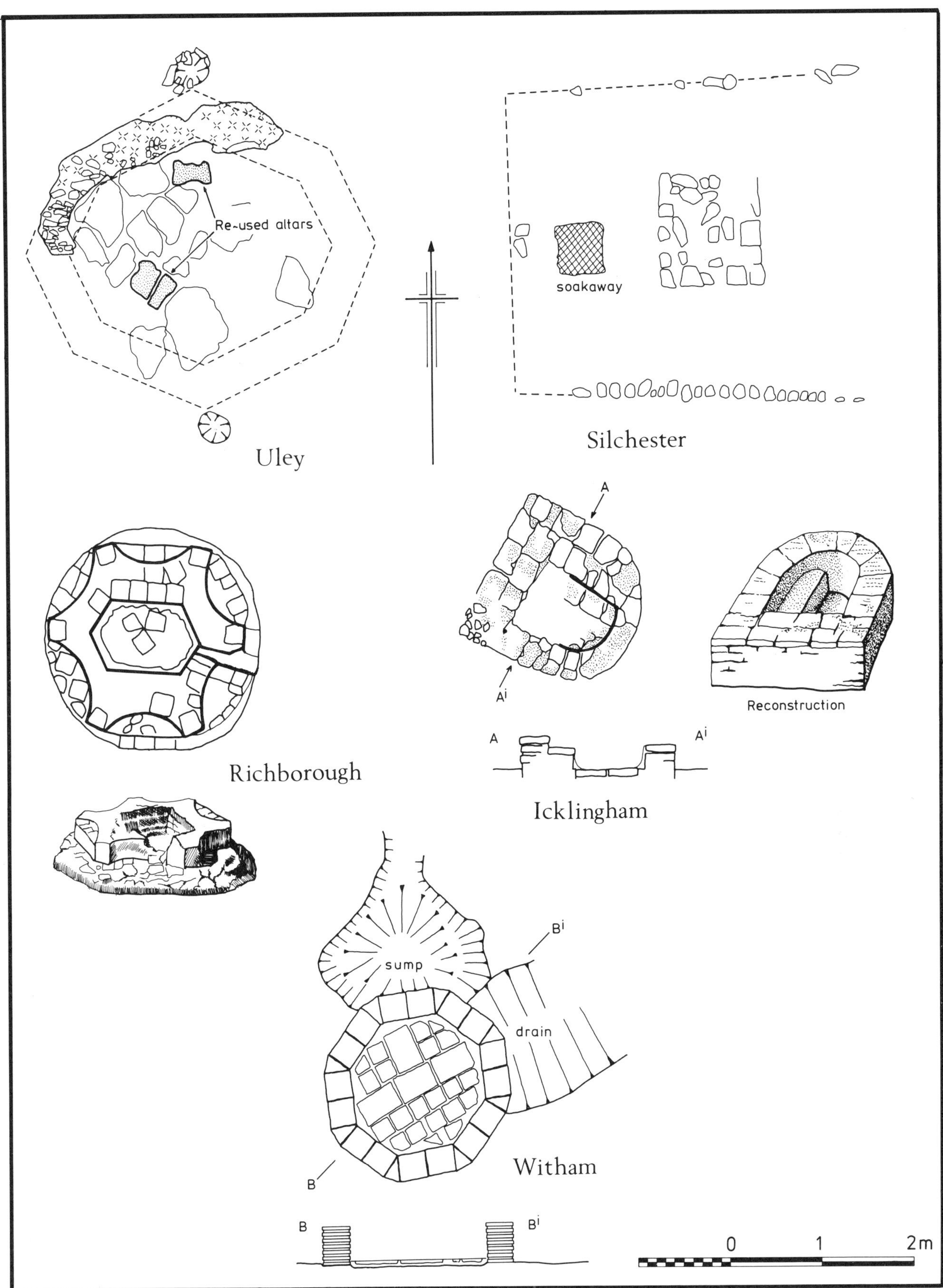

Fig 220 Baptisteries

thing similar' (Thomas 1981, 218). In this context we may recall the two copper alloy fittings (Fig 156, nos 2 and 3) associated with the baptistery at Uley. These are interpreted as vessel fittings in the catalogue but equally could have been small door hinges.

The octagonal shape of the Uley structure may be matched at no less than three further sites. Firstly, one recalls the octagonal fourth to sixth-century font, constructed of tufa and possessing red plaster facings, found outside the eastern end of the cathedral at Cologne (Brown 1971, 227 and pl xxxi A). A rather more rudimentary octagon, of three main phases, has been interpreted as a font at Ivy Chimneys, Witham, Essex (Figure 220 and Turner 1982, fig 16). The tank was constructed of brick rising from a floor fabricated from Roman tiles set in *opus signinum*. The two later phases incorporated marginal postholes which may have supported a covering shelter, and a sump lay adjacent to it. The structure lay on a site where a possible Iron Age shrine, a Roman temple and post-Roman buildings have been identified. Finally, in northern Gloucestershire, the octagonal spring-fed basin of Richmond's suggested *Nymphaeum* at Chedworth may have been converted to use as a baptismal tank late in the fourth century. Certainly some of the marginal slabs were inscribed with chi-rho symbols at that time (Goodburn 1972, pl 11). A theological context for the octagonal shape had been discussed by Morris (1983, 15, citing Davies 1964). Ideological links between baptism and death with Christ (see Colossians 2.12) are echoed by the provision of an octagon which expresses the co-resurrection of the baptismal candidate with Christ 'who was raised from the dead on what the Fathers call the eighth day, the first day of the new week' (Davies 1964, 5).

The stone church

In the late sixth or early seventh century the timber basilica was dismantled and was replaced by a much smaller structure in stone. This new building was erected over the former north-eastern corner of the basilica and of the preceding temple, and directly over the much earlier post and pit structure that had occupied the hollow over the deep Iron Age ditch (Fig 29). The structure was of two main phases, firstly a simple rectangular two-celled building, possibly with an entrance midway along the eastern side, and, in a later phase, a larger structure, extended by the addition of an apse at the north-eastern end. The doorway may have been moved to the south-western end at this stage. The building is interpreted as a two-cell chapel, initially with an altar at the 'west' end. When the structure was increased in size the altar would have been moved to the apsidal 'east' end and thus the orientation became reversed. This second phase of construction may have followed very rapidly upon the first. The building would have been tall, with a roof of reused Roman stone tiles, and with round-headed windows located high up in the walls (Fig 221). Possible voussoirs from such a window were found in the rubble lying above the weathered floor of the structure. Only the cobbled floor of the apse survived, and the superstructure may have been flimsy in nature, or founded on horizontal beams. Its wall may have been faced with stone; certainly Roman building materials must have been still available in abundance. The apse roof may have been shingled, and its apex would have rendered the high east window architecturally inappropriate; this window might therefore have been replaced by a lower east window in the apse wall. The later church is shown with a string course, and other architectural embellishments may have existed. The presence of red-streaked and other window glass on the site (Colour Plate II), glass which is of seventh to ninth century type, may derive from this building, thus suggesting the existence of a sophisticated church in a surprisingly rustic setting. Alternatively the 'window' glass may have been set originally within a piece of furniture or box. In a Christian context, these could have been an altar or a reliquary.

Both phases of church construction were accompanied by the deliberate burial of parts of the dismembered Roman cult statue (Fig 76). Two portions of the legs were incorporated in the foundations for the original north-eastern wall, and the head of Mercury was

Fig 221 Reconstructions of the stone church: Phase 7b. (Drawn by Joanna Richards)

deposited in a pit just outside the eastern junction of chapel and apse. Some parallels for such acts of ritual cleansing have been mentioned above, and it is interesting to consider where these statue fragments could have been between the act of dismembering the statue, which must have occurred prior to the construction of the timber basilica, and the construction of the stone church. The leg fragments (Fig 73), which were fairly weathered, may have been recovered from Roman demolition rubble, or from the packing around posts supporting the basilica at the time of its destruction. However, the statue head (Fig 72) was crisp and totally unweathered. Indeed it does not seem to have been exposed at all to the elements, and may have been protected by a cloth, a bag, or a box. The implication is that the statue head had been curated, preserved, and possibly venerated, during the lifetime of the timber basilica. As Dr Rodwell has suggested, the head may have been placed in a recess within the basilica, hidden in a chest, or even placed or sealed inside the altar itself. Christian doctrine has often attempted to subsume pagan elements rather than eradicate them, and the cult of the head which was so widespread in the Celtic world is known to have been reflected both in medieval church art and the cult of relics. However, the head of Mercury himself may have seemed a too dangerous and profane item in the eyes of these early Christians. They did not possess sufficient courage to destroy it, for it was instead carefully hidden by burial next to the new sacred focus. Alternatively the head may have been rescued by individuals of pagan leanings and buried secretly next to the new Christian shrine, or more radically, as Philip Rahtz has suggested, the head may have been perceived or presented as representing the head of Christ himself, or of a local saint or martyr.

The plan and morphology of the stone church at Uley may be compared to those of three different groups of structures: small rectangular buildings found adjacent to some Roman temples in south-western England, the early Christian oratories of Ireland and west Scotland, and the earliest stone churches of Anglo-Saxon England (Fig 222). The small buildings outside the Roman temples at Brean Down (Apsimon 1965) and Lamyatt Beacon (Leech 1986) are simple rectangular structures with eastern entrances. The building at Brean was constructed towards the end of the fourth century, or a little later (ApSimon 1965, 214–220, 224 and 226–7). It was built without mortar, from material robbed from the temple, and wear of the floor suggested a long period of use. The single room contained a hearth and small objects indicative of domestic occupation. But ApSimon was aware of the problems associated with such an interpretation

> 'why was it built when a building of similar area could have been obtained by walling off part of one of the annexes or part of the ambulatory? [of the temple]. If an unencumbered site was desired, use of the corner formed by the south wall of the ambulatory and the east wall of the south annexe would have saved half the work. This refusal to make use of standing structures and the choice of a different orientation look like a deliberate rejection of what had gone before'
>
> (*ibid*, 231–2)

ApSimon discussed the possibility of a Christian context for the building, but rejected it. In the light of the discovery of a further similar building at Lamyatt Beacon, a religious function is preferred, but whether both or either served to house Christian or pagan worshippers cannot be ascertained. The structure excavated at Lamyatt Beacon could not be dated closely, but may have been built with materials looted from the temple. It post-dated one of a series of nine burials of antlers, and may or may not have been contemporary with the post-Roman inhumation cemetery located immediately north of it. In terms of date, these two buildings are likely to have been rather earlier than the stone structure at Uley, and in terms of function and date they may belong more fittingly to our group of compartmentalised late Roman shrines discussed above. Such rooms may be viewed as further compartments which have become separated from the former temple building and can be compared indirectly with the eastern room at Lydney which was attached to the temple itself. This interpretation might imply a pagan context for such rooms, but at Witham, Essex, Turner has suggested that a small, two phase rectangular building with mortared walls may have possessed glass windows, and functioned as a chapel in association with the octagonal baptistery found on the same site (Fig 222 and Turner 1982, figs 14 and 17). The chapel was located on the site of a Roman temple.

The rectangular buildings discussed above are smaller than that at Uley, and also than the earliest known early Christian stone chapels or oratories of the Celtic west (Fig 222). The buildings at Church Island, Co Wexford (after O'Kelly 1958) and Ardwall Island, Kirkudbrightshire (after Thomas 1967) are of late seventh to eighth-century date and possess western entrances. However, they are preceded by smaller shrines in timber (Fig 222 after Thomas 1981, fig 18) which better match in size the rectangular buildings at Brean Down and Lamyatt Beacon. The timber shrines date from the seventh century, although that on Ardwall Island may have been constructed a little earlier. The stone versions may have been inspired by influence from Anglo- Saxon churches in England and Thomas is inclined to view them as cemetery based *memoriae* or *martyria*: cult shrines associated with the graves of prominent local Christians (Thomas 1981, 152). Any similar function for the Brean Down and Lamyatt Beacon buildings cannot be argued on the present evidence, but the stone structure at Uley, with its evidence for a western cell and a subsidiary eastern apse, can be compared with the earliest Christian buildings in another geographical zone, the churches of Anglo- Saxon England.

The earliest known Saxon churches were small timber chapels like those excavated at Wharram Percy, Yorks (Fig 222); Burnham, Lincs, and Thetford St Michael, Norfolk (Rodwell 1981, 109). (For further discussion of the phase I features at Wharram Percy, see Bell *et al* 1987, 55–7 and fig 34A). Some of these were encased later by stone walled churches which were of one or two cells. Early stone churches include Wharram Percy (Fig 222, after Hurst 1976, fig 13, and now see Bell *et al* 1987, fig 34B); Wells (after Rodwell 1981, fig 68 and 142–3); and St Helen-on-the-Walls, York (Rodwell 1981, 111, after Magilton 1980). The last two examples were erected over *foci* of Roman date: a mosaic roundel at York and a mausoleum at Wells. At St Helen-on-the-

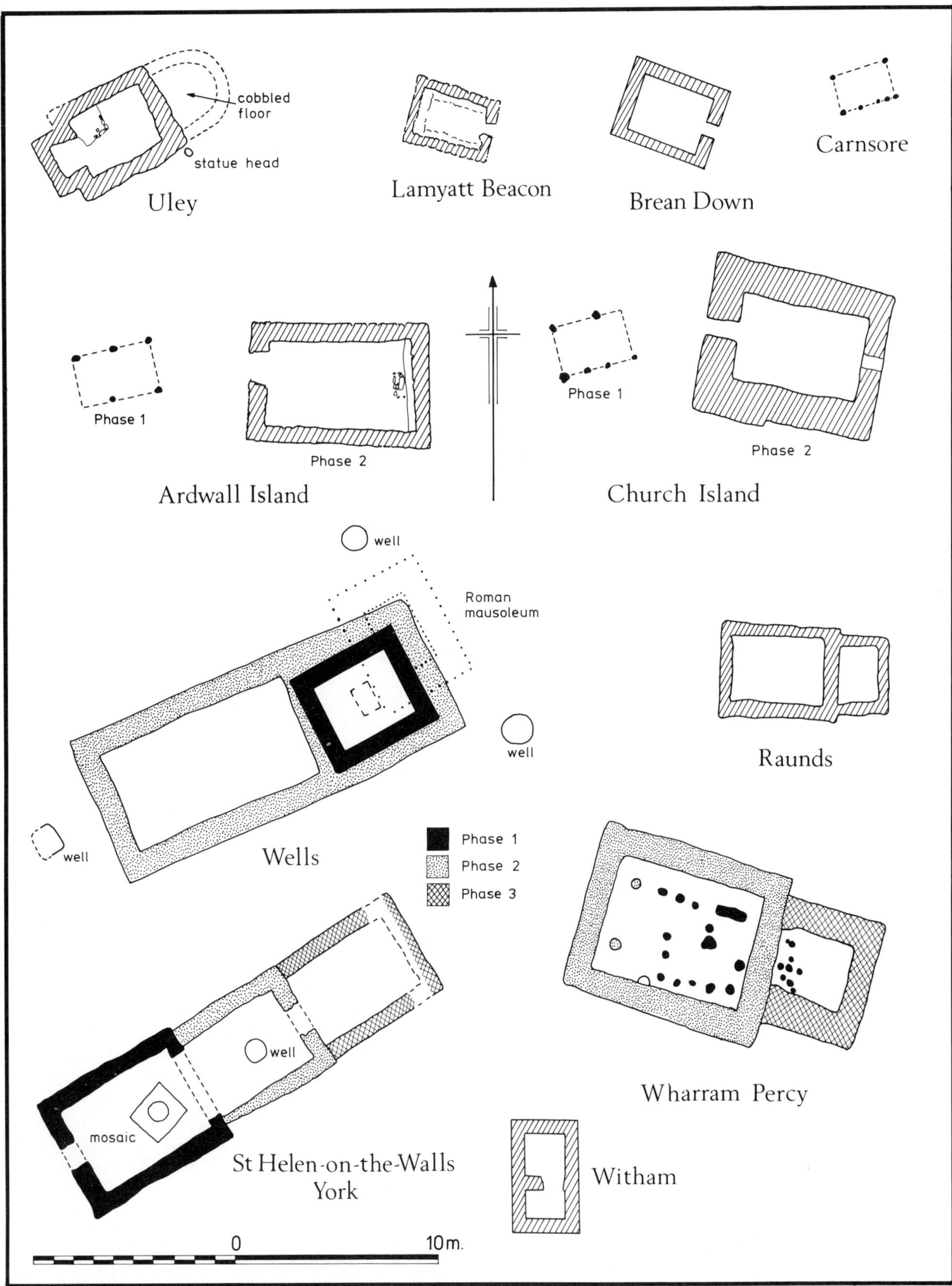

Fig 222 Rectangular shrines and churches

Walls the mosaic roundel depicting a female face belonged probably to a corridor within a town-house (and not to the house-church suggested in Rodwell 1981), but Magilton concluded that 'it may be that the rediscovery of the mosaic inspired the erection of the first church and its dedication' (Magilton 1986, 46–7). In its first phase the Uley building best matches in size the phase 1 church at Raunds, Northants (Fig 222, after Boddington 1980, 373 and fig 25.1). All these simple stone churches date from the eighth to tenth centuries, but seem to provide the best group of parallels for the stone building at Uley. Simple buildings with an early eastern apse are also well known in the Anglo-Saxon east, ranging from St Paul-in-the-Bail, Lincoln (Morris 1983, fig 11), located within the former Roman forum, to Angmering in Sussex (Rodwell 1981, 109).

Possibly connected with the stone church at Uley, by stratigraphic evidence, was the polygonal open-sided structure lying immediately to the south (Figs 29 and 64). The stone footings of the four sided foundation were uneven but mortared, and resembled the surviving first horizontal course of the foundations belonging to the church itself. Associated finds were virtually absent, and the structure has been depicted as an open sided stone screen, roofed, like the church, with reused Roman roofing tiles (Fig 221). The screen may have housed a water container, a seat, or pictorial representations in a medium such as wall plaster, but no evidence for any such internal arrangements survived. Similar screen foundations have been recorded in Roman contexts; at Silchester, Hants (Boon 1974), near to the 'priest's house'; possibly next to the temple on Chanctonbury, Sussex (Lewis 1966, 85), and nine metres south of the temple at Coleshill, Warks (Carver 1979 and Magilton, forthcoming). Another screen structure, situated in the angle between rooms 9 and 10 of the ancillary buildings at Pagan's Hill, was interpreted as an exterior altar or shrine by the excavators (Rahtz and Harris 1957, fig 1). These parallels are of Roman date and it remains to be considered whether the screen at Uley originated in this earlier period. If so, any associated deposits of the Roman period had been removed during construction of the platforms around the stone church; but the wall footings themselves were not removed, and crucial dating evidence may remain sealed beneath them. The only later parallel known to the authors is the three sided foundation trench located within the post-Roman settlement at Poundbury, Dorset (Green 1987, fig 56), but the date and function of that structure also remains elusive.

The polygonal timber building, Structure XII, of the final phase, may have been open to the south and probably was roofed. If so, it may have reflected the stone screen, Structure III, in form and function. The postholes cutting the former site of the temple and basilica do not form a clear structural pattern, but the pit F57, containing a large fragment of antler recalls the series of buried antlers found north of the temple at Lamyatt Beacon (Leech 1986, fig 8). One pit at Lamyatt, containing an antler, was sealed by the wall of the rectangular building 2, in which case the antler deposits may have been contemporary with the temple. However, at Uley the antler must have been buried after the demolition of the stone church, possibly in the eighth century or beyond.

The finds assemblage

An important aspect of the excavation programme has been the recovery of a considerable array of finds including objects of metal, stone, bone and antler, baked clay, glass, and pottery. The categories represented may be divided into three groups, those that were of undoubtedly votive character (chapters 6–8), objects which may have assumed a ritual or a secular function (chapters 5 and 9), and items of structural, domestic, or industrial function (chapters 10–11).

Groups of finds which fall most appropriately into this structural, domestic, or everyday category are the building materials, tools, querns, whetstones, whorls, styli, knives, and points, the major bulk assemblages of vessel glass, and most of the pottery. However, even in this context, it needs to be noted that many of the domestic and industrial activities represented by these objects may well have been connected closely with the ritual function of the site. Thus metalworking could have included the production of simple votive offerings, and the styli may have been employed in the inscribing of lead tablets. Apart from the early ceramic assemblages and the miniature clay pots, the pottery from the site presents similar characteristics to other assemblages from other local late-Roman settlement sites. However, table wares predominate, and this may reflect a more extensive use of containers, in connection with ritual feasting associated with the temple cult, than was normal on domestic sites. The existence of a domestic animal bone assemblage has been referred to above (see also chapter 12).

In the first century AD tools and pottery formed a significant component of the votive assemblages. These categories include heavy tools manufactured from bone and antler and almost complete ceramic vessels, several of which possessed groups of holes drilled through the lower wall or base. The groups of later Roman finds of a probable votive character are the very many coins, the stone sculpture, the inscribed items (including an altar), the copper alloy plaques and figurines, the lead tablets, miniature weapons, flat copper alloy rings, miniature clay vessels, and the ceramic 'altar'. In the early phases, full-size weapons of iron were deposited ritually, and for the later Roman period, the various groups of objects derived from furnishings and fittings may be ascribed a ritual function. These include the elaborate metal bosses and terminals, decorated studs and antler box-inlay, as well as more portable items, such as the candlesticks and metal vessels, the latter represented only by fragments. A very large number of the diagnostic finds belong to the categories of jewellery and personal items: brooches, beads, bracelets, pins and rings, spoons, toilet articles, counters, and shoe fittings. Such objects occur commonly on most later Roman sites excavated and none can be ascribed a votive function on their individual characteristics. Nevertheless it can be argued that personal objects were used as *ex votos* at Roman sanctuaries, and it will be seen below that certain categories of small personal trinkets can be linked to specific types of cult.

Table 19: The occurrence of finds categories by phase

Phase	2	3	4	5	6	7	U/S	*total*
Date AD	0	50	100	*c*310	380	420	*c*800	
Category								
Coins*	5	4	425	2154	282	-	-	2870
Figurines & *caducei*	-	-	-	4	8	6	3	21
Miniature spearheads	-	-	-	3	4	4	3	14
Plaques & leaves	-	-	-	4	8	14	3	29
Votive rings	-	1	1	8	17	9	16	52
Miniature pots	-	-	9	45	3	1	36	94
Lead tablets	-	-	5	62	15	11	47	140
Antler or bone tools	6	1	-	-	-	-	-	7
Weapons	17	15	-	5	-	4	3	44
Metal vessels	-	-	-	3	1	3	8	15
Brooches:								
dates	5	9	15	6	-	-	-	35
contexts	5	5	5	7	7	6	5	40
Glass beads	-	1	4	15	21	18	29	88
Bracelets:								
Cu alloy	-	-	2	2	11	10	8	33
shale/jet	2	-	8	4	5	3	8	30
Pins:								
jet	-	-	2	1	-	-	1	4
metal	-	1	-	1	-	1	5	8
antler	-	-	3	7	1	1	2	14
Finger rings:								
Cu alloy	-	-	2	3	10	6	9	30
jet	-	-	2	-	1	-	4	7
Spoons	-	-	1	6	1	5	13	
Toilet articles	-	-	2	1	-	-	3	6

*using dates not contexts

Table 19 shows the occurrence of selected classes of votive finds and personal items by phase. Firstly, it is important to appreciate that the degree of disturbance and reuse experienced within the excavated area will have led to the incidence of many residual finds within phased assemblages. This aspect has been highlighted within the report on the pottery (chapter 11) and can be appreciated readily by an appraisal of the differences between the distribution of brooches by phase, and their suggested time span according to expected date of manufacture (chapter 9). In spite of this, some clear chronological patterns emerge. The early Roman Phases 2 and 3, focused on the timber shrines and votive pits around them, show concentrations of full-size weapons (iron spearheads and bolt heads) and tools of bone and antler, together with a few coins and brooches. It will be recalled that individual human bones and some partly articulated animal remains derived from these same deposits. Full sized tools and weapons were not utilised as *ex votos* from the second century onwards, the weapons in contexts of later phases being largely fragmentary and apparently residual. During the main *floruit* of the stone temple, during Phases 4 and 5, the most popular forms of votive object can be seen to have been the miniature clay vessels, coins, antler pins, spoons, and toilet articles. Other categories which were employed in Phases 4 and 5 were offered also in Phase 6. Some of these categories, such as the brooches or shale bracelets, apparently were still in use during Phase 6 rather than present merely as residual items. However, several other categories occur only sporadically prior to Phase 6, and hardly at all before Phase 5. These types were objects offered up at the temple during the fourth century, and at the converted temple ruin in the early fifth century. They include the copper alloy figurines and *caducei*, the miniature weapons, sheet plaques, flat copper alloy rings, metal vessels, glass beads, the copper alloy bracelets, and the finger rings. It should be noted that the concentrations of objects in Phase 7 result from their redeposition within the make-up of the perimeter bank; they do not represent a revival of usage of votive items during the post-Roman period. In fact these concentrations are more akin to those recorded within the ploughsoil (Phase 8), an observation which should cause no surprise if the hypothesis of a Phase 7 bank, constructed from turves lifted from around the former temple, is accepted.

It is likely that objects of particular value or complexity will have been curated carefully and perhaps reused several times. Thus some of the figurines current in Phase 5, and particularly Phase 6, were manufactured most probably during Phase 4 and, as we have seen, the stone cult image was probably carved in the second century, but remained in use as a complete figure at least until the opening years of the fifth century. Amongst the simpler objects certain trends can be deduced. The only categories of finds that appear throughout the life of the shrines and temple are coins and brooches, and the brooches do not occur in large numbers. The first-century assemblage is dominated by ceramic jars and iron projectile heads, the latter possibly suggestive of a cult possessing martial aspects. In the later Roman period these categories are also represented, but only in the form of miniatures. The miniature clay vessels and the lead tablets are the most numerous find categories recovered from contexts dating to Phases 4 and 5, and all the miniature weapons from Phases 5 and 6 were spears. This trend towards miniaturisation goes hand in hand with two other processes – a tendency towards simplification; and a diversification of types. The complex full-sized tools, weapons, lead tablets, spoons, toilet articles, and brooches, are replaced through time by simpler items involving less elaborate methods of manufacture: miniature spears, sheet metal plaques, flat copper alloy rings, simple finger rings, bracelets, and some of the glass beads. This process of diversification is mainly seen to be the result of the growing practice of making offerings of small items of jewellery during the fourth century. This is not due entirely to the general increase in the occurrence of such flimsy trinkets during this period, as we shall see when some other fourth-century assemblages are considered below. It can be concluded that the votive objects deposited at Uley became smaller, simpler, and more numerous through time. Also that the distinctly martial aspect apparent in the first-century assemblage became subsumed to a great extent within the more personal aura of the fourth-century offerings, with their remarkable concentrations of circular and ring-shaped objects: coins, flat copper alloy rings, bracelets and finger rings. The potential significance of these changes will be discussed further below in relation to an assessment of the cults indicated by the inscriptions, sculptures and figurines.

One of the major aims of the excavation programme was to record the finds in such a way that detailed distributions of different categories of material could be plotted, and the occurrence of finds amongst the different structures assessed. The data is stored in a computer archive and thus will be available to future researchers (see Appendix A). In the present report it is proposed to present selected distribution plots in order to highlight particular aspects of some of the arguments essential to the interpretation of the site sequence, and to indicate the possible potential of future studies. Figures 223 and 224 show the distributions of one group of late fourth-century coins, current in site Phase 5, and of the Theodosian issues, lost initially in period 6. The coins are plotted in two dimensions, and by the phase of the contexts within which they occurred.

The main concentrations of the *Fel Temp Reparatio* copies lay within the cella of the temple, over Structure I, in Structure XIV (over Structure IX, north-west of the

Fig 223 Distribution of Fel Temp Reparatio coins

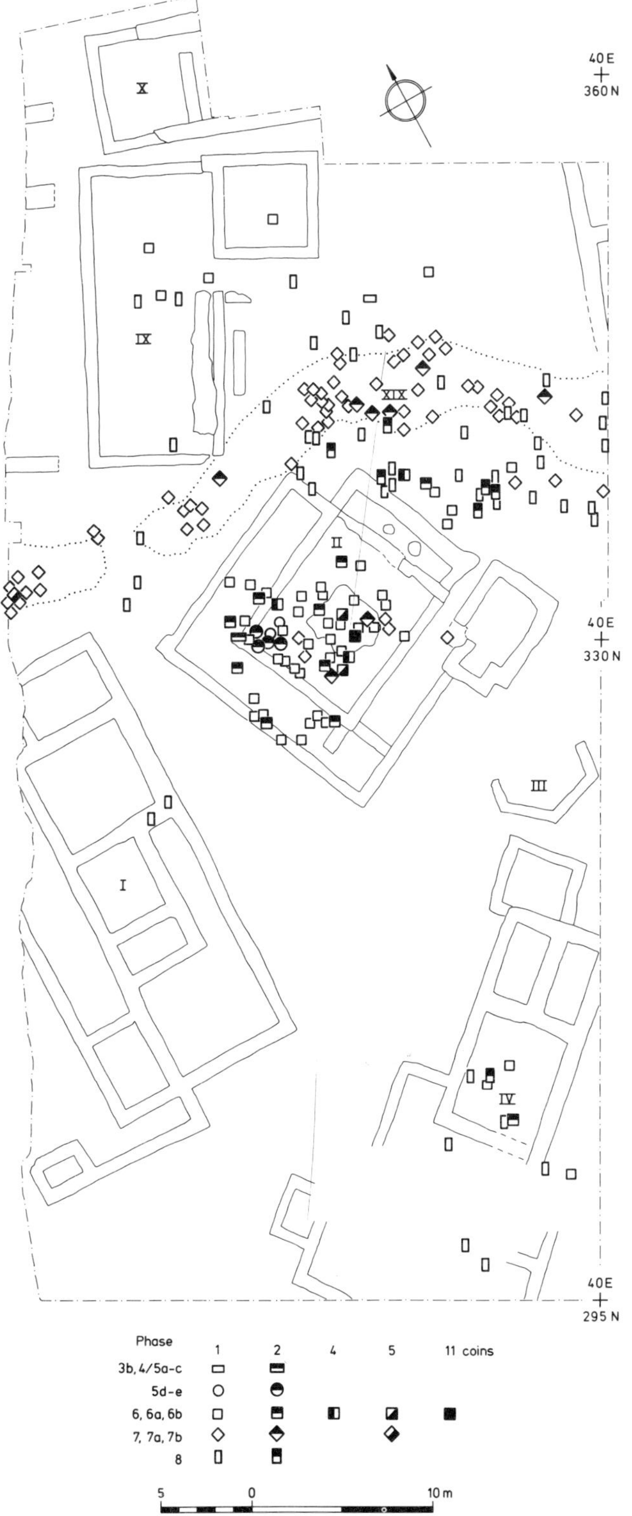

Fig 224 Distribution of Theodosian coins

temple), in the bank material, and within the modern hillwash north-east of the temple. In contexts of Phases 5d–e the coins derive from the final use of the temple and from deposits spread over the demolished remains of Structure I. Few of these findspots lay within the temple itself because very few layers of Phase 5 date survived there. The Phase 6 findspots lay in the temple cella and the south-west and north-western ambulatories; they may represent a hoard of coins scattered during the use of the converted temple. Also in Phase 6 a few of this class of coin became scattered above the remains of Structure IV, and more abundantly within Structure XIV, which was probably still in use during Phase 6. The Phase 7 findspots represent residual occurrences within the make-up of the perimeter bank. The Theodosian coins display a much more restricted distribution (Fig 224). Major concentrations occurred only in the temple area, in the bank make-up, and in the hillwash deposits between the site of the temple and the perimeter bank. Most were found in contexts belonging to Phase 6 and their restricted distribution within the cella area and the south-western and north-

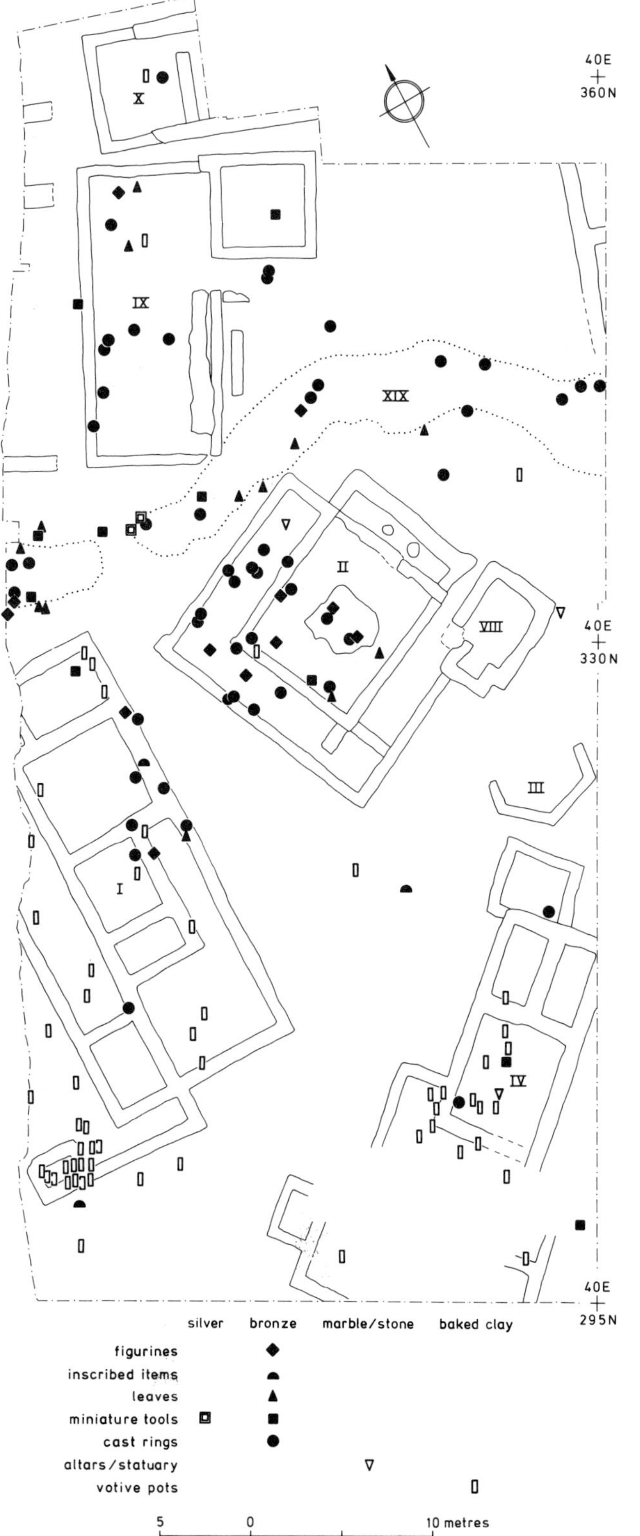

Fig 225 *Distribution of votive objects*

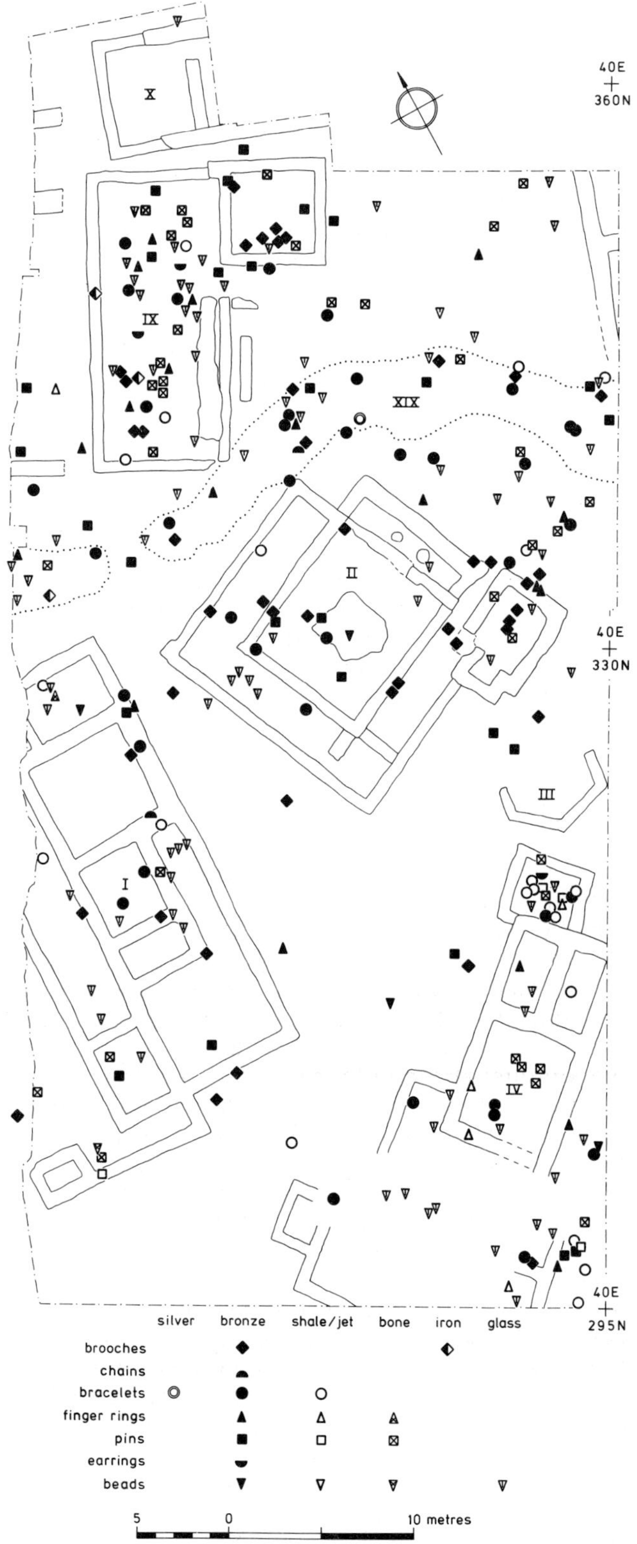

Fig 226 *Distribution of jewellery*

western ambulatories has been used as evidence to assist in the interpretation of the converted temple ruin. Also in Phase 6, a few Theodosian issues derived from Structure XIV (above Structure IX), which may have been still in use, and over the demolished remains of Structure IV. Phase 7 occurrences were located in the perimeter bank material, where they were residual within the turf make-up.

Three further plots demonstrate the distribution of various categories of diagnostic finds, grouped by function and raw material, but not separated by chronological divisions (Figs 225–27). In spite of the widespread occurrence of secondary votive deposits on the site, the greatest concentration of votive objects is centred on the temple building itself (Fig 225), and most of the copper alloy figurines and stone sculpture fragments were found within or very close to it. Examination of the distribution of other votive categories leads to two sets of conclusions: one functional and one chronological. Occupation deposits in Structure IX contained copper alloy leaves and flat rings in abundance. As some rings have casting flanges still attached it has been inferred that production took place on site. Structure IX also contained some evidence for bronze and lead working, and may therefore have formed a manufacturing focus within the complex. The distributions of objects over Structures I and IV represents the spreads of votive material deposited over the demolished and robbed remains of Structure I, and in the demolition material belonging to Structure IV. These deposits were dated by coins to before 380 AD, and the spreads of miniature pots in these locations suggest a relatively early date for this class of material. On the other hand, sheet leaves and flat copper alloy rings derived mainly from deposits of Phase 6 or 7, within the temple, Structure IX/XIV, and the make-up of the perimeter bank.

The distribution of jewellery is both more dense, and more widespread, than that of votive objects (Fig 226). Most of the brooches recovered from Uley relate to the early Roman structural phases. In the main period of temple use there is an overall paucity of brooches, but their findspots do cluster in and around the temple building. Other classes of jewellery plotted in Figure 226 include bracelets, finger rings, pins of copper alloy, antler and jet, shale armlets, and beads of shale, bone, and glass. Simple copper alloy finger rings were common in Structure IX and may reflect the copper alloy working area already adduced for votive objects. Bracelet fragments of copper alloy derived largely from the bank material, and therefore belonged mainly to the later phases of temple use. By contrast, items in antler or bone, shale, and jet were concentrated in Structure IV, not in votive deposits over it (as was the case with the miniature pots and lead tablets), but in layers related to its period of use. It is unlikely that shale and jet objects were manufactured on site but they may have been sold to visiting pilgrims, along with antler pins, from these rooms. Only the glass beads were spread evenly across the excavated area. A further set of finds categories includes various types of furniture and fittings which may have graced the temple: metal rivets and studs from stools, tables, or wooden boxes, copper alloy stripwork, plaques, and iron catches, plates, and corner fittings from boxes or chests; keys and door-fittings (Fig 227). There is a marked concentration of fittings within the temple building itself, and occurrences within Structures IX/XIV add further weight to the hypothesis of on-site metal working. The lack of finds over Structures I and IV denotes, of course, not the absence of fittings in the earlier phases of temple use, but the late date for the final destruction of its fabric. In other words, the fittings probably remained in use until the late fourth century at least. The concentration of stud finds and pieces of matching antler inlay at the westernmost excavated sector of the perimeter bank may indicate the deposition of a complete box within the bank material.

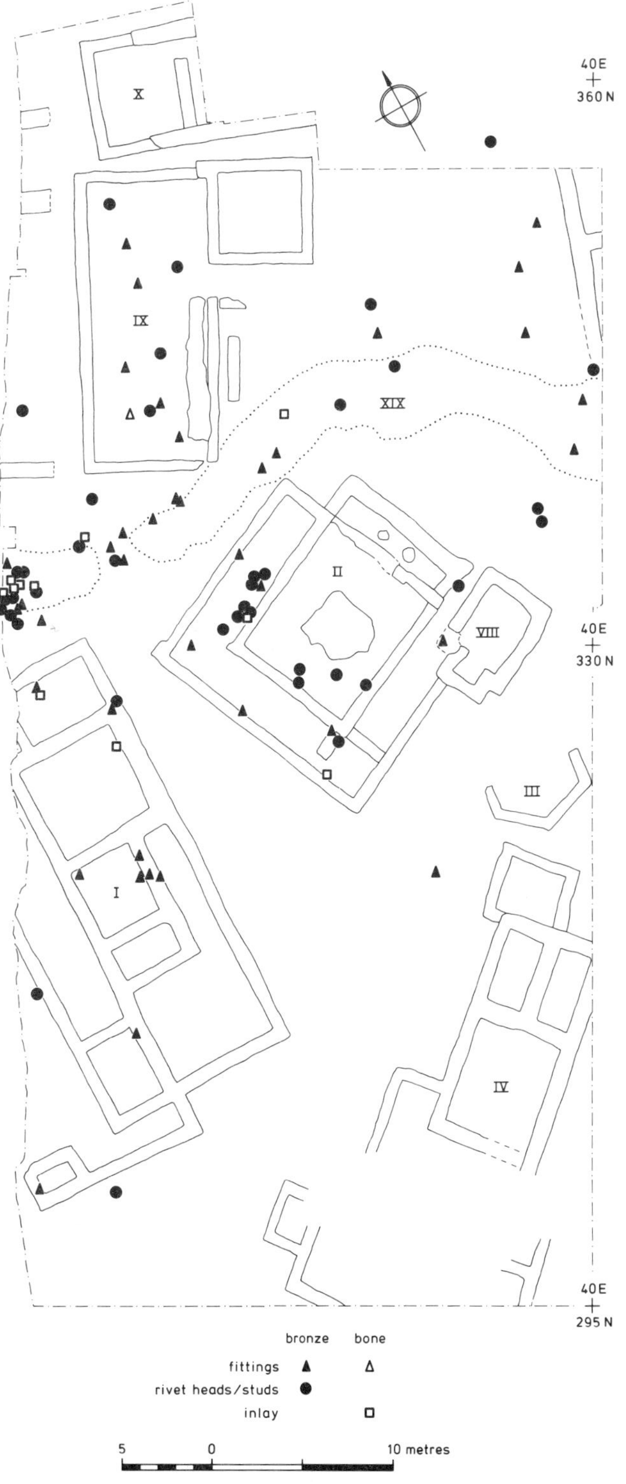

Fig 227 Distribution of fittings

A comparison of votive assemblages

In order to investigate the nature and ideological components of the finds assemblage more fully, the incidence of selected categories of material has been compared with that known for a series of other temple sites, mainly located in western England, and two contemporary domestic sites from the Cotswold region. The results of this comparison are presented in Table 20.

The finds have been quantified from the published reports as follows: from Lydney, Gloucestershire, Wheeler and Wheeler 1932; from Nettleton, Wiltshire, Wedlake 1982; from Henley Wood, Avon, Watts and Leach, forthcoming; from Woodeaton, Oxfordshire, Kirk 1949; from Harlow, Essex, France and Gobel 1985; from Lamyatt Beacon, Somerset, Leech 1986; from Marshfield, Avon, Blockley 1985; and from Frocester Court, Gloucester, Gracie 1970, Gracie and Price 1980. The counts have been limited to drawn or described diagnostic items, and do not include unpublished fragments, except in the case of Lydney where the stated totals for copper alloy bracelets and bone or metal pins have been employed, as only a small selection were illustrated or described in the Wheelers' report.

Firstly, it may be noted that the categories of votive objects and fittings listed seldom occur on the two domestic sites, Marshfield and Frocester. However, all classes of jewellery and personal items occur on both religious and secular sites. What distinguishes the temple site assemblages of personal items and trinkets from the secular groups is the occurrence of certain types in particularly large numbers on specific temple sites. This same peaking effect is also detectable amongst the categories of votive objects and fittings. Thus, each temple assemblage appears to be characterised by the occurrence of sharp peaks in the numbers of one, two, three, or in two cases, four, specific categories of object. The peaks are as follows:

Uley: votive copper alloy rings, miniature pots, finger rings
Lydney: bracelets, pins, spoons
Nettleton: brooches, pins, spoons, finger rings
Henley Wood: brooches, counters
Woodeaton: plaques, brooches, toilet articles, miniature tools and weapons
Harlow: brooches
Lamyatt: miniature tools and weapons

It could be argued in the case of the smaller assemblages, such as those from Henley Wood, Harlow and Lamyatt, that the surviving array of objects may not have been representative of the original assemblage of objects in use on the site. However, for the larger

Table 20: The occurrence of finds categories within votive and domestic assemblages

	Uley	*Lydney*	*Nettleton*	*Henley Wood*	*Wood-eaton*	*Harlow*	*Lamyatt Beacon*	*Marsh-field*	*Fro-cester*
Votive									
Stone altars/statues	12	6	6	1	-	-	8	-	-
Cu alloy figurines	18	10	-	1	7	-	7	-	-
'Rings'	52	-	-	-	-	7	-	-	-
Leaves	11	1	-	-	2	-	1	-	-
Plaques	18	9	1	-	19	-	2	-	-
Parts of body	3	2	-	-	-	-	2	-	-
Letters	-	14	-	-	3	-	1	-	-
Miniature tools/weapons	14	-	-	poss 1	11	-	23	-	-
Miniature pots	94	-	-	-	-	-	-	-	-
Clay vessels	9	-	-	-	-	-	-	-	2
total	231	37	7	3	42	7	44	-	2
Fittings									
Boss/terminal	11	-	-	-	-	-	4	-	-
Iron rings	6	-	-	3	-	-	2	-	-
Metal vessels	15	-	-	-	-	-	-	-	-
Candlesticks	2	3	2	-	-	1	?2	-	-
Bone inlay	11	5	1	-	-	-	-	-	1
total	48	8	3	3	-	1	8	-	1
Jewellery									
Brooches	40	33	68	33	>100	96	10	39	27
Bracelets:									
Cu alloy	33	*c*300	58	5	16	4	3	24	62
shale/jet	30	1	11	1	-	3	1	3	-
Pins:									
metal	8	320	63	14	29	15	2	4	9
antler	14	-	75	12	-	7	14	11	33
jet	4	3	1	2	-	-	-	-	-
Finger rings:									
Cu alloy	38	6	30	12	23	19	4	13	11
jet	7	1	1	-	-	-	-	-	-
total	174	664	307	79	168	144	34	94	142
Personal items	-	-	-	-	-	-	-	-	-
Spoons	14	>40	30	-	7	-	2	3	7
Toilet articles	6	3	19	5	29	19	2	7	15
Counters	12	?	11	60	-	-	1	5	10
total	32	43	60	65	36	19	5	15	32

assemblages at least, the differences of detailed numerical composition do seem to be real, and they are of considerable importance to any discussion of possible cults represented. The incidence of brooches may be due to chronological, rather than ideological factors, as they were in fashion mainly during the earlier Roman period, and thus would be expected to be more commonly found on temple sites that were occupied in the early centuries of Roman rule. This argument might apply particularly in the cases of Harlow and Nettleton. Otherwise it does seem likely that the concentration of particular object classes relates to the cult or cults practised at the individual temples. The prevalent finds categories identified seem to fall into three groups – objects of martial aspect (weapons); different types of ring and disc, possibly including coins; and finally, personal trinkets: bracelets, pins, spoons and toilet articles. These groups of objects may be linked to our knowledge of cults practised at the various temples, gleaned from inscriptions and representations of identifiable deities.

At Uley the evidence from stone sculpture, figurines, and inscriptions demonstrates that the main deity worshipped was Mercury, along with his associates the goat and cockerel. This direct evidence includes two statues, two altars, six figurines, six separate *caducei*, one depiction of the god on a sheet plaque, and the name of Mercury inscribed on two copper alloy items and on at least 20 of the inscribed lead tablets. Martin Henig has suggested also that several other categories of finds could be associated with the cult of Mercury. In connection with Mercury's caring for trade and markets, the coins and all the rings may be suitable offerings, and furthermore, the simple projections on some of the key rings may have represented *caducei*. The incidence of votive legs, and the plaque fragment bearing a foot, may also be linked to the cult of Mercury, but in this case relating to his role as a god of travellers, who also was effective in the cure of disease impeding movement. The supremacy of the cult of Mercury is confirmed by the animal bone evidence. The high percentage of sheep/goat bones, with male goats generally in the majority, and the large numbers of adult male domestic fowl bones, relate very neatly to a cult which involved the veneration of the goat and cockerel. The skulls and lower leg bones of the fowl were underrepresented, suggesting that the birds were prepared away from the site, while butchery evidence indicated that goat horncores were removed near the temple and that the carcasses were probably eaten after sacrifice. The ageing results show that the main concentration of sacrifices lay in August/September. Finally, the evidence from deposits within the latrine shaft (F188) showed that the goats had been fed on hay, probably whilst they were stalled in buildings not far removed from the excavated area.

Other deities represented once only amongst the Uley finds include Sol and Jupiter, possibly signifying days of the week, Cupid or Victory, and a naked child, interpreted by Martin Henig as Bacchus succoured by Mercury. However, one further deity is signified four times in the inscribed lead tablets. This is the god Mars, whose single name occurs twice on tablets, while inscriptions addressed to Mars Silvanus also occur twice, in both cases overwritten by the name of Mercury. The miniature spears could also be linked with the equestrian warrior cult of Mars. As we have seen, the miniature spears may reflect the earlier deposition of full-sized weapons in the votive deposits of the first century AD. Although sheep/goat bones were dominant in these early deposits, the goat was not prominent until around 100 AD. It may be therefore that an existing warrior cult was gradually subsumed by the cult of Mercury as time progressed. Miranda Green has pointed out that the Celtic role of Mars in Gaul was partially similar to that of Mercury. Silvanus was a Roman nature-deity who was fairly commonly mentioned in Gaul and often associated with Sucellus, who was, like Mercury, a god of prosperity (Green 1976, 11–12).

Evidence for a martial cult is also available from Lamyatt Beacon where Leech has suggested (Leech 1986, 272) that the survival of three depictions of Mars (two in stone and one a copper alloy figurine), the five horseman brooches, and the array of model weapons (spears, axes, and sickles) might signify that Mars was the supreme deity worshipped at the temple. He further notes that the antler deposits may be indicative of a conflation with a deity of Cernunnos type. Other deities represented by figurines at Lamyatt are Apollo (in stone), Jupiter, Mercury (twice), Minerva, Hercules, and a genius (Henig in Leech 1986, 274–7). At Nettleton it has been suggested that the major cult figure was Apollo, who was represented on an inscribed bronze plaque and on an intalgio, and referred to as Apollo Cunomaglos ('Hound Prince') on a reused stone altar (Toynbee in Wedlake 1982, 135–50). Other deities represented once each were Silvanus and Diana, whilst four items could be indicative of a subsidiary cult of Mercury; a relief of Mercury and Rosmerta, a further relief possibly depicting Mercury, and two cockerels, one a terracotta head and the other in the form of a copper alloy candlestick.

The name of the god venerated at Lydney is known to have been Nodens. This Celtic name may refer to a god of hunting or fishing, and depictions of sea-monsters, fish, and anchors on various copper alloy objects and the mosaic frieze, were indicative of marine connections (Wheeler and Wheeler 1932, 39–43). The figures of dogs, six in stone, and nine in copper alloy, were linked by the Wheelers (*ibid*) to a cult of healing, similar to those known from the classical world. The occurrence of a dog's head above the inscription on a votive tablet addressed to Nodens further indicated that he may have possessed a healing aspect. The large numbers of pins and bracelets were envisaged as offerings in connection with the healing cult and equivalent to those given at Greek temples by women at the time of childbirth (*ibid*, 41–2). The cult of Nodens therefore appears to have combined a simple nature cult, possibly with an element of hunting or fishing, with a major healing cult served by the guest house, specialist bath house, and long building or *abaton*.

No clear indication of specific cults has been recovered at Harlow, Woodeaton, or Henley Wood. At Woodeaton there were depictions of Venus, a Celtic goddess, Minerva, Cupid, possibly Hercules, and three representations of Mars. The miniature weapons and tools could be related to the worship of Mars, but the seven bronze eagles would more properly be associated with Jupiter. In addition, the presence of bronze snakes, a possible childbirth charm, the feminine toilet articles, and miniature bracelets would suggest the existence of a cult of healing (the finds from Woodeaton are usefully summarised in Green 1976, 175–6). No depictions of known deities have been found at Harlow or Henley Wood, but the figurine of a Celtic goddess from the latter site has been linked with the finding of many personal items, especially the brooches and animal bone deposits, to suggest the former presence of a cult possibly connected with fertility and fecundity (Watts in Watts and Leach, forthcoming).

The three groups of small *ex votos* isolated above, namely miniature weapons and tools, personal trinkets, and the coincidence of rings, discs, and money can be seen to represent three major cult forms present in the Romano-Celtic religion of Britain. The miniature weapons denote a martial cult, the personal trinkets are indicative of cults devoted to the realms of fecundity and healing, whilst the incidence of large numbers of coins, rings and discs is seen to be typical of the cult of Mercury. The Mercury cult is best exemplified at Uley, where additional evidence from the faunal remains has confirmed the primary dedication beyond doubt. A subsidiary cult of Mars has been identified also; this may have been more prevalent prior to the second century AD and related more closely to the preceding Celtic cult practised on the site. Lamyatt and Woodeaton were other temples probably dedicated to Mars. At Lamyatt the major cult was suggested by the presence of depictions of Mars and of Minerva goddess of war, along with miniature weapons and the horseman brooches. The antler deposits may be indicative of a hunting aspect, while other gods were represented by further figurines. At Woodeaton, representations of Mars and Minerva were associated once again with miniature weapons, but here also there were strong indications of a secondary cult or aspect. These indications were depictions of Venus, a female fertility goddess in the Celtic world, and her son Cupid, along with considerable quantities of toilet articles and miniature bracelets. These objects suggest a cult concerned with feminine fecundity, rather than a generalised healing aspect. A similar cult has been suggested for Henley Wood on the basis of an unidentified, but definitely female figurine, and the occurrence of many personal trinkets and food deposits.

The great healing complex at Lydney was dedicated to Nodens, possibly a god of hunting and fishing, and the extent of the healing aspect of the cult was evidenced by the representations of dogs, and the many hundreds of pins and bracelets. Apparently spoons were also connected with the rituals enacted there. The octagonal temple at Nettleton was also dedicated to a hunter, but in the more classical form of Apollo, the archer. Other hunters depicted at Nettleton included Silvanus and Diana. The epithet Cunomaglos, applied to Apollo on the stone altar, may indicate that the great god was worshipped there in his guise of archer and healer (Green 1986, 160), in which case the large numbers of pins and spoons could be interpreted in this context, as at Lydney. On the other hand, the high occurrence of finger rings at Nettleton might suggest that Mercury was being venerated also, as at Uley, and indeed we find at Nettleton that Mercury himself was represented twice on stone reliefs and his associate, possibly, by two depictions of cockerels.

Post-Roman finds

Deposits belonging to the structures of Phase 7 were generally characterised by an almost total absence of diagnostic finds. In the case of the timber basilica, few sealed levels survived and most finds derived from the filling of post pits or beam slots. Within and around the stone church, contemporary cobbled surfaces did survive, but finds were very few indeed. The cleanliness of these contexts tends to indicate a dating for the church well beyond the final deposition and burying of the mass of Roman material present on the site. On the other hand many Roman finds (especially votive objects derived from the use of the converted temple in Phase 6 according to the dating of the coins) were incorporated as residual material within the make-up of the Phase 7 perimeter bank. This assemblage included votive copper alloy rings, two figurines, miniature spears, leaves, box and furniture fittings, and items of jewellery. All these categories were current during Phases 6 and none can be ascribed any definite date of use beyond the date of bank construction, possibly in the mid-fifth century AD.

Although the assemblages of animal bones from Phase 7 contexts were much smaller than those belonging to previous phases, their contrasting nature proved striking. It is quite certain that the dominance of goats ceased at the end of Phase 6. The post-Roman bones may reflect a domestic assemblage only, signifying the demise of animal sacrifice on the site, and thus in accord with the suggested sudden change to Christian practices. One innovative aspect was the presence of red deer antler in Phase 7b, the only such fragments identified on the site. These were associated with the relatively very late timber Structure XII which post-dated the stone church.

The pottery analyses have demonstrated peaks in the occurrence of shell-tempered wares (fabric type 9) and Oxfordshire ware (fabric type 23) relating to Phase 7 deposits. The latter is a fine ware type which may have been carefully preserved, or for other reasons possessed good survival value. Fragments of handmade post-Roman wares were relatively few, comprising sherds from a handful of crudely made vessels of limestone and grass tempered fabrics. The bulk of this was recovered from contexts of Phases 6 and 7, in and around Structures VII and VIII, with smaller concentrations in association with Structure III, Structure XIX the bank, and above Structures I and XIV. Grass tempered wares are recorded at other rural sites in Gloucestershire in fifth-century or later contexts, notably at neighbouring Frocester and on Crickley Hill (Dixon 1988, 78), but rarely in the former Roman towns. No post-Roman imported wares were recognised in the Uley assemblage, and this conforms well with their virtual absence (so far) from elsewhere in the county (Heighway 1987, 4–12).

Other categories of container which may have survived are vessels of glass and metal. The glass drinking cups commonly found at Uley are of standard fourth-century types, but these are known to have survived to later dates elsewhere, as in the Anglo- Saxon cemeteries of eastern England. It is possible that some of these glass cups, like some of the pottery, survived through the fifth, sixth, and even seventh centuries at Uley.

Indeed, they may have served some liturgical use. The same may apply to the vessels of iron, copper alloy, lead or pewter, which survived as fragments mainly in contexts belonging to Phases 7 and 8.

The only items of definite post-Roman character, apart from the fragments of grass tempered pottery, were the pieces of plain and red-streaked window glass described by Jennifer Price and Mike Heyworth in chapter 10. Although unstratified at Uley, parallels suggest a seventh to ninth-century date for the panes represented. As discussed above, this glass may have filled one or more windows belonging to the stone church, or have derived from the front of a reliquary box or the altar table housed within the stone edifice.

Postscript

This volume has presented the evidence for a reconstruction of a remarkable sequence of events, which took place at a long lived ritual centre situated alongside one of the major hillforts of southern Britain. Prior to 1976 its existence was virtually unknown, but the detailed dissection of structures and deposits preserved there has allowed the articulation of a developmental hypothesis which is both exciting and provocative. However, it must be emphasised that the interpretation is only a hypothesis – the best-fit story devised by archaeologists of the later 1980s. We have attempted to separate interpretation from the presentation of data, and much more detail is recorded in the archives. Alternative suggestions and refuted ideas survive as manuscript annotation throughout the archive and some of these options seem almost as likely as those selected for presentation in this volume.

For example, the instance of the enigmatic clay layers below the floor of Structure VIII may be cited. It is argued (chapter 3) that the surviving stratification in this area could have related to a small building or room of Roman date, occupying the later site of, and totally destroyed by Structure VIII, the stone church. Its potential plan is shown in Figure 33. Owing to the lack of parallels for such asymmetrically placed annexes in Britain, this hypothesis was not followed during preparation of the main series of reconstruction drawings, but an alternative front elevation for the temple in Phase 5d is presented in Figure 228 below.

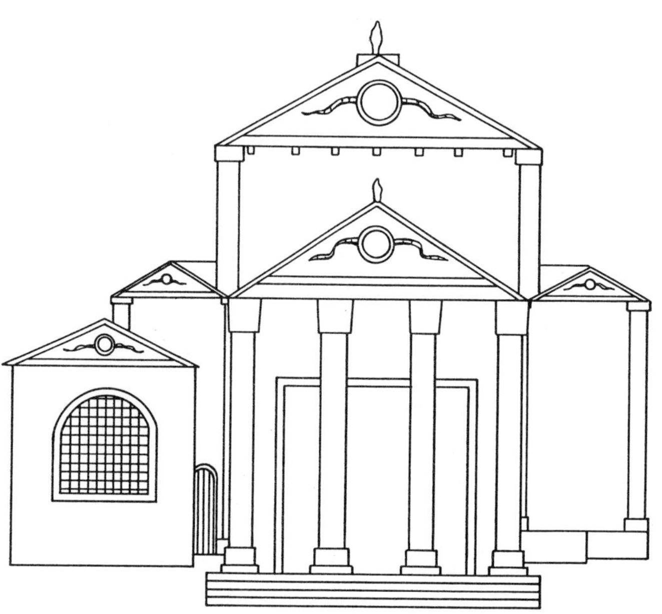

Fig 228 Alternative front elevation for the Phase 5d temple

Appendix A

Index to archive

The site archive and finds are housed in the Department of Prehistoric and Romano-British Antiquities of the British Museum. The computer files are held at the Birmingham University Field Archaeology Unit, PO Box 363, Birmingham B15 2TT.

File index

1–10	site context records
11	phasing lists, graphics register, sieving analysis
12–14	small finds index, classified by material
15	identified small finds, classified by function
16	level III trench reports, by site area and by phase
17	level IV analysis and drawing notes, level IV synopsis
18	specialist reports: bound items
19–20	specialist research and correspondence
21	published text: manuscript
22	published text, as submitted 12/88
23	publication illustrations, as submitted 12/88
24	notes for bibliography, microfiche text, as submitted 6/89
25	black/white negatives
26–30	pottery analysis
31–33	finds registers

Filing cabinet inserts

correspondence
colour slides

Card indices

phased coins
black/white print index
colour slide index
illustrated small finds
wallplaster

Notebooks

level books, site finds books and miscellaneous

Computer files

context summary descriptions
pottery statistics
painted wall plaster
small finds index

Paper archive

faunal remains data and analysis sheets

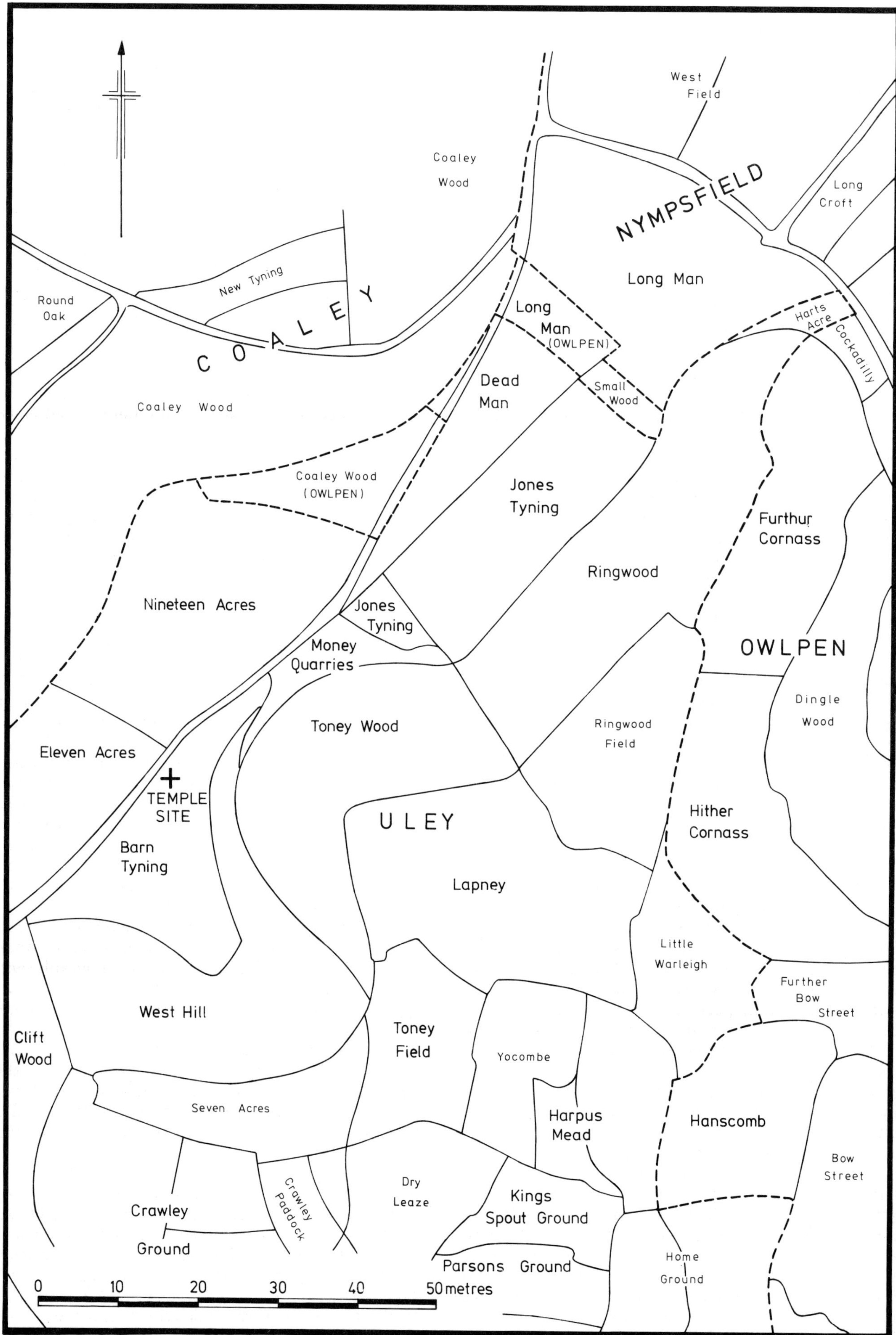

Fig 229 Uley: 16th-century topography

Appendix B

Saxon, medieval, and post-medieval Uley

by John Drinkwater

There are no references to Uley in the published Saxon charters. Prior to the Norman conquest the manor of Berkeley, of which Uley was a part, was the property of Edward the Confessor. At the conquest, it was seized by William I who rented the manor to Roger Berkeley. The first reference to Uley (Euulege) is in Domesday Book where it is shown as possessing two hides of land (Moore 1982).

From the 13th century Uley was divided between three separate manorial estates, White Court, Bassetts and Bencombe. White Court, the title of the original Berkeley manor of Uley, had been constructed soon after the conquest; its site at the western end of the modern village is still known as White Court (Fig 229). In 1240 a daughter of the Berkeley house, Margaret, married Sir Anslem Bassett. As her dowry she took to her husband half of the White Court manor to create Bassetts Manor. The site of the original house was below and to the east of the White Court on the opposite side of the road through the village. The White Court manor was sold by Richard Berkeley in 1566 to thirteen separate purchasers. Bassetts manor survived until 1780 when its lands were sold and dispersed.

The third manor, Bencombe lay in the south-eastern sector of the parish. Originally held by the de Uley family, an offshoot of Roger Berkeley I, this manor became de Bencombe by marriage in 1220. Bencombe Place, the capital mansion, formed the focus of a small manorial estate which later became the property of the Clavilles, then of the Dorney family. It remained intact until the last member of the family, Miss Elizabeth Dorney, died in 1846.

Between the conquest and the 16th century the references and records of Uley are fragmentary and dispersed. In 1639 John Smyth of Nibley compiled a History of the Hundred of Berkeley. This remained unpublished until 1883 (Smyth 1883–5). In that account each parish in the Berkeley holdings, including Uley and its surrounding parishes, has an entry which outlines its manorial structure, together with a list of pre 17th-century documentary references. Amongst these, Inquisitions post mortem, examinations conducted by representatives of the Crown after the death of tenants in chief, can provide useful background information, although their use as sources of place-names is limited. A typical example is the Inquisition held at Uley in 1312 on the death of Walter of Gloucester. He held extensive lands in Uley, some directly with his wife Hawise and some by tenants in villeinage. The document is predominantly a list of duties and dues owed by the tenants. Among the duties to be performed were ploughing, mowing and turning the lord's hay, with the provision of wheat at the winter sowing. The dues included cumin, corn, wheat, and the usual 'hen at Christmas'. Walter and Hawise held a house, garden and curtilage, together with a dovecot, directly from Thomas de Berkeley. It is tempting to regard this dovecot as the same (or the predecessor) of the White Court pigeon house purchased by Richard Payne in 1566 (Gloucestershire Record Office, D979 A T2). Three water mills are mentioned in the document, beech was the predominant woodland, and pasture land was worth eight times the value of arable.

Apart from two variant spellings of Uley (Yweleye, Ywel) no place or field names are mentioned. The document's value can only be fully exploited by contrast and comparison with other Inquisitions from Uley and its neighbouring parishes. Smyth drew much of his information from the Berkeley muniments. It would be from this archive, especially the court rolls of the Berkeley Hundred that information for the pre-Tudor parish might be obtained. A single published court roll for 1543 (Gloucestershire Notes and Queries, 1891–3, 88) illustrates the potential of such a source, providing six place-names and six personal names together with other information. In the absence of any estate survey or manorial plan, with the earliest detailed map of the parish being the 1838 tithe map, field or place-name evidence has to be gleaned from written sources. With the dismemberment of the White Court manor in 1566 and the subsequent numerous private land transactions a considerable volume of documentary material was generated. Fortunately much has survived, in the Gloucestershire Records Office. The Lloyd Baker collection (Gloucestershire Records Office, D3549) and the Daunt archives (Gloucestershire Records Office, D979) are two major sources for Uley. The majority of the indentures for the White Court manor sale in 1566 exist in the Kingscote collection (Gloucestershire Records Office, D471). Using these, together with later indentures and the tithe map, it is possible to construct a map of Uley for the 16th century on which the major fields can be shown (Fig 229). The place and field names for Uley have been published in the English Place-name Series (Smith 1965). Ten years' research into the Uley documents in the Gloucester Records Office however has considerably expanded the list given in that account, and has enabled most to be located in the parish.

Uley did not possess the normal three field common field system. The influence of uneven topography with interspersed streams and extreme variability in soil type produced a landscape of numerous, unevenly sized fields. The thin soils of the escarpment top were initially the rough grazing but by the 16th century were increasingly turned over to arable (Fig 229). The arable land lay predominantly on the higher slopes with permanent pasture occupying the lower wetter ground. A belt of beech wood hangers encircled most of the parish.

The largest arable field was West Field (Fig 229). It lay around Downham Hill bounded by Cames Brook on the west, the river Ewelme on the south and Dulkin Stream on the east. It was not a simple undifferentiated common field; prior to 1566 some enclosure had taken place especially around Wresden where a precursor to the later farm existed. To the north of West Field lay Hyde Field where early enclosure is evidenced by the mention of the New Tyning in the 1566 indentures. The arable field called Bircom or Birkem lay between the

Dulkin Stream and The Beyre (Uley Bury). To the west of White Court lay Shibley Field (the sheep ley or clearing) where early inclosure is indicated by a reference in 1543 to 'the hedge around le whete field in Shybley' and around Newbrooke the site of a later farm. Angeston (gerstun – the pasture or paddock) lay on the eastern side of Shibley Field.

To the south of Shibley's Brook (the modern River Ewelme) were the pasture fields of Lully (Lulla's ley) and Bynley (Beonna's ley). These were separated from the meadowland around Elcomb by a low ridge of drier, arable land called the Lynch (hlinc – a ridge). Shadwell (the shady well) formed the focus of a later small hamlet. The whole of the southern boundary of the parish lay inside a belt of woodland which ran from Waterley (now in the parish of North Nibley) through the Lye Wood to Owlpen. To the north of the arable Lye Field lay Bencomb which, until recent times retained an enclave of demesne land, arable, pasture and woodland. It is tempting to see Stouts Hill (from Adam le Stut 1214) as the focus of the area emparked by the early Berkeleys; a number of fields have the designation park incorporated in their field names. By 1566 enclosure had occurred with numerous references to 'the lands enclosed by the Carvers at Stouts Hill'. South-east of the village across the river, here called Netherfields Brook, lay the arable Netherfield. The former extent of this common field is difficult to determine. The western boundary lay in an area later called Great Grounds, which prior to the 19th century was divided into a number of personally named 'leazes'. One of these, Shills Leaze, on a map of the late 18th century, is almost certainly the lease of John Sheles, named as a lease holder in the Will of Richard Payne in 1588 (Gloucestershire Records Office 1588,155), again indicating early private land tenure. Evidence for a late assart in this area is provided by a reference in 1628 to Netherfield Stocking (the term stocking refers to tree stumps), presumably an area of woodland converted to arable land.

Above the village the ridge of Uley Bury hillfort, the Beyre dominates the landscape. Initially the interior of the fort was rough grazing, but by 1566 it had become arable land. Beech woods crowned the upper slopes of the Bury as hangers, the hanging lands, and quarries or 'gravell pitts' were cut into the face of the scarp. The lower slopes provided good arable land of which the field called Uleys Brideway is a frequently quoted example. The top of the escarpment at West Hill, the site of the Roman temple, had long been arable land. As will be discussed later, apart from the Deadman place or field names are scarce for this area. The dip in the escarpment between Uley Bury and West Hill gives its name to Crawleys Shard (sceard – a cleft or gap). Crawley Field (the crow's clearing) formed an area of arable land on the upper slopes of the valley. Along the base of the valley adjacent to the Owlpen boundary lay the pasture lands Smally, Lordsley and Warley all of which were separate fields by 1566. The later farmstead Mutteral Farm was created next to Plaincroft (Fig 229).

The River Ewelme (aewelm – a spring, source of a river) with its ancillary springs and streams has always been the economic heart of the parish. From the time when Uley – the yew tree clearing, was first settled it has provided water for the flocks which grazed Shibley, and a motive force for grist mills in the medieval period and for the post-medieval woollen industry (Smith 1965, 1, 7). Among the earliest records an Inquisition post mortem of 1312 includes a reference to a water mill, and later, in 1543, Roger Redying is named as the owner of a water corn mill. In the same document a reference to 'le Whetefield in Shybley' indicates corn was grown and 'le Chassenett', a net for taking crows, suggests either crop protection or a possible source of food. The keeping of pigeons and rabbits (coneys) provided a valuable supply of fresh meat in winter. The White Court manor pigeon house lay between the manor house and le Courte Garden, with the Coneygree or rabbit warren in the adjacent field. Fieldwalking of the Coneygree area in 1978 did not reveal any visible features. However the field survey indicated the survival of four pillow mounds (artificial rabbit warrens) on the north face of Downham Hill. This interpretation is confirmed by documentary sources, the Will of John Arundell in 1722 wherein 'my conigre' is given to his son John (Gloucestershire Record Office, D 2957.319.137) and a lease of 1739 which concerns 'Downham alias the Conigre and the house or lodge erected thereon' (Gloucestershire Record Office, D 2957.319.99). Although not stated, this lodge was probably for a warrener; no trace of any structure exists today. On the early Ordnance Survey maps Downham is named as Warren Hill.

In spite of the long tradition for Uley as a weaving centre few indentures before the late 18th century concern the sale or rent of mill buildings. The peak of industrial prosperity came during the 'golden years' of the woollen industry in the 18th century and a major rebuilding of the village can be ascribed to this time. The importance of weaving in the village is attested by a census in 1608 of all able bodied men, when 60% of the male inhabitants were weavers (Smyth 1608). Few tangible remains of the industry now remain. Most of the mills and their ancillary buildings have been demolished or converted to dwelling houses. A singular exception is the collection of buildings at Wresden Farm, the home of John Eyles 'the first that ever made Spanish cloth in this parish', where some original features are still visible. Numerous landscape features belonging to the former water regulation and management system: banks, leats, and mill ponds lie along the river valley south of the village. References to the river bank can be found in the indentures. As would be expected several fields in this area were entitled Rack Grounds.

By the 18th century most of the common fields were already subdivided into discrete parcels of land in private ownership and therefore the parish was not subject to parliamentary enclosure. The frequent references to 'tynings' in the 1566 indentures show that by this date the process of inclosure had started. With the sale of the White Court lands the rate of inclosure rapidly increased and indentures of exchange now occur. By these means a landowner exchanged strips or parcels of land in one field for land in another adjacent to his own, thereby providing a sufficient area of ground to be demarcated by a tyning hedge. By the late 17th century personalised tyning place names have been ascribed to these new fields, often with their boundaries defined by a 'new quick sett hedge'.

The modern parish of Uley is homogeneous in composition in that all the land within the parish boundary belongs to the parish. However this has not always been the case. The 1838 tithe map (Gloucestershire Record Office, T1/187) shows a number of fields, some deep within the parish which belonged to neighbouring parishes. Probably a similar situation existed at Uley with its fields lying inside other parishes, although examination of the tithe maps of the surrounding parishes does not indicate the presence of Uley land within them by 1840. In 1312 a reference to 'salt meadows' as part of the Uley holdings of Walter of Gloucester must refer to land outside the parish nearer the Severn, likewise the early indentures list woodland 'situate at Waterly in Uley'. At the present time Waterley lies in the parish of North Nibley, outside the south-western edge of the Uley boundary.

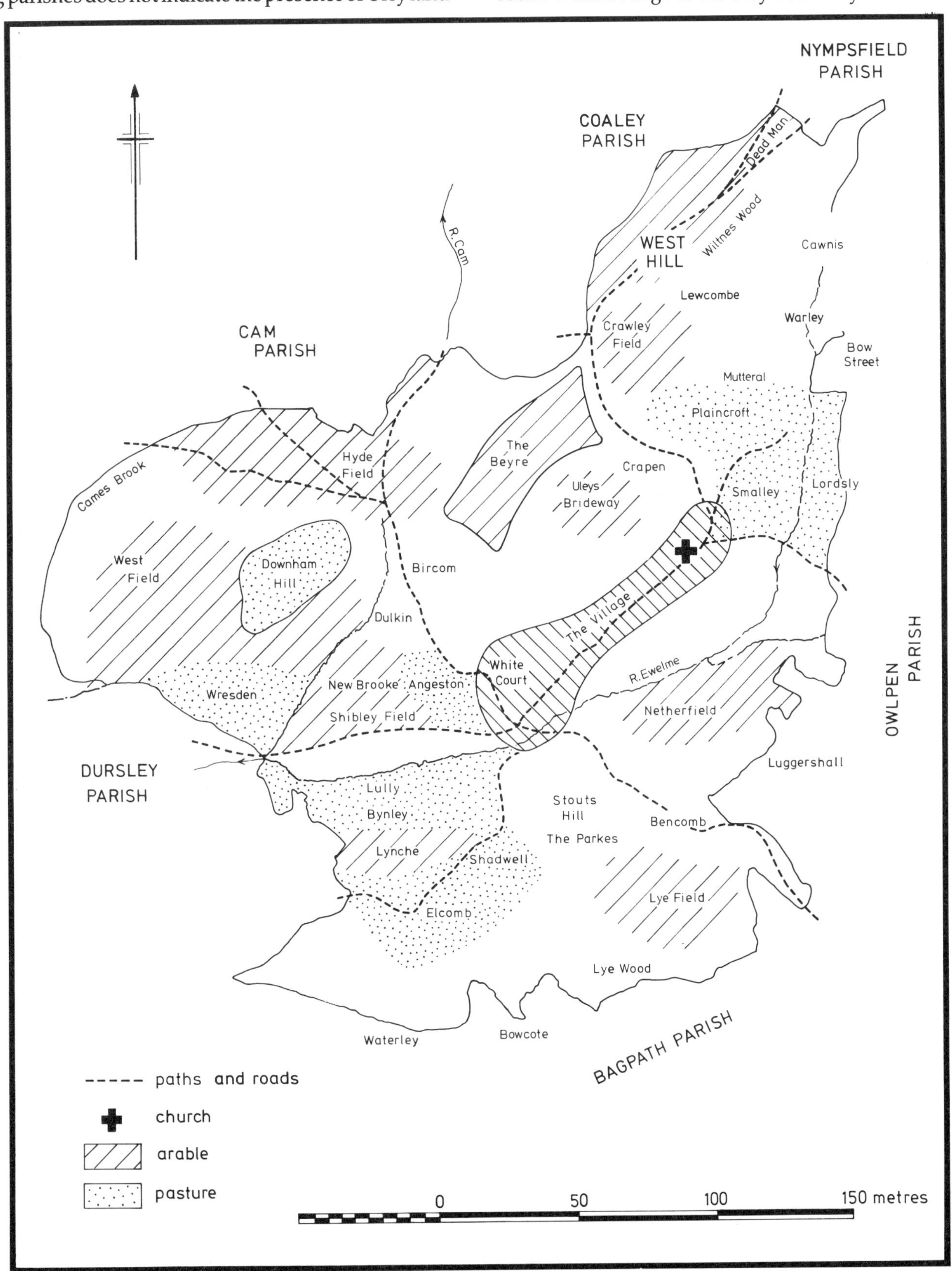

Fig 230 Tithe map, field and place names, 1838

The Uley-Owlpen boundary is discontinuous on the tithe map (Fig 230). Alternate fields lie in one parish or the other, a confusion echoed in the indentures where the phrase 'situate in Uley or in Owlpen' often occurs. A similar indented boundary existed between Uley and Cam. Even in the region of a finite natural boundary, such as is provided by the River Ewelme between Uley and Dursley, a few detached fields across the river occurred. In the absence of early charters or maps, definite boundary points are difficult to establish. The indentures make no reference to the parish boundary even if the strip or field abuts it. On the rare occasion a careful interpretation of the information provided by a sequence of indentures may indicate a precise location for a lost feature. For instance the Richard Payne indenture of 1566, in reference to a parcel of wood in Hyde Cliffe, gives the location as 'shooting southward to the upper ditches of the Bearye and extending eastwards to the Gospel place'. A subsequent indenture for the same parcel of wood provides an additional piece of information'... extending eastward to the Crossways, formerly called the Gospel Place'. The Crossways was the place where the former Uley-Coaley and Nympsfield-Dursley roads crossed at Crawleys Shard (ST 628994) on the Uley-Coaley boundary. The path leading along the boundary was called the Gospel Way and the Gospel place is almost certainly the spot at where the gospel was expounded during the ceremony of 'beating the bounds' (the term Gospel is found in common usage in this context, Smith 1965, 4 201). Above Crawley, on the escarpment where the temple site lies, the parish of Uley narrows to a point thrusting towards Nympsfield (Fig 230). The general name for this region in the medieval period was West Hill, which is inconsistent with regard to both the village and parish of Uley and is more correctly the West Hill of Nympsfield. In the 16th century indentures West Hill is sometimes given an alias 'Bald Hill' and this designation was probably the name commonly used by the Uley parishioners. The probability that West Hill owes its allegiance to Nympsfield rather than Uley is strengthened by considering the origins of the place name Nympsfield. Smith sees its derivation as the tract of open country belonging to a place called Nymed, where *nymed* is the Celtic word for a shrine, sacred grove or holy place (Smith 1965, 2 244). With the continuity of sanctity established for the temple, its predecessor and successors, the probability that its site was the *nymed* would seem almost certain.

The late 18th century probably represents the apogee of the subdivision of the former common fields into small individually-owned parcels of land. Over 200 fields are shown on the tithe map, many of which are less than five acres in extent and only a few as large as 15 acres. The name of each field in the parish is provided in the accompanying apportionment, together with the area and condition of the parcel. A list of most of these names has been published, with an interpretation of their derivation (Smith, 1965). The wealth of documentary material for Uley, held in the Gloucester Records Office, has provided both a considerable number of additional field names and allowed the vagaries of phonological and literary influences to be studied. Using the tithe map, in conjunction with the other sources it is possible to examine the West Hill region and attempt an interpretation of the place/field name evidence (Fig 230). The map of West Hill and its surrounding area has been derived from the tithe maps of Uley, Coaley, Nympsfield and Owlpen. By 1838 West Hill is the name of a single field situated on the slope of the escarpment, below Barn Tyning, which covers the site of the temple. Previously, West Hill was the name applied to all the land in this area including the modern fields called the Eleven Acres, Nineteen Acres, Barn Tyning, Money Quarries, Jones Tyning and West Hill itself. With the notable exception of Hetty Pegler's Tump, referred to as 'the barrowe on West Hill' from 1566 onwards, there is a distinct absence of localised places or field names in this area prior to the late 18th century. Uncharacteristically the indentures are non-specific in details of the location of parcels of land with expressions such as 'several parcels of arable land, by estimation 40 acres on West Hill' (1670). This may indicate a late date for the breaking up of a commonly held area of land. Disputes over common rights, in this case the depasturing of sheep on the hill, were occurring as late as 1794. The testimony of four septuagenarian inhabitants indicated that although the land on the top of the hill was freehold it was unfenced, and that during their lifetimes two flocks at a time were frequently allowed to depasture thereon (Gloucestershire Record Office, D 471.T 63). The suggestion of continued commonality is supported by the earlier field names. Both Deadman and Long Man may derive from (ge)maene, Old English for common or communal (Smith 1965, 4 153) and the three fields Deadman (Uley), Long Man (Owlpen) and Long Man (Nympsfield), are adjacent to one another and could represent the vestiges of an area of common land shared between the three parishes. With the long-established sanctity of the temple site demonstrated, it is possible that this could represent a focal place with an area of 'no man's land' surrounding it. The name Money Quarries may refer to the finding of Roman coins immediately north of the temple site.

A belt of woodland lay along the southern slope of the escarpment from Ringwood through Toney wood to Crawleys Clift wood. The early indentures provide a generic name for this woodland, variously Wiltness (1566), Wilkness (1655) or Wilderness (1820). Below the wood lay a common arable field called Lewcomb in 1566 and later occupied by Lapney and Toney Field. The place name Toney would appear to be of recent origin; there are no references to it before the late 18th century, and it derives probably from a local personal name (Smith 1965, 3 167). This area contains a number of personalised field names from the post-medieval period, Kings Spout Ground, Jones Tyning and Harpus Mead, a corruption of Harpers land. The Parsons Ground, next to Crawley, is a long-standing parcel of glebe land. Running along the base of the valley lay a complex of small pasture fields, Warleigh, Yocombe, and Crawley, whose names indicate pre-medieval origins. Across the parish boundary in Owlpen the two Cornass fields probably derive their names from Cawnis (1670, Fig 230), or originally Calueness (*c* 1250) the calf headland (Smith 1965, 2 245). Hanscombe was previously Homescombe (1676) and would correspond with the adjacent Home Ground.

The present-day field pattern of the parish is essentially that shown on the tithe map. The major change in the landscape lies in the considerable increase in the area of pasture land. Prior to this century a considerable proportion of the parish was arable land, in sharp contrast to the picture presented by the 1939 land utilisation map (sheet 103) where only a small area of arable is indicated. A superficial examination of the Uley landscape during the early months of the year would indicate a fair number of fields under the plough, but this would lead to an entirely erroneous assumption that widespread arable husbandry is being practised. Many of these fields are permanent pasture, the quality of which is improved by occasional ploughing. This practice has caused the insidious erosion of most low-profile field monuments. Only two fields, Uleys Brideway and Plaincroft, retain visible remains of the ridge and furrow which once would have been widespread throughout the parish. Apart from the features associated with the water management system, few other field monuments have survived. A scatter of denuded lynchets lie along the interface between the cultivated land and the rise of the scarp slopes; the most obvious examples are beneath Crawleys Shard and below the south face of Downham Hill. One lynchet of considerable proportions delineates the field called Castle Vernals (the Castle Furlong/Acre in 1566) south of Shadwell.

A fine set of strip lynchets are cut into the south-eastern edge of Cam Long Down just outside the parish on the northern side. No such features exist inside Uley but the medieval indentures indicate that the terraces around the Bury were cultivated. The lower slopes of the Bury and Bury Bower have been quarried extensively, obscuring any pre-19th-century features. Likewise the edge of the field called Great Grounds next to the river shows a number of features which look like old quarries.

In summary, apart from Uley Bury and Hetty Pegler's Tump, the parish is devoid of upstanding ancient field monuments. Apart from the escarpment top there is a noticeable paucity of both prehistoric and Roman find spots within the parish. It is probable that this condition could be remedied by a comprehensive air photographic survey of the parish, coupled with a programme of systematic field walking.

Appendix C

Illustrations of animal bones referred to in fiche

Fig 231 Goat horncore with large notch-like depression. (Photo: Bruce Levitan)

Fig 232 Goat radii: greenstick fracture (top), compound fracture (middle). normal (bottom). (Photo: Bruce Levitan)

Fig 233 Two goat metacarpals with additional bone growth along shaft, suggestive of tethering. (Photo: Bruce Levitan)

Bibliography

All Ancient Monuments Laboratory reports related to the site have been included below even if not cited in the text or fiche

Alcock, L, 1972 *By South Cadbury is that Camelot: The excavation of Cadbury Castle 1968–70*

Allason-Jones, L, and McKay, B, 1985 *Coventina's Well. A shrine on Hadrian's Wall*, Chesters Museum

——, and Miket, R, 1984 *The catalogue of small finds from South Shields Roman fort*, Soc Antiq Newcastle upon Tyne Mono **2**, Newcastle upon Tyne

Allen, D F, 1961 A study of the Dobunnic coinage, in Clifford, E, M, (ed) *Bagendon: a Belgic oppidum. A record of the excavations 1954–6*, 75–146, Cambridge

Ancient Monument Lab Rep 2879 David, A, 1979, *Geophysics: West Hill, Uley Gloucs*

—— 3340 Bell, M, 1981, *Preliminary examination of soil samples from the Romano-British temple, West Hill, Uley*

—— 3377 Girling, M, 1981, *Interim report on the anthropod remains from West Hill, Uley*

—— 3389 Bell, M, 1981, *Geological specimens from Uley*

—— 25/87 Bayley, J, 1987, *Metalworking evidence from West Hull, Uley*

—— 65/87 ——, 1987, *Qualitative analyses of bracelets and rings from West Hill, Uley*

—— 85/87 ——, 1987, *Analytical results for the brooches from West Hill, Uley*

—— 39/88 Roe, F, 1988, *Worked stone from West Hill, Uley*

—— 117/88 Bayley, J, 1988, *Qualitative analysis of figurines from West Hill, Uley*

—— 45/89 Girling, M, and Straker, V, 1989, *Plant macrofossils, arthropods, and charcoal from West Hill, Uley*

—— 53/89 Heyworth, M P, 1989, *Analysis of window glass from West Hill, Uley*

—— 10/93 Meddens, B, 1993, *West Hill, Uley: snail report*

Anderson, A S, 1979 *The Roman pottery industry in north Wiltshire*, Swindon Archaeol Soc Rep **2**

Andrews, J, and Noddle, B, 1975 Absence of premolar teeth from ruminant mandibles found at archaeological sites, *J Archaeol Sci* **2**, 137–44

Apicius, *The art of cookery* (see *The Roman cookery book, a critical translation of 'The art of cooking' by Apicius, for use in the study and the kitchen* trans Flower, B, and Rosenbaum, E, 1958)

Apsimon, A M, *et al*, 1961 The stratigraphy and archaeology of the late glacial and post-glacial deposits on Brean Down, Somerset, *Proc Univ Bristol Spelaeol Soc* **9**, 67–136

——, 1965 The Roman temple on Brean Down, Somerset, *Proc Univ Bristol Spelaeol Soc* **10.3**, 195–258

Armitage, P L, 1977 The mammalian remains from the Tudor site of Baynard's Castle, London: a biometrical and historical analysis, unpubl PhD thesis, Univ London

Ashbee, P, 1970 *The earthen long barrow in Britain*

Atkinson, D, 1916 *The Romano-British site on Lowbury Hill in Berkshire*, Reading

—— 1942 *Excavations at Wroxeter 1923–7*, Oxford

Atkinson, R J C, 1965 Wayland's Smithy, *Antiquity* **39**, 126–33

Audollent, A, 1904 *Defixionum Tabellae*, Paris

Babelon, E, 1916 *Le Trésor d'Argenterie de Berthouville près Bernay (Eure)*, Paris

Baker, J, and Brothwell, D, 1980 *Animal diseases in archaeology*

Bang, P, and Dahlstrom, P, 1972 *Animal tracks and signs*

Bathurst, W H, and King, C W, 1879 *Roman antiquities at Lydney Park, Gloucestershire*

La Baume, P, 1977 Signumsheibe und Merkurrelief von Niederbieber, *Bonner Jahrbüch* **177**, 565–8

Bayley, J, 1985 What's what in ancient technology: an introduction to high temperature processes, in Phillips, P, ed, *The archaeologist and the laboratory*, Counc Brit Archaeol Res Rep **58**, 41–4

——, 1987 The examination of enamelled objects, in Bacon L, and Knight, B, eds, *From pinheads to hanging bowls*, UKIC Occ Pap **7**, 8–9

——, 1990 The production and use of brass in antiquity – with particular reference to Britain, in Craddock, P T, ed, *2000 years of zinc and brass*, Brit Mus Occ Pap, **50**, 7–27

——, forthcoming The brooch analyses, in Darling, M J, with Gurney, D, *Caister-on-Sea: Excavations by Charles Green 1951–5* E Anglian Archaeol Mono

——, and Butcher, S, 1981 Variations in alloy composition of Roman brooches, *Revue d'Archéométrie* supp, 29–36

——, and ——, forthcoming Romano-British plate brooches: their composition and decoration, *Jewellery Stud* **3**

——, ——, and Cross, I, 1980 The analysis of Roman brooches from Richborough Fort, Kent, in Slater, E A, and Tate, J O, eds, *Proc 16th Internat Symposium on Archaeometry*, 239–47, Edinburgh

Beasley, M J, Brown, V A, and Legge, A J, 1987 Ageing cattle by their teeth, *Ark* **14.1**, 22–4

Beck, F, Menu, M, Berthoud, T, and Hurtel, L-P, 1985 Metallurgie des Bronzes, *Recherches Gallo-Romaines* **1**, 69–139

Bedwin, O R, 1980 Excavations at Chanctonbury Ring, Wiston, West Sussex, 1977, *Britannia* **11**, 173–222

Bell, M, 1990 *Brean Down: excavations 1983–7*, HBMC Archaeol Rep **15**

Bell, R D, Beresford, M W, *et al* 1987 *Wharram Percy: the Church of St Martin*, Soc Med Archaeol Mono **11**

Bennett, J, 1980 *A Romano-British settlement at Cattybrook*, Com Rescue Archaeol in Avon Gloucester and Somerset, Occ Pap **5**

Bertin, D, 1977 Le Sanctuaire Celto-Romain du Mesnil de Baron-sur-Odon (Calvados), *Gallia* **35**, 75–88

Biddle, M, and Hunter, J R, 1990 Early medieval window glass, in Biddle, M, ed, *The craft industries, art, and daily life in early Winchester*, Winchester Stud **7.2**

Bidwell, P T, 1979 *The Legionary bath-house, basilica and forum at Exeter*, Exeter Archaeol Rep **1**

——, 1985 *The Roman fort of Vindolanda at Chesterholm, Northumberland*, HBMC Archaeol Rep **1**

Bieber, M, 1977 *Ancient copies. Contributions to the history of Greek and Roman art*, New York

Birley, R, 1973 Vindolanda – Chesterholm 1969–72, some important material from the vicus, *Archaeol Aeliana*, 4 Ser **51**, 111–22

Blockley, K, 1985 *Marshfield: Ironmongers Piece excavations 1982–3*, Brit Archaeol Rep **141**, Oxford

Boddington, A, 1980 A Christian Anglo-Saxon graveyard at Raunds, Northamptonshire, in Rahtz, P, Dickinson, T, and Watts, L, eds, *Anglo-Saxon Cemeteries 1979*, Brit Archaeol Rep **82**, 373–8, Oxford

Boessneck, J A, Muller, H-H, and Teichert, M, 1964 Unterscheidungsmerkmale zwischen schaf u ziege, *Kuhn-Archiv* **78.1–2**, 1–129

Boesterd, M H P den, 1956 *Description of the collections of the Rijksmuseum G M Kam at Nijmegen 5: the bronze vessels*, Nijmegen

Böhme, A, 1972 Die Fibeln der Kastelle Saalburg und Zugmantel, *Saalburg Jahrbuch* **29** 5–112

Boon, G C, 1966 Roman window glass from Wales, *J Glass Stud* **8**, 41–5

——, 1969 Belgic and Roman Silchester: The excavations of 1954–8, *Archaeologia* **102**, 1–81

——, 1974 *Silchester: the Roman town of Calleva*

——, 1979 Wookey Four cemetery, a description of the finds, *Proc Univ Bristol Spelaeol Soc* **15**, no 1, 39–48

——, and Savory, H N, 1975 A silver trumpet-brooch from Carmarthen, *Antiq J* **55**, 41–61

Booth, P M, forthcoming The pottery, in *Excavations at Coleshill Warks*

——, and Green, S 1989 The nature and distribution of certain pink grog tempered vessels, *J Roman Pottery Stud* **2**, 77–84

Boucher, S, 1976 *Recherches sur les bronzes figures de Gaule Pre-Romaine et Romaine*, Ecole Francaise de Rome

Bourdillon, J, and Coy, J, 1980 The animal bones, in Holdsworth, P, ed, *Excavations at Melbourne Street, Southampton 1971–6*, Counc Brit Archaeol Res Rep **33**, 79–137

Bradley, R, and Holgate, R, 1984 The Neolithic sequence in the Upper Thames Valley, in Bradley R, and Gardiner J, eds, *Neolithic Studies*, Brit Archaeol Rep **133**, Oxford 107–34

Brailsford, J W, 1962 *Antiquities from Hod Hill in the Durden collection*, Hod Hill **1**, British Museum

Branigan, K, 1977 *Gatcombe Roman villa*, Brit Archaeol Rep, Brit Ser **44**, Oxford

Braun-Blanquet, J, and Tüxen, R, 1952 Irische Pflanzenge sellschaften, in Ludi, W, ed, Die Pflanzenwelt Irlands, *Veröff, Geobot Inst Rübel* **25**, 224–421

Brickstock, R, 1987 *Copies of the* Fel Temp Reparatio *coinage in Britain*, Brit Archaeol Rep, Brit Ser **176**, Oxford

Brighton, T, and Newton, R, 1986 William Peckitt's red glasses, *Stained Glass Quarterly* **81**, 213–20

British Museum Catalogue 1958 *Guide to the antiquities of Roman Britain*

Brothwell, D R, 1972 *Digging up bones*

——, 1979 Roman evidence of a crested form of domestic fowl, as indicated by a skull showing associated cerebral hernia, *J Archaeol Sci* **6**, 291–3

Brown, P D C, 1971 The church at Richborough, *Britannia* **2**, 225–31

Brown, R A, 1986 The Iron Age and Romano-British settlement at Woodcock Hall, Saham Toney, Norfolk, *Britannia* **17**, 1–58

Bulleid, A, and Gray, H St G, 1917 *The Glastonbury lake village vol 2*, Glastonbury

Burstow and Holleyman, 1957 Excavations at Muntham Court, Findon, Sussex, *Archaeol News Letter* **6**, no 4, 101–2

Buschhausen, H, 1971 *Die Spätrömischen Metallscrinia und Frühchristlichen Reliquiare 1 Teil: Katalog*, Wiener Byzantinistische Studien **9**, Vienna

Bushe-Fox, J P, 1913 *First report on the excavations of the site of the Roman town at Wroxeter, Shropshire*, Res Rep Soc Antiq of London **1**

——,1914 *Second report on the excavations of the site of the Roman town at Wroxeter, Shropshire*, Res Rep Soc Antiq of London **2**

——,1932 *Third report on the excavations of the Roman Fort at Richborough, Kent*, Oxford

——,1949 *Fourth report on the excavations of the Roman Fort at Richborough, Kent*, Res Rep Soc Antiq of London **16**

Butcher, S A, 1977 Enamels from Roman Britain, in Apted, M, Gilyard-Beer, R, and Saunders, A D, eds, *Ancient monuments and their interpretation*, 40–70

——, 1978 Excavations at Nornour, Isles of Scilly 1969–73, *Cornish Archaeol* **17**, 29–112

Carey, G, 1982 Ageing and sexing domestic bird bones from some late medieval deposits at Baynards Castle, City of London, in Wilson B, *et al*, eds, 263–8

Carlyon, P M, 1987 Finds from the earthwork at Carvossa, Probus, *Cornish Archaeol* **26**, 103–41

Carruthers, W J, forthcoming The mineralised plant remains from Potterne, Wilts

Carver, M O H, 1979 Training excavation, Coleshill, Warwickshire, *Birmingham Univ Field Archaeol Rep* **2**, 22

Chaplin, R, 1971 *The study of animal bones from archaeological sites*

Charlesworth, D, 1972 The glass, in Frere, S S, 1972, 196–215

Charlton, J, 1934 Small objects from Housesteads and other sites, *Archaeol Aeliana*, 4 Ser **11**, 185–205

CIL *Corpus Inscriptionum Latinarum*, 1863, Berlin

Clapham, *et al* 1962 *Flora of the British Isles*, Cambridge

Clarke, G, 1979 *Pre-Roman and Roman Winchester part II: The Roman cemetery at Lankhills*, Winchester Stud **3**, Oxford

Clifford, E M, 1937 The Beaker folk in the Cotswolds, *Proc Prehist Soc* **3**, 159–63

——, 1938 The soldier's grave, Frocester, Gloucestershire, *Proc Prehist Soc* **4**, 214–17

——, 1939 Roman altars in Gloucestershire, *Trans Bristol and Gloucestershire Archaeol Soc* **60**, 297–307

——, 1961 *Bagendon: A Belgic Oppidum*, Cambridge

——, 1966 Hetty Pegler's Tump, *Antiquity* **40**, 129–32

Clutton-Brock, J, 1981 *Domesticated animals from early times*

Comstock, M B, and Vermeule, C C, 1976 *Sculpture in stone: the Greek, Roman, and Etruscan collections of the Museum of Fine Arts, Boston*, Boston

Cook, A, and Dacre, M, 1985 *Excavations at Portway, Andover, 1973–5*, Oxford Univ Comm Archaeol Mono **4**

Cole, H, 1966 Analyses and discussion of the Caerleon window glass, *J Glass Stud* **8**, 46–7

Colyer, C, and Jones M J, 1979 Excavations at Lincoln, second interim report: Excavations in the lower town 1972–8, *Antiq J* **59**, 50–91

Condamin, J, and Boucher, S, 1973 Recherches techniques sur des bronzes de Gaule Romaine, IV, *Gallia* **31**, 157–83

Cool, H E M, and Price, J, forthcoming a *The Roman glass from excavations in Colchester, 1971–85*

——, and ——, forthcoming b The Roman glass, in Webster G, *Excavations at Wroxeter*

——, and ——, forthcoming c *The glass from the Romano-British villa at Atworth, Wiltshire*

Craddock, P T, 1978 The composition of the copper alloys used by the Greek, Etruscan, and Roman civilisations 3: The origins and early use of brass, *J Archaeol Sci* **5.1**, 1–16

Cram, L, and Fulford, M, 1979 Silchester tile making – the faunal environment, in McWhirr, A, ed, *Roman brick and tile. Studies in manufacture, distribution, and use in the western Empire*, Brit Archaeol Rep, Internat Ser **68**, 201–9, Oxford

Cramp, R, 1970a Glass finds from the Anglo-Saxon monastery of Monkwearmouth and Jarrow, in Charleston, R J, *et al* eds, *Studies in glass history and design: papers read to committee B sessions of the 8th international congress on glass, held in London 1st–6th July 1968*, 16–19

——, 1970b Decorated window-glass and millefiori from Monkwearmouth, *Antiq J* **50**, 327–35

——, 1975 Window glass from the monastic site of Jarrow: problems of interpretation, *J Glass Stud* **17**, 88–96

Crawford, O G S, 1925 *Long barrows of the Cotswolds*, Gloucester

Crummy, N, 1983 *The Roman small finds from excavations in Colchester 1971–9*, Colchester

Crummy, P, 1980 The temples of Roman Colchester, in Rodwell 1980, 243–84

CSEL 3, 1868 *Corpus Scriptorum Ecclesiasticorum Latinorum*, **3** *Cypriani Opera*, Hartel, W, ed, Vienna

Cunliffe, B W, 1964 *Winchester Excavations 1949–60* **1**, Winchester

——, 1968 *Fifth report on the excavation of the Roman fort at Richborough, Kent*, Res Rep Soc Antiq of London **23**,

——, 1971 *Excavations at Fishbourne 1961–9*, Res Rep Soc Antiq of London **27**

——, 1974 *Iron Age communities in Britain*

——, 1984 *Danebury: an Iron Age hillfort in Hampshire. Vol 1, the excavations 1969–78: the site. Vol 2, the finds*, Counc Brit Archaeol Res Rep **52**

——, ed, 1988 *The temple of Sulis Minerva at Bath, vol 2: finds from the sacred spring*, Oxford

——, and Davenport, P, 1985 *The temple of Sulis Minerva at Bath, vol 1(1): the site*, Oxford

——, and Fulford, M H, 1982 *Corpus Signorum Imperii Romani: Great Britain 1,2, Bath and the rest of Wessex*

Curle, J, 1911 *A Roman frontier post and its people: the fort of Newstead*, Glasgow

Darvill, T, 1982 *The Neolithic chambered tombs of the Cotswold-Severn region*, Highworth

——, 1987 *Prehistoric Gloucestershire*, Gloucester

Davies, J G, 1964 Baptismal architecture, in Lockett, W E A, ed, *The modern architectural setting of the liturgy. Papers read at a conference held in Liverpool, September 1962*, 1–12

Debnath, R, and Das, S K, 1986 Photo-luminescence and the structure of colour centers in the copper-ruby glass, in *Collected papers of the 14th International Congress on Glass, 1986, New Delhi, India* **1**, 220–6

De Boe, G, 1982 Le Sanctuaire Gallo-Romain dans la plaine de Bieure a Matagne-la-Petite, *Archaeologia Belgica* **251**, Brussels

Déchelette, J, 1904 *Les Vases Céramiques Ornés de la Gaul Romaine* **2**, Paris

Deniz, E, and Payne, S, 1982 Eruption and wear in the mandibular dentition as a guide to ageing Turkish goats, in Wilson B, *et al* eds, 155–206

Deonna, W, 1912 *L'Archéologie sa valeur, ses Méthodes, I*, Paris

Devizes Museum, 1934 *Catalogue of antiquities in the museum of the Wiltshire Archaeol and Natur Hist Soc at Devizes*, second edition, Devizes

Dixon, P W, 1979 A Neolithic and Iron Age site on a hilltop in Southern England, *Scientific American* **241.5**, 142–50

——, 1988 Crickley Hill 1969–87 *Current Archaeol* **110**, 73–8

Dollfuss, M A, 1973 Catalogue des fibules de bronze Gallo-Romaines de Haute-Normandie, *Mémoires de l'Académie de l'Institut de France* **16**, 9–261

Donovan, H E, 1938 Adlestrop Hill barrow, Gloucestershire, *Trans Bristol and Gloucestershire Archaeol Soc* **60**, 152–64

Dove, S, 1981 Conservation of glass-inlaid bronze and lead curses from Uley, Gloucestershire, *The Conservator* **5**, 31–5

Down, A, 1979 *Chichester Excavations* **4**, Chichester

Downey, R, King, A, and Soffe, G, 1980 The Hayling Island temple and religious connections across the Channel, in Rodwell, W J, ed, 289–304

Dreisch, A, von den, 1976 *A guide to the measurement of animal bones from archaeological sites*, Peabody Mus Bull **1**, Harvard

Drew, C D, and Piggott, S, 1936 The Excavation of long barrow 163a on Thickthorn Down, Dorset, *Proc Prehist Soc* **2**, 77–96

Driver, J C, 1982 Medullary bone as an indicator of sex in bird remains from archaeological sites, in Wilson B, *et al* eds, 251–4

Drury, P J, 1980 Non-classical religious buildings in Iron Age and Roman Britain: a review, in Rodwell, W J, ed, 45–78

Duran, A, *et al* 1984 Study of the colouring process in copper ruby glass by optical and ESR spectroscopy, *J Materials Sci* **19**, 1468–76

Elcook, W D, 1975 *The Romance languages*

Ellis, P, 1987 Sea Mills, Bristol: the 1965–8 excavations in the Roman town of Abonae, *Trans Bristol and Gloucestershire Archaeol Soc* **105**, 1987, 15–108

Ellison, A B, 1978 *Excavations at West Hill, Uley: 1977, the Romano-British temple*, Com Rescue Archaeol in Avon Gloucestershire and Somerset, Occ Pap **3**, Bristol

——, 1980 Natives, Romans and Christians on West Hill, Uley: an interim report on the excavation of a ritual complex of the 1st millennium AD, in Rodwell, W J, ed, 305–28

——, and Henig, M, 1981 Head of Mercury from Uley, Gloucestershire, *Antiquity* **55**, 43–4

Espérandieu, E, 1922 *Recueil général des bas-reliefs, statues et bustes de la Gaule Romaine* **8**, Paris

Ettlinger, E, 1973 *Die römischen Fibeln in der Schweiz*, Berne

Evans J G, 1972 *Land snails in archaeology*

Ewbank, J M, Phillipson, D W, and Whitehouse, R D, 1964 Sheep from the Iron Age: a method of study, *Proc Prehist Soc* **30**, 423–6

Exner, K, 1939 Die provinzialrömischen emailfibeln der Rheinlande **29** *Bericht der Römisch-Germanischen Kommission*, 31–121

Eygun, F, 1968 Les secrets de Civaux, *Archéologia* **21**, 79–83

Faider-Feytmans, G, 1979 *Les bronzes Romains de Belgique*, Mainz

Fleischer, R, 1967 *Die Römischen Bronzen aus Osterreich*, Mainz

Fleming, A, 1973 Tombs for the living, *Man* New Ser **8**, 177–93

France, N E, and Gobel, B M, 1985 *The Romano-British temple at Harlow, Essex*, West Essex Archaeol Group

Frayn, J M, 1984 *Sheep rearing and the wool trade in Italy during the Roman period*, Liverpool

Frere, S S, 1972 *Verulamium excavations vol I*, Res Rep Soc Antiq of London **28**

——, 1975 The Silchester Church: The excavation by Sir Ian Richmond in 1961, *Archaeol J* **105**, 277–302

Fulford, M G, 1971 The coarse pottery, in Cunliffe, B, 1971, 158-259

——, 1975 *New Forest Roman pottery: manufacture and distribution, with a corpus of the pottery types*, Brit Archaeol Rep **17**, Oxford

Giacchero, M, ed, 1974 *Edictum Diocletiani et Collegarum de pretiis rerum venalium*, Genoa

Gilbert, H M, 1978 The Felmingham Hall hoard, Norfolk, *Bull Board Celtic Stud* **28.1**, 159–87

Girling, M A, 1979 Calcium carbonate-replaced arthropods from archaeological deposits, *J Archaeol Sci* **6**, 309–20

Goodburn, R, 1976 *The Roman villa, Chedworth*

Gracie, H S, 1970 Frocester Court Roman Villa; first report, *Trans Bristol and Gloucestershire Archaeol Soc* **89**, 15–86

——, and Price, E G, 1979 Frocester Court Roman villa; second report, 1968–77: the courtyard, *Trans Bristol and Gloucestershire Archaeol Soc* **97**, 9–64

Grant, A, 1975a The animals bones in Cunliffe, B, ed, *Excavations at Porchester Castle, vol 1, Roman*, Res Rep Soc Antiq of London **32**, 378–408,

——, 1975b The use of tooth wear as a guide to the age of domestic animals – a brief explanation, in Cunliffe, B, ed, *Excavations at Porchester Castle, vol 1, Roman*, Res Rep Soc Antiq of London **32**, 437–50

——, 1978 Variation in dental attrition in mammals and its relevance to age estimation, in Brothwell, D R, *et al*, eds, *Research problems in zooarchaeology*, Inst Archaeol Occ Bull **3**, 103–6

——, 1982 The use of tooth wear as a guide to the age of domestic ungulates, in Wilson B, *et al*, eds, 91–108

Gray, H, St G, and Bulleid, A, 1953 *The Meare lake village, vol 2*, Taunton

Green, C S, 1987 *Excavations at Poundbury, vol 1: the settlements*, Dorchester

Green, F, 1979 Phosphatic mineralisation of seeds from archaeological sites, *J Archaeol Sci* **6**, 279–84

Green, H S, 1984 Flint arrowheads: typology and interpretation, *Lithics* **5**, 19–39

Green, M J, 1975 Romano-British non-ceramic model objects in south-east Britain, *Archaeol J* **82**, 54–70

——, 1976 *The religions of civilian Roman Britain*, Brit Archaeol Rep **24**, Oxford

——, 1977 Theriomorphism, in Munby, J, and Henig, M, eds, *Roman life and art in Britain*, Brit Archaeol Rep, Brit Ser **41.2**, 297–326, Oxford

——, 1978 *Small cult objects from the military areas of Roman Britain*, Brit Archaeol Rep, Brit Ser **52**, Oxford

——, 1986 *The gods of the Celts*, Gloucester

Green, S, forthcoming in Allen, T, *Excavations at Rough Ground Farm, Lechlade by M U Jones*

Greene, K T, 1978 Imported fine wares in Britain to AD 250: a guide to identification, in Arthur, P, and March, G, eds, *Early fine wares in Roman Britain*, Brit Archaeol Rep, Brit Ser **57**, Oxford 15–30

Greenfield, E, 1963 The Romano-British shrines at Brigstock, Northants, *Antiq J* **43**, 228–59

Greig, J, 1983 Plant foods in the past: review of the evidence from northern Europe, *J Plant Foods* **5**, 179–214

——, 1984 The palaeoecology of some British hay meadow types, in van Zeist, W, and Casparie, W A, eds, *Plants and ancient man*, 213–26, Rotterdam

Grimes, W F, 1930 Pottery and tilery of the XXth Legion at Holt, *Y Cymrodor* **41**

——, 1961 Draughton, Colsterworth and Heathrow, in Frere, S S, ed, *Problems of the Iron Age in Southern Britain*

Guido, M, 1978 *The glass beads of the prehistoric and Roman periods in Britain and Ireland*

——, Henderson, *et al*, 1984 A Bronze Age glass bead from Wilsford, Wiltshire: Barrow G.42 in the Lake Group, *Proc Prehist Soc* **50**, 245–54

Guisan, M, 1975 Bijoux romains d'Avenches, *Bull de l'Association pro Aventico* **23**, 5–39

Gurney, D, 1986 Settlement, religion, and industry on the Fenedge; three Romano-British sites in Norfolk, *E Anglian Archaeol* **31**

Halstead, P, Hodder, I, and Jones, G, 1978 Behavioural archaeology and refuse patterns: a case study, *Norwegian Archaeol Rev* **11.2**, 118–31

Hamp, E P, 1975 Social gradience in British spoken latin, *Britannia* **6**, 150–62

Hampton, J N, and Palmer, R, 1977 Implications of aerial photography for archaeology, *Archaeol J* **134**, 157–93

Harden, D B, 1956 Glass vessels in Britain and Ireland, AD 400–1000, in Harden, D B, ed, *Dark Age Britain*, 132–67

——, 1975 The glass, in Cunliffe, B, 1975, 368–74

——, 1979 Glass vessels, in Clarke G, 1979, 209–20

——, 1983 The glass hoard, in *Burgh Castle: excavations by Charles Green*, Johnson, S, E Anglian Archaeol **20**, 81–8

Harding, D W, 1972 *The Iron Age in the upper Thames basin*, Oxford

——, 1974 *The Iron Age in lowland Britain*

——, 1987 *Excavations in Oxfordshire 1964–6*, Univ Edinburgh Occ Pap **15**, Edinburgh

Harrison, A C, 1973 Rochester east-gate 1969, *Archaeol Cantiana* **87**, 121–57

Hawkes, C F C, 1947 Britons, Romans, and Saxons round Salisbury and in Cranborne Chase, *Archaeol J* **104**, 30–81

——, and Hull, M R, 1947 *Camulodunum*, Res Rep Soc Antiq of London **25**

Heighway, C, 1983 *The east and north gates of Gloucester*, Western Archaeol Trust Mono **4**, Bristol

——, 1987 *Anglo-Saxon Gloucestershire*, Gloucester

Henig, M, 1970 Zoomorphic supports of cast bronze from Roman sites in Britain, *Archaeol J* **127**, 182–7

——, 1972 Bronze rings with intaglios, appendix 3, 84–5 in Eagles, B W, and Swan, V G, The Chessalls, a Romano-British settlement at Kingscote, *Trans Bristol and Gloucestershire Archaeol Soc* **91**, 60–91

——, 1978 *A corpus of Roman engraved gemstones from British sites*, Brit Archaeol Rep, Brit Ser **8**, 2 edn, Oxford

——, 1980a Fragments of a stone cult-statue of Mercury from West Hill, Uley: an interim note, in Rodwell, W J, ed, 321–2

——, 1980b Art and cult in the temples of Roman Britain, in Rodwell, W J, ed, 91–114

——, 1983a The Maiden Castle "Diana": a case of mistaken identity, *Proc Dorset Natur Hist Archaeol Soc* **105**, 160–2

——, ed, 1983b *A handbook of Roman art: a survey of the visual arts of the Roman world*, Oxford

——, 1984 *Religion in Roman Britain*

——, 1986 *Ita intellexit numine indictus tvo*: some personal interpretations of deity in Roman religion, in Henig M, and King A, 159–69

——, 1989 The Crookhorn stand, in Soffe, *et al* eds, The Roman tilery and aisled building at Crookhorn, Hants, excavations 1974–5, *Proc Hampshire Fld Club Archaeol Soc* **45**, 83–5

——, and King, A, eds, 1986 *Pagan gods and shrines of the Roman Empire*, Oxford Univ Comm Archaeol Mono **8**

Henry, F, 1933 Emailleurs d'Occident, *Préhistoire* **2**, fasc 1, 65–146
Heyworth, M P, *et al*, 1988 The analysis of archaeological materials using inductively coupled plasma spectrometry, in Slater, E A, and Tate, J O, eds, *Science and Archaeology: proceedings of a conference on the application of scientific techniques to archaeology, Glasgow, September 1987*, Brit Archaeol Rep, Brit Ser **196**, 27–40, Oxford
Hillson, S, 1986 *Teeth*, Cambridge manuals in archaeology, Cambridge
Horne, P D, and King, A C, 1980 Romano-Celtic temples in continental Europe: A gazetteer of those with known plans, in Rodwell, W J, ed, 369–556
Howe, M D, Perrin, J R, and Mackreth, D F, 1980 *Roman pottery from the Nene Valley, a guide*, Peterborough City Museum Occ Pap **2**
Hughes, M J, Cowell, M R, and Craddock, P T, 1976 Atomic absorption techniques in archaeology, *Archaeometry* **18.1**, 19–37
Hull, M R, 1968 The brooches, in Dudley, D, Excavations on Nornour in the Isles of Scilly 1962–6, *Archaeol J* **124**, 1–64
Hunter, A G, and Kirk, J R, 1954 Excavations at Campsfield, Kidlington, *Oxoniensia* **17/18**, 36–62
Hunter, J R, and Heyworth, M P, forthcoming The glass from Hamwic, in Morton, A D, ed, *Southampton finds, vol 2: The glass and copper alloys*
Hurst, H R, 1986 *Gloucester, the Roman and later defences*, Gloucester Archaeol Rep **2**
Hurst J G, 1976 Wharram Percy: St Martin's Church, in Addyman and Morris *The archaeological study of churches*, Counc Brit Archaeol Res Rep **13**, 36–9

ILS, 1892–1916 *Inscriptiones Latinae Selectae*, Dessau, H, ed, Berlin
Isings, C, 1957 *Roman glass from dated finds*, Groningen

Jackson, K H, 1953 *Language and history in early Britain*, Edinburgh
Jenkins, F, 1976 Preliminary report on the excavations at the church of St Pancras at Canterbury, *Canterbury Archaeol* **4–5**
Jensen, R, 1974 *Diseases of sheep*, New York
Jones, G D B, 1974 *Roman Manchester*, Manchester Excavation Comm

Kaufmann-Heinimann, A, 1977 *Die Römischen Bronzen der Schweiz 1 Augst*, Mainz
Kemp, R L, undated *Nettleton Scrubb: excavations of the shrine of Apollo. A review of the published report*, unpublished typescript, University of York
Kilbride-Jones, H E, 1980 *Zoomorphic penannular brooches*, Res Rep Soc Antiq of London **39**
King, A, 1978 A comparative study of bone assemblages from Roman sites in Britain, *Bull Inst Archaeol, London* **15**, 207–32
——, 1984 Animal bones and the dietary identity of military and civilian groups in Roman Britain, Germany and Gaul, in Blagg, T F C, and King, A C, eds, *Military and civilian in Roman Britain. Cultural relationships in a frontier province*, Brit Archaeol Rep, Brit Ser **136**, 187–217, Oxford
Kirk, J R,1949 Bronzes from Woodeaton, Oxon, *Oxoniensia* **14**, 1–45
Krüger, P, ed, 1963 *Codex Iustinianus*, 13 edn, Berlin

Lambrick, G, and Robinson, M, 1988 The development of floodplain grassland in the upper Thames Valley, in Jones, M, ed, *Archaeology and the flora of the British Isles*, BSBI
Lawrence, A W, 1972 *Greek and Roman sculpture*
Lawson, A J, 1976 Shale and jet objects from Silchester, *Archaeologia* **105**, 241–75
Leach, P, ed, 1982 *Ilchester vol 1, excavations 1974–5*, Western Archaeol Trust Mono **3**, Bristol
——, forthcoming Excavations at Great Witcombe Roman villa by Ernest Greenfield 1960–73, *Trans Bristol and Gloucestershire Archaeol Soc*
Leahy, K, 1980 Votive models from Kirmington, South Humberside, *Britannia* **11**, 326–30
Leclercq, H, and Cabrol, F, 1925 *Dictionnaire d'archeólogie-chrétienne et de liturgie* II
Leech, R H, 1980 Religion and burial in south Somerset and north Dorset, in Rodwell, W J, ed, 1980, 329–68
——, 1981 The excavation of a Romano-British farmstead and cemetery on Bradley Hill, Somerset, *Britannia* **12**, 177–252
——, 1982 *Excavations at Catsgore 1970–73*, Western Archaeol Trust Mono **2**, Bristol
——, 1986 The Excavation of a Romano-Celtic temple and a later cemetery on Lamyatt Beacon, Somerset, *Britannia* **17**, 259–328
Legge, A J, and Dorrington, E J, 1985 The animal bones, in France and Gobels, 1985, 122–33
Leibundgut, A, 1980 *Die Römischen Bronzen der Schweiz III, Westschweiz, Bern und Wallis*, Mainz
Levitan, B, 1977 Pathological anomalies in sheep mandibles: a methodological approach, unpublished undergrad dissertation, Univ of London
——, 1982a *Excavations at West Hill, Uley, 1979. The sieving and sampling programme*, Western Archaeol Trust Occ Pap **10**, Bristol
——, 1982b Errors in recording tooth wear in ovicaprid mandibles at different speeds, in Wilson B, *et al*, eds, 207–14
——, 1983a The animal bones, in Saville, A and Ellison, A, fiche C6–D5
——, 1983b Reducing the work load: sub-sampling animal bone assemblages, *Circaea* **1.1**, 7–12
——, 1984 The vertebrate remains, in Rahtz S, and Rowley T, *Middleton Stoney: excavation and survey in a north Oxfordshire parish 1970–82*, Oxford, 108–48
——, 1985 A methodology for recording the pathology and other anomalies of ungulate mandibles from archaeological sites, in Fieller, N, *et al*, eds, *Palaeobiological investigations. Research design, methods, and data analysis*, Brit Archaeol Rep, Internat Ser **266**, 41–54, Oxford
——, 1989 The vertebrate remains from Chichester Cattle Market, in Down, A, *Chichester excavations* **6**, 242–76
——, 1990 A method for investigating bone fragmentation and anatomical representation, *Circaea* **7.2**, 95–102
Lewis, M J T, 1966 *Temples in Roman Britain*, Oxford
Lindgren, C, 1980 *Classical art forms and Celtic mutations. Figural art in Roman Britain*, New Jersey
Liversidge, J, 1968 *Britain in the Roman Empire*
Ludowici, W, 1929 *Katalog V Stempel-namen und Bilder römischer Töpfer aus meinen Ausgrabungen in Rheinzabern 1901–14*
Luff, R M, 1982 *A zooarchaeological study of the Roman North-west provinces*, Brit Archaeol Rep, Internat Ser **137**, Oxford

Mack, R P, 1975 *The coinage of ancient Britain*
MacKenzie, D, 1980 *Goat husbandry*, 4 edn
Mackreth, D F, 1966 A Romano-British brooch from Willoughby-on-the-Wolds, *Trans Thoroton Soc Nottinghamshire* **70**, 9–10
——, 1977 Brooches, in Rogerson A, *Excavations at Scole, 1973*, E Anglian Archaeol **5**, 129–34
McWhirr, A, 1981 *Roman Gloucestershire*, Gloucester
Magilton, J R, 1980 *The Church of St Helen-on-the-Walls, Aldwark*, The Archaeology of York **10/1**, Counc Brit Archaeol
——, 1986 A Roman building and Roman roads in Aldwark, in Brinklow, D, Hall, R A, Magilton, J R, and Donaghey, S, *Coney Street, Aldwark and Clementhorpe, minor sites, and Roman roads*, The Archaeology of York **6/1**, Counc Brit Archaeol
Maltby, M, 1979 *Faunal studies on urban sites. The animal bones from Exeter 1971–5*, Exeter Archaeol Rep **2**, Sheffield
——, 1981 Iron Age, Romano-British, and Anglo-Saxon animal husbandry: a review of the faunal evidence, in Jones, M, and Dimbleby, G, eds, *The environment of man: the Iron Age to the Anglo-Saxon period*, Brit Archaeol Rep, Brit Ser **87**, 155–204, Oxford
——, 1982 The variability of faunal samples and their effects upon ageing data, in Wilson B, *et al*, eds, 81–90
Manning, W H, 1985 *Catalogue of the Romano-British tools, fittings and weapons in the British Museum*
Massy, J L, 1986 Circonscription de Lorraine, *Gallia* **44**, fasc 2, 287–307
Meates, G W, 1987 *The Roman villa at Lullingstone, Kent, vol 2: the wall paintings and finds*, Kent Archaeol Soc Mono **3**
Megaw, J V S, 1970 *Art of the European Iron Age, a study of the elusive image*, Bath
Mercer, R, 1980 *Hambledon Hill – a Neolithic landscape*, Edinburgh
Merrifield, R, 1987 *The archaeology of ritual and magic*
Millett, M and James, S, 1983 Excavations at Cowdery's Down, Basingstoke, Hampshire, 1978–81, *Archaeol J* **140**, 151–279
Moore, D T, 1978 The petrography and archaeology of English honestones, *J Archaeol Sci* **5**, 61–73
——, 1982 Whetstones, in Leach, P J, ed, 1982, 224
Moore, J S, 1982 *Domesday Book of Gloucestershire*
Morgan, F de M, 1959 The excavation of a long barrow at Nutbane, Hants, *Proc Prehist Soc* **25**, 15–51
Morris, R, 1983 *The church in British archaeology*, Counc Brit Archaeol Res Rep **47**
Munby, J, 1975 A figurine of jet from Westmoreland, *Britannia* **6**, 216–18

Nash-Williams, V E, 1924 Roman remains found at Liswerry, near Newport, Monmouthshire, *Archaeol Cambrensis* **79**, 389–91
——, 1930 Further excavation at Caerwent, Monmouthshire, 1923–5, *Archaeologia* **80**, 229–88
Neal, D S, 1974 *The excavation of the Roman villa in Gadebridge Park, Hemel Hempstead, 1963–8*, Res Rep Soc Antiq of London **31**
Neville, Hon R C, 1852 Account of excavations near the Fleam Dyke, Cambridgeshire, April 1852, *Archaeol J* **9**, 226–30
Newton, R G, 1978 Colouring agents used by medieval glass-makers, *Glass Technology* **19**, 59–60
Niblett, R, 1985 *Sheepen: an early Roman industrial site at Camulodunum*, Counc Brit Archaeol Res Rep **57**
Noddle, B, 1977 The animal bones, in Ritchie, A, ed, Pictish and Viking age farmsteads at Buckquoy, Orkney, *Proc Soc Antiq Scot* **108**, 201–9
——, 1983 Size and shape, time and place: skeletal variations in cattle and sheep, in Jones, M, ed, *Integrating the subsistence economy*, Brit Archaeol Rep, Internat Ser **181**, 211–38, Oxford
——, 1987 Mammalian remains from the Cotswold region: a survey of the literature from Paleolithic to Roman times, and a more detailed account of the larger domestic mammals from some recent Romano-British excavations, in Balaam, *et al*, eds, *Studies in palaeo-environment and economy in south west England*, Brit Archaeol Rep, Brit Ser **181**, 31–50, Oxford

O'Connor, T P, 1982 *Animal bones from Flaxengate, Lincoln c870–1500* The archaeology of Lincoln **18.1**, Counc Brit Archaeol
——, 1984 *Selected groups of bones from Skeldergate and Walmgate* The Archaeology of York **15.1**, Counc Brit Archaeol
——, T P, 1985 On quantifying vertebrates – some sceptical observations, *Circaea* **3.1**, 27–30
Oddy, W A, and Craddock, P T, 1986 Report on the scientific examination of the fragment of horse's leg, in Lawson, A K, A fragment of life-size bronze equine statuary from Ashill Norfolk, *Britannia* **17**, 338–9
O'Kelly, C, 1977 Notes on the coins and related finds from New Grange, Co Meath, *Proc Royal Ir Acad* **77**, C, 2, 43–55
O'Kelly, M J, 1958 Church Island near Valencia, Co Kerry, *Proc Royal Ir Acad* **59**, C, 57–136
Oldenstein, J, 1976 Zur Ausrustüng römischer Auxiliareinheiten, *Bericht der Römisch-Germanischen Kommission* **57**, 49–284
O'Neil, B St J, 1928 Excavations at Mancetter, 1927, *Birmingham Archaeol Soc Trans* **58**, 173–95
——, 1952 Whittington Court Roman villa, a report of the excavations undertaken from 1948–51, *Trans Bristol and Gloucestershire Archaeol Soc* **71**, 13–87
——, 1966 Sale's Lot long barrow, Withington, Gloucestershire, *Trans Bristol and Gloucestershire Archaeol Soc* **85**, 5–35
——, and Grinsell, L V, 1960 Gloucestershire barrows, *Trans Bristol and Gloucestershire Archaeol Soc* **79**, 1–149
Orton, C R, 1975 Quantitative pottery studies, *Sci Archaeol* **16**, 30–5

Painter, K, and Sax, M, 1970 The British Museum collection of Roman head-stud brooches, *Brit Mus Quart* **34**, 153–74
Parker, A J, 1988 The birds of Roman Britain, *Oxford J of Archaeol* **7.2**, 197–226
Paul, A, 1982 *Chemistry of glasses*
Payne, S, 1969 A metrical distinction between sheep and goat metacarpals, in Ucko, P, and Dimbleby, G, eds, *The domestication and exploitation of plants and animals*, 295–306
——, 1973 Kill-off patterns in sheep and goats: the mandibles from Asvan Kale, *Anatolian Stud* **23**, 281–303
——, 1985 Morphological distinctions between the mandibular teeth of young sheep, *Ovis*, and goats, *Capra*, *J Archaeol Sci* **12**, 139–47
——, 1987 Reference codes for wear states in the mandibular cheek teeth of sheep and goats, *J Archaeol Sci* **14**, 609–14
Peacock, D P S, 1968 A petrological study of certain Iron Age pottery from western England, *Proc Prehist Soc* **34**, 414–27
——, 1977 *Pottery and early commerce: characterisation and trade in Roman and later ceramics*
——, 1980 The Roman millstone trade: a petrological sketch, *World Archaeol* **12.1**, 43–63
——, and Williams, D F, 1987 *Amphorae and the Roman economy*
Penn, W S, 1960 Springhead, temple I, *Archaeol Cantiana* **75**, 1–61
——, 1962 Springhead: temples II and V *Archaeol Cantiana* **77**, 110–32
Philp, B, 1981 *The excavation of the Roman forts of the Classis Britannica at Dover 1970–77*
Picon, M, Boucher, S, and Condamin, J, 1966 Recherches techniques sur des bronzes de Gaule Romaine, I, *Gallia* **24**, 189–215
——, Condamin, J, and Boucher, S, 1967 Recherches techniques sur des bronzes de Gaule Romaine, II, *Gallia* **25**, 153–68
——, ——, and ——, 1968 Recherches techniques sur des bronzes de Gaule Romaine, III, *Gallia* **26**, 245–78
Piggott, C D, and Taylor, K, 1964 The distribution of some woodland herbs in relation to the supply of nitrogen and phosphorus in the soil, *J Ecol* **52**, 175–86
Piggott, S, 1962 *The West Kennet long barrow: excavations 1955–6*,
——, 1965, *Ancient Europe from the beginnings of agriculture to Classical antiquity*, Edinburgh
——, 1968 *The Druids*
Pitt Rivers, A L F, 1887 *Excavations in Cranborne Chase* **1**
Pitts, L F, 1979 *Roman bronze figures from the civitates of the Catuvellauni and Trinovantes*, Brit Archaeol Rep, Brit Ser **60**, Oxford
Price, E G, 1983 Frocester, *Current Archaeol* **8**, 139–45
——, 1984 Frocester Court Roman villa, third report 1980: the well, *Trans Bristol and Gloucestershire Archaeol Soc* **101**, 49–76
Price, J, 1979 The glass, in Gracie, H S, and Price, E G, eds, 37–46
——, 1982 The glass, in Webster, G, and Smith, L, eds, The excavation of a Romano-British rural establishment at Barnsley Park, Gloucestershire, 1961–79, part II cAD 360–400+, *Trans Bristol and Gloucestershire Archaeol Soc* **100**, 174–85
——, 1984 Objects of glass, in Fulford, M, ed, *Silchester Defences 1974–80*, Britannia Mono **5**, 116–18
——, 1987 Glass from Felmongers, Harlow in Essex: a dated deposit of vessel glass found in an Antonine pit, *Annales du 10 Congrès de l'Association Internationale pour l'Histoire du Verre*, 185–206
——, and Cool, H E M, 1983 Glass from the excavations of 1974–6, in Brown, A E, and Woodfield, C, eds, Excavations at Towcester, Northamptonshire: the Alchester Road suburb, *Northants Archaeol* **18**, 115–24
Price, R, and Watts, L, 1980 Rescue excavations at Combe Hay, Somerset 1968–73, *Proc Somerset Archaeol Natur Hist Soc* **124**, 1–49
P Oxy, 1898 on *The Oxyrhynchus Papyri*

Rabeisen, E, and Menu, M, 1985 Métaux et alliages des bronziers d'Alesia, *Recherches Gallo-Romaines* **1**, 141–81
Rackham, O, 1980 *Ancient woodland*
Rahtz, P A, 1951 The Roman temple at Pagan's Hill, Chew Stoke, north Somerset, *Proc Somerset Archaeol Natur Hist Soc* **96**, 112–42
——, and Greenfield, E, 1977 *Excavations at Chew Valley Lake, Somerset*, DOE Archaeol Rep **8**
——, and Harris, L G, 1957 The temple well and other buildings at Pagan's Hill, Chew Stoke, north Somerset, *Proc Somerset Archaeol and Natur Hist Soc* **101/2**, 15–51
——, and Watts, L, 1979 The end of Roman temples in the west of Britain, in Casey, P J, ed, *The end of Roman Britain*, Brit Archaeol Rep, Brit Ser **71**, 193–210, Oxford
Rawes, B, 1987 The Romano-British settlement at Haymes, Cleeve Hill, near Cheltenham, *Trans Bristol and Gloucestershire Archaeol Soc* **104**, 61–93
RIB, Collingwood, R G, and Wright, R P, 1965 *The Roman inscriptions of Britain: 1 inscriptions on stone*, Oxford
RCHM 1976 *Ancient and historic monuments in the county of Gloucester, vol I: Iron age and Romano-British monuments in Gloucestershire and the Cotswolds*
Reeder E, 1987 The mother of the gods and a Hellenistic bronze matrix, *American J of Archaeol* **91**, 423–40
Richmond, I A, and Gillam, J P, 1951 The temple of Mithras at Carrawburgh, *Archaeol Aeliana*, 4 Ser **29**, 1–92
Richter, G M A, 1970 *The sculpture and sculptors of the Greeks*, 4 edn, New Haven
——, 1971 *Engraved gems of the Romans*
Rieckhoff, S, 1975 Münzen und Fibeln aus dem vicus des Kastells Hüfingen, *Saalburg Jahrbuch* **32**, 6–104
Riha, E, 1979 *Die römischen Fibeln aus Augst und Kaiseraugst*, Forschungen in Augst 3, Basel
Rivet, A L F, 1964 *Town and country in Roman Britain*, 2 edn
Rizzo, G, 1932 *Prassitele*, Rome
Rober, A, 1983 Le Sanctuaire Gallo-Romaine de Matagre-la-Grande, *Archaeologia Belgica* **252**, Brussels
Robinson, P, 1977 A local Iron Age coinage in silver and perhaps gold in Wiltshire, *British Numismatic J* **47**, 5-21
Rodwell, J S, 1992 *British plant communities: grassland and montane communities* **3**, Cambridge
Rodwell, W J, ed, 1980 *Temples, churches and religion in Roman Britain*, Brit Archaeol Rep, Brit Ser **77**, Oxford

——, 1981 *The archaeology of the English church*
——, and Bentley, J, 1984 *Our Christian heritage*
Roe, F E S, 1987a Identification of the utilized stone, in Cunliffe, B, *et al*, eds, *Hengistbury Head, Dorset vol 1*, Oxford Univ Comm Archaeol Mono **13**, 174–6
——, 1987b *Report on worked stone from Beckford, Worcestershire*, Ancient Monuments Lab Rep 154/87
——, forthcoming a Worked stone in Woodiwiss, S, ed, *Report on The Old Bowling Green, Droitwich*
——, forthcoming b Report on smaller pieces of utilized stone, in Sharples, N, *Report on Maiden Castle Excavations 1985 and 1986*, HBMC Archaeol Rep **19** (pub 1991)
—— forthcoming c Worked Stone, in Barfield, L, ed, *Report on Bay's Meadow Roman villa, Droitwich*
——, forthcoming d Report on smaller pieces of utilised stone, in Cunliffe, B, and Poole, C, 1991, *Danebury. An Iron Age hillfort in Hampshire, vol 5. The excavations 1979–88: the finds*, CBA Res Rep **73**, 382
Rogers, G B, 1974 *Poteries sigillés de la Gaule Centrale, Tome 1: les motifs non figurés*, (27th Supplèment á Gallia, Paris
Ross, A, 1968 Shafts, pits, wells – sanctuaries of the Belgic Britons?, in Coles, J M, and Simpson, D D A, eds, *Studies in ancient Europe*, Leicester
Ryder, M L, 1983 *Sheep and man*

Saville, A, 1979 Further excavations at Nympsfield chambered tomb, Gloucestershire, 1974, *Proc Prehist Soc* **45**, 53–92
——, 1984 Preliminary report on the excavation of a Cotswold-Severn tomb at Hazleton, Gloucestershire, *Antiq J* **64**, 10–24
——, 1990 *Hazleton North, Gloucestershire, 1979–82: the excavation of a Neolithic long cairn of the Cotswold-Severn Group*, HBMC Archaeol Rep **13**
——, and Ellison, A, 1983 Excavations at Uley Bury hillfort, Gloucestershire 1976, in Saville, A, ed, *Uley Bury and Norbury hillforts*, 1–24, Western Archaeol Trust Mono **5**, Bristol
Seeck, O, ed, 1883 *Q Aureli Symmachi quae supersunt*, Berlin
Sellwood, L, C, unpublished D Phil research *An archaeological and numismatic study of the Dobunni; 50 BC – 50 AD*, Oxford
Sellye, I G, 1939 Les bronzes émaillés de la Pannonie romaine, *Dissertationes Pannonicae*, 2 Ser **8**, Budapest
Shimwell, D W, 1971 Festuco-Brometea Br-B1 and R Tx 1943 in the British Isles: the phytogeography and phytosociology of limestone grasslands. Part 1(a) general information; (b) Xerobromion in England. Part II, Eu-Mesobromion in the British Isles, *Vegetatio* **23**, 1–60
Silver, I A, 1969 The ageing of domestic animals, in Brothwell, D, and Higgs, E, eds, *Science in archaeology*, 2 edn, 283–302
Smith, A H, 1965 *The place names of Gloucestershire*, Cambridge
Smith, C, 1972 Vulgar Latin in Roman Britain: epigraphic and other evidence, in Temporini, H, and Haase, W, eds, *Austiegund Neidergang der römishen welt* 2 Ser **29.2**, 893–948
Smith, I F, 1968 Report on late neolithic pits at Cam, Gloucestershire, *Trans Bristol and Gloucestershire Archaeol Soc* **87**, 14–28
Smyth, J, 1608 *Men and armour for Gloucestershire*, reprinted 1980, Gloucester
Smyth, J, 1883–5 *The Berkeley manuscripts. A description of the Hundred of Berkeley and of its inhabitants*, Sir John Maclean ed, Gloucester
Sorrell, A, 1981 *Reconstructing the past*
Stanfield, J A, and Simpson, G, 1958 *Central Gaulish Potters*
Stead, I M, 1968 An Iron Age hill-fort at Grimthorpe, Yorkshire, *Proc Prehist Soc* **34**, 148–90
——, 1970 A trial excavation at Braughing, 1969, *Hertfordshire Archaeol* **2**, 37–47
——, 1971a The reconstruction of Iron Age buckets from Aylesford and Baldock in Sieveking, G, ed, *Prehistoric and Roman studies*, 250–82
——, 1971b Yorkshire before the Romans: some recent discoveries, in Butler, R M, ed, *Soldier and civilian in Roman Yorkshire*, Leicester
——, 1976 *Excavations at Winterton Roman villa and other Roman sites in north Lincolnshire 1958–67*, DOE Archaeol Rep **9**
——, and Rigby, V, 1986 *Baldock: the excavation of a Roman and Pre-Roman settlement, 1968–72*, Britannia Mono **7**
——, and ——, 1989 *Verulamium: the King Harry Lane site*, HBMC Archaeol Rep **12**
Sunter, N, and Brown, D, 1988 Metal vessels, in Cunliffe, B, ed, 9–21
Swain, E J, 1975–9 *Excavations at the Chessals, Kingscote*, Interim reports
Swan, V G, 1975 Oare reconsidered and the origins of Savernake ware in Wiltshire, *Britannia* **6**, 37–61

Tann, J, 1967 *Gloucestershire woollen mills*
Tansley, A G, 1939 *The British islands and their vegetation*, Cambridge
Taylor, A, 1985 Prehistoric, Roman, Saxon, and Medieval artefacts from the southern fen edge, Cambridgeshire, *Proc Cambridge Antiq Soc* **74**, 31
Taylor, M V, 1963 Statuettes of horsemen and horses and other votive objects from Brigstock, Northants, *Antiq J* **43**, 246–68
Thomas, C, 1967 An early Christian cemetery and chapel on Ardwall Isle, Kirkcudbright, *Medieval Archaeol* **11**, 127–88
——, 1971 *The early Christian archaeology of north Britain*, Oxford
——, 1981 *Christianity in Roman Britain to AD 500*
Thompson, F H, 1965 *Roman Cheshire*, Chester
Thompson, M, and Walsh, J N, 1983 *A handbook of inductively coupled plasma spectrometry*, Glasgow
Thurnam, J, 1854 Description of a chambered tumulus, near Uley, Gloucestershire, *Archaeol J* **11**, 315–27
TLL *Thesaurus Linguae Latinae*, 1900 on Leipzig
Tomlin, R S O, 1988 *Tabellae Sulis. Roman inscribed tablets of tin and lead from the sacred spring at Bath*, part 4 (the curse tablets) of Cuiffe, B, ed, *The Temple of Sulis Minerva at Bath, 2: finds from the Sacred Spring*, Oxford Univ Comm Archeaol **16.1**, Oxford
Toynbee, J M C, 1962 *Art in Roman Britain*
——, 1964 *Art in Britain under the Romans*, Oxford
——, 1978 A Londinium votive leaf or feather and its fellows, in Bird, J, Chapman, H, and Clark, J, eds, Collecteana Londiniensia: *Studies presented to Ralph Merrifield*, 129–47
——, 1982 The inscribed altars, statuary, terracottas, intaglios, and special bronze objects, in Wedlake 1982, 135–43
Turner, R, 1982 *Ivy Chimneys, Witham, an interim report*, Chelmsford
Tylecote, R F, 1986 Litharge from a second century pit, in Buckland, P C, and Magilton, J R, eds, *The archaeology of Doncaster. 1 The Roman civil settlement*, Brit Archaeol Rep, Brit Ser **148**, Oxford

Uerpmann, H-P, 1973 Animal bone finds and economic archaeology: a critical study of "osteo-archaeological" method, *World Archaeol* **4.3**, 307–22

Van Arsdell, R D, 1989 *Celtic coinage of Britain*

Wacher, J 1980 *Roman Britain*
Wait, G A, 1985 *Ritual and religion in Iron Age Britain*, Brit Archaeol Rep, Brit Ser **149**, Oxford
Walden, H W, 1976 Nomenclatural list of the land mollusca of the British Isles, *Trans Conch* **29**, 21–5
Walters, H B, 1908 *Catalogue of the Roman pottery in the Department of Antiquities, British Museum*
Watson, J P N, 1979 The estimation of the relative frequencies of mammalian species: Khirokitia 1972, J Archaeol Sci **6**, 127–37
Watts, L, and Leach, P J, forthcoming *Henley Wood: the Romano-British temples and a post-Roman cemetery: excavations by E Greenfield and others between 1960–68*, Counc Brit Archaeol Res Rep
Waugh, H, 1961 The Romano-British burial at Weston Turville, *Records of Bucks* **17**, 107–14
——, 1966 The hoard of Roman silver from Great Horwood, Buckinghamshire, *Antiq J* **46**, 60–71
Webster, G A, 1981 The excavation of a Romano-British rural establishment at Barnsley Park, Gloucestershire, 1961–79: part 1, *Trans Bristol and Glouc Archaeol Soc* **99**, 21–77
Webster P V, 1976 Severn Valley ware: a preliminary study, *Trans Bristol and Gloucestershire Archaeol Soc* **94**, 18–46
Wedlake, W J, 1958 *Excavations at Camerton, Somerset*, Camerton
——, 1982 *The excavation of the shrine of Apollo at Nettleton, Wiltshire, 1956–71*, Res Rep Soc Antiq of London **40**
Wegner, M, 1939 *Die Herrscherbildnisse in antoninischer Zeit*, Berlin
Welch, F B A, and Trotter, F M, 1961 *Geology of the country around Monmouth and Chepstow*, Mem Geol Survey Gt Brit, (for sheets 233 and 250)
West, S C, and Plouviez, J, 1976 The Roman site at Icklingham, *E Anglian Archaeol* **3**, 63–126
Wheeler, R E M, 1928 The Roman amphitheatre at Caerleon, Monmouthshire, *Archaeologia* **78**, 112–218
——, 1930 *London in Roman times*
——, 1943 *Maiden Castle, Dorset*, Res Rep Soc Antiq of London **12**

——, and Wheeler, T V, 1932 *Report on the excavation of the prehistoric, Roman and post-Roman site in Lydney Park, Gloucestershire*, Res Rep Soc Antiq of London **9**, Oxford

——, and ——, 1936 *Verulamium. A Belgic and two Roman cities*, Res Rep Soc Antiq of London **11**

White, K D, 1970 *Roman farming*

Willcox, G H, 1977 Exotic plants from Roman waterlogged sites in London, *J Archaeol Sci* **4**, 269–82

Williams, D F, 1977 The Romano-British black burnished ware industry: An essay on characterisation by heavy mineral analysis, in Peacock, D, ed, 163–220

Wilson, B, 1978a Methods and results of bone analysis, in Parrington, M, ed, The excavation of an Iron Age settlement, Bronze Age ring ditches, and Roman features at Ashville Trading Estate, Abingdon (Oxon) 1974–6, Oxford Archaeol Unit Rep **1**, Counc Brit Archaeol Res Rep **28**, 110–26, 133–8

——, 1978b Sampling bone densities of Mingies Ditch, in Cherry, J F, Gamble, C, and Shennan, S, eds, *Sampling in contemporary British archaeology*, Brit Archaeol Rep, Brit Ser **50**, 355–61, Oxford

——, 1985 Degraded bones, feature type and spatial patterning on an Iron Age occupation site in Oxfordshire, England, in Fieller, N, *et al*, eds, *Palaeobiological investigations. Research design, methods, and analysis*, Brit Archaeol Rep, Internat Ser **266**, 81–93, Oxford

—, Grigson C, and Payne S, eds, 1982, *Ageing and sexing animal bones from archaeological sites*, Brit Archaeol Rep, Brit Ser **109**, Oxford

Wilson, D G, 1979 Horse dung from Roman Lancaster: a botanical report, *Archaeo-Physica* **8**, 331–49

Wilson, D R, 1975 Romano-Celtic temple architecture, *J Brit Archaeol Assoc*, 3 Ser **38**, 3–27

Young, C J, 1977 *The Roman pottery industry of the Oxfordshire region*, Brit Archaeol Rep, Brit Ser **43**, Oxford

Zadoks-Josephus-Jitta, A N, Peters, W J T, and van Es, W A, 1967 *Roman bronze statuettes from the Netherlands I, statuettes found north of the Limes*, Groningen

Zadoks-Josephus-Jitta, A N, Peters, W J T, and van Es, W A, 1969 *Roman bronze statuettes from the Netherlands II, statuettes found south of the Limes*, Groningen

Zadoks-Josephus-Jitta, A N, Peters, W J T, and Witteveen, A M, 1973 *Description of the collections in the Rijksmuseum G M Kam at Nijmegen: VII, the figural bronzes*, Nijmegen

Index

by Isobel Thompson